contents

acknowledgments

Numerous people have helped us in the preparation of this book. Special thanks go to Michelle Golder and Simon Cauchi for their editorial work. Thanks also to Gerry Fleming and Pauline Ngan for providing research assistance and compiling the bibliography. We would also like to acknowledge the valuable secretarial assistance provided by Pat Cumming, Jessie Johnston, and Kath Myers.

Further, we would like to thank the State Services Commission for providing a grant to cover some of the costs of research, editing, and indexing. Without such assistance, books of this nature would be much more difficult to produce. It should be emphasised that the views expressed in this book are those of the authors; members of the Commission at no stage sought to influence our judgments and conclusions. They did, however, offer much valuable guidance and support, and supplied numerous comments on various draft chapters.

Substantial sections of this book, in draft form, were circulated to students undertaking a Master of Public Policy course on Public Sector Management (MAPP 510) in 1995. We would like to thank all those students who offered comments, identified gaps in the analysis, and pointed to new lines of inquiry.

Finally, we would like to thank the numerous people—including academics, public servants, trade union officials, and politicians—who contributed to the writing of this book by way of interviews, assistance with material, or comments on draft chapters: Jonathan Ayto, Carl Bakker, Ian Ball, Margaret Bazley, Joanna Beresford, Tom Berthold, Kevin Brady, Janet Brown, Jim Brumby, Jane Bryson, Janice Burns, Graham Bush, Alan Cameron, Paul Carpinter, David Caygill, Julie Craig, Christopher Cripps, Colin Davies, Richard Dunford, Lew Evans, Howard Fancy, Bill Frith, Bob Gregory, Manuka Henare, Gerald Hensley, Colin Hicks, Wes ten Hove, Philippa Howden-Chapman, Derek Howell, David Hutton, Michael Hyndman, Kerry Jacobs, Colin James, Sir Kenneth Keith, Jane Kelsey, Sally Kincaid, Andrew Ladley, Rob Laking, Miriam Laugeson, Judy Lawrence, Chris Lovelace, Peter Martin, Alex Matheson, Martin Matthews, Tony McConnell, Jas McKenzie, Peter McKinlay, Maria McKinley, Grant McLean, Elizabeth McLeay, Peter McRae, Rex Morton, Mark Neeson, Alan Nixon, Richard Norman, Maris O'Rourke, Sir Geoffrey Palmer, Ian Powell, Michael Powell, David Preston, Lyn Provost, Sue Richards, Michael Reid, Donald Riezobos, Karen Roper, Trish Sarr, Jeanette Schollum, Stuart Shepherd, Gay Simpkin, Mary Slater, Verna Smith, Alan Spencer, Michael Taggart, Brenda Tahi, Rae Torrie, Jeremy Traylen, Ian Trotman, Simon Upton, Alex Watson, Michael Webster, Michael Wearne, Charlotte Williams, Amanda Wolf, and Richard Wood.

J.B., J.M., J.P., and P.W.

abbreviations

ACC	Accident Compensation Corporation (now Accident Rehabilitation and Compensation Insurance Corporation)
AGA	annual general adjustment
AJHR	*Appendix to the Journals of the House of Representatives*
CCMAU	Crown Company Monitoring Advisory Unit
CE	chief executive
CHE	Crown Health Enterprise
CRI	Crown Research Institute
CTU	Council of Trade Unions
DMO	Debt Management Office
DPMC	Department of Prime Minister and Cabinet
DSW	Department of Social Welfare
EEO	equal employment opportunities
ERO	Education Review Office
FASAB	Federal Accounting Standards Advisory Board
FEC	Finance and Expenditure Committee
FGRS	Federal Government Reporting Study
FMI	Financial Management Initiative (United Kingdom)
FoRST	Foundation for Research, Science and Technology
GAAP	generally accepted accounting practice
GDP	gross domestic product
GST	goods and services tax
HRM	human resource management
HSC	Higher Salaries Commission
ITA	Iwi Transition Agency
KRA	key result area
LATE	local authority trading enterprise
MFAT	Ministry of Foreign Affairs and Trade
MMP	mixed member proportional (electoral system)
NPM	new public management
NZDF	New Zealand Defence Force
NZEI	New Zealand Educational Institute
NZQA	New Zealand Qualifications Authority
NZSA	New Zealand Society of Accountants
NZSIC	New Zealand Standard Industry Classification
OAG	Office of the Auditor-General
OECD	Organisation for Economic Cooperation and Development
OIA	Official Information Act
OPC	Officers of Parliament Committee
PAC	Public Accounts Committee
PHC	Public Health Commission
PPBS	Planning Programming Budgeting System
PPTA	Post Primary Teachers Association
PQ	Parliamentary Question
PSA	Public Service Association
RHA	Regional Health Authority
RMA	Resource Management Act
SCI	Statement of Corporate Intent
SES	Senior Executive Service
SOE	state-owned enterprise

SPA	Social Policy Agency
SPSAC	*Statement of Public Sector Accounting Concepts*
SRA	strategic result area
SSC	State Services Commission
TCE	transaction-cost economics
TGB-4	Technical Guidance Bulletin
TPK	Te Puni Kōkiri
TQM	total quality management
VFM	value for money
ZBB	zero-based budgeting

preface

This book is about public management in New Zealand. In particular, it documents and analyses the sweeping public sector reforms introduced since the mid 1980s. These reforms, initiated by the fourth Labour government and continued by the subsequent National administration, have radically altered the institutions, operations, management, and accountability of the public sector at both the central and local government levels. Although many of the reforms have close parallels in other OECD countries, others—especially those in the area of financial management—are relatively distinctive, if not unique. In combination, they have created, albeit unintentionally, a new model of public management, now referred to internationally as the 'New Zealand model'. This model has attracted widespread interest, and stimulated no little enthusiasm, among practitioners, scholars, and students of public management in many parts of the world. Indeed, some policy-makers elsewhere have been so impressed by aspects of the model that they have sought to introduce reforms of a similar nature in their own jurisdictions. Despite this high level of interest, there is no up-to-date, systematic, comprehensive, and authoritative account of the New Zealand model.

This book endeavours to rectify this deficiency. We have thus set out to describe the defining features of the new model, identify the principles and administrative doctrines upon which it is based, and evaluate its merits. In so doing, specific attention is given to the model's origins, including the economic and political pressures to which it was a response and its theoretical and conceptual underpinnings. We have also sought to describe how the new model actually operates in practice, how its outcomes compare with the stated aims of its originators, and what impact it has had, both positive and negative, on the governance of New Zealand.

For various reasons, we have devoted most of our attention to the reforms of the *core* public sector (i.e. departments and ministries) at the *national* level. Developments at the sub-national level (i.e. regional and territorial government) are outlined and discussed in several chapters, but are not explored in great depth. With respect to the core public sector, particular emphasis is given to the following topics: institutional design; the role, selection and assessment of departmental chief executives; the organisation and purchasing of policy advice; the impact of cultural diversity and the commitment to biculturalism; human resource management, including the process and outcomes of employment contract negotiations and the pursuit of equal employment opportunities;

financial management, including the departmental management of resources, account-ability and the collective interest, and the role of the Audit Office; the impact of the reforms on the culture, ethics, and ethos of the public sector; and the current provisions for administrative review and redress.

We are mindful, of course, that even in a book of this length it has not been possible to address every issue in the depth that would be desirable. Hence, while the book is reasonably comprehensive, there are many subjects that, of necessity, have been covered in a relatively fleeting fashion. One such topic is the role and performance of state-owned enterprises and Crown entities. Another is the day-to-day micro-management of public organisations. Other topics to receive relatively limited attention include the following: the political economy of public sector reform; the scope and application of administrative discretion; the contracting out of publicly funded services; the pro-gramme of asset sales; the changing structure and level of public expenditure; the man-agement of change; the impact of new technologies on the nature and organisation of work within the public sector; and the way various public agencies have responded to the demands for a more customer or client-oriented focus. In some cases, we have eschewed a detailed analysis because the relevant issues have been adequately covered elsewhere. In other cases, we have been limited in our observations and assessments by the current state of knowledge. It is to be hoped that this book contributes to an identification of those matters requiring further research and that it will encourage other scholars to undertake relevant projects in these areas.

It must be emphasised that this is a book about public management; it is not specifically about administrative law, constitutional law, public finance, public economics, economic liberalisation, politics, or private-sector management—although each of these fields is touched upon at various times. Nevertheless, we have provided a brief overview of the framework of government within which the New Zealand public sector operates and indi-cated some of the changes occurring as a result of the introduction of proportional repre-sentation (particularly those that relate to public management). However, readers seeking a detailed treatment of the broader governmental system, including Parliament, cabinet, and the electoral system, will need to draw on other sources—of which there is no short-age.

But what is public management? In brief, the term refers to both the location and nature of management activity. *Management*, whether in the public or private sectors, is about the optimal utilisation of resources towards desired results; that is, the creation of things of value. When the management activity is located in the public sector (how-ever defined) these values differ from those in the private sector. The main reason for this is that the management of public sector organisations takes place in a political con-text and within political constraints, such as parliamentary control over the use of tax-payer funds. Bear in mind also that public management involves both managing *within* public sector organisations and the macro-level management *of the public sector as a whole*. This latter activity involves, among other things, the fostering of cooperation and coordination among interdependent organisations in the pursuit of collectively deter-mined goals. Steering such a network requires a delicate balance to be struck between shared public interests and the interests of individual public sector organisations and the individuals who manage them. Some parts of this book (e.g. the chapters on human resource management and financial management) are about the task of management *within* government agencies, including the management of the interface between this task and the political process. Much of the book, however, is concerned with managing the public sector as a whole, and thus deals with questions of institutional design, the organisation of policy advice, and the protection of the government's collective interests.

Although the focus of this book is primarily on public sector developments in New Zealand, specifically those since the mid 1980s, reference is made (wherever possible and appropriate) to public management practices and reforms in other jurisdictions. The intention here is to provide readers with an indication of how the New Zealand model compares (e.g. in terms of machinery of government matters, human resource management, and financial management) with the policies and practices adopted in other countries, especially those with a Westminster heritage. No attempt, however, has been made to furnish detailed comparative data; this would require another book.

The sources upon which we have drawn are many and varied. To begin with, we have made considerable use of the material contained in our previous volume, *Reshaping the State*, published in early 1991. It outlined the key public sector reforms of the mid to late 1980s and described the manner of their introduction and their initial impact, particularly on the core public sector. Inevitably, some of the discussion and assessments in that volume have been superseded by more recent developments. Nevertheless, a few chapters have proved reasonably durable, and they—suitably revised and updated—have provided the basis for Chapters 2, 4 and 5 in this current volume. Aside from *Reshaping the State*, we have drawn on many of the academic papers and articles that we have written (in our respective areas of interest) on aspects of the New Zealand model since the late 1980s. In addition, of course, we have made use of the published work of other academic researchers, as well as the numerous papers and articles produced by various senior public servants since the mid-1980s on aspects of the reforms. We have also drawn on the findings of various research papers and theses, especially those of students in the Master of Public Policy programme at Victoria University. Finally, we have made extensive use of material contained in various government or departmental publications (e.g. reviews, annual reports, and the regular reports of the Controller and Auditor-General).

Quite apart from this, most of our draft chapters were circulated to a range of people for comment—academics, trade union officials, public servants, local government officers, and politicians. This process of review produced a wealth of new material— observations, insights, reflections, evaluations, and data of various kinds. We have endeavoured to incorporate as much of this material as possible into our revised drafts and are deeply indebted to the many people who have assisted us in this process. Given the wide audience for which this book is intended, we have endeavoured to write in a manner and style that, we hope, will be found accessible by both New Zealand and international audiences.

As is normal in a co-authored volume, particular chapters were the primary responsibility of individual authors with allocations depending, in the main, on our respective fields of competence and areas of interest. Nevertheless, we have all contributed to the writing of each chapter and we jointly accept responsibility, including errors and omissions, for what is contained in the whole book.

Jonathan Boston
John Martin
June Pallot
Pat Walsh
September 1995

the revolution in public management

---

1 the new zealand model: key features and continuing dilemmas

Since the early to mid 1980s, the quest for smarter as well as smaller government has led numerous countries to embark upon major public sector reforms. In Britain, the 'Next Steps' initiative has radically overhauled the structure and operations of much of the civil service. In Australia, there have been important financial management reforms and machinery of government changes at the federal, state, and local government levels. And in the USA, the Clinton administration has made the quest for a government that 'works better and costs less' one of its top priorities. Although the rhetoric might have varied around the world, most of the recent efforts at governmental reinvention, restructuring, and renewal have shared similar goals—to improve the effectiveness and efficiency of the public sector, enhance the responsiveness of public agencies to their clients and customers, reduce public expenditure, and improve managerial accountability. The choice of policy instruments has also been remarkably similar: commercialisation, corporatisation, and privatisation; the devolution of management responsibilities; a shift from input controls to output and outcome measures; tighter performance specification; and more extensive contracting out.

New Zealand's model of public management—the product of an extraordinary succession of governmental reforms commencing in the mid 1980s—has without doubt been the most widely acclaimed and celebrated. Not only has it drawn high commendations from international agencies and leading academics, but it has also figured prominently in the debates over public sector reform in numerous countries—Australia, Britain, Canada, Ireland, and the USA, to name but a few. Among those most enthusiastic about the new approach to public management pioneered in New Zealand are David Osborne and Ted Gaebler. In their influential and widely read book, *Reinventing Government*, they note that:

> New Zealand has gone the farthest along the entrepreneurial path . . . In one fell swoop, New Zealand did away with its old civil service system, freeing department managers to negotiate their own contracts with their employees. It eliminated regulations that inhibited competition in both the private and public sectors—forcing government-owned businesses . . . into more competitive markets. And it adopted a budget system focused on performance . . . and an accrual accounting system modeled on business accounting (1993, p. 330).

Such has been the interest in the New Zealand model that many government agencies around the world have sent senior officials, and in some cases sizeable delegations, to Wellington to explore first hand the nature of the reforms and assess their possible application in other jurisdictions. Detailed reports on New Zealand's reforms have also been commissioned by various international agencies and governmental organisations (e.g. Office of the Auditor General of Canada, 1995; Scott, 1995). And there has been a steady stream of invitations for senior New Zealand public servants and academics to explain the New Zealand model at international conferences, in scholarly journals and before legislative inquiries into public sector reform (see, for example, Treasury and Civil Service Committee, 1994, pp. xlix–li).

Almost without exception, those who have studied the bureaucratic 'revolution' in New Zealand have come away favourably impressed. The 'experiment' has been praised for its radicalism, boldness, coherence, and innovative methods. The remarkable scope and scale of the changes, their speed of introduction, and their ambitious objectives have also drawn much comment. While most observers have identified areas of concern with the new approach to public management, including the transitional costs associated with its introduction, most assessments have been extremely positive. It was thus no great surprise when the World Competitiveness Report in 1993 ranked New Zealand first for its quality of government (World Economic Forum, 1993).

KEY FEATURES

What, then, are the key features of the New Zealand model? First of all, it is important to note that many, if not most of New Zealand's public management reforms are in broad conformity with the ideas, principles and practices of 'managerialism' or the 'new public management' (see Chapter 2). It would be quite wrong, however, to see the New Zealand model as simply a radical, uncompromising, or extreme version of managerialism. The picture is much more complicated than this. For one thing, managerialist doctrines have been combined and applied in relatively novel and imaginative ways. For another, the reforms were based on a range of theoretical traditions, political imperatives, and pragmatic judgments by ministers. Managerialism was thus only one of the intellectual ingredients.

A further feature distinguishing the New Zealand model—and one of the main reasons why it has attracted such enthusiastic reviews internationally—is its conceptual rigour and intellectual coherence. Unlike most previous administrative reforms, which tended to be discrete and relatively *ad hoc* responses to perceived problems, those between the mid 1980s and early 1990s were part of a carefully crafted, integrated, and mutually reinforcing reform agenda. Although no government White Paper was ever published, the central features of the new model were enunciated in the Treasury's postelection briefing papers in late 1987, published under the title *Government Management.* This remarkable document, described by Christopher Hood (1990b, p. 210) as the 'manifesto' of the new public management, catalogued the weaknesses of the existing administrative order and provided the analytical framework upon which many of the subsequent reforms were based. Whether or not ministers in the fourth Labour government conceived of these reforms as a distinctive model is uncertain. Nevertheless, convinced of the need to improve the performance of the public sector, they readily embraced the main elements of the Treasury's framework.

The central components of the New Zealand model have been variously summarised by different commentators (e.g. Ball, 1994; Boston, Martin, Pallot, and Walsh, 1991; Boston, 1995b; Scott, Bushnell, and Sallee, 1990; State Services Commission, 1993; Wistrich, 1992). In the interests of clarity, it is perhaps helpful to distinguish three separate aspects of the model: the broad objectives that it was designed to achieve; the key administrative principles or doctrines that guided its overall development; and the specific policies that form its superstructure.

Objectives

From the outset, the main objectives lying behind the development of the new model of public management were:

a. to improve allocative and productive efficiency;
b. to enhance the effectiveness of governmental programmes;
c. to improve the accountability of public sector institutions and the accountability of the executive to Parliament;
d. to reduce the level of government expenditure and the size of the core public sector;
e. to minimise the opportunities for the non-transparent use of public power;
f. to improve the quality of the goods and services produced by public agencies; and
g. to make public services more accessible and responsive to consumers, as well as more culturally sensitive.

Principles

Among the key principles underpinning the new model are the following:

a. The government should only be involved in those activities that cannot be more efficiently and effectively carried out by non-governmental bodies (e.g. private businesses, voluntary agencies, etc.).
b. Any commercial enterprises retained within the public sector should be structured along the lines of private sector companies.
c. The goals of governments, departments, Crown agencies and individual public servants should be stated as precisely and clearly as possible.
d. Potentially conflicting responsibilities should, wherever possible, be placed in separate institutions.
e. There should be a clear separation of the responsibilities of ministers and departmental chief executives (CEs): ministers should be responsible for selecting the outcomes they wish to achieve and purchasing their desired outputs; CEs should be responsible for selecting the inputs required to produce the desired outputs with the minimum practicable interference from ministers and central agencies.

f. Wherever possible, publicly funded services, including the purchasing of policy advice, should be made contestable and subject to competitive tendering; the quality, quantity, and cost of publicly funded services should be determined by the purchaser's (i.e. minister's) requirements rather than the producer's preferences.

g. Institutional arrangements should be designed to minimise the scope for provider capture.

h. Preference should be given to governance structures that minimise agency costs and transaction costs.

i. In the interests of administrative efficiency and consumer responsiveness, decision-making powers should be located as close as possible to the place of implementation.

Policies

In more specific policy terms, the New Zealand model in the mid 1990s embraces the following elements:

a. A preference for retaining key governmental powers and responsibilities at the central government level with only limited devolution to sub-national government, despite considerable rhetoric about devolution in the 1980s.

b. A strong emphasis on the use of incentives to enhance performance, at both the institutional and the individual level (e.g. short-term employment contracts, performance-based remuneration systems, promotion systems, etc.).

c. An extensive use of explicit, generally written 'contracts' of various kinds, which specify the nature of the performance required and the respective obligations of agents and principals (e.g. performance agreements between ministers and departmental CEs, purchase agreements between ministers and departments, and contracts between funders and purchasers and between purchasers and providers). In addition to the emphasis on *ex ante* performance specification, more exacting monitoring and reporting systems have been introduced.

d. The development of integrated and relatively sophisticated strategic planning and performance management systems throughout the public sector. Key elements include the specification by ministers of strategic result areas and key result areas and the integration of these into CEs' performance agreements and departmental purchase agreements.

e. The removal, wherever possible, of dual or multiple accountability relationships within the public sector, and the avoidance of joint central and local democratic control of public services.

f. The institutional separation of commercial and non-commercial functions; the separation of advisory, delivery, and regulatory functions; and the related separation of the roles of funder, purchaser, and provider.

g. The maximum decentralisation of production and management decision-making, especially with respect to the selection and purchase of inputs and the management of human resources.

h. The implementation of a financial management system based on accrual accounting and including capital charging, a distinction between the Crown's ownership and purchaser interests, a distinction between outcomes and outputs, an accrual-based appropriations system, and legislation requiring economic policies that are deemed to be 'fiscally responsible'.
i. Strong encouragement for, and extensive use of, competitive tendering and contracting out, but few mandatory requirements for market testing or competitive tendering.

The main public sector reforms, including the legislative changes, between 1984 and 1995 are described more fully in subsequent chapters. They are also summarised in Appendix 1. It would, of course, be misleading to suggest that the reforms are complete. Although the central legislative building blocks—the State-Owned Enterprises Act 1986, the State Sector Act 1988, the Public Finance Act 1989, and the Fiscal Responsibility Act 1994—are firmly in place and are unlikely to undergo substantial modifications, changes around the margins are continuing. Hence, the New Zealand model is evolving and being constantly refined. For instance, the programme of state asset sales is ongoing, the fiscal restraints on departments are being tightened still further, and the strategic management system is continuing to develop. There is also pressure for further changes in various parts of the state sector, including the funding and regulation of tertiary education, the accountability of Crown entities, the monitoring of local government, and the contracting out of prison management.

New Zealand's reforms have meant not just a change in the instruments or techniques of public management; they have also brought significant changes in the style and mode of governance and the culture of the public service. This has been reflected, among other things, in the adoption of a new language of discourse. Various terms, most of them largely unknown in New Zealand's state sector prior to the mid 1980s, have now become commonplace: contestability, contracting, customised services, outputs, outcomes, ownership interest, performance agreements, purchase agreements, stakeholders, strategic planning, transparency, transaction costs, agent–principal relations, and so on. The constant focus on 'management', rather than the older term 'administration', is equally evident. 'Management' is now applied in many and varied forms—case management, change management, collective management, contract management, financial management, human resource management, performance management, risk management, strategic management, and management development.

The remarkable transformation of public management in New Zealand did not occur in isolation. Rather it was part of a comprehensive strategy of economic, social, and political reform, the chief aim of which was to improve the country's economic performance and thus end almost three decades of relative decline. At the microeconomic level, for instance, the fourth Labour government commenced a vigorous liberalisation programme covering almost every sector of the economy (Bollard, 1992, 1994). At the macroeconomic level, Labour pursued a stabilisation programme based on tight monetary and fiscal policies. With National's election victory in late 1990, the quest for expenditure cuts was intensified and major changes were made to labour market policies and most areas of social policy—including accident compensation, education, health care, housing and income maintenance. In broad terms these changes were designed to extend the targeting of social assistance, increase the reliance on cash transfers rather than in-kind assistance, cut the real value of most welfare benefits, and separate the state's roles as a funder, purchaser, and provider (see Boston and Dalziel, 1992; James, 1992; Kelsey, 1993). Important constitutional changes have also occurred since the mid 1980s: the passage of the New Zealand Bill of Rights Act 1990, the introduction of proportional representation, and greater political and legal recognition of the Treaty of Waitangi (1840). The full impact of these and other changes on public management remains to be seen.

CONTINUING DILEMMAS

Although New Zealand's public management reforms have been dramatic and far-reaching, many of the underlying issues that confront those responsible for managing the public sector have changed little. The physical contours of the public sector have been fundamentally and perhaps irrevocably altered, but many of the perennial tensions and dilemmas of governance remain. This should come as no surprise. In essence, public management is about the clarification and realisation of certain values—the common good, distributive and procedural justice, liberty, democratic responsiveness, the wise stewardship of scarce resources, openness, privacy, uniform service standards, cultural sensitivity, national security, and so on. Most, if not all, of these values are open to varying interpretations. Moreover, they frequently conflict. Bureaucratic reorganisations, however grand, rarely resolve such conflicts. Admittedly, they might alter the context within which these conflicts are articulated, mediated, and experienced; they might also reflect, as well as affect, the relative weight accorded to particular concerns and objectives. But although new balances might be struck, they are unlikely to prove enduring; a particular institutional reform might resolve a long-standing tension, but in doing so it is just as likely to create or expose a new one. Hence, the art and craft of public management is less about realising the *maximum* number of values than determining *which* values should be given precedence and which should be sacrificed. This is not to suggest that governance is always and everywhere a zero-sum game. Frequently, however, it is.

So what are the perennial issues that face those concerned with the management of the public sector? Clearly, there are many. It is not possible or necessary to catalogue them all here. But listed below are some of the more important ones:

• Where should the boundary be drawn between the public and private sectors?
• Where is the proper boundary between politics and administration?
• What are the proper limits to administrative discretion?
• How should public institutions be designed so as to meet the special needs and interests of cultural minorities?
• What is the appropriate balance between centralisation and decentralisation?
• Is it necessarily best for agents to serve only one principal?

- How can the multitude of formally autonomous yet functionally interdependent organisations that constitute the public sector be effectively coordinated?
- How should performance be measured in the absence of a bottom line?
- What are the duties of public servants?

Public versus private

Policy-makers constantly face the question of the state's proper role in society and where to draw the boundary between the public and private sectors. What should be the state's role, for example, in terms of regulation, ownership, funding, provision, and moral suasion? Are certain functions or activities inherently public or inherently governmental (see Boston, 1995a)? Furthermore, what does it mean to call something 'public'? Is it purely a question of ownership or agency? Or does it include broader ideas relating to the public interest and public access to the policy-making process? Such questions are essentially philosophical and political in nature. They are not amenable to scientific or technocratic solutions. They depend for their answers on the values of those elected to political office and those they represent.

Of course, how these questions are answered has important implications for the nature and scope of public management. Relevant here is the distinction, which Henry (1975) drew in his analysis of public administration, between 'locus' (the institutional 'where' of the field) and 'focus' (the specialised 'what' of the field). The issue of 'where' depends on the location of the boundary between the public and private sectors. By contrast, the issue of 'what' concerns not only where to draw the boundary but also what tasks the government should undertake.

Under New Zealand's new model of public management, the distinction between public and private has been conceived of primarily in terms of *ownership*. Put simply, something is deemed to be in the public sector if it is government-owned; if not, it is in the private sector. Whether this constitutes an adequate criterion for differentiation is a matter of debate. Other possible criteria include legal status, the receipt of public funds, the nature of the service being provided, and the public effects of an activity. The varying dimensions of what constitutes something 'public' are highlighted by the continuing debate surrounding prison management (see Trebilcock, 1995). Advocates of contracting out argue that public ownership and control tends to be wasteful and inefficient—characterised by rigid work practices, excessive staffing levels, and provider capture. They contend that exposing prison management to the rigours of competition will yield significant gains in productive efficiency, as well as more innovative and humane penal management practices. Critics of this view, however, point to the problems of specifying desired outcomes, establishing appropriate performance targets, monitoring subsequent performance, and enforcing the relevant contractual obligations. Given these difficulties, they note the potential risks of opportunistic behaviour on the part of commercially oriented prison managers. Many critics of the contracting out of prison management also argue that, as a matter of principle, the imposition of punishment on behalf of the community should be undertaken by institutions of a wholly public nature. Only in this way, it is contended, can the community signify, directly and unequivocally, its abhorrence of actions that violate commonly accepted norms.

Politics versus administration

The question of the appropriate relationship between the political executive and the administrative arms of the state is no less contentious. On the one hand, it is in the interests of democratic control and political accountability for public servants to be under the clear direction of, and responsible to, the elected government. Autonomous bureaucratic empires and unlimited managerial prerogatives are simply incompatible with the requirements of representative democracy. On the other hand, competent, efficient, fair and impartial administration demands that the public service be non-partisan; above all, the recruitment of public employees must be based on merit rather than political acceptability. At some point these twin imperatives of political control and neutral competence will conflict.

Under the conventions and practices of the Westminster system—a system within which the New Zealand model is still embedded—this conflict is focused in, and mediated through, the relationship between ministers and departmental CEs. The nature of this conflict is readily apparent in the provisions of the State Sector Act. Under this Act, CEs are responsible to the appropriate minister for 'carrying out the functions and duties' of their department (s. 32), but are quite explicitly not responsible to their minister for 'matters relating to decisions on individual employees' (s. 33). The problem, of course, is that matters concerning appointments, promotions, and dismissals can have political consequences—as was highlighted by the events surrounding the appointment of Frank Sharp in late 1994 to a position within Civil Defence by Perry Cameron (the CE of the Department of Internal Affairs). The details of this case need not concern us here (see Boston, 1994f). It is sufficient to note that tensions between matters of politics and matters of administration are as much a feature of the new model of public management as they were of the one it replaced. Moreover, such tensions are not limited to the central government. They arise equally in local government and in areas like school governance and health administration (see Chapters 8 and 9).

Control versus flexibility: the limits to discretion

The exercise of discretion is a fundamental and necessary feature of public management. In many areas it is impossible to draw up rules that can cover every contingency or direct officials on precisely how to behave in every situation they confront. And even where detailed rules can be devised, it might well be desirable—in terms of efficiency, flexibility, and sensitivity to the needs and circumstances of particular individuals—to provide substantial scope for individual discretion. After all, the exercise of professional judgment is a crucial feature of the delivery of many public services (e.g. education, health care, and social work services). Clinicians simply could not do their job if they were unable to exercise their personal judgment in diagnosing and treating patients. Quite apart from this, the use of discretion is an integral and desirable feature of regulation and law enforcement. If police officers are to operate independently of ministers, they must be allowed to make judgments about how to allocate the resources available to them, which offences should be investigated, which offenders should be prosecuted, and so on. And it goes without saying that judicial bodies must be able to act independently of the executive.

But if the use of discretion is unavoidable and often desirable, it also poses serious problems. To begin with, there is the issue of precisely how much discretion officials should be allowed to exercise (e.g. over the use of taxpayer funds). If parliamentary control over public expenditure is to be maximised, there are obvious limits to managerial discretion. Yet this might reduce efficiency and stifle innovation (see Chapter 13). Or to take another issue: while there is doubtless merit in allowing teachers to determine how a particular subject should be taught, should teachers be permitted to use any teaching technique? And how much discretion should they have in regard to *what* is taught? Another crucial difficulty relates to how those who exercise discretion should be held accountable. What kinds of monitoring and reporting mechanisms should there be? Should professional conduct be monitored solely by professionals or should lay people be involved? Furthermore, what appeal provisions should there be for those who believe that public officials have exercised their discretion unfairly or improperly? These problems arise irrespective of how a bureaucracy is structured, and regardless of the degree of centralisation or decentralisation of service provision. They remain abiding and important issues under New Zealand's new approach to public management (see Chapters 16 and 17).

Public services: diversity versus uniformity

All societies are pluralistic to one degree or another. They comprise people of different ethnic origins, languages, religious convictions, and ideological commitments. New Zealand is no exception. It provides a home for people from many different cultural backgrounds. Of particular importance is the Treaty of Waitangi (1840) and the obligations that it imposes on the Crown to respect and protect Māori customs, rights, and interests (see Chapters 3 and 7). Precisely how the state should fulfil these obligations has been the subject of intense and protracted public debate; doubtless this debate will continue for many years to come. At a minimum, however, the Treaty implies that Māori cultural norms and practices should be given greater weight and recognition in the public domain than those of non-indigenous minorities. It also imposes obligations on the state to ensure that Māori interests are properly represented in the policy-making process and that those responsible for delivering public services are adequately responsive to the specific requirements of their Māori clients.

Yet such conclusions raise immediate problems. What are the specific requirements of Māori clients and how can they best be met? Should the state rely on 'mainstream' public agencies to deliver services to Māori or should it establish separate (or parallel) public institutions for this purpose? Alternatively, should it contract with Māori tribes (iwi) to deliver publicly funded services? Irrespective of which option is chosen, should those charged with providing public services be required to meet certain standards of 'cultural safety', and if so, what standards should apply? More generally, is it possible for public organisations to cater for the needs of a particular cultural minority while simultaneously ensuring that all citizens are treated equitably, irrespective of their cultural background? In other words, is there not a conflict between the principle that all citizens should have equal rights and the principle that some citizens, by virtue of their particular ethnic origins, should receive different entitlements or at least entitlements delivered in different ways? If it is accepted that there is a conflict here—that it is impossible to marry uniformity and diversity, or equal citizenship rights and differential treatment—then, logically, trade-offs must be struck. But determining these trade-offs and doing so in a manner that maintains public confidence in the integrity and legitimacy of public institutions is no mean feat. The attempts of various New Zealand governments to address such problems will be considered in Chapter 7.

Centralisation versus decentralisation

The relative merits of centralisation and decentralisation have been long debated (see Chapter 8). The issues here are multiple and complex. At the broadest level, there are important constitutional questions concerning how many levels of government there should be. For example, does a unitary state have net advantages or disadvantages relative to a federal state? And regardless of whether the state is of a unitary or federal nature, is there a need for both regional and territorial government? Further, if it is decided, as in New Zealand, to have two tiers of government—central and local (the latter comprising regional and territorial)—which public functions should be assigned to each tier, which tier(s) should have taxing powers, and should overlapping responsibilities be encouraged or discouraged? More narrowly, there is the question of how individual public agencies should be structured, and in particular whether they should be relatively centralised or decentralised in their management practices.

In determining the appropriate degree of centralisation, various values are in tension. Advocates of centralisation, for example, point to its advantages in terms of ensuring uniform and consistent national standards, minimising regional, ethnic and social inequalities, minimising the duplication of services, and enabling the twin political responsibilities of taxation and expenditure to be closely coupled. By contrast, advocates of decentralisation contend that it enhances local (and regional) autonomy, facilitates greater diversity and choice, avoids undue concentrations of power, and enables citizens to participate more fully in the conduct of public affairs.

Since the abolition of the provinces in 1876, New Zealand has been a unitary state and highly centralised by international standards. Most major state functions are the responsibility of the central government, including social welfare, health care, and education. Despite the reforms since the mid 1980s, little has changed in this regard. Most public funds are still raised and expended at the national level, and the central government provides little funding to sub-national government. But if genuine devolution to sub-national government has not been a significant feature of the new model of public management, there has been considerable administrative decentralisation *within* the central government. Responsibility for human resources management, for instance, has been transferred from the State Services Commission to individual departments and most departments have, in turn, devolved their personnel functions to lower administrative levels (see Chapters 8 and 10).

Straight-line versus dual accountability

It is a widely accepted maxim, certainly among proponents of agency theory, that agents should never be accountable to more than one principal. Dual accountability, it is argued, places agents in the invidious position of having to balance the often conflicting demands and expectations of their respective principals. It can also exacerbate the problems facing principals with regard to contract specification, monitoring, and enforcement. In short, dual accountability is seen as inimical to clear lines of accountability and efficient management. Accordingly, New Zealand's public sector reforms were designed, wherever possible, to eliminate multiple accountability relationships. Thus, for example, area health boards—which were simultaneously accountable to their constituents and their principal funder, the central government—were abolished (see Chapter 8). But the quest for straight-line principal–agent relationships has not been a complete success; nor has it been possible to implement in a thoroughgoing fashion.

To start with, New Zealand's constitutional arrangements make it impossible to completely avoid dual or overlapping accountability relationships. Departmental CEs may be primarily accountable to a single portfolio minister, but they operate within a collective system of government and hence are accountable to the Prime Minister and cabinet (see Chapter 5). What is more, they are also subject to the scrutiny of the three central agencies (the Department of Prime Minister and Cabinet, the Treasury, and the State Services Commission), the Audit Office, and parliamentary select committees (see Chapters 15 and 17).

Another problem with the drive to root out all forms of dual accountability is that certain public functions are best undertaken in partnership with the relevant stakeholders. Schools, for example, have much to gain from close parental involvement and support. There is thus a strong case for parental representation on school boards. Yet if schools are to remain publicly funded, there will inevitably be tensions between the wishes of the democratically elected boards and the objectives of their paymaster—the central government (see Chapter 8).

The design of governance structures, therefore, must take a variety of considerations into account. Straight-line accountability relationships clearly have their merits, but to impose them universally throughout the public sector might undermine important constitutional principles and social objectives. The crucial question, then, is not how to eliminate dual accountability but how public organisations can be structured and managed so as to secure the benefits of multiple accountabilities while avoiding, or at least minimising, their drawbacks.

Strategic coherence versus fragmentation

Coordination among organisations that are formally autonomous but functionally interdependent is one of the keys to ensuring effectiveness in public management. Managing an *interorganisational* network is a complex task. The challenge of building interorganisational cooperation in a turbulent and complex environment 'implies a very significant expansion of the role of management in government beyond the sphere where existing business management methods can be applied more or less directly' (Metcalfe, 1993, p. 303). In particular, it requires strategic thinking, comprehensive rather than piecemeal actions, and processes of organisational learning that help policy-makers to cope with complexity (see Chapter 6).

One of the distinctive features of the New Zealand model has been the preference for single-mission organisations. Many of them have taken the form of Crown entities, one step removed from ministerial oversight, and placed in competition with private providers. The rationale is that single-purpose agencies, particularly if operating in a contestable environment, are more focused, efficient, and effective and the risks of provider capture are minimised. However, contracting out to a host of single-purpose entities in a competitive market tends to encourage separateness rather than interdependence. Within the remaining 'core' public service, the contract-based reporting framework—with its emphasis on individual ministers and CEs, and on the outputs of individual departments (not to mention competition for human resources heightened by the new CE responsibilities in this area)—might reinforce any trends towards 'departmentalism' (i.e. the breakdown of a hitherto unified public service into atomistic units). Left to itself, a 'market' approach to operating the public sector might not deal adequately with problems of collective action such as macroeconomic management, environmental protection, regional development, the advancement of knowledge, or determining trade-offs in the supply of social services such as health care or education. The challenge is to secure the advantages of single-purpose organisations and distancing from political interference while maintaining strategic coherence and protecting the government's collective interests.

Measuring performance in the absence of a bottom line

The new model of public management is built largely around the notion of performance. Improving the efficiency and effectiveness of public institutions was a central plank of the reforms. An organisation's effectiveness is measured by the extent to which it accomplishes its objectives, while its efficiency is measured by the relationship between inputs and outputs. In a purely commercial organisation, the amount of profit incorporates within it a great many separate aspects of performance that have been translated into a common denominator (i.e. dollars) to provide a single overall measure of both efficiency and effectiveness. Furthermore, it provides a single criterion that can be used to evaluate alternative courses of action, permits a quantitative analysis of those proposals in which benefits can be compared with costs, and facilitates comparison among entities that are performing dissimilar functions.

In non-profit organisations, where objectives cannot be expressed primarily in monetary terms, performance measurement is much more difficult. Throughout the world, governmental activities have been found hard to quantify or measure in a manner that would enable performance to be assessed and governments and their agents to be held accountable. In New Zealand, much effort has been expended, especially since the late 1980s, in devising meaningful performance measures for public agencies. Departmental programmes, for instance, have been reclassified as outputs and the nature of these outputs has been specified with increasing clarity and sophistication (see Chapter 13). Despite this, serious performance assessment issues remain. A good example is the provision of policy advice. Departmental policy outputs are now assessed in terms of their quantity, quality, and cost. But even if quantity and cost can be measured (and the latter is difficult enough, given cost allocation problems in situations of interdependency), assessing the quality of a piece of policy advice is even more subjective. Measuring the performance of the government as a whole presents theoretical and practical difficulties that severely limit the extent to which a rational measurement-based approach can be followed. In short, while the New Zealand model demonstrates the potential for greatly improved performance specification within the public sector, it also highlights the limitations of measurement for accountability purposes. Moreover, it explains some of the difficulties we have encountered in preparing this book in trying to evaluate the success of the new model.

The duties of public servants

It is sometimes suggested that the sole duty of public servants is to serve their minister (or ministers). Hence, if their minister asks for something to be done, the officials should perform the required task, and do so efficiently, expeditiously, and to the best of their ability. Such a view, however, requires qualification (see Chapter 16). Public servants have a range of duties, and sometimes these duties conflict. They have a responsibility not merely to serve their individual portfolio minister (or ministers) but also to serve the government as a whole. And sometimes the requirements of particular ministers might conflict with those of their cabinet colleagues. As with other citizens, public servants have an obligation to obey the law. Thus, if a minister requests that something be done that is unlawful, public servants must draw this to the minister's attention and refuse to carry out the instruction. Many writers on public administration have also argued that officials have an obligation to serve the 'public interest' or the 'common good'. Needless to say, such a suggestion immediately prompts various questions: What is the public interest? Is it not the task of the government to determine what is in the public interest? And does a public servant have a right to challenge the government's view as to what is in the public interest? There are no easy answers to such questions. Yet they are as pertinent for those serving under the new model of public management as under the old.

CONCLUSION

Despite the massive changes in the principles and practice of public management in New Zealand since the mid 1980s, the central issues of governance remain fundamentally the same. The preceding discussion has highlighted just a few of these continuing themes and dilemmas. There are, of course, many others: How can adequate political control of the bureaucracy be achieved? How should departmental CEs be appointed, remunerated, and assessed? How can the strategic management capabilities of the government be strengthened? What are the limits to contracting out? How can corruption be minimised? And how can values such as justice or equity be adequately protected in a public management environment characterised by ever-present fiscal constraints and an overriding emphasis on efficiency?

In addition to addressing questions of this nature, subsequent chapters outline and assess the origins, nature, and implications of New Zealand's new model of public management. As well as describing the details of the reforms, particular attention is given to the theories that influenced their development and the constitutional framework within which public management is conducted. The overall objective is to provide a balanced analysis of the New Zealand model—its strengths and weaknesses, benefits and costs, successes and failures. The book concludes with a brief discussion of the lessons of the New Zealand model for other countries.

2 the ideas and theories underpinning the new zealand model

New Zealand's remarkable wave of public sector reform during the mid to late 1980s was the product of a unique convergence of economic pressures and political opportunities. As in many other advanced industrialised democracies, public indebtedness, fiscal imperatives, and the resultant need for a much more efficient public sector were decisive influences (Schwartz, 1994). Also important was the general ideological shift to the Right and the consequent preference for a smaller public sector and a more extensive reliance on market mechanisms—contracting out, commercialisation, corporatisation, and privatisation. Yet another influence was the quest for greater political control over the bureaucracy and greater accountability of the executive to Parliament (see Palmer, 1979).

But while the political desire for bureaucratic reform was strong and the economic imperatives undeniable, one of the distinctive and most striking features of New Zealand's public management reforms was the way they were shaped by certain bodies of economic and administrative theory. Particularly influential in this regard were public choice theory, organisational economics—especially agency theory and transaction-cost economics (TCE)—and managerialism or the new public management (NPM) (Althaus, 1994; Boston, 1988a, 1995b; Hood, 1990b; Scott and Gorringe, 1989). The chief institution for the mediation and advocacy of these ideas, and their translation into specific policy proposals, was the Treasury (1984, 1987). This is not to suggest that other theoretical traditions had no influence on the nature of the reforms. Property-rights theory, neo-classical theory, game theory, and the burgeoning field of law and economics, for instance, also shaped the Treasury's analytical framework and policy proposals. Nor should the influence of the Treasury be exaggerated. Other departments, most notably the State Services Commission, also made important contributions to the reform agenda, as did various politicians, academics, and business leaders. Moreover, although theories of the kind mentioned played a crucial role, numerous other factors also influenced the scope, nature, and timing of the reforms: pragmatic judgments by ministers about what was likely to be feasible and politically acceptable, parliamentary and interest group pressures, the experience of other countries (particularly Australia and Britain), and New Zealand's political traditions, constitutional conventions, cultural heritage, and administrative history.

Although public choice theory and managerialism have influenced policy developments in many other countries since the early 1980s, the same is less true of organisational economics (or the new institutional economics, as it is sometimes called). In this respect, the intellectual origins of New Zealand's reforms are distinctive and deserve careful scrutiny. Hence, this chapter examines the main theories that influenced the reforms and considers their strengths and weaknesses.

Public Choice Theory

Public choice theory, variously referred to as social choice theory, rational choice theory, the economics of politics, and the Virginia School, has had an immense impact on political science, public policy and public administration during the past three decades (Mitchell, 1988; Self, 1993). Among the seminal works in the field are those by James Buchanan and Gordon Tullock (1962), Anthony Downs (1957, 1967), William Niskanen (1971), Mancur Olson (1965) and Gordon Tullock (1965). As McLean (1986) notes, public choice theory has focused on four major themes: the problem of aggregating individual preferences; studies of formal social choice, focusing particularly on the spatial theory of voting; studies that focus on individuals as rational actors (voters, politicians, bureaucrats, lobbyists, etc.) and seek to explain how these actors will behave in different institutional settings with different incentive structures; and the analysis of collective action problems (i.e. problems that arise because the pursuit of individual interests produces suboptimal outcomes for the collectivity).

The central tenet of the public choice approach is that all human behaviour is dominated by self-interest. Individuals, in other words, are rational utility maximisers. As Buchanan puts it:

> . . . in one sense, all of public choice or the economic theory of politics, may be summarized as the 'discovery' or 'rediscovery' that people should be treated as rational utility maximizers of all their behavioural capacities (1978, p. 17).

Hence, just as businesses supposedly seek to maximise their profits, government officials are believed to maximise their departmental budgets (Niskanen, 1971), while politicians seek to maximise their votes (Downs, 1957). To quote Self:

> Following this approach, voters can be likened to consumers; pressure groups can be seen as political consumer associations or sometimes as co-operatives; political parties become entrepreneurs who offer competing packages of services and taxes in exchange for votes; political propaganda equates with commercial advertising; and government agencies are public firms dependent upon receiving or drumming up adequate political support to cover their costs (1985, p. 51).

Accordingly, suggestions that politicians are primarily concerned with societal well-being or the common good, or that they and their advisers are guided by fundamental ethical precepts, are treated with scepticism by many public choice theorists. Further, concepts like 'public spirit', 'public service', and the 'public interest have not figured very prominently in the public choice literature (see Kelman, 1987; Mansbridge, 1990;

Tullock, 1984). This is partly because they are thought to lack meaning or relevance and partly because they can too readily be used to give legitimacy to the demands of sectional interest groups.

While public choice theorists accept that the pursuit of self-interest in the *economic* marketplace can be expected (with a few notable exceptions) to yield socially desirable outcomes, many argue that similar behaviour in the *political* marketplace can have damaging consequences. For example, politicians will pursue their own particular objectives at the expense of many of their constituents. Interest groups will engage in rent-seeking behaviour to the disadvantage of the wider community. And government officials, in their attempts to expand their budgets, will acquire an ever-increasing quantity of resources (Niskanen, 1971). As a result, the state will grow well beyond what is necessary to guarantee national security, maintain law and order, and satisfy voter preferences. Individual liberty will be undermined. Powerful interest groups will capture a disproportionate share of national income. And institutional rigidities will be created, thereby reducing economic growth (see Olson, 1982).

Such analyses have led many public choice theorists to endorse relatively conservative political agendas (e.g. minimising the role of the state, selling the state's commercial assets, curbing the functions of government agencies, and maximising liberty—understood in the limited sense of freedom from state coercion).[1] Further, because politicians can be expected to abuse their power, it is argued that they should be prevented, if necessary through constitutional changes, from running budget deficits or imposing taxes beyond a certain level (Brennan and Buchanan, 1980, 1985; Buchanan, 1987). Similarly, because departments have a vested interest in their own survival, they should not both tender advice and implement policy (Treasury, 1987, pp. 75–6). Otherwise, their advice will be biased and bureaucratic capture might occur (see Chapter 4). Finally, all services provided by the state should be made as contestable as possible.

Agency Theory

Agency theory rests on the notion that social and political life can be understood as a series of 'contracts' (or agreed relationships) in which one party, referred to as the principal, enters into exchanges with another party, referred to as the agent.[2] In accordance with such contracts, the agent undertakes to perform various tasks on behalf of the prin-

---

1. While the 'mainstream' public choice literature has tended to advocate a diminished role for the state, a small but growing body of scholars have used public choice assumptions to draw quite different policy conclusions (see Self, 1993, pp. 16–20).
2. The literature on agency theory, including that directly related to the public sector, is now extensive. See, for instance, Althäus (1994), Bendor (1988), Bergman and Lane (1990), Braun (1993), Chan and Rosenbloom (1994), Heymann (1988), Jennings and Cameron (1987), Jensen and Meckling (1976), Kay (1992), Levinthal (1988), Moe (1984, 1990, 1991), Palmer (1993), Perrow (1986a, 1986b), Petersen (1993), Pratt and Zeckhauser (1985), Rees (1985a, 1985b), Simon (1991), Thompson and Wright (1988), Trebilcock (1995), Weingast (1984), and B. Wood (1989).

cipal and in exchange the principal agrees to reward the agent in a mutually acceptable way. A principal might seek out an agent for many reasons. Perhaps the principal lacks the skills, expertise, or specialised knowledge required to perform a task. Alternatively, the very nature of the task might demand a team effort. Whatever the precise reason, it is generally connected to the efficiencies which arise from specialisation and the division of labour.

Initially, agency theory was applied primarily to the problems arising from the separation of ownership and control in firms, especially the difficulty of ensuring that managers act in the interests of their shareholders. However, it was soon recognised that agency problems of this nature are a central feature of social, economic, and political life. As Jensen and Meckling observe:

> The problem of inducing an 'agent' to behave as if he [or she] were maximizing the 'principal's' welfare is quite general. It exists in all organizations and in all co-operative efforts—at every level of management in firms, in universities, in mutual companies, in co-operatives, in governmental authorities and bureaus, in unions, and in relationships normally classified as agency relationships such as are common in the performing arts and the market for real estate (1976, p. 309).

To mention a few examples: in an employer–employee relationship, the employer is the principal and the worker is the agent; in a lawyer–client relationship, the client is the principal and the lawyer is the agent; and in the political realm, voters can be regarded as principals who contract with politicians (their agents) to undertake a range of tasks and activities on their behalf (Weingast, 1984). Indeed, as Moe observes:

> . . . the whole of politics can be seen as a chain of principal–agent relationships, from citizen to politician to bureaucratic superior to bureaucratic subordinate and on down the hierarchy of government to the lowest-level bureaucrats who actually deliver services directly to citizens. Aside from the ultimate principal and the ultimate agent, each actor in the hierarchy occupies a dual role in which he [or she] serves both as principal and as agent (1984, p. 765).

Agency theory, like public choice theory and neo-classical economic theory, assumes that individuals are rational, self-interested, utility maximisers. Hence, the interests of agents and principals are bound to conflict. Moreover, the management of many principal–agent relationships is complicated by incomplete information, asymmetrical information, and various uncertainties: agents generally have access to information that principals do not (and vice versa) and have an incentive to exploit this situation to their advantage; the behaviour of agents is often difficult for principals to observe; and there are frequently uncertainties surrounding the way an agent's actions are translated into the outputs (or outcomes) sought by a principal. A good deal of agency theory, therefore, is concerned with determining—given various assumptions about the information available to the respective parties and the nature of the task to be undertaken—the optimal form of contracting, including the best way of motivating agents (e.g. via rewards and sanctions) (Rees, 1985a). Put differently, the aim is to find the most satisfactory way of negotiating, specifying, and monitoring contracts so as to minimise the likelihood of violations resulting from opportunism on the part of the agent (e.g. due to shirking, deception, cheating, and collusion). Interestingly, despite the fact that principals are also thought to be opportunistic, agency theorists have paid much less attention to this side of the equation (Gorringe, 1987).

Note that the term 'contract' is interpreted very broadly by agency theorists. For instance, it may refer to a 'classical' (or arms-length) contract—i.e. a formal, explicit, often comprehensive, and legally binding contract, such as a lease agreement or an insurance policy (see Martin, 1995a, p. 39). Alternatively, it may refer to an implicit, obligational, or 'relational' contract (Williamson, 1985, p. 72). Such contracts tend to be relatively open-ended and incomplete (e.g. a marriage); in fact, they may amount to little more than a loose understanding. They usually assume a high degree of cooperation between the parties and a commitment to a long-term (trading) relationship. Mutual trust, rather than legal sanctions, is thus a crucial ingredient.

Principals have a number of options available to them in trying to ensure that an agent acts in accordance with their interests: they can use various kinds of incentives and sanctions to align the agent's interests more closely with their own; they can closely monitor the behaviour of the agent; or they can enter into a bonding arrangement whereby the agent gives a guarantee to act in line with the principals' interests or provide compensation if the contract is breached (Heymann, 1988, p. 17). The crucial point is that each of these methods—incentives, monitoring, and bonding—imposes costs on the principal (referred to as agency costs).[3] Such costs will obviously rise according to the extent of the divergence between the interests of the agent and those of the principal.

Two concepts have received particular emphasis in the literature on agency problems: adverse selection and moral hazard. Adverse selection arises from a particular kind of information asymmetry that might exist prior to the negotiation of a contract. The essential problem is that some of the information that a principal wants to know about an agent is difficult to observe. Consequently, the agent has an information advantage over the principal. Choosing people to fill job vacancies provides a good illustration of this phenomenon. In such cases many crucial aspects of the applicant's ability and character will be unknown to the employer (e.g. his or her intelligence, beliefs, values, attitude, work habits, and creativity). To be sure, the employer might have access to various indicators of the applicant's capability (e.g. qualifications, work record, references, etc.), but they might provide an inadequate, or even inaccurate, guide. Thus, the employer cannot know for certain each applicant's true 'type' and cannot be sure of choosing the best person for the job. Conversely, the best applicant is not in a position to demonstrate that they are in fact the best because all the applicants have an incentive to present themselves in a positive light in order to secure the job. In this situation, then, the employer risks making an adverse selection. Of course, employees also face the dilemma of not knowing the employer's true 'type'. Hence, they might also make an adverse selection.

---

3. Agency costs also include the cost of enforcing contracts and residual losses arising from the fact that agents invariably fail to act as a perfect proxy for the principal.

Whereas adverse selection arises because of asymmetrical information in the pre-contract situation, moral hazard derives from the unobservability of the agent's behaviour once a contract has been negotiated (Moe, 1984, p. 755). For example, in most jobs, certainly in the core public sector, it is impossible to measure accurately the marginal product of each worker. Employers might attempt to measure their employees' output by relying on proxies of performance, such as the reports of supervisors. However, this might generate goal-displacing behaviour; that is to say, employees will have an incentive to do well in those aspects of the job that are rigorously monitored but shirk where the monitoring is less rigorous. There is no easy or complete solution to this problem.

Agency theory is useful in analysing a range of policy issues, particularly those concerned with the selection of agents, the design of remuneration systems (e.g. output-based versus input-based reward systems, direct incentives like piece-rates versus indirect incentives like career structures, etc.), and the choice of institutional arrangements (e.g. in-house provision versus contracting out). Consider, for instance, the question of how police services should be provided (Moe, 1984, p. 760). Plainly, the problems of adverse selection, moral hazard, and monitoring outputs are severe in the area of policing: it is difficult to assess the merits and motivation of those wishing to serve in a police force; many of the outputs of the job are hard to measure; many of the tasks undertaken are difficult to monitor; and the state's objectives (such as good race relations, keeping the peace, and effective crime detection) are difficult to operationalise and sometimes conflict. Given this situation, it would be risky to contract out basic law enforcement functions to private organisations. Instead, there is a strong case for creating a public agency to provide policing services. This will not solve the problems mentioned above, but will certainly help to minimise them (e.g. through rigorous screening of recruits, comprehensive training programmes, and detailed monitoring of outputs by both internal and external units).

Transaction-Cost Economics

Although transaction-cost economics (TC
approaches differ somewhat in their focus
is primarily concerned with the contract f
focuses on the selection and motivation of
optimal governance structures for various l
of organising the production and exchang
is concerned with the governance of persc
focus is the exchange of physical goods. Tc
(1985, p. 2), TCE entails 'an examination
and monitoring task completion under alt
versus markets). Rational agents, he conte
imise their aggregate production and tran

The concept of transaction costs is clo:
(1985, p. 20, p. 388) distinguishes two
Ex ante transaction costs are those arisin

due to asset specificity (see below) and opportunism, including drafting, negotiating, and safeguarding a contract. By contrast, *ex post* transaction costs are the costs of altering contracts to correct *ex post* misalignments, the costs of setting up and maintaining governance structures, and the costs of bonding to guarantee contractual commitments. These costs are in turn distinguished from normal production costs (although the distinction is not always tightly drawn).

Like agency theory, TCE assumes that principals and agents are opportunistic: that is to say, they are prone to 'self-interest seeking with guile' (Williamson, 1985, p. 45). As a result, the parties to a contract might be unreliable, and might engage in rent-seeking behaviour and other forms of self-interested behaviour (cheating, shirking, lying, deceiving, promise breaking, the incomplete or distorted disclosure of information, etc.). The danger posed by opportunism will depend on the *willingness* and *capacity* of the contracting parties to pursue private gain (e.g. by breaching the terms of a contract, by exploiting their bargaining power in the event that the contract fails to cover all the possible contingencies, or by exploiting their bargaining power when a new contract falls due (Vining and Weimer, 1990, p. 6). Whether individuals are *willing* to act opportunistically will no doubt be influenced, at least in part, by their normative commitments and values system. Hence, where shirking or cheating are regarded as acceptable forms of behaviour, they are more likely to occur. The *capacity* of principals and agents to behave opportunistically, on the other hand, will depend on a range of structural or environmental conditions. They include the degree of uncertainty and the existence (or otherwise) of information asymmetries, bounded rationality, asset specificity, and small-numbers bargaining. It might be desirable at this juncture to clarify the meaning of some of these concepts.

Williamson (1985, p. 58) identifies two types of uncertainty: general uncertainty (which refers to the absence of perfect information and difficulties in measuring organisational performance) and behavioural uncertainty (which refers to a lack of confidence in the reliability of one of the parties to a contract). The concept of bounded rationality, which owes its origins to the work of Simon (1947), rests on the observation that individuals neither have the capacity to gather all the information and knowledge necessary for optimal decision-making nor the cognitive ability to process such information as is available. Hence, rather than making optimal choices, boundedly rational individuals ge in what Simon refers to as 'satisficing' behaviour. That is to say, the inherent ns on decision-making encourage people to behave according to well-outines, patterns, and rules, to seek predictability and certainty in organised vironments, and to be highly selective in the range of information upon n making choices. As the complexity and uncertainty of a situation he limits imposed on individuals by their bounded rationality and

erature on transaction-cost analysis see Boston (1994a), Bryson 1987), Vining and Weimer (1990), and Williamson (1975, of transaction costs arising from contracting within the nd Ashton (1994).

trees exhaustively in advance, and deriving the corresponding contingent prices, events are permitted to unfold and attention is restricted to only the actual rather than all possible outcomes (1975, p. 25).

Hood and Jackson (1991, p. 86) advance a similar view. Direct provision, they claim, 'allows for greater flexibility because informal evidence can be used, a quasi-moral element can be introduced into relationships among producers, nuances of direction can be developed which it would be impossible to put into a written contract, and otherwise costly litigation can be avoided'.

To the extent that in-house provision lessens the risk of opportunism, it can be expected to enhance product reliability and dependability. Accordingly, direct provision may well be preferable wherever maintaining the quality of a good or service is critical (i.e. in terms of human health and safety, or national security) and opportunism poses a serious risk. Such considerations help explain why governments are normally reluctant to contract out certain tasks like security patrols, the gathering of military intelligence, the transportation of dangerous goods (e.g. nuclear weapons), and the collection of taxes and customs (Hood and Jackson, 1991, p. 87).

Of course, in-house provision does not guarantee a satisfactory outcome. The risks of opportunism may be reduced but not eliminated entirely. To compound matters, large, hierarchical organisations like public bureaucracies can encounter a range of problems, including poor coordination, organisational slack, and the distortion of information, either accidentally or deliberately, as it flows up and down the hierarchy. Ministers also face a range of problems monitoring the behaviour of, and exercising effective control over, their bureaucratic agents (Banks and Weingast, 1992; Bergman and Lane, 1990; McCubbins, Noll, and Weingast, 1987; Niskanen, 1971; B. Wood, 1989). Difficulties of this nature could negate the possible efficiency gains from in-house provision. Finally, if there are economies of scope, scale, or learning from contracting out, then vertical integration might entail higher production costs.

Managerialism and the New Public Management

Driven primarily by practitioners and private sector consultants rather than academics or theoreticians, managerialism has had a significant impact, especially since the mid to late 1980s, on public administration in many OECD countries, not least New Zealand (see Aucoin, 1990; Caiden, 1988; Davis, Weller, and Lewis, 1989; Gunn, 1988; Hood, 1995). Its slogans include the now familiar 'Let the Managers Manage' and 'Managing for Results'. The essence of managerialism lies in the assumption that there is 'something called "management" which is a generic, purely instrumental activity, embodying a set of principles that can be applied to the public business, as well as in private business' (Painter, 1988, p. 1). Such an assumption is not new. Its origins can be traced to at least the late nineteenth century and the pioneering work of Frederick Winslow Taylor— the founder of 'scientific' management or Taylorism. Since the mid 1980s, the ideas of the older managerialist tradition have received new life and have been influenced in various ways by, among other things, public choice theory and organisational economics.

The resulting convergence of intellectual currents has produced what Aucoin (1990) and Hood (1990a, 1990b, 1995) have referred to as the 'New Public Management' (NPM). The features of the NPM have been variously catalogued by different scholars. However, they are generally thought to embrace the following:

a. a belief that, at least from the standpoint of management, the differences between the public and private sectors are not generally significant; hence public and private organisations can, and should, be managed on more or less the same basis;

b. a shift in emphasis from process accountability to accountability for results (e.g. a move away from input controls and bureaucratic procedures, rules, and standards to a greater reliance on quantifiable output (or outcome) measures and performance targets);

c. an emphasis on management rather than policy, in particular a new stress on generic management skills;

d. the devolution of management control coupled with the development of improved reporting, monitoring, and accountability mechanisms;

e. the disaggregation of large bureaucratic structures into quasi-autonomous agencies, in particular the separation of commercial from non-commercial functions and policy advice from delivery and regulatory functions;

f. a preference for private ownership, contestable provision, and the contracting out of most publicly funded services;

g. a shift from relational to classical modes of contracting (i.e. from long-term and generally poorly specified contracts to shorter-term and much more tightly specified contracts);

h. the imitation of certain private sector management practices such as the use of short-term labour contracts, the development of strategic plans, corporate plans, performance agreements, and mission statements, the introduction of performance-linked remuneration systems, the development of new management information systems, and a greater concern for corporate image;

i. a preference for monetary incentives rather than non-monetary incentives, such as ethics, ethos, and status; and

j. a stress on cost-cutting, efficiency, and cutback management.[5]

Of course, many of these ideas have a long pedigree, some having their origins in the works of Bentham and Chadwick in the nineteenth century. What is new about the NPM is the way in which these ideas have been combined, the manner of their implementation and the vigour with which they have been pursued.

THE INFLUENCE OF THESE THEORIES IN NEW ZEALAND

Assessing the influence of particular ideas, assumptions, theories, and models on a series of policy changes poses many difficulties. In any given policy setting there are usually numerous forces at work, not to mention a range of political, institutional, and technical constraints.

---

5. A more detailed list of the doctrines of the NPM is set out in Hood and Jackson (1991, pp. 182–3).

In most situations, therefore, it is impossible to ascertain with any precision the impact of specific ideas, theoretical insights, or schools of thought on the process of policy development and implementation. This is certainly the case when it comes to assessing the influence of the various theoretical approaches outlined above on New Zealand's public sector reforms. That they were influential there can be no doubt (Althaus, 1994; Johnson, 1994). But precisely when, where, and to what extent they made a difference is much harder to determine. Having said this, the following tentative judgments can be offered.

To start with, public choice theory—with its emphasis on the budget-maximising behaviour of bureaucrats, its suspicion of politicians' motives, and its concern over provider capture—undoubtedly influenced the climate of opinion within which the development of the New Zealand model occurred. For instance, the drive to separate the provision of policy advice from policy implementation and regulation was inspired at least partly by the public choice tradition (see Chapter 4). The same is probably also true of the creation, especially during the fourth Labour government, of larger political staffs in ministerial offices and the subsequent appointment of purchase advisers (so that ministers have alternative sources of policy advice and an enhanced capacity to monitor their departments).

Other signs of the influence of public choice theory include the emphasis on transparency (e.g. in the area of state subsidies and other political interventions), the various attempts to curb the role of vested interests in governmental policy-making (Treasury, 1987, pp. 44–5), and the efforts to reduce the scope for political interference in certain policy domains (e.g. monetary policy). Arguably, both the Reserve Bank Act 1989 and the Fiscal Responsibility Act 1994 (see Chapter 14) were prompted at least partly by public choice considerations.

Similarly, agency theory played an important role in developing the policy framework that underpinned the corporatisation and privatisation programmes (see Jennings and Cameron, 1987). It also influenced thinking on matters relating to employment relations, incentive structures, remuneration systems, and performance management, contributing, for instance, to the move to fixed-term employment contracts for senior public servants, the emphasis on the relationship between ministers and departmental CEs (Scott and Gorringe, 1989), and the introduction of CE performance agreements and monitoring arrangements (see Chapter 5; Boston, 1992c). In addition, insights drawn from agency theory have helped fashion policies relating to institutional design and governance arrangements. A good example was the reliance placed on agency theory in developing an analytical framework to evaluate the role and structure of the Audit Office (see Chapter 15). The specific influence of TCE is harder to discern, but arguably the heightened interest in various forms of contracting stems partly from this source. Also, the concepts underpinning TCE, such as asset specificity, bounded rationality, opportunism and transaction costs, have been widely used, especially by the Treasury, in formulating policy on issues of institutional design.

Finally, the influence of the NPM has been evident both in the way policy debates over public sector reform have been conducted and in the specific policies which have been advocated and/or introduced. Policy discourse, for instance, has been characterised by a frequent resort to private sector analogies and commercial models to explain or critique public sector arrangements. Thus, government agencies have been seen as businesses; ministers have been likened to board chairpersons and departmental heads to chief executives; the central agencies have been depicted as a firm's corporate office; and taxpayers have been seen as shareholders. In terms of policy decisions, there is a remarkably close fit between the doctrines of the NPM and the New Zealand model—the shift from process to output accountability (see Chapter 13); the devolution of managerial control (see Chapters 8 and 10); the disaggregation of large bureaucratic structures (see Chapter 4); the preference for private ownership and contracting out (see Chapters 3, 4, 6 and 8); the emphasis on consumers (see Chapter 16); the emulation of many private sector management practices (see Chapters 5 and 11); and the emphasis on cost-cutting and labour discipline.

Of course, NPM doctrines have not been adopted willy-nilly or in an uncompromising fashion. Moreover, the manner in which some NPM doctrines have been applied in New Zealand differs significantly from their application in other countries. To illustrate, both Britain and New Zealand have embarked on machinery of government changes that are consistent with NPM doctrines (e.g. the separation of policy advice functions from operational responsibilities). However, the changes have taken very different forms. Under the 'Next Steps' programme in Britain, the new delivery agencies have generally remained within the umbrella of their parent department. In New Zealand, by contrast, there has been a preference for a clear-cut institutional separation. To take another example: the changes in public sector financial management in both Britain and New Zealand have been consistent with the NPM preference for output accountability over process accountability. Despite this, the reforms contain important conceptual differences. Britain's financial management changes, for instance, have not embraced some of the concepts that are at the heart of New Zealand's reforms (e.g. the distinction between outputs and outcomes, and the distinction between the Crown's purchase and ownership interests). For such reasons, many of the criticisms that have been levelled at the British version of the NPM do not necessarily apply to the New Zealand model.

Exactly why the various theories and approaches outlined above were embraced with such enthusiasm in New Zealand is a fascinating question. Clearly, part of the answer lies in the gathering together of a group of reform-minded policy analysts in the Treasury, their familiarity with the new institutional economics and public choice, and their sustained efforts to apply this literature to the problems of governance in the public sector (see Boston, 1995b; Choat, 1993). Of course, these efforts might well have been in vain had it not been for the openness of senior ministers to the Treasury's proposals and their willingness to implement them, notwithstanding the political risks involved.

A BRIEF ASSESSMENT OF THE FOUR APPROACHES

The remainder of this chapter offers a brief evaluation of each of the four approaches outlined above. In undertaking this task, it important to distinguish between, on the one hand, the merits of the ideas and theories in question and, on the other, the merits of the reforms that they influenced, prompted or inspired. Where criticisms are made of particular theories, it does not automatically follow that the policies to which they contributed are thereby flawed. After all, there are many steps in the causal chain between a theoretical insight and its eventual expression in a specific policy decision. Moreover, as indicated above, the policies comprising the New Zealand model were shaped by a multitude of factors; the theories under examination were but one set of influences.

Without doubt, public choice, agency theory, TCE, and the NPM have each contributed to our understanding of political and bureaucratic behaviour. As with all theoretical models and perspectives, they pose questions that might otherwise have been ignored. They provide a range of interesting insights and explanations as to why certain institutions exist and why they operate the way they do. And they have generated a substantial amount of research and empirical data. In New Zealand's case, one of their most positive affects has been to force policy-makers to rethink some of their previous assumptions and to explore new ways of organising and conducting the activities of the state. This is evident from the way that various policy questions have been redefined and the burden of proof has shifted. To take one example: instead of assuming that the bureaucracy should be designed to minimise competition and avoid duplication, it is now assumed that contestability and multiple supply arrangements are generally desirable.

Other insights and contributions which have flowed from the four approaches include:

a. the recognition of the importance of transaction costs (both within and between organisations) and the need to consider such costs in determining the relative merits of in-house provision versus contracting out;

b. the stress on institutional design, especially the need to consider such things as information asymmetries, uncertainty, opportunism, and incentives in devising appropriate governance structures;

c. the emphasis on improving managerial and political accountability, via greater clarity and transparency of ministerial goals and interventions, the tighter *ex ante* specification of desired departmental outputs, and improved *ex post* reporting and monitoring of performance;

d. the recognition of the dangers of producer capture, client capture, and rent-seeking behaviour, and of the need to employ countervailing strategies;

e. the recognition of the need to give greater attention to the consumers of public services and, where possible and appropriate, to satisfy their preferences; and

f. the need to rethink some of our existing constitutional arrangements and conventions and enhance the checks on the executive.

At the same time, each of the theories under consideration has important limitations and weaknesses. Some of them are discussed below.

Public Choice Theory

Public choice theory has been challenged on numerous grounds (see especially Barry, 1965; Dunleavy, 1991; Hoogerwerf, 1992; Self, 1993). Two criticisms deserve particular mention: the theory's implausible behavioural assumptions and its limited predictive power. First, the idea that competitive self-interest dominates human nature and that broader normative considerations, such as concern for others, are virtually irrelevant is highly questionable. To be sure, self-interest is a powerful, and sometimes dominant, motivation. Individuals, on occasion, can be opportunistic, guileful, self-serving, lazy, and quick to exploit others. But human beings are also influenced by many other motivations and values. Frequently people do not act opportunistically or violate contracts, even when the potential gains (both short and long-term) from shirking or free-riding are great. Bureaucrats are not solely interested in maximising their departmental budgets (if indeed this interests them at all). They are also influenced by such things as credibility, reputation, integrity, duty, professional standards, and doing a good job. Invariably, too, they have a wide range of policy preferences, and often these are strongly held. Similarly, the evidence does not support the claim that politicians are simply vote maximisers, untroubled and untouched by considerations of ideology, ethics, or the quest for a just society.

In short, human beings are not merely economic beings, but also political, cultural, and moral beings who inhabit an economic system that is profoundly influenced by, and in a sense dependent upon, the attitudes, habits, beliefs, aspirations, ideals, and ethical standards of its members. Any theory that downplays or ignores these broader contextual factors, social relations, and normative commitments is at best incomplete, and at worst misleading and damaging (see Aaron, 1994; Dore, 1983; Granovetter, 1985; Mansbridge, 1990; Sen, 1977, 1987; Stewart, 1993a). Thankfully, this is increasingly being recognised within the public choice tradition.

Another issue sometimes ignored by public choice theorists is whether it is better to limit opportunism or to take opportunism for granted and organise institutional and monitoring arrangements accordingly (Hood, 1986, pp. 109–13; Horn, 1988). Some argue that we have no choice: human behaviour, they contend, is immutable; it is not dependent upon or conditioned by contextual and environmental factors; it is not structurally determined. Therefore, we must take opportunism for granted and design our institutions accordingly. But empirical support for such a view is thin (Perrow, 1986a). Rather, the evidence suggests that while opportunistic behaviour cannot be eliminated, it can certainly be reduced, or at least modified, by a variety of institutional mechanisms. These include, to quote Hood:

(a) Accepting as employees only people who show signs of vocation or permanent calling to the work in question, as tested by rigorous scrutiny, screening and probation procedures, not casual job-hoppers momentarily attracted to the pay or the job.

(b) Lifetime career service (another facet of 'vocation'). This may encourage people to take a 'long view' which may limit opportunism, especially if allied to more or less automatic progression by seniority and 'cradle to grave' benefits from the employer. . . .

(c) Long induction and training procedures, to cultivate a sense of enterprise solidarity and to limit the grosser aspects of self-serving behaviour (1986, p. 110).

Needless to say, such measures might have negative side-effects. They might, as Hood puts it, exchange competence for loyalty, effectiveness for honesty, independent thought for group-think, analytic capacity for piety, capability for seniority. It may mean being too kind to employees with burnout, declining competence, skill obsolescence (or who are just plain fail-ures)—in short, to do without all the potential benefits of opportunism, in terms of dyna-mism, quick-wittedness, adaptivity (1986, pp. 111–12).

Doubtless, these negative aspects of traditional bureaucratic practices and procedures contributed to the quest for public sector reform in New Zealand. But a possible danger under the new order of things—particularly with the shift in emphasis from obligational or relational contracts to classical contracts, the growing reliance on short-term employ-ment contracts, the introduction of performance-related pay, the much greater use of outside consultants, the exalted position of managers, and so forth—is that the ethos of public service employment may be changed and narrowly self-interested behaviour encouraged (see Gregory, 1995a). The point here, as Hood (1992, p. 156) observes, is that replacing relational modes of contracting (based on high levels of trust) with classical contracts (which assume lower levels of trust) may actually reduce the degree of trust and commitment. Consequently, higher agency costs and transaction costs may be incurred. To compound problems, whereas trust can be quickly undermined, it can take years to rebuild (Sako, 1991). Thus, while it may be relatively easy to move from relational to classical contracting, it may be much more difficult to move back the other way.

For such reasons, policy-makers need to understand the role of intangible governance mechanisms, such as culture and ethics, and the way such mechanisms may be affected—positively or negatively—by changes in the mode of contracting. More gen-erally, it can be argued (see Jacobs, 1994; Ouchi, 1979) that organisations have at least three separate mechanisms available to them as they seek to achieve their goals and main-tain control: markets, hierarchies, and culture (or clans). By 'culture' one means, for example, employing individuals who have a strong commitment to the values, objec-tives, or mission of the organisation in question. Cultural mechanisms are arguably most important when it is difficult to measure individual or organisational performance—as is the case in many of the professions and large parts of the core public sector.

Ironically, the current intellectual ascendancy of public choice theory comes at a time when its explanatory power is declining. As many observers have noted, the policies of liberalisation and deregulation pursued by OECD countries during the 1980s run counter to the predictions of many public choice models (which generally assume that it is in the short-term electoral interests of politicians to promote tight regulation). Nor does a public choice perspective readily explain New Zealand's recent bureaucratic rev-olution (i.e. it is doubtful whether the reforms were solely, or even primarily, the prod-uct of self-interested politicians, advised by self-interested bureaucrats, seeking to please a self-interested electorate by self-interested means). Quite apart from this, the predic-tive power of public choice theory has been found wanting in many areas of social and political life.[6] For instance, it has difficulty explaining why people bother to vote, why they give to charities or donate blood, why they join 'public-regarding' cause groups which are devoted to the promotion of common interests, and why legislators often act contrary to the expressed preferences of their constituents. Niskanen's budget maximisation hypothesis has attracted particularly rigorous analysis and has received relatively little empirical support (Blais and Dion, 1991; Conybeare, 1984; Dollery and Hamburger, 1993). Contrary to Niskanen's analysis, the evidence suggests that in most bureaucracies there is little connection between the size of a department and its status or between the growth of departments and the salaries of their employees.

The implications of such conclusions for the study and conduct of public policy are open to debate. One clear inference, however, is the need for theories that take into account a wider range of considerations, particularly the importance of ideas and values, in explaining human behaviour and policy choices. Further, once the assumption that politicians, bureaucrats, and voters are wholly or exclusively self-interested is abandoned, the problem of provider capture need no longer occupy centre stage (though, of course, it should not be ignored). Thus, rather than focusing primarily on how to immunise the political system against the dangers posed by vested interests, more attention should be given to ensuring that the decision-making arrangements are open, democratic, and fair (i.e. that they provide an opportunity for all interests to be adequately represented). This has important implications for constitutional arrangements, the machinery of government, and the role of pressure groups in the policy-making process.

Agency Theory

Just as there are problems with the public choice model, so too there are weaknesses with agency theory (see Althaus, 1994; Bendor, 1988, 1990; Davis and Gardner, 1995; Donaldson, 1990a, 1990b; Moe, 1984, 1990; Perrow, 1986a, 1986b; Petersen, 1993). Some of them are identical to those affecting public choice theory (e.g. the limitations of the assumption that agents are self-interested and dislike effort, the failure to take contextual factors—such as ethics and culture—sufficiently into account, and the tendency to treat politics as if it were identical to, or simply an extension of, economics). But there are also many other areas of criticism:

a. Agency theorists have tended to ignore the question of power and authority in human relationships. They have also focused much more on the problems posed by opportunistic agents than opportunistic principals. Thus, little attention has been given to how principals might misrepresent their 'type' and thereby mislead or exploit their agents.
b. The use of simple agent–principal models to describe and analyse complex social interactions and constitutional relationships can be misleading and inappropriate. In particular, such models cope poorly with situations where agents serve multiple and

---

6. See, for instance, Barry (1970), Bendor and Moe (1985), Blais and Dion (1991), Borins (1988), Boyne (1987), Conybeare (1984), Foster (1994), Heymann (1988), Hood, Huby and Dunsire (1984), Lane (1987), Mansbridge (1990), McGuire (1981), Miller and Moe (1983), Quiggan (1987), and Self (1985, 1989, 1993).

competing principals or where there is disagreement over who the principal ought to be.

c. Many principal–agent relationships in the public sector have a distinctive character. This is partly because the managerial disciplines supplied by private capital markets do not usually apply; it is also because public authority and coercive power play a crucial role within the governmental sphere such that many exchanges and 'contracts' are involuntary. For these reasons, familiar principal–agent relationships are transformed into 'something that is provocatively different from . . . straightforward applications' (Moe, 1990, p. 232).

d. Even where agent–principal models are relevant to the interactions under examination, the policy implications of agency theory are often unclear. Further, one of the key policy recommendations arising out of the theory—that managerial opportunism in the private sector is best controlled by separating the roles of board chairperson and CE—remains contentious. Empirical evidence suggests that returns to shareholders tend to be higher when the two roles are combined rather than separated (Donaldson and Davis, 1991).

It may be desirable to clarify a few of these issues. The first problem is that agency theory gives insufficient attention to the unequal distribution of power within organisations and society generally. Hence, principal–agent models often assume that the parties to a contract are on equal terms, with equal rights and capacities. In reality, however, many relationships are asymmetrical in nature. The labour market provides plenty of evidence concerning inequalities of power in contractual relationships. In most cases employers are in a much stronger bargaining position than their employees. While they are free to hire and fire their employees, for example, their employees cannot usually get rid of the owners and run the firm themselves. Some might object that if an employer behaves unjustly and breaks a contract, employees are free to take their labour elsewhere. But this ignores numerous factors: the possible absence of alternative sources of work due to high unemployment; the search costs involved in securing alternative employment; and the costs to the employees of terminating their contracts (what Gorringe (1988) calls 'hostages'). Hence, leaving the parties in the labour market to sort out their own contractual arrangements on a 'voluntary' basis in the absence of any legislative protection for workers and unions is likely to generate a range of injustices.

Second, agency theory is not sufficiently sophisticated to handle complex social and constitutional relationships. There is a world of difference between the relationships of parents and children, employers and employees, politicians and voters, and ministers and public servants, yet agency theory must use the same language and framework to deal with all these interactions. Consider the question of whether public servants should always do what the government dictates. Most democratic theorists would respond negatively, arguing that there are clear limits to the responsibility of public servants to implement government policy and that the state cannot require unquestioned allegiance. Further, as Heymann points out:

It could be argued that part of the rationale for systems that allow for little formal intervention by the government—in appointing senior bureaucrats and in setting their salaries—is that the bureaucracy should provide some sort of 'check and balance' on the government's actions—in other words, that the bureaucracy has a valid objective other than to carry out government policies, broadly defined. In this case, the principal–agent model breaks down, as the problem is no longer to induce the bureaucracy, as agent, to act in the government's interests (1988, p. 34).

This is no trivial point. It has been long accepted that the interests of liberty, procedural justice and good government are best served by having mechanisms that limit the power of the executive branch and curb the potential for opportunistic behaviour by ministers. For example, in order to avoid corruption, patronage, nepotism, and favouritism, politicians in most democratic countries are not permitted to intervene in the hiring and firing of civil servants (except with respect to departmental heads). Similarly, a range of competitive, multiple-principal arrangements have been developed whereby public servants usually serve as the 'partial agents' of various principals—their portfolio minister, cabinet, Parliament, a public service employing authority, and so on (Moe, 1984, p. 768).

Fortunately, the need to be cautious in applying agency theory to complex constitutional relationships has been recognised by most of the New Zealand reformers, and hence the use of simple agent–principal models was rejected by the architects of the State Sector Act. Nevertheless, the general view among proponents of agency theory seems to be, to quote Bushnell and Scott, that 'each agent must have only one principal with respect to each set of activities' (1988, p. 22). Yet if applied as an overriding principle, such an assumption could have potentially anti-democratic and illiberal consequences (see Chapters 1 and 8).

Finally, while agency theory provides a useful framework for analysing certain kinds of policy questions and highlights the role of incentives in influencing the behaviour of agents, it provides policy-makers with only limited practical guidance. Consider the question of the optimal level of delegation in the core public sector. Agency theory informs us that the answer, to quote Heymann, 'is a function of the correlation between the bureaucrat's utility maximising behaviour and the government's utility' (1988, p. 33). Put differently, the answer depends partly on the ease with which a minister (the principal) can monitor and assess the performance of his or her officials (the agents) and partly on the costs to the minister of maintaining strict controls over inputs. The ease of assessing performance depends, in turn, on such variables as the size of the agency, the nature and geographic spread of its operations, the ease of measuring its outputs and outcomes, the extent of any moral hazard problems, the extent to which the (policy) preferences (or discount rates) of officials differ from those of the minister, and so forth. Various moral and cultural factors—such as the bureaucratic ethos, notions of loyalty and duty, the degree of trust, and the extent of corruption and nepotism—are also likely to be relevant, but these tend to be ignored by agency theorists. Having outlined the relevant considerations, numerous questions then arise. How far should the delegation of responsibility go? Should input controls remain and, if so, over what kinds of inputs? What kinds of incentives (and sanctions) should be used? What forms of monitoring should be adopted? How much transparency is desirable? What role should Parliament and the Controller and Auditor-General play? Anyone hoping to find the answers to such questions in agency theory will be disappointed. Rather, they will need to consult other bodies of literature such as constitutional law, political philosophy, and administrative theory.

Transaction-Cost Economics

Like public choice theory and agency theory, the merits of TCE have been vigorously contested (Dore, 1983; Granovetter, 1985; Perrow, 1986b). On the one hand, the theory has been commended for its contribution to our understanding of alternative governance structures, particularly the differences between the nature of markets (inter-organisational relationships) and firms (intra-organisational relationships); its attention to authority relations (and not just contracts); and the importance it attaches to asset specificity, information asymmetries, and bounded rationality.

On the other hand, the theory's behavioural assumptions (which parallel those of public choice theory and agency theory) have attracted the standard criticism that they give insufficient attention to the social, cultural, and moral constraints that govern human relationships. The theory's limited predictive and explanatory power has also been criticised. Another problem is the loose definition of a transaction cost (in particular, the blurred distinction between production costs and transaction costs), which makes the theory hard to test. Further, as Williamson (1985) acknowledges, the internal transaction costs of hierarchy or vertical integration may often be greater than the external transaction costs of markets. This is because of such things as the costs of acquisition, the higher internal costs of coordinating and controlling a wider range of business activities, the additional costs of surveillance and accounting, the possibility of generating new industrial relations problems, and the difficulties of establishing internal cost systems and pricing arrangements. Thus, as Perrow (1986b, p. 245) notes, it may only be sensible to integrate forwards or backwards in certain circumstances (e.g. when there is a likelihood of acquiring a very profitable asset for a relatively low price or when one will secure additional market power as a result).

For this reason, TCE provides only a partial explanation for the development of large firms and the pronounced variations in industry structure that exist between countries and sectors of the economy, and over time. Instead, the evidence suggests that in many cases the growth of large firms during the past century can be attributed not so much to any organisational efficiencies resulting from vertical integration but to the acquisition of market power and various forms of governmental support (including subsidies, industry regulation, trade protection, etc.) (see Perrow, 1986b).

Given such considerations, a transaction-cost framework for analysing the issues of public management (such as the organisation of the bureaucracy, the structure of departments, and the contracting out of services) needs to be applied with care. At best, it offers only a partial understanding of the issues and needs to be supplemented with other perspectives.

The New Public Management

Managerialism, the NPM, and their related administrative doctrines have been the subject of numerous critiques (see Considine, 1988; Hood, 1990b; Painter, 1988; Yeatman, 1987). In particular, the NPM has been challenged on the grounds that it enjoys neither a secure philosophical base nor a solid empirical foundation. Equally, it has been criticised for its constitutional illiteracy, its lack of attention to the need for probity and due process within government, its insensitivity to varying organisational cultures and political constraints, and its potential for reducing the capacity of governments to deal with catastrophes—i.e. because of the loss of bureaucratic expertise and increasing institutional fragmentation (see Hood, 1990a; Hood and Jackson, 1992).

Critics have also pointed to the tensions between the various strands of thought that comprise the NPM. Whereas the managerialist tradition recommends a degree of centralised control and top-down implementation, public choice theory puts a strong emphasis on devolution and decentralisation (Hood, 1990b). Similarly, whereas managerialism stresses the need for bureaucrats to be responsive to their customers and clients, some public choice theorists argue that responsiveness can be but a thin disguise for interest-group capture.

Another keen focus for debate centres on the claims that public management is simply a sub-set of general management, that the same management principles can be applied equally to both the private and public sectors, and that private sector management techniques are generally superior to, and hence provide a benchmark for, those in the public sector. Critics of managerialism readily acknowledge that many, if not most, of the *tasks* or *functions* of management (as well as the available *tools*) are similar in both sectors (e.g. providing leadership; recruiting, managing and remunerating staff; selecting and deploying resources; managing an organisation's finances; monitoring performance, etc.). However, not all the tasks of public management are identical to those in the private sector. For example, the provision of policy advice, and the whole business of policy-making, law-making, and law enforcement are distinctive to the public sector. Equally if not more important, the *context* in which public sector managers must operate is usually very different from that facing their private sector counterparts (Alford, 1993; Allison, 1982; Gunn, 1988; Lane, 1988; Moe, 1987). As a result, some of the managerialist principles and techniques applicable to the private sector are less appropriate to the public sector. In short, critics of managerialism contend that public management is different in kind from private sector management; hence, it is not simply a branch or sub-set of general management. On the contrary, it is *sui generis*.

Given the importance of these claims and counter-claims, it may be useful to clarify the nature of the differences between the two sectors. To this end, Table 2.1 outlines some of the central differences between the attributes of public and private sector organisations grouped under three broad headings: environmental factors, organisation–environment transactions, and internal structures and processes. Drawing on Table 2.1, a number of points are worth highlighting and amplifying:

Table 2.1   How public and private organisations differ

Topic	Proposition
I. Environmental Factors	
1. Degree of market exposure (reliance on appropriations)	• Less market exposure results in less incentive to cost reduction, operating efficiency, effective performance. • Less market exposure results in lower allocative efficiency (reflection of consumer preferences, proportioning supply to demand, etc.). • Less market exposure means lower availability of market indicators and information (prices, profits, etc.)
2. Legal, formal constraints (courts, legislature, hierarchy)	• More constraints on procedures, spheres of operations (less autonomy of managers in making such choices). • Greater tendency to proliferation of formal specific action controls. • More external sources of formal influence, and greater fragmentation of those sources
3. Political influences	• Greater diversity and intensity of external informal influences on decisions (bargaining, public opinion, interest group reactions).
II. Organisation–Environment Transactions	
4. Coerciveness (coercive, monopolistic, unavoidable nature of many government activities)	• More likely that participation in consumption and financing of services will be unavoidable or mandatory—government has unique sanctions and coercive power.
5. Breadth of impact	• Broader impact, greater symbolic significance of actions of public administration. Wider scope of concern, such as the public interest.
6. Public scrutiny	• Greater public scrutiny of public officials and their actions.
7. Public expectations	• Greater public expectations that public officials will act with fairness, responsiveness, accountability and honesty.
III. Internal Structures and Processes	
8. Complexity of objectives, evaluation and decision criteria	• Greater multiplicity and diversity of objectives and criteria. • Greater vagueness and intangibility of objectives and criteria. • Greater tendency of goals to be conflicting (more 'tradeoffs').
9. Authority relations and the role of managers	• Less decision-making autonomy and flexibility on the part of public sector managers. • Weaker, more fragmented authority over subordinates and lower levels. (1. Subordinates can appeal to alternative authorities. 2. Merit systems constraints.) • Greater reluctance to delegate, more levels of review, and greater use of formal regulations—due to difficulties in supervision and delegation, resulting from vague objectives. • More political, expository role for top managers.

Table 2.1   How public and private organisations differ *(continued)*

10. Organisational performance	• Greater cautiousness, rigidity; less innovativeness.
	• More frequent turnover of top leaders due to elections and political appointments results in greater disruption of implementation of plans.
11. Incentives and incentive structures	• Greater difficulty in devising incentives for effective and efficient performance.
	• Lower valuation of pecuniary incentives by employees.
12. Personal characteristics of employees	• Variations in personality traits and needs, such as higher dominance and flexibility, higher need for achievement, on the part of government managers.

Source: Based on Allison (1982), pp. 19–21.

a. The state, by definition, has a monopoly over the legitimate use of force within a society and undertakes various functions that are neither fully replicated in the private sector nor subject to competition or ownership transfer. Moreover, some of these functions are highly problematical, and are characterised by limited and uncertain technologies (see Gregory, 1995b).

b. Unlike private firms, as Shepherd (1994, p. 30) observes, 'The public sector does not allow for trading in its equity by citizens, leading to an absence of market prices that reflect the market's assessment of the quality of management'. Instead, governments are held accountable via the legislature, elections, and constitutional conventions such as ministerial responsibility. Such accountability mechanisms are very different from those in the private sector, and agents not infrequently serve multiple principals.

c. The context within which public officials work differs significantly from that of their private sector counterparts. For instance, they are bound by different loyalties and obligations, their conduct is governed by a range of important constitutional principles, and they must sometimes work amid high levels of political controversy, not to mention an often uncertain and rapidly changing political environment. Such contextual differences are highlighted by the fact that there is no equivalent in the private sector to the relationship between ministers and departmental CEs.

d. There is no performance measure in the core public sector equivalent to the role that profit plays in the private sector. Rather, departments are required to implement programmes with multiple and sometimes conflicting objectives, many of which cannot be measured or quantified.

e. Because non-commercial public sector organisations do not generate a 'residual' or profit, incentive schemes based on profit sharing are difficult to apply. Likewise, the use of sanctions against wayward public servants is difficult because their application will tend to embarrass and damage the government as much as the officials concerned (at least assuming a degree of transparency).

f. Finally, the functional interdependencies between government agencies are greater and more complex than those encountered in the private sector, even in the case of large, multi-divisional firms (see Alford, 1993).

Overall, then, despite the recent efforts to bring the principles and practices of public management much more into line with those of the private sector, there remain important differences between the two sectors (especially in relation to the operating environment, governance structures, and accountability relationships). Arguably, these differences have significant implications for the way organisations within the two sectors ought to be managed. Having said this, the boundaries between the public and private sectors are sometimes very blurred (see Emmert and Crow, 1988; Musolf and Seidman, 1980). Moreover, commercially oriented public sector organisations (e.g. state-owned enterprises and other Crown-owned companies) have more in common with private sector firms than non-commercial public sector organisations (e.g. departments and ministries). Consequently, the relevance and appropriateness of managerialist principles are likely to vary across the public sector according to the nature and functions of the organisation in question. This suggests that private sector management practices are not equally applicable to *all* public organisations. Nor should it be assumed *a priori* that private sector organisations are better managed than public sector ones. Against this, it is equally wrong to assume that private sector practices should have no role in the public sector or that managerialist doctrines have no relevance to public sector organisations.

Although the New Zealand model of public management embraces many features of the NPM, it was never assumed by those guiding the reforms that private sector management practices should be applied automatically, uncritically, or comprehensively to the public sector. On the contrary, the distinctiveness of the public sector was well recognised—as was the organisational diversity within the public sector—and policies were shaped accordingly. Nonetheless, the private sector was often held up as providing a benchmark for public sector practice; hence, where it was deemed appropriate, successful private sector arrangements were treated as a model for the public sector.

CONCLUSION

This chapter has provided a brief overview of some of the intellectual currents that influenced the development of the New Zealand model. Of course, many other ideas, theories, values, and considerations also contributed to the reforms. For example, the principles of the Treaty of Waitangi and the quest for a bicultural society have had a significant bearing on the public sector since the mid 1980s (see Chapter 7), as have a range of equity-related issues (see Chapter 12). Nevertheless, the impact of the four distinct, yet related, sets of ideas examined here has been considerable. Not merely have they changed the language of policy discourse, but they have also altered the way in which public management issues are defined, analysed, and debated. As a result, the policy agenda has been dominated by issues relating to the appropriate design of incentive structures and governance arrangements, the avoidance of provider capture, the pursuit of contestability and external contracting, the application of principal–agent models to a variety of interpersonal and interorganisational relationships, the minimisation of transaction costs and agency costs, and the tighter specification of outputs and outcomes.

As highlighted in subsequent chapters, the insights furnished by the four approaches under consideration have made important contributions to improving public management in New Zealand. And notwithstanding their limitations, they have given the New Zealand model coherence and rigour. This is particular true of the financial management reforms, which have won international acclaim.

Finally, while some of the ideas discussed in this chapter have been influential in other OECD countries since the early to mid 1980s, the resulting policy changes have been anything but uniform. Hence, the claim that the New Zealand model is consistent with many of the administrative doctrines central to the NPM does not thereby imply that it is equivalent to, say, the Australian or British models of public management. As is so often the case, broad, overarching terms, such as the NPM, can shelter within them a wealth of policy diversity.

the structure of new zealand's public sector

3   the framework of government and the evolution of the public sector

The remainder of this book seeks to explain how the New Zealand public sector is managed. The aim of this chapter is to establish the political and institutional context in which public sector management takes place. This chapter outlines the key institutions of the framework of government in New Zealand. It provides a general context for the chapters which follow. It is necessarily a brief introduction to many complex structures and procedures. Further explanations and analysis may be found in any of the standard political texts (e.g. Chen and Palmer, 1993; Gold, 1992; Harris and Levine, 1992; McLeay, 1995; Mulgan, 1994; Palmer, 1992; Ringer, 1991).

New Zealand's constitutional structure derives from four principal sources:

1. *The Treaty of Waitangi:* Mulgan (1994, p. 51) describes it as New Zealand's 'founding constitutional charter'. In his view, the Treaty 'plays a crucial part in determining the legitimacy of New Zealand governments and their right to command the allegiance of New Zealand citizens, both Māori and Pākehā'.
2. *Parliamentary statutes:* some statutes establish rules and procedures governing the structure and operation of the constitutional framework. Many statutes have some bearing on aspects of the constitutional framework, but among the most important are the Local Government Act 1974, the Ombudsmen Act 1975, the Official Information Act 1982, the Constitution Act 1986, the New Zealand Bill of Rights Act 1990, the State Sector Act 1988, the Public Finance Act 1989, the Electoral Act 1993, and the Fiscal Responsibility Act 1994.
3. *The common law:* this is law made over time by the decisions of judges and includes some of our basic civil liberties, although many of these are now incorporated in the Bill of Rights Act.
4. *Constitutional conventions:* these 'are not recognised by the courts as strict law capable of judicial enforcement. They are, however, an important part of the country's constitution, using that expression in its broad sense' (Harris, 1992, p. 59). They include institutions such as the cabinet and conventions such as the doctrine of ministerial responsibility and the impartiality of the Speaker.

New Zealand governments have been reluctant to divest themselves of the capacity to change the basic rules of the political system. The Electoral Act, in s. 268, entrenches a small number of provisions by making necessary either a 75 per cent majority in the House of Representatives or a majority in a referendum for them to be amended. The entrenched clauses are s. 28, constituting the Representation Commission, an independent body that decides on the boundaries for parliamentary electorates; ss. 35–6, which establish the formula for the division of the country into electoral districts (but not the corresponding sections, which do the same for Māori representation); s. 60 and s. 74, which establish the qualifications of electors; and s. 168, which determines the method of voting in elections. This clause also entrenches s. 17(1) of the Constitution Act, which sets the term of Parliament at three years. It should be noted, however, that the entrenching clause is not itself entrenched and requires only a simple majority to be changed. On the other hand, the entrenched clauses were first enacted in the Electoral Act 1956 and have been respected since then. Other seemingly fundamental constitutional legislation has no particular protection. Harris (1992, p. 61) observes, 'Even statutes such as the Constitution Act 1986 and the New Zealand Bill of Rights Act 1990 have no greater legal status than the Margarine Act 1908.'

THE GOVERNMENTAL STRUCTURE

The Constitution Act 1986 organises the governmental structure in New Zealand into four parts: the sovereign, the executive, the legislature, and the judiciary.

The Sovereign

New Zealand is a constitutional monarchy and the powers of the sovereign are normally exercised by the Governor-General. The Governor-General has no day-to-day influence over the process of government. Harris (1992, p. 59) argues that the obligation upon the Governor-General to act on ministerial advice is 'probably the most important' of our constitutional conventions.

The powers of the Governor-General are defined in the Constitution Act and in the Letters Patent 1983. The chief powers of the Governor-General (Brookfield, 1992, p. 78; Mulgan, 1994, p. 53; Ringer, 1991, p. 56) are:

a. To appoint as Prime Minister the leader of the party with the confidence of the House of Representatives.
b. To appoint or remove ministers on the recommendation of the Prime Minister.
c. To summon, prorogue, or dissolve Parliament on the advice of the Prime Minister.
d. To assent to legislation.
e. To make statutory regulations by Order in Council on the recommendation of ministers.
f. To grant pardons.

These powers could become more significant under MMP. If there is no party with a clear majority following an election, the Governor-General will issue an invitation to form a government to the party leader whom the Governor-General judges to be best placed to command a simple majority on a vote of confidence in the House. There is some constitutional debate over the ability of the Governor-General in certain circumstances to exercise 'reserve powers' beyond those authorities noted above. Brookfield argues that the Governor-General may refuse to dissolve Parliament in the event of a Prime Minister whose party has lost its majority in an election recommending a further dissolution and a second election (Brookfield, 1992, p. 81). The Governor-General will only agree to this request when he or she considers that there is no other person or party which can command the confidence of the House. The Governor-General can dismiss a Prime Minister who has lost support in Parliament but will not resign and one who has broken a constitutional convention or acted unlawfully (Ringer, 1991, p. 57). In extreme circumstances, an 'ultimate reserve power' allows a Governor-General to act to restore constitutional order in an emergency even by going beyond the limits of statute or common law (Brookfield, 1992, p. 83). That these powers are available to the Governor-General in exceptional circumstances does not undermine the general principle of parliamentary sovereignty and the subordinate position of the Governor-General in the process of government.

The Executive

The political executive is established by convention rather than by statute. It comprises the Prime Minister and the cabinet (and ministers not in cabinet). The Constitution Act provides (s. 6(1)) that membership of the cabinet is drawn only from elected Members of Parliament.

The Prime Minister and cabinet

Under the first-past-the-post electoral system, the cabinet was historically dominant over the government caucus because it had virtually an inbuilt majority in caucus (McLeay, 1995). Recent governments have tended to have about twenty ministers in cabinet, and this, combined with ministers and/or under-secretaries outside cabinet, was usually enough to secure a guaranteed majority for the cabinet position in caucus. There were exactly twenty ministers in the National cabinet in March 1995, with four ministers outside cabinet and three under-secretaries. Unusually, one of those under-secretaries, Ross Meurant, was no longer a member of the National caucus, having withdrawn to form his own party, the Right of Centre party.[1] This foreshadows the shape of cabinets and related offices under MMP. Equally unusually, one minister, Bruce Cliffe, resigned from the cabinet in July 1995 to become a founding member of the new United New Zealand party.

Cabinet selection is a difficult issue for any government. Labour and National, the predominant political parties since the 1930s under the first-past-the-post system, have used different methods of choosing cabinet ministers. National prime ministers have selected the cabinet themselves, whereas Labour governments have relied on a ballot by the parliamentary caucus. The Prime Minister has decided on portfolios and cabinet ranking in both Labour and National governments. This has been a major source of

---

1. Meurant was dismissed from this post by the Prime Minister in August 1995.

prime ministerial power. As Mulgan (1994, p. 85) observes, the process of cabinet formation and portfolio allocation is likely to be more complicated under MMP since
prime ministers may have to deal with coalition partners who are likely to have very firm
ideas about cabinet membership, preferred portfolios, and rankings. Indeed, their participation in the government may be dependent upon their securing specific portfolios.
The Prime Minister's capacity to dismiss or otherwise discipline a dissident minister
from a coalition partner may also be more complicated under MMP (Boston, 1994c).

The Prime Minister has often been seen as exercising great power in the New Zealand
system of government and having the resources to secure his or her objectives. More
recently, doubt has been cast on the notion of the omnipotent Prime Minister. The tasks
asked of the Prime Minister are sufficiently complex and onerous that Sir Geoffrey
Palmer, a former incumbent, has observed: 'It is my conclusion that it is impossible for
any individual to perform adequately all the duties of Prime Minister in New Zealand
. . . no one can perform that range of functions with anything remotely approaching
sufficient attention to every element of them. It is a mission impossible from the start'
(Palmer, 1992, p. 171). Similarly, Alley has argued that the Prime Minister can no
longer be as confident as some predecessors were that he or she can exercise power effectively. He observes: 'The outward trappings of collective cabinet and ministerial responsibility, along with assumed party loyalty, secrecy and discipline exercised by
parliamentary whips and caucus procedures, might appear intact. But as codes and doctrines supporting effective prime ministerial influence, these principles and practices are
now strained to a point where their durability is in real doubt' (Alley, 1992, p. 175).

Ministerial responsibility

Cabinet government has been based upon the doctrine of ministerial responsibility,
which has two dimensions—collective and individual responsibility. Collective responsibility has been the linchpin of cabinet government. The collective responsibility of
ministers obliges them to support cabinet decisions outside the cabinet and to protect
the confidentiality of cabinet discussions. Ministers or under-secretaries outside cabinet
are usually seen as being bound by collective responsibility even though they may not
have participated in making the decisions. This is not completely beyond doubt, however (Martin, 1991a). Palmer argues (1992, pp. 153–4) that the functions served by
collective responsibility are that:

a. It avoids confusion as to what the government's policy is.
b It enables the people to know who is responsible for government policies and to hold
   them accountable.
c. It facilitates the cohesion of cabinet and the collective nature of government.
d. It facilitates executive control over Parliament.

Individual ministerial responsibility, on the other hand, has had a more chequered
career in New Zealand. The practice has been that ministers are only held to blame for
their own actions or inaction. They are *responsible* for departmental errors, however, in
the wider sense that they are answerable to Parliament, to the public, and to their

colleagues (Martin, 1994a, p. 49). Nonetheless, some maintain that individual ministerial responsibility has become increasingly attenuated. Martin (1994a, p. 46) has observed that ministers have in recent years become 'decoupled'—separated—from what their agencies do. Many examples could be adduced but probably the most important derive from the new relationships between ministers and the chief executives of state-owned enterprises, Crown entities, and government departments. Ministers are decoupled from the governance of SOEs and Crown entities by boards, while ministers contract to purchase outputs from departmental CEs. As Martin observes: 'The picture which emerges is one in which power and responsibility for the actions of the state is diffused and distanced from ministers' (Martin, 1994a, p. 48).

Cabinet committees

Underpinning cabinet government is a system of cabinet committees. It may be argued that this is where real power lies in the New Zealand political system. As Table 3.1 shows, cabinet committees are established on a sectoral basis. Each committee has about eight members and normally meets weekly. The purpose of cabinet committees is to ensure that matters going to cabinet have been fully considered beforehand and to permit a wide range of input for issues whose implications run across a range of cabinet portfolios. In principle, the cabinet committee system should encourage a more coordinated approach to policy development. All cabinet committee recommendations must be ratified by cabinet. The most important committee is the Cabinet Strategy Committee (the equivalent under the fourth Labour government was the Policy Committee), whose terms of reference give it responsibility for establishing 'a coherent framework, strategic policy directions and initiatives across the entire range of government activity' (Eaddy, 1992, p. 169). Under the National government, its membership comprises the twelve most senior ministers. The Cabinet Strategy Committee evaluates major social, economic, and environmental policy proposals that lie outside the specific sectoral responsibilities of the other committees.

Officials' committees may also be established to advise cabinet committees. Table 3.3 lists the standing officials' committees and their composition under the National government. *Ad hoc* officials' committees are also established from time to time. Their role is to coordinate officials' advice and to ensure that officials look beyond the concerns of their own departments. Officials' committees encourage compromises and pragmatic recommendations to ministers. The other side of this is that options considered and rejected by officials' committees may not get presented to ministers. Thus, they may play a powerful and important gatekeeper role. Officials' committees were used much less frequently under the Labour government between 1984 and 1990 but have enjoyed something of a revival under National (Boston, 1990a; SSC, 1993).

The Legislature

The Constitution Act (s. 10) constitutes a House of Representatives as those persons elected as Members of Parliament by the procedures laid down in the Electoral Act 1993. In 1993, New Zealanders opted by referendum to shift from the traditional first-past-

Table 3.1 Cabinet committees

CABINET STRATEGY COMMITTEE
    Subcommittee on Defence and External Issues
    Subcommittee on Intelligence and Security
    Subcommittee on Civil Defence/Terrorism

CABINET COMMITTEE ON ENTERPRISE, INDUSTRY AND ENVIRONMENT

CABINET COMMITTEE ON EXPENDITURE CONTROL AND REVENUE

CABINET COMMITTEE ON LEGISLATION AND HOUSE BUSINESS

CABINET COMMITTEE ON EDUCATION, TRAINING AND EMPLOYMENT

CABINET STATE SECTOR COMMITTEE
    Subcommittee on State Wages

CABINET APPOINTMENTS AND HONOURS COMMITTEE

CABINET SOCIAL POLICY COMMITTEE

CABINET COMMITTEE ON TREATY OF WAITANGI ISSUES

AD HOC CABINET COMMITTEE ON IMPLEMENTATION OF PROPORTIONAL REPRESENTATION

Source: Cabinet Office

Table 3.2 Officials' committees (September 1995)

OFFICIALS' COMMITTEE (STRATEGY)
- Chief Executive, Department of the Prime Minister and Cabinet
- Secretary to the Treasury
- State Services Commissioner
- Secretary of the Cabinet

OFFICIALS' COMMITTEE ON EDUCATION, TRAINING, AND EMPLOYMENT
- Chief Executive, Department of Prime Minister and Cabinet (Convenor)
- Secretary to the Treasury
- Secretary of Labour
- Chief Executive, Ministry of Education
- Director-General of Social Welfare
- State Services Commission
- Te Puni Kōkiri

OFFICIALS' COMMITTEE ON EXPENDITURE CONTROL
- Treasury (Convenor)
- Department of the Prime Minister and Cabinet
- State Services Commission
- Ministry of Commerce (senior official currently appointed on a personal rather than departmental basis)

Source: Cabinet Office

the-post electoral system to MMP (Hawke, 1993a). Support for this change was prompted at least in part by the belief that the first-past-the-post system's delivery of complete command over the governmental process to the political party that gained a simple (and possibly very narrow) electoral majority had made the political system increasingly unresponsive to citizens. Mulgan has described the associated capacity and inclination of recent governments to break their election promises as an 'elective dictatorship' (Mulgan, 1990). The MMP system takes effect from the 1996 general election. The Electoral Act 1993 requires (s. 264) that its operation be reviewed by a parliamentary select committee convened in 2000 and which is to report by 1 June 2002. The committee is to recommend whether there should be any amendment to the system of determining the number and distribution of general seats (ss. 35–6) or to the system of Māori representation and whether there should be another referendum on the electoral system.

The Electoral Act 1993 divides the seats in Parliament between constituency and party list seats. There are sixteen general constituency seats in the South Island, and the number of North Island general constituency seats is set according to the average population size of the South Island general seats. The number of Māori seats varies according to the numbers on the Māori electoral roll and is set on the basis of the average size of the non-Māori seats. It is expected that the first MMP Parliament will have 120 seats. Each elector has a constituency vote and a party list vote. Each party puts up a list of candidates. Its representation in Parliament is set in proportion to the votes it receives for its party list, provided its list vote is above a 5 per cent threshold or it succeeds in winning one or more constituency seats. Thus, a party that receives 25 per cent of the list vote secures approximately 25 per cent of the seats in Parliament, which entitles it to about 30 seats on the basis of a total of 120 seats (it will not be precisely 30 seats since some parties will get less than 5 per cent of the vote and will have no representation). Those seats may be all list seats or, if the party wins one or more constituency seats, will be made up of constituency and party list seats. The former take precedence over the latter. Thus, to continue the previous example, if a party entitled to 30 seats on the basis of its list vote wins 18 constituency seats, then 12 list seats would be added to its 18 constituency seats in Parliament. In the event that a party wins more constituency seats than those it is 'entitled to' by virtue of its list vote, it of course retains those seats and the total number of MPs increases accordingly.

The functions of Parliament

The Constitution Act provides in s. 14(2) that Parliament itself is the Governor-General and the House of Representatives, but common terminology (followed in this book) uses the terms House of Representatives and Parliament interchangeably. The Electoral Act 1993 prescribes the rules governing the size of Parliament, its composition, and the election of its members. New Zealand is relatively unusual in being a unitary state with a unicameral legislature and no entrenched constitution or Bill of Rights. The upper house, the Legislative Council, was established in 1854. Its members were appointed by the Governor (later the Governor-General) and could amend or reject legislation from the House of Representatives (although not money bills). The Council was abolished in 1951 (Jackson, 1972) and although the need for an upper house is occasionally suggested, most recently by the Prime Minister, Jim Bolger, there has been no significant public pressure for its restoration.

Skene (1992, pp. 250–8) identifies six key functions of Parliament:

a. It supports the government: the parliamentary process confers legitimacy on government actions.
b. It enacts legislation and authorises public expenditure.

c. It scrutinises the actions of the executive.
d. It is a crucial arena for creating party leaders and sustaining them in office.
e. It serves as a forum for a 'continuous election campaign' and as an arena for conflict among the parties.
f. It is the arena in which MPs can perform their duties of constituency representation.

The two classic functions of Parliament are to enact laws and to scrutinise the actions of the executive. Parliament authorises the government to spend public money and to incur costs. As Skene observes, Parliament is formally supreme as a law-maker, but 'in practice, it has ceded the power to legislate and thus to govern to the ministry' (1992, p. 248). In an MMP system, especially under minority governments, Parliament will retrieve a good deal of its influence over legislation. Governments will need to pay close and continuing attention to the balance of opinion among their formal and informal coalition partners and on occasions to wider parliamentary opinion. However, the balance of power between the executive and the legislature is tilted by the Constitution Act, which provides (s. 21) that the House of Representatives can only pass bills involving the expenditure or collection of public money on the recommendation of the Crown.

In Skene's formulation, Parliament also serves as a crucial arena for creating and sustaining party leaders and for a 'continuous election campaign' among the parties. Skene (1992, p. 255) considers that this function of Parliament is 'by far its most important'. Parliament is a key forum where parties compete for popular support. Palmer (1992, p. 110) comments: 'The New Zealand House of Representatives is a bearpit of ill-mannered and vituperative political debate to the exclusion of nearly everything else.' This portrayal was a product of the adversarial nature of the traditional two-party dominance of Parliament in which almost everything the government did or proposed was automatically resisted to the hilt by the opposition party. Since there was no point of contact or common cause between the parties there was no need to establish a cooperative or even civil relationship. In practice, of course, party leaders cooperated in running the business of the House but presented themselves to the public, both in Parliament and in election campaigns, as bitter opponents. Under MMP, when parties are potential or even actual coalition partners, and where the legislative process is likely to be more cooperative, it may be expected that the 'bearpit of ill-mannered and vituperative political debate' will give way to a more reasoned and civil environment. Constituency representation is the final function performed by Parliament. MPs in New Zealand have always been remarkably accessible to their constituents and have always placed great emphasis upon this aspect of their role.

The parliamentary process

Each bill that becomes law receives three readings in Parliament as well as examination in two different kinds of committee stages. Under single-party majorities, the typical legislative process has involved a government bill, initiated within the executive, developed through cabinet and caucus and their committee systems with the aid of detailed analysis by officials, and assured of the support of the members of the majority party before it reached the floor of the House. Under MMP, the pre-parliamentary stage of legislative development will depend on whether the government has a majority in Parliament and the nature of any coalition arrangements. The weaker the government's position, the more consultation will be required and the more compromises it may need to make. Coalition partners will need to be given a genuine opportunity for input into a bill before it goes before the House. This is likely to involve advice from officials to caucus committees. Indeed, on some measures opposition party caucuses may also be consulted in an effort to secure as wide a supporting consensus as possible.

Table 3.3   Select committees of the House of Representatives (March 1995)

Standing ('subject') committees	Other committees set up pursuant to standing order	Ad hoc committees (set up by order of the house for a particular purpose)
Commerce	Broadcasting of Parliament	Electoral law
Finance and expenditure	Privileges	Standing orders
Foreign affairs and defence	Regulations review	State enterprises
Government administration		Committee on the hazardous substances and new organisms bill
Internal affairs and local government		
Justice and law reform		
Labour		
Māori affairs		
Planning and development		
Primary production		
Social services		
Transport		

Source: Cabinet Office

The select committee process was always the key stage for MPs in the legislative process under a single-party majority. As noted above, the key decisions were taken in cabinet and the government caucus. While it was rare for major amendments to succeed on the floor of the House, MPs argued that their most effective opportunity to influence legislation was in select committees. Select committees combine the law-making and executive scrutiny functions of Parliament. As Table 3.3 shows, in March 1995 there were thirteen standing committees, organised on a sector basis, plus several dealing with matters to do with the operation of Parliament itself. *Ad hoc* committees are also established from time to time. Select committees have usually had 5–7 members but may become larger with more parties represented in Parliament. In the two-party system, select committees always operated with a government majority and normally a government MP as chairperson. Ministers usually did not sit on select committees. It is not clear what the composition and party balance of select committees will be under MMP, but parties are likely to be represented in proportion to their numbers in Parliament. Select committees examine all bills, except money bills and those introduced under urgency, and hear public submissions from individuals and groups. They examine the budget estimates and consider petitions, and may investigate the policy, administration, and expenditure of departments and many other public agencies (Skene, 1992). Their work combines genuine effort to improve legislation and remedy problems with serving as a forum for party conflict and as an opportunity to secure partisan advantage. Select committees are serviced by the Select Committee Office, which is in the Office of the Clerk, but departmental officials are also involved in advising committees on bills under consideration and in commenting on submissions.

The capacity of select committees to act as a check on executive power under single-party majority governments was constrained by a number of factors. One was the heavy workload shouldered by MPs, including the caucus committee system where government MPs felt they had a better chance of influencing legislation at an early stage in the legislative process. Another key factor under the first-past-the-post system was the tightness of party discipline, which limited the willingness of government MPs to investigate too closely the actions of ministers or officials acting on their behalf (Skene, 1992). By the time a bill reached the select committee stage, governments were typically reluctant to contemplate major changes to its basic thrust. Notwithstanding this, there were notable cases of major bills, such as the Resource Management Act, which were substantially amended in the select committee process. Normally, however, the most important contribution that select committees made tended to be in technical areas. By and large, rather than making major changes to bills, select committees have ensured that the bills better achieve their stated objectives. Select committees are likely to exercise more influence over the key provisions and objectives of legislation under MMP. They may become a key arena for the forging of majority alliances on legislative proposals.

Caucus

Historically, the parties with substantial representation in Parliament have formed a caucus consisting of all MPs and perhaps a small number of key officials from outside Parliament. The National and Labour party caucuses have met regularly, usually weekly. Attendance is required of all MPs, and debate in caucus is confidential. The party caucuses discuss major political issues but focus particularly on current and pending legislation in the House and decide the position to be taken by the party on any matter before the House. The caucuses of the major parties are underpinned by a caucus committee system, where key issues and legislative proposals are examined. For the governing party or the parties in a governing coalition, the caucus committee system is a crucial forum in the policy development process. Under MMP, it is more likely that officials will provide information and advice to caucus committees, including opposition committees.

Under the first-past-the-post system, the majority decision of the government caucus on a legislative proposal effectively decided the parliamentary outcome. Jackson (1992) has argued that, in these circumstances, the parliamentary caucus system operated as an anti-Parliament system. It had the effect of downgrading the policy debate in Parliament to the status of meaningless ritual but of heightening inter-party conflict in Parliament.

Change is likely under MMP. If coalition or minority governments are elected, then the negotiations and policy compromises required among parties will rule out the kind of dominance traditionally exercised by the majority party caucus. Indeed, although New Zealand has traditionally been regarded as having one of the most tightly disciplined parliamentary parties of any Westminster system, cracks have appeared since the early 1980s with internal policy dissension in successive governments.

The Judiciary

The judiciary comprises the fourth component of the constitutional structure. The judicial system arranges the courts in a clear hierarchy:

a. There are about a hundred District Courts with both a civil and criminal jurisdiction. District Court judges are appointed by the Governor-General.
b. The High Court is a court of inherent jurisdiction. It hears both civil and criminal cases. High Court judges are appointed by the Governor-General and hold office until retirement. The Constitution Act provides (s. 23) that they may be removed on grounds of misbehaviour or incapacity only by the Governor-General acting upon an address of Parliament.
c. There are also a number of specialist courts—the Employment Court, Family Court, Youth Court, Māori Land Court and Appellate Court.
d. The Court of Appeal is at the peak of the court structure in New Zealand. It hears appeals from the High Court and from some specialist courts such as the Employment Court.
e. The Court of Appeal may grant leave to appeal one of its own decisions to the Judicial Committee of the Privy Council in London. The Privy Council hears on average about one or two New Zealand cases per year and it tends not to overturn the Court of Appeal on distinctively New Zealand issues. However, it shows less compunction about reversing the Court of Appeal on 'lawyers' law' regardless of the policy implications (Hodder, 1992, p. 411). Other Commonwealth countries such as Australia and Canada have abolished the right of appeal to the Privy Council, but although this has been proposed from time to time, New Zealand has not yet followed suit. In 1995 the government raised this possibility yet again and indicated its support for abolition.

It is a very strong convention that the appointment of judges be entirely non-political. This convention, and the responsibility of judges to administer the law impartially and objectively, gives rise to the sense that the judiciary is not a part of the political system. There are, however, at least three ways in which judges act politically. The first is through their willingness to preside over or to act as members of commissions of inquiry on a very wide range of issues. Judges may not see this as a political role but 'These reports have a direct impact on public opinion when published and also have an impact upon the general policy-making process within the executive government' (Hodder, 1992, p. 424). Secondly, the courts make law as well as apply it. Despite the supremacy of statute law, many areas of commercial law and civil liberties are governed by principles derived from the common law, while the detailed application and interpretation of statute often derives from court decisions (Mulgan, 1994, p. 161). The third opportunity for judges to exercise a political role is through their interpretation of parliamentary statutes. Traditionally the courts in New Zealand have tended to be conservative and to respect the sovereignty of Parliament. But in the last decade, the Court of Appeal has adopted a more activist stance. As Hodder comments,

> More recently, the Court of Appeal has expressly described its role in interpreting apparently hastily drafted legislation as one of making 'the Act work as Parliament must have intended'. As with other exercises in statutory interpretation, there is scope in this approach for judicial deductions of legislative policies which either surprise the legislators or lead to the bypassing of the language of the legislation itself.

Even more controversially the courts 'have articulated power for themselves to intervene when a decision has been made that is so unreasonable that no reasonable agency could have made it' (Hodder, 1992, p. 422). The New Zealand Bill of Rights Act 1990 provides a setting for a potential fourth path to a political role for the judiciary. Where more than one interpretation of an Act might be possible, the courts are required by s. 6 of the Bill of Rights Act to favour an interpretation consistent with the Bill of Rights.

THE PUBLIC SERVICE

The key issue in the development of the public service in New Zealand, as elsewhere, has been the tension between conflicting pressures for political control over the unelected bureaucracy and the desire for a non-political public service. The best of both worlds is sought: a democratically accountable bureaucracy but one sufficiently independent from politicians that it is still able to offer 'free and frank advice' and to act in the public interest. Public bureaucracies must not simply be the political agents of the incumbent government but neither can they be autonomous baronies acting independently of the government.

The Development of the New Zealand Public Service

In the development of the New Zealand public service during the nineteenth century there was at first no thought that public officials were anything other than the direct servants of their ministerial masters. From 1856, ministers controlled their departments and made their own decisions about appointments, promotions, discipline, and pay. A commission of inquiry in 1866 found that the civil service 'consisted of a number of independent departments which had neither common policies nor procedures. Staff were chosen and salaries and wages set by politicians. Patronage was therefore a problem, with many appointments being made by influence rather than on merit' (Ringer, 1991, p. 73). The introduction of competitive entry by examination in the Civil Service Act 1866 was ineffective. Despite its being re-established by the Civil Service Reform Act 1887, a subsequent amendment allowed the government to make 'temporary' appointments of staff who had not passed the examination. This became a major source of political patronage (Ringer, 1991, p. 74). The consequences of these arrangements were not unexpected. The public service was plagued by low morale and poor performance. As Robertson (1974, p. 108) observes, the four decades after the Civil Service Act 1866 were 'an incredibly dark and dismal period for the career service, for efficient government administration and for personnel policies'.

The Liberal government (1890–1912) greatly expanded the role of the state in the society and economy and, correspondingly, the number of government departments and employees. But growing concern over the operation of the public service led it to establish the Hunt Public Service Commission to report on recommendations for change. Before the Hunt Commission could report, the Liberal government fell, to be replaced in government by the Reform party, which quickly introduced the Public Service Act 1912. This Act established the office of the Public Service Commissioner, who was charged with two chief responsibilities: first, to ensure the efficient and economical operation of the public service, and second, to act as an employing authority for the public service. In the exercise of the second role, the Commissioner was made independent of cabinet and given authority over all personnel and industrial relations matters—appointments, grading, promotions, suspensions, dismissals, and pay and conditions (Henderson, 1990). Merit was to be the basis of the new personnel regime. The Act introduced a system of job classification based on analysis of job content with a regradings exercise to be conducted every five years by the Commissioner. A Public Service Appeal Board was established to hear appeals over grading and against non-promotion. Public servants were given priority rights of appointment to any position within the public service (above the entry grades) over any outsider and could appeal to the Appeal Board over their non-appointment to any position, regardless of whether or not the appointee came from outside the public service.

By putting stress upon the development of a unified, career-oriented service, enjoying standard conditions of employment under the jurisdiction of senior and independent public servants rather than politicians, the 1912 Act laid the basis for the modern public service. There were criticisms of the system established in 1912 but they were outweighed by a widespread consensus in its support, which lasted by and large until 1988. Pay-fixing became the most controversial part of the 1912 settlement. Public servants had no bargaining rights with the Public Service Commissioner and no access to compulsory arbitration. Not surprisingly, pressure grew from state sector unions for a different system of pay-fixing and in 1948 the Labour government reluctantly enacted the Government Services Tribunal Act (Walsh, 1991b). The Act provided that pay and employment conditions in the public sector should be fairly comparable with those prevailing in the private sector and established compulsory arbitration to enforce this obligation. Although this system was perennially controversial and endured repeated attacks from many quarters, it survived with minor amendments until the State Sector Act 1988.

The public sector grew steadily in size and diversity throughout the twentieth century (Polaschek, 1958). Table 3.4 charts the growth in the number of employees. It shows that the single biggest jump in the numbers of employees occurred under the first Labour government (1935–49), a period in which the activities of the state expanded

Table 3.4   Public service staffing 1913–94

	Permanent staff[1]	Females as proportion of permanent staff[2]	Temporary staff[3]	Casual wage worker
1913	4,918	–	–	–
1918	6,519	–	–	–
1923	6,946	–	487	–
1928	7,707	–	1,400	–
1933	7,720	–	1,783	–
1938	10,437	–	5,788	–
1944[4]	13,188	–	17,415	
1948[5]	26,784	–	3,022	–
1953	32,177	28.0	1,960	19,756
1958	36,659	28.8	2,141	19,118
1963	41,306	28.8	2,227	20,724
1968	47,948	29.7	2,161	19,169
1973[6]	51,013	28.9	1,816	16,886
1978	62,017	33.0	1,677	19,548
1983	66,102	36.0	1,388	17,739
1988	59,082	46.7	1,858	–
1993[7]	35,829	52.5	–	–
1994	34,505	52.7	–	–

1. Excludes Administrative Division, 1914–47.
2. Until 1963, this includes Clerical, General and Professional Divisions only; from 1968 includes all permanent staff.
3. Employed under regulation 150 of Public Service Regulations 1913, regulation 130 of Public Service Regulations, 1951 and s.49 of State Services Act 1962.
4. Figures for 1943 unavailable.
5. In 1947, 9,349 temporary staff were made permanent.
6. The 1973 figures reflect the transfer of more than 5,000 Health Department staff to hospital boards.
7. The figures for 1993 and 1994 are full-time equivalents.

Sources: Henderson (1990) pp. 397–9 (for 1913–88); SSC, pers. comm. 1994 (for 1993–94)
Note: Blank spaces mean data were not included in the reports from which this table was compiled

swiftly. Not only did employee numbers increase but also between 1936 and 1946 ten new government departments were established (Public Service Consultative Committee, 1946, p. 19). The office of Public Service Commissioner gave way in 1946 to a Public Service Commission of three persons, later increased to four. In 1963, following the recommendation of a Royal Commission in 1962, the Public Service Commission was replaced by a four-person State Services Commission (SSC). The Royal Commission was highly critical of the failure of the Public Service Commission to provide the 'imaginative leadership' needed in the public service (Royal Commission, 1962, p. 46). The Royal Commission argued that the Public Service Commission had become preoccupied with its personnel responsibilities to the detriment of its performance in its other chief area of responsibility, which was to ensure the efficient and economical management of the public service (Royal Commission, 1962, pp. 48–9). In strong terms—'we cannot overemphasise the importance we attach to the recommendations which follow'—the Royal Commission urged the government to establish a State Services Commission which, while continuing to carry out its personnel role, would make the efficient management of the public service a principal focus of its activity (Royal Commission, 1962, p. 58). It proposed that the SSC would be engaged in 'reviewing continually the machinery of government' and would satisfy itself that 'Permanent Heads continually review their departmental structure' (Royal Commission, 1962, p. 54).

Notwithstanding these recommendations, the SSC largely continued the tradition set by its predecessor. Personnel and industrial relations matters became its main concerns. Indeed, considering the general volatility of industrial relations in New Zealand during the first twenty years of the SSC's life, it could hardly do anything else. The increasing frequency and intensity of industrial disputes in the public service and wider state sector preoccupied the SSC, as state employees, including teachers, nurses, doctors, and other professionals, joined the growing militancy. Under these pressures, the task of 'reviewing continually the machinery of government' tended to be put to one side as the duties of being central employer crowded in.

Pressures for Reform

Under the legislative structures in place from 1912 until the 1980s, a particular type of public service emerged. It was an apolitical career public service, staffed by independent and permanent officials who, at least at more senior levels, tended to take a broad service-wide perspective at least as much as a narrow departmental focus. Their orientation towards a lifelong career within the public service encouraged a long-term perspective on policy-making, tempered by their responsibility to serve the interests of the government of the day. The obligation to be non-political required officials to be non-partisan; it was not a licence to be insensitive to the political constraints facing ministers. A distinctive public service culture emerged. It was heavily rule-governed, 'bureaucratic' in the technical sense of the term, and a complex plethora of rules, variously sourced from determinations, manuals, circulars, and Treasury instructions, closely constrained the behaviour of public servants in almost every conceivable situation. There was of course more discretion at upper levels, but even senior officials, having served their time at lower levels, did not readily shed the caution imbued in them by that experience.

The influence exercised by senior officials, their independence, their durability, their security, and their long-term and broad orientation gave rise in some quarters to the belief that the public sector balance had shifted too far away from political control. It was argued by critics of the public service that it had become politically non-responsive and impervious to the views of elected governments. In particular, it was argued by members of the third Labour government (1972–75) that the combination of an entrenched conservative public service culture and the policy inclinations of senior officials had frustrated and even subverted their policy objectives (Hayward, 1981; Bassett, 1976). Even before their victory in the 1984 election, senior figures in the Labour party had already made clear their determination to radically reorganise the public sector; indeed, David Lange had spoken of requiring senior officials to undertake loyalty tests (Martin, 1988a, p. 15). This political motive for reform fuelled other pressures for change that had been building from various quarters. The discussion in Chapter 2 identified the key ideas and theories that influenced the reform programme in New Zealand. These ideas and theories were used to find solutions to the wide range of concerns that had emerged over the structure and operation of the public sector, namely:

a. The already noted concern over the accountability of officials to ministers.

b. Concern over accountability linkages down through public sector agencies: were public servants properly responsive to their superiors?

c. Concern over effectiveness: did public sector agencies achieve the objectives set for them?

d. Concerns over efficiency: increasingly it was believed that where public sector agencies did achieve their objectives, they did not do so at anything like a satisfactory level of efficiency. Efficiency concerns were linked to, but not exclusively driven by, anxieties over the growth of public expenditure as a proportion of GDP.

e. The belief that personnel and industrial relations arrangements had become an impediment to the efficient and effective operation of the public sector.

f. The belief that public sector agencies had failed to address equity concerns and specifically bicultural issues. This was related to concern over personnel arrangements, but was also linked to more fundamental concerns over organisational culture.

The Treasury's briefing papers to the incoming Labour government in 1984, *Economic Management*, was a clear statement of these concerns. It offered a searching and highly influential critique of the structure and activities of state trading enterprises and government departments. The Treasury concluded that it was vital to reorganise departmental structures and operations in a manner that would allow them to emulate the claimed efficiency of private sector firms: 'The aim of management should be the implementation of systems in the public service that can perform broadly the same role for the public service as the price system does in the private sector' (Treasury, 1984, p. 287). During Labour's first term, structural reform in the state sector was confined largely to the corporatisation of state trading enterprises through the State-Owned Enterprises Act 1986.[2] The issue of departmental management structures was revived again with the publication of *Government Management*, the Treasury's briefing papers to the Labour government following the 1987 election. There, the Treasury (1987, pp. 55–6) identified the key elements of the management process as clarity of objectives, freedom to manage, accountability, effective assessment and adequate information flows. These pressures for reform led into the restructuring programme begun under the Labour government and continued under National.

Key Legislative Components of the Reform Programme

Only part of the restructuring programme was implemented through legislation. A major component came through the comprehensive reorganisation of government

---

2. The process of state sector reform is discussed at much greater length in Boston, Martin, Pallot and Walsh (1991).

departments and other public sector agencies. Much of that reorganisation was a consequence of efforts to achieve the policy objectives set down in the principal reform legislation. The three most important Acts were the State-Owned Enterprises Act 1986, the State Sector Act 1988, and the Public Finance Act 1989.

The State-Owned Enterprises Act established a number of state trading organisations as autonomous state-owned enterprises and obliged them to operate as profitably as companies not owned by the Crown. The SOEs are constrained by a limited social responsibility obligation and are required to be 'good employers'. Their CEs are appointed by, and responsible to, a board of directors appointed by the shareholding ministers. The shareholding ministers also have the capacity to alter an SOE's annual statement of corporate intent. However, the intention of the legislation was to separate ministers from the running of trading enterprises, and to date ministers in both Labour and National governments have largely resisted any temptation to intervene in the jurisdiction of either SOE managements or their boards.

The State Sector Act reorganised the public service and changed the relationship between ministers and heads of departments. It replaced the office of permanent heads of government departments with that of chief executives, appointed on a limited term contract with the possibility of renewal. It also established the Senior Executive Service, a small cadre of senior officials to act as a force for cohesion across the whole public service. This was prompted in part by another key aspect of the State Sector Act—the dissolution of the unified service. CEs were made employers of their staff and required to be 'good employers'. Departments were constituted as separate organisations for employing purposes with priority rights of appointment to other departments lost and the appeals system replaced by a modified reviews process of more limited jurisdiction.

The Public Finance Act introduced new financial management procedures into the public service. Accrual accounting replaced cash accounting, and departments had a thorough system of financial reporting imposed upon them. The emphasis in the financial management system shifted from input controls to output and outcome measures.

THE CONTEMPORARY PUBLIC SECTOR

The contemporary public sector in New Zealand is the product of a period of remarkable convulsion since the mid 1980s. Its architecture has been redesigned on a scale and at a pace that in earlier times would have been thought impossible. The remainder of this chapter sketches a very broad picture of the New Zealand public sector in the mid 1990s. Chapter 4 provides a more detailed analysis of the changes that have taken place to the machinery of government.

Table 3.4 shows the rapid fall in the numbers of central government employees in recent years. Indeed the number of employees has almost halved in the last decade. This fall has been due to a combination of factors, of which the most important have been fiscal constraints, corporatisation, privatisation, contracting out of central government functions, and general departmental restructuring. The pace and scope of restructuring have been such that it can be difficult to define the public sector. A pragmatic approach is to define the public sector as those agencies that come within the jurisdiction of the Audit Office. Table 3.5 shows the range and variety of the categories of those agencies as at April 1995. In this classification, public sector agencies come under three main headings: central government, Crown entities, and local government. Tables 4.2, 4.3, and 4.4 in Chapter 4 outline the changing identity of government departments since 1984.

Central Government

Central government consists chiefly of the departments of the public service, but it also includes three offices of Parliament: the office of the Ombudsmen, the Parliamentary Commissioner for the Environment, and the office of the Controller and Auditor-General (this is not yet formally an office of Parliament but should become so under proposed legislation). There are also five organisations, which form part of central government but do not fit easily into these categories. These are the Defence Force, the Police, the Office of the Clerk of the House of Representatives, the Parliamentary Counsel's Office, and the Parliamentary Service.

The public service is defined in s. 27 of the State Sector Act as 'the departments specified in the first schedule to this Act'. As Table 3.5 shows, by April 1995, there were forty-one government departments.[3] Three of these, the Department of Prime Minister and Cabinet (DPMC), the Treasury, and the SSC, are central agencies. Table 4.5 classifies other departments according to whether their main responsibility is policy advice, service delivery, taxation, review and audit functions, or trading operations.

Central agencies

Central agencies perform functions in some ways analogous to those carried out by the corporate office of a large private sector company. The size and complexity of the public sector, the magnitude of the financial and human resources it commands and the diverse and overlapping responsibilities of its many components make the need for some degree of central coordination imperative (Logan, 1991). The central agencies seek to protect 'the collective interests of the Crown'.

The Department of Prime Minister and Cabinet (DPMC) 'has an interest in any matter that is likely to carry implications for the Government as a whole' (SSC, 1993, p. 9). DPMC operates as a key institutional base for the Prime Minister. Its existence reflects an awareness that the Prime Minister needs officials' support in the same way

---

3. This number differs from the figure of thirty-nine departments in Chapter 4. The difference is partly accounted for by the inclusion of the new departments established as a consequence of the restructuring of the Department of Justice and the Ministry of Agriculture and Fisheries in 1995. Also, the Audit Office includes the Office of the Clerk, the Parliamentary Counsel's Office, and the Parliamentary Service in its list of departments, although these offices are not 'departments' under the State Sector Act.

Table 3.5   Public sector entities subject to audit by the Audit Office (April 1995)

Central Government		
The Crown Financial Statements	1	
Government Departments	41	
Offices of Parliament	3	45
Crown Entities and Other Public Bodies		
Education—		
Colleges of Education	5	
Technical Institutes	25	
Universities	7	
Primary Schools	2,099	
Intermediate Schools	148	
Secondary Schools	314	
Area Schools	37	
Special Schools	56	
Rural Education Activity Programmes	12	2,703
Health—		
Public Health Commission	1	
Regional Health Authorities	4	
Crown Health Enterprises	23	28
Business Development Boards	21	
Reserve Boards	79	
Other Crown Entities	76	
State-Owned Enterprises	16	
Māori Trust Boards	19	
Patriotic Councils and War Funds	16	
Primary Producer Boards	13	
Other Public Corporations	39	279
Local Government		
Regional Councils	12	
City Councils	15	
District Councils	59	86
Airport Companies	7	
Energy Companies	33	
Fish and Game Councils	13	
Licensing Trusts	27	
Local Authority Trading Enterprises	64	
Port Companies	13	
Sinking Fund Commissioners	61	
Cemetery Trustees	169	
Miscellaneous	5	392
Pacific Islands		
Tokelau Administration		1
		3,534

Note: These numbers do not include subsidiaries unless Parliament has established them as a special class of entity, e.g., LATEs.

Source: Office of the Controller and Auditor-General

as other ministers do, probably more so. Until the mid 1970s, the Prime Minister's Department was a small unit providing the Prime Minister with foreign policy advice only. This seemed to suit successive prime ministers until Robert Muldoon reorganised it into five sections. One of them was the Advisory Group whose role was to be the Prime Minister's 'eyes and ears' and to provide independent policy advice (Galvin, 1991). In 1989, a major review led to the establishment of the Department of Prime Minister and Cabinet (Hunn and Lang, 1989). The review grew out of rising concern over the policy dominance of the Treasury and a desire to ensure contestable policy advice within the government. There was also concern over policy coordination problems. The DPMC operates as any government department, providing the Prime Minister with professional policy advice. It is also responsible for the coordination of government operations. The 1989 review also established the Prime Minister's Office with responsibility for political, press, and secretarial services for the Prime Minister. These arrangements thus separate the partisan political services required by any Prime Minister from professional policy advice and coordination functions (Eaddy, 1992, pp. 170–2; Alley, 1992, pp. 183–6; McLeay, 1995, pp. 149–59).

The Treasury is the government's principal financial and economic adviser. It exercises oversight over public expenditure, manages the budgetary process and advises the government on economic policy and on many other policy areas as well. Treasury reports on all departmental expenditure proposals before cabinet. A critical Treasury report can substantially diminish the likelihood of securing approval. Treasury has a considerable influence on virtually all areas of domestic policy (Boston, 1992b, pp. 204–11).

The State Services Commissioner has an overall responsibility for the public sector as a collectivity. The Commissioner and Deputy Commissioner are appointed by the Governor-General in Council on the recommendation of the Prime Minister for five-year terms. They may only be dismissed by the Governor-General following a resolution of the House of Representatives. The formal responsibilities of the State Services Commissioner, as set out in s. 6 of the State Sector Act, are to:

a. review the machinery of government, including the allocation of functions to and between departments, the need to establish new departments or amalgamate existing ones and the coordination of functions among departments,
b. review the performance of departments and chief executives,
c. appoint chief executives of departments and negotiate their employment contracts,
d. maintain a Senior Executive Service,
e. negotiate collective employment contracts for public servants,
f. promote and develop personnel policies at an appropriate level of quality,
g. promote, develop and monitor equal employment opportunities policies and programmes in the public service,
h. furnish advice on the training and career development of staff,
i. provide advice on management systems, structures and organisations, and
j. carry out other tasks with regard to the management of the public service as requested by the Prime Minister.

It should be noted that not only does the Commissioner appoint CEs and evaluate their performance but he or she may also dismiss them with the agreement of the Governor-General in Council. In addition, although the SSC retains formal responsibility for the

Table 3.6   Crown entities (April 1995)

Accident Rehabilitation and Compensation Insurance Corporation.

Accounting Standards Review Board.

Agricultural and Marketing Research and Development Trust.

Alcoholic Liquor Advisory Council.

Animal Control Products Limited.

Asia 2000 Foundation of New Zealand.

Auckland International Airport Limited.

The Blood Transfusion Trust established under Section 92j of the Health Act 1956.

Boards as defined in Section 2 of the Reserves Act 1977.

Boards of Trustees constituted under Part IX of the Education Act 1989.

Broadcasting Commission.

Broadcasting Standards Authority.

Building Industry Authority.

Business Development Boards.

Careers Service

Casino Control Authority.

Civil Aviation Authority.

Commerce Commission.

Commissioner for Children.

Crown Health Enterprises.

Crown Research Institutes.

Early Childhood Development Unit.

Earthquake Commission.

Education and Training Support Agency.

Electoral Commission.

Fish and Game Councils.

Foundation for Research, Science, and Technology.

Government Superannuation Board.

Health and Disability Commissioner.

Health Research Council of New Zealand.

Health Sponsorship Council.

Hillary Commission for Sport, Fitness, and Leisure.

Housing Corporation of New Zealand.

Housing New Zealand Limited.

Human Rights Commission.

Institutions established under Part XIV of the Education Act 1989.

International Year of the Family Trust.

Land Transport Safety Authority of New Zealand.

Law Commission.

Learning Media Limited.

Legal Services Board.

Management Development Centre Trust.

Maritime Safety Authority of New Zealand.

Museum of New Zealand Te Papa Tongarewa.

New Zealand Artificial Limb Board.

Table 3.6   Crown entities (April 1995) *(continued)*

New Zealand Film Commission.

New Zealand Fire Service Commission.

New Zealand Fish and Game Council.

New Zealand Game Bird Habitat Trust Board.

New Zealand Government Property Corporation.

New Zealand Lotteries Commission.

New Zealand Lottery Grants Board.

New Zealand Qualifications Authority.

Every transferee company under the New Zealand Railways Corporation Restructuring
   Act 1990 in which the Crown holds 50 per cent or more of the issued ordinary shares.

New Zealand Sports Drug Agency.

New Zealand Symphony Orchestra Limited.

New Zealand Tourism Board.

New Zealand Trade Development Board.

The Office of Films and Literature Classification.

Pacific Islands Employment Development Board.

Police Complaints Authority.

The Power Company Limited.

Privacy Commissioner.

Public Health Commission.

Race Relations Conciliator.

Regional Health Authorities.

Residual Health Management Unit.

The Retirement Commissioner.

Road Safety Trust.

Securities Commission.

Special Education Service.

Standards Council.

Takeovers Panel.

Te Reo Whakapuaki Iriranga.

Te Taura Whiri I Te Reo Māori (Māori Language Commission).

Teacher Registration Board.

Tertiary Research Board.

Testing Laboratory Registration Council.

Transit New Zealand.

Transport Accident Investigation Commission.

Trustees of the National Library.

Wellington International Airport Limited.

Source: Office of the Controller and Auditor-General

negotiation of collective (but not individual) employment contracts for public servants, it has delegated operational responsibility for that to CEs.

The State Services Commissioner has a number of specific authorities with regard to government departments which may be used to carry out these functions. These authorities are set out in ss. 7–10 of the State Sector Act and include the right to conduct investigations, the right to obtain information from departments, and the right to enter departmental premises and require the production of documents or files and to question departmental employees in connection with that. Under s. 11 of the Act, the Prime Minister may direct the Commissioner to exercise any of the roles set out in ss. 6–10 over any part of the wider state services, such as the education or health sectors or Crown entities. The wording of these sections implies a much more directive role for the SSC than is actually the case. Understandably, the SSC seeks to avoid using these powers coercively, except in highly unusual circumstances.

It is clear that the modern SSC would not be as liable to the criticisms made of its predecessor, the Public Service Commission, by the Royal Commission in 1962. It now pays considerable attention to machinery of government issues, as would be expected given the restructuring programme. Moreover, the SSC has shed the responsibilities of central employer, and its interest in employment, industrial, and human resource management issues is to guard the government's collective interests and to provide strategic policy advice.

Crown entities

As Table 3.6 shows, Crown entities comprise a very wide range of organisational categories. A Crown entity is defined in s. 3(7) of the Public Finance Act as 'a body or statutory officer named or described in the Fourth Schedule to this Act'. The list in Table 3.6 gives some idea of the enormous variety of bodies that fall into this category and the scope of the activities they undertake. The concept of Crown entities was introduced in 1992 to bring this category of agencies within the provisions of the Public Finance Act. They replaced the traditional organisational form known as quangos. Crown entities are organisations established and generally funded by the government to perform certain functions. Most are governed by a board appointed by the government and managed by a chief executive and staff. Some operate as companies. The government has established a Crown Company Monitoring Advisory Unit (CCMAU) to monitor its ownership interest in them.

Crown entities undertake advisory, regulatory, purchasing, and service provision functions or a combination thereof. Their establishment and the imposition of financial management and accountability obligations upon them was an effort to rationalise this particular kind of public sector agency. The structure and procedures established are consistent with the general model of reform in New Zealand.

Local Government

Table 3.5 lists 392 local government agencies that are audited by the Audit Office. Many of them are not very significant in size or responsibilities—almost half are cemetery trustees—but some form an important component of the governmental system. The twelve regional councils have responsibility for the management of natural resources and civil defence, while the fifteen city councils and fifty-nine district councils have a wide

Table 3.7   The changing status of public sector trading enterprises

	Original Activity	Current Status (1995)
1. Corporate forms pre-dating 1987		
New Zealand Railways Corporation	Train, bus, ferry services	Privatised as separate companies
Housing Corporation	Concessional mortgages and rented property	Prime mortgages sold and rental properties assigned to Housing NZ. Residual HC and Ministry of Housing
Development Finance Corporation	Development bank	Privatised
Bank of New Zealand	Trading bank	Privatised
Air New Zealand	Air services	Privatised
Petroleum Corporation of NZ	Oil and gas production	Privatised
Tourist Hotel Corporation of NZ	Hotels	Privatised
Shipping Corporation of NZ	Shipping services	Privatised
Rural Bank	Agriculture bank	Privatised
Government Life Insurance Corp.	Life insurance	Now owned by policy holders
State Insurance	Insurance services	Privatised
2. Corporations established under State Owned Enterprises Act 1986		
a. Established in 1987		
Airways Corporation of NZ	Air traffic control	SOE
Coal Corporation of NZ	Coal mining	SOE
Electricity Corporation of NZ	Electricity generation	SOE—Transpower and Contact Energy since hived off
Government Property Services	Govt property holdings	SOE—selling assets
Land Corporation	Govt rural land-holdings and leases, property consultancy	SOE—some mortgages and licences sold
New Zealand Forestry Corporation	Forestry management	SOE
New Zealand Post	Postal services	SOE
PostBank	Savings bank	Privatised
Telecom Corporation	Telephone services	Privatised
b. Established since 1987		
Works and Development Services Corporation	Civil engineering and consultancy	SOE
Government Computing Services	Computer systems	Privatised
Government Supply Brokerage Corporation	Govt purchasing company	Privatised
NZ Liquid Fuels Investment	Crown company owning shares in synthetic fuel firms	Privatised
Radio New Zealand	National radio services	Commercial stations being privatised
Television New Zealand	Two national TV channels	SOE
Forestry Corporation of NZ	Production and harvesting of exotic forests	SOE
Timberlands West Coast	Production and harvesting of indigenous and exotic South Island forests	SOE
Meteorological Services	Weather forecasting	SOE
Transpower	Electricity transmission	SOE

Table 3.7   The changing status of public sector trading enterprises *(continued)*

Contact Energy	Electricity generation	SOE
3. Uncorporatised trading bodies		
Health Computing Services	Health computing	Privatised
Government Print	Printing services	Privatised
National Film Unit	Film making	Sold to TVNZ
Communicate New Zealand	Publicity Services	Privatised
4. Corporatised trading bodies		
Learning Media	Curriculum material	Crown entity
Animal Control Products	Manufacturing and distribution	Crown entity
Housing NZ	Rental housing	Crown entity
5. Other Crown companies		
9 Crown Research Institutes	Scientific research	Crown entities
23 Crown Health Enterprises	Health services	Crown entities
3 international airport companies	Airport management	Crown entities
6. Local authority corporations, etc.		
Electrical supply authorities	Local electricity distribution	Mix of private investor and local authority ownership
Port companies	Port operations	Mix of private investor and local authority ownership
Domestic airport companies	Airport management	Mix of Crown entities and joint ventures
Other LATEs	Buses, garbage collection, etc.	Some contracting out

Source: Based on Duncan and Bollard (1992), pp. 12–13, and updated by the authors

range of responsibilities ranging from roads, parks, and buildings to sewage, water, and rubbish collection and disposal (Bush, 1992).

The Health and Education Sectors

By far the biggest category of Crown entities is the 2,703 educational agencies, of which 2,561 are the boards of trustees of New Zealand's primary and secondary schools. The health sector restructuring has seen the establishment of Regional Health Authorities and Crown Health Enterprises, which are also categorised as Crown entities. Restructuring in both education and health was motivated by many of the concerns that drove the wider programme of state restructuring in New Zealand—concerns over efficiency, effectiveness, and fiscal exposure, as well as industrial relations and personnel issues.

State Trading Enterprises

Establishing appropriate structures and modes of operation for state trading enterprises was a major policy focus for both the Labour and National governments. Their programme of corporatisation and privatisation redrew the map of state enterprises in New Zealand. Table 3.7 sets out the original status and eventual fate of these enterprises between 1986 and 1995. It can be seen that some trading enterprises have been established as Crown companies, while some local authority corporations have been constituted as a mix of private investor and local authority ownership.

Corporatisation began with the State-Owned Enterprises Act 1986, which established nine new SOEs and provided for further SOEs to be established. The focus then shifted to privatisation, which began in Labour's first term and then gathered pace after 1987, despite an election commitment to the contrary. Privatisation has continued under National. Some privatisations have been very large with Telecom alone bringing in $4.25 billion, Petrocorp $801 million, State Insurance $735 million, Postbank $665 million and Air New Zealand $660 million. Others have been small scale—the sale of Communicate NZ (a public relations organisation) reaped only $200,000 and the National Film Unit was sold for $1.5 million (Mascarenhas, 1991, p. 47). In total more than twenty state organisations or assets have been privatised for a value of about two-thirds of the state's previous commercial assets (Boston, 1995b).

CONCLUSION

This chapter has sought to establish the wider context in which public sector management operates and to review the objectives of public sector management. Public agencies are established to serve a public purpose and that purpose, for the time being, is defined by ministers within the law. Public servants exist to serve the government. Although these statements may have an archaic ring, they remain the constitutionally correct formulation and the political reality. In the case of departments, the relationship with ministers is mediated through the chief executive, as it always has been, although since the State Sector Act it has acquired a much more formal character. Moreover, the departmental head's new status as employer has altered the nature of the direct relationship between the two. But the management of a government department is designed to ensure that the objectives established by the minister through various accountability documents are met. Inevitably, this gives public sector management a political character that is lacking in the private sector. Certainly, there are internal politics within any business organisation and any employee who ignores them is foolish in the extreme. But this is quite different from the political dimension attached to the work carried out in the public sector and to the management of that work.

The New Zealand public servant has for many years worked in an environment dominated by the executive. The power wielded by the executive in New Zealand under single-party majority governments was quite possibly without parallel in democratic systems. This chapter has shown that historically the institutional configuration of New Zealand politics placed few impediments in the way of an executive determined to carry out its objectives. The historical landscape displays a series of strong prime ministers used to, and comfortable with, the exercise of power and unaccustomed to opposition of any significance. Public servants and their managers have long operated in a context in which the Prime Minister and cabinet could, if they wished, ride roughshod over any opposition. Ironically, these very institutional arrangements facilitated the public sector reforms of the mid to late 1980s, which were in some respects a reaction against that style of government.

MMP may well change that. Indeed, the change has begun before the first MMP election, partly as a result of the parliamentary balance following the 1993 election and partly in anticipation of MMP. For public servants, the new environment creates new issues to be dealt with (see SSC, 1995d). The implications of the shift to MMP are explored further in other chapters of this book. But for public servants, the shift will be another chapter in a long-running process of fundamental change that has gripped the public sector since the mid 1980s. The changes to date and those looming combine to make the task of management in the public sector a demanding one.

4 institutional design in the public sector

One of my pet hates is ideological assertions or value judgements tarted up as serious analysis . . . As one example, I cite the arguable thesis that there should be a total separation between policy formulation and the delivery of services. Experience in areas like Defence and Māori Affairs suggest that a realist would . . . have to question this particular doctrine (Bolger, 1991, p. 13).

The previous chapter outlined the framework of government in New Zealand and noted some of the key changes to the organisation and management of the public sector since the mid 1980s. This chapter focuses on the issue of institutional design in the public sector. It begins with an account of the various administrative 'doctrines' (i.e. principles or rules of thumb) which have guided policy-makers around the world in their choice of organisational forms. It then considers the machinery of government changes in New Zealand since the mid 1980s and examines the doctrines upon which they were based.[1] Finally, it assesses the strengths and weaknesses of the new bureaucratic order.

New Zealand has not been alone in undertaking major machinery of government changes in recent times. Australia and Britain, in particular, have also made substantial institutional reforms (Halligan, 1987; Kemp, 1990; O'Toole and Jordan, 1995). In neither case, however, have these matched the scale or scope of the bureaucratic reorganisation in New Zealand. Moreover, while some of the structural changes in New Zealand have had their parallels elsewhere (e.g. the separation of commercial from non-commercial functions), others have been more distinctive. Among these are the preference for single-purpose rather than multi-purpose organisations, the separation of responsibilities for funding, purchasing and provision (e.g. in health care), and the attempt to separate (at both the ministerial and organisational levels) responsibilities for the Crown's ownership interests and purchase interests. Broadly speaking, New Zealand's machinery of government changes have brought it much closer to the Swedish model (sometimes referred to as the 'functional' model) in accordance with which the tasks of policy advice and implementation are generally carried out by separate agencies

---

1. The term 'machinery of government' refers to the systems and structures of government, the allocation of governmental functions among departments and other agencies, and mechanisms for coordinating departmental operations.

(see Ewart and Boston, 1993; Gustafsson, 1987; Vinde, 1967; Vinde and Petri, 1978). By contrast, many other OECD countries have continued to rely, at least to date, on more inclusive organisational arrangements. Under this approach (sometimes referred to as the 'sectoral' model), advisory and delivery functions are generally combined, or vertically integrated, within the same organisation.

INSTITUTIONAL DESIGN

Issues, Doctrines, and Justifications

Despite continuing debate over the best way of organising public bureaucracies, no scholarly consensus has emerged on many of the fundamental issues of institutional design.[2] There is thus no agreement on what organisational forms are the most effective for carrying out particular functions; nor is there even agreement on the criteria that should guide decisions on machinery of government matters. Against this, it is generally accepted that the study of institutional design is not an exact science and that the quest for a unified or general theory of organisational choice is misplaced. Equally, it is agreed that the design of public sector institutions should not be thought of primarily in mechanistic terms; departments and agencies are not so much bits of governmental machinery but rather the limbs of an integrated and constantly evolving organism. It is thus essential to adopt a 'whole of government' perspective; agencies must be seen as part of a larger canvas rather than as isolated, independent, self-contained units. Moreover, if they are to remain effective over time they must be adaptable and responsive to changing circumstances.

Over the centuries countries have developed their own unique range and combination of public sector institutions (and blend of public and private modes of delivering publicly funded services), reflecting their history, culture, values, bureaucratic traditions, constitutional arrangements, and economic imperatives. Among the many factors influencing the machinery of government, three deserve particular note: the role of the state, the constitutional framework, and the prevailing administrative doctrines and theories of organisational design.

Clearly, the nature, scope, and scale of a public bureaucracy will reflect the outcome of broader philosophical debates over the state's proper role. There is no point, for instance, worrying about how to organise and manage the delivery of health services if the state is deemed to have no responsibility for the funding, provision, or regulation of health care. Similarly, the structure of a country's bureaucracy will be influenced by

---

2. See, for example, Campbell (1983), Campbell and Peters (1988), Chapman (1972), Clarke (1972), Craswell and Davis (1993), Doig (1979), Dunleavy (1989a, 1989b), Dunsire (1990), Egeberg (1988), Halligan (1987), Hammond (1990), Hood and Dunsire (1981), Hood and Jackson (1991), Mansfield (1969), McLaren (1989), Painter (1987), Pitt and Smith (1981), Pollitt (1984), Review Committee (1994), Rowat (1963), Schaffer (1958, 1962), Self (1977), Smith, Marsh, and Richards (1993), Spann (1973), Treasury (1987), Weller (1991), Wettenhall (1986), and Wilson (1989).

the constitutional framework within which the institutions of the state must operate (e.g. federal versus unitary, presidential versus parliamentary, etc.). Under a parliamentary system, for instance, key considerations include the size and organisation of the cabinet, the conventions governing the provision of advice to ministers, and the nature and scope of the doctrine of ministerial responsibility. If the cabinet is large, then in all likelihood there will be correspondingly more ministerial departments—especially if each minister expects to have a separate portfolio (or group of advisers) and if each portfolio responsibility is thought best handled by a separate ministry. Although the size of the cabinet is only one of the factors influencing bureaucratic arrangements, it is interesting to observe that countries with relatively large cabinets, like Canada and New Zealand, have tended to have a large number of departments, whereas those with much smaller cabinets, like Switzerland and the USA, have correspondingly favoured a small number.

Having decided that the state has a responsibility for a particular task (e.g. policing, civil defence, environmental protection, or the provision of low-cost housing), at least three further questions arise. What kind of organisation should be chosen to undertake it (e.g. public or private, departmental or non-departmental, etc.)? How should the organisation be structured internally? And to whom should it be accountable? Such questions are often thought to be relatively mundane and largely technical in nature, but this is not the case. Institutional design poses important normative, political, and symbolic issues; it is thus centrally about values, and their relative importance. To quote Cameron:

> Organization is not merely a technical arrangement of work, authority, resources, and relationships. Alternative ways of organizing an institution represent choices among competing values. This applies to all organizations, governmental or non-governmental. . . . Organization is instrumental of values in two respects. First, values may be secured or rejected directly, insofar as they are or are not embodied in the organization itself. Values such as participation or professional autonomy, for example, are related directly to the way in which an institution is organized. Second, values may be advanced or retarded indirectly, insofar as the organization is or is not conducive to their attainment (1992, p. 167).

Many different values are potentially relevant to the issue of institutional design. This is reflected in the diversity of administrative doctrines that have been espoused over the years by rival schools of organisational theorists. Such doctrines have been usefully summarised and categorised by Hood and Jackson (1991). Drawing on this analysis, at least ten competing sets of doctrines can be identified. These, together with a brief summary of some of the typical normative justifications for each doctrine, are outlined in Table 4.1.

The Justification Paradox

Paradoxically, the same justifications are often used to recommend radically different organisational arrangements. Efficiency considerations, for example, provide a central justification for both public and private ownership and both large-scale and small-scale organisations. Contradictory recommendations of this nature are explicable in a variety of ways. Contextual factors provide part of the answer: there may be a strong efficiency case for large-scale organisations in some contexts but an equally good case for small-scale organisations in others. Indeed, most, if not all, of the administrative doctrines listed in Table 4.1 are to some extent context-dependent. For instance, relatively long hierarchies may be appropriate (for reasons of effective command and control) in the case of the police and the military but counter-productive for policy ministries. Like-wise, profit-making organisations may be best when self-interest can be adequately con-strained by the pressures of competition and objectives are strictly commercial but less advantageous when the provision of a good or service requires a high degree of altruism and dedication, when there is a substantial risk of opportunism, and when the specificat-ion and monitoring of performance are difficult and costly.

Another explanation for the justification paradox is the limited and ambiguous evi-dence supporting the merits of particular organisational arrangements. Partly for this reason, debates over machinery of government matters are notable for their rapid shifts in fashion (Peters, 1992). Particular institutional forms may be favoured by policy mak-ers at one point in time, only to fall into disfavour shortly afterwards. 'Bureaucratic giantism', for example, was favoured in the 1960s and 1970s in many countries, result-ing in the creation of super-departments and the amalgamation of local authorities into larger units. More recently, however, the 'bigger is better' approach has been balanced, if not superseded, by the notion that 'small is beautiful'. Likewise, the contingency school of organisation theory—which argues that the best or optimal institutional form depends on the particular context and task to be undertaken (or that form should follow function)—has been much in vogue in recent decades. Before this, the prevailing wis-dom favoured organisational uniformity and the standardisation of procedures and processes throughout the public sector. Another set of administrative doctrines that have been subject to the changing tides of fashion are those associated with the length of organisational hierarchies. Whereas long hierarchies were once generally favoured, the current wisdom supports relatively short hierarchies. The incentives provided by long hierarchies have been replaced, at least to some extent, by more flexible remuneration systems and performance-related pay.

Sectoral Versus Functional Approaches

One of the most significant shifts in administrative doctrine since the mid 1980s, cer-tainly in New Zealand, has been the gradual rejection of the sectoral model based on inclusive organisational modes (especially vertically integrated organisations). Tradi-tionally, the idea of placing advisory and delivery functions (or policy and execution) under a 'single roof' (i.e. within the same organisational boundaries) has been defended on the grounds that it improves interaction and feedback between those responsible for the provision of advice and those responsible for implementing the government's decisions (see Table 4.1). It is claimed, for instance, that vertical integration enables policy advisers to have a better feel for the problems of policy implementation, as well as more up-to-date knowledge about the changing needs and preferences of client groups; their advice is thus likely to be better informed. Further, if good feedback mechanisms exist within the organisation, advisers can act promptly when a policy proves difficult to implement or produces unanticipated consequences. Another justification for vertically integrated organisations is that they facilitate better administrative oversight and minimise transaction costs. Costly interorganisational negotiations and external contracting are avoided, with reliance being placed on relational contracts and the traditional modes of hierarchical control. Similar arguments, of course, are used to defend in-house provision against the claimed advantages of contracting out. In short, the case for a sectoral model, based on vertically integrated organisations, is that it yields better, more informed policy advice, enhances coordination, facilitates the quicker and easier identification and rectification of error, and improves accountability and control.

Critics of the sectoral approach, on the other hand, contend that it often leads to bureaucratic or producer 'capture' (Strategos, 1989a, 1989b, 1989c, 1989d; Treasury, 1987). This occurs when the operational interests within a department dominate the decision-making process, with the result that policy options with adverse consequences for existing departmental providers are not given adequate weight. As the Strategos Report on Defence puts it:

> Policy and advisory roles ought to be separated from the administrative and operational aspects of each department. The importance of this principle is to ensure that there is no monopoly on policy advice, and more importantly to ensure that policy is not the exclusive preserve of the operational agency. This principle does not preclude ongoing feedback to the policy agency, but tries to prevent advice being tailored to meet the needs of the operational agency rather than the needs of the consumer of the service (1989b, p. 76).

The SSC provides a similar rationale:

> In terms of the risk of policy capture, if operational interests and perspectives control or dominate the department, then those interests will pose a high risk to the development of the full range of policy advice options. This is because they (operations):

- [may] consider that the development of policy options which involve using means of service delivery other than themselves will damage their interests;
- may genuinely be unable to see the advantages of other options;
- generally believe that they are doing well and prefer options which strengthen, not weaken, their functioning;
- dislike options which support competitors or potential competitors or the view of groups they oppose;
- may be reluctant to support change if it means extra work;
- may be reluctant to change because of the costs of disruption and a preference for stability (1991, pp. 49–50).

By contrast, where the functions of policy advice and delivery are separate, it is argued that the advisers will be freed from 'the stultifying influences of bureaucracy' (Wildavsky, quoted in SSC, 1991, p. 50). They are thus likely to explore a wider range of

Table 4.1   Institutional design: key administrative doctrines and their justifications

Administrative Doctrines	Typical Justifications
1. Public versus private organisation	
1.1 Prefer public	Enhances public control and accountability Enhances allocative and productive efficiency Improves long-term planning and investment
1.2 Prefer private	Enhances allocative and productive efficiency Minimises political interference Enhances economic freedom
2. Kinds of public organisation	
2.1 Prefer ministerial department (classical public bureaucracy)	Increases ministerial control and responsibility Enhances parliamentary oversight and political accountability for administrative action Highly adaptable organisational form
2.2 Prefer non-departmental forms (statutory boards, commissions, publicly owned companies, trusts, universities etc.)	Reduces ministerial control and responsibility; facilitates local democratic control Facilitates recruitment of specialist or more representative personnel Increases managerial autonomy and administrative flexibility, thereby enhancing efficiency and effectiveness Facilitates organisational autonomy and independence from government
3. Kinds of private organisation	
3.1 Prefer for-profit organisation	Enhances managerial incentives and financial accountability Efficiency benefits of transferable property rights
3.2 Prefer non-profit, independent or voluntary organisation	Reduces opportunism Enables more diverse delivery of services and greater client sensitivity Use of volunteers reduces costs
4. Scale of organisation	
4.1 Prefer large scale	Enhances systematic learning and innovation Enhances coordination, priority setting and integrated planning Reduces influence of narrow, parochial interests Enhances productive efficiency (due to economies of scale)
4.2 Prefer small scale	More 'human', improves worker motivation Better administrative oversight; minimises span of control problems Enhances productive efficiency (due to diseconomies of scale and greater contestability of supply) Greater adaptivity and responsiveness
5. Functional scope of organisation	
5.1 Prefer multi-purpose	Enhances coordination and a holistic approach More efficient due to economies of scope
5.2 Prefer single-purpose	Narrower and sharper focus improves managerial oversight, external monitoring, and accountability Facilitates a more unified organisational culture and and mission

Table 4.1   Institutional design: key administrative doctrines and their justifications *(continued)*

6.	*Degree of uniformity*	
	6.1 Prefer uniform administrative structures	Enhances predictability and uniformity for customers Facilitates inter-agency comparisons, enhances monitoring, performance assessment and control
	6.2 Prefer pluriform administrative structures	Optimal organisational form depends on function and context
7.	*Inclusive versus divided responsibility*	
	7.1. Prefer inclusive ('single roof') organisation 7.11 via horizontal integration across related activities (or across the portfolio)	Enhances productive efficiency and flexibility Facilitates unified political responsibility Minimises transaction costs and improves consumer convenience via 'one-stop shops' Improves policy coordination
	7.12 via vertical integration (e.g. of policy-making and execution, purchasing and provision etc.)	Minimises transaction costs Enhances oversight and control Improves security of supply Improves policy coordination and quality of advice
	7.2 Prefer divided responsibility	Minimises conflicts of interest Minimises bureaucratic 'capture' Reduces the concentration of power; facilitates more checks and balances Enhances clarity of organisational mission Facilitates contestable provision, decentralisation of responsibility and greater client responsiveness
8.	*Single-source supply versus multi-source supply*	
	8.1 Prefer single-source supply	Enhances productive efficiency by minimising duplication, waste and transaction costs Facilitates specialisation and scale economies Enhances effectiveness by minimising potential confusion, deadlocks and inter-agency rivalry
	8.2 Prefer multi-source supply	Enhances productive efficiency by facilitating contestable supply Facilitates multiple advocacy
9.	*Combine like activities versus combine unlike activities*	
	9.1 Prefer like with like (e.g. on the basis of purpose, process, clientele or area)	Homogeneous organisations operate more effectively Facilitates greater specialisation
	9.2 Prefer administrative pluralism	Diversity facilitates creative synergies Avoids excessive concentrations of power over sensitive functions
10.	*Long versus short hierarchies*	
	10.1 Prefer long	Enhances motivation by providing more incentives Enhances command and control functions
	10.2 Prefer short	Improves information flows Reduces duplication Improves accountability and reduces buck-passing up the chain of command

Source: Based on Hood and Jackson (1991, pp. 71–100).

policy options and advance different policy positions. More specifically, it is claimed that they will be less inclined to favour public provision over private provision and in-kind assistance over cash transfers.

The functional model, then, is seen as one way to reduce the risk of capture. But it is also defended on the grounds that it offers the prospect of more contestable service delivery and sharper (as well as narrower) organisational objectives, thereby enhancing accountability. Further, where organisations have multiple, and often diverse, tasks—as under the sectoral model—it is claimed that they will have greater difficulty developing a unified culture or common sense of mission. Vertically distinct and more narrowly focused organisations, by contrast, can concentrate their whole energies on the central task in hand and, where properly managed, can develop a cohesive organisational culture. This is said to enhance their effectiveness and the quality of the outputs produced.

At the same time, advocates of the functional approach recognise that it might allow policy ministries to tender advice that lacks sensitivity to the practicalities and complex-ities of implementation. Indeed, as the Treasury acknowledges, 'Too rigorous a separa-tion would . . . be likely to impose costs at the expense of little gain' (1987, p. 77). Nevertheless, it is argued that policy analysts will usually have an incentive to build a strong relationship with the relevant operational agencies, thus reducing the dangers of the government receiving 'ivory tower' advice. Also, the inclusion of operational per-spectives in advice to ministers can be encouraged through the use of appropriate quality assurance mechanisms.

Some Other Design Issues

Vertical integration, of course, is not the only way to achieve the benefits of inclusiveness. Inclusiveness can also be secured horizontally (see Table 4.1). For example, a single organ-isation can be made responsible for providing policy advice across a related set of issues, such as all education-related matters (including tertiary and early childhood education). A key justification for an 'across-the-portfolio' approach such as this is that it improves policy coordination and priority setting within a particular policy domain. Although arguments in favour of horizontal inclusiveness have a certain intuitive appeal, they are not without their problems (Hawke, 1988). One of these is determining the proper scope of the activ-ities that should be linked horizontally within the same organisation. To take the case of education again: some might contend that education and science are closely related; hence, policy advice in respect of these activities should be combined under the same organisa-tional umbrella. Yet if education and science are linked, so too are education and employ-ment, education and the arts, and in some cases education and health care (e.g. the training of health professionals). The difficulty, of course, is that if too many related policy domains are located within the same organisation, there might be serious span-of-control problems, not to mention a massive workload for the responsible portfolio minister. Equally, there is the possibility that certain policy concerns might simply be 'lost' or ignored if placed within the confines of a large, heterogeneous department.

Yet another issue concerns the relative merits of departmental and non-departmental institutional forms. As a general rule, departmental status tends to be the preferred option when a high level of ministerial involvement, direction, and responsibility is deemed appropriate. This is generally because of the nature and significance of the government's purchase interest, in particular the difficulties of *ex ante* output specification and/or *ex post* assessment of performance. By contrast, non-departmental institutions (i.e. SOEs and Crown entities) tend to be favoured when there is less need (or political pressure) for frequent ministerial involvement, when the government has a more limited purchase interest, or when there are fewer problems of specifying and measuring organisational outputs.

Finally, there is the question of what criteria should guide the groupings of various government activities. As Spann (1973, p. 52) and Pollitt (1984, p. 159) observe, a common assumption is that similar tasks should be grouped together in the same organisation. But this begs the question of what kind of 'similarity' is relevant. According to Gulick (1937), if the principle of 'similarity' is used as the main criterion for organising the bureaucracy, four options are available. Agencies can be structured in line with: (i) the service rendered; (ii) the processes used; (iii) the people served; and (iv) the area served. A further possibility, advanced by the Treasury (1987), is to organise departments on the basis of certain key values, such as wealth maximisation, equity, and security. Predictably, there are problems with each of these proposals, and in practice the principle of similarity has not been consistently applied by public administrators in any of the major liberal democracies (Boston, 1989a; McLaren, 1989).

THE EVOLUTION OF NEW ZEALAND'S BUREAUCRATIC LANDSCAPE

In the century or so prior to the mid 1980s the structure of New Zealand's bureaucracy evolved in a more or less *ad hoc* fashion (Lipson, 1948; Polaschek, 1958; Webster, 1989). Most machinery of government changes were the result of new policy initiatives, changing societal needs, or political manoeuvrings; they were not the product of concerted efficiency drives or the application of grand bureaucratic designs. Various features of the bureaucratic landscape during this period are particularly worth of note. First, there was a heavy reliance on ministerial departments for the conduct of the business of government;[3] hence, the 'core' public sector was relatively large. Second, the sectoral model was predominant with most departments undertaking a range of advisory, delivery, and regulatory functions. Many also combined significant commercial and noncommercial responsibilities. Third, there was a relatively large number of departments: there were 31 in 1890, 49 in 1946, 41 in 1957, and 34 in 1984, prior to Labour's state sector reforms (see Table 4.2). This contrasts markedly with countries like Britain, Sweden and the USA, where it has been customary to have fewer than twenty departments. Fourth, non-departmental organisations took a wide range of forms: government-owned companies, public corporations, advisory bodies, regulatory agencies, tribunals, boards, councils, and commissions. Accordingly, accountability arrangements also varied a good deal.

The state sector reforms between the mid 1980s and the mid 1990s brought about a radical refashioning of the departmental landscape. In the eleven years to July 1995, twenty-six new departments (mainly small, sector-based policy ministries) were created, twenty-three departments were abolished, corporatised or privatised, and most of the remainder were extensively reorganised (see Tables 4.3 and 4.4).[4] As a result, the number of departments increased from thirty-four in July 1984 to thirty-nine in July 1995. More important, the nature of most departments changed significantly. Whereas in 1984 only two departments had under 100 staff, by the mid 1990s more than a dozen fell into this category. Whereas in 1984 at least eight departments had over 3,000 staff, by the mid-1990s only three (Corrections, Inland Revenue, and Social Welfare) exceeded this number. And whereas the sectoral model predominated in 1984, by the mid 1990s the functional model was much more common: fewer than half the departments in mid 1995 had significant delivery responsibilities (i.e. in addition to policy advice and contract management). Evidence of the declining role of departments as service providers is reflected in two sets of statistics: first, the total number of staff employed by departments fell from around 88,000 in 1984 to 61,000 in 1988 and to fewer than 35,000 in 1994; and second, of the outputs purchased by the government in 1994–95, $9.65 million (61.5 per cent) came from non-departmental organisations as compared with $6.05 million from departments (Hunn, 1994b, p. 11).

Many of the machinery of government changes that occurred between the mid 1980s and the mid 1990s were the product of wider policy changes that affected the role and operations of particular departments. Labour's programme of economic liberalisation (e.g. the removal of subsidies and import controls, the deregulation of financial markets,

---

3. The departments listed in the first schedule of the State Sector Act 1988 (and the State Sector Amendment Act No. 2 1989) have a variety of titles including 'department', 'ministry', 'office', and 'commission'. There is little consistency in the use of such terms. On the whole, however, the term 'ministry' has been applied in recent years in New Zealand to government agencies primarily concerned with providing policy advice to ministers and which have few, if any, delivery functions. By contrast, the term 'department' is now generally applied to government agencies mainly concerned with the delivery of services. For a systematic examination of the uses of terms like 'ministry' and 'department' see Wettenhall (1986). Note, too, that in accordance with the current policy framework, government agencies that have a direct accountability relationship between their chief executive and a minister—as provided for in Section 32 of the State Sector Act—are deemed to be departments. Those agencies that have an indirect accountability relationship between their chief executive and a minister are not departments and lie outside the core public service. This currently includes the Police and the New Zealand Defence Force, SOEs, and Crown entities. Finally, whereas SOEs and Crown entities have a separate legal status, departments do not.

4. Most of the 'new' departments are reconfigurations, or parts, of previous departments. Likewise, in many cases where departments were abolished, their functions were taken over by other departments.

Table 4.2   Departments and ministries as at July 1984

Ministry of Agriculture and Fisheries	Lands and Survey Department
Audit Department	Legislative Department
Commission for the Environment	Māori Affairs Department
Crown Law Office	Post Office
Customs Department	Prime Minister's Department
Ministry of Defence	Public Trust Office
Education Department	Department of Scientific and Industrial Research
Ministry of Energy	Social Welfare Department
Ministry of Foreign Affairs	State Insurance Office
New Zealand Forest Service	State Services Commission
Government Printing Office	Statistics Department
Health Department	Tourist and Publicity Department
Housing Corporation	Trade and Industry Department
Inland Revenue Department	Ministry of Transport
Internal Affairs Department	Treasury
Justice Department	Valuation Department
Labour Department	Ministry of Works and Development

Total: 34

Table 4.3   Departments abolished, corporatised, or privatised July 1984–July 1995

Ministry of Agriculture and Fisheries	Lands and Survey Department
Ministry of Defence	Legislative Department
Department of Education	Māori Affairs Department
Ministry of Energy	Ministry of Māori Affairs
Commission for the Environment	Post Office
Department of Foreign Affairs	Prime Minister's Department
New Zealand Forest Service	Department of Scientific and Industrial Research
Government Printing Office	State Insurance Office
Department of Health	Tourist and Publicity Department
Housing Corporation	Trade and Industry Department
Iwi Transition Agency	Ministry of Works and Development
Department of Justice	

Total: 23

Table 4.4   New or significantly reshaped departments and ministries as at 1 July 1995

Ministry of Agriculture	Ministry of Forestry
Ministry of Commerce	Ministry of Health
Department of Conservation	Ministry of Housing
Department of Corrections	Ministry of Justice
Department for Courts	Ministry of Māori Development
Ministry of Cultural Affairs	National Library of New Zealand
Ministry of Defence	Ministry of Pacific Island Affairs
Ministry of Education	Department of Prime Minister and Cabinet
Education Review Office	Ministry of Research, Science and Technology
Government Superannuation Fund	Serious Fraud Office
Ministry for the Environment	Department of Survey and Land Information
Ministry of Fisheries	Ministry of Women's Affairs
Ministry of Foreign Affairs and Trade	Ministry of Youth Affairs

Total: 26

etc.) necessitated important changes to the functions of departments like Customs, Trade and Industry, and Agriculture and Fisheries. Likewise, the restructuring of the tax system and the introduction of new income maintenance provisions, such as family support and family care, required major changes to the staffing and operations of Inland Revenue and Social Welfare. Labour's strategy of devolving or decentralising responsibility for the delivery of governmental services impacted significantly on most of the service-oriented departments like Education, Health, Labour, Māori Affairs, and Social Welfare. In the early 1990s, National's policy changes in areas like health care and housing had a major impact on the role and structure of various departments. Quite apart from this, the internal organisation of most departments was affected by the financial management reforms of the late 1980s, the introduction of new technology, and the devolution of the SSC's personnel responsibilities to individual departments. Thus, departments previously organised in accordance with the requirements of programme-based budgeting had to adjust their internal structures to accommodate the new system of appropriations based on output classes. Similarly, the corporate services branches in many departments had to be reorganised and expanded to cope with their new personnel and industrial relations functions.

The Treasury Model

A crucial influence on the nature and scale of the machinery of government changes between the mid 1980s and mid 1990s were the radical ideas for structural reform advanced by the Treasury (1987, pp. 74–5). From the Treasury's perspective, the central government bureaucracy in the mid 1980s suffered serious defects. Not merely did most government departments lack clear, consistent objectives but also the existing structures tended to generate 'provider capture' and interorganisational conflict. The Treasury gave considerable thought to how such problems might best be alleviated and, in the process, developed its own distinctive theoretical framework to guide policy-making on questions of governance structure and institutional choice. This framework drew heavily on the new institutional economics (see Chapter 2; Bushnell and Scott, 1988; Scott and Gorringe, 1989). Accordingly, the Treasury placed emphasis on minimising transaction costs and agency costs, avoiding dual or multiple accountabilities, minimising the risks of provider capture, and distancing ministers from decisions of an operational nature. It also extolled the virtues of contestability (or multi-source supply), transparency (e.g. of organisational objectives, public subsidies, and desired governmental outcomes), competitive neutrality (e.g. between public and private suppliers), and the institutional separation of potentially conflicting objectives (such as ownership and purchase interests). Broadly speaking, it favoured private ownership and non-ministerial organisational forms.

The Treasury, of course, has not been the only department providing advice on machinery of government issues. The SSC has also contributed in important ways to the debate over how best to organise the bureaucracy, as have a number of consultancy firms, such as Strategos. In addition, ministerial preferences and concerns have influenced the nature of the institutional choices made in particular cases.

THE NEW REGIME

Objectives and Key Administrative Doctrines

The decisions taken since 1984, together with the available documentary evidence, indicate that public policy on machinery of government matters has been guided by at least eight broad objectives. New Zealand's organisational choices, in other words, were designed to:

a. maximise allocative and productive efficiency;
b. reduce the range of state functions under direct ministerial control;
c. ensure clear lines of managerial and political accountability;
d. ensure that all organisations have a clear mission and that inconsistent objectives are transparent and, ideally, the responsibility of separate organisations;
e. ensure high-quality, contestable policy advice across all sectors;
f. minimise the risk of bureaucratic, provider, or regulatory capture;
g. ensure good horizontal coordination; and
h. improve the bureaucratic representation of disadvantaged or poorly represented groups (e.g. Māori, women, youth, consumers, etc.).

New Zealand's experience indicates that such objectives are not always compatible. Enhancing the contestability of policy advice or improving the representation of disadvantaged groups necessarily entails some overlapping responsibilities; yet this falls foul of the objective of productive efficiency. Similarly, endeavours to minimise the risk of provider or regulatory capture might give rise to organisational arrangements that impose relatively high transaction costs, exacerbate coordination problems, and impede information flows. Consequently, trade-offs are necessary. How these trade-offs are made and which particular administrative doctrines are ultimately embraced will be influenced, as noted earlier, by the overall climate of opinion and the prevailing ideological consensus. In New Zealand's case, the dominance of market liberalism and managerialism since the mid 1980s has had a significant bearing on the preferred administrative doctrines and practices.

In keeping with the categories outlined in Table 4.1, there has been a general preference in New Zealand for:

a. private over public organisations (especially for commercial functions);
b. non-departmental organisations over ministerial departments (especially for policy implementation rather than advice);
c. small-scale over large-scale organisations;
d. single-purpose over multi-purpose organisations;
e. pluriform over uniform administrative structures;
f. divided over inclusive responsibility (i.e. the separation of policy and operations, the separation of funder, purchaser and provider, the separation of operations and regulation, the separation of provision and review/audit, the separation of commercial and non-commercial, and the separation of responsibilities for monitoring the Crown's ownership interests and its purchase interests);

g. multi-source over single-source supply;
h. like with like (primarily on the basis of purpose or the kind of service);
i. short hierarchies;
j. straight-line accountabilities (i.e. the avoidance of multiple principals); and
k. decentralised administration for the delivery of services.

Space does not permit a detailed commentary on the extent to which each of these doctrines has been applied. However, it would be wrong to suggest that they have all been implemented in a rigorous, consistent or thoroughgoing fashion. Nor have they been pursued with a dogmatic purity. On the contrary, in many instances pragmatic judgments and political considerations have had a decisive influence on particular institutional changes. For example, despite the substantial privatisation programme during the late 1980s, a number of important commercial organisations remain in public ownership, and there has been little public or political support for privatisation in areas like education, health care, and scientific research. Similarly, although there has been a preference for single-purpose organisations on the grounds that they permit a greater clarity of objectives and unity of purpose and improved managerial oversight, there has been no attempt to reduce the scope of each organisation's activities to a single output class (let alone a single output). Hence, virtually all departments, even the smallest, supply more than one output class, and some supply a significant number (e.g. Commerce and Internal Affairs).

Similar comments apply to many other of the administrative doctrines currently in vogue. Flatter managerial structures have been adopted in most departments, but not universally. Some organisations decentralised many of their operational activities in the late 1980s and early 1990s only to partially recentralise subsequently. Likewise, the preference for straight-line accountability (or unity of command) has not been translated into practice in a thoroughgoing fashion. Indeed, numerous exceptions remain, and in some instances multiple accountability arrangements have been an inevitable, if unwanted, consequence of embracing other administrative doctrines. Examples of existing multiple accountabilities include:

a. departmental chief executives simultaneously serving a number of ministers (e.g. Commerce, Foreign Affairs and Trade, and Internal Affairs), or a minister and an advisory board (e.g. the National Library);
b. the heads of organisations that fall within a department having a direct accountability to a minister as well as to the relevant department's chief executive (e.g. the Ministry of Consumer Affairs is located within the Ministry of Commerce, the Office of Treaty Settlements is linked to the Ministry of Justice, and CCMAU falls under the umbrella of the Treasury); and
c. the heads of various Crown entities, although in theory primarily accountable to their respective boards, in practice reporting regularly to ministers (e.g. Accident Rehabilitation and Compensation Insurance Corporation [ACC] and the New Zealand Qualifications Authority).

Table 4.5   Departments and ministries as at 1 July 1995

Central agencies	*Review and audit functions*
Department of Prime Minister and Cabinet	Audit Office
State Services Commission	Education Review Office
Treasury	

Mainly policy functions	*Significant delivery and policy functions*
Agriculture	Foreign Affairs and Trade
Commerce	Labour
Cultural Affairs	Social Welfare
Defence	
Education	*Mainly delivery functions (and policy)*
Environment	
Fisheries	Conservation
Forestry	Corrections
Health	Courts
Housing	Crown Law Office
Justice	Customs
Māori Development	Inland Revenue
Pacific Island Affairs	Internal Affairs
Research, Science and Technology	National Library
Transport	Serious Fraud Office
Women's Affairs	Statistics
Youth Affairs	Survey and Land Information

Residual category—mainly trading operations
Government Superannuation Fund
Public Trust Office
Valuation New Zealand

Total: 39

The preference for divided organisational responsibilities has also been applied in a variable fashion (see Table 4.5). To illustrate: the formal institutional separation of policy and operations (and, where relevant, the separation of funder, purchaser, and provider roles) has been implemented to a greater extent in areas like defence, environmental administration, health care, housing, justice, and scientific research than in areas like labour, police, and social welfare. Probably the strictest application of the functional model is the area of scientific research. Here there is a formal split between the roles of funder, purchaser, and provider: the Ministry of Research, Science and Technology is essentially a single-purpose policy ministry, while the Foundation for Research, Science and Technology (FoRST) purchases scientific research via a competitive bidding process from a series of CRIs (currently nine), tertiary institutions and private providers and monitors the performance of providers. The monitoring of the Crown's ownership interest in the CRIs is carried out by CCMAU. Although the Ministry is the government's chief adviser on science policy, FoRST is also funded to provide policy advice. It thus has multiple advisory, purchasing, and monitoring roles.

A similar pattern, albeit more complex, is evident in health care. Here again the roles of funding, purchasing, and provision have been allocated to different organisations: the Ministry of Health provides funds to the four RHAs, which in turn purchase health services from the twenty-three CHEs and various private providers. While the RHAs monitor the performance of providers, the Crown's ownership interest in the CHEs is monitored by CCMAU. By comparison with the funding of scientific research, the funding of health care is complicated not merely by the decision to have four purchasing agencies but also by the existence of the ACC (which has independent taxing and purchasing responsibilities on behalf of accident victims). As far as the relationship between policy advice and operations is concerned, the situation in health care is even less clearcut. The Ministry of Health is the government's principal adviser on health care matters but it also has major regulatory responsibilities, including the administration of numerous Acts (such as the Medicines Act 1981, the Health Act 1956 and the Mental Health Act 1992), the licensing and inspection of health-care providers, and the provision of support services to various occupational registration boards. Further, the four RHAs all have a significant policy role and regularly supply advice to the Minister of Health, as does the ACC. And the Treasury provides advice on health matters to the Minister of Finance.

Although the objective of splitting policy and operations has been applied in many other policy domains (agriculture, defence, environment, housing, forestry, justice, etc.), the resulting organisational arrangements have been less wedded to the functional model than might be supposed. Take the case of environmental administration—which was the first area to undergo major institutional reforms in early 1987. Here the three existing departments (the Commission for the Environment, the Department of Lands and Survey, and the New Zealand Forest Service) were replaced with two SOEs (Forestry Corporation and Land Corporation), two policy ministries (the Ministry for the Environment and the Ministry of Forestry), two departments with mixed responsibilities (the Department of Conservation and the Department of Survey and Land Information), a residual Department of Lands (which ceased operations in 1989) and a Parliamentary Commissioner for the Environment (Boston, 1987; Bührs, 1990; Dixon, Ericksen, and Gunn, 1989). The separation of policy and operations was a central feature of these reforms, yet it was not pressed to the maximum extent possible. The Department of Conservation, although primarily an operational department (with responsibilities for managing the conservation estate, protecting endangered species, and providing recreational facilities), also has a policy advice role and advocacy and educational functions. The Department of Survey and Land Information also has a mix of operational and advisory responsibilities. Nevertheless, the primary responsibility for providing environmental policy advice, certainly advice of a strategic nature, lies with the Ministry for the Environment.

The idea of separating regulatory (or review) responsibilities from advisory and delivery functions (e.g. to avoid the regulators being captured by, or capturing, advisers and/ or implementers) has been pursued to varying degrees in different policy domains. As already noted, the Ministry of Health combines both functions (although internally the functions are carried out by separate administrative units). Much the same is true of Commerce, Inland Revenue, Internal Affairs, Labour, and Social Welfare. In many other areas, there has been a preference for separate regulatory (or review) agencies (e.g. the Broadcasting Standards Authority, the Commerce Commission, the Education Review Office, the Police Complaints Authority, the Securities Commission and the proposed Environmental Risk Management Authority).

Arguably, the advisory/regulatory/delivery split has been pursued most vigorously in the area of transportation (see Audit Office, 1994a; Martin, 1995a; Stack, 1995). The Ministry of Transport, once a large multi-purpose department with thousands of staff, has become primarily a policy ministry with fewer than sixty staff. Its former regulatory and delivery functions are undertaken, on contract, by a range of statutory organisations. Regulatory tasks are carried out by three organisations, each overseeing a particular mode of transport: the Civil Aviation Authority, the Land Transport Safety Authority, and the Maritime Safety Authority. Responsibility for investigating aircraft, rail and maritime accidents lies with the Transport Accident Investigation Commission. In addition, several bodies are responsible for the funding and management of the state highway network. Despite the formal organisational separation of policy and regulatory activities, the three regulatory bodies are all funded to provide advice to the government. Indeed, the combined appropriations to these bodies for this purpose almost equal the funds appropriated to the Ministry of Transport for the provision of advice. To suggest, therefore, that the new institutional framework is characterised by strict policy/ regulatory or policy/delivery splits is not, in fact, correct. Rather, the aim is to separate regulatory and delivery functions (in the interests of minimising conflicts of interest) and to enhance the contestability of advice by placing responsibility for the provision of broader or more strategic advice on transport issues in an agency one step removed from the day-to-day demands of regulation and service delivery. The relative merits of such an arrangement (e.g. in terms of its impact on the quality of the advice provided and the cost-effectiveness of the various regulatory outputs) remains an open question. However, it almost certainly involves some duplication of effort and places a premium on developing effective mechanisms for inter-agency coordination.

Where departments have retained some or all of their core operational activities (e.g. Commerce, Internal Affairs, Labour, and Social Welfare), the responsibility for strategic policy development has generally been separated internally from regulatory and delivery activities. In the case of Social Welfare, for instance, separate business units (or agencies) carry out the department's responsibilities in the fields of policy advice, income support, the funding of non-departmental service delivery organisations, and the protection and care of young persons. The Social Policy Agency (SPA) has a mandate to provide advice on a wide range of social policy matters, including the provision of income support and social welfare services and the integration of social assistance programmes. In formulating advice, there is a good deal of interaction with the operational agencies within Social Welfare, as well as other government and non-government agencies. Moreover, each of the operational agencies retains some policy expertise; hence, even though the functional model has not been applied, there is still a degree of contestability (both *within*

Social Welfare and *between* the department and other agencies). There is little evidence to suggest that the nature of the advice provided by the SPA has been captured by the department's operational units.

AN EVALUATION OF THE NEW ORDER

Evaluating the merits of New Zealand's massive restructuring of the machinery of government poses numerous difficulties. For one thing, there is a dearth of published research data and solid evidence. To date, relatively few independent, systematic, in-depth studies of the various structural changes have been undertaken—the result of limited academic research and National's decision in 1991 to discontinue the regular departmental review programme initiated by the SSC in 1989 (see Trotman, 1993). For another, there is the continuing problem of determining the appropriate benchmarks for assessing the merits of particular organisational changes and securing relevant, reliable data. The relationship between organisational structure and individuals' behaviour is also poorly understood.

Assessing the changes in New Zealand against their intended objectives poses at least two problems: first, in some cases the objectives were poorly stated, conflicting, incomplete, or even deliberately concealed; and second, it is often difficult to evaluate in any meaningful way whether the stated objectives have been achieved. Changes in productive efficiency can be measured when outputs are readily quantifiable, but in the core public sector this is frequently not the case. A further complication is that many machinery of government changes occurred as part of a much broader package of reforms. Hence, the new organisations have different responsibilities from those they replaced and might be operating in a radically altered regulatory framework. This makes it all the harder to isolate the particular effects, beneficial or otherwise, of structural change. Even if it is possible to demonstrate that a specific structural reorganisation has enhanced (or reduced) productive efficiency, assessing changes in organisational responsiveness, flexibility and adaptability, the quality of advice, the degree of coordination, the risk of capture, the degree of accountability, and the morale of staff is much harder.

Partly because of the difficulties of measuring organisational effectiveness and evaluating the merits of different structural arrangements, debates over machinery of government issues have often been characterised by appeals to supposedly 'scientific' or 'rational' principles of management, a heavy reliance on anecdotal evidence, the repetition of slogans, and the transformation of useful rules of thumb into administrative dogma. Where reliable evidence has been compiled in other countries, the results have not always been encouraging for the advocates of institutional reform (Hood, Huby, and Dunsire, 1985; Peters, 1992). March and Olson, in their study of administrative reorganisations at the federal level in the USA, conclude that:

> In terms of their effects on administrative costs, size of staff, productivity, or spending, most major reorganization efforts have been described by outsiders, and frequently by participants, as substantial failures. Few efficiencies are achieved; little gain in responsiveness is recorded; control seems as elusive after the efforts as before (1983, p. 288).

A similarly disappointing record is evident at the state and local government level.

At the same time, not all machinery of government changes around the world have been negative or merely neutral in their effects; some have undoubtedly been positive (see Weller, 1991). This is certainly true in New Zealand's case where significant gains can be identified in various areas. For example:

a. There have been major improvements in productive efficiency and standards of service as a result of the separation of commercial and non-commercial operations and the establishment of the SOEs (Duncan and Bollard, 1992; Scott, Bushnell, and Sallee, 1990, pp. 148–50).
b. There have been improvements in the scope, quality, and contestability of advice available to governments as a result of the creation of policy ministries where previously departmental advice was patchy or virtually non-existent (e.g. strategic advice on the environment, science, and women's issues).
c. Departmental managers report that their organisations have a much sharper focus and a clearer organisational mission, and that there is less intra-organisational conflict over objectives; further, senior managers in policy-oriented ministries are less distracted by the demands of operational activities.

The major structural changes since the mid 1980s have also brought other benefits: they have contributed to the creation of a more enterprising public service culture, provided opportunities to remove poorly performing staff, and in some instances facilitated substantive policy reforms (e.g. by overcoming previously entrenched departmental inertia or resistance). One clear indication that the new bureaucratic order is working tolerably well is the fact that, with relatively few exceptions, policy-makers have not felt obliged to undertake major revisions of the new institutional arrangements.

Against this, the changes have generated numerous criticisms. Among these are the following:

a. Too much emphasis has been placed on the benefits of structural change and too little on their costs. Further, there has been a preoccupation with *structural* solutions to policy problems at the expense of potentially simpler and cheaper non-structural remedies. In some cases, the fiscal and social costs of the changes have been considerable, possibly outweighing any subsequent gains in productive efficiency.
b. The current allocation of functions between departments and Crown entities is, at times, puzzling and not necessarily compatible with traditional notions of ministerial responsibility. It is also claimed that the increasing reliance on contractualist modes of governance might be undermining political accountability (see Martin, 1994a, 1995a).
c. By international standards, New Zealand has a large number of departments, many of which are very small. Sector-specific and population-based ministries have certain advantages, but they also have well-known disadvantages (e.g. in terms of increasing the costs of inter-agency coordination and conflict resolution).
d. While the attempt to separate policy and operational responsibilities appears to have worked reasonably well in the majority of cases, its application in others has been

much less successful (e.g. defence). Moreover, it could result in advisers in policy ministries becoming detached from the communities or sectors about which they are providing advice and are supposed to have detailed knowledge (e.g. education, housing, and transport).

e. The preference for single-purpose organisations and the separation of potentially conflicting functions has led in some cases to the creation of a plethora of functionally distinct, but nonetheless interdependent, organisations. This in turn has led to greater problems of horizontal coordination, territoriality, and inter-agency conflict; it has also resulted in some organisations reporting to a series of monitoring and review bodies (e.g. as in the health sector) and intensified problems for consumers by abandoning the concept of a 'one-stop shop' (e.g. education and housing).

f. While multiple purchasing and/or supply arrangements might be desirable—in terms of improving productive and allocative efficiency—in some contexts, in others their advantages are more questionable. For instance, efficient and effective service delivery in areas like secondary health services and scientific research typically requires long-term supply arrangements, relative institutional stability, and inter-agency collaboration (rather than competition). Hence, the attempt to create genuine contestability and market-driven organisations might prove counter-productive.[5]

g. The idea of separating, at an institutional and ministerial level, the responsibility for the Crown's ownership interests and its purchaser interests is of dubious wisdom when the Crown is the principal purchaser (and hence the two interests are strongly interdependent).

h. The concern about bureaucratic, provider, or regulatory capture, while proper, has been exaggerated. Further, the view that the risk of capture is always best reduced via institutional separation is open to doubt.

It is not possible here to examine each of these criticisms in depth. However, brief comments on some of them are in order.

The costs of structural change

Whatever the merits of the new institutional design, the costs of the massive changes in organisation boundaries have been substantial. These include the direct financial costs of reorganisation (including the costs of consultants' reports, departmental submissions, redundancy pay, redeployment and retraining, etc.), the costs of disruption to the ongoing business of government, and the social and psychological costs (including the stresses and strains caused by extra work pressures, job insecurity, the loss of morale, redundancy, etc.) (see Lister, Rivers, and Wilkinson, 1991). To date, no comprehensive evaluations of the costs of the various machinery of government changes have been undertaken, although figures have been published from time to time on the costs of redundancy pay and consultancy fees in particular cases. For example, between Septem-

5. For various views on the merits of the organisational arrangements in the health sector see Ashton (1992), Fougere (1994), Howden-Chapman (1993), Howden-Chapman and Ashton (1994), Wakelin (1994).

ber 1986 and July 1990 redundancy pay to state employees cost more than $310 million (*Dominion Sunday Times*, 22 July 1990). In some cases the reorganisations were not well handled: departmental staff endured long periods of uncertainty over their future employment; there were high levels of staff turnover, including the loss of many experienced staff (and a resultant loss of institutional memory);[6] major transitional problems arose as a result of a failure to estimate accurately the number of personnel required to run the new organisations or to recruit adequate support staff; and there were lengthy delays in the appointment of new CEs (and other senior staff). To compound problems, some departments (e.g. Health and Māori Affairs) have been subjected to two or three major reorganisations within a relatively short period of time.

Further, some departmental reorganisations failed to achieve their promised cost savings. The changes to educational administration in the late 1980s, for example, were supposed to save approximately $100 million, largely through the downsizing of the central education bureaucracy. But the initial results were so poor that the government embarked upon another major review within months of the new administrative regime taking effect (Lough, 1990). As a result, significant cuts were made to the budgets of several of the new organisations. While National's health reforms were not primarily designed to cut the number of bureaucrats, in mid-1994—a year after their introduction—there were 50 per cent more staff in health-related agencies at the central government level (i.e. including RHAs but not CHEs) than in mid-1992 (*Evening Post*, 5 July 1994).

Given that any major reorganisation is likely to prove disruptive and costly, that certain teething problems are inevitable, and that a new organisation might take a year or more to become fully effective, it is always worth asking whether a proposed structural adjustment is really necessary or whether a change in policy or personnel might not be a better, cheaper, or simpler solution to the identified problem. After all, a major reorganisation entails serious risks. It might take a long time to bring a new management team together. Some of the best staff might leave because of the deterioration in their working environment. Some of the new recruits might be no better than their predecessors. The restructuring is likely to disrupt normal work flows and impact negatively on the policy-making capacity of the affected organisations. And in the meantime key policy issues might have to be resolved. Thus, as Scharpf has argued:

> . . . even though institutions . . . do matter as a serious constraint on policy making, institutional reform may not be a very promising strategy for the improvement of public policy. It is difficult to achieve, its outcomes are hard to predict and its benefits are likely to be realised only in the longer term while the short-term costs are not negligible. Instead, would-be policy-designers might do well to try working with (or, if need be, working around) existing institutions (1986, p. 187).

---

6. Organisations depend on both hard data (e.g. files, databases, computer records, etc.) and soft data (e.g. the accumulated knowledge and wisdom that is not recorded). It is the loss of the latter, as much as the former, that is damaging to organisational effectiveness.

The current allocation of functions

Various inconsistencies are apparent in the new configuration of departments and Crown entities. Sector-specific ministries have been established in areas like agriculture, fisheries, forestry, housing, and transport, but not in other important policy domains such as energy and mining, employment, and tourism. Whereas the Ministries of Cultural Affairs, Pacific Island Affairs, and Youth Affairs have been hived off from the Department of Internal Affairs, no such action has been taken with respect to local government or civil defence. Equally puzzling, whereas there has been a preference for single-purpose (or single port-folio) ministries in many areas, one or two departments have become virtual dumping grounds for a range of disparate functions. Likewise, the Treasury combines responsibil-ities for both economic policy and financial management, responsibilities which are sep-arate in many other jurisdictions (Boston, 1989b). Other puzzles can also be noted: the Government Superannuation Fund, the Public Trust Office, and the Valuation Depart-ment remain as departments whereas the National Provident Fund, the State Insurance Office, and the Government Printing Office have been hived off (or privatised); the Crown's heritage interests are variously divided between the National Archives (which is housed with the Department of Internal Affairs), the National Library (which is a depart-ment), the Museum of New Zealand (which is a Crown entity), and the New Zealand Film Archive (which is a charitable trust); and the Education Review Office, which because of its review and audit functions should be relatively independent of the govern-ment, is a department, whereas the New Zealand Qualifications Authority, which has a major policy role, is a Crown entity.

The merits of small, sector-specific or population-based policy ministries

As noted, a key feature of the new bureaucratic landscape has been the establishment of small policy-oriented ministries, many with fewer than 100 staff. These ministries either have advisory responsibilities for a particular section of the population (e.g. Māori, Pacific Islands, women and youth) or a relatively narrow, sector-specific brief (e.g. fishing, forestry, transport, etc.) (see also Chapter 6). Presumably the larger the number of such ministries the greater the number of streams of advice flowing to the cabinet. Although this might enhance the contestability of advice, it is bound to increase the transaction costs of decision-making on inter-sectoral issues (i.e. in terms of the number of organisations that must be consulted, the range of views that must be con-sidered, etc.) (see SSC, 1991, pp. 52–7). Moreover, since organisations tend jealously to guard their assigned responsibilities, the problems of 'patch' protection (e.g. in rela-tion to information sharing), monitoring cross-sectoral impacts and inter-agency con-flict are likely to be intensified. There is equally a risk that sector-specific policy ministries will be inclined to defend the interests of their own particular sector and lose sight of broader, national interests.

The question of the cost-effectiveness of operating a relatively large number of small ministries also arises. To date, the limited empirical research that has been undertaken overseas on the relationship between departmental size and efficiency indicates that large departments are no more efficient than small ones (Clarke, 1972; Hood, 1987). Such comparisons, however, have not involved ministries or agencies as small as those in New Zealand. The SSC examined the relative costs of operating small and large departments in 1991. Its findings indicated that

> smaller departments generally have a higher per capita overhead cost than a policy department with around 100 staff. However, when compared to larger departments, the evidence is inconsistent: some larger departments with a strong policy focus have a higher operating cost per head. This figure can be distorted by the costs incurred through using consultants (1991, p. 55).

The SSC went on to point out that costs of operating smaller and larger departments reflect many factors in addition to size (e.g. lease arrangements) and that the quality of the advice provided is an equally important issue. Here the task of evaluation is complicated by the difficulties of measuring 'quality'. Even if small ministries are as cost-effective as their larger counterparts, their capacity to attract high-quality staff might be constrained by the limited nature of the career prospects in the organisation and the potentially narrow field of policy work. This might not present major problems where a ministry can appeal to the policy commitments, social conscience or 'missionary zeal' of its staff, but arguably it poses difficulties where these conditions do not apply.

Vertically divided responsibilities

There can be no doubt that the functional model is desirable in many situations, not so much as a structural device for reducing the risk of provider capture but as a means of making the provision of services more contestable, decentralising responsibility, facilitating greater citizen participation, and enabling a wider range of cultural values to receive expression in the way services are delivered. Thus, those committed to radical democratic principles and the devolution of service delivery to local and regional government (e.g. for education and health care) will necessarily favour the decoupling of policy advice and policy implementation. Much the same applies to those who favour giving iwi greater control over the delivery of services like education, training schemes, health care, and housing.

Such decoupling, however, is not always to be recommended. A case for vertical integration could arise where one or more of the following circumstances applies:

a. where much of the policy work is of an essentially operational nature and where advisers therefore need a detailed day-to-day knowledge of operational issues in order to supply sound, relevant, and timely advice (e.g. as is the case in conservation, defence, foreign affairs, police, security intelligence, taxation, etc.);

b. where it is in the public interest (for reasons of confidentiality, security, efficiency, equity, procedural justice, etc.) for a government department directly accountable to a minister to undertake the provision of the service;

c. where there is little, if any, scope—even in the long term—for contestable provision (again for reasons of security, efficiency, etc.); and

d. more generally, where the transaction costs of decoupling and contracting out are likely to be much higher than the sectoral approach (due to environmental or behavioural uncertainty, difficulties in specifying and monitoring contracts, etc.) and compensatory savings in production costs are improbable.

Defence provides an excellent example of where many of these considerations apply. Plainly, those advising the government on defence policy require an intimate understanding of operational matters in order to give competent advice; also needed is a high degree of coordination and care in the processing of highly sensitive information. Given this situation, a strict application of the functional model is likely to be undesirable, if not unworkable. Such a conclusion is supported by New Zealand's experience in the early 1990s following the reorganisation of the Defence Department and the creation of a small policy ministry to provide advice on defence matters separate from the New Zealand Defence Force (see Rolfe, 1990, 1993; Ewart and Boston, 1993; Silver, 1995). In this case, the model was effectively abandoned—as had been anticipated by its critics (see Boston, 1991; McLean, 1989)—and new consultative and deliberative mechanisms were established between the two organisations. Policy-making is now coordinated at the highest levels and the functional model, while retained in statute, is all but a fiction in practice.

Although policy advice and operational activities might be best combined under one organisational umbrella in certain circumstances, the possibility still exists for ministers to seek alternative channels of advice from experts outside the bureaucracy or, indeed, to establish competing sources of advice within the bureaucracy (perhaps in the form of upgraded ministerial offices along the French model). If such considerations are accepted, then the choice is not between an exclusively sectoral or an exclusively functional approach, but rather a matter of finding the appropriate balance between the two models in accordance with a range of principles or criteria.

Competitive purchasing and supply arrangements

Related to the separation of advisory and operational responsibilities has been the development in some areas of multiple purchasing arrangements (e.g. health care) and multiple supply arrangements (e.g. health care and scientific research). The claimed advantages of having multiple purchasers of similar services include enhanced allocative efficiency, greater consumer responsiveness, more innovative purchasing strategies, and the opportunity to challenge the power of unified national suppliers and professional associations (i.e. by requiring them to negotiate separately with each purchaser). Against this, there are a range of potential disadvantages. In the case of health care, having four RHAs inevitably means a good deal of duplication in areas like the formulation of policy, the setting of priorities, the development of purchasing plans, and the negotiation of contracts. It also means that national suppliers have to negotiate with four separate organisations, each with its own distinctive purchasing and monitoring requirements. Quite apart from the high transaction costs entailed by such arrangements, there are also additional costs for the Ministry of Health in fulfilling its overall coordination and monitoring responsibilities.

The key advantage of competitive supply arrangements lies in the potential for improvements in productive efficiency. Such improvements, of course, might not accrue if there are significant market failures. For instance, in some situations contestability will be limited by asset specificity, small-numbers bargaining, and the need for long-term supply contracts. Likewise, competitive bidding arrangements might be constrained by the uncertainty of demand, information asymmetries, and problems of contract specification, monitoring, and enforcement. To date, no independent, systematic studies have been undertaken of the merits of the contestable supply arrangements introduced in health care and scientific research in the early 1990s. But such evidence as there is suggests that the transaction costs of the annual bidding process conducted by FoRST have been very high and that the uncertainties generated by the relatively short-term nature of the funding arrangements have been injurious for certain areas of scientific research, not to mention their negative effects, at least initially, on morale within the research community. It is unclear, however, what impact the new contestable funding arrangements have had on the quantity and quality of research outputs.

With regard to health care, there has been much debate about the merits of the current purchaser/provider split and the accompanying requirement for CHEs to operate more or less along commercial lines (see Howden-Chapman and Ashton, 1994). So far, the degree of competition between CHEs has been constrained by the purchasing strategies of RHAs, the government's overall policy guidelines, and the opposition of hospital specialists to competitive bidding arrangements (e.g. for certain kinds of elective surgery). There are also concerns that the new structural arrangements and competitive pressures might be encouraging excessive investment in, and the duplication of, expensive medical equipment by the providers of secondary services. Finally, the government's hopes that the new model of health care delivery would produce substantial fiscal savings, as well as significantly reduced waiting lists and times for elective surgery, have not so far been fulfilled.

The problem of capture

Although the 'capture' argument has been very influential within the policy community in New Zealand since the mid 1980s, it does not necessarily provide a sufficient justification for splitting the policy and operational (or regulatory) activities of a department. Admittedly, multi-purpose departments do sometimes engage in rent-seeking behaviour, or seek to expand their budgets more than is justified, or supply demonstrably self-serving policy advice. It is thus perfectly legitimate to be concerned about the possibilities of capture and to search for ways of minimising it. As Bertram has argued:

> However productive the activity, however clear the public interest in provision of some service by government, it will always be useful to keep track of the opportunities and incentives created by the structure of provision, and to seek organizational forms which reinforce, rather than erode, incentives for professional providers to deliver the right goods, of the right quality, at the right price (1988, p. 28).

Of course, various forms of 'capture' can occur in a bureaucratic context: ideological capture, client capture, provider capture, regulatory capture, and capture by professionals or technical experts. The case for separating policy advice from service delivery attempts to address only one of these—provider capture. Yet in some instances ideological, regulatory, or professional capture might be a greater risk, and separating policy advice from service delivery will not solve such problems; indeed, it might exacerbate them. A critical concern in the USA for many decades has been regulatory capture (i.e. the capture of regulatory agencies by the industries they are charged with regulating). Interestingly, regulatory agencies in the USA are generally separate from those providing policy advice or delivering services. Hence, the concern over regulatory capture has not arisen because of inclusive organisational arrangements and the supposed problem of *internal* vested interests but because of the power of *external* vested interests.

Recent overseas evidence suggests that provider (or bureaucratic) capture is less of a problem than is often claimed by some public choice theorists (see Niskanen, 1971). Dunleavy's (1989b) findings on the British central government bureaucracy indicate that, contrary to the predictions of public choice theory, there is little evidence of budget-maximising behaviour by government departments (or their senior staff). Broadly similar findings have been reported in relation to the federal bureaucracy in the USA and elsewhere (Blais and Dion, 1991). Nor has much hard evidence come to light to confirm the view that policy units within line departments are regularly 'captured' by the administrative divisions within their respective organisations.

Even where the risk of provider capture is high, the functional model might provide only a partial solution. After all, under a functional approach policy ministries will often be dependent on delivery agencies for information and advice on what is administratively feasible, sensible, and cost-effective. Such dependence gives operational agencies considerable influence and leverage. In fact, a policy ministry faces the prospect of being sidelined where operational agencies enjoy major advantages in terms of information and expertise and where much of the advice required is of an operational nature. This was highlighted in the case of the defence reorganisation in 1990 (Ewart and Boston, 1993).

In short, organisational designers need to avoid becoming fixated with the issue of provider capture or with seeing functional separation as an automatic remedy. To the extent that provider capture (or any other form of capture) is a problem, the solution lies in a combination of institutional pluralism, multiple advocacy, internal and external mechanisms for vetting departmental advice, the use of consultative arrangements, and maximum governmental openness (Schaffer, 1962).

CONCLUSION

There appears to be no ideal way of organising the machinery of government. Each structural arrangement has its advantages and disadvantages, and in many cases the arguments are finely balanced. Essentially, then, policy-makers must choose the particular advantages they want (or seek to avoid the pathologies they least want) (see Hammond, 1990). Further, while a particular administrative arrangement, such as the functional model, might be preferable in some contexts, it might be equally undesirable in others. Recognising the importance of contextual factors does not mean an abandonment of general principles of organisational design. It does suggest, however, that such principles must be applied with circumspection and that appropriate attention should be given to evidential as well as theoretical considerations.

If an eclectic approach is adopted, the structure of the bureaucracy will necessarily seem messy. But the quest for tidiness or absolute consistency should never be given an overriding priority. In fact, a simple, neat, consistent organisational framework is probably impossible to devise. As Self (1977, p. 64) points out, one must expect to discover 'untidy and awkward elements in any system', among other reasons because 'at any point in time there will always be a number of unresolved and emergent issues'. Spann (1973) makes a broadly similar point:

> The structure of government and administration is not simply a monolith of rational design, but also a political structure of competing powers and interests and a society with its own culture and subcultures (p. 57) . . . It will be clear that no simple principles are available to determine major issues concerning the machinery of government . . . there is also the need for continuous adjustment to changing circumstances (p. 60).

But what of the future? Are the trends evident in recent years—in particular the process of decoupling, decentralisation, delayering, downsizing, and the establishment of sector-specific or population-based policy ministries—likely to continue? It seems certain that the separation of commercial and non-commercial activities will endure, if only because the majority of the Crown's commercial enterprises have now been fully privatised. Likewise, the preference for a relatively large number of departments and the separation of policy and operations seems destined to persist. At the same time, having a plethora of sector-specific ministries (and single-purpose Crown entities) imposes certain costs, not the least of which are the problems of finding numerous chief executives and managing their performance (Hunn, 1994b, p. 12; Chapter 5). Hence, pressures for horizontal (but not vertical) reintegration can be expected to mount from time to time and on occasion give rise to further organisational realignments. Political pressures, too, particularly those arising from the introduction of MMP and the prospect of coalition government, might also prompt further bureaucratic reshuffling (Boston, 1994c). There is also the possibility in the longer term of a paradigm shift away from managerialism (and its related administrative doctrines) to a model emphasising 'holistic governance' (Dunsire, 1990). On the whole, however, the broad contours of the present bureaucratic order are likely to prove durable, albeit fluid around the edges.

management at the centre

5 senior management in the core public sector

INTRODUCTION

The quality of public management depends crucially on the calibre of the people recruited to serve in leadership positions in government departments, Crown entities, and other public institutions. It also depends on ensuring that senior managers are adequately accountable for their actions and that appropriate mechanisms are in place for identifying and addressing substandard performance. In New Zealand, it was argued in the mid 1980s (see Treasury, 1987) that the existing provisions for appointing, remunerating, and assessing the performance of departmental chief executives (CEs)—or 'permanent heads' as they were then called—were seriously deficient. The system of appointments was all but a closed shop giving applicants from within the public service a major advantage over external candidates. Cabinet ministers, despite their obvious interest in the values, skills, experience, and political acumen of those appointed to head their departments, had no statutory role in the selection process—though they were normally advised of the name of the preferred applicant prior to the appointment being formalised. Remuneration levels were fixed centrally by the Higher Salaries Commission (HSC) and took only limited account of the widely varying size and responsibilities of departments. Moreover, the performance appraisal system was poorly developed, and there was no linkage between CEs' performance and their financial rewards. There were also no established procedures for handling cases of substandard performance.

Agreeing with these criticisms, the fourth Labour government made significant changes to the legislative provisions relating to the appointment, conditions of employment, and powers and responsibilities of CEs. These changes were embodied in the State Sector Act 1988. The Act had at least five central objectives relating to CEs:

a. making the appointment system more open and flexible, thereby facilitating more appointments from outside the core public sector and enhancing the career opportunities of women and Māori, while at the same time minimising the risks of adverse selection;

b. clarifying the role and enhancing the accountability of the various parties involved in CE appointments;

c. preserving the political neutrality of the public service while at the same time giving ministers an explicit right, if they saw fit, to reject the recommendations of the State Services Commissioner and make their own appointments;
d. improving the incentives for CEs to perform and making it easier to remove those not performing to an acceptable standard; and
e. enhancing ministers' ability to monitor and assess the performance of their CEs and hold them to account 'for the output and efficiency of their departments' (Scott and Gorringe, 1989, p. 82).

This chapter considers whether these and related objectives have been fulfilled. It also examines the role of the State Services Commissioner and explores the nature, purpose and achievements of the Senior Executive Service (SES).

THE ROLE OF CHIEF EXECUTIVES

Departmental CEs play a pivotal managerial and advisory role in virtually all governmental systems. New Zealand's managerialist and decentralist ethos means that CEs' responsibilities—both statutory and non-statutory—are especially broad and demanding. Under the State Sector Act (s. 32), each CE is responsible to the 'appropriate Minister' for:

(a) The carrying out of the functions and duties of the Department (including those imposed by Act or by the policies of the Government);

(b) The tendering of advice to the appropriate Minister and other Ministers of the Crown;

(c) The general conduct of the Department; and

(d) The efficient, effective, and economical management of the activities of the Department.

Various other Acts also impose statutory responsibilities on CEs. For example, the Public Finance Act 1989 makes CEs responsible for 'the financial management and financial performance of the department' (s. 33(2)) and 'compliance with the financial reporting requirements of this or any other Act' (s. 33(3)). CEs are also obliged to 'comply with any lawful actions required by the Minister [of Finance] or the Responsible Minister' (s. 33(2)).

Although CEs are directly accountable to their portfolio minister(s) for most of their functions, in a number of specific areas CEs have a statutory duty to act *independently* (see Roseveare, 1994a, 1994b, 1994c). This, of course, is to protect certain vital state functions from inappropriate or improper political interference, direction, or control. Personnel matters provide one such instance (see Boston, 1994f). Under the State Sector Act (s. 33), 'in matters relating to decisions on individual employees (whether matters relating to the appointment, promotion, demotion, transfer, disciplining, or the cessation of the employment of any employee, or other matters), the chief executive of a Department shall not be responsible to the appropriate Minister but shall act independently'. The rationale for this provision is to ensure that ministers do not interfere in personnel decisions, thereby preserving the non-partisan nature of the public service and avoiding the problems of favouritism, cronyism, and nepotism. In addition to personnel matters, some CEs have particular statutory powers and responsibilities that they are required to exercise independently of their minister. Among them are the Controller and Auditor-General, the Commissioner of Inland Revenue, the Director-General of Health, the Government Statistician, the Surveyor-General, the Solicitor-General, and the State Services Commissioner. This does not mean that CEs should never inform or consult their minister about the course of action they plan to take. Nor does it imply that they should ignore or disregard the expressed policy of the government. But it does mean that they must, in the final analysis, make a genuinely independent decision.

While all departmental CEs have broadly similar managerial responsibilities, the nature of their jobs varies greatly. For example, managing small, population-based policy ministries, such as Youth Affairs or Women's Affairs, differs substantially from running large multifaceted organisations, such as Inland Revenue, Internal Affairs, or Social Welfare. Similarly, the demands on CEs in policy ministries and central agencies are quite different from those facing CEs in line departments with relatively insignificant policy roles (e.g. the Government Superannuation Fund, the Public Trust Office, and the Valuation Department). Those in policy ministries, for example, have much greater contact with ministers, parliamentarians, and sector group leaders, and accordingly require the appropriate competencies to work in an intensely political environment. Further, whereas some CE positions require particular professional expertise (e.g. in diplomacy, economics, law, and statistics), others are more easily interchangeable.

Just as the roles of departmental CEs vary, so too do the roles of public and private sector CEs. This is because, as noted in Chapter 2, the two sectors have different governance structures and accountability relationships (Earp and Brown, 1991). Also, the goals of government departments are generally less measurable and more varied than those of private sector organisations. Finally, departmental CEs must operate in a political environment and cope with the demands of parliamentary scrutiny and public criticism. As a result, public sector CEs require a different combination and range of competencies than their private sector counterparts.

THE PROCESS OF APPOINTING CHIEF EXECUTIVES

The provisions relating to the appointment of CEs are contained in s. 35 of the State Sector Act. A summary of the process is set out in Table 5.1. In comparison with the provisions that used to obtain under the State Services Act 1962, the State Sector Act gives ministers a much greater role in the appointment process. At the same time, the current legislation seeks to minimise the likelihood of party-political appointments by making direct ministerial interventions relatively transparent. The process has also been opened up: vacancies are advertised (sometimes overseas) and interview panels include at least one person (and usually more) from outside the core public service. As a result, the appointment procedures are much less likely to facilitate a self-perpetuating elite (or 'old boys' club).

Table 5.1   Summary of appointment procedures for departmental chief executives

i.	A vacancy occurs as a result of retirement, resignation, or new department.
ii.	The vacancy and job/person specification are discussed with the Minister of State Services and the relevant portfolio minister. Ministers advise the Commissioner how they see the nature of the job and what sort of skills and experience are required. The Commissioner prepares a paper for consideration by the Cabinet Appointments and Honours Committee, attaching the job description and person specification and raising any other matters to be taken into account in making the appointment. The Commissioner also asks the relevant portfolio minister about the composition of the selection panel.
iii.	The vacancy is advertised by the Commission in the main New Zealand newspapers, State Sector Circular, and sometimes overseas, generally in Australia, Canada, and the United Kingdom.
iv.	A private sector consultant is often used to assist with the initial screening of applicants. Close consultation is maintained with the Commissioner throughout the process.
v.	An initial list of applicants is reduced to about the ten best. Those ten applicants are screened more thoroughly and then a final short-list of the best candidates is decided by the Commissioner.
vi.	An interview panel is convened. The State Sector Act requires the inclusion of the Commissioner, the Deputy Commissioner, and one or more other persons appointed by the Commissioner. Generally, the panel includes at least one person with a good knowledge of the specific area of the appointment, a person with the equivalent of chief executive experience, and perhaps another person. In most cases panels only deal with one appointment.
vii.	The panel considers, and interviews, the best candidates—usually three or four persons. The aim is to reach unanimous agreement as to the best person. However, it is the Commissioner's responsibility to decide on the person to be recommended for appointment.
viii.	The name of the person recommended is forwarded to the Minister of State Services, who advises the relevant portfolio minister and refers the recommendation to a cabinet committee for consideration (currently the Cabinet Appointments and Honours Committee). The committee's decision is then referred to the cabinet and the Governor-General in Council.
ix.	The Governor-General in Council decides whether to accept or reject the recommendation. (In practice, of course, it is a cabinet decision.)
x.	If the recommendation is accepted, the Commissioner makes the appointment and obtains approval from the Minister of State Services and the Prime Minister concerning the conditions of appointment. If it is not accepted, either the government makes its own appointment or the Commissioner recommences the selection process.

Whereas under the State Services Act 1962 CEs were appointed by the SSC, the responsibility for making appointments under the current legislative framework lies squarely with the cabinet (or, strictly speaking, the Governor-General in Council). The State Services Commissioner now manages the process and makes a recommendation, which can either be accepted or rejected by the government.[1] If it is rejected, the government has the right to appoint another person of its own choice or ask the Commissioner to put forward a further recommendation. In the event that the government appoints someone other than the person recommended by the Commissioner, it is required under s. 35(11) of the State Sector Act to publish the name of the person in question in the *Gazette*. Direct politicisation of the process is thus transparent and

---

1. In the case of the Government Statistician, the Commissioner makes the appointment and the government does not have the power to intervene (see s. 37 of the State Sector Act).

subject to parliamentary scrutiny and criticism. However, the role of ministers in the appointment process is not limited to making appointments. They may also inform the Commissioner of any matters that they believe ought to be considered in making an appointment (including the nature of the job, the skills required, and the way the position is advertised). Further, they can suggest candidates for interview panels and can encourage people they deem suitable to apply for CE positions.

In determining the suitability of candidates to serve as CEs, the Act (s. 35(12)) requires the Commissioner and the Governor-General in Council to appoint a person who:

(a) Can discharge the specific responsibilities placed on that chief executive; and
(b) Will imbue the employees of the Department with a spirit of service to the community; and
(c) Will promote efficiency in the Department; and
(d) Will be a responsible manager of the Department; and
(e) Will maintain appropriate standards of integrity and conduct among the employees of the Department; and
(f) Will ensure that the Department is a good employer; and
(g) Will promote equal employment opportunities.

Overall, the appointments process under the State Sector Act appears to be working tolerably well and has found favour with most of those directly affected (see Boston, 1993; Whitcombe, 1990a). Various concerns, however, have surfaced from time to time.

Among them is the complex, slow, and bureaucratic nature of the process. If there are no major hitches, it generally takes a minimum of three months from the time that a decision is made to fill a vacancy for the Commissioner to forward a recommendation to the government. The process can, however, be much more protracted, sometimes because of the difficulty of finding suitable candidates. Consequently, departments might be managed for relatively lengthy periods by acting CEs. The Logan review (1991, p. 80) noted that during the three and a half years to September 1991 no fewer than sixteen acting CEs had been appointed and of them ten had held their positions for more than four months. Such delays in making appointments can be disruptive for departments and cause a good deal of uncertainty. Yet it is hard to see how such delays could be avoided, particularly given unexpected resignations, the need for consultation with ministers at various stages in the appointments process, and the complexities and subtleties of decision-making within a cabinet system of government.

A related issue centres on the limited pool of people suitable for departmental CE positions. By international standards, the public sector in New Zealand is small, and the number of high-calibre managers is correspondingly limited. The difficulty of finding suitable people has not been assisted by the increasing fragmentation of the machinery of government and the resultant growth in the number of CE positions in the public sector (both at a departmental and non-departmental level). Admittedly, the potential field of candidates can be broadened by recruiting from overseas. However, the distinctive nature of New Zealand's constitutional conventions, administrative arrangements, cultural context, and policy environment place inevitable limits on the extent to which reliance can be placed on overseas recruitment.

Critics of the State Sector Act in the late 1980s—among them a former Chairman of the SSC, Dr Mervyn Probine, and senior members of the then opposition National party—argued that the new procedures for appointing CEs might lead to the politicisation of the upper echelons of the public service, and that the Act should be changed to prevent such a possibility. In the event, however, there has been no evidence of politicisation and the relevant provisions remain intact, despite the change of government in late 1990. More specifically, s. 35(11) of the Act—which, in effect, enables the cabinet to reject the Commissioner's recommendation and make its own appointment—has not been used. Nor is there much prospect of any political appointments being made in the near future since both major political parties are reluctant to use s. 35(11).

At the same time, a number of the Commissioner's recommendations are reported to have caused controversy among ministers. For example, in the case of the appointment of a chief executive to head the new Ministry of External Relations and Trade in 1989, one of the portfolio ministers involved (the Minister of Overseas Trade and Marketing, Mike Moore) was reported to have opposed the Commissioner's recommendation (Graham Ansell), preferring another candidate for the position. In the event, the cabinet accepted the Commissioner's recommendation.

The most serious problem to date arose in mid-1990 when the Labour government rejected the Commissioner's recommendation to appoint Gerald Hensley (a former head of the Prime Minister's Department and Coordinator of Domestic and External Security) as Secretary of Defence (see Boston, 1990b; Hunn, 1991, pp. 6–8). In this instance, ministers decided not to make their own appointment and instead directed the Commissioner to put forward another recommendation (a procedure that has subsequently become known as the 'third way'). In the Commissioner's view, none of the other applicants had all the necessary skills, so a number of senior public servants were approached to see if they would be interested in the job. One of these, John Chetwin (a Deputy Secretary in the Treasury), was subsequently recommended to the government for appointment. At this stage, however, the Solicitor-General advised that the State Sector Act required the government to readvertise the position. This advice was accepted: in early July 1990 it was announced that Hensley had been rejected and that the Commission would readvertise the vacancy.

By this stage the matter had become the subject of considerable public speculation and controversy, with allegations being made that the government had acted contrary to the spirit and intent of the State Sector Act. In response, some of the public servants interested in the job, including John Chetwin, withdrew their names from consideration. When the second round of advertisements failed to yield a suitable appointee, the Commissioner asked the management consultant who had been advising on the appointment whether he was aware of any experienced managers who might be interested in such a position. The consultant supplied three names, one of whom (Harold Titter, an Auckland businessman and an accountant by training) was approached. Mr

Titter expressed interest and, after being interviewed for the position, the Commissioner recommended him to ministers. In late August 1990 Mr Titter was appointed as the new Secretary of Defence for a twelve-month term. Ironically, Mr Hensley was subsequently appointed by the National government, on the recommendation of the Commissioner, in late 1991.

The Hensley affair raises a number of important issues (see Boston, 1990b; Probine, 1990). For example, what is the appropriate course of action if a government rejects a Commissioner's recommendation, but has no one else in mind for the job, or at least wants to avoid an overtly political appointment under s. 35(11)? Should the Commissioner in such an instance be expected to readvertise the position and put forward a second recommendation, and if so how many times should the Commissioner be expected to submit further recommendations? Equally important, are second nominations likely to be seen as political and/or inferior appointments? Bear in mind that if a second nomination is regarded negatively, then competent public servants are likely to remove themselves from contention, thereby making it all the more difficult to find a suitable candidate. In short, even if the constitutional propriety of the 'third way' is accepted, its practicability is less certain.

Surprisingly, such issues have not attracted any serious public debate during the ensuing five years. The Logan review (1991, pp. 79–80) touched briefly on such matters, but its analysis was neither comprehensive nor rigorous. It is possible, of course, that the political costs associated with the 1990 debacle will deter politicians from seeking to use the 'third way' in the future. Nevertheless, it would be unfortunate to witness a repeat of the Hensley affair. One possibility, therefore, would be to change the Act to remove the option of the 'third way'. Ministers would then have either to accept the Commissioner's recommendation or to make their own appointment; there could be no going back to the Commissioner for a different recommendation. The difficulty with this, however, is that unless ministers were willing to politicise the process by appointing a candidate of their own choice, they would be obliged to accept the Commissioner's recommendation. What is more, they might have no other candidate in mind for the post or might have difficulty finding a suitable person who is willing to be appointed under s. 35(11). There is also the possibility that a determined Commissioner, knowing of the government's reluctance to make a 'political' appointment, could virtually force ministers to accept the candidate recommended.

Another option would be to require Commissioners to seek the government's views as to the acceptability of preferred candidates before making formal recommendations.[2] This approach, however, would reduce the transparency of the process, invite greater ministerial interference in appointments, and make it more difficult to hold Commissioners accountable for their recommendations. A better solution, therefore, might be to eliminate the option of the third way but require the Commissioner to place two

---

2. Under the current arrangements the Commissioner occasionally seeks ministers' views informally prior to making a recommendation, but generally only if there is doubt over the political acceptability of the preferred candidate.

names before ministers, ranked in order of preference (as happens in Britain). Such a procedure would have a number of advantages: it would force Commissioners to find at least two suitable candidates whom they could recommend to the government with confidence; it would give ministers a genuine choice, thereby reducing the need to resort to s. 35(11); and it would avoid the complications associated with the 'third way'. On the other hand, if Commissioners were required to put forward two names, the appointments process could, at least in some cases, become even more protracted. Nevertheless, such an approach might still be preferable to the current arrangements.

CONDITIONS OF EMPLOYMENT

Under the State Sector Act (s. 38), departmental CEs are appointed on renewable terms of up to five years. The conditions of employment for each position are negotiated between the Commissioner and the appointee and, unless otherwise approved, must be within policy guidelines set by the government. In addition to their base salary, CEs receive a car, superannuation provision, an allowance for club and professional fees (of $2,000 per annum), and an allowance for expenses (of $1,000 per annum). They are also eligible, depending on their performance, for an annual lump sum bonus of up to 10 per cent of their base salary.

The range of salaries paid to CEs has markedly increased since the late 1980s. Under the previous pay-fixing arrangements, departmental heads were grouped into five categories, with those in the top classification (such as the Secretary to the Treasury) earning about 50 per cent more than those in the bottom classification (such as the head of the Ministry of Women's Affairs). There was a single rate of pay within each category and no provision for performance-related bonuses or increments. Under current arrangements the base salary of those at the top of the range is double that of those at the bottom. For instance, in June 1994, the Secretary to the Treasury had a base salary of between $170,000 and $180,000, as did the State Services Commissioner and the Commissioner of Police whose remuneration is determined by the HSC. By contrast, the CEs of departments like Cultural Affairs, Pacific Island Affairs, and Women's Affairs earned less than $90,000 (SSC, 1994d, pp. 55–6). The average base salary of those CEs covered by the State Sector Act (excluding those whose salaries are determined by the HSC) was around $122,600 in June 1994 (ibid., p. 56).

While the majority of CEs appointed under the State Sector Act have been placed on an initial five-year contract, a growing number of appointments since the early 1990s have been for shorter periods. Factors contributing to the negotiation of terms of less than five years have included the preference of appointees for a shorter contract, the desirability of ensuring flexibility (especially when machinery of government changes have been on the horizon), and the recruitment of a person to undertake a specific, relatively short-term task, such as the management of a major policy change (e.g., Dr Russ Ballard was appointed to head the Department of Education in 1988 on a short-term contract to oversee the implementation of Labour's changes to educational administration). As far as contract extensions and reappointments are concerned, the

Commissioner has been mindful of the desirability of CEs not remaining in the same job for too long. Hence, the norm for reappointments has been a three-year term (or less).

Interestingly, a significant number of CEs have resigned before the expiry of their contract. In a few cases, uneasy working relationships with ministers have contributed to early departures. Undoubtedly the most notable such instance was that of Perry Cameron, who resigned in October 1994 after a conflict with his minister, Warren Cooper, over a personnel matter (see Boston, 1994f; Probine 1994). To date, only one CE (Graham Scott, Treasury) has chosen not to have his contract renewed, and only one CE (Jocelyn Quinnell, Ministry of Youth Affairs) has failed to have her contract renewed by the Commissioner.

It should be noted that under their employment contracts, CEs can be removed from office on the grounds of misconduct, ill health, or because of a major restructuring (or abolition) of a department. In recognition of the complex and demanding nature of the relationships that CEs must manage, contracts include a provision to deal with situations where, through no fault of the CE, there has been an irrevocable breakdown in the relationship with a portfolio minister. The terms of this provision state that:

> The Commissioner shall in the first instance seek to arrange for the Chief Executive to be appointed to another position within the state services on terms and conditions of employment that in their overall effect are no less favourable than the terms and conditions of employment under this Contract and this Contract shall terminate upon the Chief Executive being made such an offer. . . . Where the Commissioner concludes after a reasonable period that such an appointment will not be possible this Contract shall terminate at a date three (3) months after the Commissioner has advised the Chief Executive that no other appointment is possible.

Where another position cannot be found, the Commissioner is required to compensate the CE for the early termination of his or her contract.

Contracts also include provisions to deal with situations where the performance of CEs—as judged via the annual reviews of performance (see below)—is deemed to be substandard. Where such circumstances arise, the contract states that the Commissioner 'shall wherever practicable allow the Chief Executive a reasonable opportunity to meet the required standards or objectives'. The emphasis, in other words, is on rectifying the problem via management development rather than contract termination. However, where substandard performance continues, the Commissioner may terminate the contract, either by finding the CE another position within the state services (whether or not on the same terms and conditions of employment) or paying the CE a sum equivalent to six months of his or her base salary. To date, no CEs have been sacked during the term of their contract for poor performance. However, management development programmes have been undertaken in a number of cases.

New Zealand's experience since 1988 suggests that the desirability of fixed-term contracts remains an open question. The advantage of contractual arrangements of this kind is that they provide an incentive to perform and make it somewhat easier to remove a CE whose performance is demonstrably substandard. Against this, fixed-term contracts have the disadvantage of creating uncertainty, especially in the period leading up to the expiry of the contract. And such uncertainty can be troubling and demotivating for the individuals concerned and unsettling for their departments. Another potential problem with fixed-term contracts, particularly those of a very short-term nature, is that they might lead senior managers to focus primarily on immediate issues and problems and ignore longer-term concerns (such as staff development). Having said this, all employment arrangements (open-ended contracts, non-renewable, fixed-term contracts, etc.) have their disadvantages, and it is by no means clear whether the present system is demonstrably inferior to the alternatives on offer. If any changes are to be made, one possible improvement might be to strengthen the employment protection for CEs in the event that they are forced to resign their position for reasons other than substandard performance, misconduct, or ill health (see Boston, 1994f). That is to say, the Commissioner could be required to guarantee CEs employment on equivalent terms and conditions within the state services (and within the SSC if necessary) for a period of at least two years. Such a provision would have a number of advantages. Not only would it provide some protection for CEs in the event that their minister, for one reason or another, prefers to have another person heading their ministry, but also it would also give the Commissioner greater flexibility in managing the retention and deployment of senior managers within the public sector.

DEPARTMENTAL CEs UNDER THE NEW ORDER

There has been a substantial turnover of CEs since the passage of the State Sector Act. Excluding the transitional arrangements that applied to those in CE positions when the legislation came into force, more than fifty appointments were made between 1 April 1988 and 1 July 1995 under s. 35 of the Act.[3] During the same period over a dozen CEs were reappointed under s. 36 and five have had their contracts extended. On average, then, there have been around nine appointments or reappointments per year since 1988. Of the thirty-three CEs employed when the State Sector Act took effect, only six remained in mid-1995: Ballard (Agriculture), Blakeley (Internal Affairs), Hensley (Defence), McDonald (Valuation), Robertson (Survey and Land Information), and Walker (Research, Science and Technology); and only McDonald and Robertson were still in the same department (see Table 5.2). Most departments, therefore, have had a change of CE since 1988. Indeed, some (including Conservation, Education, Foreign Affairs and Trade, Forestry, Health, Internal Affairs, and Transport) have had two changes, and Defence has had three. In at least a dozen cases, new appointments have resulted primarily from machinery of government changes (including the restructuring of departments and the creation of new ones) rather than retirements or resignations.

---

3. A number of CEs are not appointed under the provisions of s. 35 of the State Sector Act—the Controller and Auditor-General, the Solicitor-General, the Commissioner of Police, and the State Services Commissioner.

Among Labour's objectives in altering the procedures for appointing departmental heads was a desire to move away from a situation in which departmental heads were almost exclusively white, male, and middle-aged (see Levine, Rainbow, and Roberts, 1987; Roberts, 1987; Thynne, 1988; Whitcombe, 1990a). There was also a desire to open up the senior ranks of the public sector to suitable people from the private sector. To what extent have these objectives been realised?

Overall, the CEs appointed since April 1988 are more highly educated and have a more varied work experience than those recruited under the previous arrangements. Significantly, in three cases overseas candidates (two Australians and a Canadian) have been favoured over local applicants. Also, there has been a notable increase in the number of women appointed to CE positions. In mid 1995, eight CEs were women, compared with two in 1987. Against this, only one CE position is currently held by a Māori—Te Puni Kōkiri (the Ministry of Māori Development)—and one by a Pacific Islander—the Ministry of Pacific Island Affairs. So far no Māori or Pacific Islander has been appointed to head a 'mainstream' ministry.

There has been a slight trend towards more youthful appointees under the State Sector Act. In the mid 1980s, the average age of permanent heads at the time of their appointment was 50. By contrast, the average age since 1988 has been around 48. There has, however, been a good deal of variation. Some of those appointed in the mid 1990s were in their mid-fifties. On the other hand, many of those appointed have been in their early forties, and Murray Horn was only 39 at the time of his appointment as Secretary to the Treasury in 1993. Interestingly, SES members and other senior public servants have generally had a better chance of being appointed to head a department other than their own. Also important to note is the growing number of CEs who have served in more than one department (e.g. Aitken, Ballard, Bazley, Belgrave, Blakeley, Hensley and Walker). With more people being appointed to CE positions in their forties, it is likely that the rotation of suitably qualified and competent CEs will become an increasingly prominent feature of succession management.

Yet it would wrong to exaggerate the changes in recruitment patterns. Most appointees, as in the past, have been senior public servants. Admittedly, around a quarter of new appointees since 1988 have come from outside the core public sector. However, at least half of these had worked for a government department during their career, either in New Zealand or overseas. Moreover, few genuine outsiders have been appointed to policy ministries. Such outcomes are unsurprising. Governments around the world have attempted since the early 1980s to recruit more senior managers from the private sector and have met with only partial success. A major reason for this is that managing a government department, as mentioned earlier, is rather different from running a private sector firm. Hence, not many private sector people are attracted to top departmental positions, and those who decide to make the transition face a steep learning curve. Relatively unattractive remuneration levels for departmental CEs have no doubt been another contributing factor. Further, whereas some ministers in the fourth Labour government were suspicious of their senior bureaucrats and believed that appointees from the private sector would be preferable, this view appears to have lost currency in

Table 5.2   Departmental chief executives at 1 September 1995

Department	Title	Name
Ministry of Agriculture	Director-General	Russ Ballard
Audit Office	Controller & Auditor-General	Malcolm McDonald
Ministry of Commerce	Secretary	Howard Fancy
Department of Conservation	Director General	Bill Mansfield
Department of Corrections	Chief Executive	Mark Byers
Department for the Courts	Chief Executive	Wilson Bailey
Crown Law Office	Solicitor-General	John McGrath QC
Ministry of Cultural Affairs	Chief Executive	Christopher Blake
Customs Department	Comptroller	Graeme Ludlow
Ministry of Defence	Secretary	Gerald Hensley
Ministry of Education	Secretary	Maris O'Rourke
Education Review Office	Chief Review Officer	Judith Aitken
Ministry for the Environment	Secretary	(appointment pending)
Ministry of Fisheries	Chief Executive	Warwick Tuck
Ministry of Foreign Affairs and Trade	Secretary	Richard Nottage
Ministry of Forestry	Secretary	John Valentine
Government Superannuation Fund	Chief Executive	Rita Evans
Ministry of Health	Director-General	Karen Poutasi
Ministry of Housing	Chief Executive	Rob Laking
Inland Revenue Department	Commissioner	Graham Holland
Department of Internal Affairs	Secretary	Roger Blakeley
Ministry of Justice	Secretary	John Belgrave
Department of Labour	Secretary	John Chetwin
National Library	National Librarian	Peter Scott
Ministry of Māori Development	Chief Executive	Wira Gardiner
Ministry of Pacific Island Affairs	Chief Executive	Apii Rongo-Raea
Department of Prime Minister and Cabinet	Chief Executive	Simon Murdoch
Public Trust Office	Public Trustee	David Hutton
Ministry of Research, Science and Technology	Chief Executive	Basil Walker
Serious Fraud Office	Director	Charles Sturt
Department of Social Welfare	Director-General	Margaret Bazley
State Services Commission	Commissioner	Don Hunn
Department of Statistics	Government Statistician	Len Cook
Department of Survey and Land Information	Director-General	Bill Robertson
Ministry of Transport	Secretary	Judi Stack
The Treasury	Secretary	Murray Horn
Valuation Department	Valuer-General	Hamish McDonald
Ministry of Women's Affairs	Chief Executive	Judy Lawrence
Ministry of Youth Affairs	Chief Executive	Catherine Gibson

the 1990s. Instead, it is increasingly recognised that departmental heads need to be trained in what Martin (1988a) calls the 'profession of statecraft' and that such training is best secured in the public sector.

THE PERFORMANCE MANAGEMENT SYSTEM

Regular, systematic assessment of CE performance is a central feature of the New Zealand model of public management, and is provided for in s. 43 of the State Sector Act. The logic here is simple: with CEs having much greater autonomy and administrative discretion, good systems of performance monitoring, reporting, and assessment are imperative, otherwise public power might be abused and the government would face unacceptable risks in relation to its ownership and purchase interests in government departments. Since 1988 the SSC has invested considerable resources in developing a workable and effective performance management system for CEs. The current system embraces four key elements:

a. the prior specification of expected performance via annual agreements between CEs and their portfolio ministers;
b. annual reviews of the performance of each CE by the State Services Commissioner;
c. the application of financial rewards (in the form of performance-based bonus payments) or sanctions (including the non-renewal of a contract of employment and the possible termination of a contract in the event of continuing substandard performance); and
d. the encouragement of personal development.

By comparison with the performance management systems in other OECD countries, New Zealand's approach is formalised, comprehensive, and exacting. Two features of this system deserve particular attention: performance agreements and the review procedures (see Boston, 1992c, 1993; Trotman and Jones, 1993; Whitcombe, 1990a).

Performance Agreements

Prior to the State Sector Act very few CEs had any form of written performance agreement with their portfolio minister. Nor was the performance of CEs reviewed on a regular, systematic basis. New Zealand was not of course alone in this. Until the late 1980s the use of performance agreements between departmental heads and ministers was extremely rare, certainly within the OECD. There were, however, various systems of performance appraisal for CEs, most notably in Canada (Osbaldeston, 1989) and in several Australian states (Radbone, 1988). Since 1988, CE performance agreements have become an accepted, important, and increasingly sophisticated accountability device within the public sector in New Zealand. Essentially, they furnish a mechanism through which ministers can specify their expectations of CEs during the forthcoming financial year and the priority they attach to particular departmental outputs and activities. They also provide agreed performance measures, which can subsequently be used to evaluate performance. To quote the SSC:

> Performance Agreements exist for the purpose of clearly identifying the responsibilities and accountabilities that exist between the parties to them. The focus of Performance Agreements is on clearly identifying the accountability relationship of a Chief Executive with one or more Ministers. This focus helps the parties to reach agreement on what their priorities are, what

range and level of performance constitutes success and how such success can be assessed. Performance Agreements are also a means for providing a formal mechanism for the parties to exchange information on the progress that is being made (SSC, 1989, Appendix 3).

Note that CE performance agreements are not a statutory requirement. Instead, they rest on a cabinet directive. Nor should they be confused with contracts of employment, departmental purchase agreements, or corporate plans. They must, however, be consistent with the contents of these documents. The intention since 1988 has been for performance agreements to be prepared on an annual basis, more or less in conjunction with the Budget. During the late 1980s and early 1990s, the usual pattern was for CEs to prepare the first draft of their agreement drawing on guidelines prepared by the SSC. These guidelines required CEs to take appropriate account of their responsibilities under s. 32 of the State Sector Act, the provisions of their department's corporate plan, and the particular concerns and priorities of the portfolio minister(s). Such drafts were then discussed with the relevant minister(s), amended as required, and signed by both parties. There was no formal vetting of the drafts by the SSC or cabinet.

Initially, there were difficulties ensuring that all CEs had agreements with their minister(s). For instance, of the thirty CEs interviewed by Whitcombe (1990a, p. 60) during the summer of 1989–90, fifteen did not have signed agreements. Six months later, in June 1990, much the same position prevailed. There were several reasons for this. Some recently appointed CEs had not had the opportunity to draft a document and secure their minister's signature, and some ministers were opposed to the idea of performance agreements. Since the early 1990s the system has become much more widely accepted, and virtually all CEs have signed agreements with their portfolio minister(s).

Significant changes to the nature and design of performance agreements have been made over the years, and this process of adjustment and refinement is continuing (see SSC, 1994a; Trotman and Jones, 1993). Some of these changes have been in response to perceived weaknesses in the previous policy framework; others have resulted from changes in the government's approach to strategic planning and priority setting. In broad terms, the aim has been to make performance agreements more specific and exacting, to give them a sharper and more strategic focus, and to ensure that their contents reflect the collective interests of the government as well as the requirements of individual ministers. In particular, a major objective has been the integration of performance agreements into the government's strategic planning system based on strategic result areas (SRAs) and related key result areas (KRAs). In other words, performance agreements have been used as a key mechanism for driving the implementation of the government's overall political strategy.

Table 5.3 summarises the process and timetable by which performance agreements are developed and illustrates the relationship between these agreements and the government's planning and budgeting system. Three features of this process are worth highlighting. First, the timetable is exacting and places substantial demands on the Commissioner and the SSC's Chief Executives Branch in ensuring that the politico-bureaucratic interface is well managed. Second, the Commissioner, with the assistance of the heads of DPMC and Treasury, plays a pivotal role in monitoring and reviewing draft performance agreements

Table 5.3   The timetable for developing performance agreements and their relationship with other planning and accountability mechanisms, 1994–95 financial year

30 June 1994:	Budget for 1994–95 financial year introduced to Parliament.
July–September:	Performance agreements for the 1994–95 financial year finalised, signed and lodged with the SSC.
July–December:	State Services Commissioner (Don Hunn) reviews the performance of each departmental CE against performance agreements for 1993–94 financial year and other relevant documents.
Sept.–December:	Ministers begin to identify priorities for their CEs in accordance with the government's SRAs, budget priorities, their own output and ownership priorities, and relevant departmental management issues.
February 1995:	SSC issues guidelines for CE performance agreements for 1995–96 financial year.
23 February 1995:	Government releases Budget Policy Statement (as required by the Fiscal Responsibility Act 1994). This sets the strategic priorities for the 1995 Budget and the government's short-term and long-term fiscal objectives.
23 February 1995:	Government announces its SRAs for the public sector for 1994–97.
Late February 1995:	Provisional performance agreements for 1995–96 completed and referred to SSC.
March–April 1995:	Commissioner reviews provisional performance agreements and KRAs in conjunction with the CEs of the Department of Prime Minister and Cabinet (Simon Murdoch) and the Treasury (Murray Horn).
May 1995:	Provisional performance agreements are amended where necessary, with the agreement of the relevant ministers and CEs, to reflect the Commissioner's advice and any adjustments arising from the budget process. Revised drafts are forwarded to the SSC.
Late May:	Commissioner reports to Prime Minister on the quality of KRAs.
1 June 1995:	Budget for 1995–96 financial year introduced to Parliament.
June/July:	Ministers and CEs sign performance agreements and forward them to the SSC.

Source: SSC (1995a), p. 4. Updated by authors.

and ensuring their consistency with the government's SRAs and overall priorities. Third, the Prime Minister maintains general oversight over the process.

Prior to the 1994–95 financial year, each performance agreement contained three main elements: the CE's personal commitments to his or her portfolio ministers (e.g. regarding the policy, legislative, or implementation matters that should be given priority); the CE's responsibilities in relation to departmental outputs and operations (including financial management); and the CE's responsibilities for managing the Crown's ownership interests and protecting the collective interests of the government. In 1994 the structure of performance agreements was revised to give effect to National's new strategic management approach. The SSC's guidelines for performance agreements now require CEs to specify the SRAs to which their department will contribute and to outline a few significant KRAs that are expected to contribute to the government's

SRAs, their minister's priorities, or the strategic effectiveness of their department (SSC, 1995a, p. 5). Each KRA is expected to have a medium-term focus (i.e. around three years) and to be stated in such a way that its purpose is clear and its achievement assessable. CEs are required to specify observable and verifiable milestones so that progress towards the achievement of each KRA can be evaluated. In addition, performance agreements include a provision requiring CEs to ensure: (i) that their department fulfils the terms of its purchase agreement(s) with the relevant minister(s); (ii) that the management and policy-making activities of their department contribute to the government's collective ownership interests (including inter-agency coordination and consultation); and (iii) that they complete any major management initiatives as specified in their department's corporate plan (ibid., p. 15).

CEs are expected to report regularly to their minister on their progress in fulfilling the undertakings specified in the agreement. They are also expected to put in place the necessary internal controls and reporting systems to enable them to evaluate their own progress. Although performance agreements, once signed by both parties, are intended to remain fixed for a twelve-month period, it is recognised that they might have to be modified during their term (e.g. due to a change of policy, minister, or government). Consequently, there is provision for agreements to be revised and for such revisions to be taken into account by the Commissioner in the process of reviewing a CE's performance.

The evidence to date suggests that CE performance agreements can provide a valuable management tool. For one thing, they require both governments and individual ministers to be more specific about their objectives and priorities. As a result, CEs gain a better understanding of what the government (as well as their portfolio minister(s)) is trying to achieve, which in turn assists them in organising their department's work programme (Scott, 1990). Conversely, in the process of discussing the contents of their CE's performance agreement, individual ministers gain a better appreciation of what outputs their department can deliver and of the strategic choices and allocative decisions that must be made. In this way, they are in a better position to exercise control over their departments—should they wish to do so. Another advantage is that performance agreements provide CEs with a useful management tool (i.e. they can be used as a basis for developing a series of performance agreements with their senior managers). Further, in some cases a performance agreement might help protect a chief executive from a rapacious minister. Finally, such documents, if well designed, provide a useful benchmark against which a CE's performance can be monitored and reviewed.

As is well recognised, not everything of importance can be incorporated into a written document. A good working relationship between ministers and their CEs requires trust and mutual respect, and these ingredients cannot be manufactured via performance agreements. Moreover, for the system to operate in an optimal fashion, certain reasonably exacting conditions must be fulfilled. Ideally, the political environment needs to be relatively stable, with infrequent changes of government and ministers and a stable policy framework, allowing ministers and CEs to work together in the same portfolio area for several years or more. Likewise, ministers must be willing to specify their strategic objectives, assist with the process of determining KRAs, and take an active interest in the performance of their department. Unfortunately, the nature of politics under a parliamentary system of government is not always conducive to the satisfaction of these requirements. With the introduction of proportional representation in 1996, strategic planning might become more difficult and governments less stable. This is not to suggest that performance agreements will be rendered unworkable, but their effectiveness as a management tool might be diminished.

The Performance Review Process

Under s. 43(1) of the State Sector Act, the SSC is 'responsible to the appropriate Minister or appropriate Ministers for reviewing, either generally or in respect of any particular matter, the performance of each chief executive'. Subsection 2 states that:

> In carrying out its functions under subsection (1) of this Section, the Commission shall report to the appropriate Minister or appropriate Ministers on the manner and extent to which the chief executive is fulfilling all of the requirements imposed upon that chief executive, whether under this Act or otherwise.

Section 43 applies to all CEs with the exception of the Solicitor-General, the Controller and Auditor-General, the Commissioner of Police, and the State Services Commissioner. The SSC, therefore, has the responsibility to monitor and review the performance of about thirty-six CEs. The Commission is also required under s. 6(b) of the State Sector Amendment Act (No. 2) 1989 'to review the performance of each Department, including the discharge by the chief executive of his or her functions'. The contracts of employment signed by CEs make further mention of these review functions and require CEs to 'assist the Commissioner to conduct any review of performance'.

The assessment procedures followed by the SSC have changed a good deal over the years, partly as a result of the continuing refinements to performance agreements (see Trotman and Jones, 1993). Initially, assessments relied heavily on the views of the relevant portfolio minister(s), with performance agreements providing the primary evaluative benchmarks. This approach was criticised, among other things, for giving too little weight to the government's collective interests (Boston, 1992c). By the early 1990s, therefore, the Commissioner was seeking assessments from a wider range of sources, including nominated referees and the other central agencies. Another change has been the placement of more emphasis on concepts like self-management and self-review in line with the idea that responsibility lies with CEs to demonstrate that they have performed to their portfolio minister's satisfaction and in accordance with agreed specifications. This requires CEs to put in place appropriate management information systems capable of verifying that agreed targets and requirements have been met. The onus is also on CEs to account for any failure to meet the agreed performance targets and standards.

By mid 1995, CE assessments were based on the following sources of information:

a. regular reports to ministers by each CE (and copied to the Commissioner) on their performance (based primarily on the requirements in the CE's performance agree-

ment), CEs being asked to account for any failure by their department to fulfil the requirements of its purchase agreement or failure to meet the milestones set with regard to particular KRAs;
b. brief self-assessments supplied by CEs in confidence to the Commissioner, covering their successes, failures, and principal areas of focus during the year;
c. comments on each CE from up to six referees (nominated equally by CEs and ministers);
d. assessments by the Prime Minister and the Minister of State Services regarding each CE's performance in relation to the collective interests of the government;
e. assessments of each CE by the relevant portfolio minister(s);
f. comments by each of the central agencies on relevant areas of each department's performance—the Treasury on compliance with financial management requirements, the DPMC on policy coordination and consultation, and the SSC on management, EEO, and human resource issues; and
g. other such information as is deemed relevant (e.g. the contents of departmental corporate plans and annual reports).

Once this information has been collated, the Commissioner prepares an overall evaluation of each CE and this forms the basis for an interview between each CE and the Commissioner. A three-point performance rating scale is used: failing to meet expectations, meeting expectations, and exceeding expectations. To date, few CEs have received an unfavourable rating.

The introduction of annual performance reviews in 1988–89 has undoubtedly brought significant benefits. Moreover, the review process has improved over the years (particularly as a result of the increasing clarity and specificity of performance standards and the growing acceptance of performance agreements). According to Whitcombe (1990a), CEs have found the reviews useful in giving them feedback on their performance, including of course an insight into the views of their portfolio minister. They also believe that the review process enhances their incentive to perform well and produce results. In addition, the Commissioner has found the reviews useful in identifying problems within the core public sector and in securing a better understanding of what departments are doing and where improvements are needed.

Against this, the review process has attracted a range of criticisms and concerns (see Boston, 1993; Trotman and Jones, 1993). At a conceptual level, there is the on-going problem of determining what constitutes a 'successful' CE (Osbaldeston, 1989; R. Wood, 1989). Good departmental leadership is plainly a key ingredient, yet it is inherently difficult to assess. Maintaining a close working relationship with ministers is equally important, yet it depends as much on ministers as on CEs. Another issue centres on the extent to which CEs should be judged on the basis of their department's performance. Plainly, the performance of a CE and his or her department cannot be viewed in isolation, yet it might be unfair to hold a CE wholly responsible for an underperforming department, especially in the case of relatively new appointees. A further concern centres on the demanding nature of the current performance management system; it entails high transaction costs and imposes significant burdens on CEs and the central agencies. Performance reviews, for instance, can take up to six months to complete. This is partly because of the numerous parties who must be consulted and partly because so much of the consultation process rests on the shoulders of one person—the State Services Commissioner.

Initial indications suggest that the quality of performance specification has improved as a result of the introduction of SRAs and KRAs and the incorporation of KRAs (with appropriate milestones) into CE performance agreements. Nevertheless, the new strategic planning system has drawbacks and limitations. Irrespective of how tightly KRAs are specified, it is not always easy to assess the magnitude or effectiveness of a particular CE's contribution to a KRA. Nor is it always clear to what extent particular KRAs contribute to SRAs. For such reasons, it would be unwise—in relation to CE performance reviews—to place excessive reliance on a department's fulfilment of its KRA targets. Another difficulty centres on the sequencing of the various steps in the performance management system and the significant lags that occur in the feedback loop. As it stands, SRAs and KRAs for the forthcoming financial year (beginning 1 July) must be set well before the completion of the existing financial year. This means, for example, that any problems that come to light towards the end of the first year of a planning cycle cannot be dealt with within the performance management system until the third year. While such problems highlight the limitations of an *annual* system of performance reviews, other difficulties would arise if reviews were less frequent.

The application of rewards and sanctions under the new performance management system has been a continuing bone of contention. When the State Sector Act was passed it was assumed that CEs would receive an enhanced level of remuneration—more in line with comparable positions in the private sector—as a *quid pro quo* for their relative loss of job security, their greater responsibilities, and the more exacting system of performance appraisal. It was also assumed that high achievers would be appropriately rewarded via a performance-based remuneration system.[4] In practice, political and fiscal constraints have limited the Commissioner's capacity to meet these expectations. Indeed, not only have the base-line salaries of CEs deteriorated relative to their counterparts in the private sector, they have also been asked by the government on several occasions to forego recommended pay increases. To be sure, a system of bonus payments has been introduced (as noted earlier), but at present the maximum bonus represents only a relatively small proportion of CEs' salaries. If financial incentives are to figure less prominently in the performance management system than was originally intended, then as the current Commissioner, Don Hunn, (1992, p. 10) has observed, other behavioural motivations, such as the intrinsic

---

4. It is an open question whether performance-based remuneration systems contribute to improved managerial performance. Wood (1991, p. 35) observes that 'there is very little research which shows a strong or even significant relationship between managerial compensation and organizational performance'.

enjoyment of the job, the opportunity to help shape public policy, professional ethics, recognition and reputational factors, will need to be given greater weight.[5]

THE ROLE OF THE STATE SERVICES COMMISSIONER

The effectiveness of the current processes for appointing and reviewing CEs depends on the Commissioner. It is the Commissioner who is ultimately responsible for selecting advisory panels, consulting ministers, making a recommendation on whom to appoint, negotiating remuneration, reviewing performance, managing substandard performance, and dealing with the numerous political and other tensions that inevitably surround such activities. These are significant statutory responsibilities. The way they are carried out is important not merely for ensuring good quality management but also for preserving the integrity and non-partisan character of the public service. Furthermore, the responsibilities are onerous—especially given the increasingly demanding nature of the performance management system and the growth in the number of CE positions. These considerations lead to the question of whether all these responsibilities should be located in one person, regardless of the competency, professionalism, and trustworthiness of the individual in question.

In both the public and private sectors important responsibilities are frequently shared among a number of individuals (e.g. via a cabinet, committee, board, or council). The standard objection to this approach is that it undermines accountability by dispersing it among a number of people. However, this argument—even if true—must be weighed against the considerations outlined above. Given the nature and importance of the Commissioner's statutory responsibilities, and the workload these responsibilities generate, a good case can be made for moving back in the direction of the previous arrangements, under which a small group of individuals (perhaps three Commissioners) would undertake the business of recommending appointments and reviewing performance on a collective basis. An arrangement along these lines would be perfectly consistent with the central principles of the current policy framework.

THE SENIOR EXECUTIVE SERVICE

Among other important changes to departmental management as a result of the State Sector Act was the creation of a Senior Executive Service (SES). It consists of senior managers at the level immediately below the CE. The principal aim of the SES was to provide, in the words of the Act (s. 46(b)), 'a unifying force at the most senior levels of the Public Service'. In this way, it was hoped to mitigate any negative implications that the abandonment of a single, unified, career service might have on interdepartmental cooperation and policy coordination. It was also hoped that the SES would provide a focus for man-

---

5. At the time of writing (mid-1995), the Commissioner was reviewing CEs' pay policy and to this end had established a remuneration advisory group to assist him in developing proposals to put to the government.

agement development, a source of talent to meet particular governmental objectives, and a vehicle for CE succession planning (Logan, 1991; Whitcombe, 1990b).

In keeping with the principles of straight-line accountability and managerial autonomy, the Act gives CEs the right to appoint members of the SES, to determine their conditions of appointment, to monitor their performance, and to reward them accordingly. However, in the interests of maintaining the integrity, unity, and cohesion of the public service, the Act constrains CEs in a variety of ways. For example, the power to designate which positions (or alternatively to declare which persons) in each department will form part of the SES lies with the SSC (though the Commission cannot act without the concurrence of CEs). Similarly, CEs must consult with the SSC before making appointments and before finalising the employment conditions of SES officers. Furthermore, under the Act the responsibility for arranging the training of SES officers (and those who have the potential to be appointed to positions in the SES) lies with the SSC rather than with CEs. Consequently, CEs are constrained by the SSC with respect to their conduct of certain personnel and management practices, and such limitations have been an unwelcome feature of the new policy framework (Laughrin, 1988, pp. 25–6; Logan, 1991, p. 83).

This is not the only problem to beset the SES. Like CEs, SES members are employed on contracts for periods of up to five years. But unlike CEs there is no provision for reappointment at the end of their term. Hence, SES members must reapply for their jobs when their contract expires. Employment conditions of this nature are not in keeping with good management practices (Logan, 1991, p. 85). At the same time, it should be noted that in the event that a person is not reappointed to a SES position, there are provisions in the State Sector Act (s. 54) for them to be employed for at least two years within the SSC. The objective here is to avoid competent managers being lost to the public sector (e.g. because of departmental restructuring, etc.). Another problem centres on remuneration levels. As it stands, salary packages are determined following consultation with the SSC in accordance with government guidelines. The nature and demands of each SES position are assessed, and a median remuneration level is set according to the 'job size'. CEs can pay the relevant SES officer between 85 per cent and 120 per cent of the median rate. The main difficulty is that governments have been reluctant to increase CE remuneration, which guides SES levels, with the result that membership of the SES has become less attractive. In fact, it has not been uncommon for CEs to resist placing particular individuals and positions within the SES in order to avoid the resulting remuneration constraints.

New Zealand's establishment of an SES follows similar moves in other OECD countries (Caiden, 1988; Cullen, 1986; Hede, 1991; Renfrow, 1989; Uhr, 1987). The first SES was created in the late 1970s in the USA as part of President Carter's reforms of the federal civil service. Subsequently the concept spread to Canada and Australia. In each case the motivating force was the desire to improve the quality of management in the public service and thereby enhance the overall operation of the state sector. To this end, the SESs were designed to bring qualified people from the private sector into the senior ranks of the bureaucracy and often entailed a move away from traditional public sector personnel practices such as tenure and relatively fixed pay scales. Moreover, in line with managerialist principles, they placed much greater emphasis on performance monitoring and assessment and the use of financial incentives and sanctions.

While the existing SESs share certain characteristics, they also exhibit important differences in regard to size, employment conditions, and the degree of central agency control over appointments. New Zealand's SES, for instance, is by far the smallest of those mentioned, with fewer than 130 members. This is barely a third of the total number of senior management positions within the core public sector (i.e. including third-tier managers). Whereas SES membership in New Zealand is basically limited to the tier of management directly below the CE, elsewhere membership generally covers three or more management tiers.

The SES experiments in Australia, Canada, and the USA have produced mixed results (Hede, 1991; Renfrow, 1989). With the exception of Victoria (Cullen, 1986), recruitment from the private sector into senior positions in the public sector has not markedly increased. Nor has there been a dramatic improvement in the representation of women and those from minority ethnic groups among the senior echelons of the public service. Internal mobility at the top levels within the public sector has remained largely unchanged. Merit pay arrangements have generally proved difficult to implement, partly because of the inherent problems of performance assessment and partly because of poor design features and fiscal constraints (Perry, 1988). Despite much rhetoric about executive training programmes, the evidence suggests that training opportunities have not greatly improved. Finally, the quest for a unified and cohesive group of top-flight managers with a distinct identity and common mission remains an elusive goal.

The results in New Zealand have been similarly mixed. As in Victoria, direct recruitment of senior managers from the private sector appears to have increased quite significantly. According to a survey in late 1994 of senior departmental managers (excluding CEs, but including SES and non-SES members), 19 per cent were recruited from the private sector (all but two from within New Zealand) (Laking, 1994). Although comparable figures are not available for the mid 1980s, there can be little doubt that recruitment patterns have changed. The representation of women in SES positions has also improved significantly, but not that of Māori. Job mobility within the senior echelons of the public service since the late 1980s has been considerable. However, this has been due to organisational changes and flatter management structures rather than the creation of the SES. More important, the SES has not succeeded in its primary objectives of creating a unifying force in the public sector and providing a vehicle for senior management development across the public sector (Hunn, 1993, p. 10; Logan, 1991, p. 75). If anything, the public service has become less cohesive since the State Sector Act. It would be misleading, however, to lay such problems at the door of the SES. Rather, they have to do with the difficulties created by rapid structural and administrative change, together with the decentralist philosophy underpinning the State Sector Act. Nevertheless, it is difficult to see how the SES as currently constituted and operated could ever act as a powerful unifying force within the bureaucracy.

Various attempts have been made since 1991 to reshape the SES and to enhance senior management development and succession planning. However, to date relatively little has been achieved. Legislative changes were proposed in 1993 but have so far remained at the drafting stage. Likewise, the idea of a Management Development Centre, first mooted in 1992, has made very slow progress.

CONCLUSION

Senior managers in the public sector have generally welcomed the changes in management philosophy and accountability procedures brought about by the State Sector Act and believe that they represent a marked improvement on the old system (Whitcombe, 1990a; Logan 1991; Norman, 1995). Of the thirty CEs interviewed by Whitcombe in late 1989, for example, most favoured the new appointment procedures, 80 per cent supported the idea of contract employment, most accepted the need for a performance appraisal system, more than two-thirds favoured some kind of performance-linked remuneration system, and many felt that they were now more accountable than they had been previously. Our more informal investigations during the early to mid 1990s indicate that CEs continue to support the reforms of the late 1980s.

Against this, not all the effects of the State Sector Act have been positive. In particular, some of the CEs interviewed by Whitcombe argued that the new incentive structure and accountability arrangements had encouraged CEs and their departments to act independently of each other and made interdepartmental coordination more difficult. Vertical relationships, in other words, had been emphasised at the expense of horizontal ones. Changes to CE performance agreements and review procedures during the early to mid 1990s, together with a renewed emphasis on strategic management, have attempted to rectify these problems, but it is not yet clear whether the centrifugal forces inherent in the Act have been fully negated.

As argued, various aspects of the current policy framework relating to senior department managers require further analysis and possible refinement. One of these is the system for appointing CEs. Plainly, the goals of the new arrangements are commendable (i.e. in terms of maximising transparency and accountability, clarifying the role of ministers and giving them a choice, while at the same time minimising the likelihood of partisan appointments). Nevertheless, the 'third way' has drawbacks and a case can be made for the Commissioner putting forward two names to ministers rather than a single name as at present. Another issue centres on the increasingly onerous nature of the Commissioner's responsibilities and the possible desirability of reinstating a collective leadership structure. Further, there are grounds for reviewing the current employment conditions for both CEs and SES members with a view to granting more flexible remuneration arrangements. Finally, an effective senior management development strategy is long overdue, and it is unlikely to be assisted by the present SES arrangements.

6 the organisation
and purchasing of policy advice

Governments need advice on a great many issues—from whether to close a small rural school or hospital to the much broader questions of how best to fund education or health care. Paradoxically, not only do they require wise counsel on a whole raft of specific policy matters but they also need guidance on from whom advice should be sought. At the heart of public management, then, is the question of how those charged with the task of governing can secure the best possible advice in the most cost-effective manner and ensure that decisions based on this advice are implemented efficiently and effectively. This in turn raises important issues about the relevant criteria for assessing the quality of advice, the best institutional arrangements for generating and delivering good advice, and, more specifically, from whom advice should be purchased.

At present, the organisation and purchasing of policy advice in New Zealand are based on the principles and practices of the Westminster model. Hence, governments rely largely on in-house advisers employed in more or less permanent public organisations (primarily policy ministries and departments). Such advisers are required to offer impartial advice without 'fear or favour' and to serve governments of varying ideological persuasions with equal dedication and loyalty. Institutional arrangements of this nature are not immutable or sacrosanct. Governments could, if they wished, adopt alternative purchasing strategies (see SSC, 1991; West, 1994). For instance, they could purchase much, if not all, of their advice from private firms and think tanks. Whether such an approach would be desirable, however, is open to serious doubt.

The provision of advice is intensely political. Ministers, quite rightly, have a keen interest in the qualities of their senior advisers. They want people who are reliable, trustworthy, and loyal. Equally, they are interested in what kind of advice they receive—how good it is, how much it costs, whether it is timely, and whether it serves their political purposes. Furthermore, the way advice to governments is organised and purchased has significant implications for the role and power of ministers, and in particular for the scope of their patronage (as highlighted by the American political system). It also influences who has the ear of decision makers, the nature and content of the advice that is provided, and ultimately the location of public power. Accordingly, how policy advice should be purchased and from whom are not matters that ought to be decided solely on the basis of efficiency criteria, let alone party-political considerations. Rather, such matters must also be judged from the standpoint of sound constitutional principles.

This chapter describes and evaluates the arrangements in New Zealand for the organisation and purchasing of policy advice. It begins by outlining the nature of policy advice and the sources from which advice is currently secured. It then explores the arrangements for purchasing advice under the Public Finance Act 1989, how much advice costs to obtain, and how its quality is monitored and assured. Next, the chapter addresses some of the ongoing issues that face public sector managers in delivering high-quality advice and examines some of the criticisms that have been levelled against the current institutional arrangements. No attempt has been made here to describe the policy-making process in any detail (see Chapter 3; McLeay, 1995; Mulgan, 1994; Nethercote, Galligan, and Walsh, 1993).

THE NATURE OF POLICY ADVICE

Policy advice can be defined and categorised in various ways. Although it has been common in New Zealand to distinguish between only two main types of advice, 'strategic' and 'operational' (see Boston, 1994d; Corban, 1994; Scott, 1992), it is probably more useful to distinguish at least three types: 'strategic', 'substantive', and 'operational'.

Strategic advice has a broad, intersectoral, and longer-term focus, and involves anticipating and responding to future demands. Put in the language of the Public Finance Act 1989, such advice is concerned with the outcomes a government wants to achieve (e.g. social cohesion, justice, a sustainable environment, a healthy community, etc.), whether they are desirable or realistic, how they should be prioritised, the linkages between outputs and outcomes, and which outputs should be selected to achieve the outcomes sought. Substantive advice differs from strategic in being narrower and more sector-specific. It includes the production of systematic, in-depth, and well-researched reports on discrete policy issues, such as the role of the state as a funder, provider, and regulator in particular policy domains (e.g. education, health care, and housing). It is also concerned with the choice, specification, and monitoring of departmental outputs. Ideally, both strategic and substantive advice should include an analysis of the policy options and provide recommendations on the preferred course of action. Both, therefore, must analyse how various policy objectives might conflict and how such objectives can and should be traded off against each other. Such advice is thus fundamentally about values: which values matter, how they should be ranked, and how those given priority can be maximised (see Edwards, 1992). Operational advice, on the other hand, focuses on the more technical or practical issues relating to the implementation of policy or the administration of government programmes (e.g. legal advice on drafting or amending laws and regulations, advice on appointments to public organisations, advice on specific machinery of government issues, etc.). In practice, of course, strategic, substantive, and operational advice frequently overlap. Drawing unduly sharp distinctions, therefore, is unwise. Instead, it is probably helpful to think in terms of a continuum, with strategic advice at one end, highly specific technical or operational advice at the other, and substantive advice on discrete policy issues somewhere in the middle.

The three categories of advice identified here can, in turn, be distinguished from many other activities often carried out by policy advisers. Such activities encompass, for example, social science research, including modelling and forecasting (which might or might not generate policy-oriented conclusions); provision of regular statistical reports and surveys; advice of a party-political nature; and provision of day-to-day administrative services for individual policy-makers (e.g. the preparation of speeches, the handling of correspondence, the management of appointments and public engagements, etc.). Many of these activities, of course, are interrelated and mutually dependent (Plumptre, 1988, p. 112). They are also closely connected with the provision of policy advice. Good strategic and substantive advice, for instance, depends on sound research.

A final point to make about the nature of policy advice is that it means more than the provision of a certain number of suggested outputs (e.g. background briefings, option papers, drafting instructions, etc.). When ministers seek advice on issues like unemployment, education, immigration, or defence, they also expect and require an integrated, carefully coordinated, ongoing servicing capacity. This will include the day-to-day provision of oral advice, assistance with the task of negotiating policy trade-offs and explain policy proposals to the various interested parties (both inside and outside the government), advice on implementation issues (including subsequent monitoring, review, and policy adaptation), advice on how to deal with anticipated and unanticipated problems, the capacity to undertake negotiations with foreign governments and sub-national governments, and so on. The need for a diverse and competently managed servicing capacity has important implications for the provision of advice. Not only does it highlight the need for senior policy advisers to have a close working relationship with ministers, but also it suggests that the system of policy advice must be able to ensure that policy formulation can be appropriately coordinated both vertically (i.e. within departments and other agencies) and horizontally (i.e. across the government as a whole).

POLICY ADVICE: THE PROVIDERS

In New Zealand, as in most countries, governments secure policy advice from a wide range of sources. Although most of the advice that is publicly funded is supplied by policy advisers and analysts employed within government departments and agencies, ministers secure advice from numerous other quarters—Royal Commissions, committees of inquiry, taskforces, expert advisory panels, political advisers, caucus committees, select committees, academics, party members, lobby groups, and members of the public. At any one time there are likely to be over 100 non-departmental advisory bodies providing advice to the government on various policy issues (Legislation Advisory Committee, 1990). Many of these are independent statutory bodies, and some are very influential (e.g. the Law Commission). Additionally, at any given time there are usually many *ad hoc*, short-term, government-appointed advisory bodies. The extent to which such 'external' sources of advice are used varies from one minister to another and between governments. It also varies across policy domains. It is much greater, for example, in areas like social and environmental policy than, say, foreign policy or defence policy. A notable development since the early 1990s has been the appointment of so-called 'purchase advisers' in some ministerial offices to advise ministers on their purchase of departmental outputs, including policy advice. Whether the use of such advisers becomes the norm remains to be seen.

By virtue of its relatively small population, New Zealand's 'policy community' (i.e. those people with a day-to-day involvement in advising upon, or making, policy decisions at the central government level) is correspondingly limited in size. Only a small proportion of the approximately 35,000 people employed in the core public service are closely involved in the preparation and provision of policy advice. For example, in 1993 it was estimated—on the basis of government expenditure on policy advice (see below)—that no more than 1,450 person years were devoted to the provision of advice by departments and ministries (Morris, 1994, p. 8). Allowing for a reasonable margin of error, together with the fact that some departmental policy advisers are employed on a part-time basis, such figures suggest that in the early to mid 1990s fewer than 2,000 people were employed as, or in effect undertook the role of, policy advisers. Of course, many departmental employees who are not designated as policy analysts contribute in various ways to the formulation of policy advice. Likewise, many Crown entities (e.g. RHAs) employ policy analysts, and there are growing numbers of private sector consultants employed in a policy role. Various sectoral organisations and interest groups also retain the services of policy analysts. Beyond this, however, relatively few people in the private sector have a close involvement with the formulation of public policy advice.

As noted in Chapter 4, most of the public organisations with a primary responsibility for the provision of policy advice have been decoupled from, or have gradually lost, their delivery and/or regulatory functions. Of the thirty-nine departments and ministries in mid-1995, only about twenty employed more than ten policy analysts, and only one department, the Treasury, employed more than 100 (see Bradford, 1993). Interestingly, too, about a dozen departments accounted for more than 80 per cent of total government expenditure on policy advice. The main business of policy formulation is thus concentrated in a small number of organisations.

One of the key distinguishing features of departmental advisers is that they serve a single client (i.e. the cabinet or, more specifically, a portfolio minister). They are not at liberty to sell their advisory services to non-governmental clients. This characteristic makes public sector advisory bodies radically different from private consultancy firms. There are various reasons why departments serve only the government, such as minimising conflicts of interest, maintaining confidentiality, and preserving a relationship of trust between ministers and their advisers. But it must not be forgotten that within any state the government is the dominant purchaser of policy advice. Hence, even if departments were able to sell their expertise elsewhere there would be few domestic buyers; their main potential clients would be foreign governments.

As in other bureaucracies, each department in New Zealand has primary responsibility for a particular ministerial portfolio (or related group of portfolios) and its respective policy domain (e.g. education, health care, employment, or housing). Departmental advisers are generally not permitted to go beyond their designated domain or offer their services to ministers other than their own. Of course, policy domains frequently overlap. Indeed, sometimes this overlap is deliberate (e.g. in order to promote contestability). Furthermore, the domains of some departments (most notably the central agencies, but also ministries like Environment and Women's Affairs) are relatively broad, thus enabling them to comment on a wide range of issues. Typically, departments develop well-defined, clearly recognised, and sometimes deeply entrenched policy positions (see Walsh, 1989; Brosnan, Smith, and Walsh, 1989). This, together with the inevitability of overlapping policy boundaries, generates a measure of interdepartmental rivalry and conflict. It also facilitates a degree of ideological pluralism and competition in the market for ideas (or what is sometimes called 'multiple advocacy').

The Dominance of the Treasury

A notable feature of many of the policy debates in New Zealand since the mid 1980s has been the dominance of the Treasury and its market-liberal paradigm (Boston, 1989b). To be sure, finance ministries tend to be among the more powerful departments in most bureaucracies. This is because of the vital and abiding importance of fiscal policy (of which finance ministries are the guardian) and the opportunity for economics ministries to comment on all matters with 'economic' or 'financial' implications—which invariably covers most domestic and foreign policy issues. In New Zealand's case, additional factors have significantly strengthened the Treasury's hand and given it a commanding position in the policy community:

a. the relative robustness of its philosophical framework rooted in neo-classical economics and organisational economics, the absence of a widely accepted alternative framework, and the conscious decision to apply its framework to policy matters that had not previously been seen to fall within the Treasury's immediate area of responsibility (e.g. the organisation and administration of education, health care, scientific research, etc.);

b. its close relationship with a series of powerful and determined finance ministers;

c. the gradual removal or downgrading of institutional rivals (such as the Ministry of Works and Development), and the absence of a large and powerful Prime Minister's Department;

d. its capacity to recruit and retain a large team of generally highly trained policy analysts (mainly economists);

e. the support of key individuals in other influential departments, sectoral groups, and the financial community; and

f. the boldness with which it has advanced its policy prescriptions (which included the publication of book-length treatises in 1984 and 1987 setting out its blueprint for the liberalisation of the New Zealand economy and the reform of the public sector).

The Treasury's capacity to produce high-quality policy advice has been greatly assisted by its generous level of funding by comparison with other policy ministries. In 1994–95, the Treasury was appropriated nearly $50 million to provide policy advice. This was around a sixth of the total appropriated by Parliament for the purchase of policy advice (see below), and more than double the amount appropriated for the purchase of advice to any other department.

The Use of Consultants

Most policy analysts working within the core public sector are employed on open-ended contracts. Since the passage of the State Sector Act, however, many departments have placed an increasing reliance on relatively short, fixed-term appointments. They have also made much more extensive use of private consultants. Indeed, quite a number of middle-level and senior public servants have resigned to take up positions in consultancy firms, and in some cases have been almost immediately re-hired on contract by their former employer. It has been calculated that in 1992–93 departments spent about $48.5 million on advice supplied by third parties (Morris, 1994, p. 5). Thus, expenditure on consultants was almost a sixth of total government expenditure on policy advice. Interestingly, three departments (including the Treasury) accounted for over half of this expenditure, suggesting that the use of consultants has been much more extensive in some areas of policy than in others. Advice on health care is one area where there has undoubtedly been a strong demand for consultants. Between late 1990 and mid 1993, the Ministry of Health engaged no fewer than 377 consultants at a cost of over $11 million (*Dominion*, 22 June 1993). Other departments also made extensive use of consultants to provide advice on health-related matters during this period, most notably the Treasury, the DPMC, and Te Puni Kōkiri (TPK). The main direct beneficiaries of this growing reliance on consultants have been accounting and stockbroking firms, merchant banks, and the burgeoning number of policy-oriented consultancy firms. Interestingly, policy think tanks, of which there are hardly any in New Zealand, do not appear to have gained from the growing reliance on consultants. By comparison, think tanks have played an increasingly important policy role in a number of other countries, such as Britain, Canada, and the United States (see James, 1993; Jarman and Kouzmin, 1993).

In 1994, prompted by public concerns, the Audit Office investigated the use of consultants by departments. This review (which covered all consultants and not just those providing policy advice) confirmed that some departments rely heavily on consultants and attributed their use to two main reasons: to provide skills that are either not available in the department at the time required or cannot be obtained economically via the recruitment of permanent staff (Audit Office, 1994b, p. 15). Although the Controller and Auditor-General accepted that 'under appropriate conditions, consultants are a normal, legitimate and economical way to obtain the needed services' (p. 15), he identified numerous weaknesses in the way consultants were often engaged. These included: a lack of written specifications or terms of reference relating to the nature of the task to be undertaken; a failure to estimate at the pre-engagement stage the likely costs and time-scale for assignments; a failure to use competitive selection methods (i.e. where there is more than one recognised expert in the field); a lack of specificity in contracts with respect to such matters as the ownership of material and the requirement for confidentiality; and a failure to state explicitly the standard of performance required.

Of particular concern was the general failure of departments to review or evaluate the work undertaken by consultants. Departments were thus 'unable to show that they had achieved a cost-effective result and learned lessons for the future' (p. 31). In order to rectify these deficiencies, the Audit Office outlined a detailed checklist of good management practices, which, it argued, ought to be followed by departments when engaging consultants (pp. 32–41).

PURCHASING POLICY ADVICE

Prior to the Public Finance Act 1989, departments were funded for the inputs they required to provide policy advice (e.g. personnel, travel, materials, maintenance, capital, etc.). From 1989, however, advice has been treated as an output in exactly the same way as are other departmental outputs, such as the administration of grants, the issuing of licenses, the maintenance of buildings, and so forth. In keeping with the new output-based appropriations system, the advice supplied by departments and non-departmental organisations is categorised into various 'output classes'. Most departments receive a parliamentary appropriation to supply at least one policy output class (exceptions include the Customs Department, the Serious Fraud Office, and the Valuation Department). This is usually designated in the Estimates of Appropriations as 'policy advice' or 'policy advice and ministerial servicing'. Ministerial servicing is generally treated as a separate output class when it is a relatively expensive departmental activity—as is the case in Education, Justice, and Social Welfare. Occasionally, policy advice is funded as part of a broader output class. For instance, the policy advice supplied by the Ministry of Cultural Affairs is funded as part of an output class called 'policy advice and grants administration', and the foreign policy advice supplied by the Ministry of Foreign Affairs and Trade falls within an output class entitled 'management of New Zealand's relations with other countries'.

Departments with substantial or wide-ranging advisory responsibilities (e.g. Commerce, Internal Affairs, Labour, TPK, and the Treasury) typically have three or more policy output classes. The Ministry of Commerce, for instance, had no fewer than seven policy output classes in 1994–95: business environment, competitive markets and business issues, business development, communications, consumer issues, energy and resource issues, and tourism. Similarly, TPK had six policy output classes in 1994–95: Māori education, Māori health, Māori assets management, Māori labour resources, Māori potential, and relationships between Māori people and the Crown. Altogether, in 1994–95 there were sixty-five departmental policy output classes and thirty non-departmental policy output classes.

Generally, the funds appropriated by Parliament to the various departmental (and non-departmental) policy output classes fall between $1 million and $4 million. But the amounts can vary greatly. In 1994–95, for instance, Parliament appropriated to the Department of Internal Affairs the princely sum of $90,000 to provide the government with advice on racing issues. By contrast, there were appropriations to other departments of $3.45 million for advice to the Prime Minister, $4.04 million for advice on competitive markets and business issues, $16.9 million for advice on the agricultural, horticultural and seafood sectors, and almost $21 million for advice on the financial performance of the Crown and its sub-entities.

It is common, especially where a policy output class is fairly general in nature and where the funds appropriated are relatively large, for many specific policy outputs to be listed in the Estimates (and the related departmental corporate plans). A good example is furnished by the Ministry for the Environment. In 1994–95 the Ministry (which is almost exclusively an advisory organisation) had a single policy output class, 'environmental policy advice'. The Ministry was allocated almost $12 million to undertake this function. Under this output class, twenty-four specific outputs were listed in the Estimates. They included policy advice on such issues as the following: hazardous substances and new organisms reform; pollution, waste, and hazardous substances; ozone layer protection; energy and the environment; climate change; trade and the environment; and Treaty claims and environmental issues. Provision was also made for the handling of ministerial correspondence and parliamentary questions. The nature of the work programme for each output was specified in the Estimates, as was the cost of each output.

Whether it is necessary or desirable to specify policy outputs in such detail in the Estimates (or purchase agreements) is open to debate. Potential benefits include greater transparency and accountability. Against this, there is the problem of uncertainty: departments do not know precisely the matters upon which a government may need advice during the year ahead. After all, even the most sophisticated system of strategic planning cannot predict all the policy issues that will arise twelve months in advance. Nor can it predict a government's decisions on key issues and how they will affect its subsequent need for advice. Hence, attempting to specify precisely a department's work programme so far in advance might reduce flexibility and result in excessive time being spent on planning, and then subsequently renegotiating, the work programme to accommodate unexpected developments (e.g. a change of minister, a change of government, or a change in the government's priorities).

THE COST OF POLICY ADVICE

High-quality policy advice is expensive. Precisely how costly, however, is hard to determine. This is because policy advice is one of the most difficult departmental services or 'outputs' to measure, assess and price. Various efforts have been made to calculate how much New Zealand governments spend on the provision of policy advice from departments and other agencies. According to the SSC (1991, p. 2), public expenditure on policy advice was around $343 million in the 1991–92 financial year. However, this figure is somewhat exaggerated since it included expenditure in the region of $50–70 million on ministerial servicing, such as the preparation of speeches and the handling of ministerial correspondence and parliamentary questions. It also included various other activities, such as policy-oriented research, which are not policy advice in the strict sense. Subsequently, as part of the so-called 'Pricing Policy Benchmark' exercise undertaken by the SSC and the Treasury in 1993, it was estimated that the government purchased approximately $386 million of

Table 6.1   The cost of different types of policy advice, 1992–93

Types of advice	Days	Total cost ($000)
Business Issues	47,000	56,650
Environment	15,000	14,040
Human Resources and Knowledge	35,000	42,780
Health and Welfare	38,000	40,200
Law and Order	14,000	16,290
Foreign Relations	51,000	156,760
Public Sector Management & Misc	46,000	59,560

Source: Morris (1994).

policy advice from thirty-two departments during the 1992–93 financial year (Morris, 1994, p. 5). Again, however, this figure is an overestimate since it included the costs of diplomatic services supplied by the Ministry of Foreign Affairs and Trade. If such costs are excluded, expenditure on policy advice from departments is reduced to around $245 million. To this figure there needs to be added $48.5 million spent on advice from consultants, giving a total of almost $300 million. This is under 1 per cent of total government expenditure, and less than 0.3 per cent of GDP. How this compares with other countries is uncertain since reliable comparative data are not available. Nevertheless, it would be surprising if the proportion of public expenditure devoted to the purchase of policy advice in New Zealand were radically different from the practice elsewhere in the developed world.

The aggregate figures on the cost of policy advice provide only part of the picture. Also relevant are the costs of employing policy advisers. As part of the 'Pricing Policy Benchmark' exercise, officials sought to estimate the full costs of employing a policy adviser on a market salary in 1993 (including the costs of office space, support staff, provision for training and an allowance for fixed assets and overheads) (see Hawke, 1993b, pp. 23–6). These estimates were then compared with data supplied by individual departments. The results are revealing. Officials estimated the full costs of employing an adviser at between $121,000 and $171,000 per annum, or between $710 and $1,040 per day (assuming around 170 'productive' days per annum—i.e. allowing for holidays, training, sickness, etc.) (Morris, 1994, p. 2). The data provided by departments were roughly in line with this, with the average across thirty-one departments being $952 per day and 41 per cent of departments falling within the expected range. The average, however, masks substantial variation: the actual range was between $466 per day and $3,550 per day (Morris, 1994, p. 4).[1] As expected, those departments employing a high proportion of experienced and senior advisers, such as the DPMC, tended to be the most expensive. Nonetheless, part of the variation is probably due to methodological differences, especially in relation to the treatment of overhead costs. At a cost of almost $1,000 per day it might be thought that departmental policy advisers are very expensive.

---

1. The most expensive department was the Ministry of Foreign Affairs and Trade. The reason for this lies in the inclusion of the costs of overseas representation in the costs of employing policy advisers.

Yet when compared with the fees charged by many private sector consultants (which can exceed $2,000 a day), most of the departmental estimates appear more modest.

The relative costs of the various kinds of policy advice are also of interest to this discussion. Table 6.1 sets out the level of public expenditure on seven broad categories of advice in 1992–93 (see also SSC, 1991, pp. 135–8). These figures have been derived by aggregating the expenditure on policy advice of departments operating in a roughly similar area. For instance, the category 'human resources' includes the cost of policy advice provided by the Department of Labour, TPK, and the Ministries of Education, Pacific Island Affairs, Women's Affairs, and Youth Affairs. The figures should be treated with caution since in practice the categories overlap and the advice supplied by most departments falls into more than one category. Nevertheless, they provide a rough indication of the allocation of public expenditure across different areas of policy advice. Notice, in particular, that expenditure on environmental policy (which incorporates the advice of the Ministry for the Environment and the Department of Conservation) is low when compared with the other categories (with the exception of advice on law and order). It is also relatively cheap on a per-day basis. The expenditure on foreign relations (which incorporates the advice provided by the Ministry of Foreign Affairs and Trade, the Ministry of Defence, and the New Zealand Defence Force) is very high, partly because it includes expenditure on diplomatic services.

Whether governments in New Zealand spend too much or too little on policy advice—or too much or too little on specific kinds of advice—is ultimately a matter for political judgment rather than precise 'scientific' analysis. Necessarily, governments need advice on a great many issues. Breadth, as well as depth, of expertise is therefore essential. Maintaining such breadth is expensive, all the more so—at least in relative terms—in a small polity like New Zealand. It has been claimed that there might be too few incentives for governments to limit their expenditure on policy advice (SSC, 1991, p. 20). This is because policy advice represents a minor part of many departmental votes. It thus attracts little attention during annual budget rounds. Another reason is that each minister has an incentive to increase the policy capacity of his or her department in the interests of receiving better advice and being able to challenge more effectively the views of political rivals. By contrast, there are few transparent benefits from reducing expenditure on policy advice (other than the fiscal savings). Cumulatively, the result might be a tendency for governments to spend too much on policy advice.

It is doubtful whether the available evidence in New Zealand supports this analysis. Judging by the tiny size of many policy ministries, the limited number of policy advisers employed in some specialised fields (e.g. science policy), and the stress that many advisers and policy managers have been under since the commencement of the bureaucratic revolution, it could be argued that governments have been getting the advice they require on the cheap. It can also be argued that too little is spent on policy-oriented research, especially in the broad area of social policy (Boston, 1994e). The conduct of such research has not been helped by the abolition of the Planning Council in 1991, the collapse of the Institute for Social Research and Development in 1994, and the limited funds earmarked for social science research by the Foundation for Research, Science and Technology.

ENSURING HIGH-QUALITY ADVICE

Ultimately, the cost of a piece of advice is not as important as its quality. In New Zealand, much effort has been expended since the late 1980s on determining how to assess, and how best to improve, the quality of advice to ministers (see Blakeley, 1993; Bushnell, 1991; Hawke, 1993b; Hunn, 1994c; Scott, 1992; SSC, 1992b). The resulting delibera-tions have led to the adoption of a performance management framework for policy advice incorporating three main elements: performance measures, product quality characteris-tics, and quality management processes. An outline of these measures, characteristics and processes, drawn from the 1994–95 corporate plan of the Ministry of Commerce, is presented in Table 6.2.[2]

Under the new framework, the policy outputs purchased by ministers must meet cer-tain specified performance measures (i.e. quantity, coverage, quality, timeliness, and cost). These measures are set out in the Estimates for each policy output class and are incorporated into departmental corporate plans and purchase agreements. As to the quality of advice, the new framework places emphasis on seven specific quality charac-teristics (see Table 6.2):

- purpose
- logic
- accuracy
- options
- consultation
- practicality
- presentation.

In addition, ministers are asked every three months to indicate their level of satisfaction with the relevance and quality of the advice they receive. Such assessments form part of the performance management regime for CEs. Of course, whether ministers are always the best judges of what constitutes good advice is questionable. Many ministers have little expertise in policy analysis and, as Hunn (1994c, p. 32) puts it, 'advice can be good without being welcome' or well received by the government. Nevertheless, given that ministers are the main 'clients' of departmental advice, their evaluations should never be ignored.

The Public Finance Act 1989 requires departments to furnish statements of service performance setting out the level of service provided against that specified in the relevant purchase agreement. This provision applies to all policy output classes. Accordingly, departments have introduced new quality assurance systems and renewed their efforts to produce advice of the highest possible quality. Better databases have been developed. The use of external and internal peer review has been greatly extended. And new con-sultative mechanisms have been put in place. The fact that virtually all policy papers are

---

2. The performance management system set out in the Table 6.2 was originally developed by the SSC and the Ministry of Housing.

Table 6.2   Policy advice: performance measures, quality characteristics and quality management

---

Performance Measures

Quantity

Project work is advanced to the position agreed in the year's work programme, as modified by agreement between ministers and the Secretary in the course of the year, and assessed by comparison against the programme agreed to in the Secretary's Performance Agreement and Purchase Agreements with each minister and subsequent amendments.

Coverage

Provision of a comprehensive service; the capacity to react urgently; the regular evaluation of government policy impacts on outcomes, and timely and relevant briefings on significant issues; support for ministers as required in cabinet committees, select committees and in the House. Performance will be assessed by ministers' satisfaction. In most cases this will be done by regular surveys of ministerial satisfaction levels.

Quality

Supply of individual products of a high quality, as defined by the Quality Characteristics outlined below and assessed by ministers' satisfaction as reported in the quarterly response sheet.

Timeliness

Specified reporting deadlines are met. Assessed by comparison against deadlines set in the written work programme as modified in the course of the year.

Cost

The out-turn is within budget. Assessed by comparison of out-turn with Estimates.

Quality Characteristics

Purpose: The aim of the advice is clearly stated and it answers the questions set.

Logic: The assumptions behind the advice are explicit, and argument is logical and supported by the facts.

Accuracy: The facts in the papers are accurate and all material facts are included.

Options: An adequate range of options is presented, and the benefits, costs and consequences of each option are assessed.

Consultation: The ministry has consulted with other government agencies and other affected parties, and possible objections to proposals are identified.

Practicality: The problems of implementation, technical feasibility, timing and consistency of recommendations have been considered.

Presentation: The format meets Cabinet Office and ministerial requirements; the material is effectively, consistently and clearly presented; has short sentences in plain English; and is free of spelling, grammatical and numerical errors.

Quality Management

Product quality will be supported by a quality management process including:
- external review of scope and methodology for major analytical work;
- circulation of drafts for critiquing by other government agencies and other parties as appropriate;
- internal peer review and checking procedures; and
- adherence to the ministry's Policy Framework.

Source: Based on Ministry of Commerce, *Corporate Plan 1994–95*, pp. 22–3.

publicly available under the Official Information Act (albeit after the relevant policy decisions have been taken) also places an incentive on departments to perform and provides another check on the quality of their advice.

Although undoubtedly useful, requiring policy advice to conform to certain quality characteristics (such as logic, accuracy, and practicality) does not guarantee its soundness or quality. The seven characteristics listed above are neither self-interpreting nor uncontroversial. Nor are they complete. Another possible test of the merits of a piece of policy advice is whether, if adopted, it yields the expected and desired outcomes. Yet applying such a test raises numerous methodological and empirical difficulties. After all, assessing the relationship between a series of policy recommendations and their consequences once implemented (or assessing the relationship between specific outputs and the resulting outcomes) requires considerable skill—and such evidence as may be available is frequently open to a range of interpretations (due to intervening variables, incomplete data, etc.). Assessing the quality of policy advice, therefore, is an art rather than a science (see Waller, 1992; Wildavsky, 1979). Moreover, much depends on the professional judgment of individual advisers. And the quality of this judgment depends, in turn, on the competency, experience, knowledge, political acumen, and ethical standards of the advisers in question (see Martin, 1988a; Chapter 16).

The provision of good advice is greatly assisted by the presence of strong, relatively stable, multi-disciplinary teams of advisers. Such teams, of course, do not just materialise; they must be nurtured (see Blakeley, 1993; D. Preston, 1994). Key ingredients include the recruitment of appropriately qualified and motivated personnel, adequate investment in staff training and development, the wise deployment of the skills available within the team, good technical and clerical support, and fostering an environment in which advisers take a professional pride in their work and are encouraged to engage in rigorous debate, think creatively, and challenge entrenched opinions (see Plumptre, 1988, pp. 309-17). The recruitment of good advisers depends in turn on the reputation of the relevant policy managers, adequate financial rewards, interesting work, and reasonable career prospects.

Informal evidence suggests that the performance of departments in the provision of policy advice varies considerably. Some have acquired a well-deserved reputation for producing excellent work, whereas others have been much less successful. In some instances, poor management has almost certainly contributed to the problems encountered. However, there are a number of general, sector-wide issues that cannot be ignored: the lack of investment in policy-related research and the dearth of reliable statistical information in some areas; the relatively small pool of top-line policy managers and analysts; the difficulties faced by small policy ministries in investing in expensive, long-term staff training; the lack of adequate financial resources resulting from the continuing expenditure reductions across the core public sector; and the numerous reorganisations, some of dubious merit, to which various departments have been subjected. Unless or until such problems are addressed, significant weaknesses in the advisory system are bound to persist.

POLICY COORDINATION

Ensuring good policy coordination is one of the hardest tasks of public management (see Bührs, 1991; Minnery, 1988; OECD, 1987b; Painter, 1981). Coordination problems can arise for a host of reasons: organisational fragmentation, sectoral interdependence, policy complexity, competing interests, conflicting values, poor consultation, and the sheer scope and scale of governmental activity. On any particular issue there are invariably a number of competing streams of departmental advice, not to mention the conflicting views of external advisers and interest groups. Quite apart from this, there is the continuing problem of translating complex policy decisions into practical reality. Regardless of how the machinery of government is organised, therefore, policy coordination will present difficulties.

In New Zealand, the public sector reforms in the late 1980s generated various concerns about coordination within the government machine (Boston, 1992a; Galvin, 1991; Hunn and Lang, 1989). One of these was that the State Sector Act had encouraged 'departmentalism'. This is because it emphasises the vertical relationship between a departmental CE and his or her minister while largely ignoring the horizontal relationship between departments and the collective nature of government a cabinet system. Another concern related to the relative weakness of the coordinating machinery at the centre of government, in particular the limited resources of the Prime Minister's Department.

Such concerns prompted a number of governmental responses (Boston, 1992a; McLeay, 1995). The advisory resources available to the Prime Minister were strengthened. CE performance agreements were amended to include a specific requirement for them to consider the collective interest. New standing officials' committees were established to 'shadow' various cabinet committees and oversee the formulation and implementation of policies of an intersectoral nature (see Hawke, 1993b, p. 35; Tanner, 1993). And the provisions in the *Cabinet Office Manual* relating to interdepartmental consultation were strengthened.

Under current arrangements, for instance, departments preparing a cabinet paper are obliged to 'consider', in the words of the *Cabinet Office Manual*, 'all the implications for other Government agencies and consult them at the earliest possible stage' (Cabinet Office, 1994, Ch. 4, A11). Further, when making submissions to cabinet, departments must certify (on a CAB 100 form) that they have followed the required consultation process. Ministers must likewise certify, on the same form, whether consultation with other departments and ministers has taken place and whether there has already been (or should be in the future) consultation with the government caucus, opposition parties and other interested groups. The *Cabinet Office Manual* provides guidance on the range of policy issues that fall within the responsibility of each department and specifies for certain departments the issues on which they must be consulted. For instance, the Crown Law Office must be consulted on all proposals having 'legal implications for the Crown', the Ministry for the Environment on all matters having 'significant environmental implications', and the DPMC on all matters 'which are likely to have implications for the government as a whole or for the coordination of the activities of two or more departments' (Ch. 4, Appendix 2). The Cabinet Office reserves the right to reject submissions where the necessary consultation does not appear to have occurred.

Having good formal processes and appropriate incentives for consultation is one thing. Ensuring that these systems work as intended is quite another. Equally important, the degree of consultation that is possible beyond official circles will often be limited by political imperatives and the need, at least under Westminster conventions, to protect the confidentiality of the ministerial–adviser relationship. It is thus not always possible for departments to consult extensively during the process of policy development.

How well the current coordination mechanisms are working is difficult to assess. Plainly, the whole policy-making apparatus was placed under great strain between the mid 1980s and early 1990s as a result of the bureaucratic revolution during these years. Almost inevitably this led to consultation failures and resulting coordination problems, some of them serious (see Boston, 1994b). Since the end of the revolution, policy-making has followed a more ordered path, the pressures on the cabinet system have eased, and coordination problems have been less evident. The introduction of SRAs and KRAs also appears to have assisted interdepartmental coordination (e.g. by focusing attention on key intersectoral linkages). Equally, the development of close informal relationships among the CEs of the central agencies, particularly since the 1993 general election, seems to be contributing to a greater sense of common purpose among senior officials.

THE PROVISION OF STRATEGIC POLICY ADVICE

It is often claimed that governments focus too heavily on politically sensitive, urgent or pressing day-to-day issues at the expense of broader, long-term issues. Yet these latter issues are often more important. And if cabinet ministers are generally overwhelmed by the needs of the moment, so too are their advisers. As a consequence, departments might spend too little time thinking about issues of a longer-term or intersectoral nature and devote few resources to in-depth policy research and 'blue-skies' analysis.

A related concern is whether the current arrangements for the purchasing of policy advice discourage departments from undertaking policy work of a more strategic nature. For example, it has been suggested that, in accordance with the Public Finance Act, departments should only provide advice that falls within their specified output classes (or outputs). Likewise, unless a department's purchase agreement specifies that the provision of its policy outputs should include strategic advice, officials lack a mandate to supply such advice. Another point that is sometimes made is that ministers should decide outcomes, and public servants should advise on the outputs required to achieve these outcomes. From this perspective, the provision of advice on the merits of the government's chosen outcomes goes beyond the legitimate role of public servants.

These arguments carry little force. Not merely are they wrong in principle, they conflict with recent research evidence (see Corban, 1994). Public servants under current conventions in New Zealand have a right and a duty to tender advice on both outcomes and outputs. As previously noted, CEs have an unambiguous obligation, stated in their contracts of employment, 'to provide free and frank advice . . . without fear or favour'. Such an obligation gives departments a mandate to comment on outcomes, to suggest changes in governmental priorities, and to propose courses of action that ministers might have overlooked or previously rejected. In any case, the way policy output classes are currently defined does not significantly limit the nature of the advice tendered. And according to Corban (1994, p. 93), the government's 'outcome statements' are not treated by departmental advisers as the main determinant or constraint on their policy work. Of course, if the specificity of purchase agreements were to increase still further, and if outcome statements (together with SRAs and KRAs) were to be more tightly defined, such observations would no longer hold.

It is worth noting that departments have an incentive in a contestable environment to undertake policy work that goes beyond the government's immediate priorities and policy preferences in order to maintain their effectiveness, responsiveness, and credibility as policy advisers in the longer term. After all, if they do not, they run the risk of finding themselves on the back foot *vis-à-vis* other departments or advisers, especially in the event of a change in government or a significant policy shift. In other words, it is in the interests of a department to think ahead and have the capacity to respond in the event of major changes in the policy context. As one official put it: 'The department has to be in a position to provide informed advice not only to the present Government, but also to future governments—and this requires prior investment in policy analysis' (p. 103).

However, Corban's research revealed marked differences in the way departments perceived their policy functions and obligations. Some were much more proactive than others and felt less constrained by the wording of their respective outcome statements and purchase agreements. Furthermore, some departments reported difficulties in ensuring that longer-run or more substantial policy projects were included in their work programmes. The problems included the scarcity of resources (especially in the case of small policy ministries) and a lack of political interest or support (p. 105). Nevertheless, Corban found that many agencies undertook at least some policy development work that went beyond that directly related to the outcomes desired by the government or was additional to the priorities indicated by their portfolio minister (p. 97). This was more likely to be the case in respect of departments with a strong policy orientation. In some cases such work occurred without the direct approval (or even knowledge) of a minister; in other cases it was part of a programme of work agreed upon at ministerial level (pp. 105–6).

In the interests of developing and clarifying its strategic goals and priorities, the National government instituted a new planning system in the early to mid 1990s. This involves the identification of SRAs and KRAs and their integration with the Budget cycle, departmental planning systems, and various accountability documents. The nature and merits of the new approach to strategising are discussed elsewhere (see Chapters 5 and 14).

ALTERNATIVE METHODS OF PURCHASING POLICY ADVICE

From time to time the current arrangements for the purchasing of policy advice have been criticised for being insufficiently contestable and placing public providers (especially departmental policy analysts) in a relatively privileged position compared to their private sector counterparts. As a result, it is claimed, the advice required by governments is not being provided in a cost-effective manner. In order to free up the market for policy advice, a number of radical proposals have been suggested. Two such proposals were considered, and subsequently rejected, by the SSC in the early 1990s. The first entailed creating a market for policy advice within the public sector (SSC, 1991, pp. 28–30). Under this approach, government agencies would be required to compete for contracts to supply policy outputs (or output classes). The second proposal went even further. It involved creating an open market in which public and private organisations would compete, on more or less equal terms, for contracts to supply policy outputs. Under such an approach, an in-house advisory capacity in particular policy areas would not necessarily be retained.

Similarly radical proposals have been advanced by Andrew West (1994). West questions whether it is desirable for governments to depend so heavily on departmental advisers and argues that advice would be more efficiently provided by the private sector. Under his proposals, the provision of policy advice would operate as follows:

> each Minister might employ a highly capable resource of personal advisors within their Office to develop purchase contracts and tender them out on a contestable basis. The Minister would seek to contract the best skills available so as to purchase the most effective and efficient outputs. To lower transaction costs and secure continuity of supply these contracts would probably be let for the term of the Government. Each would have clear performance measures for quality of output. The Minister's Office would monitor the performance of the contracted agents. The advisors in Ministerial Offices would most probably prepare the final policy papers for their Ministers, based on information purchased by contract . . . Initially departments would compete with any other provider in the market for public policy advice. Private sector providers would seek to employ public servants with key advisory skills (already occurring). Some individuals would resign to establish their own consultancies (already occurring). Ultimately, the Government would review its need to own departments (pp. 27–8).

West accepts that contracting out all the functions of the central agencies, especially the Treasury, might not be desirable. He admits, for instance, that it is 'open to debate' whether the integrity of the budget process could be maintained if all Treasury's outputs were undertaken by private sector suppliers (p. 28). Similarly, he acknowledges that if most policy outputs were provided by the private sector it would be necessary for governments to develop coordinated annual strategic plans and coordinate their purchasing strategies across portfolios. But such problems, in his view, should not be 'insurmountable' (ibid.). He also dismisses the possibility that his proposals would politicise the purchasing of advice or reduce the extent to which governments received impartial advice. Finally, he claims that the transaction costs involved in purchasing advice under his model would be reduced because 'compliance with the Public Finance Act . . . would be removed and the relationship between purchaser and provider reformatted around bona fide contractual law' (p. 27).

This is not the place to provide a detailed analysis of the merits of such proposals (see Boston, 1994a; 1995a). However, a number of points need to be made. The provision of policy advice is not an 'inherently governmental function', in the sense that it should only be supplied by employees of the state (US General Accounting Office, 1991). Clearly, the private sector can provide advice on most issues that is equal in terms of quality, timeliness, political sensitivity and so forth to anything provided by policy analysts working in the public sector. There is no reason in principle, therefore, why a significant proportion of the advice required by ministers should not be purchased from the private sector. At the same time, there is good case for governments retaining in-house advisers across the broad sweep of policy issues that they are likely to face.

First, there are important constitutional issues at stake. Despite suggestions to the contrary, West's model could give ministers an undesirable degree of power and politicise the whole advisory system, especially if ministers were directly involved in selecting their advisers and allocating contracts for policy outputs. Not merely would such an approach raise the possibility of corruption, cronyism, and nepotism, it would also undermine the tradition of providing advice without 'fear or favour'. In other words, advisers would have an incentive—assuming they wished to retain their contract—to fashion their advice to suit the policy preferences of their particular minister (or government). If direct ministerial involvement in selecting successful bidders were to be avoided, an independent agency would need to be established to manage the bidding process, ensure that bids were properly coordinated, allocate contracts, and monitor the performance of successful bidders. The problem with this approach, of course, is that such a body would itself have considerable power since it would determine who received the contracts to supply advice to ministers.

Second, competitive arrangements for purchasing advice as proposed by West are likely to be more costly and generate numerous administrative problems. The findings of the new institutional economics are particularly instructive in this respect. The relevant literature indicates that contracting out or the use of market-type arrangements is not generally desirable (i.e. in the sense of minimising production and transaction costs) when the following conditions apply: there is a high degree of general and/or behavioural uncertainty, and in particular a high risk of adverse selection of agents by the principal; there is only limited contestability due to the existence of specific assets; there is a high likelihood of opportunism by at least one of the parties to the contract; and the relevant transactions are frequent and complex (see Bryson and Smith-Ring, 1990; Weimer and Vining, 1990). Most, if not all, of these conditions are likely to apply under West's model. Uncertainty over the advisory needs of ministers will make contract specification very difficult. This, in turn, will generate considerable problems in the area of contract monitoring and enforcement. External contracting will be further hampered by uncertainty over how long a particular minister or government is likely to remain in office. Meanwhile, the degree of contestability between suppliers in many policy domains will be constrained by the small size of New Zealand's policy community. Hence, there is a risk of opportunistic behaviour (e.g. suppliers might seek to generate additional demand for their advice) with consequent difficulties for maintaining trust between ministers and their advisers, and between the competing advisory bodies.

To compound matters, policy coordination would be more difficult (due to a greater turnover of policy advisers and less sharing of information as teams of advisers compete with each other for contracts) and changes of government would provoke major problems (due to the need for new teams of advisers to be selected). Also, West's proposals could well reduce the incentive for advisory bodies to invest in policy-oriented research, engage in strategic or long-term policy development, and undertake transaction-specific investments in policy expertise. For all these reasons, the quality of the advice provided is likely to be impaired. Hence, competitive tendering arrangements under which public and private sector organisations would be required to compete for the right to provide policy outputs would almost certainly be contrary to the public interest. It is thus no accident that proposals of the kind advanced by West have never been implemented and that virtually all governments around the world maintain long-term, in-house advisory services.

In short, the present institutional arrangements for providing advice to New Zealand policy-makers—which rely heavily on more or less permanent teams of advisers willing and able to serve governments of varying ideological persuasions—have a clear logic. They facilitate the competition of ideas while at the same time minimising the problems of opportunism, whether by agents or principals, in an environment characterised by considerable uncertainty, complexity, asset specificity, and information asymmetries.

CONCLUSION

The current arrangements for the organisation and purchasing of policy advice have many positive features. Flexibility is one: a government can readily seek new sources of advice, or expand, combine, or abolish existing departmental advisory structures. Contestability is another: departmental advice is almost always subject to the scrutiny of other departments and is open to external critique—if not always at the time when decisions are taken, then shortly afterwards (e.g. via the Official Information Act). This is not to deny that departmental advisers have certain advantages over their external rivals. But at least the advisory system is relatively open and structured to ensure a degree of multiple advocacy. Other positive aspects of the current arrangements include the conventions guiding the conduct of departmental advisers, including the requirement to offer 'free and frank' advice; the greater specificity and clarity with respect to the nature and cost of policy outputs provided by the new appropriations framework; the commitment of departments to providing quality advice, and the introduction of new procedures for improving quality assurance; and the development of improved procedures and incentives for interdepartmental coordination and consultation.

Whether or not the new structures and processes for the delivery of policy advice constitute a major advance in the techniques of public management remains an open question. As yet there has been relatively little systematic research on the consequences of the separation of policy advice from implementation, especially its effects on operational agencies, policy-feedback mechanisms, formal and informal inter-agency relationships, transaction costs, and the duplication of effort. That there are drawbacks and limitations associated with the new arrangements, however, is readily acknowledged by senior advisers. To quote Don Hunn, the State Services Commissioner:

> Greater contestability in policy advice has undoubtedly reinforced various partisan positions. The separation of policy advice and implementation has engendered some fragmentation in the policy sphere, and perhaps a lack of overall coordination. Costing policy outputs has focused attention on costs but it remains unclear whether this process has improved the quality of policy advice. It is also difficult to gauge whether present day policy advice has dramatically improved compared with previously . . . we have yet to establish a method to determine whether and how the outputs contribute positively to the stated outcomes (1994c, p. 33).

Additional problems can also be identified. There remains a dearth of expertise in some policy fields, and the quality of advice from certain departments is a continuing source of concern to the central agencies and various ministers. In some areas there is a poverty of good data, insufficient policy-oriented research, and little systematic policy evaluation. The relative dominance of the Treasury in the policy community has also generated disquiet (even among some of those sympathetic to its views), as has the hegemony of the market-liberal paradigm. Quite apart from this, the frequent redrawing of departmental boundaries since the mid 1980s has placed considerable strains on many policy advisers. High-quality advice depends primarily on having competent, professional advisers, and such people operate best as part of collegial, motivated, and relatively stable teams. When such teams are regularly reshuffled and disbanded, the whole advisory system suffers (e.g. due to a loss of morale, institutional memory, and experience). A period of relative institutional stability would thus not go amiss.

The introduction of proportional representation will pose new challenges for policy advisers and might herald important changes to the policy-making process (SSC, 1995d). For one thing, there is the possibility of more frequent changes of government (and of the parties forming the government) and longer periods of caretaker government. For another, single-party majority governments—which have been the norm in New Zealand since the Great Depression—are likely to be rare. Instead, majority coalitions or single-party minority governments are the most probable outcomes. In either case, there will be implications for the relationships between the executive and Parliament, between the various parliamentary parties, and between public servants and opposition parties. Policy-making is likely to be slower, the sources of advice more numerous and fluid, and parliamentary scrutiny of the bureaucracy more intense. This, in turn, will have implications for the kind and quantity of advice sought by ministers (e.g. there may be greater demand for political advice and advice that takes into account the political feasibility of proposed policy options). If the non-partisan nature of the public service is to be protected in these circumstances, it will be important to ensure that there are clear and generally accepted protocols concerning the proper role of departmental advisers. It will be equally vital to ensure that any changes to the principles and procedures governing the purchase of policy advice do not undermine the tradition of 'neutral competence' and the provision of 'free and frank' advice.

7 public management in a bicultural society

Public management is shaped by many diverse forces. Among them are a nation's ethnic composition and cultural heritage. Since colonisation, New Zealand has been the home of at least two distinct peoples—Māori and Pākehā (i.e. Europeans). The signing of the Treaty of Waitangi in 1840 (see Orange, 1987) signalled a commitment to a partnership between these two peoples. But this commitment was not enduring. Indeed, between the mid-nineteenth century and the 1980s the state, dominated by the Pākehā majority, largely neglected Māori interests and did little to nurture or promote Māori language, values, customs, and economic development. Since the mid 1980s, however, governments have given much greater attention to the Treaty of Waitangi and renewed the quest for partnership. One sign of this has been the emergence of a new policy of biculturalism. Another has been the attempt to resolve long-standing Māori grievances.

This chapter begins by exploring some of the policy issues that arise as a result of cultural pluralism. It then examines the nature of biculturalism and how recent New Zealand governments have interpreted the requirements of biculturalism in the context of public sector management. Particular attention is given to Labour's strategies of 'devolution' and 'responsiveness' and National's strategy of 'mainstreaming'. No attempt is made here to provide a detailed analysis of the wider constitutional issues concerning Māori political representation and demands for Māori sovereignty (see Durie, 1995; Kelsey, 1990; Mulgan, 1989; Sharp, 1990). Nor does the chapter discuss the current institutional arrangements for settling claims under the Treaty of Waitangi or the outcome of these processes (see Morton, 1995).

CULTURAL PLURALISM AND PUBLIC POLICY

Cultural pluralism poses serious philosophical conundrums, political challenges, and policy dilemmas. To start with, there are the problems of reconciling individual and collective rights and balancing the various competing principles of justice (see Kymlicka, 1989; McLeay, 1991; Williams, 1995). On the one hand, liberal theories of justice have traditionally placed great weight on ideals such as equality of opportunity, impartiality, universal citizenship, and uniform rights for all; they have also tended to give priority to individual rights over the rights of groups or collectivities. On the other hand, there are various other ideals, more often associated with communitarianism than liberalism, like the maintenance of cultural diversity and cultural options, and in particular the nurturing and protection of minority cultures (including their distinctive values, language, art, customs, traditions, ceremonies, symbols, etc.). The central problem is that in order to protect these latter ideals, special collective rights might be required; yet such rights are likely to be in tension, if not inconsistent, with a system of uniform rights for all citizens.

Handling these issues raises many challenges for the conduct of public management. Take, for example, the area of institutional design. One immediate question that arises is whether, and if so how, a country's political, legal, administrative, and other public institutions should reflect the range of cultures represented in that society. For instance, should the members of a country's democratic institutions, such as Parliament, be chosen via a common electoral roll or should there be separate systems of representation for each significant cultural group? Likewise, should a country's administrative and social institutions (e.g. schools, hospitals, etc.) be organised so as to provide services for all citizens, irrespective of cultural background, or should parallel institutions be established with each major cultural group being serviced by separate agencies? If the former option is chosen, is it possible to ensure that 'mainstream' agencies adequately reflect the values of the non-dominant cultures (e.g. in the way they are organised and managed) and provide public services in a culturally sensitive, appropriate, and responsive fashion? And if the latter option is chosen, is it possible to guarantee equal citizenship rights or does administrative pluralism, however well intentioned, necessarily result in equivalent cases being treated differently?

In New Zealand, issues of this nature have been at the centre of public debate for many years, especially since the mid 1980s. This reflects at least two key developments. First, the constitutional significance, legal status, and policy implications of the Treaty of Waitangi have received increasing recognition (see Chen and Palmer, 1993, pp. 295–436). Under Article I, the Māori tribes ceded 'all the rights and powers of sovereignty' to the British Crown (in the English version) or 'complete government over their land' (in the Māori version).[1] In return, the Crown guaranteed in Article II that Māori would enjoy the 'full exclusive and undisturbed possession of their lands and estates, forests, fisheries and other properties'. Further, in Article III, Māori were granted 'all the rights and privileges of British subjects'. The Crown's commitments, particularly under Article II of the Treaty, were not fulfilled. In fact, a large proportion of Māori land was unjustly seized by the Crown during the mid to late nineteenth century. In response to growing Māori legal and political action, governments since the mid 1980s have finally begun the difficult and complex task of rectifying past injustices and resolving resource

---

1. Clearly, these differences in the English and Māori versions of the Treaty are important and have potentially significant policy implications. Broadly speaking, the Māori version secured more for Māori (e.g. the sharing rather than ceding of sovereignty) while the English version gave more to the Crown. As it stands, there is continuing debate over which version of the Treaty should be accorded priority. Likewise, there is debate about whether Article I should have precedence over Article II.

and taonga (treasure or property) grievances based on the Treaty. They have also responded in various ways to the mounting evidence of racial inequality, increasing pressure by iwi (tribe) and hapu (tribe/clan) for greater autonomy, and demands for Māori values and beliefs to become an integral part of the nation's public life.

Second, changing immigration patterns have made New Zealand society increasingly heterogeneous. Whereas the vast majority of immigrants prior to the 1960s were of European origin (mainly British), in recent decades a growing proportion of immigrants have come from the South Pacific (e.g. the Cook Islands, Niue, Samoa, Tonga, etc.) and Asia (e.g. Cambodia, Hong Kong, Taiwan, Vietnam, etc.) (see Earle, 1995). Consequently, there are now large non-European immigrant communities, especially in Auckland. Nevertheless, Māori remain the largest minority ethnic group, making up around 13 per cent of the total population.

BICULTURALISM

Such developments have made it politically impractical to base public policy, including the management of the public sector, on a presumption of monoculturalism. At the same time, they have raised the issue of what precisely the policy of the government should be. For instance, should it endorse some form of biculturalism (which at the very least must entail official or state recognition of, if not preferential treatment for, two cultures, namely Māori and Pākehā)? Alternatively, should it embrace multiculturalism (which could entail the official recognition of more than two cultures and/or the equal treatment of all minority cultures)? Or should it attempt some combination of the two (e.g. by adopting a bicultural approach in some policy spheres and a multicultural approach in others)?

Two immediate difficulties arise in any analysis of the relative virtues of biculturalism and multiculturalism. First, there is no agreement on what these terms actually mean (see Benton, 1990; Culpitt, 1994; Durie, 1993; Earle, 1995; Ministerial Advisory Committee, 1986; Sharp, 1990, 1995). For some, biculturalism means—at least in the New Zealand context—a partnership between Māori and Pākehā where responsibility and authority for policy decisions is shared and where Māori values, perspectives, and terminology are incorporated into the design, management, and operation of public institutions. At a minimum this entails the adaptation of essentially Pākehā institutions to satisfy Māori requirements and aspirations. For others, biculturalism requires the development of separate Māori institutions—preferably of comparable authority and status to their Pākehā counterparts—to provide specifically for Māori needs. Sharp (1990) refers to this as 'bicultural distributivism'. Still others maintain that biculturalism requires a commitment to bilingualism and a policy framework in which Māori and Pākehā culture enjoy an equal status, both officially and practically, in all spheres of public life.

Durie (1993) provides a helpful perspective by noting that the goals of biculturalism are varied and its policy implications depend a good deal on the context in which the term is being applied. More specifically, he argues that biculturalism can be viewed along two continuums, one concerned with goals and the other with organisational structures (pp. 7–8). With respect to bicultural goals, the relevant continuum ranges from the acquisition of a basic knowledge and appreciation of Māori culture at one end to the establishment of joint ventures between the Crown and Māori based on agreed policy frameworks at the other. With respect to structural arrangements, the relevant continuum ranges from unmodified mainstream institutions at one end to independent and relatively autonomous Māori institutions at the other. Between these two poles is a range of possible arrangements including the inclusion of explicit Māori perspectives and practices into the operations of existing public institutions, the establishment of Māori units within public agencies, and the creation of parallel Māori agencies.

Second, regardless of their precise meanings, both biculturalism and multiculturalism are politically loaded terms; both tend to alienate various groups within the community. For instance, many Pacific Islanders living in New Zealand find the term biculturalism unattractive because of the implication that those whose origins are neither European nor Māori are second-class citizens. Equally, many Māori dislike the term multiculturalism because it implies that all minority cultures, including Māori, are of equal status.

Despite such sensitivities, recent governments have made an explicit, albeit reticent, commitment to biculturalism. In broad terms, this has meant giving Māori values and perspectives more weight than (but not absolute priority over) the claims of other *minority* cultures. This has been particularly evident in areas like education policy, language policy, broadcasting policy, and arts funding, but less so in many other policy domains. The preference for biculturalism over multiculturalism has been justified on two main grounds: the Crown's Treaty obligations (especially under Article II) and the position of Māori as New Zealand's indigenous people (or tangata whenua). No attempt has been made to give Māori culture an equivalent status to Pākehā culture (e.g. via a policy of bilingualism). Also, National's endorsement of biculturalism has been much more reticent and ambivalent than Labour's.

MĀORI AFFAIRS: THE POLICY FRAMEWORK PRIOR TO THE MID 1980s

New Zealand has had a separate department responsible for Māori affairs for most of the period since 1840: first the Protectorate of Aborigines, next the Native Department, and subsequently the Department of Māori Affairs, Manatu Māori (the Ministry of Māori Affairs) and Te Puni Kōkiri (the Ministry of Māori Development). The size, purpose, and responsibilities of these departments have varied a good deal. The Department of Māori Affairs, for instance, was a large organisation with a strong regional presence. It undertook a wide range of operational activities, such as providing loans for the purchase of new or existing homes, managing educational and vocational training programmes, and providing grants for land development, business development, and cultural activities. By contrast, Te Puni Kōkiri (TPK) is a relatively small policy ministry, as was its immediate predecessor—Manatu Māori. Despite the long existence of a separate department with specific responsibilities for Māori affairs, most publicly funded services (such as education, health care, accident compensation, and income support) have usually been delivered to Māori and Pākehā in the same way (i.e. via mainstream agencies) and in accordance with the same criteria. Furthermore, many of the programmes once administered or funded by the Department of Māori Affairs were little different from those operated by mainstream departments (i.e. in terms of their policy prescriptions and funding arrangements). Hence, they were not examples of affirmative action or positive discrimination. They simply had Māori names and, for the most part, were delivered by Māori public servants. Little attention was given to ensuring that these programmes satisfied the distinctive requirements of Māori. Nor was there much support for giving Māori, and more specifically iwi, greater autonomy or a larger role in policy development.

One reason for this was that policy-makers had, from the mid 1800s, placed relatively little value on the protection or enhancement of Māori culture. On the contrary, Māori culture was generally regarded as backward and unsophisticated, and the learning of te reo Māori was actively discouraged. Instead of fostering cultural diversity, the aim was to integrate Māori into mainstream Pākehā society (Hunn, 1961). Essentially, this meant turning Māori into brown-skinned Pākehā. As part of this objective, it was hoped that Māori and Pākehā would eventually enjoy a broadly similar standard of living and socio-economic status.

By the late 1970s, it was plain that the policy of assimilation was not working; nor was it any longer acceptable to Māori. Indeed, Māori leaders were becoming increasingly impatient with the state's failure to recognise, let alone encourage, Māori values and traditions, and to provide adequate resources for Māori development. They were bolstered in their convictions by the increasing recognition being given in various United Nations covenants and international law to the rights of indigenous peoples and the rights of cultural minorities. Widening, and seemingly entrenched, racial inequalities also served to heighten Māori demands for significant policy changes. As the Ministerial Advisory Committee (1986, Appendix, p. 26) pointed out, for 'virtually every negative statistic in education, crime, child abuse, infant mortality, health and unemployment, the Māori figures' were 'overwhelmingly dominant'.

LABOUR'S STRATEGY

Against this backdrop, the fourth Labour government made a determined effort to rethink the state's whole approach to protecting Māori culture, alleviating racial inequality, and resolving Treaty grievances. The net result was the adoption of a more explicitly bicultural policy stance and a much greater emphasis on the Crown's obligations under the Treaty (see Kelsey, 1990, 1991, 1993; Mulgan, 1989; Sharp, 1990). Early in its term, Labour extended the jurisdiction of the Waitangi Tribunal to allow for the investigation of Treaty claims back to 1840 (instead of 1975), and substantially increased the Tribunal's membership. Subsequently, it gave statutory recognition to the 'principles of the Treaty of Waitangi' in a number of important pieces of legislation, including the State-Owned Enterprises Act 1986, the Environment Act 1986, the

Conservation Act 1987, and the Education Act 1989 (see Joseph, 1993).[2] It made Māori an official New Zealand language and established the Māori Language Commission to promote the use of te reo Māori. And it consulted widely with Māori leaders on the best way of making public services more responsive to their needs, aspirations, and cultural norms. As a result, a two-pronged strategy was adopted: devolving the funding and control of many of the services provided by the Department of Māori Affairs to tribally based institutions, and enhancing the responsiveness of 'mainstream' public agencies to their Māori clients and customers.

Devolution

The impetus for devolution came from a variety of sources. First, it reflected growing disillusionment during the 1980s—both in New Zealand and many other advanced industrialised democracies—with the capacity of large, centralised, and often paternalistic state bureaucracies to respond effectively and appropriately to the diversity of human needs, especially within the context of an increasingly heterogeneous society. Advocates of more participative modes of decision-making argued for institutional arrangements that empowered citizens, enhanced local accountability, and ensured that public services were more responsive to the needs of particular communities and cultural groups.

Second, and more specifically, there was considerable disenchantment among both policy-makers and the wider Māori community with the Department of Māori Affairs. The Department was regarded as neither a good advocate for Māori interests nor an effective instrument for the delivery of public services. Matters came to a head in late 1986 as a result of the so-called 'Māori Loans Affair'. This centred on an attempt by senior staff in the Department to arrange a loan of $600 million from overseas financial interests for Māori development (Palmer, 1987, pp. 53–6). In the event, the loan did not proceed. An inquiry by the SSC (1986) was highly critical of the Department's conduct and the quality of its advice.

Third, the impetus for devolution also reflected a growing acceptance (or at least assertion) of the tribally based nature of the Māori community and a recognition that the Treaty of Waitangi was signed by chiefs on behalf of their iwi or hapu, rather than on behalf of a Māori nation—for no such collective identity existed (Booth, 1989; Sullivan, 1990). The idea of devolving various state responsibilities to iwi received firm support from many Māori leaders at an important Māori Economic Summit, or Hui Taumata, in late 1984. It was argued, for example, that iwi would make more effective use of the available state resources (in terms of achieving better outcomes for Māori) and that they would deliver services in a more culturally appropriate manner. Subsequently, devolution was strongly endorsed in an influential report—*Puao-te-Ata-Tu* (*Day Break*)—prepared by the Māori Perspective Advisory Committee for the Minister

---

2. The nature and scope of the 'principles of the Treaty of Waitangi' have been the subject of much debate. One authoritative statement of the 'principles' during the fourth Labour Government is contained in a document entitled *Principles for Crown Action on the Treaty of Waitangi*, published by the Department of Justice in 1989.

of Social Welfare in 1986 (see Ministerial Advisory Committee, 1986). The report (which dealt primarily with how the Department of Social Welfare might best meet the needs of Māori in the areas of policy formulation, planning, and service delivery) was unequivocal in calling for public institutions to adopt genuinely bicultural policies, in particular policies that gave iwi greater power to direct and allocate resources currently controlled by the state. It should be borne in mind that moves to devolve services had commenced as early as 1977 under the 'Tu Tangata' philosophy introduced by the Secretary for Māori Affairs, Kara Puketapu (Fleras, 1985; Puketapu, 1982). This had seen the development of community-based programmes, most notably Te Kōhanga Reo, Maatua Whāngai and Kōkiri Centres.[3]

Labour's policy for devolution was first outlined in 1988 in a discussion paper, *He Tirohanga Rangapū* (*Partnership Perspectives*) (Minister of Māori Affairs, 1988a). This document readily acknowledged the many deficiencies in the existing policy framework:

a. the programmes administered by mainstream departments failed to meet the needs of Māori;
b. the Department of Māori Affairs had insufficient influence to bring about many of the improvements the community desired;
c. most mainstream departments had little interaction with Māori communities, and their ministers lacked access to high-quality advice on Māori issues; and
d. iwi lacked an adequate role in shaping and delivering programmes of importance to Māori.

To rectify these problems, Labour proposed abolishing the Department of Māori Affairs and transferring many of its responsibilities to other departments (i.e. mainstreaming). It also proposed giving iwi a greater role in delivering certain publicly funded services. A new policy ministry would be established to provide a 'strong, unified, coherent' source of advice to the government on Māori issues and to ensure that Māori values were 'considered in all policy development' (p. 12).

Both the idea of mainstreaming and the dismantling of the department were questioned, if not rejected, by Māori (Jones, 1990). However, the principle of partnership and devolving many departmental functions to iwi received strong support. Labour's revised policy, outlined in *Te Urupare Rangapū* (*Partnership Response*) (Minister of Māori Affairs, 1988b), entailed the establishment of a new policy ministry (Manatu Māori) and a separate delivery agency, Te Tira Ahu Iwi (the Iwi Transition Agency or ITA). The latter body would be temporary and would be responsible for transferring various government programmes (such as Māori housing, land development, Te Kōhanga Reo,

---

3. Te Kōhanga Reo is a programme that funds early childhood learning centres specifically designed to encourage the learning of te reo Māori. Maatua Whāngai was a programme designed to reduce the numbers of young Māori offenders in government institutions by placing them in the care of whanau and hapu. Kōkiri Centres were created as drop-in centres or community centres and were used as sites for training schemes, such as Māori ACCESS, and pre-school education, such as Te Kōhanga Reo.

Māori ACCESS, and the MANA Enterprise scheme) to iwi organisations over a five-year period.[4] Both new departments commenced operations in mid to late 1989.

In December 1989, the government introduced the Runanga Iwi Bill (see Palmer, 1992, pp. 96–8). Its main aim was to give legal recognition to Māori institutions by providing for the establishment and incorporation of runanga to represent iwi. Such runanga would then become vehicles through which public funds could be channelled. More specifically, the legislation identified the essential characteristics of an iwi, established rules for the incorporation and operation of runanga, and established procedures for the resolution of conflicts within an iwi or between incorporated runanga. The Bill was eventually enacted in August 1990—one of Labour's final legislative initiatives.

Although the principle of devolution received broad support from the Māori community, many aspects of Labour's approach attracted considerable criticism and suspicion (Jones, 1990; McLeay, 1991). It was feared, for instance, that the new policy would be used as a means of cutting public expenditure on Māori programmes. Likewise, many claimed that devolution, although ostensibly about iwi exercising tino rangatiratanga (tribal control), was really about the government exercising kawanatanga (governorship). A particular concern was that iwi authorities would simply become instruments of the state, responsible for delivering prescribed outputs, and directly accountable to a Minister of the Crown. Put differently, Māori were concerned that new policy was essentially a form of 'delegation', 'administrative decentralisation' or 'contracting' rather than 'devolution'. Whereas delegation involves a principal–agent relationship, devolution entails a genuine transfer of power, authority and responsibility (see Boston, 1988b). If the policy were no more than a form of delegation, iwi authorities would be primarily, if not exclusively, accountable to the government. If, however, genuine devolution were to occur, the question arose as to how Parliament was to be assured that public funds were being wisely and properly spent. An alternative was to see the policy as a form of partial devolution similar in kind to Labour's education reforms.

Whatever the appropriate characterisation of the policy, it faced numerous problems of implementation. These included: establishing iwi authorities and determining their membership; resolving how services would be delivered to Māori living in urban areas where iwi structures had broken down; determining what services should be transferred to iwi and how much discretion iwi should have in using public funds; and the fact that most iwi lacked the experience and administrative skills to undertake the role expected of them—as evidenced by the difficulties encountered when MANA, Māori ACCESS, and Maatua Whāngai funds were first devolved (Kawharu, 1989). Also, notwithstanding the broad support within Māoridom for devolution, there was no consensus on how much effort should be expended on rebuilding tribal structures and identities as opposed

---

4. Māori ACCESS was a programme that funded training courses for young Māori and attempted to place them in secure employment positions. It was modelled on the ACCESS programme operated by the Department of Labour. The MANA Enterprise scheme was concerned with the development of viable, subsidised enterprises and the provision of increased employment for Māori.

to fostering pan-Māori structures and a corporate sense of Māori identity (see Levine and Henare, 1994). Lastly, the social and economic problems facing Māori were such that even well-run and adequately financed programmes would take many years to bring improvements. In the event, Labour's policy was not put to the test. At the 1990 election the government was resoundingly defeated by National, which was firmly opposed to devolution.

Enhancing Responsiveness

The second prong of Labour's approach was to make public agencies more responsive to Māori needs and cultural traditions and ensure that departmental programmes were more accommodating of cultural differences. The policy gradually took shape during the mid 1980s and was eventually enunciated with greater clarity in *Te Urupare Rangapū*. At least four separate streams of thought contributed to the new policy framework (see O'Reilly and Wood, 1991):

a. the growing international quest for greater consumer responsiveness and client sensitivity on the part of public sector organisations (OECD, 1987a; SSC, 1988);
b. the drive to eliminate institutional racism;
c. the desire to reduce the socio-economic inequalities of disadvantaged minority groups; and
d. the imperatives of the Treaty of Waitangi.

Note that the first three of these rationales for greater responsiveness are more consistent with multiculturalism than biculturalism. Only the last, the imperatives of the Treaty, provides a basis for a strictly bicultural approach to public management.

In line with the growing international emphasis on 'administrative responsiveness', the policy required departments to adopt new approaches towards the users (consumers or clients) of their services. This requirement had at least five aspects:

a. ensuring that the Māori clients of public agencies were better informed about what government services were available;
b. ensuring that public agencies became more aware of the social, economic and cultural influences affecting Māori and developed a better appreciation of tikanga Māori and the Treaty;[5]
c. ensuring that government services were more relevant to the needs of their Māori clients;
d. ensuring that Māori clients had more of a sense of 'ownership' (i.e. that they had an opportunity to participate in the design and delivery of public services); and
e. improving client access to services through the removal of various social, physical and psychological impediments.

---

5. Tikanga Māori is an all-embracing term that encompasses the values, beliefs, customs, and practices of iwi.

With respect to Labour's goal of enhancing Māori input into policy development and service delivery, government agencies adopted a range of approaches during the mid to late 1980s. More Māori staff were employed, often on an *ad hoc* basis. New consultative arrangements with iwi and pan-Māori organisations were instituted. Some departments established Māori advisory committees or appointed iwi liaison officers in regional offices. Advice on various matters, including cultural protocol, was regularly sought from individual kaumatua (elders). Further, most departments adapted their structures to reflect the new emphasis on biculturalism and partnership (see O'Reilly and Wood, 1991). For example, many departments, including Conservation, Education, Environment, Health, Inland Revenue, Justice, Labour, Social Welfare, and Women's Affairs, created specific Māori divisions, units, or secretariats to serve as repositories of expertise and advice on issues relating to Māori affairs, to promote tikanga Māori, to undertake liaison with iwi, and to coordinate the implementation of *Te Urupare Rangapū*.[6] Other departments (e.g. Commerce, Housing, and External Relations and Trade) appointed individual staff, rather than units, to undertake similar functions. In a few cases, departments created separate Māori units while also retaining (or instituting) tagged Māori advisory positions within their mainstream branches. Since the late 1980s various other central government agencies (e.g. the Human Rights Commission), as well as many local councils, have also created separate Māori units.

Another aim of the responsiveness policy was to enhance the employment opportunities of Māori in the public sector. A particular aim was to ensure that more Māori were appointed to positions of influence and responsibility, thereby overcoming the long-standing tendency for Māori to occupy predominantly low-status positions. The SSC was charged with monitoring the levels of recruitment, training and promotion of Māori in the public sector. Under the State Sector Act 1988 (s. 56), chief executives are required to operate a personnel policy that complies with the principle of being a 'good employer'. Among other requirements, a good employer is required to recognise the aims, aspirations and employment requirements of Māori, and seek their greater involvement in the public service (s. 56(2)(d)). Further, s. 6(e) requires the SSC to 'promote, develop, and monitor in each Department equal employment opportunities policies and programmes'.

Unlike devolution, Labour's responsiveness strategy has been continued, albeit with less enthusiasm, by National. Such evidence as there is suggests that the strategy has made departments and other public agencies more aware of, and more sensitive to, the Crown's obligations under the Treaty (see O'Reilly and Wood, 1991; Sarr, 1993). Large numbers of public servants have attended courses on tikanga Māori. This has not only instilled greater cultural awareness but also given Māori staff more pride in their cultural heritage and lessened their sense of inferiority. Some of the new Māori units have provided a positive working environment and a good training ground for young Māori analysts; they have also made a significant contribution to policy development in certain

---

6. Some of the Māori units have subsequently been dismantled (e.g. Education) in favour of alternative structural arrangements.

areas (Tahi, 1995). Additionally, many departments have made a genuine effort to incorporate Māori values and perspectives into their operating procedures and management styles. Examples include the publication of documents in English and Māori, the opportunity for whanau (family) support at job interviews, karakia (prayers) before meetings, the regular use of hui (conferences), and the inclusion of Māori on selection panels. The Department of Conservation provides a good illustration (Sarr, 1993). Since it was established in 1987 it has worked hard to enhance Māori representation within the organisation, to build active and effective relationships with iwi, and to ensure that Māori perspectives are reflected in its management of the nation's conservation estate. Given that the bulk of this estate is currently subject to Treaty claims and the open antagonism of many claimants to the Department, the fostering and maintenance of a close partnership with iwi will be even more important in the future.

While the responsiveness strategy has gone at least some way to making government agencies more culturally inclusive and less alien to Māori (whether in their roles as public servants, citizens or clients), it has also exposed deficiencies within the management of the public sector and highlighted the tensions implicit in the commitment to biculturalism. The development of responsive corporate cultures has been uneven, in part reflecting the varying levels of enthusiasm among chief executives (and ministers). Māori perspectives on policy issues continue to be treated as 'add-ons' rather than as central components of departments' analytical frameworks (Parata, 1994). Similarly, Māori culture, needs, and outcomes still receive only limited attention in departmental planning and performance management systems (e.g. corporate plans, internal resource allocation, performance measures, information systems, etc.). Despite the heightened emphasis on EEO, there are still very few Māori in senior departmental positions. In part, this reflects the limited pool of professional Māori policy analysts and middle managers. But whatever the reasons, until significantly more Māori acquire senior status within the public sector, there will be little justification in talking of 'bicultural policy development or bicultural implementation of policy or of a bicultural policy environment' (Parata, 1994, p. 49).

At another level, the responsiveness policy (coupled with the Treaty settlements' policy) has drawn attention to some of the ethical tensions faced by Māori public servants. On the one hand, they are increasingly expected by their own people to defend and promote Māori interests and to display loyalty to their respective iwi or hapu. On the other hand, they are expected, as public servants, to serve the government with dedication and loyalty (see Durie, 1993; Martin, 1991a). Of course, most public servants face conflicting obligations at times, but those confronting Māori in recent years have been especially acute.

Not surprisingly, many Māori, as well as Pākehā (see Kelsey, 1990), have regarded the responsiveness policy as a form of tokenism, if not a charade. As Durie (1993) observes, there is a suspicion that the pursuit of cultural sensitivity is simply a vehicle for placating Māori and avoiding the central issues, such as the quest for self-determination and a resolution of Treaty grievances. The aim, in other words, appears to be 'to create an impression of responsiveness to Māori issues but without any demonstrable evidence that the Māori position was well understood or addressed in the core business' of each public agency (ibid., pp. 10–11). Whether or not these perceptions are accurate, the new policy has certainly not been characterised by any genuine sharing of power, resources or responsibilities with iwi. Whatever the official commitment to biculturalism, Māori have remained very much the junior partner.

NATIONAL'S STRATEGY

The National government since 1990 has had considerable difficulty in developing a coherent, consistent policy framework for the conduct of public management in the context of cultural pluralism (see Morton, 1994; Parata, 1994). This difficulty reflects not only the inherent complexity of the issues but also the tensions within the cabinet and caucus on race relations and the increasing divisions within the wider community over the state's handling of Treaty issues.

Philosophical Issues

National's approach has been strongly influenced by its commitment to traditional liberal principles, such as democratic equality, uniform citizenship rights, and individual choice. From this viewpoint, as noted earlier, individual rights are generally accorded priority over collective rights. Likewise, to the extent that collective rights are justified, all ethnic or cultural groups should be treated equally; giving special rights, a distinctive status, or preferential treatment to one group is seen as unfair discrimination. Similarly, while it is legitimate for the state to assist individuals in various ways (e.g. via the provision of education, health care, or income support), such assistance should be based on a person's (or a family's) needs rather than considerations of race, gender, or cultural background. The presumption, then, is that Māori and Pākehā should be treated on equal terms by government agencies; Māori should not receive favourable treatment on the basis of their racial origins or status as tangata whenua. Only if their needs are greater—because of significant socio-economic inequalities—can greater state assistance be justified. Moreover, from a liberal standpoint, any social assistance provided by the state should be delivered in a manner that maximises individual choice. This implies a preference for cash transfers rather than in-kind assistance since individuals are then at liberty to purchase the services they need from a provider of their choice. Such an approach is necessarily at odds with a more collectivist or communitarian framework under which there might be a case for channelling certain forms of social assistance via tribal structures.

Given this philosophical stance, the National government has been reluctant to support policies that give Māori preferential treatment. It has tended to oppose the development of parallel public institutions and proposals that smack of 'tribalism', separate development, or apartheid. At the same time, it has accepted the Treaty as the nation's founding document and has acknowledged the failure of the Crown to honour its Treaty obligations. For this reason, it devoted considerable effort to the settlement of Treaty claims. Such an approach, of course, is fully consistent with liberal principles.

After all, liberal theories of justice place great weight on the protection of property rights and the honouring of contracts. But while accepting the constitutional significance of the Treaty, National has tended to place more emphasis on Article III (which is concerned with citizenship rights) than Article II (which deals with tino rangatiratanga or self-determination). It has also given priority to the English version of the Treaty and claimed that Article I should take precedence over Article II. Accordingly, it has dismissed calls from various Māori groups for the return of (some measure of) sovereignty to iwi (and/or Māori).

Notwithstanding its liberal heritage, National has recognised the importance of other ethical principles and political imperatives. For instance, it has acknowledged that the policy framework that existed before the mid 1980s tended to undermine Māori culture and demonstrably failed to address the problems of racial inequality. Furthermore, it has recognised that the needs of individuals can vary according to their cultural background and that a 'needs-based approach' founded on the premise that 'one size fits all' might therefore be flawed. Hence, although National's general instinct has been to embrace multiculturalism rather than biculturalism, in practice it has remained officially committed to the latter.

From *Ka Awatea* to Mainstreaming

National's 1990 election manifesto committed it to 'work towards a united society' in which Māori could 'participate equally in the newly created competitive environment' (quoted in Henare, 1995, pp. 48–9). Since Labour's devolution strategy was considered incompatible with this vision, the repeal of the Runanga Iwi Act was one of the new government's early legislative initiatives. But if National's opposition to statutory devolution was firm, there was no consensus within the party on a replacement policy. Moreover, while iwi autonomy and self-determination were unacceptable, National was not averse to the idea of public agencies entering into contracts with established and competent Māori organisations (ideally on the basis of competitive tendering) to provide various services (e.g. vocational training and primary health care).

In order to develop a more coherent policy framework, but also to pre-empt the Treasury's attempts to impose its market-liberal philosophy on the delivery of state assistance to Māori, the new Minister of Māori Affairs, Winston Peters, appointed a three-person Ministerial Planning Group to review the policy options and objectives in the area of Māori affairs and to make recommendations on strategies for improving the position of Māori in New Zealand society (see Henare, 1995). The Planning Group's report, *Ka Awatea (It is Day)* was published in March 1991. It provided a detailed analysis of the disadvantaged position of Māori, giving particular attention to low educational attainment, poor health status, high levels of unemployment, and income inequalities. According to *Ka Awatea*, a key objective of government policy should be to ensure that the 'distinctive and unique place' of Māori in New Zealand society is 'preserved and enhanced' and that they are able to 'participate fully' in the nation's future development (p. 64). In order to achieve this goal, the report made numerous recommendations. The most important, at least from the standpoint of public management, was the establishment of a new, specialist Māori agency to replace Manatu Māori and ITA. It was envisaged that the agency would have a staff of around 350 and would undertake a range of tasks including the provision of policy advice and the monitoring of services provided to Māori by other agencies. It would also undertake various operational activities. For instance, it was suggested that the new agency should include a Māori Education Commission, a Health Promotion Unit, a Training Unit, and an Economic Resource Development Unit. It was envisaged that the new agency would have a strong regional presence and would work with local communities and iwi to encourage Māori development. The overall aim, to quote one of the report's authors, was to 'shift the focus from a department servicing a dependent people to a ministry facilitating their development' (Henare, 1995, p. 54).

For political reasons, the authors of *Ka Awatea* put relatively little emphasis on the Treaty and said even less about Māori aspirations for rangatiratanga. As to the future development and role of iwi, the report accepted that there would be no major transfer of resources or government programmes, as some had previously envisaged. However, it recommended that iwi should be given the opportunity to form legal corporate entities and negotiate contracts with public agencies to deliver services to their people. This implied a principal–agent relationship with the Crown rather than devolution.

The government accepted the report's broad analysis of the problems facing Māori and endorsed the idea of replacing Manatu Māori and ITA with a new streamlined ministry. The new agency—to be known as Te Puni Kōkiri (TPK)—would focus on Māori development and provide advice on all matters relating to Māori affairs. At the same time, in line with the principle that policy and delivery functions should be split, ministers rejected any suggestion that TPK should operate substantive programmes of its own in priority areas such as education, training, health care, and resource development. Instead, TPK would be a policy ministry, with certain supplementary liaison and monitoring responsibilities. Accordingly, it would be much smaller (around 200 staff) than envisaged by the authors of *Ka Awatea*, and in many ways similar in function and status to Manatu Māori. The new ministry was established under the Ministry of Māori Development Act 1991 and commenced operations in January 1992.

As part of the move to create TPK, it was decided that the programmes administered by ITA (e.g. pre-school education, training, enterprise development and housing) should be transferred to other public agencies or contracted out (see Morton, 1994; Parata, 1994). The new approach, known as 'mainstreaming', had received little attention in *Ka Awatea* and did not form part of the report's recommendations. Arguably, however, the idea was implicit in the report, particularly given the rejection of devolution and the proposal to abolish ITA. As with devolution, mainstreaming was greeted with scepticism by many Māori. Some feared that it represented a return to assimilationism. Others were concerned that public funds, previously earmarked for Māori, would either be cut on fiscal grounds or dissipated into existing departmental programmes. It was pointed out that many departments had demonstrated an incapacity to respond adequately to Māori needs and aspirations and had made little real effort to improve Māori outcomes; it would thus be risky, to say the least, to give them substantial new responsibilities for serving

Māori customers and clients. Quite apart from this, it was unclear whether mainstreaming meant that specific Māori programmes would be fully integrated into existing departmental structures or continue to be funded and administered separately. Another issue was how the new arrangements would affect the ability of iwi to bid for contracts to provide services directly to their members.

More generally, at no stage did the government indicate whether the main aim of mainstreaming was to achieve better outcomes for Māori (i.e. greater policy effectiveness) or simply the same outcomes at a lower cost (i.e. greater productive efficiency). And if the aim was—in line with the goal of *Ka Awatea*—to reduce racial disparities and lessen Māori dependency on the state, it was by no means clear how mainstreaming would achieve these ends. The government, it seems, was not unduly worried by the vagueness of its objectives or the failure to undertake a careful assessment of how mainstreaming would affect Māori. Instead, its main concern was to get the new policy implemented as quickly as possible. To this end, the Residual Services Unit in TPK was required to transfer all ITA programmes to mainstream agencies by mid 1993. This meant, of course, that there was virtually no time for consultation. Yet again, therefore, Māori were given little opportunity to participant in the decision-making process. To compound matters, despite the best efforts of TPK, most programmes were transferred to mainstream agencies in the absence of any 'transfer contract containing safeguards, sanctions or transparent auditing mechanisms' (Parata, 1994, p. 42). This has generated continuing problems for TPK in undertaking its monitoring responsibilities.

As it happens, not all of the programmes administered by ITA (and previously the Department of Māori Affairs) were fully mainstreamed. Nor in many cases were their funding levels protected. In fact, five different destinations can be identified (see Morton, 1994; TPK, 1994a). First, a number of smaller programmes were scaled down and in some cases discontinued (e.g. rural lending, economic development grants, Kōkiri Centres, the Māori and Pacific Island recruitment scheme, and certain grants to Māori organisations). Second, a few residual programmes were transferred to TPK. They include grants (largely to cover administrative costs) to the New Zealand Māori Council, Māori Trust Boards and the Māori Wardens Association, together with a small number of grants for the promotion of Māori health, education, social welfare, and the learning of te reo Māori. Third, a number of activities and resources were transferred or sold to iwi—e.g. kaumatua (pensioner) flats. Fourth, some activities (and the related funds) were transferred to other public agencies but were then amalgamated with existing programmes. For instance, the funding for Māori ACCESS was transferred to the Education, Training and Support Agency and is now used to purchase training services under the Training Opportunities Programme. As a result, there are no longer tagged funds specifically for Māori clients or training providers. Much the same occurred with respect to Māori housing assistance. ITA's mortgages were transferred to the Housing Corporation, and the provision of concessional housing assistance specifically for Māori was largely discontinued. Finally, in a few cases separate Māori programmes were either retained by mainstream agencies or specific funds were 'ring-fenced' primarily for Māori clients or providers—e.g. Te Kōhanga Reo and loans for papakainga home ownership (i.e. on ancestral lands). As an indication of the magnitude of the impact of mainstreaming, whereas the Department of Māori Affairs received an appropriation of around $265 million in 1988–89 (the financial year immediately prior to its abolition), TPK was appropriated around $48 million in 1995–96.

Although National has not generally favoured the idea of maintaining, let alone developing, separate programmes for the exclusive benefit of Māori, a number of new initiatives that involve a degree of separatism or positive discrimination have been launched since the early 1990s. For example, two new scholarship programmes specifically for Māori students were introduced in 1992 in order to encourage Māori participation in education and reward academic achievement. Manaaki Akonga Rua provides scholarships for Māori senior secondary students while Manaaki Tauira provides scholarships for Māori tertiary students. Another development was the establishment of Te Māngai Pāho (the Māori Broadcasting Funding Agency) under the Broadcasting Amendment Act 1993. This body has a mandate to promote Māori language and culture by providing funds for the production and broadcasting of Māori programmes. It is funded primarily via income from the Public Broadcasting Fee. Finally, in 1994 National restructured the administration and funding of the arts. Under the new arrangements, funding for Māori arts and culture has been separated from the funding of the non-Māori population and is allocated by a separate body (Te Waka Toi Board) under the umbrella of Creative New Zealand (formerly the Arts Council of New Zealand).

An Evaluation of the Changes to Māori Administration

It is too early to provide a detailed or comprehensive assessment of the consequences of the restructuring of Māori affairs and the effectiveness of mainstreaming. Nevertheless, from the evidence currently available (see Morton, 1994; Parata, 1994; SSC, 1994b; TPK, 1994b), the following broad observations can be made.

1. The creation of Manatu Māori and ITA in 1989 and their subsequent abolition in 1991 was disruptive for the Māori policy community. It resulted in many redundancies and led to much effort being expended on administrative reorganisation instead of the development of new initiatives to assist Māori.

2. As with Manatu Māori and ITA, TPK has had difficulty recruiting and retaining top-flight policy analysts and thereby contributing high-quality policy advice across the spectrum of issues for which it is responsible. For one thing, it has had to compete with the Māori policy units in other government agencies for competent Māori advisers. For another, the Ministry has failed, at least to date, to achieve the status and influence within the Wellington policy community hoped for by the authors of *Ka Awatea*.

3. For much of the period since 1992, TPK has enjoyed neither a high level of political backing within the cabinet nor a strong presence on key officials committees, such as those servicing the Cabinet Committee on the Implementation of Social Assistance Reforms and the Cabinet Committee on Education, Training and Employment. Inevitably, this has limited its input in a number of important policy domains and left its staff feeling marginalised. A further complicating factor also deserves mention. As Parata has pointed out, TPK

by virtue of the issues it must deal with, and the constituency for which it is responsible, is often seen by other government agencies as the representative of Māori. The Māori community (or at least most of it) on the other hand recognize that the Ministry is an agent of the State. Clearly the latter situation is correct. Nevertheless, Te Puni Kōkiri is frequently forced onto the margins of policy making, even the areas for which it clearly has expertise (advice on the Treaty), because of this debilitating ambivalence (1994, p. 41).

4. The policy context within which TPK has operated has been dominated by National's attempts to settle Treaty claims and its subsequent development of the so-called 'fiscal envelope' designed to limit public expenditure on Treaty settlements to around $1 billion (see Office of Treaty Settlements, 1994). The fiscal envelope proposals provoked a very negative response from iwi—as, indeed, TPK had warned. While TPK took some of the flak for National's policy initiatives, ironically the events surrounding the fiscal envelope strengthened TPK's hand by highlighting the accuracy of its advice and the quality of its networks within the Māori community.

5. TPK has encountered significant difficulties in undertaking its statutory responsibilities to monitor mainstream programmes relevant to Māori development (see Maori Affairs Committee, 1994). Reasons for this include: the hurried transfer process mentioned earlier; the absence of clear policy objectives; poor consultative mechanisms between TPK and certain departments; an understandable reluctance by departments to have their performance scrutinised by yet another agency; TPK's lack of legislative authority to require agencies to provide the necessary information; and the failure of many agencies to collect data relevant for the purposes of assessing the impact of their services on Māori.

6. Of course, the problems of evaluating the effectiveness of mainstream programmes (in terms of improving outcomes for Māori) extend well beyond the difficulties of obtaining useful quantitative or qualitative data. In many cases the causal relationship between departmental outputs and subsequent outcomes is extremely complex and hard to establish. Even so, the government should make analyses of the impact of mainstreaming a priority. The current lack of thoroughgoing studies is lamentable.

7. More generally, the programme of mainstreaming coincided with a period of severe fiscal constraint and radical changes in social policy. Many of these changes, such as the reduction in benefit rates, higher student fees, and the charging of market rentals for state houses, have had an adverse affect on the poor, including Māori (see Boston and Dalziel, 1992). Rather, therefore, than alleviating socio-economic disparities between Māori and Pākehā, the overall policy context since the early 1990s has been inimical to this objective. To compound problems, from the perspective of many Māori, the radical refashioning of the state sector from the mid 1980s to the early 1990s, together with the fragmentation of Māori programmes across a range of departments, has made it more difficult for them to access public resources.

8. More positively, with public agencies contracting out an increasing range of services, Māori have the opportunity to develop services specially geared to their needs. Already there has been an expansion in the number of contracts negotiated with iwi and other Māori organisations by government agencies, such as Regional Health Authorities

and the Community Funding Agency (within the Department of Social Welfare). Of course, such contracting must not be confused with devolution, let alone tino rangatiratanga. Nor is the idea of competitive tendering—which entails iwi competing for public funds against each other and non-Māori providers—consistent with the ideal of a cooperative partnership sought by many Māori. On the other hand, under some of the new contractual arrangements iwi have secured a reasonable degree of flexibility over the use of the resources provided. There is thus scope under the current policy framework for iwi to develop their infrastructure, secure additional public funding, and undertake more ambitious policy initiatives.

Recognising the problems faced by TPK, the government launched an internal review of the Ministry's role in mid 1994 (see SSC, 1994b). In brief, this review reaffirmed the importance of having a separate ministry dedicated to the provision of high-quality advice on matters relating to Māori and confirmed TPK's advisory, monitoring, consultation, and communication responsibilities. However, in order to strengthen TPK's strategic policy role, the review recommended that the Ministry be recognised as the government's principal adviser on the Crown's relationship with iwi, hapu, and Māori. Further, the review proposed that TPK's monitoring role be enhanced and recommended that the Ministry develop protocols with key departments, most notably Commerce, Education, Health, and Labour, covering the development of joint projects, the formulation of auditable performance indicators, and the enhancement of information sharing and policy coordination. The inclusion of TPK on key officials' committees was also proposed. The cabinet accepted the findings of the review in April 1995. However, it remains to be seen what impact the review will have on TPK's influence and effectiveness.

CONCLUSION

No consensus has yet emerged on the best way to organise and operate public agencies to meet the imperatives of the Treaty of Waitangi and the requirements of an increasingly pluralistic society. Although there has been much talk of biculturalism, including a bicultural public service, there has been no definitive governmental statement, and certainly no agreement, on what biculturalism means or how it should be achieved. This is reflected, for example, in the varying attitudes towards the development of separate legal, administrative, and social institutions for Māori (Culpitt, 1994). For many, parallel structures and devolution to iwi are not only inimical to core liberal values but also a threat to national unity and social cohesion. Moreover, even those within the policy community sympathetic to the idea of greater iwi self-government remain sceptical about the capacity of iwi to deliver publicly funded programmes efficiently and effectively.[7] Thus, as Parata (1994, p. 46) laments, the only 'attempt by a government to

---

7. Note that the quest for greater Māori autonomy is characterised by a variety of terms (sovereignty, self-management, self-government, self-determination, self-reliance, etc.) each with subtle differences in meaning. There is no agreement amongst Māori on which term should

work with the resilient Māori cultural structures of whanau, hapu, iwi and marae, was the brief flirtation with iwi self-management and departmental responsiveness outlined in *Te Urupare Rangapū*.' And, as this chapter notes, the devolution policy was never implemented and the responsiveness initiative has been, at best, only a partial success.

Despite National's rejection of devolution, large sections of the Māori community have not abandoned their quest for a greater sharing of public power and resources. Indeed, prompted by increasing racial inequalities, the demands for iwi self-government have become more pressing. As a first step towards addressing these demands, there is a need for an informed public debate about the implications of tino rangatiratanga, the possible forms of self-government (or self-management), and the relative merits of the available policy options (see Bolger, 1995). In this context, more recognition must be given to the fact that it is difficult for a minority indigenous culture—such as Māori—to develop and flourish when everything is mainstreamed and everything is shared with the dominant (Pākehā) culture. After all, if there are no separate spheres of corporate life and activity, where is there the scope for an open display and celebration of cultural differences? In short, only if Māori have the opportunity to manage some of their own affairs and initiate their own programmes, at least in a number of domains, will they have the freedom to develop and express their distinctive values and preferences.

Questions of iwi self-government aside, public sector managers face many difficulties as they grapple with the reality of increasing cultural diversity and the challenge of biculturalism. One of these is how to be sensitive to the needs and interests of all citizens (customers, consumers, and clients) irrespective of their cultural background, while at the same time acknowledging the special place and distinctive aspirations of the tangata whenua. Responding to the needs of the various communities of Pacific Islanders living in New Zealand poses particularly significant challenges (i.e. given the problems of high unemployment, economic deprivation, and the dislocation of traditional social structures). Another pressing issue for departmental managers is how to incorporate pertinent Māori values into the mainstream work and culture of their organisations, including the formulation of policy, while at the same time avoiding the dangers of cultural relativism. Yet another challenge is developing more effective programmes for enhancing outcomes for Māori and reducing the entrenched socio-economic inequalities between Māori and Pākehā. Finally, the Treaty settlements process will involve many departments in resolving thorny policy issues over the future ownership and management of key public resources.

---

be used. Nor is there agreement on precisely what, in policy terms, is being sought. Furthermore, there is disagreement about whether the objective of greater autonomy should focus solely on iwi or whether it should embrace self-government by pan-iwi (or pan-Māori) authorities (e.g. in urban areas).

part four

management
beyond the centre

8 the centre and the periphery: the continuing game

Centralisation [is] the death blow of public freedom (Disraeli).

This chapter reviews the changing nature of the relationship between the centre and the periphery in New Zealand since the mid 1980s. It considers the theoretical case for devolution and decentralisation. Structural developments in local government, environmental administration, health, and education are briefly described. Also outlined are changes in the structure of the Department of Social Welfare (DSW), which exemplify decentralisation within a central government department. The move to 'third party government' or 'government by proxy' (Kettl, 1988) and more generally to 'contracting'— and indeed to 'contractualism' (Martin, 1995a)—is also discussed. The focus is not on the policies followed but on the structures and such issues as the location of responsibility within them. (Issues relating to the management of local government are dealt with in more detail in Chapter 9.)

New Zealand is usually described as having a unitary government. Unlike some other Westminster-style governments (e.g. Australia and Canada), or countries such as the USA, there are no provinces or states. To that extent, the checks and balances imposed on a national government by having to share power with other authorities which gain their legitimacy from fundamental law—the constitution—are absent. In this respect, New Zealand is like the United Kingdom. And, for the same reasons as those advanced by scholars such as Jones and Stewart (1983) in the British context, such sub-national government as there is should be highly valued.

Since the mid 1980s, much attention has been focused on the performance of local government, the health service and the education system. Are they efficiently delivering outputs that accord with the preferences of citizens and the views of the central government? Wider issues about the constitutional and societal significance of local institutions have been rather overshadowed. Perhaps the dominant motivation behind much reform at the sub-national level was best captured in the following statement (later disowned by some ministers: Palmer, 1988, p. 7) about local government reform:

As a fundamental principle it is agreed that local or regional government should be selected *only* where the net benefits of such an option exceed all other institutional arrangements (Bassett, 1987, p. 63, emphasis added).

In short, the traditional place in New Zealand society of elected local authorities, elected hospital boards (more recently area health boards), and the system of educational administration that had evolved over more than a hundred years was under challenge for the same reasons that lay behind the bureaucratic revolution at the centre.

At the same time, delivery mechanisms through the district offices of the sectoral government departments were also massively changed by the restructuring at the centre. Although the central government formerly had a presence throughout New Zealand in the form of regional and district offices of most departments, this presence has been severely reduced (through corporatisation and internal reorganisations). Few departments now have extensive representation nationwide. For some, Link centres are the point of contact with local citizens: established recently by the Department of Internal Affairs, these centres represent fifteen government agencies in eighteen locations. It is interesting to note, however, that organisations such as the Ministry of Education and the regional health authorities (RHAs) have found it necessary to establish a presence away from their headquarters. The dilemma of centralisation versus decentralisation noted in Chapter 1 remains an issue for the design and management of public organisations.

THE CASE FOR DECENTRALISATION

'Decentralisation' is an umbrella word that shelters a number of meanings. For political scientists it connotes 'the territorial distribution of power' (Smith, 1985, p. 1). For writers about management it means the delegation of authority and reduction of control in organisations—'letting go' and 'invisible-from-the-top' management (see Peters, 1993, p. 566). Indeed, there is a cluster of words often employed interchangeably in everyday discourse: decentralisation, delegation, devolution, deconcentration, dispersal. What they all have in common is a rejection of 'centralisation'—whether it be the concentration of political authority in the capital city or the all-pervasive bureaucratic reach of 'head office' down through the hierarchy and out to the branches. While others' definitions might be different, it is convenient, and probably in accordance with New Zealand usage (Boston, 1988b; Martin, 1988b, 1991b), to ascribe particular meanings to two key expressions, viz.:

- *devolution:* the *transfer* of power, authority and responsibility from a national to a sub-national level;
- *decentralisation:* the *delegation* of power and authority to lower levels with ultimate responsibility remaining at the national level (Martin, 1988b, p. vii).

Thus defined, 'devolution' describes the vesting of statutory power and functions in local government, for example under the Resource Management Act 1991. Similarly, 'decentralisation' applies to the internal organisation of, for example, DSW, where ultimate responsibility remains with the minister and the chief executive. While these two cases are probably uncontroversial, other arrangements of public authority are more problematic. Does the health system in place since 1 July 1993, or the post-Picot administration of education, manifest the characteristics of devolution or decentralisation? These issues are explored in more depth later, but it is probably helpful to suggest some conditions to be attached to 'devolution'. They may be framed as questions, which will be revisited at the end of this chapter:

- Does the public organisation in question derive its authority or legitimacy from statute?
- Is the governing body (council or board) locally chosen?[1]
- Does the organisation have the capacity to raise its own revenue?

Such questions direct our attention to the degree of 'distance' there is between the central government and organisations at the periphery. If an organisation is the creature of statute (rather than of ministers), is headed by a locally elected group of citizens (rather than a ministerially appointed board), and finances its activities from money raised locally (rather than receiving a grant from central government), then it exemplifies 'devolution' as defined earlier. Only local government in New Zealand meets these criteria. Nonetheless, as will be discussed, 'devolution' is still a useful framework within which to consider the important issues of accountability that are so prominent in discussions of the health and education systems. 'Devolution' and 'decentralisation' should be seen not as the elements of a dichotomy but as poles on a continuum.

Decentralisation, in the all-embracing sense used at the beginning of this section, is a description of what happens within every state (and, indeed, in supranational groupings: the discussion of 'subsidiarity' in the European Union is an example). It is simply not practicable to administer from the centre in all respects all activities of government—even in states with minimal functions (e.g. Switzerland) or where the area or population is minuscule (e.g. Tokelau). But beyond descriptive statements, decentralisation is the subject of normative judgments from various political, economic, and managerial positions. In some countries (the former Yugoslavia, for example), questions of ethnic or national self-determination are crucial in these judgments. Until recently, few New Zealanders would have thought such discourse relevant to their future constitutional arrangements. In the 1990s te tino rangatiratanga is a salient consideration. Usually, however, arguments about the desirability of more or less decentralisation turn around the weighting attached to the values of liberal democracy and economic efficiency.

For some twentieth-century political theorists in the liberal tradition, local forms of government constitute an important check on the power of central government.[2] The preservation of individual freedom is paramount (Schumpeter, 1979; Hayek, 1979).

---

1. In most cases 'chosen' means 'election', but the Runanga Iwi Act 1990 (repealed 1991) provided that *runanga*—the governing bodies of proposed statutory iwi authorities—should be chosen according to established Māori protocol.
2. For a discussion of democratic theory and decentralisation see Boston (1988b).

This view is to be contrasted with the arguments of radical democratic theorists such as Barber (1984) who seek greater *participation*[3] in the political process by citizens—a goal more likely to be achieved through local rather than national institutions. For the advocates of 'strong' democracy (whose nineteenth-century precursors were J. S. Mill and de Tocqueville) the 'town meeting' or 'city state' form of government is the ideal. Participation, it is argued, has an intrinsic value beyond the instrumental achievement of effective and efficient public policies.

Economists, on the other hand, are more likely to direct attention to the end-product of local public agencies (Helm and Smith, 1989). Where economists favour decentralisation it is because local agencies are considered to be better placed to respond efficiently to local demands. Different preferences are respected; information about preferences is more effectively transmitted and interpreted; and redress ought to be quicker. In short, local agencies may be expected to be more responsive to consumer demands. And if they do not respond appropriately, consumers—who are also citizens—may move to a locality where public services better meet their mix of needs (Tiebout, 1956).

None of these arguments is self-evident or conclusive. They involve the weighting individuals place on particular values. But they indicate the very different perspectives from which the decentralisation debate may be approached. All, as is later discussed, have been advanced in New Zealand over the past decade.

COMMUNITY

One notion prominent in discussion of decentralisation in New Zealand is that of 'community'. It is given statutory recognition in a number of Acts including the Local Government Act 1974, the Children, Young Persons, and Their Families Act 1989, the Education Act 1989, the Health and Disability Services Act 1993, and the Electoral Act 1993. Like 'decentralisation', it is a slippery expression (see Pearson, 1990). For many it is a spatial term; but it also conveys a sense of 'belonging', a social dimension.

At one level 'community' might merely denote the population of a geographically defined area. But in public policy discourse there is sometimes an assumption, as in the Picot report on educational administration (Taskforce to Review Education Administration, 1988), that there is a 'broad-based community view' or 'community educational needs'. Similarly, the provision for community boards under the Local Government Act assumes the existence of 'communities', which might (as some in local government would suggest) sometimes be the artificial constructs of the Local Government Commission. Logan Moss, in a sharp critique of Picot, questions the notion that geographical residence 'implies both a commonality of interests and a consequent unity of purpose' (Moss, 1990, p. 140).

---

3. For general discussions of participation see Nagel (1987) and Parry, Moyser, and Day (1992). Hayward (1994) has considered the application of participation theory to environmental management in New Zealand.

No longer are our social relationships dictated by geographical proximity (if they ever were) and there are few local institutions which might provide a focus for them. Our friends often live in distant suburbs and our family in more distant towns, cities and even countries. Few people work in the locality in which they live and most no longer even shop there. Indeed many routinely visit supermarkets which may be further from their homes than the average inhabitant of the villages of [William] Morris' imagination would have travelled in a lifetime (ibid, p. 142).

On the other hand, it could be suggested that the strong commitment to local identity that emerges when local government boundaries are threatened (as well as in sporting allegiances) demonstrates that in particular contexts—noting that citizens will usually identify with several 'communities'—the concept has meaning. Clearly, its problematic nature has practical implications for those charged with establishing the boundaries of statutory areas (such as the Local Government Commission) and establishing such statutory bodies as community boards. It also raises questions about the case for participation. If citizens are viewed primarily as consumers of public services, their primary relationships are with the various providers of those services (which, of course, include both local and central government). As citizens, however, allegiance is felt only to the national government, not to any sub-national authority. New Zealanders have lost—if they ever had—a sense of 'community' in a wider belonging sense, or so this line of argument goes. Such an interpretation is supported perhaps by what some would see as the continued apathy demonstrated at local authority elections and, in some areas, to school boards of trustees. By contrast, the Māori renaissance has seen an emphasis on 'community' in the form of iwi.

Such an interpretation of the way in which New Zealanders relate to the levels of government suggests that the focus of attention in future debates about the centre and the periphery will be on the dimensions of consumerism: access, choice, information, redress, and representation (Potter, 1988, p. 150). What is the place of local institutions in the delivery of services? This perspective is in contrast to an active concept of citizenship, which focuses attention on the interdependence of rights and duties underpinned by democratic processes at the local level. The apparent tension between citizenship and consumerism joins the relationship between the centre and the periphery as the themes around which the chapter is organised.

LOCAL GOVERNMENT

Management in local government is discussed in the next chapter. Here the concern is principally with the relationship between central government and local government as it is now organised, and with the extent of citizen participation. After several false starts (most recently by Henry May in the third Labour government: see Bush, 1980), Michael Bassett, Minister of Local Government in the fourth Labour government, succeeded in rationalising the structure of local government (Local Government Amendment Act (No. 2) 1989):

- the number of regions was reduced from twenty-two to thirteen (not including the Gisborne 'region', which was administered by the Gisborne District Council acting as a unitary authority), and all councils are now directly elected;[4]
- territorial authorities were reduced in number from more than 200 to seventy-four;
- the number of *ad hoc* or special purpose bodies—pest destruction boards, catchment boards, etc.—were reduced from more than 400 to seven, leaving aside the health service and energy retail organisations, both of which were subject to separate review, and a large number of local reserve boards. (Most *ad hoc* functions were transferred to regional councils.)

The provisions of the Local Government Act 1974, amended in 1989 to extend the role of regional government, were again amended in 1992 to reduce the scope of activity that regional councils could undertake. The principal functions of regional councils (except in Auckland and Wellington, where special arrangements apply)[5] are now those they carry out under the Resource Management Act 1991 (discussed later in this chapter) and the Soil Conservation and Rivers Control Act 1941. They also control pests and noxious plants; administer harbour regulations and control marine pollution; are responsible for regional aspects of civil defence; have a statutory overview of transport planning; and control passenger transport operators.

Over the decades territorial authorities (which have a much longer history than regional councils) acquired in a process similar to that of central government (by accretion rather than plan) a multiplicity of functions. Importantly, these functions have been within the gift of Parliament: local authorities may exercise only those powers and functions specifically provided in statute. A 'power of general competence' has been discussed over the years but never enacted (Officials Coordinating Committee on Local Government, 1988a, p. 58). Few functions are mandatory (resource planning, civil defence, and public health responsibilities are among the exceptions); some are taken for granted (sewage collection and rubbish disposal); others are a reflection of the collective decision-making of elected representatives in power from time to time, and might be expected to represent the preferences of citizens—housing schemes, for example (see Bush, 1980, pp. 89, 90; Bush, 1992, p. 109). Despite the lack of a power of general competence, territorial authorities have, in practice, rarely been inhibited by the doctrine of *ultra vires* from undertaking functions. Rather, it has been the reluctance of either rate payers or central government to provide finance that has been the limiting factor. There are, however, some signs that, in cities at least (Manukau and Christchurch have perhaps been the most prominent but there are others), a more positive role for territorial local government has been favoured during the 1992–95 electoral triennium.

---

4. Subsequent changes have resulted in the following structure: 12 regional councils; 74 territorial authorities; 154 community boards (Department of Internal Affairs, 1994b).
5. In 1992 various operational services of the Auckland Regional council were transferred to a new body, the Auckland Regional Services Trust. The Wellington Regional Council has, however, retained responsibility for bulk water supply, forestry, and regional parks and reserves (this last also remaining with the Auckland Regional Council).

It might have been expected that the government in Wellington would look to the now more solidly based local government level to carry out functions previously undertaken by central government; that is, that devolution would take place. The following are areas in which a transfer of functions, power, and responsibility has recently occurred (sometimes building on arrangements already in place):

a. *Resource management:* responsibility for 'sustainable management' of New Zealand's resources, under the Resource Management Act, is vested in regional councils and territorial authorities.
b. *Transport:* the Transit New Zealand Act 1989 and Transport Services Licensing Act 1989 assigned to regional and territorial councils important planning and regulatory functions in respect of roading, passenger transport, and safety (although within a framework that some in local government regard as centralist and bureaucratic).
c. *Crime prevention:* under a 'safer communities' programme initiated by the Department of Justice and now the responsibility of DPMC, pilot projects are in place in several areas, under which territorial authorities are playing a leading role in coordinating local crime prevention strategies as an example of 'partnership' between central government and 'communities' .
d. *Recreation and sport:* a number of schemes administered by the Hillary Commission and Creative New Zealand (formerly the Arts Council) involve local government.

Against this small but not unimportant list of examples of at least the rhetoric of 'partnership' must be set the sanction on local government possessed since 1992 by the Minister of Local Government. Under Part XLIIIB of the Local Government Act 1974 the minister may now initiate a review of a local authority if it is believed that there has been 'significant and persistent failure' of a local authority to meet its statutory obligations; if there has been 'significant and identifiable mismanagement'; or if there has been a 'significant and identifiable deficiency in the management or decision-making processes of a local authority' (s. 692M). The minister may require the local authority to implement recommendations that arise from the review. Past cases of mismanagement seem to provide justification for such an element of central intervention, rare as its use is likely to be; the new provisions could also be seen as a lack of faith in the ability of local government to run its own affairs despite the 1989 reforms and the undoubted improvements in performance that have followed.

As indicated earlier, the Local Government Act 1974, as amended in 1989, is predicated upon the existence of 'communities': local government is *inter alia* to recognise 'the existence of different communities'; to define and enforce 'appropriate rights within those communities'; to recognise 'communities of interest'; and to provide for 'the effective participation of local persons in local government' (s. 37K). To give effect to those purposes the Act requires 'active dialogue between councils and their publics' (McKinlay, 1990, p. 55). The annual planning process (soon to be supplemented by strategic planning over ten years) provides for both participation of citizens in the process by which local authorities determine their activities and for *ex post* accountability. The basis was thus laid by the reforms of 1989 for a participatory system of local governance. The consultative process is discussed at more length in Chapter 9, but this statutory emphasis on 'community' might suggest that local government would find a particular role within the new governance structures.[6]

'Building strong communities' is also one of the National Government's Strategic Results Areas (Bolger, 1995a). As a consequence of policy and institutional changes in recent years, there has been some pressure on local authorities, particularly from voluntary welfare organisations, to expand their 'community welfare' activities. There has, however, been little encouragement from the centre for local authorities to move beyond 'essential services'. The Local Government Association in 1992 convened a Poverty and Social Services Forum and followed up with a Charter for Local Government on Social Justice Issues, Community Development and Social Services (Local Government Association, 1993a). Clearly disavowing any interest in 'equitable income distribution . . . a central government responsibility', this document asserts that '[local government] is the most appropriate level of government to recognise and effectively respond to local needs and aspirations'. An attempt to build on this and to negotiate a 'protocol' with central government has so far been unsuccessful. The draft protocol sought an integral role for local government in the social policy-making process, and that it should be recognised as 'the primary agent' for the coordination of the local delivery of services where several agencies are involved (Local Government Association, 1993b). One reason why such an initiative was unlikely to succeed, at least in the short term, is that territorial authorities themselves range across a wide spectrum in their perceptions of their role. At the same time, they might be well advised to be wary of central government in 'load-shedding mode'.

Local government has an important place in New Zealand's constitutional arrangements. It continues to be responsible for (if not for the actual delivery of) key services; it has an important regulatory role, especially under the Resource Management and Building Acts; and it has the capacity, and arguably an obligation, to take a positive stance in the development of localities—what in the next chapter is called the 'governance' function. One possibility is that local government will increasingly become the 'voice' of citizens in dealing with the central government, taking the place vacated by the formerly elected power, harbour, and area health boards. This tendency is likely to be encouraged by the remoteness of 'local' MPs that some believe will follow the first MMP election.

THE RESOURCE MANAGEMENT ACT 1991

The Resource Management Act 1991 (RMA) became law after an extensive consultation process involving both Labour and National governments (Bührs and Bartlett, 1993; Memon, 1993). Its development in the early stages paralleled consideration of

---

6. It should be noted that the Local Government Act, in s. 598 and s. 601 respectively, empowers authorities to undertake both 'community welfare' and 'community development' activities.

local government reform; and without the structural remaking of local government it is difficult to believe that such radical change in environmental administration could have taken place. The Act allocates various functions of both a policy and regulatory nature to different levels of government. There are elements of both decentralisation and devolution, but certainly an 'assumption that decisions should be made as close as possible to the appropriate level of community of interest where the effects and benefits accrue' (Memon, 1993, p. 95).

The purpose of the Act is to promote the sustainable management of natural and physical resources. 'The net effect of the purposes and principles of the Act is to provide a formal framework against which standards, policy statements and plans can be formulated, and development proposals (consents) evaluated' (New Zealand Institute of Local Government Managers, 1992). It replaced a large number of Acts, including the Town and Country Planning Act 1977, and rather than laying down prescriptive codes, directs attention to the effects of resource use on the environment. Essentially, the Act provides for a hierarchy of decision-making—national, regional, and district—as follows (after Memon, 1993):

- *Central Government:* overview; policy development; performance and quality standards; national policy statements; mineral allocation; aspects of coastal management; management of hazardous substances.
- *Regional Councils:* overview/coordination; regional policy statements; regional plans (optional); water and soil management; management of geothermal resources; natural hazards mitigation/planning; regional aspects of hazardous substances; pollution management and air pollution control; aspects of coastal management.
- *Territorial Councils:* district plans; control of land use and subdivision; noise control; control of natural hazards, avoidance and mitigation; local control of hazardous substances use.

Central government's principal role is oversight and supervision. Functions formerly the responsibility of departments are now devolved to local government. For example, under the highly prescriptive Clean Air Act 1972, permits for discharge into the atmosphere were issued by the Department of Health at head office or by its Regional and District Air Pollution Control Officers; consents are now the responsibility of regional councils under the broad provisions of s. 15(1)c of the RMA. This is clearly an example of devolution as defined earlier. Nonetheless, the Minister for the Environment retains direct responsibility for the allocation of mineral, energy, and coastal resources vested in the Crown and may issue National Policy Statements (s. 45 *et seq.*). In addition, the minister may 'call in' matters of national importance and in 1994 did so in the case of the proposed Stratford power station. To the extent that important powers remain with the minister the RMA is an exercise in 'decentralisation'; but overall, successive ministers since 1991 have acted in a 'light-handed' manner.

Public participation processes were strengthened in the RMA. The Act requires local authorities to consult widely when preparing policy statements or plans or when considering applications for resource consents. (These consultation procedures are quite distinct from those required under the Local Government Act, discussed in Chapter 9.) Participation can, in this area, quickly acquire a legalistic form (particularly when the Planning Tribunal becomes involved) and thus become very costly for citizens concerned about the environmental impacts of development.

EDUCATION

Two characteristics of the organisation of New Zealand's public education system over the past hundred years are highlighted for the purposes of this chapter. First, it is a prime example of the historical tendency in New Zealand government to rely on *ad hoc* authorities. This is in contrast to the British practice, which it might have been expected that the colony would follow. Local government in Britain has always been multi-purpose, with responsibilities in respect of health, welfare and police as well as education. However, far more than in New Zealand, British local government has depended on central government grants and has therefore been vulnerable to intervention from London, which since the end of the 1970s has drastically limited its autonomy (Rhodes, 1988; Stoker, 1991).

Second, despite elements of local participation—but perhaps because, like British local government, funding has come from the departmental Vote—New Zealand's education system, as Barrington (1990) has amply demonstrated, has long been marked by control and direction from Wellington.

> The [Education] department's pre-eminence, its role of triton among the minnows, is assured since it channels from funds appropriated by parliament for education the approved expenditures of its local partners (McLaren, 1974, p. 8, quoted by Barrington, 1990, p. 191).

The fourth Labour government gave a high priority to education policy. Much political attention focused on the performance of the education system in preparing New Zealand to participate fully in an internationally competitive economy and society. Poor educational outcomes were associated, it was claimed, with deficiencies in educational administration. As Moss (1990, p. 144) encapsulates the message of the Picot report: 'the problem of educational administration is how to free communities from the yoke of the system.'

The Treasury, which devoted to educational administration a complete volume of its 1987 brief to the incoming government (Treasury, 1987, Vol. 2), had identified 'a high degree of centralisation of control' over 'input mixes, staff conditions of service, capital works, curricula or assessment' as a principal cause of 'considerable strains on the state system' (ibid., p. 10). This was echoed in the Picot report as 'a common theme of powerlessness' (Taskforce to Review Education Administration, 1988, p. 35). The remedy lay in:

> ... an appropriate balance of responsibilities between the local level and central government. We acknowledge that complete devolution carries certain dangers. New Zealand, for instance, has a small but highly mobile population which makes a certain amount of stand-

ardisation desirable; and it is also worth noting that one of the main reasons for establishing a central Department of Education in 1877 was the prevention of parochialism. . . . In essence, our views are that the government should take only those administrative decisions it needs to take; and that all other administrative decisions it should pass to the learning institution (Taskforce to Review Education Administration, 1988, p. 5).

The main features (with one exception—so-called 'bulk funding') of the Picot report were adopted by the Labour government in its policy statement *Tomorrow's Schools* (Lange, 1988) and given legislative form in the Education Act 1989. Five years on the changes were well summed up by the Education Review Office (1994, p. 5):

The aim [of increasing the responsiveness of the education system and the satisfaction of all significant stakeholders] was to be achieved by altering the incentive structure within the administration of education through two major structural changes. The first was to abolish all layers of administration between the central state agencies and the local school in order to locate decision making as close as possible to the point of implementation and thereby achieve greater administrative efficiency and responsiveness.

The second was to alter the balance of power between the providers and the clients of education by providing communities with the means for a greater say in the running of their schools and for expressing their expectations about children's education.

The key 'stakeholders' in the governance of the public education system are the minister and the parent-elected board of trustees. The minister is responsible to Parliament for the discharge of the functions of the office. Boards of trustees look to the minister (from whom funds are derived and who has considerable powers) on the one hand and, on the other, to their local communities. The instrument that links these parties together is the charter, which 'defines the agreement between the Board and the Crown (in the form of a non-negotiable standardised set of National Education Guidelines), and between the Board and the local community (in the form of a set of locally negotiated goals and requirements)' (Education Review Office, 1994, p. 6).

The minister, of course, has significant powers under the Education Act 1989, which may be (and have been) exercised over boards of trustees. These include the power (s. 107) to remove a board of trustees if, in the minister's judgment, it fails to perform adequately. The minister may then appoint a commissioner to manage the school until the next board elections. This authority, together with the minister's power (s. 61) to require amendment or withhold approval of charters, explains why Barrington (1990, p. 208) suggested that 'in this respect, the education reforms appear to involve some change more like decentralisation or delegation than devolution, combined with some trends towards recentralisation'. Subsequent experience confirms this view.

On the other hand, boards of trustees are separate legal entities, which employ staff under the terms and conditions negotiated by the State Service Commissioner under the State Sector Act 1988. A board has 'complete discretion to control the management of the school as it thinks fit' (Education Act 1989, s. 75). That authority, which has survived challenge in the courts,[7] is nonetheless constrained in two ways. The first of these is the National Education Guidelines (a revised version of the initial 1990 guide-lines was gazetted in 1993), which cover the desired outcomes for education, administrative guidelines for boards, and national curriculum statements. These guidelines recognise the minister's emphasis on learning and achievement, but leave boards with a wide discretion in how they handle their relationships with their communities.

Second, schools at present (except for around seventy in a trial scheme) have discretion only over about twenty-five per cent of expenditure on activities other than teacher salaries (except principals).There is a widespread view—but not one shared by the teacher unions—that the continuation of central payment for teachers (except in limited circumstances) and collective contracts prevent the full 'empowerment' of local boards envisaged by Picot. The debate about bulk funding is dominated by differences over the purpose for which the added flexibility will be used. The proponents of bulk funding claim that the ability to decide how many teachers should be employed and how they should be deployed is an essential element if local site management is to be achieved. Opponents are fearful that local autonomy will be used inappropriately (as well as making it easier for governments to reduce the level of grants in future).

Three elections have now taken place for boards of trustees (1989, 1992, and 1995). Information about the turn out of eligible voters (parents) is hard to come by, but the pattern across the country at the last election was variable. The centrality to Picot of 'community' has been weakened not only by the failure to form the recommended community education forums but also by decisions taken by National in relation to zoning. As Gordon (1994) notes, the 1988 Taskforce report highlighted 'choice' but presented two ways in which it could be exercised. Parents and communities could have a say about the development of their local school (voice) and they could make choices among schools (exit). In the event, Gordon concludes (ibid., p. 11) that 'exit' has been emphasised, forcing schools to compete with one another in an 'education market', leading to significant impacts upon the socio-economic composition of school populations.

HEALTH

The delivery of health care in New Zealand from 1938 has been an important element of a comprehensive welfare system (Laugesen and Salmond, 1994). Leaving aside primary health care (privately provided by general practitioners but publicly subsidised), institutional care was delivered principally through elected local authorities. Originally known as hospital boards, by 1989 all had become area health boards assuming the population health responsibilities of the former district offices of the Department of Health. From the 1950s funding of these bodies was almost entirely through Vote Health.

In 1991 the newly elected National government perceived that 'by the end of 1990, concern about health care had reached an unprecedented level, with fresh evidence coming to light almost daily of failures in the system' (Upton, 1991, p. 8). The economic

---

7. See, for example, *Ludke and Ors* v. *Attorney-General*, High Court, Wellington, CP No. 336/ 93, 15 December 1993, Doogue J.

situation, demographic factors (the aging population), and technological innovation also contributed to these concerns. But the fundamental problem, it was suggested, was that the area health board system—in place only since 1989 and supported by National at the 1990 general election—was 'structurally flawed' (ibid., p. 9). The new minister, Simon Upton, proposed to replace it with a comprehensive 'grand design' integrating primary and secondary care funding; separating the roles of purchasers (four regional health authorities (RHAs)) and providers; establishing Crown Health Enterprises (CHEs) based on major hospitals to act, *inter alia*, as 'successful businesses'; and giving individuals the opportunity to opt out of their RHA and choose an alternative health care plan as their purchasing agency (see Upton, 1991; Ashton, 1992; C. Scott, 1994). Not all of these proposals have proceeded. Nonetheless, under the Health and Disability Services Act 1993 major structural changes took place on 1 July 1993:

a. Four RHAs situated in Auckland, Hamilton, Wellington, and Dunedin were established to purchase health and disability services on behalf of their 'communities'. For this purpose they are funded by the Minister of Health from monies voted by Parliament, and are required to act in accordance with guidelines set by the Minister of Health. Their performance is monitored by the Ministry of Health.
b. Twenty-three CHEs were created to take over the assets of fourteen area health boards to compete with other health providers for the contracts for services awarded by RHAs. CHEs were set up in the form of companies under the Companies Act 1993. Under s. 11 of the 1993 Act, CHEs are enjoined to be 'successful and efficient businesses' and to exhibit 'social responsibility'. The boards of CHEs—largely comprising people with business experience—are appointed by the Minister of Crown Health Enterprises (who, with the Minister of Finance, is a 'shareholding minister').
c. A Public Health Commission (PHC) was established to advise the minister and to purchase population health services but has since been disbanded.[8]

By comparison with the system it replaced, the new health system is notable for:

a. The absence of any locally elected participation in its governance: boards elected at the 1989 local authority elections were replaced overnight by appointed commissioners in July 1991, themselves now replaced by appointed boards.
b. The creation of two ministerial portfolios: Health and Crown Health Enterprises. These represent, respectively, the Crown's purchase and ownership interests.
c. Reliance on a network of contracts from ministers, through RHAs, to an array of public, private, and voluntary providers, to integrate and coordinate services.

For the purposes of this chapter only two aspects of a complex mechanism for the delivery of publicly funded services are considered: the question of accountability and the notion of 'community'.

---

8. The PHC has been disestablished from 1 July 1995 (Health and Disability Services Amendment Act 1995) and its functions divided between the Ministry of Health and the RHAs.

Figure 8.1

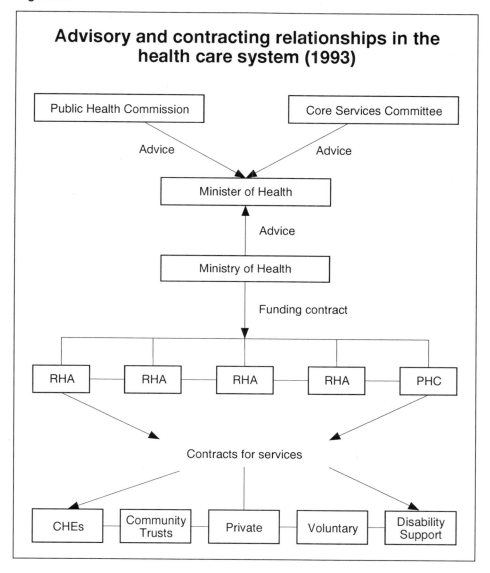

Advisory and contracting relationships in the health care system (1993)

In early 1995 the unfortunate case of Mr James McKeown, a patient in Middlemore Hospital in Auckland, focused attention on accountability (Gleisner and Paterson, 1995). Where did responsibility truly lie for a decision initially not to provide dialysis treatment to a 76-year-old patient? From the nature of public comment—both by the parties directly affected and the general public—there was clearly confusion about the respective roles of the minister(s), the Northern RHA, the South Auckland CHE responsible for Middlemore Hospital, and the medical professionals treating Mr McKeown. The physicians, when the issue entered the public domain, explained that given the level of funding available from the RHA and the guidance previously prom-ulgated by the Core Health Services Committee,[9] their ability to treat Mr McKeown was severely constrained. The issue was one of priorities and opportunity costs, not a denial that Mr McKeown could benefit from dialysis. The Minister of Health, Jenny Shipley, initially took the view that the matter was one for clinical decision, not a ques-tion of funding, and that the clinicians were guilty of the lobbying technique widely known as 'shroud waving'. In the event, the clinical decision was reviewed and Mr McKeown received treatment. While this was no doubt a welcome outcome for Mr McKeown, the issue of responsibility was hardly resolved in the public mind.

The rationing of health care in line with 'capped' funding inevitably gives promi-nence to hard cases. To the extent that the separation of purchaser and provider roles and the detailed specification of contracts injects transparency into the previously opaque process of clinical decision-making, there has been a gain for those who believe that accountability matters. On the other hand, responsibilities within relationships in a complex service cannot easily be compartmentalised. Mistakes at the delivery point are not the issue: they should be capable of resolution through professional disciplinary procedures. (The Health and Disability Commissioner appointed in 1994 will also have a role.) The problems arise when individual cases intersect with systemic questions of resources, structures, or policies.

The RHAs are the sole purchasers for the people of their region of all health services funded by the government. They are expected to reflect the strategic priorities of the Minister of Health; but they are also expected to be agents of their communities. These communities, by definition, are very widespread and diverse. They do not reflect the same degree of community of interest—however defined—as local authorities or the area health boards that they replaced. For example, it is difficult to conceive of the Southern RHA in Dunedin effectively representing the consumers of mental health care in the Buller area. Almost inevitably CHEs will move beyond their strict role as provid-ers, and indeed Malcolm and Barnett (1994, p. 91) report that:

> virtually all CHEs indicated that they identified with a geographically defined population and
> attached importance to that population's perception of their services.
>
> . . . In the same way that CHEs cannot escape the community perception of their respon-
> sibility for meeting local needs, CHEs are unable to distance themselves from health status
> and access issues, properly the responsibility of the RHA.

The complexities of the accountability chain—intended to be 'clearer and stronger' (Hawkins, 1995, p. 7) than what went before—were further illustrated by the highly public resignation in April 1995 of the chair of the Auckland CHE, at the request of the Minister of Crown Health Enterprises, Paul East. At the centre of the dispute was

---

9. The Core Health Services Committee was established by Simon Upton to lay down the range of services, treatment, and procedures that could be expected from the reshaped public health system. In the event the committee has provided guidance rather than a prescriptive list of eligible services.

a difference in judgment about whether sufficient progress was being made in bringing Auckland Healthcare to financial viability. In the background was the question of future development of Auckland health services (of major interest not only to the CHE but also to the relevant RHA, North Health, and the Ministers of Health and Crown Health Enterprises—both of whom were notably silent during the public exchanges), the adequacy of funding, and the weight that the Minister of Crown Health Enterprises should give to advice from 'Wellington advisers' against the views of the local business people whom he had appointed to the board. This is unlikely to be the last incident in which local interests, albeit in this case unelected, clash with the control system, which reaches its apex in the person of one or other of the two ministers with health responsibilities.

This case illustrates the power of ministers over the various elements of the health service: boards appointed by ministers may be dismissed by ministers. Under the Health and Disability Services Act 1993 ministers have further powers (including the power to require services from CHEs), which tend to support the view that these arrangements are nearer to 'decentralisation' than 'devolution' as these terms were defined earlier in this chapter.

The evidence of persistent local support for the retention of services under threat suggests that the notion of community and of political 'voice' (Hirschman, 1970) cannot lightly be legislated away in designing systems for the delivery of public services. Or, put another way, 'enthusiasm in some quarters for balancing taxpayer and consumer interests through a highly explicit national process of rationing health services has proved uninfectious' (Hawkins, 1995, p. 8). It is optimistic to believe that health services can be depoliticised at either the local or national levels. Leaving aside questions about the location of accountability, claim and counterclaim about the efficiency and effectiveness of the new arrangements continue. Much depends on the indicators used—financial viability and/or health status—but this debate is outside the scope of this chapter (see Ashton, 1992; Blank, 1994; Consumers Institute, 1995; Spicer, Trlin, and Walton, 1994; and Salmond, Mooney, and Laugesen, 1994).

SOCIAL WELFARE

As suggested above in the discussion of the role of local government, the essence of effective delivery of statutory social services would seem to lie in their responsiveness to individuals and families. It might, therefore, be expected that notions of 'devolution' and 'decentralisation' would figure prominently in the design of these services. In New Zealand the principal provider of welfare services is the state acting through a central department: the Department of Social Welfare (DSW). In other jurisdictions statutory welfare services are frequently the responsibility of local government.[10] The question addressed in this section is the extent to which considerations of devolution and decentralisation

---

10. Statutory social services do not include, for the purposes of this chapter, the provision of income support to which there is an entitlement.

(as defined earlier) have informed the development of structures in New Zealand's statutory social services.

The mid 1980s saw considerable debate about 'devolution' in respect of the services of DSW (R. Laking, 1987; Nixon, 1988; Cody, 1990). For example, the department's 1988–89 draft management plan (quoted by Nixon, 1988, p. 124) included a statement that the DSW would improve service delivery by 'devolving to the community greater control of programmes and services currently administered by the Department, where such power sharing would result in a better client service.'

Influential in the development of the department during this period was the report of a Ministerial Advisory Committee headed by John Rangihau. The report, *Puao-te-Ata-tu*, presented in 1986, reflected strong Māori dissatisfaction with the department, including the claim of 'institutionalised racism'. Substantial changes in the organisation and staffing of the department followed, including moves towards 'devolution'. The principal manifestation of devolution was the Community Organisation Grants Scheme (COGS) administered by DSW, under which around $10 million annually was allocated for distribution by forty-nine distribution committees elected locally (Nixon, 1988, p. 126; Levett, 1988). Experience with this scheme, later transferred to the Department of Internal Affairs, illustrated the inherent conflict between community decision-makers and ministerial responsibility for funds voted by Parliament. Ministers of Social Welfare were uncomfortable with public criticism of decisions taken by people beyond their control. At the same time, DSW was coming to terms with District Executive Committees (DECs)—ministerially appointed committees (comprising seven community representatives and an official each from DSW and the then Department of Māori Affairs). The role of DECs was to monitor and, from time to time, to review the effectiveness and appropriateness of DSW's services in each of its nearly fifty districts.

The internal structure of this large department of state, employing around 7,000 people, was at the end of the 1980s built around three levels: head office, regions (at first six; from 1990 four) and districts. The organisation was multifunctional: at both regional and district level, DSW offices undertook functions in respect of income support, welfare services, and relationships with the private and voluntary sectors. One innovation in service delivery was the establishment in 1988 of community service teams, and in 1989 the Children, Young Persons, and Their Families Act brought a further new dimension to the relations between the DSW and the community.

Cody, in a perceptive comment (1990, p. 159), reaches the conclusion that:

> public discussion of 'devolution' was one element in a strategy to regain control of the Department and to disengage government and its agents from increasingly complex conflicts of interest, as well as to provide the Minister with positive initiatives to promote.

Certainly, Cody's discussion of the DSW's travails during the 1980s documents the difficulties that a government department faces in reconciling community responsiveness and ministerial responsibility. During the 1990s a radically different approach has been followed, which might be described as 'managerialist' (the term is not meant pejoratively) and which was in response to a situation frankly described in a 1991 internal document in these terms:

> The Department as it is currently structured is becoming difficult to manage as a single business, it is struggling to meet the Government's requirements for delivery of welfare services, its vote has been subject to drift and blow-out over the past decade, the organisation is subject to increasing stress, managers at all levels are overstretched and accountability lines for delivery of outputs are at best muddled (quoted by Smith, 1995, p. 45).

The solution, in effect from 1 May 1992, was to create three separate business units: the New Zealand Income Support Service (NZISS), the New Zealand Children and Young Persons Service (NZCYPS), and the New Zealand Community Funding Agency (NZCFA). (They are now supported at the centre by the Director-General's corporate office and the Social Policy Agency.) The rationale for this major change, apart from taking advantage of the managerial flexibility provided by the State Sector and Public Finance Acts, was that 'each area of work has grown in flexibility to a degree that each needs its own management focus . . . Asking District Managers to take responsibility across the board for all those demanding tasks has become unrealistic in the face of increasing complexity and volume of work' (DSW, 1992, p. 5). Fears that the vertical separation of the Department's functions in districts would result in fragmentation, with damaging effects on its 'customers', do not appear to have been borne out. The Department's annual report for the year ended 30 June 1994 (DSW, 1994) records achievements in the delivery of quality services in a timely manner, particularly by the NZISS. As at 30 June 1995 the NZISS had forty district offices, the NZCYPS fifteen area offices, and the NZCFA eight area teams (as well as eighty-four outreach workers).

Notwithstanding this extensive coverage, there remains a question that goes beyond the scope of this chapter, namely, whether the business units could be decoupled from head office and translated into separate departments or Crown entities. At the same time, the social work services delivered by the NZCYPS, together perhaps with at least some NZCFA contracts, might be devolved to territorial local authorities. Prior to the 1992 statutory restrictions on the role of regional authorities, these organisations might have been seen as the appropriate bodies to which social work functions could have been transferred. Now, if there are doubts about the critical mass of territorial authorities generally, a selective process of devolution by contracting to individual authorities—notably in the cities—could be considered.

Already DSW has considerable experience in contracting, particularly since restructuring, with 'third party' providers. Grant funding of various organisations had long been the practice. But, in accordance with the increased requirements for both effectiveness in and accountability for the expenditure of public monies contained in the Public Finance Act 1989, these arrangements have now generally been superseded by contracts specifying the outputs expected, monitoring processes and sanctions. These developments are discussed in detail by Smith (1995).

'THIRD PARTY' GOVERNMENT AND CONTRACTING

The cases discussed so far in this chapter have illustrated ways in which publicly funded services are delivered by statutory authorities in either devolved (local government), decentralised (DSW), or mixed (education and health) models.

A further option to which reference has been made under both health and social welfare is the contracting out of service provision to the private or voluntary sector—a further variant of decentralisation in the umbrella sense. This is not a new development in New Zealand; the DSW has long funded the IHC (now brought within the ambit of the health service), and the Department of Health was for many years the dominant funder of Plunket's activities, a function now delegated to RHAs (Martin, 1995a). (The Plunket Society's clinics and nurses advise mothers about baby care.) Contracting is, however, playing an increasingly important role in a wide range of public activities at both central and local level.

The 'new contractualism' as it is being implemented in New Zealand has been the subject of considerable discussion. The principal arguments advanced for its widespread attraction internationally (see, for example, Osborne and Gaebler, 1993) are threefold:

a. It means that clear objectives or specifications are necessary to meaningfully compare alternatives. This means that providers are results driven and performance focused, because there is little scope for fudging results.
b. It requires information to be provided to allow the assessment of options. Improved transparency, accountability and learning are a consequence of more relevant and better focused information.
c. It improves responsiveness to voice. Feedback on performance carries more weight where it is assessable and meaningful. This rich source of information is vital to the incentives operating in both external and internal competition for the production of public services (Caffery, 1995, p. 4).

There is little doubt that there are attractions in contracting for service delivery where contestable supply is a practical possibility, where the desired outputs can be adequately specified, and where monitoring does not present major difficulties. In these cases efficiency gains are very likely. Respected commentators such as Stewart (1993b) have, however, directed attention to the possible disadvantages of contracting out public functions. These include the difficulties of specification and the provision of information; the adequacy of *ex post* sanctions; the location of political responsibility; the protection of values such as fairness, justice and due process; and the advantages of flexibility provided by command relationships. Overshadowing all these is the fundamental question of the extent to which we are prepared to 'depoliticise' public functions as a trade-off for efficiency gains (Boston, 1995a; Caffery, 1995; Martin, 1995a; Trebilcock, 1995). An associated point of some relevance is that most contracts within the public sector— but also in the contracting out of public services—might be presumed to be of a relational character (Kay, 1993). They are not dealings on a spot market but elements in continuing relationships in which trust and long-term mutual benefit are of the essence—not only for the two parties to the contract (often, as in the health service, funder and provider) but also for third parties, whether they be called consumers, clients, or customers.

A persuasive case can be made for specific applications of 'government by contract': for example, performance agreements between ministers and CEs, 'Statements of Corporate Intent' for SOEs, school charters, the performance agreement between the Civil Aviation Authority and the Minister of Transport (Martin, 1995a), and local government contracting out of services. Nonetheless, it would be unwise to slide over some of the legitimate questions about accountability, and indeed effectiveness and efficiency, that require answers in each case.

CONCLUSION

This chapter began by considering some of the theoretical arguments for decentralising (in the general sense) public activities. It has then reviewed the principal developments since the mid 1980s in relations between the centre—the government in Wellington— and the periphery, represented by local government, elected boards of school trustees, appointed boards of health organisations (CHEs and RHAs), the district offices of DSW, and contracted 'third parties'. It is useful now to return to the three tests earlier suggested as being relevant to questions about the degree to which there has been a tendency in the direction of devolution—a *transfer* of power to sub-national organisations. To recall, the three questions were whether an organisation at the periphery has statutory legitimacy (bluntly, whether the Parliament or the executive has the power of life or death over its continuation), whether the governing body is locally chosen, and whether the organisation has a significant local source of revenue.

On the first point, local government, boards of trustees, and health organisations all derive their powers, functions, and authority from Parliament. Experience, has, however, suggested that this is not a status greatly respected by the executive. The dismissal of elected area health boards in 1991 (and their later abolition) and the 1992 removal of certain functions of the Auckland Regional Council illustrate the reality of executive power—at least under the former first-past-the-post electoral system. The fact that in neither case was there a major public outcry is no doubt explained by the public perception at the time of the performance of these particular elected bodies. Depending on individual values, these developments could be seen as the triumph of the instrumental view of local organisations or as warnings to be vigilant in protecting the remaining opportunities for local electoral participation.

The previous paragraph largely disposes of the second test, local choice, as well. There are undoubtedly those who wish to return to local representation in the health system; and, indeed, opposition parties in Parliament have indicated that they will move in this direction. While there has been dissatisfaction, both in local communities and in the Ministry of Education and ERO, with the performance of some boards of trustees (sometimes leading to the dismissal of boards and their replacement by ministerially appointed commissioners), there seems to be no disposition to move away from elected site management in education (Wylie, 1994).

Finally, there is the vexed question of funding. The 'pure' view (Scott, 1988) is that only where there is a robust system of local revenue-raising can devolution be said to exist. Dependence on central government for funding leaves locally elected organisations, whether or not their powers and functions are derived from statute, highly exposed to central intervention. This position is well based in logic and experience. But for those who remain persuaded that participation is an important value in the modern state, it is not impossible to conceive of satisfactory contractual relationships between the centre and local public organisations based on a form of revenue-sharing. At present, it must be acknowledged, the trend is in the other direction. Leaving aside roading expenditure funded by Transit New Zealand, local authorities collectively derive only about 1 per cent of their revenue from central government; and schools are turning to parents and their communities increasingly to supplement funds from Vote Education. But at a time when contracting and 'third-party government' are becoming so widespread, an antipathy to 'government', in the National administration at least, seems to have ruled out local government as a respectable contracting party in the cause of devolution of power to local communities. This, as the next chapter demonstrates, has a certain irony given the rhetoric of the late 1980s about the 'partnership' between central and local government that could be built upon 'modernised' local government (Bassett, 1989).

9 management in local government

Many years ago, R. J. Polaschek (1956, p. 5) posed the question: 'if electors do not agree to reform local government, one must consider seriously whether its continued existence serves any useful purpose at all'. Until the late 1980s there was little obvious response to this blunt challenge; and then the initiative came not from local electors but from the central government. Emboldened by their success in carrying through reform of public management in central government, ministers of the fourth Labour government, in their second term, turned their attention to local government.[1]

The previous chapter reviewed recent changes in the relationship between the centre and the periphery and considered the place of community participation in the New Zealand system of government. This chapter looks in greater detail at the way in which local government is organised and attempts to assess its capacity to play whatever role is expected of it in the years ahead. That role is problematic. Statements made by the Minister of Local Government who presided over the reform process, Michael Bassett, suggested that a more streamlined local government structure and improved management were the prelude to a transfer of functions to local government—true 'devolution' as defined in the previous chapter.[2] On the other hand, Warren Cooper, minister in the National government after the 1990 general election, seemed to espouse a minimalist view of local government; this sentiment reflected community feeling at the time, sharpened by recent memories of much-publicised, but not necessarily typical, examples of local

---

1. Michael Bassett, a former Auckland City Councillor and MP in the third Labour government (1972–75), was Minister of Local Government between 1984 and 1990. A comprehensive programme of reform of local government was promised in the *Economic Statement* made on 17 December 1987 by the recently returned Lange Government (Bassett, 1987). Bassett's commitment to reform, his appointment of (later Sir) Brian Elwood—a former National Party candidate and Mayor of Palmerston North—as chair of a newly mandated Local Government Commission (Local Government Amendment Act (No. 3) 1988), and the dedication of officials in the Department of Internal Affairs were key factors in the achievement of the first radical change in the structure of local government for over 100 years.
2. For example, in a statement in 1989 Bassett claimed that 'local government's role as a *true partner* in the governance of the country is a reality' (Bassett, 1989, emphasis added). See Chapter 8 for a discussion of the meaning of 'devolution'.

government mismanagement.[3] According to this view, rates should be cut (or at least the rate of increase halted), services should be contracted out, and 'government' generally should be reduced. At the same time, paradoxically, there was a movement in some localities for local government to take a more positive leadership position both in promoting economic development and, less widespread, in responding to visible social ills in the community. These were responses to 'felt needs' in different communities, whether or not functions were 'devolved' from central government. Later in this chapter it is suggested that this 'governance' role is likely to be the way of the future for local government.

Overlying all these perspectives on the proper role of local government has been agreement on the need to 'modernise' the management of local authorities. As in central government there is no apparent wish to turn the clock back to the systems and structures ushered out by the Local Government Amendment Act (No. 2) 1989. There are, nonetheless, issues which are worthy of closer attention from practitioners and students of public management. This chapter identifies and assesses the key changes in local government management since the late 1980s and looks to the future.

THE STATUS OF LOCAL GOVERNMENT

A principal achievement of the reforms of local government in the late 1980s was the reduction in the number and variety of local bodies. Essentially, local government now consists of regional councils and city and district councils (replacing boroughs and counties). Since 1989 the number of regional councils has been reduced to twelve, with the formation of further unitary authorities in Marlborough, Nelson and Tasman (1992) to add to the one—Gisborne—that emerged from the 1989 reorganisation. Unitary authorities are district councils that undertake the statutory functions of regional councils. Functions under the Resource Management Act 1991 are a principal responsibility of regional government. Special arrangements apply in Auckland, where the main assets of the Auckland Regional Council were transferred under the Local Government Amendment Act 1992 to a new body, the Auckland Regional Services Trust, and in Wellington to a lesser extent.

Local government should be regarded as an entity in which regional councils and territorial authorities have separate but complementary functions, rather than as two levels of sub-national government where one is subordinate to the other. Both regional councils and territorial authorities are created by Parliament and derive their functions and powers from statute. Section 37K of the Local Government Act 1974 (as amended in 1989) states that the purposes of local government are to provide:

(a) Recognition of the existence of different communities in New Zealand;

(b) Recognition of the identities and values of those communities;

(c) Definition and enforcement of appropriate rights within those communities;

---

3. The administration of Waitemata (now Waitakere) City was the subject of a highly critical Audit Office report in 1989 (Audit Office, 1989a), and various aspects of management in the Wellington City Council attracted unfavourable attention in the early 1990s.

(d) Scope for communities to make choices between different kinds of local public facilities and services;

(e) For the operation of trading undertakings of local authorities on a competitively neutral basis;

(f) For the delivery of appropriate facilities and services on behalf of central government;

(g) Recognition of communities of interest;

(h) For the efficient and effective exercise of the functions, duties, and powers of the components of local government;

(i) For the effective participation of local persons in local government.

Later in the same section the functions of regional councils (s. 37S, as amended by s. 7 of the Local Government Amendment Act 1992) and territorial authorities (s. 37T) are spelled out.

General legislation (e.g. the Health Act 1956) confers functions, duties, and powers on local government. In addition, some 1500 local acts either empower named local authorities to carry out particular functions or validate various unauthorised acts of local authorities. Some functions are mandatory (e.g. civil defence), while others are permissive (e.g. libraries and museums). In respect of some functions (e.g. providing drainage—a permissive power) Parliament has enacted detailed statutory provisions about how the activity is to be carried out. In other areas, the empowering provisions are general and the local authority may make by-laws to deal with detailed administration (Palmer, 1993).

Every regional council and territorial authority is a body corporate (s. 37L(4)) and not simply an agent of the Crown. Nonetheless, Bush is undoubtedly right to emphasise (1992, p. 104) that 'Parliament [is] the constitutional architect of our local government systems' and that as 'occupiers of a malleable part of the constitutional spectrum [local bodies] may be abolished or modified as Parliament or those acting in its name dictate'. On the other hand, as Bush also notes, by and large 'governments of whatever political hue have always generally refrained from interfering in the formulating of local bodies' policies or from pinpricking regulating of their behaviour ...' (ibid.). There have been signs that this tolerance might be declining, for example, in some elements of the amendments to financial provisions of the Local Government Act introduced into Parliament in 1994 (discussed later in this chapter). Nonetheless, in a Parliament elected under an MMP system major change of the structure of local government, opposed by a significant proportion of elected local body representatives, would be difficult to pass.

GOVERNANCE

Representation

'Governance', or the set of arrangements by which the affairs of an institution are ordered, is in the case of local government underpinned by the legitimacy conferred by the democratic process. Local body politics have, however, rarely inspired the citizenry. Personalities, particularly at the mayoral level in the cities, and occasionally issues (such as sewage disposal in Auckland in the 1950s and in Wellington in the 1980s, or Queen Elizabeth II Park in Christchurch in the early 1970s) have stimulated sporadic interest. But if voter turnout is taken as the indicator, it is hard to avoid the conclusion that local authorities do not feature highly in local consciousness. Despite the introduction of postal voting for all elections except Hutt City in 1989 and the encouragement of ward (rather than 'at large') elections,[4] the average turnout in 1992 in regional council elections was only 52 per cent; for city councils the comparable figure was 48 per cent and for district councils 61 per cent. Although these figures would be quite respectable in other jurisdictions (e.g. the USA), they are well below the turnout at New Zealand general elections (85 per cent in 1993).

Voting is on a first-past-the-post system (although the move to MMP at the national level has led to renewed talk of proportional representation). Any citizen over the age of 18 and on any parliamentary, and hence local authority, electoral roll may stand for election; since 1991 ratepayers (who are not always residents) may also vote, although the numbers in 1992 were proportionately very small. (For discussion of the law governing local government elections see Palmer, 1993.)[5]

Political parties seem to be playing a declining role in local body affairs. Labour, in the cities, has a long tradition of participation in local politics (although this appears to be weakening); some of its prominent national politicians, including Michael Bassett and David Caygill in the fourth Labour government, had local government experience. National has never explicitly backed candidates for local authorities, but Citizens and Ratepayers Associations in the cities have usually been seen as closely associated with National interests. 'Environmental' candidates have been prominent since the 1970s (when Tony Brunt, founder of the Values Party, became a Wellington city councillor). Greens of various hues, as well as Alliance members, have more recently seen local government as an important arena. But outside the cities the great majority of candidates have always stood as independents.

It is tempting to draw parallels between the structures of central and local government. Both have a representative dimension: like MPs, regional and territorial councillors are elected. However, there the similarity ends. At the centre, the nature of responsible government is that the executive is selected from and must command a majority in the legislature; but it is clearly a separate arm of government. In local government, by contrast, councils are both legislature and executive—effectively Parliament and the cabinet. This constitutional difference is reflected at the political level where, in the absence of political parties—and even where they feature—few issues divide the electorate in such a way that a group of councillors could claim an electoral

---

4. In 1992 in only three out of fifty-nine districts (including the Chatham Islands) were elections conducted 'at large'. In cities the comparable figure was three out of fifteen. All regional councils are elected by 'constituencies'. In territorial authorities mayors are elected 'at large'; the chair of a regional council is, however, elected by the members collectively.
5. For analysis of results see *Local Authority Election Statistics, 1992* (Department of Internal Affairs, 1994a) and its predecesor publications.

mandate. (There are, of course, exceptions such as the Labour commitment in 1986 in Wellington to construct a new sewage plant at Moa Point.) As a consequence, the resolution of issues before councils features what in European legislatures are known as 'jumping majorities'.

A developing tendency in local government representation is to seek to reduce the number of councillors. In part this is a reflection of the transfer of activities to local authority trading enterprises (LATEs) and to contracting out of functions. But it is also a manifestation of the tendency throughout the public sector to 'depoliticise' the management of services. Equally, there are those who oppose such an apparent loss of representation; and the Local Government Commission has been conservative in its decisions. A related issue is the ability and willingness of citizens to make themselves available to serve as councillors. Some reluctance is probably attributable both to the increased participation of women in the workforce and to more exacting requirements of employers.

The relatively low turnout in 'at large' elections and the collective nature of decision-making led Halligan and Harris (1978, p. 249) to conclude that 'there is lacking in New Zealand local government any concept of *responsibility*' (emphasis in original). Despite the prevalence now of ward elections, the operation of the representation process does not, of itself, provide reason to dissent from that view. It does, however, provide a rationale for the attempt to promote both accountability and participation by way of the statutory consultation processes described below, as well as the other statutory mechanisms such as the Local Government Official Information and Meetings Act 1987. To that extent it could be claimed that the concept of responsibility has been both broadened and deepened.

Council Committees

Council committees have an important place in the governance structure of local authorities. Much of the council's business is effectively done in these committees and, importantly, they are the meeting-point for the exchange of information between elected representatives and officers. As a consequence, the role of chairperson of particular committees can be one of authority and influence. Relationships between committee chairpersons and officers can be significant in the conduct of an authority's affairs. Whatever the roles of committees—and there is sometimes a lack of clarity in terms of reference—the task of coordination must assume a high priority for mayors (or council chairpersons) and CEs.

The Local Government Act (ss. 114 P and S) provides for the establishment of standing, special, and joint committees (this last providing a means for two or more local authorities to deal with issues in which they have a common interest, such as a sewage treatment plant serving more than one district). Committee members, of whom there must be at least three, are appointed by the council—but they need not necessarily all be councillors. Officers may not be members of a committee. Committees may exercise the delegated authority of the council except in respect of matters listed in s. 114Q of the Act (principally the powers to make rates or by-laws or to borrow money).

Community Boards [6]

Community boards, introduced by the 1989 Amendment Act, are not 'local authorities' in law—although territorial authorities may delegate to them certain powers and functions. 'Neighbourhood' representation had already existed under the 1974 Act, which provided for community councils in both urban and rural areas. By amendment in 1976 community councils could no longer be established in urban areas, except when those urban areas were part of a larger rural area. The verdict on the operation of community councils, whether as a vehicle for participation or an enhancement of service delivery, was at best patchy (Bush, 1980).[7]

In part, the motivation behind the establishment of community boards in 1989 was the same as that behind the establishment of community councils in 1974. If local authorities were to be amalgamated so as to capture economies of scale, there was both a political and an administrative case for the voice of smaller 'communities' to be heard. On the other hand, too loud a neighbourhood voice could inhibit the integration of the new larger authorities. Indeed, a considerable body of opinion in local government was inclined towards 'ward committees' with an advisory role only.

In the event, quite late in the reform process, Michael Bassett introduced legislation that gave community boards wide powers to communicate, consult and advise without decision-making power (s. 101ZY). However, it also authorised parent councils to delegate their powers other than those listed—to borrow, to hold property, and to deal with staff (s. 101ZZ). On 1 November 1989, 159 community boards took office in 49 of the 74 territorial authority districts (Department of Internal Affairs, 1991, p. 1). Subsequent establishments and disestablishments meant that by 1994 there were 154 (Department of Internal Affairs, 1994b). Community boards may consist of up to 12 members, at least half of whom are directly elected by residents; the remainder are appointed by the council.

Activities undertaken by community boards vary widely but may extend into every aspect of territorial local government. The official description (Department of Internal Affairs, 1994b) is that their general purpose is twofold: first, to promote greater community involvement in decision-making by helping to make sure the 'parent' territorial authority knows and meets the community's needs; and second, to carry out those functions delegated to the board by the territorial authority. More community board activity is of an advisory nature (s. 101ZY) than of a decision-making character (s. 101ZZ); many councils give no decision-making power to community boards. Decision-making functions frequently relate to service delivery; few regulatory functions are delegated, although community boards in many areas have a major advisory role in planning functions.

In a few districts the tensions of amalgamation in 1989 have not yet been forgotten, and the transitional 'political' role of community boards remains. It is, however, possible

---

6. We are indebted to Elizabeth Brown for much of the material on which this discussion is based
7. A second edition of Graham Bush's important *Local Government and Politics in New Zealand* was published by Auckland University Press in late 1995.

to reflect upon the experience so far. The key variables appear to be: (a) the size of the community area—for instance, Christchurch boards represent around 50,000 people; (b) the nature of the community of interest represented by the board; and (c) the extent to which decision-making power is delegated by the council. The views of a small defined geographical locality are easier to represent to a board than those of a large area in which many diverse interests are included. Similarly, a board that is perceived to affect the community by its actions is likely to attract more support than one that is a 'voice' only. Of course, community boards, from the point of view of the parent council, might suffer from 'second chamber syndrome': if they agree they are redundant; if they disagree they are obstructive. Community boards might also be seen to be especially prone to 'capture' by interest groups.

The Openness of Local Government

One of the characteristics of local government is its availability to citizens. Access to elected representatives should be relatively easy. The meetings of councils and their committees are, except in very limited circumstances, open to the public. Since 1975 the Ombudsmen have had jurisdiction in respect of matters of administration in local government (under Part III of the First Schedule to the Ombudsmen Act 1975). Further, since 1987 the availability of information has been provided for (in accordance with the same principles that apply at other levels of government) under the Local Government Official Information and Meetings Act 1987.

One important aim of 'open government' is to enhance accountability. The other principal purpose of the legislation mentioned in the previous paragraph is to encourage participation. On both counts, according to Brown (1995, p. 74), 'the local government reforms have led to a very great increase in the opportunities available for the public to participate in the processes of local territorial authorities and to hold authorities accountable for the results'. There are, however, some reservations. Some councils (although fewer since an amendment to the Local Government Official Information and Meetings Act in 1991) on occasion exclude the public from their meetings, or at least from parts thereof, in circumstances that might not always be justified under the statute. A desire for confidentiality is not enough. A further problem is the 'meeting that is not a meeting', where substantive issues are discussed in private with only the necessary resolutions being passed in public session.

Another way in which the intent of 'open government' legislation can be thwarted is when matters are devolved to LATEs—see below—or contracted out to the private sector. LATEs, unlike their counterparts at the national level, SOEs, are not within the jurisdiction of either the Ombudsmen or the statute providing for the availability of official information. At least there is provision (Local Government Act 1974, s. 594F) for councils to consult with their communities before the divestment of interests in LATEs; but the Treasury is understood to have questioned the appropriateness of this provision. The 'openness' of local government is, despite these reservations, an important factor in any consideration of its future role.

COUNCILS AND CHIEF EXECUTIVES

Crucial to the 1989 reforms, and congruent with changes in central government, was the clarification of the roles of the elected council on the one hand and the appointed CE on the other. Essentially, the council is 'decoupled' from the day-to-day management of the authority. The council-appointed CE, like counterparts in central government, is on a performance-based contract for up to five years and is the employer of all other staff. The council's job is to set 'policy' and to monitor the performance of the chief executive; the CE and other officers are to manage within that policy. Section 119D of the Local Government Act 1974 provides that the functions of a CE include:

(a) Implementing the decisions of the local authority;

(b) Providing advice to members of the local authority and any community boards;

(c) Ensuring that all functions, duties and powers delegated to him or her or to any person employed by the local authority, or imposed or conferred by an Act, regulation or bylaw are properly performed or exercised;

(d) Ensuring the effective, efficient and economic management of the activities and planning of the local authority.

The 'policy–administration dichotomy', and especially the difficulty of delineating a sharp boundary between the two aspects of government, has been a staple of public administration literature for more than a hundred years. The task of establishing the 'proper' role of elected and appointed officials is, if anything, more difficult in local government than it is at the national level. The relative absence of electoral commitments and of cabinet collective responsibility leaves a policy vacuum into which officers can be expected to move. On the other hand, elected members, particularly those who served before 1989 and those who are accustomed to a more active role in their private employment, have not found it easy to distance themselves from day-to-day management.

Policy advice is clearly a principal function of the CE and other senior officers. This can range from questions of statutory powers to feasibility studies of development proposals. But since the late 1980s, matters of management have loomed large in the affairs of local authorities as they 'modernise'. To the extent that these achieve high salience publicly they become 'political' and, by extension, 'policy'; and thus a concern to elected members.

Clearly, there has been managerial advantage in distancing elected members from detailed staffing and organisational matters. Equally, however, a CE who alienates a mayor (or chair of a regional council) or significant group of elected members is in an exposed position. Elected members are answerable to the ratepayers and the electorate, and for the funding of the authority's activities. The very 'localness' of local government encourages expectations on the part of citizens (which they might not have of MPs) that their elected representatives can 'get things done'. The president of the Local Government Association summed up well what he called 'the grey area':

Clearly, councils rely on a wide range of managerial, professional and technical advice to process policy, decide on it and then to implement it. There is no question, therefore, that man-

titioners in local government were inclined, however, to see it literally as 'an imposition'. In a survey of the consultative process in respect of 1991–92 plans commissioned by the Local Government Group in Internal Affairs (Deloitte Touche Tohmatsu, 1993), local authorities were reported as regarding the consultative process as poor value for money. The number of submissions was neither high nor of the quality sought, and changes in plans made as a consequence were few in number. Not surprisingly, the response varied across the country, reflecting predominantly the investment in the process made by individual authorities and the existence of issues of high salience. Anecdotal evidence suggests that in subsequent years there has been some increase in interest in the community and in the assessment of value on the part of local authorities. To some extent this can be attributed to the way in which almost all authorities, no doubt recognising the complexity of council business, have gone beyond the minimal requirements of statute in conducting public consultation. Fliers in letterboxes, radio interviews with mayors and councillors, as well as public meetings have provided ample opportunities for citizen input. At the same time, the complexity of issues and the appearance of some councils to be unwilling to change direction despite the expressed views of those citizens participating in the consultation processes have left a sense of dissatisfaction in some districts. Compliance costs are not insignificant, but the price of 'local democracy' is worth paying. (The important issue of consultation with tangata whenua, whether under the Resource Management Act or in respect of other council activities, has proved to be a particularly difficult responsibility for local government to discharge. This issue cannot be discussed adequately in a chapter of this length: see Te Puni Kōkiri, 1993.)

FINANCIAL MANAGEMENT

McKinlay's judgment of the accounts of local authorities prior to 1989 is harsh but probably not unfair: 'Accounts were prepared on a cash basis for the entity as a whole, and were virtually meaningless as a source of information on its activities' (McKinlay, 1994, p. 21). The 1989 Act's provisions, in essence, follow the reforms introduced into financial management in central government by the Public Finance Act 1989. At the local level, too, they were motivated by the mutually supporting aims of improved management of public resources and a higher standard of public accountability of local authorities. Accrual accounting was introduced; every local authority is required to adopt 'financial systems and reporting and record keeping procedures that are consistent with generally accepted accounting practices recognised by the New Zealand accounting profession as appropriate and relevant for the reporting of financial information in the public sector' (s. 223F).

This requirement, taken together with the annual planning process, has greatly improved the quality of financial information available to decision-makers and to citizens. Indeed, the Controller and Auditor-General considered that 'the framework for financial accountability of local authorities now surpasses that of publicly listed companies' (Audit Office, 1993b, p. 15). A major gap was, however, the treatment of assets in local government accounting. The Audit Office noted that before the 1989 reforms there was no requirement for local authorities to disclose the value of fixed and infrastructural assets in their published financial statements.[10] Indeed, the value of infrastructural assets was usually unknown; accounting for funds was the priority. While most councils were already developing asset management plans, the financial provisions of the Local Government Law Reform Bill (currently before a select committee) go much further in imposing on local government a strategic framework in which to conduct their financial affairs (not dissimilar in purpose to the Fiscal Responsibility Act 1994 at central government level). They would represent the most significant change in the way in which local government business is conducted since 1989. The main provisions are:

a. local authorities are now to be required to manage their financial affairs (including debt) 'prudently' in the interests of the district of the local authority or its inhabitants and ratepayers;
b. all relevant information including 'an assessment of the costs and benefits of different options' is to be considered;
c. where appropriate the costs of expenditure should be recovered 'in the year in which the direct benefits of the expenditure will, or can reasonably be expected to, accrue to any persons or groups or categories of persons';
d. more generally, funding sources should be matched to the direct benefits of expenditure or, where there is a general benefit to the district, costs should be allocated on a fair and equitable basis;
e. local authorities are to be required, every three years from 1997, to adopt (after consultation with the community and concurrently with the annual plan) a long-term financial strategy related to a period of ten or more years;
f. the long-term strategy is to be required to cover expenditure (including the cost of capital) and revenue, cashflow projections, asset management, and borrowing requirements;
g. the Local Authorities Loans Act 1956 is to be revoked and a much less prescriptive regime applied to local government borrowing (although loan polls would still be required).

The proposed funding principles centre on the matching of funding sources to functions. While this is a proposition supported in both central and local government, it raises numerous issues of definition and, indeed, the purpose of local government. 'User-pays' implies a clear identification of the user. Whether or not some local body services are truly 'public goods' in the economists' use of the term—and thus by definition incapable of being allocated to identifiable users—is often a matter for debate (New Zealand Business Roundtable, 1995). Similarly, the introduction of user charges for rubbish disposal might be a relatively straightforward exercise, but agreement on the

---

10. Infrastructural assets include floodbanks, roading networks, cemeteries, recreational reserves, landfill sites, footpaths, kerbs, and reticulation systems such as water supply, sewage disposal, and drainage (Audit Office, 1993b, p. 30).

beneficiaries of libraries is a much more difficult and value-laden matter. Some authorities, quite legitimately, might decide that the availability of publicly funded library services is a 'merit' good; that is, one for which a charge could be made, but in respect of which the elected council interprets the collective community preference as being in favour of free provision. It is not surprising that the assessment and allocation of benefits differs among communities; that is surely the *raison d'être* of local government.

The proposed amendments to the financial provisions of the Local Government Act represent a further stage in the process of requiring transparency in New Zealand government at all levels. It is, therefore, to be welcomed. It would, however, be unfortunate if this commendable ambition were to constrain the freedom of local authorities, in possession of the available facts, to make decisions about the nature of the services they provide and the way they are funded. At some point if this route is followed the purpose of democratically elected local government—to resolve issues of conflicting values and citizens' preferences—is itself called in question.

SOURCES OF FINANCE

The financing of local government has been the subject, over the years, of recurring investigation (Scott, 1988), and was included in the 'comprehensive' review initiated by Bassett in 1987. The Officials' Coordinating Committee examined the options while emphasising the need for fiscal discipline on the part of local government. Various possibilities for revenue sharing with central government were discussed, including grants, local taxation on goods and services, and a share of GST. No new initiatives emerged, however, from the fourth Labour government's otherwise radical reforms, and since National assumed office the underlining of 'fiscal responsibility' has (as the Local Government Law Reform Bill demonstrates) become even sharper. The trend is clearly to 'user-pays'. Pressure on councils to minimise 'the rates burden', coupled with the new transparency and better quality information now available, has provided an environment in which councils have been able to establish the 'true cost' of activities, and thus to justify more easily a shift in costs from ratepayer to consumer (in this regard Alam and Lawrence (1994) usefully report on the experience of the Hamilton City Council). Nonetheless, as Table 9.1 shows, rates remain the principal source of funding for local government.

In 1991 it could be said that 'in this area [of rating] there is a considerable gulf between the principles of economic rationality espoused by the Treasury and local government's desire for flexibility' (Martin, 1991b, p. 276). By 1995 that gulf was not so great. Councils throughout the country, responding to the clear views of ratepayers (albeit not as quickly in some cases as vocal groups demand) have acknowledged that increased expenditure (with, in consequence, higher rates) is a significant issue. The focus is now increasingly on the share of rates to be met by different categories of ratepayers—the problem of differential rating. This issue is one in which the courts have so far determined the course of events as much as, if not more than, the legislature or the executive at national or local level.[11] The key issues are the extent to which taxpayers

Table 9.1　Local authority revenue 1992–93[1]

Source	%
Rates [2]	32
User charges [3]	23
Asset sales	13
Other [4]	11
Loans	9
Central government grants	6
Reserves	3

1. Figures are rounded and do not add to 100 per cent.
2. This includes general, separate, and special rates, separate uniform annual charges, and uniform annual general charges.
3. This includes fees, charges, water by meter, water race charges, 'bag' charges, pan tax, and trade waste charges.
4. This category includes income from investments, lump sums under the Rating Powers Act, and 'other' revenue.

Source: New Zealand Local Government Association
(pers. comm.; latest available figures)

have benefited from services provided by local authorities, and whether the rates levied fairly reflect that allocation of benefits.

HUMAN RESOURCE MANAGEMENT

Perhaps the greatest manifestation of the changed culture of local government is evident in councils' employment practices. Prior to 1989 local government, like central government, provided a career. This was largely within one authority, although appointments at the senior level often resulted in promotion of officers from other authorities.[12] Elected members were involved in appointments down to the third level of the permanent staff. Conditions of employment were negotiated under the Labour Relations Act 1987. Tradespeople were employed under the relevant award or agreement and clerical officers by instruments negotiated with authorities by the regional Local Government Officers Unions. Others in the industrial relations community tended to regard local authorities as 'soft' employers, and a 'state sector linkage', which assured local government employees of at least the movement in state rates of pay, was a perennial problem (Minister of State Services, 1986).

The 1989 legislation removed councillors from the employment function except in respect of the CE who, like counterparts in central government, acquired the employer

---

11. Key cases are *MacKenzie District Council* v. *Electricity Corporation of New Zealand (ECNZ)* [1992] 3 NZLR 41; *South Waikato District Council* v. *ECNZ*, High Court, Wellington, CP 16-93, 18 August 1994, Heron J; and *Woolworths (NZ) Ltd* v. *Wellington City Council*, High Court, Wellington, CP 385–94, 15 May 1995, Ellis J.
12. The Joint Council for Local Authorities Services, established in 1977, was a largely unsuccessful attempt to impose on local government elements of a national career service.

role in respect of all employees of the council. Under s. 119C of the Local Government Act, the chief executive is responsible to the local authority 'for employing, on behalf of the local authority, within his or her area of responsibility, staff of the local authority and negotiating their terms of employment'.

Local authorities are significant employers in their communities. In April 1993 (*Management*, April 1993), ten authorities employed over 500 staff, with the largest approaching 2000. Authorities formed by amalgamation were required under the Local Authorities (Employment Protection) Act 1963[13] to carry over existing pay levels and, for employees with more than five years' continuous service, to maintain them for at least two years. In the early years after the 1989 Act many of the new local authorities, as they reviewed their role in service delivery, significantly reduced staff numbers, often leading to personal grievance proceedings over employment terminations.[14] In this environment pay negotiations were, for many councils, more difficult than in the past. Since the Employment Contracts Act 1991, as collective agreements expired, there has been a marked shift from coverage by a collective agreement to individual employment contracts. From another perspective, generalised pay increases have been replaced by individual arrangements based on performance. (For movement in local government pay rates see Table 11.2).

As in central government the last few years have seen some tensions between the emphasis on performance (marked by more rigorous evaluation and performance pay arrangements) and the 'good employer' provision. CEs are required to operate a personnel policy containing provisions generally agreed as necessary for the fair and proper treatment of employees in all aspects of their employment including an EEO programme, recognition of the aims and aspirations of Māori, ethnic and minority groups, women, and people with disabilities (s. 119, Local Government Act 1974).

In the absence of a central agency to play the monitoring role that the SSC performs in central government, a council's 'good employer' performance is subject to scrutiny through the statutory planning process (here, the annual report must contain a summary of the EEO programme and performance). Evidence, other than anecdotal, is limited, and performance over so many authorities could be expected to vary. But it is unquestionable that the employment culture of local authorities, by and large, is now both more performance-oriented and less restrictive than it was before the reforms.

AN APPRAISAL

If the second half of the 1980s saw a 'revolution' (Boston, Martin, Pallot, and Walsh, 1991) in central government, the transformation of local government—structure, func-

---

13. The 1963 Act was repealed by the Local Government Amendment Act (No. 2) 1989 (s. 55), but its provisions applied to existing staff who transferred to the newly formed authorities before 1 November 1990.

14. Severance agreements for senior officers attracted considerable media attention, for example, in Wellington.

tions and culture—has since 1989 been at least as traumatic. Polaschek's question of 1956, recalled at the beginning of this chapter, was not effectively addressed for almost forty years. This review of the changes since 1989 does not, of itself, answer the question. Rather, it suggests that the 'modernisation' of local government has cleared the decks for it to play a more positive role, if that is the preference of citizens. The management systems are now in place both to identify the diversity of local issues across the country and to respond to them.

It is useful, after McKinlay, to reflect on 'what was ordered, what was delivered and what is still to come' in local government reform. McKinlay (1994, p. 6) notes that the framework underpinning the reforms of central government, when applied to local government, revealed five immediate problems:

a. confusion between councillors and senior management about their roles;
b. a built-in bias towards inefficiency resulting from the absence of contestability in the provision of council services, most of which were provided 'in-house';
c. confusion between commercial and non-commercial objectives in the management of council trading activities;
d. the lack of appropriate incentives and accountability arrangements to enable elected representatives to hold managers accountable for resource use; and
e. the diseconomies of scale—in resource use and recruitment and retention of quality management—of too many small authorities.

To what extent have the reforms solved these problems? In answering this question, a distinction has to be made between statutory requirements and performance. Broadly speaking, the Local Government Amendment Act of 1989 and its successors did not go as far as some advisers to the fourth Labour government might have initially hoped; but the experience since 1989 has been inexorably in the direction then set. To summarise:

1. The 'policy' and 'implementation' roles of the council and the CE respectively have been clarified and, by and large, accepted. Forbearance is required on the part of elected representatives, and sensitivity on the part of officers. A purist insistence on the CE's autonomy, not tempered by good communication with councillors, would be to ignore the essentially local nature of the environment. Equally, attempts at 'political interference' in matters of management carry risks for councillors and the interest of the community.

2. 'Contestability' with consequent gains in efficiency in service delivery has proceeded apace since 1989. Although, as McKinlay notes (1994, p. 17), there was no 'compulsory corporatisation' (except in respect of transport authorities), the use of LATEs and 'business units' has exposed the activities of local government to an increasing degree of competition. Similarly, although contracting out of services has not been made mandatory, in practice there has been an increasing propensity to contract out (note, though, the position of regional councils and activities funded by Transit New Zealand).

3. New employment arrangements (the position of the CE and individual performance-related contracts) and the move to output-based, accrual accounting linked to a transparent planning process have introduced appropriate incentives and accountabil-

ities for management. Proposals in the Local Government Law Reform Bill enhance these.

4. Despite setbacks in the 1992 Amendment Act's adjustments to regional government (reducing its potential role) and to the reorganisation process (making possible easier local 'triggering' of boundary changes),[15] most local authorities have had the critical mass to support new systems of management.

The changes yet to come fall into two categories: first, those major financial reforms now before Parliament; and second, the direction chosen by the councils elected in October 1995.

As has already been indicated, the new financial proposals have the potential to assist both the performance and accountability of local government, but could place unreasonable inhibitions on the ability of territorial authorities to govern in accordance with the wishes of citizens in their districts. They do, however, focus the attention of local authorities on the long-term and the intergenerational implications of their decisions. Deferred maintenance on local infrastructural assets together with the need to meet higher standards (for example, with waste water treatment) is probably the most dramatic challenge facing local government in the remaining years of the twentieth century. Estimates—probably conservative—of the cost of new infrastructure 'range upwards from $2000 million over the next 10–20 years' (Audit Office, 1995a, p. 23).

During the term of the councils elected in October 1995 the rethinking already well under way about the proper role of local authorities will undoubtedly continue. A case can be made that recent developments in local government—charging for services, for example—have been regressive in their social impact (particularly when coupled with central government policy changes). The foreseeable future is, however, unlikely to see a growth on any large scale of social service provision by local government. Rather, the debate about the role of local government is likely to focus on what Reid labels governance. 'Local governance' is a function, in his interpretation, with at least four elements (Reid, 1994, p. 2):

- the guardianship of difference;
- the protection of future selves;
- the advancement of 'positive rights';
- the provision of civic leadership.

In a stimulating contribution to debate about the role of the public sector, Reid makes the point that collective choice and 'the public interest' are more than simply a

---

15. Amendments to s. 37 of the Local Government Act in 1992 substantially changed the 1989 procedures for constituting new districts and regions, providing *inter alia* for a poll of electors in the area of the proposed new district and reducing the minimum population of a new district from 50,000 to 20,000 (Department of Internal Affairs, 1992b). This has led to a reawakening of interest in 'de-amalgamation' on the part of areas that lost their statutory identity in 1989; none have so far been successful in separating from their parent district.

reflection of the majority will; they recognise that there is more than one 'public'. Good local governance is about managing the diverse interests reflected in the wider community; it is concerned with the future needs of citizens beyond this generation; and it embraces an obligation to assist citizens to participate meaningfully in the life of their communities (even if this participation runs counter to the policies of central government). Above all, the governance role is synonymous with leadership. As Reid observes, 'the question of which services are best delivered by local government is ultimately a technical decision made within the context of specific spatial and temporal conditions' (ibid., p. 5). By contrast 'governance', involving leadership and a vision for a community, cannot be 'contracted out, delegated to appointed boards of management or ultimately privatised'. This is not a notion in good currency in central government at present.[16] Ironically, though, the search for efficiency in local government promoted from the centre since 1989, coupled with load shedding in such areas as housing, has provided the conditions in which the governance role can develop.

---

16. An interesting development has been the formation of the Local Government Forum, including interest group associations such as the Business Roundtable, Federated Farmers, and the Manufacturers' Association, and 'corporates' such as ECNZ, Fletcher Challenge, and Telecom.

human resource management

10   managing the employment relationship

This chapter and the next two consider the policies and practices adopted by government departments in the management of staff since 1988.[1] This chapter assesses the continuing management of the employment relationship. Chapter 11 examines the process of contract negotiation that establishes the terms and conditions under which people are employed. Chapter 12 examines the development and implementation of EEO policies. Ideally, EEO would not be considered separately as it is a vital component of any strategic approach to HRM. However, the introduction of the good employer obligation in the State Sector Act and the implementation of EEO programmes has involved such substantial changes in the management of people in public agencies that a satisfactory account requires a separate chapter.

THE PARADOX OF HUMAN RESOURCE MANAGEMENT

Since the 1980s, the language of human resource management (HRM) has dominated discussions about employment relations and the management of people in organisations. The HRM tide has rolled over competing discourses; the new orthodoxy has, it seems, established itself securely in a relatively short period of time. The New Zealand public sector has been no exception. Increasingly, public sector agencies are trying to adopt a strategic approach to the management of human resources. To the extent that this model is put into practice, it has significant implications for the conduct of employment relations in the public sector and for the day-to-day work experience of public employees. It is necessary then to begin with some consideration of the theory and practice of HRM and some of the difficulties associated with it.

There are two brands of HRM on offer: the 'hard' and the 'soft' versions. As Hendry and Pettigrew (1990) put it, the former represents a 'utilitarian instrumentalism' and the latter a 'developmental humanism'. In Legge's definition, the hard model 'stresses HRM's focus on the crucial importance of the close integration of human resource policies, systems and activities with business strategy . . .' (Legge, 1995, p. 34). She goes on to quote Storey's often cited observation that the hard model emphasises the

---

1. The focus of this and the next two chapters is on developments in the central government sector. Where appropriate specific reference will be made to the health and education sectors.

'quantitative, calculative and business strategic aspects of managing the headcount resource in as "rational" a way as for any other economic factor' (Storey, 1987, p. 6). The soft developmental humanism model, 'while still emphasizing the importance of integrating HR policies with business objectives, sees this as involving treating employees as valued assets, a source of competitive advantage through their commitment, adaptability and high quality (of skills, performance and so on)' (Legge, 1995, p. 35). Legge sums up the difference in terms of the hard model's focus on 'human *resource management*' in contrast to the soft model's focus on '*human resource* management' (ibid., p. 35, emphasis in original).

Although both strands run through most conceptualisations of HRM, the soft model, the 'nicer face' of HRM, predominates in the academic and practitioner literature. Storey (1995a, p. 5) sets out a clear definition of the soft model of HRM as 'a distinctive approach to employment management which seeks to achieve competitive advantage through the strategic deployment of a highly committed and capable workforce using an integrated array of cultural, structural and personnel techniques'. Storey (1995a, pp. 5–8) identifies five central premises of HRM:

a. Employees are a source of competitive advantage.
b. Therefore HRM has strategic implications and HRM strategy must be the concern of senior management, and particularly of the CE.
c. HRM policies must be based on an alignment of the competitive environment, business strategy, and HRM strategy.
d. HRM is far too important to be left to HRM specialists. It becomes part of the responsibility of line managers.
e. The key levers for the effective delivery of HRM are the management of corporate culture, the design of integrated HRM policies and practices, and an organisational structure that devolves responsibility and empowers employees.

Storey (1995a, p. 5) observes that the most important of these premises 'is the idea that at bottom, it is the human resource among all the factors of production which really makes the difference. It is human capability and commitment which in the final analysis distinguishes successful organisations from the rest.' Even the most cursory perusal of the practitioner literature shows that it is now an article of management faith that effective strategic HRM is the key to organisational success. Yet, there are theoretical, epistemological and empirical problems associated with the HRM model that should—but seem not to—induce caution.

In a recent major review of the strategic HRM literature, Wright and McMahan (1992, p. 297) conclude that the field has been poorly theorised. They note a preoccupation with descriptive typologies, practical advice and the atheoretical presentation of empirical data. Second, Legge (1995, pp. 38–9) observes that the hard and soft models of HRM are both plagued by significant epistemological problems. The key concept of integration, so vital to the hard model, has two different meanings within the model itself. These two meanings are not easily reconcilable and imply quite different practical prescriptions. The dominant soft model is beset by contradictions in its 'conceptual scaffolding' between commitment and flexibility, flexibility and quality, individuality and teamwork, strong culture and flexibility, and quality and commitment (Legge, 1995, p. 35). These concepts do not always sit easily together. Indeed, in some cases, it might be concluded that they never sit easily together and yet they form the conceptual core of orthodox HRM theory and practice. The third issue is that of implementation. To what extent is HRM a reality in modern organisations? Has it replaced the traditional personnel management approach? The heavily empirical tradition of UK industrial relations/personnel management research has provided a solid survey base for a judgment there. Having reviewed the empirical evidence, Sisson is in no doubt:

> Remarkable as it may seem, HRM seems to have had little or no impact on the personnel function in the UK in the decade or so in which the thinking associated with it has been so pervasive. Hopes that HRM would lead to a more strategic approach to the management of human resources have been largely frustrated (1995, p. 105).

Legge reaches a slightly more cautious conclusion:

> What evidence we have is of a patchy implementation of practices designed to achieve flexibility, quality and commitment, often constrained by the contradictions inherent in enacting these slippery concepts, and motivated more by the opportunities afforded by high levels of unemployment and the constraints of recession and enhanced competition rather than by any long-term strategic considerations (1995, p. 47).

The US evidence is based more on case studies than surveys but, as Guest observes, the same cases tend to recur again and again in the literature. He concludes that HRM's emphasis on the potential for human growth, on the desire to make things better for people in organisations, and the key role of leadership and culture fitted neatly into the political values of the Reagan years in which HRM rose to orthodoxy. HRM, says Guest, is 'yet another manifestation of the American Dream and its popularity and attractiveness must be understood in this context' (Guest, 1990, p. 377).

The paradox of HRM is that it has acquired its current status among academics and practitioners despite significant theoretical and epistemological deficiencies in its conceptual formulation and notwithstanding its at best patchy implementation in organisations. Explaining this paradox would take us further into the sociology of knowledge than we can go. But the paradox is itself important; HRM has taken hold at least as an ideal throughout modern economies. It is not only an American dream.

THE EVOLUTION OF EMPLOYMENT RELATIONS IN THE NEW ZEALAND PUBLIC SECTOR

Managers in the New Zealand public sector have embraced HRM with considerable enthusiasm. Statutory arrangements have encouraged this trend. Not only have CEs become employers of their staff but also they are obliged to be 'good employers' (see below). The SSC maintains a statutory responsibility to monitor personnel and equal employment opportunity policies. But the embracing of HRM itself was not required by legislation; that owes more to the general growth of HRM since the 1980s. Thus, personnel and industrial relations managers have given way to human resource managers; departments have acquired HRM divisions at a corporate level and, where appropriate, at the level of the business unit. The SSC has established a Strategic Human Resource Development Branch. The branch has developed a strategic HRM model for the New Zealand public sector (SSC, undated), which it encourages departments to adopt and to modify for their own needs. As the manager of the branch has put it, the SSC is

> striving for a common understanding and commitment to strategic HR management. The purpose is to develop processes that will facilitate the integration of human resource policies into the organisation's strategic thinking and planning processes—as opposed to HR policies which sit separately, to the side of that process (Craig, 1994, p. 1).

The language and culture of HRM permeates the management of employment relations in the public sector.

This is a substantial departure from the traditional management of employment relations in the public sector, which was organised around principles of centralised and uniform bureaucratic control (Friedman, 1977). Rules were prescribed and their application monitored from the centre. In departments, superiors applied these rules so as to control the behaviour of subordinates. These rules limited the discretion and constrained the behaviour of managers and employees at an individual level and union and management at a collective level. In New Zealand, these rules were embodied in the Public Service Manual, Treasury Instructions, SSC circulars, and determinations that prescribed pay and working conditions. The flexible deployment of staff, the harnessing of the creative potential of employees, the use of initiative and lateral thinking were, as in all bureaucratic control systems, assigned less priority than the certainties of clear-cut responsibilities, the advantages of known and methodical procedures, and the commitment engendered by employment security and the existence of diverse and well-understood opportunities for promotion.

Employment Relations, 1912–88

To understand the scope of the changes to employment relations in the public sector, it is necessary to set them in their historical context. Prior to the Public Service Act 1912, governments directly controlled the pay and conditions of state employees, as well as their appointment, promotion, and dismissal. The 1912 Act established an independent career service with personnel procedures insulated from political influence. The basic structure of the public service personnel system did not change greatly between 1912 and 1988. By the 1980s, its key features were as follows:

a. The SSC was the employing authority of all staff in the public service and held all HRM authorities. There was some limited devolution prior to the State Sector Act 1988. As the public sector grew in size and complexity, it had become impossible for the SSC to carry out all the HR responsibilities assigned to it. It had begun to delegate many of the day-to-day HR authorities to departments, but these remained delegations and could be withdrawn. Moreover, these delegations were limited, and the SSC retained a determinant role in the management of the employment relationship in the public sector.

b. The public service operated as a unified career service. Public servants were eligible for appointment to any position in any department. The internal labour market, the tradition of job security, and a superannuation system superior to almost any in the private sector (and which required forty years' service for maximum benefit) encouraged a lifetime public sector career.

c. Public servants were protected against rivals from outside the public sector by the requirement that for any position above the entry grades an outsider had to demonstrate 'clearly more merit' than an applicant from anywhere in the service. This criterion also applied to the appointment of a public servant above a more senior internal applicant for a position. An appeals system enforced this provision. The effect was to discourage the appointment of outsiders and the swift elevation of able junior staff.

d. An occupational classification system applied across the entire public service and categorised all positions into about 150 occupational classes. Positions were standardised across the service, and the qualifications and experience required for a position, the job description, and the pay and conditions applying to it varied hardly at all from one department to another.

e. A standard public-service-wide performance appraisal system assessed the performance of staff.

Pay-fixing procedures, however, did change between 1912 and 1988, and they were perennially controversial. Following the 1912 Act, pay-fixing remained subject to political influence despite being formally under the control of the Public Service Commissioner. Until the passage of the Government Services Tribunal Act 1948, public sector unions, unlike their private sector counterparts, had no bargaining rights and no access to compulsory arbitration. The 1948 Act established a pay-fixing system based upon fair relativity with the private sector, achieved, if need be, through compulsory arbitration by an independent tribunal (Walsh, 1991b). Although particular details changed from time to time, the basic structure of the pay-fixing system remained fairly constant from the 1948 Act to the 1980s (Powell, 1989):

a. General wage adjustments were the chief instrument for the determination of state sector pay. They were based upon a survey of private sector pay rates, from which was calculated the average private sector pay increase for the period of the survey. This average increase was then applied to all state employees.

b. Occupational class pay claims permitted an occupational class which felt that its private sector equivalent had moved ahead faster than the private sector average or which for any other reason believed it was experiencing particular recruitment and retention difficulties to lodge its own pay claim.

c. Statutory pay-fixing criteria were designed to ensure fair relativity with the private sector and to take account of recruitment and retention factors.

d. Compulsory arbitration by the appropriate tribunal resolved deadlocked negotiations.

e. Salaries for permanent heads and some deputies were set separately by the HSC based on relativity with the private sector. Their triennial adjustments had consequential margins implications for the rest of the state sector. (The HSC also set salaries for a variety of other positions including MPs, judges, doctors in public hospitals, academics, and some local authority positions.)

f. Non-remuneration conditions of employment were determined by a series of block negotiations, which covered the whole of the state sector.

Trade unions and state employing authorities were centralised and bureaucratic. It was a non-participatory system whose operation was exceedingly remote from those whose fate was being decided. Trade unions only infrequently relied upon participation by their members to achieve their objectives. Equally, state employing authorities felt only infrequent need to communicate with their employees about the conditions under which they would employ them. Senior managers of individual departments and other public agencies had no role in these negotiations. It was an indulgent system. The formal rules governing negotiations meant that it was literally certain that there would be a wage increase. In the case of general wage adjustments, the size of the increase was broadly known before the negotiations began once the survey results were known. Pay increases had no negative funding implications for departments. Supplementary adjustments were made to compensate departments. This gave officials little or no incentive to resist occupational class pay claims. On the other hand, it was an efficient system. Transaction costs and levels of industrial conflict were low.

Bargaining, whether over the general wage adjustment or an occupational class pay claim, was normally remote from the workplace. The exceptions were departments like the Forest Service, the Ministry of Works and Development, and the New Zealand Electricity Department, which negotiated directly with some of their employees, usually their 'wage-workers'. For other workers and managers, pay structures, pay levels, and employment conditions were imposed from the centre and arrived by a process that did not involve them. Neither managers nor employees had any sense of ownership of pay and conditions. Indeed, many had only a limited understanding of the process by which they were determined. When a dispute arose over the application or interpretation of employment conditions in a workplace, it was quickly removed to the centre where union and SSC officials fixed things in ways of which workers and managers were only dimly aware. In due course, a ruling would be handed down to apply not only to the workplace where the dispute originated but also to all public sector workplaces.

Industrial relations were highly politicised. In major disputes, unions tended to look either for an arbitrated solution or a political deal. Governments took an active interest in the outcome of industrial relations issues in the state sector, and unions frequently appealed to the electoral sensitivities of ministers when other avenues had proved fruitless. Ministers were always consulted by employing authorities about negotiations over major occupational class pay claims, and on many occasions these were resolved one way or another by cabinet direction. In this environment there was no possibility of a strategic approach to the management of human resources.

Pressures for Reform

The fourth Labour government's assessment of this system was set out in the ministerial discussion paper, *Pay-fixing in the State Sector* (Minister of State Services, 1986). The principal criticisms made by the Buff Paper, as it came to be called, were that:

a. The stress upon employment and income security had, in the absence of market pressures for continuous change, generated rigidities that limited individual and departmental performance. Employment relations were seen as significant impediments to public sector efficiency.

b. Centralisation and uniformity ensured that personnel and industrial relations arrangements took no account of the management, financial, and policy goals of departments.

c. The priority given to occupational relativities above market factors or other factors specific to the occupational class ensured a rigid system of determining pay and employment conditions.

d. The annual general adjustment (AGA) gave the impression of state pay leadership and encouraged catch-up claims in the private sector.

e. Among state employees, the AGA was seen as an automatic entitlement, to be supplemented by an occupational class claim. Many employees argued that they had received a nil increase in years when they received 'only' the AGA.

f. National pay rates based on survey averages guaranteed both occupational and regional labour market distortions.

g. The HSC's salary ceiling limited the ability of state employers to respond to changing market conditions, especially for specialist skills and for salaries just below the ceiling. In addition, the Commission's ceiling compressed salary margins just below the ceiling.

h. Margins reviews to restore vertical relativities at lower levels following a HSC determination could have major implications throughout the state sector, as happened in 1985.

This analysis, combined with the outcomes of a series of state sector industrial disputes and the 1985 HSC determination, convinced the Labour government that reform was needed.[2]

---

2. The events that were the catalyst for convincing the Labour Government of the need for reform, especially the 1985 HSC determination, are discussed in more detail in Boston, Martin, Pallot, and Walsh, 1991, Ch. 5.

THE STATE SECTOR ACT 1988

The State Sector Act 1988 made radical changes to employment relations in the public sector.

a. CEs were established as employers of their own staff and exercised all the responsibilities of an employer, with the exception of the negotiation of employment conditions.

b. The SSC was established as the 'employer party' for the purposes of negotiating conditions of employment. The SSC was required to consult with CEs in carrying out this task and was empowered to delegate this responsibility to CEs.

c. CEs and the SSC had joint employer party status for any disputes over the interpretation or application of employment conditions.

d. CEs had the status of employer party for any personal grievances taken by a member of their staff.

e. The unified service was replaced by departments operating independently of each other as employers in line with the new status of CEs as employers. The appeals system was replaced by a review process applying within each department.

f. The AGA and the public-service-wide negotiations of non-remuneration conditions of employment were abolished.

g. Statutory criteria to govern collective bargaining were eliminated.

h. Compulsory arbitration to resolve disputes over the negotiation of employment conditions was abolished (a three-year transitional provision made compulsory final offer arbitration available in return for giving up the right to strike; very few unions made use of this).

i. The public sector came under the provisions of the Labour Relations Act, which previously had applied only to the private sector.

HUMAN RESOURCE MANAGEMENT UNDER THE STATE SECTOR ACT

The Integration of HRM with Corporate Strategy

It is difficult to assess the degree to which the strategic integration of HRM with corporate strategy has been achieved in the New Zealand public sector. The research evidence does not exist. Evidence from other quarters suggests that success is likely to have been limited. Although the integration with corporate strategy is vital to the strategic HRM model, available empirical evidence suggests that this objective is not widely achieved. Storey's case studies of fifteen major UK companies led him to conclude that 'most cases failed to offer much in the way of an integrated approach to employment management, and still less was there evidence of strategic integration with the corporate plan' (Storey, 1995a, p. 14). Survey evidence reaches similar conclusions. Marginson's analysis of the UK company level survey concluded that 'if one of the defining characteristics of human resource management is the explicit link with corporate and business strategies then this survey has failed to find it for the majority of large companies' (Marginson et al., 1993, p. 71).

It is doubtful that the situation is very different in the New Zealand public sector. This is despite the fact that the State Sector Act gave CEs ownership of their employment relations and thus made it possible for departments to take a strategic approach to HRM. Public sector HR managers and CEs interviewed in 1994 conceded that their organisations had not yet achieved strategic integration.[3] Although HR objectives are included in departmental corporate plans (few departments have a separate HRM plan), it is unusual to discern any strategic focus in the HRM sections of departmental corporate plans. Most are relentlessly operational in their focus.

The planning and performance management process is one route by which strategic integration might be achieved. In many departments there is a top-down/bottom-up planning process, which is intended to ensure that the work of every member of the department contributes to the achievement of the outputs within established budget limits. This has brought major change to the manner in which managers think about the use of human resources. In earlier days, line managers tended to be unconcerned with budget limits and if they needed new staff they would apply for it. Now line managers are ruled by their budget; their first question is 'can I afford it?' New staff can only be employed if staff or services are cut elsewhere. Budget constraints mean that managers must always be consulting with staff to get their input. The emphasis is on 'working smarter' and staying inside budget. Thus, departments put considerable emphasis upon developing performance management systems designed to ensure that the performance targets of each employee are aimed at contributing to those outputs. But this emphasis on the more efficient deployment of human resources does not itself constitute strategic integration.

The difficulties in achieving strategic integration have not been due to a lack of emphasis on the HR function. In most departments, the corporate HR division has grown in size since 1988. Just as importantly, the corporate HR division tends now to be staffed by HR professionals and have a policy focus in contrast to the heavily operational focus taken by personnel staff before 1988. Organisational charts indicate that HR appears to carry sufficient status and influence in departments, with corporate HR managers by and large reporting either directly to the chief executive or to the second management tier.

The inability to achieve strategic integration of HRM in the New Zealand public sector is likely to derive from factors similar to those identified in the international research literature. It is argued, drawing upon Chandler's (1962) classic formulation, that the chief reason is that HRM issues only enter strategic decision-making as downstream consequences of higher-order decisions about organisational strategy and structure (Purcell, 1989; Purcell and Ahlstrand, 1989). These decisions place severe constraints on the range of HRM policies that can be pursued. The exclusion of HRM

---

3. These interviews were undertaken as part of a wider OECD project comparing the level of decentralisation in public sector HRM in a number of countries. The data from those interviews are drawn on in the analysis in this and the following two chapters.

specialists and therefore HRM considerations from these decision-making processes makes it highly unlikely that HRM can play a strategic role in the achievement of business objectives. Moreover, the 1980s and 1990s have been marked by market instability and cost stringency in the public and private sectors. Intense pressure on management to achieve short-term financial economies has made it much harder for organisations to take HRM issues into account in strategic decision-making. The concerns of employees, their need for personal development and training, and the importance of a caring, nurturing environment have taken a lower priority than basic bottom-line decisions.

This explanation fits well with experience in the public sector in New Zealand. The relentless pace and scope of restructuring have meant that higher-order decisions of strategy and structure have been almost continuously to the fore since the mid 1980s. Where HRM considerations have played any role in this, it has tended to be within the utilitarian instrumentalist framework of the hard HRM model. Although the key precepts of the developmental humanist model of HRM have been adopted and promoted by departments, it has in fact been the hard model of HRM that has been central to much of the HRM policies and practices of public sector agencies since 1988. This has been most evident in the wider programme of public sector restructuring. Departmental reorganisation and associated huge job losses have seen thousands of careers abruptly terminated or unwillingly redirected. Many of those remaining have seen workloads increase almost beyond endurance to compensate for staff reductions and the wider impact of funding restrictions. The drive to cut back existing employment conditions and the virtual pay freeze for the first half of the 1990s are other aspects of the hard model of HRM. These changes have been justified by the fundamental principles of the model of utilitarian instrumentalism: departments must deploy their human resources in as rational and economically efficient a manner as possible. For many of those who have experienced the sharp edge of the hard HRM model, morale is low and insecurity high. Equally, however, there are many employees who have done well out of the changes in the last decade. Their assessment and accordingly their morale and commitment would be considerably higher. A major problem for HRM policies is to reconcile the widespread emphasis in departments on the attractive humanistic principles of the soft HRM model with continuing employment insecurity and lack of improvement in employment conditions. Notwithstanding other substantial advances in the management of human resources in the public service, this sets limits to the degree of commitment that can reasonably be expected of employees. Commitment can only be sustained if it is reciprocal.

The Decentralisation of HRM

Two key strategic developments in public sector HRM since 1988 have been, first, the decentralisation of responsibility for HRM out from the SSC to CEs, and, second, within departments, the decentralisation of day-to-day responsibility for people management down to line managers. They will be discussed in turn.

Under the Public Finance Act 1989 the government allocates inputs in order to buy specific outputs from departments. The efficient production of outputs by departmental staff is the responsibility of departmental CEs. If CEs were to be held accountable for what their staff do, they had to be made employers and given the rights and responsibilities associated with that. Thus, the decentralisation of authority for HRM out from the SSC to CEs was a consequence of wider reforms rather than pursued in its own right, but it was central to the reform programme. The wider programme of reform could not have been implemented without it.

The State Sector Act does not cut departments loose entirely. The Act places some constraints on the CE in an effort to ensure equitable HR policies and practices:

a. Vacancies must be advertised in a manner that allows suitably qualified persons to apply.
b. CEs are obliged to appoint the person 'best suited' to the position and to notify all appointments to existing departmental staff.
c. Departments are required to establish an appointments review process available to any unsuccessful candidate from within the department. This process must be approved by the SSC, although the department conducts the review itself.
d. The Act obliges CEs to be a 'good employer'. This requires them to provide good and safe working conditions, to appoint staff impartially, and to provide opportunities for staff to develop their abilities. It also obliges CEs to develop and implement an EEO programme and to have particular regard to the needs of women, Māori, ethnic minorities, and workers with disabilities.
e. The SSC is obliged to promote and develop personnel policies for the whole of the public service and to promote, develop, *and* monitor EEO policies and programmes.
f. The SSC also retained responsibility for negotiating conditions of employment.
g. The Employment Contracts Act and the Human Rights Act set substantive and procedural standards in the area of discipline and dismissal. Other legislation applying to all employers regulates areas such as occupational health and safety, minimum wage levels, minimum leave entitlements, and public holidays.

With the exception of the specific areas noted here, the SSC has no role to play in HRM in departments. There is no provision for any reporting to the SSC of day-to-day HRM, nor any provision for complaints or appeals to the SSC. CEs are able within these constraints to develop policies tailored specifically to their own needs and circumstances.

The decentralisation of HRM out from the SSC to CEs has been followed by the devolution of responsibility for HRM within departments down to line managers. Departments vary in the degree to which they have done this, but there is a clear trend towards the devolution of responsibility for the main HR functions to line managers. This development is fundamental not only to new models of HRM but also to new models of devolved financial management. As organisations devolve cost centres, line managers take responsibility for meeting financial targets. Storey's case studies of fifteen large UK organisations show that the old-style reactive line manager has given way to a proactive commercially oriented manager charged with ensuring the achievement of business objectives (Storey, 1992, p. 198). Legge observes that these changes reflect the 'crucial fusion' of devolved management and the non-proceduralised approach of HRM, with its emphasis on direct communications with employees, participation and involvement, hands-on management style, on-the-job coaching and development. . . . This transformation, in itself, has given line management the responsibility for a wider matrix of employees and for the management of change. This in turn brings human resource issues higher up the line manager's agenda. . . . (Legge, 1995, p. 51).

Authority to make appointments in government departments has by and large been decentralised to line managers or their recommendations are rubber-stamped at corporate office; responsibility for implementing performance management systems has been assigned to line managers, and where the system includes performance-based pay, they make recommendations for pay increases; promotion recommendations are made by line managers, although final decisions might be made in consultation with senior management; but training responsibility tends to be shared between regional and corporate offices. Decisions about dismissals and other forms of discipline tend to be the most centralised of the HR functions. This is partly due to equity considerations but also because getting it wrong can be very costly for a department if an employee makes a successful personal grievance claim for unjustifiable dismissal.

These developments raise important issues about the appropriate role for a corporate HRM office and the nature of its relationship with line managers in a decentralised environment. Is there even any need for corporate HRM? In departments that have adopted a business unit structure, the relationship operates at two levels—the relationship between the departmental corporate office and the business units, and within business units the relationship between their own corporate office and line managers. Ideally, the role of a corporate HRM division in a decentralised system is chiefly a policy one, although one that draws upon line management expertise in policy formulation. Line managers exercise their HRM authority within the framework of departmental policy. Thus, the parameters and the criteria for HR decisions are the responsibility of the corporate HR office, whereas particular decisions about an employee are the responsibility of line managers. As decentralisation of HRM proceeds further within departments, the role of the corporate HRM office is becoming similar to that of SSC with regard to the public service as a whole. The corporate HRM office functions more and more as a consultant to line managers throughout the department. It ensures that departmental policies are complied with, and outside those policy responsibilities its role is advisory and supportive.

The key issue brought to the fore by the decentralisation of HRM is the competence of line managers. In practice, the competence of line managers varies so much within and across departments that it is difficult to make general statements about it. Line managers do not necessarily have skills in the management of people. For the most part, they advanced to management level because of their expertise in the subject area of the organisation. The lack of people management skills is particularly the case where line managers come from a highly technical background and where the legislation administered was highly prescriptive and allowed little discretion or flexibility in its application. For line managers with this kind of background, the very different approach required by their new-found HRM responsibilities poses a distinctive set of difficulties. These managers might prefer more prescription from the centre. All line managers require considerable support and training in HRM. Corporate HRM divisions accept a responsibility for training line managers in new HRM policies. Thus, line managers are supported but are responsible for delivery. This is a radical change from the situation prior to 1988, when line managers made virtually no staffing decisions. Then, HRM was easy for line managers; the answer to any question was in the personnel manual, or the question was referred to Head Office who either dealt with it or sent it on to the SSC. In practice, of course, the decentralisation of HRM to line managers is not fully operational in all departments. Departments vary in the degree to which they are willing to cede authority to line managers. In most departments, there are some line managers not yet comfortable with their new role. Some are reluctant to take the hard decisions as well as the popular ones. Where line managers do not accept responsibility for HRM, the corporate office finds itself drawn into operational matters rather more than it would like. But some departments maintain a degree of operational control at the centre to ensure consistency and equity of treatment. This reflects a lack of confidence in the HRM expertise of line managers and a strong need for line manager training.

The decentralisation of HRM gives rise to another important issue for CEs: whether and, if so, to what degree they want to ensure standard HR policies and practices throughout the organisation. One view is that sufficient standardisation comes from the development at a central level of HR policies that apply across the department. These policies might permit some variation in their application, according to different regional or functional circumstances and so particular practices might differ throughout the department. This variation might be acceptable so long as overall policy parameters are not breached. Another view might be that there is a secular trend towards decentralised HR practices. For seventy-five years following the Public Service Act 1912, it was considered important that all departments had the same HRM policies and practices. Since then, it has been accepted that departments will differ from each other in their HR policies and practices. In this view, it is then but a short step to argue that considerable differences in HRM policy and practice can be tolerated within a department. Adoption of a business unit structure will make this development more likely. A business unit model grows out of a recognition of difference and of the need for separate paths of development to accommodate difference. Different HRM policies and practices seem to flow logically out of that.

The difficulty in the public sector is that CE accountabilities differ from those in the private sector. A CE of a private sector multi-divisional company is accountable for bottom-line outcomes. So long as they are satisfactory, the range of HR policies and practices within the company might not be of vital importance. In the public sector, at least in New Zealand, the 'good employer' obligation in the State Sector Act and the review process for CEs means that they are directly accountable for HR policies and practices. This does not necessarily rule out wide variation within the department, but the greater the variation then the greater the monitoring difficulties for corporate HR and the greater the likelihood that policies and practices incompatible with the good employer obligation might develop.

OPERATIONAL HUMAN RESOURCE MANAGEMENT

An assessment of HRM in government departments under the State Sector Act must of necessity tend to focus at a strategic rather than an operational level. The empirical database upon which to make a public-sector-wide assessment of the operational side of HRM does not exist. Case studies provide some evidence, but there is a pressing need for survey data on HRM policies and practices across the public sector. However, it is clear that there have been substantial changes to HRM policies and practices since 1988. The public-service-wide systems in place then have been swept away and replaced by a range of policies appropriate to the circumstances of different departments. In this section, the main HRM policy areas will be considered briefly.

Any organisation has to decide how many people it will employ. This is not a decision consciously made and remade frequently, but massive restructuring has meant that every public agency has had to address this issue since the mid 1980s. Chapter 3 documented the huge job losses that have occurred in the central government sector. During this period, the emphasis in the literature has shifted from a traditional 'manpower planning' focus and from a reactive 'downsizing' model to a more strategic 're-engineering' approach. Dakin and Smith (1995, pp. 114–15) observe that re-engineering involves a systematic consideration of the organisation's strategic objectives, the structure needed to achieve those objectives, the work design and the number and type of employees appropriate for that, and the value system to support it. The restructuring of government departments in New Zealand has had elements of both approaches, although earlier restructurings tended to be more of the reflexive 'downsizing' variety. But certainly, no major restructuring of recent years would have taken place without a careful consideration of the overall strategic and structural needs of the organisation.

Having decided on its employee needs, an organisation has to find employees and persuade them to come and work for it. Recruitment and selection is an area in which any organisation must proceed carefully. One reason is that the procedures and terms by which employees enter and leave an organisation are the most heavily regulated of the chief HRM functions. In the public sector, not only does the Human Rights Act 1993 constrain these processes but the good employer provisions of the State Sector Act also set limits to how these should be handled. As a result, the recruitment and selection procedures of government departments are heavily shaped by the provisions of their own EEO programmes. For example, departments make a strong effort to recruit from non-traditional backgrounds and to ensure that their selection criteria are open and fair to all potential employees. The other reason to take recruitment and selection seriously is the cost of getting it wrong. Not only is there the lost investment in the new employee, but also it is not always a straightforward matter to dismiss or otherwise get rid of an incompetent worker. The Employment Court has set clear substantive and procedural requirements to be met in the case of dismissals (Hughes, 1993). Employers who breach those standards pay the monetary price, which in the case of senior employees is substantial. More positively, as Iles and Salaman observe, 'as one way of delivering behaviours seen as necessary to support organisational strategies, recruitment and selection initiatives have become increasingly important alongside training and development and large-scale cultural change and total quality management initiatives' (1995, p. 207). A central concern of HRM is to get the right person in the right job. This is particularly important if an organisation has established autonomous work group systems as some government departments have. The more autonomy, and therefore power, employees have, the more important it is to have hired the right ones. In recognition of this, and as a consequence of their EEO programmes, departments have formalised their recruitment and selection procedures. Clear job descriptions and person specifications are standard. Departments make more use of external recruitment agencies than in the past, particularly for management positions. Departments presumably do this because they feel they lack the expertise themselves despite the high cost (30 per cent to 40 per cent of the recruit's salary (Dakin and Smith, 1995, p. 119)). More worryingly, Dakin and Smith report research evidence from both New Zealand and the United States showing that recruitment consultants have little faith in cognitive tests as a selection method and considerable faith in personality tests despite the strong research consensus in the reverse direction (1995, pp. 136–7). This raises the question of whether departments get value for money from recruitment consultants.

Once staff are employed, the next stage is to assign them tasks and set them to work. Most departments have made major changes to their grading and classification structure. One approach has been to reduce substantially the number of occupational classes and to collapse a number of grades into one with a long salary range. One indirect and unintended consequence has been reduced opportunities for incremental progression, and this has negatively affected staff perception of career structure and possible career development. The wider issue of setting employees to work raises fundamental questions about the labour process itself, the organisation of work, and the nature of hierarchy and authority in the workplace. The desire to make the best use of the skills and knowledge of employees is central to HRM. This means that employees must have a structured involvement in the decisions that affect the work they do. The Harvard model of HRM identifies employee influence as its most important operational requirement (Beer et al., 1984). A longstanding formal opportunity for employee influence in most government departments is the consultative provisions in collective employment contracts in which CEs agree to consult the PSA over any proposals for organisational change. This often involves the formation of joint working parties on a range of issues, most commonly job evaluation, ranges of rates and performance appraisal. Opportunities for employee influence are bound up in wider efforts to transform organisational culture in the public sector. There is no doubt that many departments have tried to establish a participatory culture. Departments also use a range of other communication mechanisms, such as attitude surveys, to solicit employee opinions. Whether these translate in practice into effective employee influence is unclear. Commitments in principle to the rhetoric of employee influence run up against the limits established by the strategic dominance of utilitarian instrumentalism.

These considerations lead into the contemporary debate about workplace reform (Ryan, 1995) or, as it tends to be called outside Australia and New Zealand, total quality management (TQM).[4] Johnson describes TQM as 'based on the tenet that given the opportunity to participate in planning their work and given appropriate training and management support, employees will be motivated to produce quality products and services' (1995, p. 268). This of course raises a series of fundamental questions: what opportunities will employees be given to participate in planning their work; will a team-based system be introduced where appropriate; if so, how will teams be chosen and their leaders selected and changed; how much authority will teams exercise over which issues; will management genuinely cede power to workers or is it a game of deception to lure workers into cooperation on management's terms; what training and support is offered to further develop the skills of employees; and do these production systems in fact lead to improved quality? There is no doubt that the language of TQM has become very prominent in the public sector since the late 1980s, and a number of departments have introduced teamworking, but the extent to which production systems that meet the standards of TQM are in place is not known.

TQM and other similar approaches to organisational design imply a strong commitment to employee development. If organisations value the contribution employees can make, they will want them to further develop their skills and expertise. The concepts of the learning organisation and continuous improvement reflect commitment to education and training and to the general development of staff. Elkin and Inkson (1995) observe that many large government departments have adopted competency-based learning models that involve the setting of educational objectives and the measurement of outcomes: 'The measure of learning completion becomes not elapsed time or material covered but the achievement of an outcome. These approaches are likely to grow in popularity and are supportive of the move towards individual-centred learning' (Elkin and Inkson, 1995, p. 169). Data to assess whether public sector organisations have increased or decreased their commitment to education and training are not readily available. Elkin and Inkson conclude (1995, p. 161) that private sector investment in human resource development has decreased, and it seems doubtful that the public sector would have done any better in a time of great budget stringency.

Competitive and budgetary pressures have made the effective management of performance a vital issue for all organisations. Storey and Sisson observe that 'arguably the whole point about the concept of performance management is that it promises or offers a way to link the micro activities of managing individuals and groups to the macro issue of corporate objectives' (1993, p. 132). They identify the key elements of a performance management system as:

1. The setting of clear objectives for individual employees (these objectives are derived from the organization's strategy and a series of departmental purpose analyses (DPAs)).
2. Formal monitoring and review of progress towards meeting objectives.
3. Utilisation of the outcomes of the review process to reinforce desired behaviour through differential rewards and/or to identify training and development needs (1993, p. 132).

---

4. Some commentators would wish to draw a distinction between workplace reform and TQM, and for a specialist analysis of workplace organisation distinction that would be important.

All or nearly all government departments would meet these standards. Most departments have made major changes to their performance management systems since 1988. They have been driven by the need to achieve corporate objectives, to improve staff performance and to develop staff. The focus on efficiency—achieving the same or better result for less input—means that improving staff performance and developing the future performance capacity of staff are both important. Corporate HR divisions provide the tools for line managers to carry out performance management, but line managers are responsible for its implementation. As noted earlier, there is a major effort made to ensure coherence among individual, branch, or regional and corporate objectives through a top-down/bottom-up planning process. There is lively debate about the degree to which departments succeed in this aim. Ideally, job descriptions for each position personalise corporate objectives. Individual targets are combined with that and staff are rated on the achievement of both sets of objectives. Despite the emphasis on teamwork in many departments, few departments have yet developed a working system of group performance appraisal or rewards, although a number of departments are starting to examine this issue. In DSW, two of the business unit collective contracts contain provision for reward to be on the basis of team performance. The performance appraisal outcome may make staff eligible for pay increases, incremental progression, accelerated increases or bonuses. The outcome of the performance appraisal process is one of the inputs in the pay setting process for individual employees.

The use of performance pay is more controversial. It has been a major source of industrial dispute in the education sector. Despite the unresolved debate in the research literature about its impact, public sector managers in New Zealand, as elsewhere, show considerable faith in performance pay. Kessler (1993) has identified two different logics used by managers to introduce performance pay. One is a contingency approach in which management chooses a system appropriate to the circumstances facing that organisation and for reasons that will further the organisation's objectives. The second logic is a political or ideological one, in which management intends to 'send a message' to the workforce. It is as much a tool of cultural change as it is directly an instrument to achieve organisational goals. One common example of performance-based pay in government departments has been bonuses or 'at risk components' for managers. Laking (1995, p. 12) observes that departments are typically reluctant to reveal much about their reward structures as they see them as a source of competitive advantage but notes that about half of departments have bonuses for managers and other staff. But the most important element of an organisation's reward structure is not the performance-based pay component of total remuneration; it is the basic pay structure. Employees judge their worth in terms of their pay in relation to others. As Brown (1989, pp. 252–3) puts it: 'The most ingenious of bonus systems and the best of supervision are of little use if the underlying pay structure is felt to be unfair. Consequently, the prudent personnel manager devotes far less time to devising new pay incentives than to tending old notions of fairness.' Despite the removal of the legislative obligation to maintain relativity with the private sector, this remains a continuing issue of practical importance for CEs. If the public sector gets too far out of line with the 'going rate' in the private sector, it will be unable to recruit and retain able staff. It is often conceded that the public sector will never be able wholly to match the private sector, especially at senior management, and that career public servants accept a 'salary discount' for the distinctive character of senior public sector employment. Laking (1995, p. 10) estimates this discount presently at about 25 per cent.

Pay structures and remuneration systems have changed in all departments. Pay scales were replaced by ranges of pay rates soon after the State Sector Act was passed in 1988. They were presented as a move towards performance-based pay, although it was always intended that other factors such as service, qualifications and market scarcity would also affect placement within the range. Six years on, many are critical of aspects of the role of ranges of pay rates. The computer payroll systems required the informal insertion of pay levels, which became *de facto* steps; the possibility of regression was ruled out by a clause in collective agreements prohibiting it; although many positions seemed to offer a long salary range to the holder, in practice many employees were unable to progress beyond a certain point; and, despite the ostensible link with performance appraisal, the system soon seemed in some departments to generate annual progression just as its predecessor had done. Where it did not, perhaps because of budget constraints, it became a target for staff dissatisfaction. This has given some urgency to the development of new remuneration systems and new systems of performance management. The length of the salary ranges is an important source of flexibility for line managers. It allows them to make their own decisions about the mix of staff and pay levels provided they stay within budgets. The length of the pay ranges also takes away much of the pressure for occupational reclassification. Where prior to 1988 most positions were located in bands of $3,000–$4,000, now most are in a range three or four times that in length. Provided no glass ceilings apply, and in many cases they do, staff do not need such frequent reclassification in order to continue to progress in pay.

A major emerging issue for HRM in the public sector is the management of a workforce much less firmly connected to their organisation than in the past. For much of this century there was an orthodox career in the public sector. Public servants served for forty years or close to it. They were bound to their career by the opportunities for promotion made available to them through the internal public service labour market, by the superannuation system, which was not portable and which heavily penalised early withdrawal, and, for those who rose to senior positions, by the intrinsic satisfaction gained by working at senior levels of the public policy-making process. Long stable careers were not unique to the public sector. There were parallels in the careers of those in large private sector organisations. Elkin and Inkson (1995, p. 171) observe that the viability of this kind of career pattern has been brought into question since the 1970s by developments such as the globalisation of business, increased competition, technological change and organisational restructuring. A study of managerial careers in New Zealand by Cawsey and Inkson (1992) showed that between 1980 and 1991 the proportion of management job changes that were either upward or within an organisation declined compared with those that were downward, lateral, or from one organisation to another. One of the expressed purposes of the public sector reforms in New Zealand was to encourage greater movement between the public and private sectors. The traditional public sector career would be replaced with one in which tenure in public sector jobs is shorter and in which employees' immediate career aspirations might be outside the public sector. The result would tend to be a workforce in which people identified themselves as public employees less firmly than in the past. Another key factor reducing employees' connection and therefore commitment to the public sector is the growth of the contingent workforce. This might lead to a public sector workforce in which the traditional standard worker, the permanent full-time employee, is much less dominant. The growth of fixed-term contract employment in the public sector reflects this, as does the public sector's greater use than the private sector of consultants and of forms of non-standard employment such as part-time and casual employment (Anderson, Brosnan, and Walsh, 1996). Rasmussen, Deeks, and Street have developed the notion of the 'entrepreneurial worker', a person who manages their own career and is 'speculatively alert to the opportunities for his or her human capital' (1995, p. 4). The entrepreneurial worker acquires a wide range of skills and makes use of them in a variety and succession of employment settings. Although this is only an emergent trend applying to a limited group, there is no doubt that an increasing number of 'entrepreneurs' have built exactly such a career in the public sector since the mid 1980s. Elkin and Inkson liken these changes from the traditional notion of career to a shift from a cruise on an ocean liner to whitewater rafting (1995, p. 172). These changes in the nature of the connection between employees and their organisation and the shift to a contingent workforce point to the development of segmented labour market in the public sector and raise a host of problems associated with managing that kind of workforce. Ironically, just as modern HRM theory calls for mutual commitment, HRM practice sees the loss of the notion of a lifetime career and the growth of the contingent workforce and the entrepreneurial worker.

CONCLUSION

Since 1988 government departments have been trying to develop and implement a wide range of HRM initiatives. There can be no doubt that much progress has been made. The experience of the employment relationship in the public sector is quite different from what it was before 1988. It is much less rule-governed and much more subject to discretion and flexibility. Responsibility for HRM has been decentralised to departments and devolved to line managers. There is no support from either union or management for a return to the pre-1988 system. All believe that decentralisation has been vital to the achievement of a range of HRM reforms. In a general sense, these refer to the new-found capacity of departments to own their HRM policies and practices and thus to develop those appropriate to their own circumstances. Differences of opinion are mostly about the appropriate degree of devolution within departments and the ability of line managers to carry out their new responsibilities. There are considerable reservations about the extent to which departments have provided sufficient training for line managers in this radically new role for them. It is employees who deal with the negative consequences of devolution. The key issue is the combination of line management incompetence (where it occurs) with the degree of discretion and flexibility line managers enjoy under the new HR regime. Incompetence operating without prescription is a potent brew and understandably it makes employees apprehensive. In some cases, they literally do not know what will happen in particular circumstances. Many senior managers believe that the broad policies they have established should deal with this problem. But in a devolved system this will only work if there is effective monitoring of day-to-day HRM practices, and it is evident that this is not always achieved, especially in large departments. Size and complexity were of course the principal original reasons for bureaucratisation—that is, the laying down of universal and prescriptive rules and the limiting of discretion. There will continue to be a lively debate about the appropriate degree of decentralisation and the relationship between corporate HRM divisions and line managers. It is probable that the balance of opinion will swing back and forth at different times. It is also clear that the active centre of that debate has shifted substantially since 1988.

However, notwithstanding substantial changes at an operational level, there is still a consensus that strategic HRM and the integration of HRM with corporate strategy has been achieved only to a limited degree. Guest's comments on the failure to achieve strategic integration in the UK public sector reads like a template for New Zealand: 'Short-term changes have been piled one on top of the other, usually without a sufficiently coherent strategy and usually without allowing time fully to implement each initiative. This is a recipe for employee scepticism and uncertainty' (Guest, 1992, p. 13). However, achieving strategic integration might not simply be a matter of more time and calmer waters. It must be clearly shown that HRM does contribute to competitive advantage. The latter is sometimes taken for granted by HRM's academic and professional advocates, but this view is not always shared by senior management (Guest, 1992). One difficulty might lie with the models of organisational design and of HRM itself that tend to predominate in the New Zealand public sector. Earlier, Wright and McMahan's (1992) assessment was cited to indicate the theoretical weakness of the strategic HRM area. But Wright and McMahan go on to point to emerging developments that might provide the necessary theoretical foundation for strategic HRM (1992, p. 300). One of them is the resource capability school of strategic management. It directs attention to the internal resources already held by an organisation. Barney observes that 'the resource-based model suggests that sources of sustained competitive advantage are firm resources that are valuable, rare, imperfectly imitable and non-substitutable' (Barney, 1991, p. 116). Many commentators have suggested that human resources—employees—might fit these criteria rather well. In one study, CEs identified 'employee know-how' as a key resource that could contribute to competitive advantage (Hall, 1992). The CEs judged the most important form of employee know-how to be the firm-specific operational skills ('how we do things around here') that employees acquire over time. In trying to identify the organisational structure in which employee know-how could have this impact, Purcell argued that decentralised, multi-divisional structures, similar to those implemented in a number of government departments in New Zealand, limit the potential impact of employee know-how:

Organizational learning of unique attributes which make up the synergies, resources and capabilities comes to be valued across the firm, as in Porter's horizontal strategies. ... Instead of isolating each component unit of the firm in order to find its precise contribution to profits and growth (or loss and decline), horizontal strategies emphasise intangibles, learning and skill transfer and the reduction in transaction costs (Purcell, 1995, pp. 83–4).

The implication of this is that the decentralised organisational structure favoured in the New Zealand public sector, whether formally a business unit structure or not, might not be the best means of making strategic use of the human resource potential of the organisation.

Meanwhile, despite the scope of the public sector revolution, some things do not change in employment relations. The traditional public sector ethos continues to exert its influence over HRM policies and practices. Most CEs of government departments are career public servants and see themselves as keepers of the public purse. This constrains what they are prepared to do. They also remain aware that their employment policies might become subject to closer public scrutiny than would likely be applied to a private sector firm and that they must not needlessly expose their minister to political risk by unacceptable or controversial employment practices. But notwithstanding their caution, the amount of change has been enormous. It is evident that so far managers by and large assess these changes to HRM more positively than do employees. This is understandable given the managerialist thrust of recent reforms and the disturbances experienced by employees, seemingly without relief since the late 1980s. The future assessment of their employment experience by employees and, associated with that, the efficiency, productivity and integrity of the public sector will depend to a significant degree on the operation of the new regime of human resource management.

11 negotiating the employment contract

All governments encounter strong incentives to intervene in the negotiation of employment conditions in the public sector. The size of the state wage bill, the potential influence of public sector employment conditions on those in the private sector, and the consequences they might have for fiscal and other policy objectives all combine to give governments a continuing interest in this area. The essential and highly visible nature of many public services means that public sector employment relations can acquire a high public profile and industrial disputes in particular can have some electoral implications. On the other hand, governments possess powers enjoyed by no other employer. They have the capacity to change employment conditions or the rules by which the employment relationship is conducted without the consent of their employees or without negotiating those changes. Throughout the democratic world, governments accept the need to balance these roles as employer and legislator and to limit their direct or coercive intervention in the employment relationship. But governments still rightly maintain a continuing oversight of employment relations, particularly the negotiation of employment conditions, and preserve the possibility of intervention where they might need to protect their legitimate interests. The tension between these two potentially conflicting positions has been an important factor in the development of state sector employment relations in New Zealand as elsewhere.

As the discussion in Chapter 10 showed, New Zealand governments resolved this issue between 1948 and 1988 by adopting a pay-fixing system based on fair relativity with the private sector. However, over time both Labour and National governments became increasingly dissatisfied with this system. Chapter 10 reviewed a number of the reasons for this. At a general level, however, the most important reason for government unhappiness was their inability to exercise sufficient influence over the determination of employment conditions in the public sector. When the first Labour government reluctantly accepted the fair relativity system in 1948, it reassured itself with the knowledge that it would be importing the outcomes of the private sector arbitration system into the public sector. The pay levels that public employees would be seeking to emulate were not the product of an unregulated process but of a legislatively governed state arbitration system. Over the next forty years, the regulatory capacity of the private sector arbitration system progressively declined. The pay levels imported into the public sector by the fair relativity transmission mechanism were set by a far less regulated process than that which had applied in the 1940s. Moreover, the industrial context of the public sector altered greatly. Union membership levels grew in the public sector and with it came a rise in industrial militancy. Groups such as teachers and nurses and other professionals began to take a much more active and vigorous industrial posture. Governments found little that pleased them in a system where increasingly confident and effective unions pulled both industrial and political levers in pursuit of pay levels set in an unregulated private sector. Unions also made use of the system to secure non-remuneration conditions that in some cases, such as parental leave, the right to return to work after child care, and various other leave entitlements, were substantially superior to those in the private sector.

The Labour government, elected in 1984, found its inability to control events in public sector industrial relations particularly irksome. Labour was firmly set on a policy of fiscal restraint and yet at almost every turn it seemed it was beset by groups of public sector employees clamouring for pay rises. That much of this clamour was the legacy of the National government's pay freeze of 1982–84 was little consolation to Labour. From its early days in office, Labour faced claims by groups such as junior doctors, air crash fire crew, nurses, secondary teachers, police, and many others. All ended unhappily for the government with substantial pay increases being awarded by compulsory arbitration. On top of this came a very large 1985 HSC determination for senior state employees and large consequential adjustments that had to be made down through the public sector to preserve vertical pay relativities. It was clear that the key to this inability to control the state pay bill lay in the continued availability of compulsory arbitration (abolished in the private sector in 1984) and the legislative pay-fixing criteria that governed the arbitration tribunals' decisions. So long as these remained unchanged, a government bent on fiscal restraint would constantly find its policy being undone by arbitrated pay settlements over which it had no control.

The State Sector Act was designed to restore to governments some measure of control over pay-fixing in the public sector. Ironically, unlike the deregulatory policies pursued by Labour in other spheres, its public sector labour market legislation aimed to replace one form of regulation that it considered it had failed with another more to its liking. The repeal of the fair relativity provisions, including the statutory pay-fixing criteria, and the abolition of compulsory arbitration were the keys to the restoration of control over pay-fixing. They made possible the policies followed since 1988.

This chapter focuses on the negotiation of employment conditions in the public sector since 1988. The chapter will discuss this in two stages, first the period 1988–91 and second the period since the passage of the Employment Contracts Act in 1991.[1] The most important changes to industrial relations in the public sector took place in the first period but the Employment Contracts Act has also led to a number of significant developments. To facilitate a comparison of the two periods, each will be discussed in terms

---

1. There is a much fuller account of the negotiation of employment conditions in the period 1988–91 in Boston, Martin, Pallot, and Walsh (1991), ch. 5.

of four major headings: the bargaining parties, bargaining structure, bargaining process, and bargaining outcomes.

BARGAINING UNDER THE STATE SECTOR ACT (1988–91)

Representation: The Bargaining Parties

The State Sector Act changed the faces on the employer side of the bargaining table. The Act provided that the SSC would be the employer party for the purposes of employment negotiations throughout the state sector. This represented a substantial strengthening of the role of the SSC and reflected the government's determination to control public sector pay. In the public service, the SSC succeeded the State Services Coordinating Committee, a body comprising the permanent heads of all state sector employing authorities and the Secretary to the Treasury (Randle, 1985). In the health sector, the SSC took the place of the Health Services Personnel Commission, which had had responsibility for health sector negotiations. In education, it replaced the Education Services Committee, a negotiating body with combined representation from both the SSC and the Department of Education.

The identity of the bargaining parties on the union side did not change as a result of the State Sector Act. Under the Act, state sector unions became for the first time registered trade unions in terms of the union registration provisions of the Labour Relations Act. These, which had applied to private sector unions since 1894, conferred upon a union registered with the Registrar of Unions the exclusive right to represent the category of workers specified in its membership clause. Registration under the Labour Relations Act allowed public sector unions to seek a compulsory union membership clause. Union membership had always been voluntary in the state sector. In 1948, when unions were granted the same right to compulsory arbitration as private sector unions, the Labour government, thinking that compulsory arbitration and compulsory unionism went hand in hand, offered the latter to the state unions. With the exception of the Post Office Union, they had turned it down. Despite this, membership levels remained very high. Public sector unions took the same path after 1988. Again with only one major exception, this time the NZEI, they chose to retain voluntary membership. Another change was not directly related to the State Sector Act: the state sector unions dissolved their own federation, the Combined State Unions, and joined private sector unions in a new central organisation, the New Zealand Council of Trade Unions. This change had its roots in events wider and earlier than those that led to the State Sector Act, but it was appropriate that public sector unions joined private sector unions just as they came under the same legislative structure.

Bargaining Structure

The single most important industrial relations change associated with but not directly caused by the State Sector Act was to the structure of bargaining in the public service. A shift to departmental bargaining had in fact been agreed to by the SSC and the PSA just before the State Sector Act. On the union side, it reflected an awareness that increasingly the issues facing members were specific to departments. This was particularly the case as the first wave of restructuring began in 1986–87. It was an issue on the employer side also, as was the concern for more flexible and decentralised bargaining units. Following the State Sector Act, departments, now separate organisations in every respect, moved from the traditional service-wide determination system to one of individual national departmental collective agreements. (In a small number of cases, where a union other than the PSA had membership coverage, more than one collective agreement was negotiated. One example was the Department of Conservation where the Workers Union represented wage-workers). Notwithstanding the clamour in some circles for the decentralisation of bargaining units within departments on a geographical, divisional, or occupational basis, neither departments nor the SSC showed strong interest during this period in moving away from an enterprise bargaining unit. It was felt that the introduction of ranges of rates in place of salary scales gave managers the flexibility to respond to varying occupational and regional labour market situations. In the health and education sectors, the bargaining structure between 1988 and 1991 continued to be based chiefly around national occupational negotiations, and for the first time national awards were negotiated for most of the major occupational groups in those two sectors.

The most controversial issue with regard to bargaining structure in this period was the SSC's drive to exclude senior staff in all sectors from collective bargaining coverage and to shift them on to individual employment contracts. In the past, almost all state employees had been covered by collective bargaining, but this was now seen as incompatible with the new managerial ethos that underpinned the State Sector Act. It was argued that senior management, as the employer's representative, should not be involved even indirectly in negotiating an agreement in which they had a personal interest. Moreover, individual contracts were valued in their own right as contributing to the development of a new management culture and as enhancing accountability.

The outcome of this issue varied across sectors. In the health sector, there was very little change to the award coverage of health professionals between 1988 and 1991. In the education sector both the NZEI, the primary teachers' union, and the PPTA, the secondary teachers' union, resisted intensely the SSC's efforts to introduce individual employment contracts into schools (Walsh, 1988a; 1990). The Labour government, frustrated industrially, finally resorted to legislation to place principals in secondary schools on individual contracts and to provide for other senior teachers to be placed there by Order-in-Council (not yet activated). However, in the case of primary school principals, many of whom are full-time teachers rather than managers, a compromise was reached by the agreement to introduce ranges of rates for principals but to keep them under collective bargaining coverage.

In the public service, the PSA agreed to senior managers being placed on individual contracts (CEs and SES members were of course required by the Act to be on individual contracts). Gradually in some departments this was extended down to the third level of management and was widened to include staff with any involvement in the negotiating process. The main response by the PSA to coverage exclusion was to trade it for industrial democracy and union facilities clauses in most departmental agreements. These were negotiated in 1988 and continue to be included in most current collective employment contracts in the public sector. They entail an agreement that the department will consult PSA delegates where practicable, particularly over issues of major organisational change, while the PSA recognises the right of management to make ultimate decisions. Similar provisions were negotiated in the main health sector awards. Although these provisions did not entail any major sacrifice of managerial prerogative, they did involve the acceptance of a union-based participatory structure.

The other significant development in the public sector was the growth of limited-term employment contracts, which was partly a result of the continuous restructuring process that encouraged departments to appoint staff as needed for specific projects on a short-term basis. It was also a consequence of the managerialist emphasis in this period and a desire to imitate what were seen as successful private sector practices. However, it appears that the public sector was in fact more likely to use fixed-term employment contracts than the private sector (Anderson, Brosnan, and Walsh, 1996). Although the incidence of such contracts was never large, they created an impression out of proportion to their frequency and helped foster the notion that traditional concepts of lifetime service and public service loyalty were fast disappearing.

The Bargaining Process

The bargaining objectives of the parties were shaped by the managerialist thrust of the Act and by the government's tight fiscal policies. The SSC aimed explicitly to develop a management culture to reinforce the policy objectives of the Act. They translated into specific bargaining objectives such as the replacement of salary scales with ranges of rates, a shift to individual contracts of employment, and downgrading a wide range of employment conditions. Union bargaining objectives in the face of discouraging institutional, fiscal, and strategic developments were to maintain the living standards of their members, to consolidate existing conditions of employment, and to build more effective union representation.

From 1988 to 1991, the negotiation of employment conditions throughout the state sector remained under tight SSC control (Walsh, 1993b). In health, education, and the public service, collective bargaining was shaped by the key role played by the SSC as employer party. The SSC had no role to play in local government. But at all times the SSC acted as the government's agent. The Labour government established a special Cabinet Sub-Committee on State Wages, which has been continued by the National government, to lay down policy for state sector employment negotiations and to oversee their conduct. The SSC's role as employer party for the negotiation of employment conditions was seen by many as contradicting the decentralising philosophy behind the State Sector Act. But this role was similar to that played by a corporate human resource or industrial relations office in a multi-divisional organisation. It was there to protect the government's general industrial relations policy interests.

The Labour government decided in 1988 to leave the responsibility for negotiating public sector conditions of employment with the SSC because it doubted the ability of individual public sector employers to take this role on successfully immediately following the passage of the State Sector Act. In the public service, departments had very limited industrial relations experience and the government wanted to ensure that inexperienced negotiators did not jeopardise its fiscal stance. Although the SSC was required to consult with departmental CEs and area health board general managers in carrying out this role, effective authority lay with SSC. In the education sector, the accountability mechanisms that might have permitted the newly formed and similarly inexperienced School Trustees Association to negotiate employment conditions were lacking.

In the public service, the degree of directive control exerted by the SSC varied across departments. This variation reflected different assessments by the SSC of the political risk involved in permitting departments a degree of autonomy. The SSC's assessment was based on a number of factors, including the industrial relations expertise within departments, their size and the likelihood of industrial action. In the first few years following the State Sector Act, departmental views of the role played by the SSC reflected these different experiences.[2] The SSC controlled bargaining in the health sector also, but area health board general managers sought to involve themselves in negotiations. General managers had a different perspective from that of the SSC, and their at times conflicting interests gave rise to some difficulties in their relationship (Walsh and Fougere, 1989). These difficulties were also apparent in the education sector in the relationship between the SSC and the School Trustees Association (Pilgrim, 1992; Walsh, 1990), but the latter was not as substantial nor as successful a player in the industrial relations process as were general managers in health who were the employers of their staff. In the education sector, negotiations were almost completely controlled by the SSC (Rae, 1991).

In the public service, each year the SSC and the PSA would begin negotiations in a number of departments. The negotiations would continue despite deadlock, adjournments, and threats of industrial action until a settlement was reached in one department. That settlement would quickly become the standard for the whole of the public sector and be disseminated throughout all departments. There was some flexibility on particular conditions of employment, which could vary to some degree from one department to another. But overall, the process delivered by a very different route outcomes that differed little from the avowedly centralised and uniform system of the past. In both health and education, national award bargaining meant that each major award had to be negotiated to its conclusion, although in health a common pattern tended to apply in all settlements.

Bargaining Outcomes

The Labour government and its National successor were determined to send to CEs, to senior managers and to all employees the message that their tight fiscal stance set severe limits to pay increases and that annual budgets, as originally set, could no longer be increased to finance unwisely negotiated wage rises. The elimination of compulsory

---

2. Different departmental assessments of the role played by the SSC in this period are offered in Boston, Martin, Pallot, and Walsh (1991), ch. 5.

arbitration made such a policy feasible for the first time since it could no longer be undermined by an arbitrated settlement. This policy was remarkably successful. Pay outcomes in public sector collective bargaining were below those achieved in the private sector in this period. It was striking, however, that this was not the case at senior levels where salaries moved ahead very quickly and substantially. The private nature of individual employment contracts means precise information is not available on this issue. But anecdotal evidence combined with the published salary bands for CEs make it clear that senior salaries did increase considerably. Traditional vertical relativities were swept away. Interestingly, on the surface at least, this did not appear to create great resentment.

One unusual feature of the negotiations in the first two years following the State Sector Act was the SSC's attempt to 'claw back' a range of employment conditions gained by unions over the years. This attempt reflected the managerialist emphasis of the new regime. It also reflected the dominance of the hard or utilitarian instrumentalist model of HRM during this period. A similar managerialist emphasis marked employment negotiations in the SOEs established in 1987 (Walsh, 1988b; Walsh and Wetzel, 1993). In the past, negotiations had been conducted on the basis of existing conditions as a starting point from which advances would be made by unions and employees. The drive to reverse past gains was a new development. They were largely unsuccessful in terms of achieving changes to employment conditions but they did send signals about changes in the industrial climate and organisational cultures. Their value can be questioned from the perspective of developing constructive relations with employees and unions, but in circumstances of great change this objective might need to be traded off against other objectives. They can also be questioned on strategic grounds, as they appeared to mobilise employees and unions in ways that were counter-productive for management.

THE EMPLOYMENT CONTRACTS ACT 1991

Since 1991, industrial relations in the state sector have been governed by the provisions of the Employment Contracts Act. The Act was enacted by the National government shortly after its victory in the 1990 election. Labour market regulation had been a controversial issue for most of the preceding decade. Despite its deregulatory zeal in many policy areas, Labour had retained much of the traditional arbitration system in its major industrial legislation, the Labour Relations Act 1987 (Walsh, 1989). This Act preserved the bargaining monopoly that unions had enjoyed historically, permitted the inclusion of compulsory union membership clauses in awards and agreements, and provided for awards to apply to all employers in an occupation or industry regardless of whether they had been involved in its negotiation. The effect of these arrangements was to ensure a highly unionised workforce and a high level of multi-employer collective bargaining coverage. Strong criticisms of this outcome led National to commit itself to radical labour market reform in the 1990 election campaign, and this commitment was honoured in the Employment Contracts Act.

It is not intended to set out the key provisions of the Employment Contracts Act in great detail, as they are well described elsewhere (Anderson, 1991; Hince and Vranken,

1991; Walsh, 1992; Brook-Cowen, 1993; Walsh and Ryan, 1993; Deeks, Parker and Ryan, 1994). In contrast to previous industrial legislation, which applied only to workers covered by a registered award or agreement, the Employment Contracts Act applies to all employment contracts, whether of a chief executive or a part-time relieving receptionist. All matters relating to a contract of employment come within the jurisdiction of the Employment Tribunal or the Employment Court. The Tribunal was established as a low-level informal specialist tribunal providing mediation and adjudication services to ensure a speedy and fair resolution of differences between the parties to employment contracts. The Court was established to provide a specialist court to oversee the role of the Tribunal and to deal with particular legal issues. The members of the Employment Court are appointed and enjoy tenure on the same terms as High Court judges. The Act made major changes to the provisions governing trade union membership, representation, and the negotiation of employment conditions. With regard to union membership, the Act prohibits the negotiation of any compulsory union membership clause. It also provides that employees should not experience any advantage or disadvantage in their employment as a result of union membership or non-membership. The Act separates union membership from representation. Employees are free to decide who, if anyone, will negotiate on their behalf, and unions must seek individual bargaining authorisation from their members. Employers can veto who may have access to the workplace to seek representation authority but once this authority has been given, the authorised representative may have access at any reasonable time to discuss contract negotiations. The Act establishes two types of employment contracts—individual and collective. Employment contracts may be varied at any time but only by the mutual agreement of the parties. An individual contract may be negotiated where there is no applicable collective contract or where its provisions are not inconsistent with the applicable collective contract. The Act encourages enterprise collective bargaining over multi-employer bargaining. The Act prohibits any industrial action to force an employer to become a joint party to a collective contract. When a collective contract expires, employees previously covered by it are deemed to be employed on an individual contract with the same conditions as the expired collective contract. All employment contracts must contain effective procedures to settle personal grievances and disputes and, in the absence of such procedures, the procedures in the Act apply (Anderson, 1988; Hughes, 1993). The Act permits strikes and lockouts but only in support of the negotiation of a new or an expired collective contract. Any form of industrial action while a collective contract is in force is unlawful, and no industrial action may be taken in connection with an individual employment contract or, as noted above, in pursuit of a multi-employer contract.

The Act's long title is 'an Act to promote an efficient labour market'. Opponents of the Act argued that its promotion of efficiency would be at the expense of equity considerations. The National government responded to these concerns by providing a 'minimum code of employment'—a range of minimum employment conditions enjoyed by all employees delivered through other legislation (Brosnan and Rea, 1991). It is not possible for any employment contract to provide conditions inferior to these, although it is of course possible to improve on them: the Minimum Wage Act 1983 establishes a statutory minimum wage for all workers aged 20 or over and sets minimum wages for workers aged 18 or 19, calculated as a proportion of the adult rate; the Wages Protection Act 1983 prohibits employers from making unauthorised deductions from workers' wages; the Holidays Act 1981 establishes an entitlement to three weeks' annual leave, eleven public holidays and five days' domestic leave for all employees; the Parental Leave and Employment Protection Act 1987 provides that any worker employed by the same employer for a minimum of ten hours per week over the previous year may take unpaid leave at the time of their child's birth. A mother may take fourteen weeks' and a father two weeks' leave, while extended leave of up to fifty-two weeks' unpaid leave may be taken by either parent or in combination by both of them; the Human Rights Act 1993 prohibits discrimination in any matter relating to employment on grounds of a person's sex, marital status, religious or ethical belief, colour, race, ethnic or national origin, disability, age, political opinion, employment status, family status, or sexual orientation; the Equal Pay Act 1972 prohibits any employer from discriminating in any term of employment between workers doing substantially similar work on grounds of their sex; the Health and Safety in Employment Act 1992 requires employers to establish systems to ensure that their workplace is safe for employees, customers, or any legitimate visitor to the workplace; and the Accident Rehabilitation and Compensation Insurance Act 1992 provides that any worker who suffers loss of earnings through a work injury is entitled to compensation at 80 per cent of their normal earnings. These statutory provisions limit the contracting freedom of the parties to employment contracts.

BARGAINING UNDER THE EMPLOYMENT CONTRACTS ACT

This section reviews developments under the Employment Contracts Act in terms of the same headings used earlier in the discussion of the State Sector Act. There is no attempt to provide a detailed analysis of the decisions made by the Employment Tribunal and Employment Court interpreting the Employment Contracts Act. For that it is necessary to consult one of the major employment law commentaries (e.g. Mazengarb, 1995).

Representation: The Bargaining Parties

On the employer side, the bargaining parties have changed in the public service and in the health sector but not directly as a consequence of the Employment Contracts Act. In the public service, the SSC decided to delegate negotiating authority in 1992 to CEs of government departments and other public agencies. The reasons for this decision are discussed further below. The restructuring of the health sector led to the replacement of area health boards by Regional Health Authorities (RHAs) and Crown Health Enterprises (CHEs) in 1993, and in the new structure they assumed responsibility for all aspects of their employment relationships. The identity of the employer bargaining parties has not changed in the education sector.

The Employment Contracts Act broke the automatic link between trade union membership and representation and created the potential for state sector unions to be challenged as the dominant bargaining parties in the state sector. This has not happened. In the health and education sectors, the traditional unions have retained their role as exclusive bargaining agents. An effort was made to establish the Secondary Principals Association of New Zealand as a rival organisation to the PPTA, but the two organisations coexist amicably and the PPTA's bargaining role has not been jeopardised. The PSA, a large and diverse organisation, appeared potentially vulnerable to the progressive defection of dissatisfied groups, wooed away by other unions, rival bargaining agents, or by groups of members taking the initiative to defect on their own account. This has not happened to any great degree. The major organised defections have been by customs officers in Auckland, health sector workers in the South Island, staff in the Accident Rehabilitation and Compensation Insurance Corporation, Inland Revenue, and Income Support Services and, most significantly, the formation of the Penal Officers Association by prison officers. Most of these groups have negotiated their own collective contracts, in some cases with the support, covert or otherwise, of senior managers, but their combined coverage and significance is not yet substantial. There have been no other major defections from their union by groups in the state sector. Non-union bargaining agents have not made a significant impact in the state sector.

The corollary is that the membership levels of state sector unions have not fallen greatly in the wake of the Employment Contracts Act. The most important reasons for this include the long tradition of voluntary membership, the small number of employers (and even smaller number of negotiating parties), the large size (by New Zealand standards) of a high proportion of state sector workplaces, and the joint emphasis by unions on professional and employment issues. It might also reflect assessments by state employees of the need for continuing industrial representation in the difficult circumstances that have prevailed throughout this period. The small decline in union membership in the public sector in New Zealand accords well with international experience.

However, it runs counter to the private sector experience in New Zealand. Overall trade union membership in New Zealand fell, according to one estimate, by 27 per cent between December 1991 and December 1994 (Harbridge, Hince and Honeybone, 1995). But in the public service sector, union membership fell by only 13 per cent. In the education sector, the NZEI and the PPTA continue to represent almost all teachers, while coverage in the tertiary sector is also very high. A similar picture applies to professionals in the health sector, although union coverage in the large ancillary sector has declined. The PSA's membership continues to be over 67,000, a figure it has been close to for more than a decade. This figure conceals short-term rises and falls as a result of restructuring, union amalgamations, and changing patterns of representation. The amalgamation with the Northern and Central Local Government unions in 1993 brought about 17,000 members to the PSA. On the other hand, as the figures in Chapter 3 show, the number of employees in central government fell by about 30,000 since the mid 1980s, although some of them employed in SOEs are still PSA members. It does point, however, to the PSA's organisational continuity in a decade of great turbulence, involving major restructuring and massive job losses in its core sector, allied to unfavourable legislative changes and a growing climate of scepticism towards the value of trade unions.

Bargaining Structure

The Employment Contracts Act enhanced the possibility for the national bargaining established under the State Sector Act to be broken into a series of collective contracts, perhaps supported by a major extension of individual contracts. This has not happened even though individuals are now able to choose to be employed on individual employment contracts. Throughout the state sector, there are a handful of individual employees below managerial level who have exercised this option, often to the annoyance of senior management. Their employment conditions do not vary from those of the collective contract. This has happened more in the public service than in health and education.

Table 11.1 Employment contract coverage (percentage of employees) in the public sector (excludes local government)

	Awards/ agreements under Labour Relations Act	Collective employment contracts	Expired awards/ agreements under Labour Relations Act	Expired collective employment contracts	Negotiated individual contracts
1992	79	10	–	–	10
1993	–	51	24	12	12

Source: Statistics New Zealand (1995)

Table 11.1 shows that in February 1993, 12 per cent of employees in the central government sector (which includes all the state sector except local government) were employed on individual employment contracts that had actually been negotiated under the Employment Contracts Act. A large number (36 per cent) were also employed on *de facto* individual contracts as a result of their collective contracts (or awards from the Labour Relations Act) having expired and having not yet been renegotiated. But the key consideration is that for those employees, their employment conditions were determined by collective rather than individual bargaining, and it could be presumed that a high proportion of their expired collective contracts would eventually be renegotiated. Unfortunately, at the time of writing these figures had not been updated by Statistics New Zealand. Rob Laking, the CE of the Ministry of Housing, claims (but does not give supporting documentation) that by December 1994 only 16 per cent of public servants were employed on negotiated individual contracts; that is, on contracts that did not derive from expired collective contracts (Laking, 1995, p. 8). Most of them are for managers and typically are not fixed-term contracts. They are likely to differ from the collective contract by the inclusion of a range of non-salary rewards. Laking (1995, p. 12) comments that 'the original standard contract drafted by the State Services Commission in 1988 was designed to encourage the use of non-monetary rewards (and reduce publicly reported salaries) by providing a favourable rate of conversion from salary to other forms of reward'.

In the public service and in Crown entities, the pre-Employment Contracts Act bargaining structure of a single national collective document for each organisation has been largely retained. The PSA now negotiates more than 300 collective contracts, a sharp contrast to the pre-1988 days when the AGA and a small number of occupational class claims constituted the sum total of collective bargaining in the public service. Many of the PSA's collective contracts cover a small number of employees, stretching its resources even further to negotiate and service these contracts. Indeed, about fifty of the PSA's collective contracts cover fewer than ten members.

The great majority of government departments negotiate a single national collective contract. There are particular reasons for some departments having more than one collective contract. Some examples illustrate this. The Crown Law Office has negotiated one contract for its legal staff and another for its general staff. The Public Trust Office has negotiated one collective contract for its general staff and another for its managers. The Ministry of Foreign Affairs and Trade has negotiated a separate collective contract for its Antarctic Division. The Department of Internal Affairs has negotiated three collective contracts—one for most of its staff, another for VIP drivers and a third for staff working on the *Dictionary of New Zealand Biography*. The Department of Conservation sought a separate collective contract for staff at its seventy-five field centres but encountered strong resistance. A series of nationwide joint union–management problem-solving workshops led to agreement on one collective contract with a common core of conditions supplemented by separate sections for the field centre staff and other employees. The Inland Revenue Department also has three collective contracts, one for most staff, another for its managers not on individual contracts and a third negotiated by its own staff association for non-PSA members, which is identical to the PSA collective but has all references to the PSA removed. The Department of Justice has a similar 'unrepresented' collective contract, which it offers to any of its employees who do not have a bargaining agent.

There are only two major examples of bargaining decentralisation in the public service. Since 1994, the Department of Social Welfare has negotiated six collective contracts, one for each of its four business units, one for its information technology unit, and one for a corporate office collective. The department sought business unit collective contracts to reflect the autonomous operating structure of each business unit. DSW had been seeking business unit collective contracts for some time but the employees had successfully resisted it. Until 1994, the department had only managed to convince its employees to agree to a series of business unit 'add-ons' to the departmental collective contract. These 'add-ons' offered the opportunity to include conditions specific to the circumstances of each business unit. So far, however, no other department with a business unit organisational structure has adopted a business unit contract structure. They have seemingly considered it more important to retain a single departmental identity. Some may be considering a change. The other major example of the proliferation of collective contracts is in the Department of Corrections, one of the departments created in 1995 out of the Department of Justice. Prior to the new department being established, Justice had negotiated a separate collective contract for the corrections division. Now that contract is in the process of being divided into possibly as many as seven collective contracts. Some of this is due to the growing importance of the Penal Officers Association, which has secured the loyalty of about half the prison officers.

In the health sector, the combined impact of the Employment Contracts Act and the new health structure has seen bargaining decentralised from the national level to each CHE (Oxenbridge, 1994; Powell, 1995). The CHEs negotiate separate collective contracts with the unions that represent each of the major occupational groups in its employment—nurses, ancillary staff, senior doctors (specialists), junior doctors (residents), clerical staff, and a range of other smaller occupations. As noted above, union membership is very high among all these groups, and although some CHEs might aspire to discard collective bargaining, it has not been a feasible option. There are very few individual contracts.

In the education sector, national bargaining continues in schools. The NZEI has negotiated two collective contracts in the primary sector, one for basic scale teachers and another for senior teachers. For some time NZEI continued to reject the SSC's financial inducements to move primary school principals on to individual contracts. In 1995, however, NZEI accepted individual contracts for about 700 senior principals (about 25 per cent of the total) as part of the settlement to their long-running pay dispute. Other key features of the settlement were the acceptance of performance appraisal and substantial pay increases, particularly for principals and assistant and deputy principals. The most important provision in the settlement was the agreement to establish pay parity between primary and secondary teachers. At the time of writing, a working party chaired personally by the Minister of Education, Dr Lockwood Smith, was investigating the development of a unified pay scale. The chief source of resistance to pay parity appeared to be the PPTA rather than the government. The PPTA retains one collective contract that covers all teachers except principals, who, as noted earlier, are employed on individual contracts by legislation. With the exception of principals, there are virtually no individual employment contracts among primary or secondary teachers in state schools. Non-teaching staff are employed on collective contracts. In the tertiary sector, bargaining takes place at the institutional level, and a mix of individual and collective contracts apply. In the pre-school sector, kindergartens retain a national collective contract (excepting Auckland, which is to negotiate a separate collective) while child-care centres combine two major multi-employer collectives with site-based collectives and individual contracts.

The Bargaining Process

The bargaining process has changed substantially since 1991. The role of the SSC is now different in each sector. In the health sector, it retains the right to be consulted but it does not participate to any degree. However, the SSC and the CCMAU take a continuing interest in the process and outcomes of employment negotiations in the CHEs. In the education sector, the SSC continues as employer party in the schools sector but is not significantly involved in the tertiary or pre-school sector. The picture is more complex in the public service. During the period 1988–91, resentment grew at the degree of control exercised by the SSC over the negotiation of employment conditions. It was argued that this was at odds with the philosophy behind the State Sector Act and particularly with the role of CEs as employers held to account for their performance in this area. How could this be so if a major part of the employment relationship remained outside their control? Human resource managers became increasingly frustrated at their own lack of control over negotiating the employment conditions of their own staff. Moreover, it was also suggested that it was at odds with the philosophy of the Employment Contracts Act and its emphasis upon the importance of managers constructing and taking responsibility for their employment relations.

In 1991, the SSC decided to delegate negotiating authority to CEs for the negotiations in 1992. CEs were to be required to exercise that authority in consultation with the SSC, a complete reversal of the situation that had applied since 1988. The negotiating authority of CEs was a delegated one and could be withdrawn by the SSC. The SSC remained the agent of government that continued to take as close an interest as before in public sector employment conditions. In its letter of delegation to CEs, the SSC laid down the government's constraints on their negotiating freedom: bargaining outcomes had to be 'fiscally neutral' (that is, not cost any more), achieve reductions in potential redundancy liabilities, achieve savings in other areas where it was possible, and ensure there was no flow-on effect to other departments from any provisions in their collective contract. Although negotiating authority was delegated to departments, the SSC still played a watchdog role in the negotiating process itself. Departments had to get clearance before the negotiations were completed, and the SSC retained a representative on the negotiating panels.

Departments experienced some degree of frustration at these constraints. They acknowledged the existence of the collective interests of government, which it needs to protect, and appreciated that governments will always set limits to what can be negotiated. Nonetheless, the constraints remained a source of frustration, which tended to be directed at the SSC as the agency responsible for ensuring that departments comply with government policy. Opinions vary across departments as to whether the SSC took a more active role than the situation warranted. Certainly the negotiations were protracted and difficult, as was to be expected given the shape of the bargaining position that CEs were obliged to adopt.

The 1994 and 1995 negotiations operated differently. The SSC's delegation of authority to CEs in 1994 was not as specific and far less prescriptive than it had been in the 1992–93 negotiations. There were two reasons for this. One was developmental, in that it had always been intended that over time departments would become less and less constrained by direct SSC oversight. The delegation of authority to CEs in 1992 had been an important step in that direction. The terms of the 1994 delegation took that further. But, second, it was also judged that the time was tactically right. Having achieved reductions in redundancy liabilities in 1992–93, and aware of growing pressure from staff for a wage increase, the government loosened the reins for 1994 and gave departments more discretion in the negotiating process. The SSC retained its role in approving settlements or referring potentially difficult settlements to the Cabinet Sub-Committee on State Wages. It remained clear that settlements had to be within the confines of government policy. The negotiating parameters continued to insist on fiscal neutrality and on the avoidance of settlements with implications for other departments, but they were not enforced quite so directively. The SSC played a less active role in negotiations themselves. This process was continued in 1995. Departments are now more in control of their fate than they were in the first round of bargaining under the Employment Contracts Act in 1992–93.

Although the negotiating context has been difficult, it has not been marked by high levels of industrial action. Industrial conflict has declined greatly in New Zealand in recent years. The services sector, which includes private sector services, has had one of the highest incidences of industrial action, but it is still at historically low levels, as might be expected given prevailing labour market conditions (Statistics New Zealand, 1995). What conflict there has been in the state sector has tended to be in the education and health sectors. Although there have been some cases of industrial action in departments of the public service, it has usually taken the form of a go-slow or some other action short of a full stoppage when negotiations have been deadlocked. In recent years, particular emphasis has been placed on the development of what has been called a problem-solving approach to bargaining to replace the traditional conflict-ridden adversarial style. It allows a joint working towards constructive solutions to problems.

Bargaining Outcomes

In the public service, there is little variation across departmental collective contracts in terms of core non-wage conditions of employment (i.e. various forms of leave, allowances and expenses). For detailed data on the content of collective contracts it is necessary to rely on one of the major surveys of collective contracts. However, the increasing importance of individual contracts means that it is unwise to focus only on collective contracts, particularly for pay increases. Non-remuneration conditions of employment still tend to be the same across individual and collective contracts. The most useful source of aggregate pay data remains the prevailing wage rate index prepared by Statistics New Zealand. Table 11.2 sets out the index for the period 1978–93 and allows a comparison of the period leading up to the State Sector Act and the years since then.

Table 11.2 Prevailing weekly wage rates index base: December 1985 quarter = 1000

	Private sector	Local government	Private and local government combined	Central government	All sectors
1978	–	–	440	447	442
1980	–	–	608	595	603
1982	–	–	846	837	843
1984	–	–	862	840	854
1986	1098	1089	1098	1064	1085
1988	1279	1270	1278	1272	1276
1990	1382	1440	1387	1408	1394
1992	1445	1521	1451	1477	1461
1993	1463	1537	1469	1486	1476

Source: Statistics New Zealand (1995)

An assessment of the data shows that:

a. Between 1978 and 1982 a reasonable degree of comparability prevailed in the rate of pay increases in the central government sector compared with the joint private/local government sector.
b. Between 1982 and 1984, the wage freeze bit more deeply in the central government sector than elsewhere with the central government falling considerably behind the private/local government sector.
c. Between 1984 and 1988, the central government sector recovered much of this lost ground, while over the whole decade 1978–88 the fair relativity provisions of the 1977 Act were largely upheld with central government index moving at about the same level as the combined private/local government sector.

Since 1988, the data concerning private sector and local government pay outcomes have been provided both separately and in combination. If at first we continue the time series comparison of the combined sectors, it can be seen that:

d. Between 1988 and 1991, the central government sector moved ahead considerably faster than the private/local government sector, whereas the reverse is true for the period since 1991.
e. Over the whole period 1978–93, the central government sector and private/local government sectors are broadly in line although, perhaps contrary to common perception, the former is slightly ahead.

If the data are examined separately for the private sector and local government, we find that:

f. For 1988–91, the local government sector is considerably ahead of the central government sector with the private sector well behind both.
g. For 1991–93, private sector pay rates rose more quickly than the other two sectors, and at a rate more than twice that of the central government sector which was also a long way behind the local government sector.

A similar picture emerges from the recently established labour cost index. Between December 1992 and June 1994, total labour costs in the public sector rose at less than half the rate of increase in the local government sector and less than a third the rate of increase in the private sector. The differences for non-wage labour costs (leave, super-annuation, ACC premiums, medical insurance, private use of cars, and low interest loans) are huge, with the private sector rate increasing at more than seven times the rate in the public sector (Statistics New Zealand, 1995, pp. 134–5). The wage increases in the public sector between 1990 and 1994 came almost wholly from non-negotiated increases. Pay ranges themselves remained static in this period. The increases derive from changes in the composition of the workforce and on employees moving up within their pay ranges or securing promotion.

Aggregate level comparisons among the three sectors might not be the most appro-priate comparisons to make, but they do give a general indication of relative wage movements. The data discussed here include wage rates in both collective and individual contracts. The picture for collective contracts alone is different. Table 11.3 shows that wage increases negotiated in public sector collective contracts kept pace with other sectors in the first two years following the Employment Contracts Act but began to lose ground in 1994–95. Data for 1995 also allow a comparison within the state sector for the first time. In the year to June 1995, wage increases in collective contracts throughout the economy were 1.5 per cent. In the area of government administration, collective contract wage increases were 0.7 per cent but in the health sector they were 1.6 per cent and in education 1.2 per cent. By way of comparison, private sector increases ranged from 0.1 per cent in agriculture to 4.6 per cent in insurance (Harbridge and Honeybone, 1995, p. 2). In 1994 most departments granted a lump sum pay increase to their employees, which did not go on to pay rates themselves. This reflected a desire by CEs to compensate employees for substantial productivity increases but also their lack of confidence that future funding would be available to support increased pay rates.

Table 11.3: Annualised wage increases (percentage) negotiated in collective contracts

	November 1992	June 1993	November 1993	June 1994
All sectors	0.1	1.1	1.0	1.0
Public/community services	0.1	1.0	1.2	0.8

Source: Harbridge (1993, 1994).

Table 11.4 shows the percentage of employees covered by particular provisions in collective contracts. The table compares outcomes for all sectors with the public/community services sector of the NZSIC. The data do not permit a straight public/private sector comparison. The data reflect the particular composition of the public/community services workforce, which is more likely than many other sectors to be salaried rather than wage workers and thus less likely to have any need for overtime or penal rates of pay or clock hours (defined standard hours of work). Productivity clauses are slightly less frequent in the public/community services sector.

Table 11.5 shows the percentage of collective contracts that contain specified leave provisions. Public/community services collective contracts provide entitlements inferior to the all sectors category on all types of leave with the exception of parental leave. The reason for this is the preference in public/community services collective contracts for leave entitlements to be discretionary. For instance, 72 per cent of public/community services collective contracts provide discretionary bereavement leave compared with 37 per cent in all contracts while for domestic leave the figures are 86 per cent and 69 per cent. The emphasis upon reducing leave provisions to discretionary status has been a particular focus of managerialism in the public sector. Parental leave provisions in the public/community services sector are substantially superior to those in the all sectors category. It is likely that this reflects the importance given to EEO issues in the public sector in recent years.

Table 11.4   Percentage of all employees covered by specified collective contract provisions

Productivity clauses	
All sectors	15
Public/community services	10
Clock hours	
All sectors	57
Public/community services	36
Overtime rates	
All sectors	90
Public/community services	83
Penal rates	
All sectors	57
Public/community services	36

Source: Harbridge, Honeybone and Kiely (1994).

Table 11.5   Percentage of collective contract with specified provisions

Four weeks' annual leave for 7 years service	
All sectors	57
Public/community services	34
Sick leave of 10 days or fewer	
All sectors	67
Public/community services	36
Domestic leave	
All sectors	30
Public/community services	14
Bereavement leave specified	
All sectors	61
Public/community services	28
Long service leave provided	
All sectors	80
Public/community services	67
Parental leave specified	
All sectors	42
Public/community services	62
Eligibility for parental leave above legal standard	
All sectors	26
Public/community services	61
Duration of parental leave above legal standard	
All sectors	21
Public/community services	45
Payments for parental leave	
All sectors	38
Public/community services	62

Source: Harbridge, Honeybone and Kiely (1994).

One important issue since the Employment Contracts Act has been whether collective contracts provide for new employees to be offered the conditions in the collective contract. Without such a provision, it is possible for new workers to be hired on inferior employment conditions. In the public/community services sector, 62 per cent of collective contracts require employers to offer the terms of the collective contract to new employees compared with 50 per cent of all collective contracts (Harbridge, 1994, p. 43).

NEGOTIATING EMPLOYMENT CONDITIONS IN THE STATE SECTOR: AN ASSESSMENT

On any assessment, there have been remarkable changes in the negotiation of employment conditions in the state sector since 1988. One of the principal policy objectives of the new public sector bargaining system was to restore government control over pay levels. This has been achieved to some degree, although the fruits have only been apparent during the 1990s when a virtual pay freeze has been successfully applied to central government employees. Over the whole period 1988–93, central government pay rates have risen faster than those in the private sector, but since 1990 the reverse has been true. This, combined with efforts to cut back on conditions of employment, has had predictable effects on employee morale and on the character of employment relations in the public sector.

For all parties, there has been a major problem of adjustment to a new set of circumstances. The overriding development has been bargaining decentralisation, and for the SSC and for unions this has posed great difficulties as they struggle to cope with an ever-widening band of activities with similar or fewer resources than previously. For CEs in the public service and in the health sector, the task has been to adjust to new bargaining responsibilities. The SSC has faced a complex environment in this period. The broad pattern of developments raises hard questions about the role of a central agency in the new structure. The SSC has been caught between the expectations of government and those of CEs. The government has expected that the SSC would act as its agent, controlling pay increases and employment conditions, and promoting the dissemination of a new management culture. CEs and their human resource managers, especially in the public service, have felt frustrated by central constraints that limited their ownership of their employment relations. The SSC has dealt with this by a staged process in which it used its employer party status to negotiate contracts that as much as possible met the government's agenda, while over time loosening the degree of direct central control it exercised over negotiations. It is clear that the level of frustration among departments has accordingly diminished since 1994. The SSC must still meet government expectations but to do this it now relies on the terms of delegation, on the new systems of financial management, and on the final decision-making authority vested in it and the Cabinet Sub-Committee on State Wages. The nature of public sector accountabilities means that the SSC is likely to retain its role as the agent of government policy. Notwithstanding the improved relationship between departments and the SSC, it is in the nature of the different roles they play that there will always be difficulties between the two. The best route for resolving those differences is likely to be through the gradual emergence of practical accommodations and understandings. The participants learn over time what they can and cannot do and how to reconcile their different positions and responsibilities. One factor whose importance should not be underestimated is the impact of the many years of SSC direction on the culture of public sector industrial relations. In addition, of course, many human resource managers in the public sector are formerly employees of the SSC.

Employees across the state sector still belong to the same unions in about the same proportions as they did in 1988 and continue to be represented by them in negotiations. High membership does not necessarily mean high activity levels. Unions have also had trouble adapting to the new environment. Like the SSC, unions are caught, in their case between the expectations of members for improvements in employment conditions and the resource scarcity that affects all state sector employers. Quite apart from that, unions have had to cope with wave after wave of restructuring and associated job losses. For many union officials, their job in recent years has been the discouraging one of selling jobs at the highest price. Unions have also had to accept a significant reduction in collective bargaining coverage. A very high proportion of managers are now employed on individual employment contracts. The PSA does provide a consultancy service to assist members in the negotiation of individual contracts or the resolution of disputes arising out of them; however, their growth has meant a substantial loss of influence for the union over managerial employment conditions.

The managerialist thrust in the public sector and the reassertion of managerial prerogative have encouraged some managers to attempt to by-pass unions. This is not easily done, however, given union membership levels and the Employment Court's rulings on the obligations of employers to deal with properly authorised bargaining agents. However, in most public sector agencies, managers have tried to develop direct relationships with their employees, often for the first time. Management efforts to develop a collective sense of organisational identity and commitment and to build a common culture in the organisation have the potential to jeopardise the loyalty of members to their union. Unions thus face the problem of remaining relevant in the workplace. In this context developments such as ranges of rates become a two-edged sword for unions. They have been the vehicle for increased wages for many union members in a period where wage rates themselves have been static, but this means that pay increases are being delivered not through union-based collective bargaining but awarded by managers on the basis of a performance assessment of some kind. The main threat to the role of unions in the public sector comes less from a direct management assault than from an erosion of its standing with its members through its inability to be seen as delivering improved working conditions. Working in unions' favour at the present time is the continuing insecurity many employees still feel and the important role unions play not just as a defensive instrument but also in representing membership views in a time of continuing uncertainty, change, and stress. In some quarters, the reassertion of managerial prerogative has been at some expense to the relationship with the union. But overall, union/management relations remain constructive. Most significantly, they have had to develop a new relationship based on both of them representing, in their different ways, the interests of their employees or members.

Perhaps the most important change has been the shift from complete uniformity to relative or emerging diversity. Where previously employment conditions and the manner of their negotiation differed not at all across the public sector, recent changes have introduced some degree of variation. The shift from a unified service to each CE acting as an employer of staff has been the most important source of this emerging diversity. Also important has been the move from a bargaining system based almost completely on collective bargaining to one that combines individual and collective employment contracts and mixes standard permanent employment with fixed-term contracts and other non-standard arrangements, including the use of external contractors and consultants. The impact of changes to financial management and organisational culture should not be overlooked either. However, the extent of this diversity should not be overstated; most public sector employees still enjoy broadly similar conditions of employment, as is to be expected given similar labour market factors, and union-based collective bargaining remains vitally important. But in this picture of continuity and change, there can be no doubt that the centralised, unionised and collective system that prevailed before 1988 has slowly begun to unravel. Experience internationally and so far in New Zealand suggests that it will not unravel nearly as much nor as quickly as in the private sector. What is undeniable, however, is that the process has begun.

12 equal employment opportunities

Since the mid 1980s, the pursuit of equal employment opportunities (EEO) has moved firmly on to the agenda in the New Zealand public sector, as in other countries. Legislation governing the operation of central, regional, and local government and the state's trading enterprises contains a 'good employer' obligation that requires CEs to implement EEO programmes. The allocation of resources to EEO, the appointment of EEO coordinators, the development of EEO programmes, and the explicit consideration of the EEO implications of wider policies and decisions have all become regular elements of the management of public sector organisations. Long-serving employees could not but identify the development of EEO as one of the major changes of the last decade.

The development of EEO in the New Zealand public sector was tied to the intersection of two separate and opposing agendas for change. On the one hand, an EEO agenda promoted the remedying of labour market discrimination by the implementation of policies constraining and channelling managerial discretion. This reform programme ran up against a managerialist restructuring agenda that aimed to reshape the public sector in the image of successful private sector firms and to do away with bureaucratic restrictions on managerial discretion.

The two agendas were not easily reconciled. They were informed by different values, they were oriented to the achievement of conflicting objectives, and their prescriptions for managerial practices were markedly at variance. The development of EEO during a period of comprehensive managerialist-driven restructuring reflected to a considerable degree the ability of its advocates to hitch the cause of EEO to that of managerialism. But it also reflected the acquisition of independent resources by EEO advocates and their ability to resist the degeneration of EEO to the status of a mere servant of managerialism.

THE DEVELOPMENT OF EEO IN NEW ZEALAND

EEO first emerged in New Zealand as a social justice issue. As Burns (1994, p. 133) observes, EEO was promoted 'as a sort of equity product tacked on to other functions and practices'. EEO was advocated in part as a response to the evident inadequacy of existing legislation in New Zealand. Legislative provisions to prohibit employment discrimination on a wide range of grounds, including race, ethnic origin, gender, and religion, were contained in the Race Relations Act 1971 and the Human Rights Commission Act 1977 (both now incorporated in the Human Rights Act 1993), as well as in the personal grievance provisions of the Industrial Relations Act 1973 (subsequently incorporated in the Labour Relations Act 1987 and later in the Employment Contracts Act 1991). However, the impact of these three Acts was limited. A series of court decisions limited the jurisdiction of the statutory personal grievance provisions to the point where most personal grievances were concerned with claims of unjustifiable dismissal. Wider issues of personnel policy—recruitment, selection, promotion and so forth—could not be addressed satisfactorily through the personal grievance provisions. Nor could they be addressed through the anti-discrimination legislation, which focused on specific individual complaints of discrimination, mostly confined to hiring decisions. There was no statutory obligation on employers to adopt EEO policies and no effective means of ensuring changes to personnel policies to protect the collective interests of disadvantaged groups.

Government officials rather than politicians were central to the promotion of the EEO agenda in the early 1980s. Politicians from the governing National party did not support EEO but nor did they oppose it. An informal coalition of supportive managers and trade union officials advanced the issue industrially. A number of important EEO provisions had been introduced throughout the public sector by the mid 1980s. They included permanent part-time work, the right to return to employment after up to five years of childcare leave, enhanced domestic leave, and a right to tangihanga (bereavement) leave. The same coalition succeeded in persuading the SSC to issue an EEO Policy Statement in 1984, which recognised the under-representation of women, Māori, Pacific Island people and people with disabilities in the public sector, and called upon government departments to address this through the adoption of EEO policies (Tremaine, 1991, pp. 346–7). Over the next two years, EEO gradually became articulated as an issue in the public sector with the formation of an EEO Unit in the SSC in 1986. As Tremaine observes: '... in less than two years, an EEO co-ordinator had been appointed within the SSC, a network of senior liaison officers had been established covering all departments, and some departments had appointed their own internal EEO co-ordinators' (1991, p. 348).

At about this stage, the new EEO constituency encountered the agenda of managerialist restructuring for the first time. The emphasis upon managerial discretion and flexibility did not sit easily with EEO considerations. In the policy debate that led to the State-Owned Enterprises Act and the State Sector Act, the clash between managerialism and EEO was to the fore. But the prior establishment of the EEO agenda within the public sector, the committal of resources to it and the existence of influential internal and external supporters ensured that EEO could not be easily dismissed by the managerialist agenda.

Common ground, or at least a compromise between the two agendas, was found by shifting the case for EEO from a social justice or equity focus to an efficiency-based argument. This drew, whether consciously or not, upon the liberal model of EEO in which it was argued that the efficiency of labour markets and of particular organisations was enhanced by eliminating any policy or practice that permitted discrimination in any form

(Jewson and Mason, 1986). In this argument, it was important to ensure that merit was the sole basis upon which an individual entered an organisation and advanced within it. Managerialism's emphasis upon the efficient operation of markets and organisations encouraged the advocates of EEO to rely heavily upon the contribution it could make to efficiency. In particular, they emphasised its ability to widen the recruitment pool to include people with a range of knowledge, skills and experiences different from those that had traditionally predominated in the public sector but which would become increasingly important to the efficient and effective delivery of public services in the future.

But only a limited version of EEO was politically and bureaucratically sustainable in the State-Owned Enterprises Act. The approach taken was purely exhortatory. The government included in the SOE Act a requirement that the SOEs be 'a good employer'. This included a requirement that they take account of social responsibilities, but only where practicable, and that they implement an EEO programme. The latter provision was simply a bald statement. The Act was silent on what constituted the desired structure, objectives, content, or operation of this programme, nor did it include any monitoring or enforcement mechanisms. The only way to enforce the good employer obligation was in the courts. In the event, there have been no successful cases concerning EEO brought under the good employer obligation.

Within the core public service itself, the EEO agenda continued to advance slowly. By 1987 the SSC had established an EEO Unit and had issued a directive requiring government departments to establish an EEO programme by 1 April 1988. This directive was overtaken by the introduction of the State Sector Bill into Parliament in December 1987. The Bill simply replicated the EEO provisions in the SOE Act. The experience of the SOEs had not suggested that they have been effective (Walsh, 1988b; Walsh and Wetzel, 1993). The EEO provisions did not greatly restrain management, and the SOEs were not notable for their promotion of EEO concerns. A fierce policy debate was conducted and led to the inclusion of a much stronger good employer obligation in the State Sector Act (Walsh, 1991a).

The Good Employer Obligation in the State Sector Act 1988

The State Sector Act's emphasis upon the good employer obligation and EEO is reflected in the criteria for the appointment of departmental CEs (s. 35), which require the SSC to appoint a person who will ensure that the department is a good employer and who will promote EEO. The Act goes on to require each CE to be a good employer (Boxall, 1990). This is set out in s. 56:

(1) The chief executive of a Department shall operate a personnel policy that complies with the principle of being a good employer.

(2) For the purposes of this section, a 'good employer' is an employer who operates a personnel policy containing provisions generally accepted as necessary for the fair and proper treatment of employees in all aspects of their employment, including provisions requiring—

(a) Good and safe working conditions; and

(b) An equal employment opportunities programme; and

(c) The impartial selection of suitably qualified persons for appointment; and

(d) Recognition of—

    (i) The aims and aspirations of the Māori people; and

    (ii) The employment requirements of the Māori people; and

    (iii) The need for greater involvement of the Māori people in the Public Service; and

(e) Opportunities for the enhancement of the abilities of individual employees; and

(f) Recognition of the aims and aspirations, and the cultural differences of ethnic or minority groups; and

(g) Recognition of the employment requirements of women; and

(h) Recognition of the employment requirements of persons with disabilities.

(3) In addition to the requirements, specified in subsections (1) and (2) of this section, each chief executive shall ensure that all employees maintain proper standards of integrity, conduct and concern for the public interest.

(4) For the purposes of this section, 'employee' includes a member of the senior executive service.

In s. 58(3) the Act defines an EEO programme as one 'that is aimed at the identification and elimination of all aspects of policies, procedures, and other institutional barriers that cause or perpetuate, or tend to cause or perpetuate, inequality in respect to the employment of any person or group of persons'. The CE is required by s. 58(1) to develop and publish an EEO plan and ensure that it is complied with throughout the department. This obligation is enforceable through a compliance order under the Employment Contracts Act.

These provisions are much stronger than those in the SOE Act. They broaden the EEO agenda from the liberal model's focus upon individuals competing on merit to what has been called the radical model of EEO, which focuses upon groups rather than on individuals (Jewson and Mason, 1986). Moreover, a statutory obligation upon CEs to take account not just of the needs of the organisation but also of the employment needs of EEO groups and the 'aims and aspirations' of Māori and ethnic and minority groups forces upon CEs a set of considerations from outside the organisation that neither managerialism nor the liberal model of EEO would embrace.

A STRATEGIC APPROACH TO EEO

As noted above, the case for EEO shifted over time from one based on social justice or equity to one chiefly based on efficiency arguments. Since the enactment of the good employer obligation, this has been extended further to embrace the argument that EEO should be an integral component of a strategic human resource management policy; that is, of an HRM policy designed to contribute to the achievement of the strategic objectives of the organisation. The increasing pressure upon scarce resources means that it has to be shown that EEO contributes to organisations gaining a competitive edge.

In its early years, EEO tended to be seen as an add-on to the real human resource management work of a department and certainly outside the development of a business strategy for the organisation (Burns, 1994, p. 131). Departments would develop their human resource policies and practices and then modify them to make sure they complied with their EEO programme. The process might not have been as exactly sequential as this description implies, but that was what it amounted to. This is not intended to denigrate the EEO developments in this period, and the changes made to HRM policies on the basis of EEO were often substantial and had a major and durable impact. In recent years, however, the focus has shifted to arguing for the alignment of EEO with the strategic objectives of the organisation and its integration with wider HRM policy. To some degree, this has coincided with the emergence of a strategic HRM perspective in the public sector. It was not possible for EEO to be viewed strategically until HRM was seen in a strategic framework.

The SSC observed the beginnings of this change in its 1992 progress report on EEO in the public service, where it commented that many organisations were starting to locate EEO within their wider business strategy. The report suggested that 'organisations which adopt this approach are likely to become leaders in the EEO field' (SSC, 1992a, p. 29). Burns has argued also that organisations that take a strategic view of EEO are likely to be leaders in the HRM field. In turn, those organisations are more likely to be successful in achieving their business objectives (Burns, 1994, p. 137). The institutional location of EEO units and coordinators in the public service points to the new strategic approach. In the SSC, the EEO section is now located within the Strategic Human Resource Development Branch. In its 1993 progress report, the SSC observed that this 'reflects the recognition that EEO is integral to strategic human resource development' (SSC, 1994e, p. 40). The SSC further observed that, within departments, 'responsibility for coordinating EEO seems to be increasingly located within the area responsible for human resource management' (SSC, 1994e, p. 9).

A strategic approach is also clearly visible in the 'EEO Stages of Development for the New Zealand Public Service' model, which the SSC has recommended for departments (SSC, 1994e, pp. 42–5). The model sets out 'a cyclical and dynamic process for implementing EEO across a wide variety of organisations' (SSC, 1994e, p. 7). There are three stages to the process. The first stage, 'Organisational Preparation and Analysis', begins with an analysis of the department's human resource data and of how the rationale for EEO fits with the department's mission statement. It goes on through a process of consultation to secure the production of a policy statement from senior management as to how EEO will support the department in achieving its organisational objectives. It concludes by ensuring the allocation of resources to EEO at appropriate levels and devising a strategy to educate managers about EEO. In the second stage, 'Management of Change Process', an initial EEO plan is produced and an EEO database set up. The third and final stage, 'Maintenance of Change Process', produces an annual plan based on evaluation of progress and targets particular areas for change to support the department's human resource and business strategies. The SSC has developed a methodology for evaluating EEO in departments, which reflects the 'Stages of Development' framework. The evaluation is sent to the CE, and it is followed by face-to-face meetings. From 1995, the CE receives a draft evaluation, which is amended on the basis of the meeting. This ties in with the importance of commitment and leadership from senior management, especially CEs, to the success of EEO.

The SSC emphasised a strategic approach to EEO in its reporting requirements for departments in 1995 (SSC, 1995b). There the SSC observed that the medium-term future (five years) for EEO will have three strategies: 'alignment of EEO with departmental business goals; integration with strategic human resource planning and practice, and customisation or "fit" of the implementation and operation of EEO in terms of organisational culture, size, structure and systems' (SSC, 1995b, p. 3). These themes are now to inform the annual EEO plans. The SSC observes that it expects to see the following features in any EEO plan:

alignment of EEO with departmental business goals

integration with strategic human resource planning and practice, and

customisation or 'fit' of the implementation and operation of EEO in terms of organisational culture, size, structure and systems.

congruence—is the plan developmental and is there a relationship with corporate EEO and regional/business/divisional planning?

planning—are objectives clearly specified, can actions achieve them, is responsibility assigned and is monitoring process in place? (SSC, 1995b, pp. 13–14)

In line with this approach, the SSC introduced a new reporting method for departments. It is an optional EEO commentary in which departments provide information to the SSC under the three headings of alignment, integration and customisation. The SSC's evaluation of each department will be under those headings as well as the baseline practices. The importance attached to a strategic approach to EEO runs through the document outlining the reporting requirements. At the same time, however, the SSC still requires considerable information from departments. It concedes the demands that this places on departments and has tried to simplify the reporting tasks (SSC, 1995b, p. 2).

MANAGING EEO: STRUCTURES AND PROCESSES[1]

A fundamental requirement for the advancement of EEO, and certainly for the implementation of a strategic EEO approach, was to guarantee its status and its resources within departments and to provide a secure platform from which its supporters could reasonably hope to make progress. There were two aspects to this: integrating EEO within management structures, and raising the awareness of and support for EEO among all departmental staff. A perception by management and by employees that EEO had been imposed from outside and/or that it constituted interference with the 'real business' of managing the organisation would be certain to stimulate resistance. All

---

1. This assessment of EEO management plans is based upon a detailed study of EEO in nine government departments between 1988 and 1992, supplemented by more recent examination of EEO plans and SSC progress reports. For a more detailed account than that provided here see Walsh and Dickson (1994).

EEO management plans, therefore, have concerned themselves with the question of institutional security and integration. This was expressed in aiming for the appointment of EEO coordinators at appropriate levels, reporting to or actually part of senior management, and the appointment of EEO liaison staff. A key objective in a small number of plans was that management job descriptions include EEO responsibilities and that a commitment to EEO be a requirement for management appointments.

The SSC reported that the number of full-time EEO positions in departments has fallen recently from sixteen in 1991 to eight in 1992 and six in 1993. On the other hand, the number of part-time positions has doubled from five in 1991 to ten in 1993 while another eighteen positions have some responsibility for EEO. To some degree this reflects a decentralisation of responsibility for EEO to line managers or, in the case of departments such as DSW with business unit structures, to business unit HR managers. Many departments have a group with senior or middle management representation that has responsibility for coordinating or monitoring or advising on EEO policies and practices in the department. In 1992–93, three large departments, Justice, Labour and Inland Revenue, had EEO units of two to five full-time members (SSC, 1994e, pp. 8–9). At the same time as there is a focus on integration, there is also a concern about the potential it creates for the dilution of the EEO impetus or a sole preoccupation with the issues of one department and a lack of awareness of the wider picture. As part of its statutory obligation for the promotion of EEO, the SSC's EEO section convenes a monthly meeting of EEO coordinators, liaises with departments, and facilitates other meetings to discuss issues of mutual concern (SSC, 1994e, p. 40).

It was also necessary that progress towards EEO objectives, as with any management objectives, be regularly and reliably assessed. Thus, many programmes include as an objective the development of an EEO database, which includes data on advertising, job applicants, appointments, promotion, disciplining, training, dismissals, and redundancies, for systematic assessment against the principles of the EEO programme. This particular objective was vulnerable to wider corporate decisions about monitoring human resource outcomes, especially where significant capital investment was required in information technology.

The institutional security of EEO and its prospects of success depend to an important degree on support from staff throughout the organisation. A range of objectives has been identified in departmental plans to raise awareness of EEO. Common elements include publicising the department's commitment to EEO, circulating information packages among employees, banning the use of sexist and racist language in all departmental communications, and ensuring that an EEO grievance or complaints process is established and well known. All departments relied upon training as a means of raising awareness. Management plans included the objective of sending staff at all levels on general EEO courses, on Māori language and culture courses, and on courses about other community languages and cultures. The SSC's report on EEO in 1993 observes that 'departments making progress are those which have provided training for managers and established responsibility and accountability for EEO within managerial job descriptions, employment contracts and/or performance appraisals' (SSC, 1994e, p. 11).

Undoubtedly the biggest component of all EEO management plans deals specifically with HRM policies and practices. The determination to give all individuals of comparable merit a roughly equal chance of being appointed to an organisation and of progressing within it is at the heart of the liberal model of EEO. It is also central to a strategic EEO approach, which cannot be developed if the highest quality staff are not appointed, retained and promoted to positions of responsibility. These concerns are expressed in a focus on recruitment, selection, performance appraisal, and job evaluation policies. Most departments seek to ensure that all their personnel material reflects their EEO policies, that recruitment booklets are multilingual, and that recruitment methods are culturally appropriate. This involves advertising jobs widely to affirmative action target groups inside and outside the department, noting in all job advertisements the department's commitment to EEO and its desire to receive applications from EEO group members, and, where appropriate, advertising vacancies in Māori and other languages and including in job advertisements knowledge of Māori and community languages and cultures as part of the criteria for appointment and promotion. In some cases, it also entails establishing relations with community groups that might be a source of potential job applicants. This has also grown out of increased awareness of and commitment to the need to equip public sector employees to deliver services to Māori appropriately and sensitively on behalf of the Crown as a Treaty partner.

EEO plans call for job interview panels with an appropriate gender and cultural balance. Some aim to provide suitable EEO training for all interview panel members to ensure that they are free of bias in their questions and evaluations of applicants. All plans permit job applicants to bring whanau (family members) to interviews. Many plans address the need for a physical audit of the workplace to assess its suitability for people with disabilities and to make such provision, including carparking, as is necessary. Some plans emphasise the importance of incorporating EEO indicators into any performance appraisal system. They also call for the review of job descriptions and job evaluation systems to ensure that they are gender- and culturally neutral and that they specify appropriate and essential job content and relevant experience and skills. In this regard, there is particular concern not to disqualify unnecessarily workers with disabilities and to identify jobs that could be carried out by workers with disabilities (Sullivan, 1988).

Other provisions in EEO plans involve affirmative action for EEO groups rather than the universal policies described above. Affirmative action policies fit into a radical model of EEO, which seeks to alter outcomes for EEO groups. The provision of career development opportunities specifically for EEO group members is an important example of this approach. This includes career counselling, with counsellors drawn from EEO groups where possible. Deliberate efforts are made to solicit applications from EEO group members for non-traditional jobs and to introduce career structures in previously dead-end jobs. In the debate over EEO, positive discrimination policies are the best-known examples of this interventionist approach. Departments have been slow to move towards positive discrimination policies, partly no doubt because of fears of political repercussions but also because of scepticism about their effectiveness. However, over time there has been a trend towards quantitative targets for the employment of EEO group members, while other departments were committing themselves to employing 'more' EEO group members. Related to this is the objective of nominating EEO group members for management training and systematic programmes to encourage promotion applications from group members.

Another theme that runs through EEO plans is the broader issue of workplace organisation. It involves an acceptance that the success of EEO policies might require significant changes to the organisation so that it can more effectively accommodate the diverse needs of different groups of employees. Such an acceptance fits in with Cockburn's transformative model of EEO in which the objective is to change organisations to suit people rather than the reverse (Cockburn, 1989; Webb and Liff, 1991). In this vein, some departmental EEO plans include the objective of investigating the possibilities of creating more flexible work patterns, which include numerical flexibility (e.g. flexible hours, permanent part-time work, job sharing, rotation, secondment, special projects or placements in positions of greater responsibility, and child-care policy) and functional flexibility (e.g. occupational reclassification, reskilling target group members into non-traditional areas, and new ways of defining and recognising skills, especially those acquired in home, marae (Māori village-centre), or community work or other non-traditional environments). The plans also include the objective of applying affirmative action policies in selecting workers for training and reskilling opportunities.

Cockburn's transformational project is based on the notion that the traditional ways of organising work, of recognising and valuing skill and experience, and of structuring work flows are in need of redesign. This approach begins from the premise that the organisation of the labour process, in all its dimensions, is the most fundamental aspect of any organisation and shapes the range of individuals likely to be able to enter and to prosper within it. Organisations are made and remade in the image of those who have succeeded in them. Developing new winners demands a different kind of organisation. It is the most radical and challenging component of the EEO agenda.

THE OUTCOMES OF EEO PROGRAMMES IN THE PUBLIC SERVICE

The most important judgment on EEO programmes is whether they achieve their objective of securing changes in the employment experience of EEO groups. The SSC's progress reports assess these developments in terms of overall representation of EEO groups in the public service, their employment status, their salary levels, and recruitment and retention data. The information presented below is drawn from the SSC's most recent report, which deals with the 1993 year (SSC, 1994e, pp. 46–56).

Representation

The SSC's data show that women are represented in the public service at a level above their overall participation in the labour force or the total number of women aged between 15 and 59. The other EEO groups for whom this is the case are 'ethnic minority and other' and 'Pacific Island and other'. In the latter case, the total numbers are very small, and the difference between public service representation and total numbers aged 15–59 is also very small. An assessment of changing patterns of representation since 1988 for EEO ethnic categories and workers with disabilities shows that for all but two groups representation levels have not changed greatly in that period, although in the case of some groups representation did drop within this period but has now recovered to be above 1988 levels. The two groups whose representation has fallen are 'ethnic minority and other' and 'people with disabilities'.

Management Status

All EEO groups are greatly underrepresented in management positions, which are defined as positions with a salary of $60,000 or more (but excluding CEs). Of the 1596 management positions (defined in this manner) in the public service, 24 are held by ethnic minority people, 23 by Māori, 9 by persons with a disability, and 3 by Pacific Island people. The proportion of managers who are women has risen from 9 percent in 1991 to 20 percent in 1993.

Salary Distribution

The data show clearly the relative salary disadvantage suffered by EEO groups. Men are three times as likely as women to be paid more than $40,000, and this difference has not changed much since 1991. The proportion of Māori earning more than $40,000 has hardly changed since 1991, although the number of Māori women in this category has fallen sharply. More Pacific Island men earn more than $40,000 now than did so in 1991, but there has been no change for Pacific Island women. In contrast, considerably fewer ethnic minority people earn more than $40,000 than did so in 1991, and the fall affects both men and women. A similar situation applies to people with disabilities, although men have fared slightly worse than women in this regard.

Recruitment and Retention Data

Data comparing relative recruitment and retention rates for EEO groups allow some assessment of the likely future demographic profile of the public service. The data show that women are being appointed at a rate slightly higher than their rate of application for public service jobs, but are ceasing work at about the same rate as they are being appointed. Māori are also being appointed at a rate slightly higher than their rate of application but are leaving at a considerably higher rate than that. The appointment of Pacific Island people and other ethnic minority people runs ahead of their rate of application, and their cessation rate is lower than that. Data on people with disabilities are not collected until appointment, but their appointment and cessation rates for 1992–93 were about the same.

Average Salary on Appointment

All EEO groups except ethnic minority people were on average appointed at salaries below the public service average. Men were appointed well above the average salary.

EEO IN THE PUBLIC SERVICE: AN ASSESSMENT

The principal thrust of EEO management plans in the public service has been to reform HRM practices and policies in a manner consistent with the liberal model of EEO. As discussed earlier, this model could be hitched to the managerialist cause and presented as contributing to greater organisational efficiency by removing obstacles to a freely operating labour market. From this point of view, EEO ensures that organisations draw upon the widest possible pool of potential recruits and that the contribution they are able to make once employed is not negated by bias in HRM procedures or by the personal prejudices or ignorance of supervisors and managers.

Continual restructuring has shaped the environment for EEO in the public sector. Other chapters in this book document the pace and scope of that restructuring. At the same time, all government agencies have encountered fiscal stringency to a degree not previously known. Budget constraints cramped departments and compelled economy in all aspects of their operations. Time and again, departmental EEO progress reports identify restructuring and financial restraint as the key constraints on the achievement of EEO objectives. Organisational turbulence and continuing uncertainty make it difficult to implement new EEO policies effectively. This is particularly so for policies such as career development and training, which require managers to take a long-term perspective. Few could do so with much confidence. In a period of great job insecurity, policies that seemed to favour particular groups over others aroused opposition. Fiscal constraint limited the resources available for EEO-related activities. It is likely that departments on occasion found these to be convenient scapegoats for lack of success, but there can be little doubt that the task of advancing EEO in the New Zealand public sector in these years was made far more difficult by the relentless process of reorganisation and financial restrictions.

EEO coordinators must take a considerable part of the credit for the advances made in this difficult situation. They faced the usual difficulties of promoting a relatively new agenda in a bureaucratic setting where possibilities for resistance and opposition abound. In addition, they were required do so amid a process of managerialist restructuring whose very premises tended to be hostile to EEO. Messervy's study (undated) of EEO coordinators in government departments found that, although most of them held to the radical model of EEO, the majority of the measures they had implemented fitted into the liberal model. Messervy suggests that this was because the coordinators saw liberal measures as having a greater chance of being effective.

New organisational structures established as part of the restructuring process had a distinctive impact on the fate of EEO. Responsibility for EEO, as for other management functions, was decentralised. It remains a moot point whether direction from the centre under the pre-1988 structure might have achieved more and at a faster rate than working through separate and autonomous departments and divisions. The old structure had essentially one crucial veto point, and a change in the prevailing balance at the centre could have brought progress to a sudden halt. The new structure is more favourable to EEO when a particular department is strongly supportive and can move ahead at its own pace and according to its own judgment. The attitude of the departmental CE is often vital. It is less favourable to EEO when the opposite is the case. The creation of a greater number of potential veto points enhances the opportunities for successful resistance to EEO. Clearly, decentralisation has made for greater variation in EEO policies and practices. The range of departmental plans attests to that. But, in the case of some departments with autonomous divisions or service units, the differences among the EEO plans are quite marked, and hence EEO outcomes are notably uneven within a department.

CONCLUSION

The SSC's progress report on EEO in 1991 concluded that 'not all organisations have heard or absorbed the message that progress in EEO is integral to the practice of good human resource management' (SSC, 1992a, p. 17). Just two years later, the judgment was considerably more positive:

> The ongoing extension of EEO analysis and activity into the area of human resource management, and the more recent focus on developing EEO strategies or actions for a wider range of staff, signals departments' interest in more comprehensive and lasting solutions to maintaining and developing a healthy and effective workforce (1994e, p. 38).

Any judgment on the progress of EEO in the public service needs to begin from the position that the promotion of EEO is a long-term project. What is most striking is the changes wrought and progress achieved since EEO first established itself on the agenda little more than a decade ago.

The most important recent change is the development of a strategic orientation to EEO in many but as yet by no means all government departments. The universal acceptance that EEO is vital to the achievement of the business objectives of government departments and that without it organisations are less likely to succeed would be of enormous long-term significance for the employment future of members of EEO groups. Such an achievement would be of greater significance than the specific advances or lack of them made by those groups in recent years. Nonetheless, EEO groups have made steady and encouraging progress. However, it was never expected that the profile of the public service workforce would be quickly recast. It was always expected that those workforce changes would follow and be dependent upon changes to HRM structures and to human resource policies and procedures in departments. It is clear that there has been substantial progress in these areas despite an unfavourable context of managerialist restructuring and financial restraint. The conflict between managerialism's emphasis upon managerial discretion and EEO's imposition of constraining rules and procedures was resolved by a shared commitment to efficiency and merit. Out of this has come the integration of EEO as an essential component within strategic HRM. The significance for the future lies in the fact that EEO has acquired resources and status and is now firmly embedded in the organisational structures and culture of the public service.

financial management

13 departmental management of resources

The passage of a new Public Finance Act in July 1989 was a landmark event in the management of public finances. Together with the State Sector Act 1988, the Public Finance Act 1989 transformed the way government departments operate. At the departmental level, the financial management reforms can be seen as the culmination of years of *ad hoc* attempts to amend the deficiencies of the traditional bureaucratic system based largely on controls over inputs. New Zealand is not alone in its efforts to undertake such management reforms or in the managerialist approach adopted. The reforms of the late 1980s and early 1990s can be distinguished from the earlier initiatives, however, by the coherence of the conceptual framework underlying the key pieces of legislation. The Public Finance Act also set in motion pioneering reforms to financial management at the whole-of-government level; in particular, its requirements for Crown reporting in accordance with generally accepted accounting practice paved the way for new budgetary information under the Fiscal Responsibility Act 1994.

This chapter examines reforms to the management of public resources at the departmental level. It is argued that while it has been possible within departments to adopt practices from the private sector, as the day-to-day tasks of resource management are similar, innovative thinking has been required and will continue to be required once the management of individual organisations is seen in its political context. In particular, at the interface between the managerial and political spheres, certain tensions are evident, such as the appropriate balance between managerial autonomy and parliamentary control. Chapter 14 will explore public management for the whole of government. At that level, challenges not typically encountered by businesses in the private sector emerge in relation to macro-economic management, interorganisational coordination, and public control over the use of funds coercively obtained.

HISTORY OF DEPARTMENTAL FINANCIAL MANAGEMENT

Traditionally, the system of financial control in New Zealand central government, as in most other countries, focused on the annual cash cost of inputs such as personnel, travel, maintenance, and materials. Attempts to shift the emphasis in central government from the annual cash cost of inputs to the objectives of government over longer periods can be found at least as far back as the recommendations of a Treasury review team in 1967. Strongly influenced by the Planning Programming Budgeting System (PPBS) models, which had gained popularity in government budgeting in the USA, the proposals of the New Zealand review team included: setting objectives linked to the planning and budgeting process; decision-making based on analytical techniques; quantitative measures of programme achievement; better cost projections integrated with budgeting and economic planning; and improved resource management through better financial reporting, responsibility accounting, and decentralised budgetary control (Treasury, 1967).

Following the Treasury review, planning and forecasting systems were introduced in central government. In addition, the central government management information system and the Estimates were structured, at least in part, along programme lines. Ten years later, however, a report by the Controller and Auditor-General, A. C. Shailes (Audit Office, 1978) observed that practice had fallen well short of the Treasury's intentions. Focus on the cash cost of inputs and failure to develop meaningful performance measures meant that managers focused on budget and legal compliance rather than managing resources effectively and efficiently. The Shailes report advocated an accrual-based accounting system to ensure cost responsibility, encourage ongoing monitoring of assets, and enable systematic costing and charging for services.

While a cash accounting system records items when cash is received or paid, an accrual accounting system matches the resources used in the production of goods and services with the revenues or services produced in the same period. The distortion of financial performance under cash accounting, which occurs when capital assets are recorded wholly in the year in which they are purchased, is avoided under accrual accounting where the cost of capital assets is spread over their useful life. Because accrual accounting requires the keeping of asset registers, and measurement of annual resource consumption, managers are more aware of the importance of managing their capital assets efficiently. The notion of accrual accounting in the interest of better costing and asset management was echoed in a New Zealand Planning Council report (Ball, 1981). Unlike some overseas countries, then, accrual accounting in New Zealand has never been seen as a technical accounting issue in isolation but rather as an integral part of better management (McCulloch and Ball, 1992).

In the wake of the Shailes report, a number of attempts were made in the early 1980s to improve financial management in government. Departments increasingly started charging one another for services, thereby revealing the inadequacies of cash accounting systems for measuring cost. New management information systems were proposed. Senior departmental financial officers argued for a shift in emphasis from a centralised accounting system to departments owning their own data, a move facilitated by changes in computer technology. Detailed Treasury regulations were progressively dismantled and Financial Management Guidelines issued. Bulk budgets and revolving funds represented attempts to increase flexibility for managers to manage. Bulk budgets were intended to give managers more flexibility to shift spending between groups of expenditure. Revolving funds were separate funds through which management could use receipts from continuing operations to finance operating expenditure, thus removing the requirement for annual appropriation of expenditure and the incentive for year-end spending.

The loosening of controls over inputs was not, however, accompanied by an effective development of performance measures. Although departments began identifying their objectives and reporting them in the Estimates, the process was a difficult one. Objectives in government are often multiple and conflicting, and the fact that departments were structured with a mixture of administrative, service, regulatory, and commercial objectives did not help. There was confusion between types of objectives, with workload measures often being reported rather than measures of efficiency and effectiveness. Furthermore, it was often unclear whether a lack of effectiveness was due to policy or to programme implementation. Corporate planning was introduced, but not integrated with the resource allocations process. The result was that many plans, after taking up considerable management time and effort, had virtually no impact in practice. The commitment to financial management reform varied enormously from department to department, depending largely on how seriously the permanent head took his or her responsibility in this area.

The early 1980s also saw the New Zealand Society of Accountants (NZSA) start to play an active role in the public sector. A committee set up to investigate the development of accounting standards for the public sector established two important principles from the outset. The first was that adequate reporting in the non-profit sector required non-financial, as well as financial, measures of performance. The second was to shift from cash accounting to accrual accounting. Similar principles were endorsed by the Public Expenditure Committee of Parliament, which had commenced a review of the format and content of the Estimates and Public Accounts in 1982 (Public Expenditure Committee, 1984).

In the latter half of the 1980s, the government brought reform of the public sector to the forefront of its agenda. In its briefing to the incoming government, the Treasury reiterated the problems associated with management in the public sector and the possibly perverse impact of cash allocations and cash controls on decision-making (Treasury, 1987, p. 81). In contrast to overseas management reforms, however, it was specifically acknowledged that the starting-point for considering how the conduct of government could be most efficiently administered was the constitutional relationship between the electorate, Parliament, and government:

> The extent to which that constitution enables the preferences of the electorate to be transformed into action, and the strength of accountability of the government and Parliament for that action will be a determining factor shaping the nature of administration (Treasury, 1987, p. 51).

Within an overall framework in which elected representatives were to take the responsibility for deciding objectives, a set of five interrelated and mutually reinforcing elements of the management process were identified (ibid., pp. 55–6):

a. *A clear specification of the objectives* for which managers are responsible and an avoidance of multiple and conflicting objectives where possible.
b. *Freedom to make resource allocation decisions* on a basis that enables the most efficient attainment of objectives.

c. *Accountability*, i.e. incentives and sanctions in place to modify the behaviour of managers to ensure that they meet established objectives rather than pursuing independent goals of their own.

d *Effective assessment of performance* so that managers could be held accountable. In particular, a distinction should be made between results of management and results stemming from external factors over which managers have no control.

e. *Sufficient quantity of information* to make performance assessment possible.

The funding process was seen to play a major role in influencing the behaviour of public sector managers. Accordingly, several suggestions for reform were made (Treasury, 1987, p. 94):

a. Clearer specification of intended outputs.

b. Substantial relaxation of input controls.

c. Full costs of activities attributed to departments.

d. Development of accrual-based budgeting and accounting.

e. Improved reporting to government and Parliament by providing additional information.

f. Incentives and penalties for under and over achievement of budget targets.

The State Sector Act, which took effect from 1 April 1988, initiated the process of fundamental reform in the core state sector. To complete the reforms, however, it was obvious that a clearer definition of the concept of performance, together with a comprehensive overhaul of the financial management system, was required.

Overseas developments had been reviewed by the Treasury but had not been found particularly helpful. Not only had management reforms largely been viewed in isolation from the role of elected representatives but also there was little evidence that financial management projects had been successful in practice. The Treasury therefore decided to proceed from first principles, taking into account the broader context of the reforms and the particular constitutional relationships in New Zealand. The reform that had already been initiated with the SOE model was felt to be a useful starting-point, along with the set of principles that guided that process. Private sector practices were also examined to see whether there were any concepts and practices that could be usefully applied in the public sector.

The desired conceptual clarity was brought about through the adoption of two sets of ideas that would strongly influence the subsequent design of proposals. The first key notion was a distinction between *inputs, outputs,* and *outcomes.* Inputs were defined as the resources (e.g. labour, materials, electricity) used in the production of outputs. The goods and services produced by departments were described as outputs. The notion of outputs encompassed a variety of types including policy advice, the administration of regulations, and the administration of transfer payments, as well as the provision of specific services such as education or prison management. The term 'outcomes' was adopted for the impact of the activities of government on the community (e.g. a lowered incidence of disease, a lowered crime rate, an increase in economic welfare). It was envisaged that the government would determine the outcomes it wished to achieve and use policy advice, based on analysis of the relationship between outputs and outcomes, to make trade-offs between outcomes and to select the appropriate outputs. For example, if the government wished to reduce the level of serious crime, it would require advice about which outputs or combination of outputs would be most likely to achieve the desired outcome.

The distinction between outputs and outcomes thus meshed with a new, clearer definition of the respective roles of the government and departments, and made it possible to hold the chief executive of a department accountable, as envisaged under the State Sector Act. For accountability to operate effectively the individuals held accountable must have control over their results. If a police department, for example, were to be evaluated in terms of outcomes rather than outputs, there would be a readily available set of excuses for poor performance, because the causes of serious crime include factors largely outside the control of the police, such as high levels of unemployment, drug abuse, or changing social values. On the other hand, it is easier in theory to hold the police accountable for the quantity and quality of police patrolling.

The second key notion concerned the relationship between departments and the government. Influenced by the new institutional economics, it viewed relationships as *contractual* and identified two types of contract, corresponding to two different relationships between the government and the department. First, the government was seen as a *purchaser* of outputs from departments or, alternatively, from organisations in the private sector. Accountability would be in terms of a purchase contract, which would be as specific as possible about the nature and quantity of the output to be produced, the quality desired in the outputs, delivery time and place, and price. Second, the government was viewed as *owner* of its agencies. As owner, it would wish to ensure that it is getting the best possible return on the assets invested. The government as owner was presumed to be interested in changes to the capital stock of the agency and the capacity of the agency to perform in the future. This concept of government as separate from its individual departments was to be applied in many areas of financial management and reporting. For example: departmental bank accounts were distinguished from the Crown bank account; certain assets (e.g. national parks) were deemed to be owned by the Crown and merely managed by departments and hence to be excluded from departmental balance sheets; certain revenues and expenditures, such as transfer payments and taxation receipts, were identified as belonging to the operating statement of the Crown rather than of departments.

THE PUBLIC FINANCE ACT 1989

The Public Finance Act obtained the royal assent on 26 July 1989, with its provisions effective from 1 July 1989. Significant amendment Acts were passed in 1992 and in 1994. Major changes associated with the Public Finance Act and amendments are as follows:

Appropriations

The Act continues the long-established constitutional principle of no spending of public money except in terms of an appropriation.

In line with the purchase/ownership distinction, the first major type of appropriation to departments under the Public Finance Act, as enacted in 1989, was for classes of outputs. As these covered the full costs of outputs, including depreciation, there was an incentive for departments to move to accrual accounting. The ownership interest was reflected in appropriations for capital contributions where the government chooses to increase its level of investment in departments, while appropriations for transfer payments formed a third category.

Appropriations for 'other expenses', such as asset write-downs and restructuring costs, were introduced in 1992. The 1994 amendment to the Public Finance Act 1989 specified additional types of appropriation, to accommodate better the increasing proportion of government expenditure undertaken outside departments, and placed all appropriations on an accruals basis. The classifications are now all according to their purpose rather than according to whether they are for departmental or Crown transactions. The seven types of appropriation are for:

a. classes of outputs
b. benefits and other unrequited expenses
c. borrowing expenses
d. other expenses
e. capital contributions
f. purchase or development of capital assets by the Crown
g. repayment of debt.

Except for offices of Parliament (whose votes are the responsibility of the Speaker of the House), each vote is the responsibility of one minister and is administered by one department. In general, the authority to spend or to incur costs lasts only to the end of the financial year to which an Appropriation Act relates. An appropriation for a class of outputs may be increased by up to 5 per cent by transfer from another class of outputs in that vote provided the total amount for the vote remains unaltered. Multi-year appropriations of up to five years are now possible if stipulated in the Appropriation Act.

The first appropriation bill for each financial year must be introduced into the House before the end of July unless the House resolves otherwise—a significant improvement on the three-to-five-month period of uncertainty under the previous regime. In 1995, the Budget was introduced a month before the start of the financial year.

Estimates

The 1994 amendment to the Public Finance Act introduced a new, more complete and consistent format for the Estimates documentation. Previously, appropriations and departmental information were published together. From 1 July 1995 the contents of the Estimates book are limited to the appropriations; information about the expected output classes and financial performance of each department is published in separate departmental reports. Separation of reporting on departmental performance from the Estimates is intended to help clarify the respective accountabilities of ministers and departments. The Estimates become a more explicitly ministerial document reflecting the purchaser/owner orientation and presenting Parliament with information that supports the appropriations being sought by each minister.

Under the 1994 amendment, the Estimates for each vote are required to identify the minister responsible and the department administering the vote, to describe each class of outputs to be purchased by the Crown and the proposed costs or expenses to be incurred, and to identify the link between them and the government's desired outcomes. The proposed expenses or liabilities to be incurred in respect of each of the other types of appropriation must also be identified. Budgeted and estimated actual figures for the previous appropriation period and comparative actual figures for each of the previous four financial years must be included. A statement of the estimated net worth at the start of the financial year and the forecast net worth at the end of that financial year are also required. Section 9A specifies the information required with respect to supplementary estimates.

Banking and Investment

The Act provides for two principal types of bank account for public money: a Crown bank account operated by the Treasury, and departmental bank accounts operated by departments. By removing the Crown bank account (formerly the Public Accounts) from the Reserve Bank, the management of the Crown's finances was separated from the operation of monetary policy.

Where a department operates a departmental bank account, money disbursed to a department by the Treasury and all receipts relating to departmental revenue or the sale of assets held by the department are to be paid into that bank account. All other money is to be paid into the Crown bank account. Money can be paid out of the Crown bank account only in terms of a warrant signed by the Governor-General after the Audit Office has ascertained that it is for a lawful purpose and has certified that the amount of the warrant may be lawfully paid. The Audit Office must also certify that each payment out of the Crown bank account is in terms of a Governor-General's warrant and there is an appropriation or other authority available against which it may properly be charged.

Reporting

The Treasury is required to prepare consolidated annual and half-yearly financial statements for the Crown in accordance with generally accepted accounting principles. These requirements will be described in more detail in Chapter 14.

The chief executive of a department is responsible to the 'Responsible Minister' for the financial management and financial performance of the department but, unless agreed with a minister, is not responsible for the financial performance of agencies and enterprises funded through a vote administered by the department. The chief executive must carry out any lawful financial actions required by the Minister of Finance or the responsible minister.

The Public Finance Act 1989 specified a new set of reporting requirements for departments, for Crown entities, and for the Crown as a whole, introducing much greater consistency across the central government sector. Departments, offices of

Parliament, and Crown entities are now required to prepare annual financial statements in accordance with generally accepted accounting practice and must include:

a. A statement of financial position at balance date.
b. An operating statement, reflecting revenue and expenditure for the year.
c. A statement of cash flows.
d. A statement of objectives, specifying outputs to be produced and financial performance to be achieved.
e. A statement of service performance, reporting on outputs produced. They can be compared with intended outputs as specified in the Budget documents so that Parliament can obtain a better view of the performance of the organisation.
f. A statement of commitments.
g. A statement of contingent liabilities.
h. A statement of accounting policies.
i. Such other statements as are necessary to fairly reflect the financial operations for the year and the financial position at the end of the financial year.
j. Comparative actual figures for the previous financial year.

Departments and offices of Parliament are also required to report on unappropriated expenditure or costs incurred in relation to their activities under s. 12 of the Act and to produce half-yearly accounts. Annual financial statements must be forwarded to the Audit Office (or, in the case of offices of Parliament, an auditor appointed by the House) within two months. Financial statements must be accompanied by a statement by management, signed by the chief executive and chief financial officer, taking responsibility for the integrity of the financial statements. The financial statements, together with the management report and the audit report, must be tabled in the House by the responsible minister not later than six sitting days after the auditor has returned the financial statements to the reporting entity concerned.

EVALUATION OF THE FINANCIAL MANAGEMENT REFORMS

Following the passage of the Public Finance Act 1989, far-reaching changes to accounting and financial management in the public sector have been accomplished in a very short time. The accounting changes have brought about a considerable improvement in the amount, the type, and the quality of information available to ministers and to Parliament. Longstanding concerns, such as focus on the cash cost of inputs, failure to integrate planning and budgeting, poorly defined notions of performance, inappropriate incentives and lack of transparency (e.g. between current and capital expenditure), have at last been addressed.

The changes have, on the whole, been very well received by departments, particularly at senior management levels, and by politicians (Logan, 1991). Transitional problems with the new regime mostly related to the time skills and resources required for implementation (Horne, 1992). T ere has been a major shift in emphasis from *controls* over *inputs* to *control* over *outputs*. As a result, both politicians and departments themselves have begun asking serious questions about their activities, why they do them, and whether they should continue doing them or whether they should be doing something else.

The accounting and financial management reforms have at least two notable strengths. First, they have a coherent and well-thought-out conceptual foundation; in particular, the input/output/outcome and purchaser/owner distinctions that form the basis for appropriations and for reporting on performance. Second, accounting reforms have not been addressed in isolation from management reforms generally or from wider constitutional relationships. Thus the State Sector Act and the Public Finance Act cannot be viewed in isolation from one another; they form an integrated whole. New legislation was necessary because of the major changes in constitutional relationships and parliamentary processes that were involved. Legislation also gave teeth to recommendations on accounting and financial management, forcing hitherto recalcitrant departments to make the necessary changes.

While it is easy to point to dramatic improvements in New Zealand's overall economic performance by 1994, and expenditure by government departments has reduced, it is difficult to demonstrate how much of this is due to efficiency gains by departmental managers, particularly as many activities have been shifted outside the core public service. Anecdotal evidence, however, suggests that departments are providing better services with fewer resources and ministers believe that they are able to make more informed choices about outputs. The Logan review of the state sector reforms concluded that senior managers and ministers were very supportive of the changes and the improvements in performance that had resulted (Logan, 1991). Issues that the Logan review identified in relation to financial management included:

a. The number and structure of appropriations.
b. The need for further clarification of the process for specifying outputs and the need for further development of cost allocation systems to support decisions about outputs.
c. The support available to MPs to use fully the improved level and quality of information now available to them to assess performance.
d. Perceptions on the part of ministers that the reforms have increased the exposure to risk from poor departmental decisions.
e. The role of central agencies, especially duplication of functions and the compliance costs associated with the new reporting requirements.
f. Lack of shared understanding of the purpose and operation of incentives and the effectiveness of incentives, such as the capital charge, in guiding resource allocation decisions.

Concerns about the cost of compliance under the new accountability regime, particularly in the case of small departments, were also identified by the Logan review. As a result, the Public Finance Amendment Act 1992 did away with the requirement for audited half-yearly departmental financial statements. Further consideration has also been given to differentiating between departments with small budget allocations, where the risk to taxpayers' funds is minimal, and larger departments where the size and significance of the activities justify the costs of sophisticated information. A working party set up to review accountability requirements reported in October 1994 (see Chapter 14).

More recently, interviews with a selection of ministers, MPs, CEs, chief financial officers, and operational managers have confirmed that they believed that financial management reforms have improved the way that central government operates, although some work remains to be done (Audit Office, 1994e). The Audit Office has signalled an intention to continue examining the following areas of concern:

a. The adequacy of contracting, monitoring, and accountability arrangements for benefits and outputs supplied by parties other than departments, given that these represent a large and increasing proportion of Parliament's appropriations.
b. The appropriateness of performance measures; in particular, the link between outputs, outcomes, and SRAs.
c. Refinement of the incentives regime for resource management, including such issues as operation of the capital charge at lower levels of management and the effects of retaining surpluses on managerial motivation, on the one hand, and parliamentary control, on the other.

The remainder of this chapter examines the experience in terms of each of the major components of the new financial management framework based on agency theory concepts: delegation of managerial freedom from principal to agent; a system of incentives and sanctions to align the interests of the agent with those of the principal (in particular, the efficient and effective utilisation of resources); and performance specification and reporting.

Managerial Autonomy

Recent public administration literature hotly debates the desirability of the new public sector management philosophy known as 'managerialism', and it is possible to identify a close association between accounting and managerialist philosophy (Guthrie, 1992). While managerialism has its strong supporters among those who view the alternative to be a return to input controls and bureaucratic structures and processes (Paterson, 1988), some of the deeper concerns about managerialism might be legitimate and worth raising in the context of the accounting reforms in New Zealand.

Two strands of concern can be detected in the criticisms of managerialism. First, there is a concern that managerialism over-emphasises the rational, the technical, and the economic at the expense of the moral, the political, and the intuitive. In this vein, it relies mechanistically on incentives and sanctions rather than internalised norms and values and is more concerned with products than processes. In such an environment, trust could be replaced by activities measured by performance indicators, and a fetishism of techniques could displace many of the requirements of good public service such as service to the community. Second, there is a concern about the *separation* of management from the political realm. Executive autonomy might be increased at the expense of parliamentary control; an emphasis on management displaces or becomes divorced from policy; and accountability is internal rather than public. This is seen as contrary to fundamental principles of parliamentary control over the use of taxpayers' funds.

Concerns about technical rationality and separatist management are clearly relevant to the accounting focus on outputs and the accountability of CEs to ministers. At first glance it would appear that the new accounting is open to the criticisms made by the anti-managerialists. The language is technical and does encourage thinking in product and market-oriented terms. There could be so much effort going into reporting by departments to individual ministers that public accountability of the government as a whole to Parliament and the public at large receives scant attention. The New Zealand reforms, however, have tried to deal with these potential problems. Constitutional relationships formed an integral part of the design of the new accounting framework, which envisages government responsibility for outcomes as well as departmental responsibility for outputs. Ministers are responsible for selecting outputs as well as having an overall responsibility for their department's delivery of these outputs. Meaningful reporting on outcomes is difficult but the effort has not been abandoned. Neither will Parliament ignore inputs or processes where it believes taxpayers' funds are exposed to too much risk or there is a perception of extravagant spending by managers. Questions about inputs have been noticeable in areas like property and accommodation, while the Auditor-General has responded to parliamentary concerns about processes, such as the employment of consultants and purchasing practices of government departments, through special investigations and reports (Audit Office, 1994b, 1995c).

One issue that illustrates the tension between managerial autonomy and parliamentary control is the proposal that departments be able to retain surpluses achieved through efficiencies and cost reductions. From a managerial standpoint, being able to retain surpluses is an incentive to be more efficient. Retained surpluses could be a source of venture capital, thus encouraging innovation and better results. From the point of view of Parliament, retention of surpluses undercuts one of the fundamental principles of public expenditure, i.e. that the money is appropriated for specific purposes. While more activity might be desirable from the point of view of an individual department, it might not be in the collective interest for government to devote additional funds to that department because priorities might lie elsewhere. Also, it is difficult to be confident that a real surplus exists until accurate specification of outputs, cost allocation, and good performance management systems are in place (Logan, 1991, p. 295).

The structure of output classes and the appropriate level of aggregation also affect the degree of parliamentary control. Appropriations are made at the level of output classes, and the specification of the output classes includes a statement of projected performance. Parliament therefore needs reasonable assurance when it votes money to an output class that neither the performance specified for that output class nor the costs of delivery will be changed beyond some acceptable margin (5 per cent under the Public Finance Act) without recourse to Parliament for a further appropriation. Some departments expressed fears that errors in forecasting the cost of an output class might be greater than the allowed 5 per cent tolerance. This creates an incentive to aggregate outputs in order to increase the degree of managerial flexibility. Some departments have also been sceptical about managing some of the smaller output classes as separate products or services. They view the divisions between them as arbitrary and as ignoring the joint nature of some of the services. There might, therefore, be strong incentives to work around output class boundaries (e.g. by fudging overhead allocations).

Parliament has also faced problems with the way output classes have been determined. Despite the incentives to aggregate outputs, the actual experience initially was that the Public Finance Act significantly increased the number of separate appropriations in the Appropriation Act (from 56 in 1988–89 to 774 in 1989–90; in 1994–95 there were 686 plus 71 in the 'other' category). The number of output classes could be reduced to facilitate better comprehension by MPs while at the same time some very big output classes could be subdivided to permit tighter parliamentary control. The problem of cost allocation has also concerned Parliament. Where arbitrarily allocated of overheads form a high proportion of total output costs, the information that Parliament receives about costs can be significantly distorted. Unless this issue is tackled, there could be little point in spending a great deal of time and effort in carefully specifying output classes.

Even a specific accounting issue such as depreciation of assets can be viewed in the context of the managerialism debate. From a managerial standpoint, it is simply a technical matter of measuring the cost of resource consumption. However, covering the cost of depreciation could result in funds being accumulated within the organisation prior to their being used to replace assets. They could be used to finance other activities in the short term, and this would tend to undermine the control taxpayers normally have over management (Rutherford, 1983, p. 8). Aiken (1994, p. 17) argues that 'there can be no ultimate delegation of powers away from elected representatives with respect to the allocation and balancing of scarce resources' (p. 17) and that 'the main issue with capital maintenance is the need for a direct statement of what exactly is to be maintained and under what authority'. He warns that current values and associated depreciation charges bearing little resemblance to present or future realities might take over the allocation roles, which should be issues for public debate.

Complaints from some departments that they do not have the flexibility of private sector counterparts in finance (e.g. they are prohibited from raising loans or entering into finance leases and new ventures) suggests that the reforms to date have not been excessively managerialist. There is still much to be gained from the principles of chief executive responsibility and accountability established under the reforms. Indeed, the major challenge now is to ensure that all chief executives and their staff fully utilise the wide range of approaches and tools available to them, whether adopted from the private sector and other organisations in the public sector or developed of their own initiative. For example, the increased emphasis in the private sector on quality, processes, learning organisations, culture, and ethics seem at least as important in the public sector.

The balance between managerial autonomy and parliamentary control will probably require continual fine-tuning. Ultimately, however, the effectiveness of parliamentary control depends on whether MPs have the skills, time, resources, and motivation to understand and use the increased volume of information coming from departments.

New Zealand has acute difficulty in this area because it has the same range of activities as other countries but a particularly small parliament (even at 120 MPs) by international standards. Whenever there has been a government with a large majority in the House, it has been very difficult therefore to find enough opposition Members of Parliament to staff all the select committees in a balanced manner. It remains to be seen whether changes to select committee processes under MMP will enhance parliamentary control over the activities of the Executive.

Incentives

Financial signals and incentives form an essential part of the new management environment. For example, the provision in the Public Finance Act that enables departments to retain receipts from the sale of assets is designed to encourage disposal of surplus assets. Interest payments by the New Zealand Debt Management Office of the Treasury (DMO) are designed to discourage departments from holding surplus cash on call and to give better information about liquidity requirements while the capital charge is intended, *inter alia*, to provide an incentive to rationalise assets.

Cash management

The financial management reforms were designed to overcome deficiencies in the traditional system of cash management resulting from the emphasis on compliance and control in terms of parliamentary appropriation of the gross cash cost of inputs. One disadvantage had been that the confusion of monetary policy and financial management objectives in the management of the government's cash created difficulties in assessing performance with respect to both objectives. A second problem was that there was no incentive to manage cash in a way that took account of the time value of money (e.g. to pay bills when they were due rather than when they were received) or to try to earn interest on idle cash balances. Also, the information provided by the central accounting system was of no use for purposes of cash management because it recorded cheques when they were written rather than when they were cashed.

Departments were assigned responsibility for day-to-day cash management and given their own bank accounts in order to be able to do so. A profile of cash outlays (on, say, a fortnightly basis) is negotiated and agreed with the Treasury, and surpluses can earn interest by being deposited with the DMO. Decentralisation of accounting systems and the shift to accrual accounting improved the information available to departments for the management of debtors and creditors. Savings from improved cash management (including better accounting for, and use of, supplier credit and improved debt collection) were some of the earliest benefits to be realised from the reforms. Morris (1995) identifies a range of benefits, including improved understanding of departmental business, savings of around $31 million a year in interest costs through the use of supplier credit and improved utilisation of cash, and unquantified savings in bank fees from more efficient transaction processing.

The responsibility for consolidating cash balances was centralised, however, enabling funds to be managed more efficiently, offset with overdrafts, and linked to overall funding and risk management. The DMO, which had the responsibility of managing the overseas and domestic debt (the latter in conjunction with the Reserve Bank), assumed the role of the central treasury function. A report by the Auditor-General in 1994 concluded that the procedures for the management of the Crown's debt portfolio by the DMO were of high quality and that there had been a growing clarity in the DMO's articulation of its conceptual framework for its debt management strategies and of its guidelines for the implementation of its strategic objectives (Audit Office, 1994c).

Capital charge

The capital charge is designed to make the cost structure faced by departments mirror that of any other producer in the economy by including the cost of capital investment. The specific objectives of capital charging are, first, to make clear the *full* costs of goods and services produced by departments and, second, to provide the information and incentives needed for efficient management of the Crown's investment in departments (McCulloch, 1991). Treasury officials view the capital charge as an integral and consistent part of the wider programme of reform and stress that it is not to be confused with the public sector discount rate. The capital charge relates to the investment in an individual department for a particular period rather than to the evaluation of public policies, which can involve several different departments and have effect over a number of years.

The capital charge is calculated by multiplying the government's investment in a department by the charge rate. The latter is based on the weighted average costs of debt and equity capital and expected future growth for private sector counterparts. Where there are no private sector comparators, a standard rate is set by the government. Once balance sheet valuations had been established, all departments were given an appropriation to cover the capital charge. If the asset base is reduced, the charge is correspondingly reduced but not the appropriation, thus providing an incentive to dispose of unproductive assets.

The regime, at least in its early stages, has not been without theoretical and practical difficulties, however. A number of managers experienced initial difficulty in understanding the capital charge system. Where it is understood, the rationale behind capital charging generally has been accepted. The problems lie with the determination of the capital base and the level at which the charge is set. With respect to the capital base, more guidance was needed in the initial stages on what to do with capital work in progress and whether items such as revaluation reserves and longstanding accruals should be included in taxpayers' funds. The adequacy of the initial valuations on which the capital charge was based has also caused some departments concern.

Designed to give correct financial signals, the capital charge regime is not able to remove all potential distortionary effects. For example, because human resources are not included, the capital charge might be understated and distort the allocation of resources between, say, human and physical capital. Or the capital charge regime might result in leasing or disposal of assets, which meets short-term objectives but is less than optimal in the longer term. Since the capital charge is based on net equity (total assets less total liabilities), the charge will not alter on sale of a fixed asset unless the cash so obtained is returned to the government. The incentive might be to spend cash arising from asset rationalisation before the end of the financial year, rather than return it to the government. This is not necessarily consistent with long-term planning or overall coordination of governmental priorities.

Several difficulties arise with respect to the level at which the charge is set and the methodology to be used. Not all public sector activities have an exact equivalent in the private sector in which case a default rate based on the Capital Asset Pricing Model, popular in finance theory, is to be applied. Pratt (1992) questions the relevance of a model centred on concepts of risk in financial markets to obligatory governmental activities like policing. Even if the Capital Asset Pricing Model is accepted as the most rational approach (Lally, 1992), the rate, which applies to a department as a whole, might not be the appropriate rate for particular activities. For example, the initial 13 per cent default rate was possibly inappropriate for land and buildings at a time of particularly low returns on property in the private sector (Lewis, 1991).

Another major area of concern is how the charge is to be passed on to third-party clients. Some government departments provide services to low-income clients who might not be able to pay the increased charges. How the government is to compensate such clients directly or to compensate departments that incur deficits by providing services at reasonable cost requires a clear policy, which is far from easy to develop. Some departments might choose to allocate costs, including the capital charge, in such a way as effectively to cross-subsidise particular outputs. Such behaviour might run counter to the original intent of capital charges, which is to provide clear signals for financial management. Questions of efficiency and questions of equity are inextricably intertwined in a way that is perhaps not envisaged in models based on private sector thinking.

In practice, there appear to have been considerable improvements in asset management overall. A 1993 survey (Price Waterhouse, 1993) found that departments had better control of working capital, undertook more rigorous reviews of surplus assets, investigated rent versus buy options, and had an improved understanding of risks and investment analysis. However, the extent to which this has been prompted by the capital charging regime is unclear (Audit Office, 1993a, p. 41); a desire to fund new asset purchases might have been a more important incentive to sell existing assets than the capital charge *per se*. Additionally, concerns have been expressed by departments that there is little awareness of the capital charge outside head offices. If this is the case, its incentive effect on the managers who actually use many of the assets might be limited.

Performance Specification and Reporting

The reforms have taken an innovative approach to some of the problems that have long plagued the setting of objectives and measurement of performance throughout the world. The accompanying structural changes—such as the separation of trading, policy advice, administration, and service delivery activities into separate agencies with their own sets of accounts—have helped to overcome the problems of multiple and conflicting objectives. Placing the departmental reporting emphasis on output specification (in

Table 13.1   Examples of quantity and quality measures for output classes

Group	Output class	Quantity measures	Quality measures
Customer oriented	Advisory or reference services	Estimated range for number of requests answered	% of clients who rank service *x* or better based on independent survey against agreed criteria
	Replies to ministerial correspondence and questions	Estimated range for number of replies	• % first drafts accepted by minister • % completed within *x* time & maximum time for completing remainder
Transactions	Issuing licences, permits or rulings	Estimated range for number of licences, permits and rulings issued	• Minimum % issued fully comply with law • Minimum % issued within *x* working days of (completed application); remainder within *x* working days • Maximum % of appeals lodged sustained
	Pest control or destruction	Estimated number of hectares cleared or completed pest destruction projects	• % pest reduction in designated area attested by post-kill assessment • Targeting designed to avoid killing endangered species. Maximum estimated number.
Professional/ managerial	Policy advice	Completion of the agreed priority policy projects	As specified by the cabinet and set out in Treasury's purchase agreement guidelines. Measures encompass: coverage of service, time, quality of individual papers (purpose, logic, accuracy, options, consultation, practicality, presentation). Assessed against criteria by minister.
	Contract management	List of contracts (or contract types) which will be managed	The measures would cover relevance, best price, risk management, accuracy, time, completeness in the content of contract negotiated
	Standard or rule setting	Completion of the list of rules or standards to be developed to what stage	• Minimum % of rules to be reviewed this year • Maximum time since rule or standard last reviewed • Minimum % of affected parties who rate consultation process, rule clarity and relevance of standards as *x* or better • Absence of successful challenges in court
Investigations	Commercial investigations	Estimated range for number of cases investigated	• % of cases initiated by provider (proactive) • Minimum % complaints acted on • Minimum % case files comply with evidential standards • Maximum number of cases subject to successful legal challenge

Table 13.1   Examples of quantity and quality measures for output classes *(continued)*

Behavioural	Case management: work interviews	Estimated range for number of individual interviews completed	• Minimum % of interviews match agreed profile • Minimum % of individuals interviewed taking one of the preferred actions (joining a job action initiative, being placed, ceasing registration) within *x* time of interview attributable of interview
Control	Prison management	Estimated range for number of prisoner days by security level (maximum, medium and minimum)	• Maximum number of escapes or improper releases (by security level) • Maximum number of complaints against prison management upheld by independent review • Minimum % of facilities complying to *x* extent with international standards for humane custody attested by independent audit • Maximum number of serious incidents or riots reported
Emergency services	Fire suppression	Resources available	• Contingency plan exists • Minimum % of fires responded to within *x* time.
Defence	Contingent military capabilities	• Levels of equipment and staffing of unit X to enable it to undertake readiness training activities to maintain its Minimum Level of Capability (MLOC) • Levels of munitions, technical and expendable stores to generate its Operational Level of Capability (OLOC) and sustain operations until supply can be arranged • Levels of personnel to sustain and replace unit X when committed to operations at OLOC	• Level of proficiency achieved by unit X on completion of readiness training activities • Ability of Unit X to be staffed and equipped to be ready to deploy for operations at the end of its degree of notice • Ability to correct (or not correct) unit X's identified critical deficiencies by the end of its degree of notice

Source: Adapted from Treasury (1995) *Purchase Agreement Guidelines with Best Practices for Output Performance Measures*, pp. 41–80

terms of quantity, quality, cost, location, and time) rather than on imponderable outcomes, which individual departments cannot control, helps to hold managers accountable. Distinguishing purchase and ownership interests of the government, the respective types of appropriation involved, and the respective forms of reporting required improves transparency of governmental activities and facilitates the switching of resources into key priority areas.

A number of the initial difficulties in specifying outputs (e.g. inclusion of goods and services that did not go outside the department or the definition of outputs in terms of existing organisational structures) have since been overcome. The Treasury provided considerable advice on these matters, which was generally found helpful, although some departments complained that the Treasury had too much influence in deciding what the definitions were to be, and there was suspicion about the motives behind output specification. Some departments claimed that improved specification decreases management flexibility and enhances the chances of the amounts appropriated being cut whereas central agencies, in contrast, argued that areas where specification was poor tended to be dealt with more severely (Logan, 1991, p. 99).

Initially, the government purchased output classes from departments on the basis of little more than the information in the Estimates. In 1992, an interdepartmental working party looking at output definition recommended that all CEs be required to specify the outputs within each output class in a purchase agreement with their responsible minister. Starting in the 1993–94 year, such purchase agreements are now incorporated into the performance agreements of all CEs, and parallel ownership agreements are to be developed. The signed purchase agreement becomes a record of the output purchase decision agreed by the minister with a department. In addition to specifying the outputs that will be purchased, the document sets out the terms and conditions surrounding the purchase such as procedures for monitoring, amending, and reporting. Ministers can still agree to changes in the output mix during the year, subject to overall appropriation constraints, but those changes must be recorded. It is envisaged that in the future ministers will increasingly make use of purchase advisers from outside the department that is party to the agreement. If prepared well, purchase agreements should assist ministers to understand the outputs the department is supplying, to determine which outputs to purchase, to compare the department with other suppliers, and to hold the provider accountable for delivery (Treasury, 1995).

Overall, the process of identifying outputs seems to have been a useful learning exercise for all concerned. There has been a rapid improvement in the ability to specify outputs, and it has led to departments and politicians asking meaningful questions about why particular activities are undertaken. The main area of difficulty has been specifying the less measurable, but often most important, aspects of performance, running the risk that the more readily measurable aspects are over-emphasised in comparison. While quality is often regarded as the least readily measurable dimension of performance, its importance has not been overlooked in specifying outputs (see Table 13.1 for examples). Of particular importance, given its role in linking government's activities to its strategic objectives, is the quality of policy advice. The ultimate test of policy advice would be whether it resulted in the achievement of desired outcomes. But given the nebulous nature of outcome measures, the difficulty of collecting valid social indicators on a current basis, the time lags involved, and the impossibility of conclusively proving cause and effect in an open and changing social system, such measurement of quality is difficult.

Cost is often viewed as one of the easier dimensions of performance to measure. In fact, it has proved to be one of the more difficult in the case of departmental outputs. The allocation of costs to outputs has been particularly difficult. Audit opinions on financial statements were often qualified because of inadequate bases for allocating costs. This is an area of ongoing development in departments. Changes envisaged include the introduction or refinement of personnel time-recording systems; more emphasis on direct costing and reduction in corporate overheads; reviews of cost allocation bases; the allocation of costs to more disaggregated levels, and improvements in management information systems and recording. The benefits of this sort of effort need to be weighed up against the cost, however, particularly in the case of smaller departments, which might not be able to absorb the costs of developing and monitoring sophisticated cost allocation processes.

Perhaps the most contentious issue in the new performance reporting regime has been whether there has been an over-emphasis on outputs to the neglect of reporting on outcomes. Initially departments tended to want to specify outcomes rather than outputs. They had often given considerable thought to why they were doing things and regarded the attention being given to outputs as a step backwards in that focusing on means might result in losing sight of ends. It is therefore necessary to stress that definition of outputs is only the first step of a two-step process. The second step involves assessing the contribution of outputs to outcomes (an important role of policy advice) so that the focus still remains on the reasons for funding outputs (Bushnell, 1989). Nonetheless, placing the reporting emphasis on outputs runs the risk of losing sight of outcomes such that managers in government simply perform to specification and walk away from the substantive issues of whether the public interest has been served. To a large extent this risk should be overcome by the new emphasis on SRAs linked to CE performance agreements.

CONCLUSION

Although the speed and scope of the recent financial management reforms have given the appearance of revolution, it needs to be recognised that these changes are built on a history of earlier attempts at financial management reform on the part of government officials, the Audit Office, and the accountancy profession. As a result, the notions of accrual accounting and non-financial performance measures were well established by the mid-1980s and accounting was viewed as an integral part of overall resource management. There has been considerable goodwill towards the reforms brought about through the State Sector Act and Public Finance Act, especially on the part of senior managers and politicians. Although the speed of the reforms has created some transitional problems, as well as considerable effort and expense, the principles underlying the reforms now seem well understood.

Outstanding issues are of two types. First, there are essentially transitional problems that arise because not all practical consequences of the proposed changes could have been anticipated in advance (e.g. specification of outputs, allocation of costs, the degree of guidance from central agencies required by departments, and the operation of incentives such as the capital charge). While these areas require some further work, some practicable solutions are likely in the near future. Other outstanding issues are of a more intractable nature; for example, the desirability and practicality of measuring outcomes and the appropriate balance between managerial autonomy and parliamentary control. For some of these questions there might never be any single correct answer.

> Public management reform is not just an apolitical quest for technical efficiency within a given institutional framework. Public management in the 1990s will have to develop new concepts and models of governance which alter political processes, redefine the criteria of policy effectiveness and transform the patterns and processes of accountability (Metcalfe, 1993, p. 292).

With the new financial management regime in individual government departments firmly established, New Zealand was able to turn its attention to planning, budgeting, and reporting for the Crown as a whole. Here the reformers faced a new series of challenges. Public management cannot be confined to the micro-level of individual organisations but 'implies a very significant expansion of the role of management in government beyond the sphere where existing business management methods can be applied more or less directly' (Metcalfe 1993 p. 303).

This chapter examines recent initiatives in planning, budgeting, and reporting for the whole of government. These initiatives in whole-of-government strategising and reporting were designed to meet several interrelated objectives. The first was to minimise the risks associated with inadequate information and lack of public awareness about the implications of immediate policies for the longer term. Such inadequacies could encourage short-term thinking and action on the part of politicians mindful of the need for popular support for re-election. Short-term thinking not only runs political and economic risks, such as over-expenditure or poorly targeted expenditure, but also it creates problems for departmental managers trying to develop strategies in an environment of constantly changing priorities and uncertainty in budgets beyond one year. A further objective was to address the need to articulate and communicate the collective interest of government with better alignment between the central agencies accompanied by better alignment between the Budget and non-financial plans. Whole-of-government initiatives might also help overcome any problems of coordination created by increased separateness of agencies within a contracting state.

COORDINATION

Coordination among organisations that are formally autonomous but functionally interdependent is one of the keys to ensuring effectiveness in public management. Metcalfe (1993) observes that public management involves the complex task of taking responsibility for managing an *interorganisational* network. However, contracting out to a host of single-purpose entities in a competitive market tends to encourage separateness rather than interdependence. Without macro-level coordination, a 'market' approach to operating the public sector cannot deal adequately with problems such as environmental protection, macro-economic management, regional development, or trade-offs in the supply of social services such as health or education. The reporting framework, with its emphasis on individual ministers and chief executives, and on outputs of individual departments, might reinforce any trends towards 'departmentalism' (Martin, 1990); that is, the breakdown of a hitherto unified public service into atomistic units.

The 1991 review of the state sector reforms (Logan, 1991) identified three issues as having emerged from the experience with the accountability relationship between ministers and chief executives and from the government's concern that the parties involved interpret that relationship in light of the collective interest.

First, there were different perspectives on the idea of the collective interest (Logan, 1991, pp. 45–6). Ministers tended to emphasise the need for a joint commitment by ministers and officials to the overall goals of the government and the need for good communication. Some ministers considered that the reforms had adversely affected elements of the collective interest, such as policy advice coordination, support for collective decision-making and efficient resource management, and advocated greater collegiality among chief executives as a means of redressing this. CEs emphasised the constitutional responsibilities of cabinet and ministers to provide leadership and strategy. Others pointed to the need for a collegial view of accountability and the importance of public service culture and procedures as a means of reinforcing the collective interest. In other words, as Roberts (1991) suggests, the underlying concept of accountability needs to shift from the present 'hierarchical' accountability, which heightens a sense of separateness, to one of 'socialising' accountability, which emphasises interdependence.

Second, there were concerns about the processes of government decision-making; in particular, strategy formulation. The reforms presumed that the government would have an agreed set of priorities in the form of policy goals or outcomes, which guide collective agreement on output purchases. In 1991, the Logan review (p. 47) found a widespread view among public servants that the structure of performance management had not been completed by the development of an integrated view of ultimate policy goals by cabinet. Some thought that ministers were disinclined to think strategically in the sense of committing themselves to outcomes, although it was recognised that prior specification of outcomes by individual ministers was difficult in the absence of a clear statement of the government's strategy. Others argued that it was neither practicable nor politically feasible to hold ministers to outcomes, particularly given difficulties in establishing clear relationships between outputs and outcomes. In practice, there tended to be a 'bottom-up' process whereby outcomes were defined to explain the purpose of outputs rather than outputs being driven from a set of outcomes.

The Logan report (p. 47) argued that ministers did in fact engage in strategic processes; in particular, the budget process was a comprehensive look at the government's priorities and a central expression of cabinet's collective responsibility. However, it acknowledged that too much government strategising was done in conditions of secrecy and haste, which were not conducive to good decision-making. In the case of the budget process, its fixed calendar deadline, its secrecy, and (in some policy areas) the small number of ministers and officials involved placed strategic thinking under great pressure. The Logan report (p. 50) suggested that the process of cabinet strategy formulation should begin prior to the budget process in order to build consensus on overall priorities and to enable members of the cabinet to discuss issues of mutual interest.

Third, the Logan report (pp. 53–8) identified policy, purchase, and ownership risks arising from devolved decision-making, inadequate consultation between departments, and insufficient consideration of the potential consequences and actions (e.g. in the use or disposal of assets) for government and other agencies. Also, certain Crown interests (such as maintaining standards of equity in the treatment of citizens, obligations to specific groups such as Maori, and being a good employer) might not be viewed by departments as in their own self-interest. The Logan report (p. 57) identified functions that even large decentralised private sector corporations retain at the centre (e.g. strategic planning, corporate accounting and treasury functions, and ensuring efficient use of overall resources). Where cabinet or ministers decide to delegate decision-making, the Logan report (p. 60) recommended that it be done under the principles of clear specification of desired results, effective monitoring of the results achieved, and the creation of incentives for the results to be achieved in the most cost-effective manner.

A considerable amount of work has since been carried out in response to the issues raised by the Logan report. The government was keen that the strategic vision set out in its 1993 document, *Path to 2010*, be given effect in the public service. During an exercise early in 1994 in which CE performance agreements were being reviewed, the SSC introduced the concept of Strategic Result Areas (SRAs) to provide a stepping down from the broad vision contained in *Path to 2010*. At the same time, the key result areas (KRAs) in CEs' annual performance were extended to cover a three-year period and be more strategic. Following consultation with the Treasury, DPMC, and CEs, DPMC took up responsibility for implementing the concept and did the development work of the actual SRAs with CEs and ministers.

The SRAs were first made public in February 1995. The published SRAs, together with the budget policy statement required by the fiscal responsibility legislation described later in this chapter, are intended to communicate to governmental managers and to the public at large what the government intends to accomplish over the next 3–5 years and how it plans to go about using its own agencies. The nine SRAs for 1994–97 were:

a. Maintaining and Accelerating Economic Growth
b. Enterprise and Innovation
c. External Linkages
d. Education and Training
e. Community Security
f. Social Assistance
g. Health and Disability Services
h. Treaty Settlement Claims
i. Protecting and Enhancing the Environment.

For each of the above, there is a description of the SRA and its objective in largely outcome terms and a listing of the activities on which particular emphasis will be placed during the next 3–5 years. The SRAs are linked to the operations of departments through the KRAs, which are developed from and take account of the SRAs for the public service as a whole. In the case of departments that do not have business directly related to SRAs, greater emphasis is given in the KRAs to the responsible minister's priorities and the strategic effectiveness of the organisation.

KRAs are not meant to encompass every aspect of a department's business but rather to focus on critical matters such as:

a. Delivery of goods and services in support of SRAs.
b. Aspects of departmental management with a high priority that are regarded as critical to a department's performance and its strategic capability to deliver its goods and services. These could include such issues as structure and governance, investment and divestment, organisational development, planning and management of financial and human resources and key relationship management.
c. Other priority areas for action (SSC, 1994a).

Although part of an annual contract, KRAs are generally expected to take a three-year focus and not to vary greatly during that time unless a major change is agreed in strategic direction. The SSC has stated that progress towards achievement must be defined in terms of observable and verifiable milestones, which will form the basis for assessing CE and departmental performance. Therefore, although the milestones will cover the three years, they will typically have a one-year focus. The three central agencies review draft KRAs in consultation with each CE. As well as reviewing how well the KRAs have been specified, this process provides an opportunity for overall coordination of strategy by examining whether the KRAs are linked to SRAs, or are of key strategic importance, and whether each KRA mutually reinforces the KRAs of other departments that contribute to the same SRA.

Central agencies such as the DPMC, the Treasury, and the SSC are an important mechanism for ensuring coordination across the various agencies of government. The Logan report had, however, identified a perceived lack of coordination between the central agencies with gaps and overlaps in the definition of their responsibilities of central agencies (Logan, 1991, pp. 69–73). Conflicts between, for example, policy and financial management roles of the Treasury, the policy advice and policy coordination roles of the DPMC, and the advisory and review roles of the SSC can result in contradictory advice, inconsistent use of terminology, and lack of knowledge about what other agencies or other parts of the same agency are doing. Furthermore, CEs considered that the advisory and monitoring functions of central agencies had an excessive impact on departments with information being requested without regard for the costs involved.

A number of the above issues were addressed in a report by the working party set up to review accountability requirements in 1994 (SSC, 1994f). The report concluded that there were no fundamental problems with the underlying elements of the accountability system and endorsed the developments in enhancing strategic direction. With respect to information requirements and processes for accountability relationships, the working party developed a list of protocols that it thought the central agencies and the Audit Office should observe:

a. the purpose of, and justification for, the information should be made clear;
b. the purpose should be consistent with the responsibilities and accountabilities of ministers, chief executives and the central agencies;
c. the information processes to be used are the most efficient and effective way to achieve that purpose;
d. issues of materiality and risk should be properly addressed;
e. duplication and overlap should be minimised; and
f. reasonable assurance should be given that benefits exceed costs, and/or that overall costs are minimised.

In turn, the report (SSC, 1994f, p. 2) suggested that chief executives provide feedback to the central agencies on the application of these protocols.

The 1992 amendment to the Public Finance Act 1989 had removed the requirement for half-yearly audits, thus reducing compliance costs. The working party noted that many corporate plans duplicated information in other accountability documents, such as the Estimates and purchase agreements. Published corporate plans have since ceased to be mandatory.

All government decisions, whether long-term or short-term, have fiscal implications. Recent efforts to bring the new longer-term focus and concern for strategic coherence into the budget process are examined below.

FISCAL RESPONSIBILITY ACT

The Budget for the government as a whole is the translation of its collective strategies into financial terms. From 1991 the Treasury had been working on the budget process to improve its strategic coherence and, about the time that the notion of SRAs was developed, began formalising the new budget approach in the form of a Fiscal Responsibility Bill. The idea behind the bill was to improve the level of the Crown's fiscal disclosure in such a way that governments would be required to state their fiscal objectives and report progress towards achieving those objectives. It was argued that such transparency would lead to more informed public decision-making and encourage governments to take a longer-term perspective to fiscal management, thereby reducing risk. In attempting to minimise the influence of short-sighted political decision-making on management of the economy, the fiscal responsibility legislation can be viewed as the equivalent for fiscal policy of the Reserve Bank Act for monetary policy.

Ruth Richardson, who was Minister of Finance at the time the Fiscal Responsibility Bill was developed, subsequently became chairperson of the Finance and Expenditure select committee (FEC), which examined the bill and therefore played a key role in both its development and enactment. During the committee examination of the bill, the main issue considered was whether the greater transparency afforded by enhanced disclosure was enough to ensure responsible fiscal policy. Concern was expressed that loosely bound governments under MMP might be less able to resist temptation to adopt short-term fiscal strategies that were inconsistent with longer-term goals. Public choice arguments were used; in particular, that excessive spending is possible in the pursuit of vote maximisation, particularly where voters' benefits are highly visible but costs are widely spread or deferred to the future. Some submissions favoured mandatory fiscal targets such as the achievement of an AAA credit rating or a balance sheet in which total debt did not exceed current assets. Mandatory targets were rejected by the committee, however, for the following reasons:

a. There is no theoretical justification for any particular fiscal target that can be maintained over a period of time. While targets are set for monetary policy, there is not the same degree of consensus for fiscal policy.
b. The inflexibility of mandatory targets makes it difficult for fiscal policy to respond appropriately to the inevitable volatility of economic circumstances.
c. Overseas experience showed that legislated targets (e.g. the Gramm-Rudman-Hollings Act in the US federal government) had failed to produce the desired results. Mandatory targets could result in window dressing, distort decision-making, or send inappropriate signals to the electorate. For example, if a mandatory balanced budget target was set, it could result in off-budget spending and policy substitution.
d. The process would depend on the vagaries of economic forecasting.
e. Governments (albeit via Parliament) should not legislate to bind future governments.

An alternative approach suggested in submissions was to specify fiscal guidelines to provide benchmarks for governments in their setting of fiscal objectives. Progress could be measured against these objectives and governments be required to explain and justify departures from the guidelines. The FEC supported the idea of guidelines and requiring the government to specify reasons for any temporary departure from them. Section 4(2) of the Fiscal Responsibility Act 1994 sets out the following principles of responsible fiscal management:

a. Reducing Crown debt to prudent levels by achieving operating surpluses every year until a prudent level of debt has been attained. The legislation does not define or prescribe what is meant by a 'prudent level of debt'. Rather, it is left to each government to determine, and justify to the public, what it considers 'prudent' and 'reasonable'.
b. Maintaining total Crown debt at a prudent level by ensuring that on average operating expenses of the Crown do not exceed operating revenue.
c. Achieving and maintaining levels of Crown net worth that provide a buffer against adverse future events.
d. Prudent management of the fiscal risks facing the Crown.
e. The pursuit of policies consistent with a reasonable degree of predicability about the level and stability of tax rates for the future.

Any departure from the above five principles must be both transparent and temporary. The FEC also considered a guideline of achieving the highest possible credit rating but decided that this was more in the nature of an outcome than an output and depended on a variety of factors, not just the level of the fiscal aggregates. A further related issue considered by the FEC was whether a particular set of broad economic and social objectives for fiscal policy, such as employment and equity goals, should be adopted. The FEC, on the advice of the Treasury, decided that the bill was not intended to prescribe the nature and scope of the ultimate objectives that fiscal policy serves, but rather to ensure that a government pursue the set of social and economic objectives it chooses in a transparent, responsible manner.

The former Secretary to the Treasury, Graham Scott, raised the question of wider strategy coordination in his submission to the FEC (G. Scott, 1994). He advocated greater integration between fiscal strategy and the overall strategy for economic and social policy and suggested a government statement early in the budget cycle announcing the parameters for the forthcoming budget cycle and relating them to the government's broader objectives. The FEC took up this suggestion with the result that the statements required by the legislation as enacted include:

a. A *budget policy statement*, setting out long-term objectives for fiscal policy, broad strategic priorities for the Budget and fiscal intentions, published by 31 March in each year. The government must assess whether they are consistent with the principles of responsible fiscal management and previous budget policy statements, disclosing and explaining any departure from them.
b. *Economic and fiscal updates*, containing economic and fiscal forecasts for the current year and each of the following two financial years. Economic information provided must include forecasts of movements in GDP, consumer prices, the current account position of the balance of payments, and a description of all significant underlying assumptions. The fiscal updates comprise forecast Crown financial statements, in the same format as the *ex post* statements, together with details of all significant underlying assumptions.

   The Act legislates for economic and fiscal updates at the time the Budget is prepared, in December of each year and between 42 and 28 days before a general election. Each economic and fiscal update must be accompanied by a statement of responsibility signed by the Minister of Finance and the Secretary to the Treasury.
c. A *fiscal strategy report*, containing projections in total revenue, expenditure, debt, and net worth over the next ten years, and assessing whether the trends and updates are consistent with the budget policy statement.

The financial information must be in accordance with generally accepted accounting practice (GAAP), enabling comparison with subsequent reports on actual financial position and performance. That the New Zealand government, unlike overseas counterparts, was prepared to bind itself to GAAP established by an independent Accounting Standards Review Board, rather than trying to determine its own accounting rules and regulations, can be attributed largely to the determination of those politicians who had fought to improve the government's financial situation to impose fiscal restraint on their successors and prevent them from manipulating accounting practices.

In tandem with the Fiscal Responsibility Act, amendments were made to the Public Finance Act to provide comparative and more timely information for accountability and decision-making. The amendments moved non-departmental appropriations to an accrual basis following what had been the practice for departmental appropriations since 1989. The amendments also introduced a more complete and consistent format for the Estimates and the accrual-based monthly Crown financial statements.

The budget cycle now consists of a series of stages, which mesh with overall processes of collective strategising and accountability. The stages of the budget cycle are now:

a. a strategic phase (October–December)
b. a budgeting phase (December–February)
c. a collective review phase (February–April)
d. a budget production phase (April–May)
e. an *ex post* review phase (July–September).

The introduction of a formal strategic phase is, as this chapter has highlighted, the major new initiative. It enables the debate on overall fiscal strategy to be separated from questions of detailed budget allocations and makes trade-offs more explicit. It anticipates a more open budget process under MMP. Preliminary meetings of senior officials are followed by an all-day meeting of cabinet at which ministers present key policy and resource issues and cabinet agrees budget parameters. These are then translated into instructions for departmental budgets and form the basis for the budget policy statement. During the same period, cabinet agrees SRAs for the public sector. Ministers and departments then prepare budgets within the overall budget strategy, agree KRAs consistent with SRAs, and arrive at purchase agreements. The future is likely to see more use of independent purchase advisers by ministers to help overcome the asymmetry of information between them and their departments.

The collective review phase in recent years has been developed to overcome traditional problems of disputes between Treasury and departments or conflicting interests of ministers and to ensure transparent dispute identification. Once the Treasury has reviewed the three-year budgets for consistency with the government's overall fiscal strategy, any disputes between the Treasury and departments are heard by the Officials' Committee on Expenditure Control, which resolves low-level disputes and clarifies issues for ministers. The budgets are then reviewed by the Cabinet Committee on Expenditure Control and Revenue (chaired by a minister other than the Minister of Finance). New initiatives are considered by senior ministers, and individual ministers are able to have their 'day in court'. Recommendations then go to the cabinet Strategy Committee, chaired by the Prime Minister. The budget decisions are turned into the budget documentation and estimates of appropriation. Once the results for the previous year are available, overspending (usually caused by inability to forecast with complete accuracy in demand-driven expenditure areas) can be examined and necessary validating legislation passed. Other significant variances, such as major underspending or major deviations from forecasts, are also examined, and the experience is fed into the next review of baselines.

Under MMP there is likely to be pressure to bring the Budget further forward in time so that it is passed prior to the start of the financial year (Fancy, 1995). Not only would this provide managers with a better planning basis for the year ahead but also it would signal that the government continues to have the confidence of the House or allow time for remedial action prior to the start of a financial year in the event that a minority government loses the confidence of Parliament or a coalition collapses. While earlier budgets would mean greater forecasting uncertainties, the medium-term focus to fiscal policy should ensure that the expenditure side at least is reasonably robust. In any event, the revenue side is influenced by many factors outside the government's control. A shift to earlier budgets could lead to a more intensive review of spending plans, and the issue then arises as to whether Parliament should be able to propose amendments to the Budget. Allowing such amendments, however, would mark a significant constitutional shift from the principle that the formulation of the Budget is the responsibility of the executive and blur accountability for overall management of fiscal policy.

Fancy (1995) also identifies a number of other issues in relation to budgeting and strategising under MMP. For example, unexpected elections or caretaker periods of government could place pressure on a longer-term strategy. As the term of a Parliament matures, it might become much more difficult for a coalition government to provide a longer-term focus to policy, particularly as the parties to the coalition increasingly seek to differentiate themselves. MMP might also bring pressure on supply. If the passage of appropriation bills becomes more difficult, government agencies will need to manage themselves very tightly against appropriation and imprest authority, highlighting the need for accurate, timely internal systems for monitoring their positions. At present, the Imprest Supply Act gives the Executive authority to spend or incur expenses or liabilities up to the limits provided for by the Act in the period between the end of the financial year and the passage of the first Appropriation Act. Under MMP, the assumption that decisions involving increases in spending will subsequently be validated by Parliament is much less assured, and each supply bill is potentially a confidence issue. Even under current arrangements it is possible to envisage situations where supply is not assured; for example, dissolution of a Parliament prior to the passage of a requisite appropriation bill. Options used in other countries to address this issue include making sure that a supply bill is the last Act of an outgoing government, creating an automatic provision in law for a certain period of supply to be maintained in such circumstances, and provisions to roll the previous year's Budget forward on a pro-rata basis.

Whatever its role in fiscal policy or its implications for day-to-day management by government agencies, the question of public finance is one of fundamental constitutional significance. Control over taxation and expenditure is intimately tied up with questions of parliamentary sovereignty. The challenge under MMP will be to balance the right of elected representatives, even if motivated by short-term considerations, to change priorities through a reasonably detailed system of appropriations and the need to ensure continuity and stability in the wider public interest. Enhanced transparency and debate made possible through the changes under the Fiscal Responsibility Act and the related work on collective strategising should help to articulate that wider public interest and ensure robustness of fiscal policy under MMP.

CROWN FINANCIAL STATEMENTS

Summary financial statements for the whole of government are one means of bringing together the many activities carried out by government in a coordinated presentation that can assist Parliament and the public at large to hold the government accountable. Internationally, the subject of accounting by sovereign states has attracted increasing interest in recent years (Dye and Bowsher, 1987; IFAC, 1991). The importance of summary financial reports by national governments was highlighted in the Federal Government Reporting Study (FGRS) carried out in the United States in the mid 1980s. The FGRS expressed the need for concise summary annual reports that provided an overview of the financial position and operating results of the federal government. Such reports, the FGRS argued, could assist users in demanding an accountability for actual results by comparison with earlier projections or budgets and provide a common database for analysis and for developing and debating policy decisions. Concerns about financial reporting by governments had also been expressed by economists (e.g. Britton, 1987; Oxley et al., 1990; Blejer and Cheasty, 1991). In their view, cash-based fiscal indicators fail to portray the sustainability of government policies. A few economists gave thought to the content and desirable characteristics of comprehensive balance sheets for national governments or developed stylised reports, but by 1990 nothing operational had been developed.

In April 1992, New Zealand became the first country in the world in recent decades[1] to produce a set of combined financial statements for its national government on a full accruals basis. Reporting on actual financial performance by the Crown was therefore the first of the whole-of-government initiatives of the early 1990s and helped pave the way to viewing government as an integrated whole, rather than a collection of separate individual entities. It also anticipated the introduction of accrual-based prospective information under the Fiscal Responsibility Act. Consistent with the view adopted for individual government departments, it was argued that accountability for the Crown as a whole requires that actual performance be compared with prior specification of performance; hence GAAP was adopted for both sets of statements. New Zealand, then, is distinctive internationally in that the same accounting practices are consistently applied to both the public and private sectors, to the whole of government as well as individual entities, and to government budgets as well as reports. Preparation of financial statements for the government as a whole on a full accruals basis had been provided for in the Public Finance Act 1989. However, it was recognised that this would be facilitated if full accruals

---

1. New Zealand produced departmental and state balance sheets and income statements during the 1930s, but this early initiative lapsed during World War II when cash accounting was resumed due to a wartime shortage of paper and accountants. In the Budget of 1930, the Minister of Finance explained that 'One of the objects in introducing the balance-sheet system was to obtain a general State balance sheet which would show accurately and in concise form all the assets held against the public debt and generally the position of the national finances from a commercial viewpoint' (*AJHR*, 1930, B. 6, p. 14, cited in New Zealand Government, 1992, p. 71).

accounting was first introduced across the individual government departments. The Crown financial statements for the half year ended 31 December 1991 began with government departments, offices of Parliament, and the Reserve Bank. The Crown reporting entity has since been extended to include SOEs and Crown entities.

The set of annual and half-yearly financial statements required under the Public Finance Act include not only an operating statement, statement of financial position (balance sheet), and statement of cashflows, but also statements of borrowings, commitments and contingent liabilities. Furthermore, there are detailed notes to the accounts and an overview in plain language accompanied by graphs and charts. There is also an extensive commentary on the statements in general and on the results for the reporting period in particular, complete with appendices and references to other sources of information. In the next few years trend data will start to emerge (for a full description see MacLeod, 1992; Pallot, 1994).

Evaluation of the Crown Financial Statements

The new Crown financial statements have produced a great deal of additional information that should help meet objectives of public accountability and usefulness for decision-making. The commentary on the first Crown financial statements (New Zealand Government, 1992, p. 72), states that their primary purpose is 'to assist Parliament and the electorate to hold governments accountable for their overall management of public resources'. Parliament now has a comprehensive set of financial statements, exceeding those provided by private sector companies, and the shift to an accrual basis of accounting gives a much more complete picture of assets, liabilities, revenues, and expenses. The range of information for assessing the government's fiscal position has been extended and provides a better view of longer-term fiscal consequences of current decision-making. Attention can be drawn to the nature of risks inherent in the balance sheet, helping to discourage governments from pursuing strategies of greater fiscal risk. Compiling and maintaining a more complete listing of Crown assets has helped to ensure that public sector managers remain conscious of the need for accurate reporting and competent management of assets under the control of the Crown.

Theoretical ideals, such as Buiter's (1982) ideal balance sheet, include such items as non-marketable social overhead capital (e.g. infrastructure assets), the present value of future tax revenue, the imputed value of the government's cash monopoly, and the present value of social insurance and other welfare programmes. While the present value of future tax revenues and welfare programmes is undoubtedly relevant in assessing the financial strength of government, the Crown financial statements exclude such assets and liabilities. As Blejer and Cheasty (1991, p. 1669) point out, 'the present value of the tax program ... presents conceptual difficulties large enough to cast doubt on the interpretation of any measure of government net worth.' Also excluded from the balance sheet are intangible assets and human resources. This is also an issue in the private sector, but it might be exacerbated in government, which is typically much more labour-intensive rather than capital-intensive as well as being information-intensive.

Several reasons were given in the commentary to the first Crown financial statements for the exclusion of these assets and liabilities. One is that their nearest equivalents in the private sector (e.g. levies on members of mutual or cooperative organisations and unfunded labour costs) are not recognised in balance sheets. However, these analogies are not exact, and there are substantial differences between the coercive power of governments and the power to levy members of cooperatives. Constitutionally, it is possible to argue instead that government does not have full control over the raising of taxes as it must obtain the approval of Parliament. In addition, as Stella (1989, p. 19) comments, 'many activities take place without the knowledge of government. . . . Transactions that imply tax obligations (for example, the earning of income) or imply future expenditure (for example, the unemployment rate) are not known with precision by government.' It is reasonable to suggest that governments should not be held accountable for that over which they cannot be expected to have knowledge or control.

A second reason for omitting these assets and liabilities involves the trade-off between relevance and reliability; that is, while the information is relevant, it is far too unreliable to meet the requirements of generally accepted accounting practice. A third reason is that if such assets and liabilities were included they would 'swamp' the balance sheet, rendering other items immaterial in comparison. Excluding them allows a more informative picture of the residual net worth and concentrates on what the government is able to manage. Yet another argument is that the present value of the taxation revenues and the present value of contingent liabilities for welfare payments offset one another. However, this argument could be extended to *all* potential reductions in government net worth in which case 'the present value of the tax programme simply replaces net worth as the balancing item in the comprehensive balance sheet' (Blejer and Cheasty, 1991, p. 1674).

Quite apart from the difficulties with intangible assets such as the right to tax, the very significant human resource in the public sector and the knowledge and information held, there are special difficulties in valuing tangible assets such infrastructure or heritage assets. The reporting of infrastructure and heritage assets in the Crown financial statements differs from the recommendations earlier put out by the New Zealand Society of Accountants in its *Statement of Public Sector Accounting Concepts* (SPSAC, 1987) and its exposure draft of a Technical Guidance Bulletin (TGB-4) on the subject. Under SPSAC and TGB-4, infrastructure and heritage assets had been referred to as 'community assets' (see Pallot, 1990) because they were used directly by the community and the community were likely to have an active interest in decisions about them (for example, their replacement or sale). Because of significant differences in both their economic characteristics (e.g. their value, nature of the benefits provided and to whom) and their 'social' characteristics (e.g. the degree of control held by the reporting entity), SPSAC and TGB-4 had recommended that community assets be reported separately from fixed assets in a Statement of Resources. The Statement of Resources was excluded from the list of statements required by the Public Finance Act 1989, although there are signs that the Federal Accounting Standards Advisory Board might advocate such an approach in the United States (FASAB, 1994). Given that reporting of community assets was still essential for accountability purposes, the effect of having no statement of resources in New Zealand was to force them on to the statement of financial position.

The commentary on the first financial statements argues that 'as in the private sector, reporting assets on the Crown balance sheet carries no implication that those assets are intended for sale. Neither does reporting the assets on the balance sheet indicate their value in non-financial terms; for example, the conservation value of a scenic reserve' (New Zealand Government, 1992, p. 79). While best efforts have been made in New Zealand to place values on these assets, it is difficult to be accurate given that they are traded less frequently than private sector assets, and public sector asset prices might be markedly different from private sector prices in a thinner market. Furthermore, the usefulness of this information can be questioned. Market (exchange) values seem irrelevant if there is no intention of liquidating the assets, and value in use cannot be represented by the present value of future cash flows since benefits are mostly non-financial. Also, because a variety of valuation bases has been adopted in the Crown balance sheet (including historic cost, market value, and replacement cost), it might not be possible to add the valuations together so as to make the net worth calculation a meaningful figure. In contrast to items like the present value of taxation revenues, where relevant but unreliable information was excluded, values of infrastructure assets are more reliable but their inclusion is possibly less relevant.

Having a mixture of valuation bases that cannot be added together in a meaningful way is, of course, a pervasive problem in the private sector as well. However, it is exacerbated when additional valuation bases for infrastructure and heritage assets are included. If a balance sheet is meant to reflect financial viability, taxation capacity is far more relevant than somewhat arbitrary values assigned to monuments and roads, which cannot, or should not, readily be sold. If balance sheets are meant to reflect physical capacity, then a report on the intended and actual quantity, quality, and capacity of infrastructure and heritage assets, along with depreciation that is a reflection of actual resource consumption rather than simply an allocation of cost, should be considered. Trying to tackle these issues in government highlights the need for accounting in both the public and private sectors to decide whether financial or physical capital maintenance (or neither or both) is the key underlying issue. Perhaps accounting in both sectors should provide not only a statement of financial position, based on value in exchange, which reflects financial viability but also a statement of resources, based on value in use, which reflects physical capacity.

The shift from a cash to an accrual-based set of accounts might be justified partly in terms of the *visibility* it gives to items such as accounts receivable, borrowings, and fixed assets, thus alerting managers, politicians, and the public at large to the need to manage these properly. Even when it is impossible to obtain completely 'accurate' figures, this increased visibility might still be very important. Also, a single net worth figure might mean little in isolation, but trends over time and comparisons with other nations might provide more meaningful information. This will require a willingness to continue with the New Zealand initiative both here and overseas.

In surveying the literature on the measurement of fiscal deficits, Blejer and Cheasty (1991, p. 1674) conclude that 'the jury is still out on the superiority of net worth calculations compared with traditional flow measures'. It is unlikely that any theoretically ideal solution to reporting by sovereign governments will ever be found. The inability to solve all theoretical problems, however, has never prevented accounting from being important and useful in the commercial sector. Furthermore, the New Zealand initiative suggests that a significant improvement in information can be obtained and much can be learned from experience if a start is made in the first place.

Pallot (1994) suggests that three major lessons can be learned about accounting from this exercise of producing Crown accounts. First, accounting is not just a technical matter. Consolidation of Crown accounts raises all manner of legal and political questions about the boundaries of the Crown's estate, the relationship between various arms of government, and the ownership of tangible and intangible assets. Because of the imperative created under the Public Finance Act 1989 to produce combined financial statements for the Crown as a whole, accounting reforms have required an examination of legal and organisational changes, particularly with respect to relationships between the Crown and its agencies and the ownership of assets. For example, Crown accounting revealed that ownership of urban motorways (e.g. between the Crown, local government, Transit New Zealand, or even the public at large) was uncertain and has required that the legal situation be clarified.

Second, the exercise has shown that the introduction of accrual accounting in government does not mean that differences between public and private sector accounting disappear. The commentary to the Crown financial statements (pp. 83–4) carefully points out that while the statements provide many of the benefits of private sector financial reporting, they differ in some important respects. For example, a government's revenue and spending are aimed at improving the welfare of the nation as a whole, rather than of the Crown entity alone. Thus, statements such as the Operating Statement and the Statement of Financial Position have to be interpreted differently from the Income Statement and Balance Sheet of private sector companies.

Revenues and expenses in the Crown's Operating Statement are different in nature from those in the private sector. Most Crown revenue arises from exercising 'sovereign powers', principally the power to tax, and much expenditure by the Crown is designed to improve national well-being in a way that has virtually no counterpart among private sector companies. The private sector concepts of profit and loss do not have a precise counterpart in the public sector. While the Crown's operating balance is an important indicator of the Crown's financial performance in a given period, it is not on its own an adequate measure of whether the government is achieving its broader goals.

Just as the Crown's Operating Statement is not entirely comparable with that of a company, neither is the Crown's Statement of Financial Position. Many assets recorded in the balance sheet are not held primarily to generate revenue but rather to provide services in the national interest (e.g. heritage assets such as national parks and national archives). Interpretation of the balance sheet is different; for example, the power to tax means that a sovereign entity is not insolvent if it has a negative net worth.

Finally, having to tackle accounting issues on which there is no generally accepted accounting practice exposes some problems in accounting theory generally. There are problems that are also pervasive in the private sector, such as when to recognise an item as an asset, the treatment of intangibles and human resources, and a mixture of valuation bases on the balance sheet that cannot be added together in any meaningful way. However, these issues are exacerbated in the public sector either because they are particularly significant or because there are additional sorts of assets and liabilities (such as infrastructure, heritage assets, and taxation capacity). The nature of assets, the meaning of balance sheets, the significance of financial versus physical capital maintenance, and the meaning of depreciation are just a few of the issues still waiting to be resolved. A cooperative venture between accountants in the private sector and accountants in government might provide the best opportunity for broad-based and innovative thinking on these perennial matters.

CONCLUSION

In the early 1990s New Zealand undertook a number of bold new initiatives in planning, budgeting, and reporting for the Crown as a whole. They sought a longer-term strategic focus and improved coherence and coordination that are particularly important, given the fragmentation that is possible in a contracting style of government. Enhanced transparency and open informed debate have been viewed as key ingredients in making governments accountable for serving the collective interest. (See Table 14.1 for a summary of Parliament's annual financial cycle.) The developments in budgeting and financial reporting for the whole of government have built on the reforms described in Chapter 13 and are unprecedented internationally.

In their emphasis on clear specification of purpose, top-down decision-making, rational analysis and the need to coordinate planning and budgeting, the recent initiatives in New Zealand seem to echo the PPBS-influenced thinking of the late 1960s. The question arises as to whether the present system will meet with some of the same problems as PPBS; in particular, the impossibility of rational comprehensive approaches to decision-making given limitations of time, knowledge, reasoning ability, and resources, and the incompatibility of technical analysis with political objectives. Given such problems, Lindblom (1979) argued that it is necessary to adopt instead a process of 'muddling through' in which change is achieved incrementally. Similarly, Wildavsky (1978) argued that incremental budgeting is technically and politically more feasible and therefore more likely to be effective than 'rational' approaches like PPBS and zero-based budgeting (ZBB).

The New Zealand approach tried to avoid some of the difficulties of PPBS by deliberately separating the political decision-making from technical decision-making and by simplifying objectives as far as departments are concerned by focusing on outputs rather than imponderable outcomes. In providing policy advice, however, which will help governments to set long-term agendas and make informed selections of outputs to meet selected outcomes, there is certain to be a shortage of adequate analytical knowledge, skills, and time. There are also questions as to whether Parliament and its select committees have the necessary skills, time, resources, and motivation to make use of the vastly increased quantity and quality of information now available. With the advent of MMP, the tension between the 'rational' and the political will perhaps become even more acute. The challenge will be to balance a much greater intensity for short-term issue management with the maintenance of longer-term strategy.

Table 14.1   Parliament's annual financial cycle

July	• On or before 31 July main Appropriation Bill introduced (s. 6, PFA), second reading (Budget debate) commences • On Budget night Minister of Finance tables report on Government's fiscal strategy (s. 7, FRA), economic and fiscal update (s. 8, FRA), and Estimates of Appropriations for the Government of New Zealand (s. 9, PFA) • FEC allocates task of conducting examinations of the Estimates to select Committees
August	• Second reading of main Appropriation Bill continues
August–September	• FEC reviews fiscal strategy report and economic and fiscal update and reports to House on or before 30 September • FEC allocates task of conducting examinations of the Estimates to select Committees
September–October	• 20-hour debate on Estimates in Committee of the Whole (Estimates debate)
October	• Main Appropriation Bill passed on or before 31 October. Third reading debate may include fiscal strategy report, economic and fiscal update and the report of the FEC on these (3-hour debate) • *Annual financial statements of the Crown (s. 31, PFA) and report of the Controller and Auditor-General on audit of these statements tabled* • *Departmental annual reports tabled (s. 39, PFA)*
November–March	• *FEC conducts review of annual financial statements of the Crown and reports to House on or before 31 March* • *Select committees conduct financial reviews of performance of departments and report to House on or before 31 March*
December	• Minister of Finance publishes half-yearly economic and fiscal update prepared by the Treasury
March	• Crown's half-year financial statements tabled or published by 7 March • Minister of Finance publishes budget policy statement on or before 31 March
April	• FEC examines and reports on budget policy statement on or before 30 April
May	• Imprest Supply Bill may be introduced for further interim supply for current year (4-hour debate) • Supplementary Estimates may be introduced • Minister of Finance tables current year fiscal update (s. 15, FRA) • FEC may allocate task of conducting examination of Supplementary Estimates to select committees • House debates budget policy statement and FEC report on statement (2-hour debate)
June	• Select committees examine Supplementary Estimates and report to the House • Appropriation Bill containing all Supplementary Estimates passed by 30 June (3-hour debate) • Imprest Supply Bill for next year's interim supply introduced and passed on or before 30 June (4-hour debate)
Throughout the year	• *Review of state enterprises and public organisations: Select committees conduct reviews of the previous financial year's performance and the current operations of state enterprises and public organisations (i.e. Crown entities named or described in the 6th schedule to the PFA 1989 plus the Reserve Bank) and report to the House within 6 months of the relevant annual report being tabled in the House. A 10-hour debate on performance and current operations is held in Committee of the Whole House each financial year*

Note: Roman type relates to appropriations for the current year. *Italic type* relates to review of the previous year.

Abbreviations: FEC Finance and Expenditure Committee; FRA Fiscal Responsibility Act 1994; PFA Public Finance Act 1989.

15 the role of the audit office

Without audit, no accountability; without accountability, no control; and if there is no control, where is the seat of power? (W. J. M. Mackenzie, 1966, p. vii)

An audit is the principal means by which stakeholders gain independent assurance about the stewardship or management of resources that they have entrusted to another party when they are unable, for reasons of complexity or distance, to satisfy themselves (Flint, 1988). Governmental accounting and auditing are as old as civilisation itself. The independent checking of fiscal receipts and public accounts is evident among the ancient Egyptians, Babylonians, Greeks, Romans, and Chinese (Chatfield, 1974). As Geist (1981) points out, state audit institutions developed over time to help legislatures implement 'the power of the purse', which had two essential elements: the granting of moneys and the supervision of their expenditure. Given the complexity of state budgets, the inelasticity of much expenditure, and the constraints on time available to legislators, the latter has come to be the more practical and feasible mechanism for control of the Executive in modern times. With its access to information and review of government activities, state audit has therefore fulfilled an increasingly important role in providing legislators with the detailed reliable information necessary for control. Nonetheless, state auditors have also typically retained some involvement in the process of control via the granting of moneys.

This chapter examines the existing role and functions of the Audit Office in New Zealand, including the challenges and changes faced by the office as a result of the state sector reforms of the 1980s and 1990s. It then identifies issues to be debated in developing new legislation, which will ensure that the office continues to serve the needs of Parliament into the next century.

CURRENT FUNCTIONS AND DUTIES OF THE AUDITOR-GENERAL

The Audit Office in New Zealand is created by Act of Parliament. It has responsibilities in all areas of the public sector including central government, local government, government trading enterprises and Crown entities. The Audit Office consists of the Controller and Auditor-General, a Deputy Controller and Auditor-General and any other person who is appointed by the Auditor-General to act on his or her behalf. The Audit Office views its roles and responsibilities as follows:

> The role and purpose of the Auditor-General is founded upon fundamental constitutional principles. In our system of government, Parliament is supreme—all authority for governmental activity ultimately stems from Parliament. Public sector organisations are therefore accountable to Parliament for their use of resources and powers conferred by Parliament. As part of its accountability arrangements for Executive government, Parliament seeks assurance from an independent source—the Auditor-General—on the performance of the instruments of government. . . . The Auditor-General's role is to provide assurance that governmental organisations are operating, and accounting for their performance, in accordance with Parliament's intentions. To be credible, such assurance must be seen to be independent and competent (Audit Office, 1995b, pp. 15–16).

The principal outcomes sought from discharging the role of Auditor-General are:

a. maintenance of the integrity of public sector accounting and reporting systems, and reporting of financial and non-financial performance by public sector bodies; and
b. better use of public resources (Audit Office, 1995b, p. 18).

Existing Legislation

The legislation that currently specifies the functions and duties of the Auditor-General is s. 25 of the Public Finance Act 1977. For each of the entities concerned, the Auditor-General is appointed to be the auditor of their money and stores and, without limiting the scope of that appointment, has the responsibility to ascertain whether:

a. the entity's books and accounts have been faithfully kept;
b. the entity's procedures, including internal controls, are sufficient to ensure that there is effective control over the revenue, expenditure, and other resources of the entity; and
c. the entity's resources have been applied effectively and efficiently in a manner that is consistent with the applicable policy of the entity.

As the above items do not really convey the full range of functions carried out by the Audit Office in practice, a brief description is provided below.

Reporting Functions

In common with private sector auditors, the Auditor-General makes a report on an audited entity's public accountability statements.[1] Although there is no reference in the Public Finance Act 1977 to reporting on the public accountability statements of the entities subject to audit, this responsibility can be found in the various statutes covering

---

1. Historically, the focus of audit was on compliance and financial management behaviour. The idea of attesting to the validity of accountability statements seems to have come later with the growing development of private sector audit.

the entities themselves. The Auditor-General is appointed by Parliament to be the auditor of all public sector entities with the exception of the Reserve Bank of New Zealand.[2] In 1995, this amounted to 3,660 entities excluding subsidiaries not established by Parliament as a special class of entity (Audit Office, 1995d).

The scope of the report is not limited by the law, but it is normally confined to what is called the 'short-form audit report' or the 'audit opinion', which is attached to the audited statements. With the introduction of statements of service performance in many parts of the public sector, the audit report commonly has to address both financial and non-financial performance.

In addition to assurance as to the validity of accountability statements, it is expected that the Auditor-General will provide independent assurance that accountability arrangements applied to public sector entities are adequate and that entities are conducting their affairs effectively and efficiently as well as lawfully and with probity. This assurance may be conveyed in reports by the Auditor-General to the House of Representatives pursuant to the reporting powers in s. 33 of the Public Finance Act 1977.

The Auditor-General is not, however, restricted to reporting to the House. Section 34 of the Public Finance Act 1977 confers the power to report to whomever and whenever the Auditor-General chooses on any matter relating to his or her auditing responsibilities. In practice, the power is constantly used to report to select committees, ministers, governing bodies, chief executives, and other interested parties.

The Auditor-General is obliged by s. 33 of the Public Finance Act 1977 to make at least one report to the House each year. The content of any report is at the Auditor-General's discretion relating to—

(i) Any accounts or transactions that are required to be audited by the Audit Office under any Act; or
(ii) The performance or exercise by the Audit Office of any of its functions, duties, or powers under any Act.

As well as reports arising out of findings of the regular annual audits, there are some reports based on special studies, often into single specific subjects. Such studies have included the results of what are known internationally as 'efficiency and effectiveness' or 'value for money' (VFM) audits—a wider approach to audit introduced in response to mounting concern over increasing government expenditure during the 1960s and 1970s. VFM auditing examines all manner of capital projects and social service functions, requiring that legislative auditors build teams of non-accountant professionals and experts, ranging from engineers to social workers.

By the mid 1980s, New Zealand had established a VFM audit group, learning from the experience of the Canadian Auditor-General's office, which had established itself as a world leader in this field. Since that time, the New Zealand Audit Office has consist-

---

2. This anomaly arises from the fact that the Reserve Bank originated in the private sector and was subsequently nationalised in 1936. The change from private sector auditors has never been made.

ently produced and presented several projects to Parliament each year on a wide range of activities from local hydroelectric power schemes and Ministry of Transport road safety to the administration of pharmaceutical benefits and control of Crown debt. In the case of government companies (e.g. SOEs, CHEs, CRIs, and port companies), however, legislation restricts the Auditor-General to giving opinions on the financial statements rather than allowing audits of their efficiency and effectiveness. Although the potential for quite extensive commentary does exist under the powers to report on any account or transaction subject to audit, this restricted mandate has been considered unsatisfactory (Audit Office, 1995d, p. 22). The Audit Office has had to decline requests from MPs to pursue public concerns (e.g. the waiting list of a particular CHE) because it did not have the expected powers.

Because it is not possible, given limited resources, to audit performance in every conceivable area of public interest, the Audit Office has adopted a process of strategic audit planning in which areas of highest financial and political risk are systematically identified and used to determine the emphasis in the Audit Office's annual work programme. In future, improved reporting of non-financial performance by departments themselves should allow the performance audit effort to concentrate mainly on areas where reporting is inadequate.

Whether the Auditor-General's reports have much effect depends on whether Parliament, or the government, takes action on the matters raised. During 1994 and 1995, the Audit Office adopted the practice of formally offering to brief relevant select committees on the particular aspects of each report that had been drawn to their attention. In most cases the offer was accepted. While this is an advance over the experience of previous years when reports resulted in limited follow-up, it still falls short of practice in other Westminster-based systems of government. The Public Accounts Committee (PAC) in the UK, for example, actively engages in the follow-up of reports by the National Audit Office. The PAC conducts a full examination of each report, including taking evidence from relevant officials, and draws its own conclusions. If it believes that remedial action is required, it makes recommendations to the government. A large proportion of the PAC's recommendations are subsequently implemented.

Assistance to Select Committees

There are a number of activities that the Audit Office currently undertakes to assist Parliament, and in particular select committees, in holding the Executive to account. While there is no specific legislative mandate for these activities, they draw on the independent knowledge gained during the audit process and are consistent with both the Auditor-General's broader reporting responsibilities and with making a constructive contribution to the public accountability process.

Select committees annually conduct a financial review of the performance of each government department and each office of Parliament. The annual report, including audited accountability statements, of these organisations forms the basis for these reviews. Based on their annual reports, statements of corporate intent, and other documents presented to the House, a similar review is undertaken of the performance and current operations of state-owned enterprises and other public organisations. Parliaments have historically had the ability to 'send for' the Auditor-General and his or her papers, and it is now commonplace for the Audit Office to be asked to appear before each select committee conducting a review to provide further details of the results of the audit of the entity, the report on the accountability statements, and any other matter on which the committee might want independent assurance.

The Audit Office also assists select committees in their examination of the Crown's estimates of expenditure. These examinations are a central part of the processes of the House in considering the Crown's budgetary proposals for the year and deciding whether to agree to the proposals and grant supply. In recent years, the assistance has taken the form of providing the committee with a report on each department's estimates. The report draws on the knowledge gained from the audit and suggests key issues and potential lines of inquiry for the committee. As a result of the increase in information available to Parliament under the new reporting regime, select committees have a very real need for technical support and advice. Given that such advice must be independent of the government, it could come from employment of staff in the office of the Clerk with particular expertise in financial analysis and management, from a new office of the House (along the lines of the Congressional Budget Office in the United States), or from *ad hoc* advisors. However, locating this function in the Audit Office is probably the most cost-effective option given the nature of the office's other responsibilities. Any move to rationalise the process of select committee scrutiny by combining the estimates review with the review of financial performance would further weaken the case for an additional advisory office.

In addition to the regular reviews of estimates and financial performance, a select committee may conduct an inquiry into any matter within its terms of reference. Again, the Auditor-General might be requested to appear before the committee or to make staff of his or her office available to assist the committee. Finally, the Auditor-General might assist select committees in their consideration of proposed legislation, particularly if issues of public sector accountability or management are involved.

Taxpayer and Ratepayer Inquiries

The Auditor-General receives many inquiries from taxpayers, ratepayers, and representatives of interest groups asking about, or expressing concern about, the use of public resources by public sector entities and officials. These inquiries are regarded as part of the public accountability process (even if not formally recognised as such) because it is usually the case that the inquirer has either not received a satisfactory response from the entity or believes that the Auditor-General is the only person who can, and will, properly and impartially address the subject of the inquiry. In responding to these inquiries, the Auditor-General performs the role of 'public watchdog'.

Controller Function

In New Zealand, the individual holding the office of Auditor-General also holds the separate office of Controller whose purpose is to verify the legality of issues of public money. The elements of the controller function are to be found in the Comptroller's Act of 1865, which built on similar legislation in the United Kingdom, and the office has continued largely unchanged since that time. That no money can be paid out of the consolidated fund of the State without the express authorisation of Parliament is an important constitutional principle long recorded in statute (the English Bill of Rights 1689) and now set out in s. 22 of the (New Zealand) Constitution Act 1986. The controller function is designed to police that principle.

The controller function is exercised under ss. 59 and 60 of the Public Finance Act 1989. Payment out of the Crown bank account is prohibited unless there is a warrant under the hand of the Governor-General bearing a certification from the Audit Office that the amount may lawfully be paid. There must also be an appropriation or other authority against which the payment may properly be charged. The Controller may refuse to certify a statement of proposed payments if not satisfied about these two conditions. Further, the Controller may refuse to certify a statement if there is a reason to believe that any money paid into a departmental bank account may be used for a purpose that is not lawful or consistent with the appropriations administered by that department. Given that this is a fairly blunt instrument in that the whole payment needs to be stopped, not just the part relating to an activity in question, this important sanction is rarely exercised. However, the threat to stop payment (as opposed to the actual stopping of payment) is in itself a powerful sanction and was effective in 1990 in causing the Ministry of Agriculture and Fisheries to rectify its position regarding the conduct of a number of business ventures in which it was engaged.

ROLE OF THE AUDIT OFFICE IN FINANCIAL MANAGEMENT REFORMS

The Audit Office has played an important part in bringing about and facilitating financial management reforms in the New Zealand public sector. Beginning with the Shailes report in 1978 (Audit Office, 1978), which advocated many of the reforms that have since been implemented, the Audit Office has actively supported the reforms generally and helped in resolving a number of particular issues.

An important role played by the Audit Office has been as advocate of accountability to Parliament. For example, the Audit Office participated in the working party set up to make proposals on the earliest central government restructure—the splitting of the Ministry of Energy into separate business enterprises. The key concern of the office was to preserve a necessary degree of accountability, including recognition of the rightful role and interest of Parliament, without unreasonably constraining the benefits to be gained from the freedom to operate on a true commercial basis. The efforts of the working party led to the development of the general framework for accountability for SOEs that underpins the State-Owned Enterprises Act and has served as a model for subsequent reforms in local government and Crown entities. The key elements of the framework included a set of goals established and agreed in consultation with the community or with the appropriate minister. The agreed goals are then made public, either through tabling in Parliament or by requiring the document to be publicly available. They are followed up by half-yearly or annual reports on financial and non-financial achievements against those agreed goals.

As the framework was implemented, the Audit Office played an active role in commenting on how well it was operating. In 1988, the Auditor-General, Brian Tyler, reported on the accountability requirements of state-owned enterprises. He pointed out that:

> One of the features of a company ownership form is the transference of authority from Parliament to the Executive. Allowing the Executive to determine the resources to be entrusted to a State-Owned Enterprise and the nature of the activities that will be undertaken with them, represents a very real reduction in the authority of Parliament. As Parliament's authority is eroded and its constitutional role diminished, so too is the effectiveness with which it can impose proper accountability. This will continue to occur until adequate mechanisms exist which allow Parliament to examine and challenge actions, both taken and proposed, of the Executive or the enterprises themselves (Audit Office, 1988, p. 22).

Tyler highlighted the importance of the Statement of Corporate Intent (SCI) as the basis of the accountability framework and noted that, in his view, the SCIs presented in 1987 did not provide adequate information about the objectives, scope of activity, performance measures, or reporting obligations of SOEs. Two years later, he again concluded that the SCIs generally did not provide sufficient information to meet legislative requirements and that 'the SOEs are consequently falling short in their obligations of accountability to Parliament and to the wider public' (Audit Office, 1990b, p. 6). By creating awareness of the need for SOEs to be accountable to Parliament, the Auditor-General was arguably instrumental in the establishment of the State Enterprises select committee.

With respect to central government departments, the Auditor-General, in his submission on the Public Finance Bill, pointed out that no provision had been made in the Bill for reporting on outcomes. While acknowledging the point being made, the Finance and Expenditure Committee 'felt unable to consider amendments to the Bill in the area of Ministerial accountability'. Undeterred, the Auditor-General, in public forums, continued to stress the need to ensure accountability:

> Currently, there are no explicit requirements for ministers to report their performance—and that of the government as a whole—against stated goals or outcomes. This is a significant omission from the current accountability arrangements. . . . If [Ministers] think that such a requirement would be unfair is it because of, for whatever reason, the belief they would be held to account for things which they cannot in fact control or influence? If so, I can understand their concern. The principle that should be adopted is that they be held to account only according to their extent of control or influence (Tyler, 1989, pp. 147–8).

Again, such comments served to maintain a level of awareness about ministerial and whole-of-government accountability and contributed to a climate for developments in whole-of-government reporting, SRAs, select committee questioning of ministers, and further work on outcome reporting. More recently, the Audit Office has commented on the adequacy of accountability and contractual arrangements for payments of Crown money to parties other than government departments (Audit Office, 1994f).

The Audit Office also had an active involvement in the development and implementation of the Public Finance Act 1989. In a small country such as New Zealand, where there is a limited pool of expertise, the Audit Office was best positioned to assist in such functions as:

a. Providing advisers to the Finance and Expenditure Committee of Parliament for its consideration of the Public Finance Bill in 1989, its inquiry into reporting by the Crown and its sub-entities, and its inquiry into the format of the Crown financial statements. It also made submissions to the FEC during its examination of the Fiscal Responsibility Bill.

b. Developing guidelines for reporting non-financial information. Since no other jurisdiction (with the exception of Western Australia) audits non-financial information, the New Zealand Audit Office was forced to fill the gap and provide criteria for devising and auditing non-financial information. The dimensions identified by the Audit Office for measuring the delivery of outputs (quantity, quality, timeliness, cost, and location) became widely accepted throughout the public sector. More recently, the Audit Office has been developing criteria for judging the appropriateness of performance measures selected by the reporting entity.

c. Facilitating the production of the Crown financial statements. This included commenting on the Crown accounting policies as they were developed and on the format of the Crown financial statements. The Audit Office also advised on the evidential standards to be met in some of the more technical valuation issues such as military assets, libraries, roads, and archives and carried out a special audit of the opening balances at 1 July 1991 for the half-year financial statements to 31 December 1991.

CHALLENGES FACING THE AUDIT OFFICE

The financial management reforms presented the Audit Office with many challenges. At the practical level, large and complex tasks had to be accomplished in a very short period of time. For example, the Public Finance Act 1989 required the Crown financial statements to be prepared within two months of the end of the financial year and the audit to be completed within a month after that. Such an audit required rigorous planning and tight project control and cooperation with the preparers of the financial statements (the Treasury) without compromising independence. In the case of the Crown financial statements, several items needed special attention in the initial years. These included: the setting of materiality levels given the size of the reporting entity, its assets, and its transactions; the degree of reliance that could be placed on accounting systems and internal control given the newness of the systems, the restructuring of many public sector organisations, and the recency of the change to accrual accounting; and the involvement of experts in such areas as the valuation of infrastructure and heritage assets, the valuation of specialist military equipment, and actuarial calculations of employee-related expenses.

Additionally, keeping up with the changes in more than 3,500 entities was, and continues to be, an enormous task. Extra work was often required to cover transitional issues such as amalgamation audits, changes in balance date, and audits of opening balance sheets (particularly on completeness and valuation aspects). The range of audit activities was suddenly expanded with the adoption of accrual accounting in place of simple cash accounting and the adoption of performance reporting in non-financial terms. Commercialisation meant that the Audit Office had to acquire skills to audit commercial, profit-oriented, and tax-paying enterprises. New risks for the office arose, for example, from the audit of financial statements of SOEs being sold and involvement in the associated due diligence processes. In a more litigious environment, it was necessary for the Audit Office to develop procedures to reduce risks from potential legal action.

More generally, questions were raised about the scope and mandate of the Audit Office. Notably, when the SOE Bill was under consideration, there were strong objections to SOEs being required to have the Audit Office as auditor. It was felt that this statutory 'monopoly' was out of place with the new philosophy of contestable markets. It was also argued that it would be more difficult to raise funds if the audits were not conducted by internationally known accounting firms. As one of the major accounting firms said in its submission:

> With the need for state-owned enterprises to meet funding arrangements from borrowings, particularly offshore borrowings, lenders will require them to produce sophisticated proposals, backed up by audited financial accounts. Lenders are familiar with the international reputation of large firms. Credibility of financial advisers and reliance placed on the work of these accounting firms are often critical to the success of a funding arrangement (Deloitte, Haskins and Sells, 1986, p. 11).

Public enterprises themselves also used possible problems in financing as an argument against auditing by the Audit Office. If these perceived problems did in fact exist, it seems unfortunate that a sovereign appointment should conflict with the needs of international business.

Although the Act with respect to dividend declaration, reporting, and audit was passed substantially in its original form, these issues have remained contentious in the SOEs' relationships with the government and the public at large. There have also been pressures on the Audit Office to restrict the amount of information made public on the grounds of commercial confidentiality. Except for those entities subject to official information legislation, in which case Parliament has set the criteria for non-disclosure, the Audit Office is faced with a dilemma as to whether the disclosure of information, regarded by the management of the entity as commercially confidential, is in the public's best interest.

A report commissioned from Strategos Consulting by the Finance and Expenditure Committee in 1988 reflected a number of views about the Audit Office that were prevalent at the time. The report (Kirk, 1988) even went as far as to suggest that the ground was being laid for the removal of the Audit Office function. As well as arguing that government corporations should be audited by private sector auditors, the report questioned whether the same office should carry out both audit and control functions and suggested that these functions be split or reallocated. It also thought that the Treasury and the Audit Department were duplicating the expenditure control function, that VFM audits were not an accounting function and of doubtful value, that advice to Parliament should become contestable and that the relevance of state-sector-specific expertise had been diminished with the convergence of state and private sector management structures and objectives.

The Strategos report, which had not undergone rigorous substantiation, contained numerous flaws. In particular, it failed to appreciate constitutional relationships in government or to distinguish between control on behalf of Parliament from control on the part of the government. It addressed neither the problems of auditor independence in the private sector, where there is strong competition for audit engagements and the client has the ability to dismiss the auditor if not satisfied, nor the effect of contestability on the independence of advice to Parliament. However, the report did reveal a need for the work of the office to be more clearly understood and for the Audit Office to ensure that it performed its functions efficiently and effectively and could demonstrate that it was doing so.

AUDIT OFFICE RESPONSE

On taking up his appointment in December 1992, the incoming Auditor-General, Jeffrey Chapman, decided to respond immediately to the pressures created by the ever-changing nature of the public sector and the demand for increased efficiency and effectiveness.

First, he significantly restructured the office, separating it (administratively although not in a formal legal sense) into two units that mirrored the purchaser/provider and policy/operations splits now common across the public sector. The new units were:

a. *The Office of the Auditor-General (OAG)*, responsible for standard setting and oversight of the provision of audit services and for parliamentary reporting, liaison, and advice. The VFM audit group (later renamed the Performance Audit Unit), although an operational function, was also included since its small size of approximately fifteen staff did not warrant its standing alone.

b. *Audit New Zealand*, responsible for carrying out regular audits on a similar basis to private sector auditors. A 'contract' was set up between the Auditor-General and Audit New Zealand for the provision of audit and related operational services.[3]

Second, Chapman introduced contestability as a means of demonstrating efficiency and value for money in the conduct of audits. Since the early 1980s the Audit Office

---

3. In 1995 the OAG, including the performance audit unit and the corporate office, had 44 staff while Audit New Zealand had 248 staff. Crown revenue—to cover reports to Parliament, special studies, advice to select committees, ratepayers and taxpayers, administration of the

had contracted out a small number of audits, initially to introduce private sector auditors to the public sector and later to enable the Auditor-General to compare in-house costs and practices with those of the private sector. The education reforms of 1989 created approximately 2,600 separately accountable bodies. As the Audit Office did not have the resources to audit them, it decided to contract these new audits to the private sector. Chapman went further and, in December 1992, introduced a new contracting philosophy and processes. The aims were, first, to demonstrate efficiency and value for money in the conduct of audits and, second, to facilitate the exchange of knowledge that would occur as a result of drawing on a wider pool of auditors and their associated knowledge and practices.

The portfolio of public sector entities was divided into two parts: those for which the provision of audit services was contestable and a 'core' that would, at least in the immediate future, be audited by Audit New Zealand. The latter are mainly those entities, such as government departments and local authorities, that rely wholly or partly on revenue from the exercise of taxing powers. The audits in the contestable part of the portfolio were to be allocated to competent service providers, including both Audit New Zealand and private sector auditors, on the basis of competitive tender. To avert potential criticism that the Auditor-General might favour Audit New Zealand, every effort was made to ensure that the tender process was unbiased and seen to be so. Tenderers are selected by a series of panels comprising a representative of the entity to be audited, a representative of the Auditor-General, and an independent chairperson. Additionally, an independent evaluator of high standing in the accountancy profession was appointed to oversee and report on the integrity of the overall process.

The contract period is for three years, with provision for the contract to be renewed for a second period of three years, subject to agreement between the Auditor-General, the service provider, and the audited entity. A shorter period would be inefficient given the investment the service provider must make in gaining an appreciation of the audit entity and the sector in which it operates. A longer period runs the perceived risk that the service provider gains so much familiarity and empathy with the audited entity and its personnel that independence is compromised.

Successful tenderers are required to comply with audit standards promulgated by the OAG and to be subject to quality assurance and monitoring processes carried out by the OAG over the contract period. Several issues made the development of audit standards and guidelines beyond those adopted in the private sector an urgent task for the OAG.

First, the rapid development of reporting on performance in the public sector, such as the requirement to publish statements of corporate intent, statements of service per-

---

Local Authorities (Members' Interests) Act and operation of the Controller function—amounted to $3.58 million. Revenue from other sources—primarily the provision of audit services—amounted to $28.6 million and covered the costs of providing audit services (Audit Office, 1995d).

formance, and other non-financial information, created an entirely new set of challenges for the scope of audits and their evidential requirements.

Second, given that most audits had been conducted by staff of Audit New Zealand, knowledge of issues about public sector audits (in particular, the audit of compliance with key legislation) had not been formalised in a way that made it readily accessible to outside parties such as the private sector auditors now contracting to provide services. Furthermore, there is much debate internationally about the very nature and scope of the audit of compliance with legislation. This, together with the fact that New Zealand is one of the few jurisdictions where auditors are required to give an opinion on non-financial information, required much innovative thinking on the part of the OAG in developing standards and guidelines.

Finally, the public sector auditor differs markedly from the private sector auditor in 'client' orientation. The private sector auditor is usually engaged by the entity to be audited and reports to its directors and shareholders. The public sector auditor, on the other hand, is engaged by the Auditor-General and has reporting responsibilities to Parliament and the public at large. Information important in reporting to Parliament might not be information that the audited entity is willing to have disclosed publicly. Indeed, it can be argued that audits in the public sector are not an end-product in themselves but more a means by which Auditors-General fulfil their reporting obligations in the interests of public accountability. A shift in orientation from the audited entity to the Auditor-General as immediate client, and to the imperatives of public accountability, might not be an easy one for many private sector auditors to make.

By 1994, approximately one third of the total annual audit workload was being undertaken by audit service providers other than Audit New Zealand (Audit Office, 1994i, p. 26). Contestability in the provision of public sector audits having now been introduced, it is hard to imagine that the process will be reversed. To date, the audits tendered have been small entities (such as schools) or those conducting commercial activities, and placed on more arm's length ownership arrangements, where the scope of audit is very similar to the audit of organisations in the private sector. These commercial entities can be viewed as lying at one end of a spectrum at the other end of which are organisations that rely largely on taxation revenues and are subject to comprehensive public accountability arrangements (e.g. government departments and local authorities). In the middle of the spectrum are Crown entities with social objectives and requirements to report service performance. The questions now to be faced are how far the tendering process should be extended along this spectrum and whether the Auditor-General needs to retain an inhouse audit capacity at all.

The Strategos report's suggestion that the Audit Office could be disestablished seems far-fetched. Given limitations on the time and relevant expertise of its members, Parliament is always likely to require a statutorily independent specialist professional agency, an arrangement which gives it the administrative convenience and economy of having to appoint and deal with only one auditing agent. Thus, at very least, there is a role for the Audit Office in selecting and engaging auditors, monitoring their performance, and dealing with their reports. In principle, auditors so engaged could all be chosen from the private sector, provided that the contracts were clearly specified and adhered to and the auditors had adequate understanding of such matters as auditing legislative compliance and non-financial information as well as the different client orientation and dynamics of public accountability. There could be reasons why the Auditor-General might nonetheless wish to retain some in-house audit capacity. Transaction cost analysis suggests that in-house provision enables a greater reliance on relational contracts and mutual trust rather than formal written contracts. In-house provision allows informal information to be used and fine nuances of direction to be developed. The advantages are not only a reduction in transaction costs but also a faster and more effective response to changing or unexpected circumstances. The Auditor-General might wish to have 'an auditor of last resort' in the event of there not being an auditor willing or available to carry out particular tasks, or it might be necessary to respond to urgent requests from Parliament for an audit or investigation without the delay of negotiating contracts. Some areas of government activity are particularly sensitive (e.g. the Inland Revenue Department, the Treasury, or the Security Intelligence Service). Additionally, an in-house capacity could provide a benchmark for the quality, efficiency, and costs of outside contractors and some safeguard against oligopolistic behaviour. This, however, would require an in-house audit capacity of sufficient size to have the necessary knowledge and expertise.

ISSUES TO BE DETERMINED IN FUTURE LEGISLATION

The current legislation governing the Audit Office is Part II of the Public Finance Act 1977. The substantial reforms in public administration since the 1977 legislation, together with the report of the Finance and Expenditure Committee on its inquiry into officers of Parliament in 1989, point to the need to review the role of Parliament's auditor with a view to reaffirming the appropriateness of its activities and ensuring it will serve the needs of Parliament into the next century. While little dissatisfaction has been expressed about the current functions of the Audit Office, matters that Parliament expects the office to examine (e.g. legislative compliance or probity) are not expressly mentioned as functions in the present legislation. Much of the terminology in the 1977 Act does not reflect contemporary thinking or usage. The appointment of the auditor is contained in a variety of specific statutes (in some cases, such as universities, not specified at all) with the result that there is no consistent and coherent approach to audit arrangements. The introduction of MMP, which could result in significantly increased demands on the Audit Office for support for Parliament, adds to the need for review and clarification.

New legislation is likely to establish the Auditor-General as an officer of Parliament and to disestablish the present department. Given the constitutional significance of the Audit Office, there is a strong case for Parliament to play a much more influential role than is customary when the government introduces new legislation. For example, the government might base its decision on the recommendations of Parliament instead of the usual process whereby it first obtains the recommendations of its key advisors, such as the Treasury, and subsequently seeks Parliament's endorsement of its policy. Provision exists in standing orders for the Officers of Parliament Committee (OPC) to consider any proposal referred to it by a minister to establish an office of Parliament. Were the government to advise the OPC of its intentions to enact new Auditor-General legislation, the OPC could consider, and make detailed recommendations about, what it believes should be the appropriate functions, duties, and powers of the new office. Since the government would need to respond to the OPC's recommendations, Parliament could have a more influential role in the process of developing the bill.

The introduction of new legislation presents an important opportunity for discussion on, and clarification of, such matters as the mandate and powers of the Auditor-General and the arrangements that best promote independence and accountability. Terms and conditions of appointment and subsequent employment of the Auditor-General are also likely to be carefully examined in the wake of Chapman's sudden resignation in October 1994.[3] The main issues to be debated in developing the proposed legislation are identified in a discussion paper produced by the Audit Office in 1994 (Audit Office, 1994g) and are outlined below.

Mandate

As a matter of principle, Parliament should appoint the auditor of any organisation that is ultimately accountable to it. Reasons for being accountable to Parliament include having the power to tax, being reliant on appropriations by Parliament, and being reliant on parliamentary authorisation for the use of public funds. The accountability is generally reflected in a requirement for an organisation's statements of account to be tabled in the House and for its performance to be subject to scrutiny by a select committee. Parliament appoints the auditor for the purpose of obtaining independent assurance about the representations and performance of those organisations that are accountable to it. Reasons for appointing the Auditor-General include statutory independence and the administrative convenience and economy of dealing with only one auditing agent (Audit Office, 1994g, p. 46).

Parliament's primary scrutiny interest is in respect of the entities that form part of the Crown. Since the Crown is defined in the Public Finance Act 1989 as including the Reserve Bank, the argument can be made that new legislation presents an opportunity

---

3. Chapman resigned office on 10 October 1994, giving as his reason for doing so that his personal financial situation was incompatible with his maintaining the independence of the Auditor-General. The Minister in charge of the Audit Department appointed accountant Bruce McCallum to undertake an audit of the administration of the Audit Office consequent on the resignation of the Controller and Auditor-General. McCallum stated in his report that 'it is my opinion that Mr Chapman is indebted to the Audit Office for a sum of $156,753' (McCallum, 1994, p. 6). He also stated (p. 12) that 'the absence of a clear and full definition of the terms and conditions of appointment contributed to the situation which led to this report.' Subsequently, an investigation by the Serious Fraud Office resulted in several charges of fraud, which, at the time of writing, have yet to be heard in court.

for the existing anomaly, in which the Auditor-General is not the auditor of the Reserve Bank (see above, note 2), to be removed. Opposition to the Auditor-General continuing to be the auditor of departments is unlikely. In the case of SOEs and some Crown entities, however, it has been suggested that Parliament should delegate its right to another party thereby removing the Auditor-General as auditor. Such a view is based on the argument that legislation has made these entities primarily accountable to their shareholding ministers who should therefore appoint the auditor. According to this view, Parliament's interest in SOEs and Crown companies should be confined to how ministers have executed their responsibilities to manage the Crown's interest. Such a view tends to ignore the accountability arrangements that Parliament has put in place in the reporting requirements of the Public Finance Act 1989 and in its standing orders. The State Enterprises Committee, with its wide powers of inquiry, clearly has interests that extend beyond reviewing the execution of the responsibilities of shareholding ministers. If anything, parliamentarians and the public at large expect the Audit Office to have a wider mandate with respect to these entities, not a reduced role. It is difficult to see why Parliament would wish to confine its interest to assessing the performance of responsible ministers and, in doing so, forego the right to obtain independent audit assurance directly.

There are also entities for which Parliament currently appoints the Auditor-General but which are not primarily accountable to Parliament. These other entities include those accountable to a particular constituency (e.g. local authorities) and those accountable to another public sector owner (e.g. airport companies, LATEs, port companies, and some energy companies). There are also entities where accountability is unclear (e.g. Maori trust boards, some energy companies). Whether the Auditor-General should be the auditor in the case of such entities is less apparent than in the case of entities that form part of the Crown estate.

While local authorities derive their powers to tax from Parliament, they are primarily accountable to their local constituents who elect their governing bodies. It is arguably the right of these constituents to appoint their own auditor. There are examples, particularly in the USA (and even briefly in New Zealand in the nineteenth century), where auditors have been elected by local citizens. However, since this is administratively burdensome and runs the risk of politicising the audit role, an independent proxy who makes the audit appointment on the public's behalf might be preferable. It would also help to ensure consistency of audit approach and coverage for all local authorities. The United Kingdom has an Audit Commission for local authorities and the National Health Service in addition to a National Audit Office at the central government level. New Zealand's small size might not warrant two separate bodies; furthermore, recent discussions in the United Kingdom suggest there could be merit in combining their two bodies.

Where entities, such as LATEs, are clearly accountable to another public sector owner, it could be argued that the owners should appoint the auditors consistent with, for example, the arrangements in the Companies Act 1993. On the other hand, it could be argued that the ultimate owners are the community, who should therefore appoint the auditor. Where a local authority has discretion over which of its activities to devolve to a LATE, it is conceivable that the community would suffer a loss of accountability for these activities if the authority also had control over the audit arrangements. In any event, there are professional and practical advantages in having the same auditor for the parent entity and its related entities.

Where accountability is unclear, any change in audit arrangements would seem to first require a fuller review of the accountability framework in each case. Some more immediate action might be required in the energy sector where two main problems have emerged. First, the Energy Companies Act 1992 provides for the Auditor-General to be the auditor until such time as joint public sector ownership ceases to be the controlling interest in an energy company. The Auditor-General cannot be reappointed at a subsequent time even if the company is again controlled by joint public sector ownership. Second, community trusts that hold equity in energy companies are responsible for the stewardship of significant public resources but, unlike local authorities, the accountability and audit arrangements have been determined by executive action rather than through legislation on behalf of the community. New Auditor-General legislation presents an opportunity to review such anomalies.

Parliament also has an interest in private sector entities that receive appropriations for the delivery of outputs (e.g. the Plunket Society, the Society for the Intellectually Handicapped). In principle, the purchasing minister will contract with a departmental CE or other agent to administer the contract and put in place mechanisms to ensure that the funds are applied for the purposes appropriated and that the outputs specified are delivered. The question then arises as to whether the Auditor-General should also have a right of access to the books of those entities. Several overseas jurisdictions (e.g. UK, Ireland, and Canada) give the Auditor-General such a power where Crown funds are 51 per cent or more of the body's income. The problem with this is that accountabilities could become mixed and there might be less incentive for ministers and departments to set up adequate monitoring and contractual arrangements. However, the Auditor-General should at the very least comment on the adequacy of those monitoring and contractual arrangements. In the event of a complete breakdown of the monitoring and accountability processes, there might be a case for the Auditor-General to have reserve powers to examine the books of non-governmental bodies in receipt of public funds. Concerns that such powers might be too readily used by an over-zealous Auditor-General could be alleviated if the Speaker, after consultation with the responsible minister, had the responsibility of determining whether the case justified the use of the inquiry powers of the Auditor-General.

Also to be considered are the other functions that stem from the audit role and the particular knowledge and skills gained through the process of conducting audits such as assisting select committees and responding to inquiries from members of the public. The main issues to be considered here are handling, prioritising, and resourcing the volume of inquiries likely to be generated, particularly under MMP. It might be unreasonable, for example, to expect the Auditor-General to respond to every inquiry from a member of the public. The role of the Auditor-General in relation to Parliament's conferral of authority—in particular, select committee examination of Estimates, consideration of proposed legislation, and even the operation of the Controller function itself—could prove more controversial. The argument here is that there is a potential risk that an audit could be compromised if it uncovered problems connected to the Auditor-General's *ex ante* activities or advice. However, as mentioned at the start of this chapter, state auditors internationally have a long history of involvement in the process of control over the granting of public money without apparent problem.

Existing legislation confers a number of powers on the Auditor-General that need to be reviewed and, where appropriate, reaffirmed in new legislation. These powers include: access to all relevant books, accounts, money, and property (including those of contractors to the government and local authorities) and to private bank accounts where the Auditor-General believes that public money has been improperly paid into them; power to take evidence on oath; power to surcharge people who are considered responsible for a deficiency or loss; and power to commence proceedings for offences under particular pieces of legislation such as the Local Authorities (Members' Interests) Act, the Public Finance Act and the Local Government Act. The Audit Office's 1994 paper discusses these powers, concluding that while some are rarely used they are probably useful reserve powers (Audit Office, 1994g, pp. 92–7). There might also be areas in which the powers of the Auditor-General could be extended. For example, local government auditors in England and Wales have statutory powers to issue prohibition orders to prevent illegal or improper acts and to initiate proceedings for judicial review. Any proposed legislation would also need to consider delegation of the Auditor-General's powers to act.

Independence

Independence is fundamental to the concept of audit and is critical to the proper and effective discharge of the Auditor-General's functions. Specifically, it means independence from the bodies subject to audit and statutory protection against improper influence. Such protection is secured through legislation that gives auditors-general unrestricted access to information required to conduct the audits adequately and which ensures that there are no restrictions on their ability to report any matter that comes to their attention during the course of exercising their functions, duties, or powers. Establishment of the Auditor-General as an officer of Parliament and abolition of the audit department will reinforce independence by severing any administrative connection with ministers or the public service. Functional and organisational independence is also best achieved by statutory protection over such matters as appointment and removal from office, salary and conditions of employment, and resources available to carry out audit work.

In the private sector, the fact that the directors of a company generally have the most influence in the appointment, remuneration, and dismissal of auditors is an ever-present threat to a truly independent audit opinion. For example, it might deter an auditor from issuing a qualified audit opinion. No citizen is ever completely independent from the government, but independence of the Auditor-General can be secured in statute. In the past the Governor-General has appointed the Auditor-General on the recommendation of the Prime Minister. Ombudsmen are appointed by the Governor-General on the recommendation of the House of Representatives, and it is likely that a similar process will be followed for the appointment of the Auditor-General once formally established as an officer of Parliament. Indeed, involvement of the Speaker in the appointment of Chapman's successor, David Macdonald, foreshadows such a development.[4]

Similarly, it is appropriate that Parliament has the sole right of removal from office. Section 20 of the Public Finance Act 1977 provides for removal only by the Governor-General upon address from the House of Representatives for disability, bankruptcy, neglect of duty, or misconduct. The same limited and specific grounds apply to members of the judiciary. Any more general grounds would create opportunities for subjective assessment and open the way for a governing majority in the House to invoke the powers of removal for reasons unrelated to the Auditor-General's real performance. However, given that auditors-general are hard to remove, care needs to be taken in specifying the term of office. Currently, the Auditor-General holds office until age 60, subject to the right to hold office for a minimum of five years. If a relatively young Auditor-General were appointed, the term could therefore be quite long. An average of overseas practices would indicate the appropriateness of a fixed term of about seven years, since any shorter term might lead to anxieties about reappointment and thus threaten the independence of the office.

The sudden illness of Tyler in 1991 and the resignation of Chapman in 1994, not to mention the many months taken to have a new Auditor-General in place, highlight the importance of unbroken leadership. The current legislation provides for this by way of a statutory office of Deputy Controller and Auditor-General with the full status and powers of the Auditor-General. An alternative arrangement might be for the Auditor-General to determine who is to be acting Auditor-General in the event of a voluntary or predetermined absence and for the Speaker to determine, on the basis of standing advice from the Auditor-General, who should act if the Auditor-General has been unable to make arrangements. An advantage of this alternative to the current arrangement is that it could encourage the Auditor-General to cultivate the appropriate competencies in more than one person.

Salary and conditions of employment also require protection from government influence and possible reduction if independence is to be preserved. Section 18 of the Public Finance Act 1977 provides permanent appropriation for the salary of the Auditor-General in a manner consistent with other officers of Parliament and members of the judiciary, and there is a case for extending this to non-salary conditions of employment. The Higher Salaries Commission currently determines the remuneration and superannuation rights of the Auditor-General, but other conditions are not specified. The circumstances surrounding Chapman's resignation highlight the need for greater clarity in this area. Protection of the salary of the Auditor-General and Deputy might be of limited use, however, if the Executive is able to constrain the resources to carry out the necessary work and report effectively to Parliament. Such a concern was addressed by the Finance and Expenditure Committee in its 1989 inquiry into officers of Parliament, with the result that resources for these officers and the Auditor-General are now allocated by the House itself upon recommendation of the Officers of Parliament Committee.

---

4. Macdonald came from a partnership in an international accounting firm, unlike previous auditors-general who had been drawn from the public sector.

The Auditor-General is given a very wide range of powers and considerable operating autonomy. It is necessary in return for there to be robust accountability procedures to enable Parliament to monitor and assess the performance of the Auditor-General. This is currently achieved through the annual report of the Auditor-General, appointment by the House of an independent party to audit and report on the statements of account of the Audit Office, and a review of the estimates of the office by Parliament. Underpinning the request for resources is the programme of work for which the Auditor-General proposes the resources be applied, including a programme of special studies. In some countries (and to some extent in the past in New Zealand) special studies have been on the initiative of the Auditor-General and viewed as consistent with his or her freedom of investigation. To ensure that the interests of Parliament and the work of the Auditor-General are attuned and thus maximise the likelihood of action on the subsequent report, the Auditor-General could be required to consult the Officers of Parliament Committee and other select committees in formulating a work programme, provided the function and independent status of the office is not undermined in any way. To go further and suggest a system of performance contracts, purchase agreements and rewards and sanctions, similar to those for CEs of government departments, would require very careful consideration of the constitutional role and independent status of the Auditor-General. Neither officers of Parliament nor members of the judiciary are subject to such arrangements.

CONCLUSION

Above and beyond the considerable challenges facing auditors in the private sector, such as rapidly changing technology and an increasingly litigious environment, the Audit Office in New Zealand has been under enormous pressure during the process of state sector reform. It has been required to keep abreast of changes in the structures, personnel, and financial management systems of some 3,500 public sector entities, to develop audit practices, techniques, and guidelines where there is no international precedent, to be an informed commentator and contributor to many innovative developments in accounting, financial management, and accountability arrangements, and to provide Parliament with advice on all these matters. All this has been accomplished with remarkably little resourcing by international standards. At the same time it has faced concerted attacks on its position, an internal examination of its role, and several changes of Auditor-General each with a distinctive operating philosophy. Given its constitutional position and relationship to Parliament, the introduction of MMP is likely to generate yet further challenges for the office. Yet, perhaps because state audit is such an ancient institution, there is an expectation among the public that it will be a constant in a sea of change. Proposed new legislation presents an opportunity to secure an effective and independent office that continues to play its vital role in the process of public accountability.

responsible management

16   ethos and ethics

... the public interest may be presumed to be what men [*sic*] would choose if they saw clearly, thought rationally, acted disinterestedly and benevolently (Lippman, 1956, p. 40).

The central concern of ethics is whether something is right or wrong. It is about what *ought* to be done. Ethos is defined by the *Concise Oxford Dictionary* as the 'characteristic spirit or attitudes of a community'. This chapter discusses some of the questions of 'right or wrong' within the bureaucracy and explores the 'spirit' of the New Zealand public service after a decade of unparalleled change in purpose, organisation, and people. Has the ethos changed too? If so, does it matter? Has such a change, if it can be identified, been for better or for worse?

For most of New Zealand's history the place of the appointed official within the country's constitutional arrangements has received little attention. The duty of the public servant was clear: within the law they owed their allegiance to the government of the day (in Whitehall parlance, G.O.D.). Public servants were 'neutral' in the sense that, with limited exceptions before 1962, they were appointed on merit without ministerial intervention (formally at least). But as Roberts (1987) reminds us, they were never neutral in the sense of being disinterested in the political fortunes of the minister whom they served. They were indeed the servants of their political masters for the time being without being partisan. The ethical standards of the public service cannot be divorced from the political context; but despite the political context people in public employment are still required to accept personal moral responsibility.

The distinctive feature of the role of officials in systems of governance derived from Westminster (and distinguished from Washington or Western European models) is that while their tenure is 'permanent', duty shifts with every change of administration. Or, to look at it another way, the presumptive duty of officials is to the office of minister (and its collective expression in the cabinet), even though office-holders change with the vicissitudes of the electoral system or prime ministerial preference. On the other hand, the work of officials, particularly in policy advice, is—or ought to be—informed by a notion of the 'public interest'.[1] Thus, one ethical dimension of the public servant's role has always been concerned with the tension between political responsiveness and the public interest. One of the aims of this chapter is to consider whether statutory changes or practice since the mid 1980s have significantly altered the conventions by which public servants operate.

The interface between politicians and public servants directly affects few public servants—those at the top of departments and, increasingly, policy analysts in policy ministries. Perhaps this relationship has received disproportionate attention in most commentaries on the recent reforms. There is, however, another aspect of public administration that impinges on the day-to-day activities of many servants of the state, whether they are employed in policy ministries or regulatory agencies or are providing services in such organisations as CHEs. This concerns the exercise of *discretion* within prescribed general rules (whether in statute or within delegated authority). What are the values and the processes by which officials choose how to act in the course of their official duties? Often, their decisions are backed by the coercive power of the state: judicial retribution might follow failure to comply. Even where the element of coercion (real or threatened) is not present, decisions by public authorities are, almost by definition, important to the lives of affected citizens. For that reason, the adequacy of the ethical norms within which officials operate and the extent to which they can be influenced by such factors as recruitment, employment sanctions, training, and education are questions worth exploring. And that is the second aim of the chapter.

The questions raised in this chapter should not, however, be considered without regard to Chapter 17 on avenues of administrative review and redress. Together, these chapters represent two sides of a perennial debate, which was given its classical expression by Herman Finer and Carl Friedrich fifty years ago (Friedrich, 1940; Finer, 1941; and discussed in Burke, 1986). On the one hand there is the view (associated with Finer) that, to the greatest extent possible, officials should be controlled by externally derived rules and procedures. On the other, Friedrich, recognising the inevitability of administrative discretion, urged the importance of complementing external controls with the inner checks of professionalism. He noted, in particular, the importance of the 'fellowship' of the professions: officials who were also members of a profession (e.g. the law or medicine) would be guided in their behaviour by the standards of that profession and would be judged by their peers. That argument can be broadened into a case for the career public service to be regarded as a profession—'a profession of statecraft' (Martin,

---

1. The 'public interest' has rather fallen out of favour in official discourse in recent years under the public choice critique (see Chapter 2). And Scott (1962, p. 140) warned of the error in claiming that 'the duty of loyalty is subject to the exception that public servants should protect the public interest from the marauding activities of politicians'. Nonetheless, the expression is found in important legislation such as the Official Information Act 1982 (see Chapter 17) and is useful, at the very least, in reminding officials that the *purpose* of their official activity goes beyond satisfying the current minister or their own ambitions. In a practical way it can be reflected in a check-list of the considerations to be taken into account in official behaviour (Martin, 1991a, pp. 9–12). The notions of stewardship, trusteeship, and guardianship on behalf of the wider community—of democratic principles, constitutional proprieties, and public resources— also contribute to an understanding of the 'public interest'.

1988a). This chapter explores the development of that notion in the New Zealand public service since the mid 1980s, together with a number of other issues of current salience. First, however, it is useful to signpost the discussion by reference to a framework for analysis conceived in the context of US government.

A FRAMEWORK FOR ANALYSIS

Pops (1988) identified four kinds of ethical judgment in the administrative process and suggests that they occur in the following sequence:

1. 'Determining whether one has *responsibility*, that is, the legal discretion and willingness to act or not upon policy, and thus the opportunity to make an ethical policy judgment' (Pops, 1988, p. 32).

This formulation directs attention to the situation that frequently faces officials. Do they have the authority to do (or not do) something? If so, should they become involved? The starting point for consideration is usually the law: have specified officials (or classes of officials) been given delegated powers to act, either on request or on their motion? Such powers might allow unfettered discretion (e.g. powers of the Director-General of Health under the Health Act 1956) or they might be restricted by criteria specified in the legislation (e.g. the powers of the Director-General of Social Welfare under the Social Security Act 1964 and other statutes). The common element is the need to make a judgment about whether a matter comes properly within an official's purview. How to act is a second-order question.

Other situations might not turn so directly on questions of specific statutory authorisation. Policy advice is an obvious example. A principal responsibility of CEs (s. 32(b), State Sector Act 1988) is to tender advice to ministers. Whether or not to initiate advice on any topic is a judgment that senior public servants make daily. What considerations should guide them in this decision? 'Self-determination by administrators that they have discretion to make or influence a policy decision, and the responsibility to do it, is the first step and a necessary precondition to normative decision-making' (Pops, 1988, p. 35). This perspective injects an ethical component into the highly political relationship between CEs and ministers.

2. 'Sorting out *pressures and obligations* that bear upon the decision-maker, determining the values attaching to them, and determining whether an ethical dilemma exists' (ibid., p. 33).

Pops portrays administrators 'at the center of a field of forces and interacting with many actors' (ibid., p. 36). Some of these actors have direct links: administrative superiors (including ministers), administrative peers, subordinates, and interest groups. Each might have differing expectations of the official in any given situation. 'The question of which actors and pressures to include or exclude from the policy process is a major ethical question, one going directly to the problem of democracy in the administrative state' (ibid., p. 37). What weight is to be attached to the views of each actor? To what extent do some have privileged access to the policy process? How 'open' should the process be? These questions, which can only be answered by reference to the values of the officials involved (whether these values are explicit or implicit), have always faced New Zealand public servants. They are likely to be even more pressing under MMP.

3. 'Choosing among *decision alternatives* and thus among the values implicit in them (i.e. resolving the dilemma)' (ibid., p. 33).

The discipline of policy analysis has developed strongly in New Zealand since the mid 1980s. A common criticism of the discourse of policy analysis is that it has tended to neglect such values as citizenship, justice, fairness, or democratic participation, favouring instead efficiency as its standard of choice to evaluate policy outcomes and the policy process itself (Anderson, 1979). The institutional dominance of the Treasury in the New Zealand policy process (Boston, 1989b) has, it can be argued, ensured that the economists' frames of reference and analytical tools have 'crowded out' other legitimate approaches to public policy-making. Gregory (1995c, p. 25) puts the point another way. He argues that the new public management with its emphasis on 'enhancing formal, structural controls, in the form of corporate plans, performance reviews, contractual appointments and efficiency audits' has created a 'new technocratic haven' (ibid., p. 29), about which critics 'may find themselves wondering whether it might not be better for managerial reformers to leaven their quest for efficient productive control with a little more concern for responsible reflective judgement'.

Further, it is sometimes suggested (although the evidence is anecdotal) that 'informed dissent' within agencies is likely to be suppressed by the strength of the dominant intellectual paradigm and organisational loyalty. This line of argument raises further questions of importance. To what extent should government agencies reflect a pluralist society? Is this not the role of elected politicians rather than officials? Is it desirable for individual agencies, headed by CEs now subject to fewer institutional checks and balances than before 1988, to develop their own distinctive ethos? To what extent does 'the collective interest' of the government as a whole require the acceptance of over-arching values?

4. 'Designing and selecting *strategies* to facilitate acceptance of ... the decision taken and to reduce the opportunity costs attached to values not embraced in the decision' (Pops, 1988, p. 33).

Pops is here directing attention to the ethical elements in *implementing* decisions. Procedural strategies involve value trade-offs as much as policy choices. To what extent, and in which circumstances, is the 'blitzkrieg' approach favoured by Sir Roger Douglas (1993) appropriate? When is 'ownership' by the community important, and how can it be achieved in the absence of local representation? Consider, for example, the case of the New Zealand health reforms (Easton, 1994).

RESPONSIBILITY IN GOVERNMENT

'Accountability' has been the term in vogue in New Zealand since the mid 1980s. Following Jones (1977) and Gregory (1995c), there is a case for regarding 'responsibility' as an ethically richer notion—one that includes 'accountability' in the sense of 'answerability', but also extends to questions of remedy and consequences. As Gregory (ibid, p. 19) puts it:

> Further, much more so than accountability, responsibility will usually place a burden of choice on a person; it may sometimes give rise to agonising moral dilemmas; it always demands a capacity for reflective judgement. A person, official or whomever, may give an account of the choices made, but responsibility requires one to contemplate reasons for those choices and to live with the consequences that flow from them. In this sense, therefore, accountability may be understood as a necessary but by no means sufficient component of responsibility.

At the heart of any discussion of systems of government is the question: where does responsibility reside? In the New Zealand system of cabinet government the first answer must be: with ministers. Ministers are certainly answerable in Parliament for all that is done by government departments, and to varying degrees, and in different ways, by SOEs and Crown entities (see McGee, 1994, pp. 368–76). And there is an expectation among citizens that ministers will take steps to remedy systemic deficiencies in policy and procedures. Where ministers do *not* appear to accept this degree of responsibility, some measure of political retribution is likely to follow—in respect of the reputation of an individual minister and/or cumulatively of the government as a whole. To that extent the classical doctrine of vicarious ministerial responsibility remains a pillar of the New Zealand constitution (see Chapter 3; Martin, 1991a).

There is, however, little doubt that there have been changes in the perception of what is appropriate behaviour by public servants in their relationships with ministers and the extent to which CEs in particular can be held to be responsible. One view, advanced by a former Chief Ombudsman (Robertson, 1990, p. 9) in 1990 and still apposite, is that:

> Given the accountability structure for senior officials in relation to outputs, it becomes much easier to transfer the accountability justification to the shoulders of Chief Executives in the 'I am responsible but not to blame' syndrome. No matter how it is done, Ministers now have every opportunity if they wish to take it to transfer accountability for outputs to officials.

This comment highlights two often-confused aspects of responsibility: *managerial accountability* and *political responsibility*. Rightly, a constant theme throughout the decade of reform has been the importance of transparency in ensuring managerial accountability. A not unjustified criticism of bureaucracies everywhere has been that accountability is fudged. A striking example in New Zealand was the so-called Maniototo case of 1984 concerning over-expenditure by the Ministry of Works and Development on an irrigation scheme. The buck was passed among ministers and officials with scant regard for administrative authority or constitutional convention (Watson, 1985; Roberts, 1987, pp. 48–50). It is a moot point whether the public was surprised that ministers sought to distance themselves from project management by engineers. Among officials in Wellington there was, however, a recognition that what Palmer (1987, p. 56) later called 'the enveloping haze' of the constitutional convention of ministerial responsibility needed to be dispersed. The combined effect of the State Sector and Public Finance Acts has been to sheet home to individual CEs the responsibility for the activities of their departments in terms of the purchase agreement with minister(s). The 'dead hand' of the central agencies is less readily available as an excuse for administrative failure, and within agencies the processes of corporate management and performance-oriented contracts specify much more clearly who should be doing what. There can be little doubt that the performance-monitoring process described in Chapter 5 is a powerful mechanism for encouraging official behaviour that is in accordance with the objectives of ministers.

If improved managerial accountability is accepted as a desired and desirable outcome of the reforms, does enhanced political responsibility inexorably follow? Or have Robertson's fears been confirmed? One response would be that the reforms—and particularly the quality and amount of financial information now available under the Public Finance and Fiscal Responsibility Acts—have so opened up to scrutiny the processes of government that ministers cannot escape their responsibilities. But that is, of course, to beg the question: for *what* are they responsible, and to *whom*? From the viewpoint of the public the answer, it is suggested, is for *everything* and to *the people*. The subtleties of outputs and outcomes are for the practitioners and the *cognoscenti*, not for the body of citizens who will wish to hold elected representatives to account through the daily toing and froing of politics and, ultimately, at the ballot box. Ministerial performance will vary as it always has, and the extent to which ministers come forward and 'take responsibility' in the full sense of the word will continue to depend as much upon the balance of political advantage (as perceived by those directly involved) as upon the views of constitutional scholars.

POLITICISATION

A related issue is whether the changes in arrangements for managerial accountability have, in themselves, the capacity to affect the attitude of officials to questions of right or wrong. At this point it is useful to return to the fears expressed when the State Sector Act was passed in 1988. Perhaps the concern most often expressed was about 'politicisation' (Walsh, 1991a, pp. 65–7). The politicisation of the appointment process for chief executives, it was argued at the time, was no more than a recognition of one clearly declared purpose of the changes: namely, to put beyond any doubt (if it were necessary) that officials are required to be responsive to the wishes of ministers. At another level there was, however, a concern that the absence of political 'bias' among New Zealand public servants would be contaminated by the new process for appointment of CEs. According to this argument, ministers would ensure the appointment of CEs with whom they were comfortable and, by extension, those who shared their political worldview. Those CEs would, it was suggested, in turn shape the ethos of their agencies in the same way. While ministers have undoubtedly had an influence on senior appointments, there is no evidence that *partisan* considerations have played a part in public service staffing since 1988. (The Hensley case in 1990—see Chapter 5—seemed to relate to the previous positions held by the SSC's preferred candidate rather than party allegiance.)

A more commonly heard argument is that adherence to the collection of ideas encapsulated by Pusey (1991) in his study of the Canberra bureaucracy as 'economic rationalism' has become a requirement for appointment at the senior level. This line of argument has been extended to suggest that the Treasury has 'colonised' the public service, given the number of CE vacancies filled by senior Treasury officers. Conspiracy theory is probably misplaced. The managerialist thrust of the reform process (with its downgrading of specialist knowledge in managerial positions), coupled with a decade that has marked a generational 'changing of the guard' in the pool of potential appointees, is sufficient explanation of the trend in appointments. The ability of the Treasury to recruit quality people and the consistent direction of economic and fiscal policy under successive governments are also relevant factors.

Another dimension of the 'politicisation' argument is that although 'responsiveness' is a reasonable expectation for ministers to have of officials, this could be translated into 'the minister is always right'. The combination of incentives and disincentives in the appointment and monitoring process can, it is sometimes suggested, have the consequence (intended or unintended) of attenuating the capacity to offer 'free and frank' advice. Formally, the position is clear: the contracts of CEs provide explicitly for the provision of 'free and frank' advice. The guidance for senior officials (State Services Commission, 1994c, p. 25) is also refreshingly straightforward:

> Free and frank advice is not always advice the Minister may wish to hear. Advice to a Minister that has been watered-down may not meet the test of being free and frank. It is inappropriate, for instance, for departmental advice to be altered, or influenced unduly, by a third party (say by ministerial staff) before it reaches a Minister.

The more problematic area is that of conflicting streams of advice within a department: in the hypothetical case of strongly held views within a department that are contrary to the government's policy—and perhaps to the position of the CE—is there a duty on the CE to ensure that they are brought to the minister's attention? The emphasis on 'professionalism' in the new public service would suggest that the answer, as it would have been before the reforms, is in the affirmative. Despite the cult of personality that now attaches itself at times to some CEs, they have no monopoly on wisdom; nor are many public policy issues clear-cut. Well-reasoned argument should be exposed to the politicians. From time to time officials in the middle of departments get the impression, rightly or wrongly, that their senior officers are reluctant to press certain positions upon the minister. While contractual considerations could influence the behaviour of senior officials, the management of relations with ministers is an important part of the 'art' of public administration: it requires judgment about the relative importance of issues (which might not be the same at different levels in an organisation) and the timing of their presentation.

One danger to which officials are exposed—and are more vulnerable to than in the past—is that of a personal identification with the minister and/or a policy. Again, this is not a new situation. Indeed, in New Zealand's history, some policies have come to be associated with prominent officials rather than ministers—for instance, 'Beebyism' in education, and 'development in depth' (of manufacturing) with W. B. Sutch. The transition of government between Labour and National was accomplished smoothly in 1990, but it is unlikely that changes of administration will always be without bureaucratic casualties.[2] Just as the 1984 Lange administration appeared to have reservations about officials who had served the Muldoon government in key positions, there will be occasions in future when a change of minister might be followed by a change of CE.

An important consideration in any discussion of politicisation is the degree to which senior officials are, or should be, visible in the public domain. One trend that can be discerned in the experience since the enactment of the State Sector and Public Finance Acts is that public servants are more visible. In many cases this is because issues of management attract public attention. A prime example, in tragic circumstances, was the way in which the Department of Conservation (DoC), and particularly the Director-General (Bill Mansfield), responded to the accident at Cave Creek where fourteen people lost their lives in April 1995. The Department showed an apparent willingness to accede to all requests for interview and an open acceptance of responsibility for any deficiencies that might be revealed. The complexity of questions of responsibility in government was, however, quickly demonstrated when issues about inadequate funding of DoC were injected into the public discussion. This would fall within the category referred to earlier as 'systemic deficiencies', for which the minister might be expected to accept responsibility. (At the time of writing a commission is investigating the circumstances of the Cave Creek tragedy.)

Such a case raises difficult issues about the role of ministers and officials. Perhaps the easier situation concerns the official's duty in respect of politically controversial policies. In the years immediately after the state sector reforms, there seemed to be a developing tendency for officials to be moving over the danger line between *explanation* and *advocacy* of policy (e.g. in respect of the purchase of frigates and the reforms of educational administration). In the MMP environment the extent to which officials become publicly identified with controversial policies will, if anything, raise even more delicate issues of judgment for all concerned.

CONSUMERISM AND THE PUBLIC SERVICE

The restructuring of the state since the mid 1980s has narrowed the areas in which government agencies deal directly with the public. Corporatisation followed by privatisation (Mascarenhas, 1991; Duncan and Bollard, 1992) has severed most trading activities from the public service. Where they have not been moved outside the public sector, they are delivered by organisations such as SOEs or CHEs, both of which, in almost every respect, are 'companies' like all others under the Companies Act 1993. Much of the ethos, and indeed the language, of these public agencies is that of the market (not surprisingly in

2. In 1991 George Salmond, Director-General of Health, chose not to complete his contract, making it clear that he found it inappropriate to continue given the sharp change in policy signalled by the new minister (Simon Upton).

the SOE case). But there is also a propensity to apply the precepts and practices of 'marketing' to the culture of Crown entities with their multiplicity of functions, and to 'core' public service departments with their predominantly policy advice role. Certainly this is true of the social service delivery agencies, whether they are Crown entities (such as the CHEs) or the Income Support Service of DSW (see McDonald and Sharma, 1994). Very broadly, this movement, which is not confined to New Zealand (see Potter, 1988), can be labelled 'consumerism'. There is a good case for public agencies to become 'user friendly'; individuals should, it goes without saying, be treated with respect and dignity (and that has not always been the case). At the same time, the emphasis on citizens as 'consumers' has ethical implications for public servants.

'Consumerism' in the market-place proceeds from the premise that 'there is an *imbalance of power* between those who provide goods and services, and those for whom they are provided' (Potter, 1988, p. 150, emphasis added). In order to shift the balance of power away from 'the big batallions' closer towards consumers, attention should be paid—it is argued—to five key factors, viz.:

- access;
- choice;
- information;
- redress; and
- representation.

This is a useful check-list for agencies reviewing their relationships with the public. Clearly, in the public sector, the implications of these terms are different from what is conveyed by them in the private sector. *Access*—who shall have access to what—is usually a matter of political choice, not of market transactions. *Choice* is, itself, a slippery notion when applied to many functions of government, e.g. the activities of the Department of Corrections, welfare entitlements, or even publicly provided health and education services. But the provision of relevant *information* will usually be an appropriate activity for even those agencies with monopoly power. *Redress*, too, in the public sector is more than simply a matter of complaints procedures and recourse ultimately to the courts; it might involve the intervention of the various statutory authorities discussed in the next chapter, or invocation of the political process. *Representation* opens up the much wider questions of consultation, participation, and 'voice' (Hirschman, 1970) in the development of policies.

In the United Kingdom and in a growing number of other countries (Pollitt, 1995), 'consumerism' has found expression in Citizen's Charters (Lovell, 1992; Lewis, 1993; Tritter, 1994). These documents purport to set minimum standards for the delivery of public services, backed by the authority—albeit rather diffuse—of ministers. While some observers see the United Kingdom Citizen's Charter as 'a sop, a legitimation device or even an attempt at deflecting criticism away from the pressing failures of government', others see it as 'a genuine move towards a new way of governing' (Lewis, 1993, p. 316). In New Zealand the degree of transparency that exists through the various accountability documents and the much greater specification of agency outputs has perhaps diverted attention away from formal charters, although there are examples of individual agencies such as the Civil Aviation Authority with its statutory Service Charter (Martin, 1995a).

At the heart of the debate about the impact of consumerism on the public sector is the confusion in terminology among 'citizen', 'consumer', 'customer', and 'client'. *Citizens* have rights as members of the polity; they participate in the political process not because they are customers of particular services but because the right to such participation is a defining characteristic of the citizen. Citizens have entitlements, for example to welfare benefits, because Parliament has determined certain criteria of eligibility. Even where an element of 'user pays' enters the equation, charges are not prices: they are not set by the market but by administrative fiat; and, further, whether or not the levy is paid is unlikely to be a matter of choice (Harden, 1992, p. 7).

As 'consumer-orientation' enters the culture of the public sector and moves beyond the quality of the relationship between the citizen and the person at the front desk, difficult questions of accountability and responsibility arise, for example, in the exercise of discretion. Officials are expected to be 'responsive' to the public, but they are 'responsible' to ministers. There is an inherent tension in this triangle between officials, ministers, and the public. This is particularly the case when the costs of a public agency are substantially funded by levy: 'user pays, user says'. (For a more detailed discussion of these issues see Martin, 1995a.)

WHISTLEBLOWING

'Whistleblowing' is to be distinguished from 'leaking'; the former is the overt provision of information to authority or the media by an identified person, while the latter refers to those cases where information enters the public domain by 'falling off the back of a truck'. To choose between them is itself to make a moral decision, but one that requires a prior decision to move beyond the norms of behaviour expected of employees, whether or not employed in a public organisation (Glazer and Glazer, 1989). Such a decision draws into sharp relief the conflicting duties with which public servants must always live, even though few might be called on to choose among them.[3] On the one hand, there is 'a strongly recognised duty of loyalty to the group, an ethical imperative we all learn very early on the school grounds, or perhaps even earlier in the family' (McDowell, 1991, p. 8). Whether 'the group' in this case is the agency in which the official is employed or the wider entity of 'the government' or the public service is a matter for later consideration. This dimension of 'loyalty' is, however, reinforced in many conceivable cases by the duty owed to superiors, including the minister. On the other hand,

---

3. The situations in which officials might consider 'blowing the whistle' are difficult to categorise and, for the individual, unpredictable. Another formulation is that of McMillan (1994, p. 115): 'There may be evidence which suggests that activity is occurring which is illegal, unethical, or a threat to public health or safety. Less dramatically, an employee may simply have a complaint about internal maladministration or financial waste.'

there is in societies like New Zealand a strong moral obligation to inform where necessary to protect other parties—particularly if those parties are not in a position, often because of a lack of knowledge, to protect themselves. 'We admire the good Samaritan and condemn the pharisee who walked by' (ibid., p. 89). For the official who becomes aware of activities within the government that violate 'procedural, policy, moral or legal bounds' (French, 1983, p. 135), there is a choice between these two ethical norms.

In New Zealand, by comparison with other jurisdictions such as the USA or, nearer home, Australia, whistleblowing has until recently received little attention. In the 1970s there were episodes of leaking, notably regarding scientific contributions to the public debate on issues such as indigenous forest policy. One documented case concerned allegations (later found to be wrong) of the case of impure anti-poliomyelitis vaccines by the Department of Health (see Martin, 1995b). It can be assumed that the arrival of the Ombudsmen from 1962 and the availability of the Official Information Act 1982 reduced the pressures to leak or blow the whistle. Nonetheless, the organisational upheavals of the late 1980s again brought the issue to the fore, and no lesser authorities than the Chief Ombudsman and the State Services Commissioner expressed some support for legislation to protect whistleblowers. In 1992, the Commissioner (Don Hunn) spoke of the need for 'safety valves in the system so that people can talk about illegal or immoral actions' in a period when 'instability and structural changes have eroded people's loyalty to the Public Service' (Morel, 1992, p. 10). Further, the then Chief Ombudsman, Sir John Robertson, warned of 'an urgent need for a person who genuinely blows the whistle to be protected from harassment and victimisation' (ibid.). The issue lay dormant until early 1994, when the case of psychiatric nurse Neil Pugmire received wide public support, largely through the agency of Opposition Justice spokesperson Phil Goff. Pugmire, employed by the Wanganui CHE, was gravely concerned about the proposed release into the community of a psychiatric patient. When this information emerged in the public domain, Pugmire became subject to disciplinary action (later withdrawn) by his employer, but received widespread public and editorial support. Goff, in the wake of this complex (and not entirely one-sided) case, introduced into the Parliament a Whistleblower Protection Bill, which aimed to facilitate disclosure in specified circumstances, to protect whistleblowers, and to ensure that remedial action would be taken. Despite an indication by the Minister of State Services that the government had in mind introducing its own legislation, the Goff bill at the time of writing is still before a select committee. (The minister has, however, established a committee to report to him on the case for whistleblowing legislation.)

Undoubtedly, such legislation raises difficult drafting issues (for the US experience see Caiden and Truelson, 1988; in respect of Australia see McMillan, 1994). But the apparent unwillingness of the National government to give any urgency to whistleblower protection in the public sector is probably related to a more fundamental scepticism about the wisdom of 'legislating for ethics'. Nonetheless, on the precedent of other jurisdictions and in the light of institutional change in New Zealand, there is a strong case to be made for acknowledgment in statute that there can be situations when duty to the public interest trumps other obligations within the system; and that officials, in prescribed circumstances, are entitled to protection from retribution. The objective would be not a licence for the disaffected but a mechanism contributing to good government.

OFFICIAL INITIATIVES

The SSC has a pivotal role to play in providing ethical leadership in the public service (and, indeed, in the wider public sector). Its mandate and its ability to do so can be found within the State Sector Act 1988. Despite the dominating thrust in favour of the managerial autonomy of CEs, the long title to the Act (retaining the words of the State Services Act 1962) speaks of: 'An Act to ensure that employees in the State Services are *imbued with a spirit of service*' (emphasis added). Indeed, the Commission's solicitor has referred to 'this element of service to the community that makes the question of ethics in the Public Service of vital importance and is essential to making our current system of government work' (Bradshaw, 1993, p. 2). Second, the Commission was specifically invited by s. 57 of the State Sector Act to issue a *Code of Conduct* 'covering the minimum standards of integrity and conduct that are to apply in the Public Service'. This the Commission did in 1990. And third, in recommending appointments to CE positions, the Commission has a heavy responsibility not only in promoting efficiency and effectiveness but also in ensuring integrity at the top of the public service.

The Code sets out the legislative obligations placed on public service employers and employees, and establishes three principles of conduct that all public servants are expected to observe (SSC, 1990, p. 6):[4]

(i) Employees should fulfil their lawful obligations to Government with professionalism and integrity.

(ii) Employees should perform their official duties honestly, faithfully and efficiently, respecting the rights of the public and their colleagues.

(iii) Employees should not bring their employer into disrepute through their private activities.

With one reservation (dealt with below) the Code develops these principles in terms of unexceptionable generality. 'In broad terms the first priority for public servants is to carry out government policy.' As well as serving the government of the day public servants must act in such a way that the department 'is able to establish the same relationship with future Ministers'. 'Honest, impartial and comprehensive advice' is urged. The 'dilemma for public servants who hold strong personal beliefs on certain issues' is recognised, but 'it is one which must be managed so as to avoid conflict with their official duties'. That officials have 'the same rights of free speech and independence in the conduct of their private affairs as other members of the public' is acknowledged.

---

4. Chief executives may issue their own codes of conduct, which may not be inconsistent with the SSC Code, and a number have done so.

Guidance is provided about the release of official information, and, in the light of the earlier discussion about whistleblowing, there must be a reservation. The Code makes the unqualified statement that '*whatever their motives* ... employees [who make unauthorised disclosure of information] betray the trust put in them, and undermine the relationship' that should exist between a minister and the public service (SSC, 1990, p. 17, emphasis added). Such unreserved commitment to the employer—more particularly to the government—is unreasonable to ask of individuals. What governments are entitled to ask is that their employees, in deciding to release unauthorised information (as in any other aspect of their official activities), do not act in a capricious manner but only after a careful weighing of the consequences for all parties.

To supplement the Code, which deals principally with issues where 'right and wrong' are clear-cut, the State Services Commissioner has devoted considerable personal attention for some years to the provision of guidance for public servants in areas where they are less easily defined: in particular, regarding the conventions that govern public servants' relationships with the public, Parliament, and ministers. The first in a series of papers, *The Senior Public Servant* (SSC, 1994c), appeared in 1994, and a number of others followed in 1995.[5] The length of time this 'Principles, Conventions and Practice' project has taken is a mark both of the complexity of the issues and of the Commissioner's strong belief that 'rules' could not be imposed. At every stage there has been discussion with CEs and other interested parties inside and outside the public service.

Mention should also be made of a *Public Service Vision Statement* approved by cabinet in 1992 and available in poster form to remind public servants of the 'principles and values' that should inform the activities of the public service. It is reprinted in Appendix 2.

'Professional management' and 'professional policy advice' are highlighted in the *Vision Statement*. Indeed, 'professionalism' is a key word in current discussions of the appropriate behaviour of public servants. One manifestation of these discussions has been the move to establish a Management Development Centre with the aim of capturing for management of the public service 'best practice' in the private sector. It will be interesting to assess the extent to which the centre, acting in accordance with this felt need of CEs, includes within its purview training in the ethics of public service.

Much of the international discussion of ethics in the public sector (Chapman, 1993; Thomas, 1993; N. Preston, 1994) has concerned such questions as: Can ethics be taught? How are we to build an ethical organisational or workplace culture? (N. Preston, 1994, p. 7; see also Kernaghan, 1993). These are questions concerning the 'institutionalisation of ethics' (ibid., p. 8). For the New Zealand public service the challenge will be to develop such an 'institutionalisation' at a time when the culture and staff of the institutions of government have been undergoing unprecedented change.

---

5. The papers in this guidance series were published in compendium form in September 1995 as *Public Service Principles, Conventions and Practice* (SSC, 1995d).

THE PROFESSIONAL PUBLIC SERVANT

As already noted, the notion of 'professionalism' is in good currency in New Zealand in the 1990s. In *The Senior Public Servant* (SSC, 1994c, p. 5) the SSC has listed the attributes of the professional public servant, viz.:

- obeying and upholding the law;
- discharging obligations to the elected government of the day in a politically impartial way;
- displaying a high level of knowledge and competence;
- delivering services and achieving results through organisational efficiency, and fiscal responsibility;
- demonstrating a strong sense of personal responsibility, personal integrity and commitment to the public good;
- preparing advice, delivering services, and making decisions reached by using analytically sound, well-rounded, informed and inclusive approaches;
- respecting people and their views both inside and outside the Public Service;
- tendering advice with courage, tenacity and independence;
- promoting and advocating the core values of the organisation, evaluating the performance of staff in the light of those values, assessing the extent to which core values are actually reflected in the organisation, and providing opportunities for general training and counselling as appropriate.

Conversely, it would be unprofessional for a public servant to:

- act out of spite or bias or favouritism;
- allow official action to be influenced by personal relationships, self-interest, or personal obligations;
- promote a particular political viewpoint or personal agenda (ibid., p. 6).

The Commission acknowledges that such a list highlights 'a strong ambiguity from which tension or conflict may arise' (ibid.). It also, by pointing to 'the core values of the organisation', recognises the importance of the individual agencies that make up the public service and the crucial role of the leadership of those organisations in developing 'professionalism' across the service. With those caveats there is little to quarrel with in this list of attributes. If such a list had been prepared in, say, 1980, it would have been unlikely to have differed very much. Nor does it seem dissimilar to the qualities other countries seek in their senior public servants (Chapman, 1993). Perhaps that suggests that there are indeed certain values which endure at all times within the governments of democratic countries and which should inform the behaviour of officials. The issue facing governments is rather how to 'institutionalise' (N. Preston, 1994, p. 7) those values in the face of major changes in organisation and (at least in the New Zealand case) people, within a political environment that in almost every country seems to be distrustful of governments.

The public service of the mid 1990s is one that has self-consciously distanced itself—in accordance with Parliament's wishes—from the culture of the 'old' public service. Concurrently, the environment in which the public service operates has itself undergone great change. The flavour of these linked changes is perhaps captured by the replacement of 'bureaucracy' by 'enterprise'. In this new situation ethical questions will continue to face public servants: in their relations with ministers (likely to be more complex following the first MMP election); in new relations with the public—whether citizens, consumers, or clients; and in wrestling with their own consciences.

It was tempting, as the media discovered, during 1994 to draw together the unrelated and disparate cases of allegations about the Commissioner of Inland Revenue and the Serious Fraud Office (in the so-called 'wine box' affair), the 'chateau Ohakea' episode concerning overexpenditure (on the base commander's house at RNZAF Ohakea), and the circumstances of the resignation of the Controller and Auditor-General (Jeff Chapman). On this basis some recalled the experience of Queensland in the 1980s, as revealed in the Fitzgerald Report, and the 'sleaze' factor in contemporary British politics, and saw parallels in New Zealand linked to the deconstruction of the 'old' public service. Such a line of argument cannot be sustained on the basis of these cases. Nonetheless, it is true that the culture has changed, that the people have changed, and that there has been a recognised need to revalidate the old norms of behaviour or to replace them with new conventions.

CONCLUSION

The usefulness of Pops' framework discussed earlier in this chapter is that it focuses attention on individuals in their role as public servant. Codes, lists of attributes and generalised guidance, whether from a central agency or from the CE, are essential components of a public service sensitive to ethical considerations. They reinforce, however, a proposition that individuals remain responsible for the acts and omissions of their behaviour as public servants. The continuing task for the SSC and CEs is to ensure that a preoccupation with technical skills and substantive knowledge does not overshadow the nurturing of understanding of the ethical dimensions of the public service. Specifically, in Pops' terminology:

a. *Responsibility:* public servants need to understand the constitutional conventions under which they operate (and their problematic nature); they need to be very clear about the authority under which they take decisions—the individual's assessment of the desirability of the end-result is not an adequate authority; and they need to be able to justify why they have acted or become involved (or vice versa).

b. *Pressures and obligations:* an awareness of, and respect for, the interests and views of others ought to be present in the intellectual armoury of every policy analyst or manager and should inform their analysis, advice, and decision-making. Elegance of policy design is not a substitute for recognition of the interests of others—within the official family or among the public—and this needs to be considered by officials as well as ministers (even if the decision-making process is slowed down).

c. *Choosing among competing values:* government is not only about the efficient delivery of services: it is about the collective choices that a society exercises in distributional issues; it is about the way in which a society treats the disadvantaged among its citizens; and it is about the decision-making process itself. In all these circumstances a number of perspectives, or what Pops (1988, p. 39) calls 'systems of thought, which give formulae or guidelines for choice' can appropriately be employed; there is an opportunity cost if only one approach (say cost–benefit analysis) is brought to bear on a decision dilemma. Officials should recognise the legitimacy of different perspectives and ensure that they are respected even though their own may be different.

d. *Choosing among implementation strategies:* in a governmental structure that has elevated the separation of policy advice from delivery to a central principle of organisational design, there is a risk that procedures for implementation will be seen as a second-order concern. It is at this point that the issues earlier discussed about consumerism import another ethical dimension into official behaviour.

If this framework is applied to the New Zealand public service in the mid 1990s a number of tentative conclusions can be suggested. First, despite the massive nature of the changes that have taken place, the continuity of certain values and constitutional conventions has enabled a 'revolution' to take place without 'barricades, bullets or Bastilles' (as a public servant quoted by the State Services Commissioner put it: see SSC, 1989, p. 6). Second, the removal of bureaucratic restraints on officials carries with it a risk that issues of authority and legitimacy—and thus responsibility—will be disregarded as unnecessary inhibitions on 'getting things done'.[6] Third, and for similar reasons, there has at times appeared to be an unwillingness to recognise legitimate interests and groups (sometimes stigmatised with the label of 'capture'); the abolition of consultative forums, both sectoral and broadly based (e.g. the New Zealand Planning Council), points in this direction. Contestability among elites is not a substitute for consultation. Fourth, the dominance of the paradigm of neo-classical economics and those whom Gregory (1995c) calls 'technocrats' has seemed to place a discount on the contribution that can be made by other approaches to public policy and management. Finally, such major policy initiatives as the reform of the health sector have demonstrated an unwillingness to appreciate the ethical questions involved in such a large implementation exercise (although it would probably be unfair to attribute any failings in this area to officials alone).

What this analysis suggests is that the ethos of the public service has been challenged and has had to be redefined to adapt enduring values to a new organisational structure and to new expectations. The leadership of the public service (particularly the State Services Commissioner throughout this period, Don Hunn) has been very mindful of the threats to ethical principles—and to citizens' trust in government—that such major change posed. Indeed, in commenting on the issues raised by the 'Chapman affair', the

---

6. An interesting insight into the priorities of some departmental managers is contained in the Controller and Auditor-General's comment that a number questioned the 'appropriateness of having me comment on their management of consultant engagements. In managers' jargon, consultants are "inputs". Commonly, managers said they were concerned with the services and products that are their "outputs", as intended by the public sector reforms' (Audit Office, 1994c, Third Report, p. 17).

Commissioner, in a somewhat Delphic remark, observed that 'there isn't any doubt there is a cost for [improved management in the public sector] and the price is the old ethic' (Kilroy, 1995, p. 7). But in New Zealand (unlike some Australian jurisdictions, for example), there has been no widespread breakdown in the standards of behaviour of public officials. There is, nonetheless, a need to 'institutionalise' ethical behaviour, or as some might say to 'reinvent' it, in the aftermath of the managerialist deconstruction (Gregory, 1995c). It is no longer possible to assume that mentors will always be available to induct public servants into the norms of the public service ethos. The turnover in staff is rapid, middle management has been greatly reduced ('flattening the pyramid'), and the fragmentation of the public service (see Chapter 4) is leading to the development of strong new agency cultures in a manner more associated in the past with the US civil service (Mosher, 1981). But there can be only one set of ethical standards for servants of the Crown. The SSC, in partnership with CEs, carries the responsibility for the behaviour of the public services as a whole. Publication of a *Code of Conduct* and the *Public Service Principles, Conventions and Practice* series represent stages in an evolutionary process.

Continued leadership from the top will need to be accompanied by structured programmes of education and training in public service ethics, about which there is now an extensive international literature (Chapman, 1993; N. Preston, 1994). If anything, the need will be greater in the post-MMP environment (Carpinter, 1993; East, 1994; Hunn, 1994d; Martin, 1994c). Ethical issues for officials cannot escape their political context. In this respect, an encouraging note on which to close this chapter is struck by the SSC in its guidance to senior public servants (1994c, p. 25):

> From time to time there has been a tendency to decry politics as an irrational and unworthy intrusion into what should be a rational and analytically pure process of public policy making. In fact, political processes are not just ways of arriving at correct resolutions of particular issues. They are an expression of democratic and representative government which is concerned as much with preserving the confidence of people in the way they are governed and building and maintaining political support as it is with resolving particular issues.

17 administrative review and redress

Administration must not only be efficient in the sense that the objectives of policy are securely attained without delay. It must also satisfy the general body of citizens that it is proceeding with reasonable regard to the balance between the public interest which it promotes and the private interests which it disturbs . . . (Franks Report, 1957, quoted by Orr, 1964, p. 7).

A principal objective of the decade of reform starting in the mid 1980s in New Zealand has been improvement in the efficiency of the public sector. At the same time there have been institutional developments that have attempted, in Franks' words, to 'satisfy the general body of citizens' that the public interest is being promoted and that the rights of citizens are being protected. These developments have not been initiated as a reaction to the recent changes in organisational structure and method. Rather, they represent a continuation of the willingness to embark on administrative innovation that began with the Parliamentary Commissioner (Ombudsman) Act 1962 (Keith, 1987).

This chapter is concerned with the various restraints that encircle officials in the conduct of their business and, seen from the other side of the fence, the avenues available to citizens seeking redress. They range from the day-to-day operation of the political process through the powers of Parliament to the activities of such institutions as the Ombudsmen and the Privacy Commissioner, and ultimately to the courts. But, as was emphasised in the previous chapter, these mechanisms should be seen as reinforcing, not replacing, the professionalism and ethical sensitivity of the public service. The aim of the chapter is modest: it is essentially to describe the avenues of administrative review now available to citizens, and to point in the direction of more detailed studies of each of its components.[1]

THE POLITICAL PROCESS

One of the distinguishing features of employment in a public organisation is the reality of being involved in 'politics'. For some (particularly those whose mandate is to run a

---

1. An avenue of 'review and redress' not covered in this chapter is the array of tribunals in particular administrative fields (e.g. the Residence Appeal and Removal Review Authorities under the Immigration Act 1991 and the Social Security Appeal Authority under the Social Security Act 1964).

'successful business') this is at best an irritant and at worst a serious inhibition on their ability to function effectively. But it is of the nature of being 'public' that those elected as the stewards of citizens' interests should monitor, criticise and even seek to have ministers intervene in the activities of public organisations. There are, of course, degrees of 'publicness': state-owned enterprises, for example, were intended by Parliament to be less subject to control by ministers than government departments (Mascarenhas, 1991). Nonetheless, the mechanisms and procedures discussed in this chapter are to a greater or lesser extent applicable to all public organisations. And certainly their activities do not escape the scrutiny of the media. The cynic might say that current affairs on television and talkback programmes on radio have taken over a principal role of the Parliament, viz. scrutiny of the executive. Nonetheless, it has long been the case that matters of administration (as much as of policy) that attain some public exposure will find their way into more formal channels.

Citizens with grievances against public organisations may raise matters with their local (or any other) MP; they may write directly to the minister or the organisation concerned; or they may have recourse to the various institutional procedures discussed in this chapter.

Parliament[2]

The Constitution Act 1986 sets out two central functions of the Parliament: 'laws and money' (Palmer, 1992, p. 109). Parliament has 'full power to make laws', and it is not lawful for the Crown, 'except by or under an Act of Parliament', to levy taxes, raise loans, or to spend public money (s. 22).[3] In practice these functions occupy the greater part of parliamentary time, a matter of concern to many observers (McGee, 1994; McRae, 1994; Palmer, 1987, 1992; Skene, 1992). One aspect of Parliament's role that has not been fully developed, because (so it is argued) of the quantity of lawmaking and the priority of the appropriation process, is that of scrutiny of the executive branch. Nonetheless, a number of reforms in the last decade—both in the House of Representatives itself and through such measures as the Public Finance Act 1989 and the Fiscal Responsibility Act 1994—have improved the capacity of Parliament to scrutinise the activities of ministers and officials, if the will is there. Equally, the mechanisms listed below are available to citizens seeking redress in respect of action (or inaction) on the part of the executive.

Petitions

The right of citizens to petition Parliament can be traced back to Magna Carta (1215) and, in New Zealand, has existed from the first meeting of the House of Representatives

---

2. Section 14 of the Constitution Act 1986 states that Parliament consists of 'the Sovereign in right of New Zealand, and the House of Representatives'. In this chapter 'Parliament' is used in the colloquial sense as a synonym for the House of Representatives.

3. The important point about s. 22 of the Constitution Act 1986 is that Parliament has the *sole* power to tax and to authorise the expenditure of public money. The Crown may not do these things except by virtue of an Act of Parliament.

in 1854. Petitions may come from single petitioners seeking relief for a personal injustice or may result from widespread concern about public issues, such as the passage of the Homosexual Law Reform Bill in 1985 (McGee, 1994, p. 384). The procedures regarding petitions are set down in the standing orders of the House, but there are few limitations on the form or contents. Petitions must, however, be in the form of a 'prayer': that is, a request that something be done (or not be done) (ibid., p. 385). Petitions will not be accepted by the Clerk of the House unless the petitioner has exhausted other relevant legal rights (for example, the right to appeal from a decision by the Commissioner of Inland Revenue, or the right to make a complaint to the Ombudsmen if the subject matter is within their competency). This does not, however, extend to judicial review (see below); the possibility that a petitioner could apply to the High Court does not preclude the House from considering the petition.

Petitions are normally presented by the petitioner's local Member of Parliament and 'laid upon the Table'. They are then referred to the Clerk of the House who distributes them to one of the select committees of the House, which is required to deal with them and to report back to the House. The select committee will determine its own procedure, but will usually seek comment from the department(s) or other public organisations involved, hear both the petitioner and department, deliberate, and report back to the House (where the petition may be debated). This report will contain either no recommendation or a recommendation that the matter be referred to the government for 'consideration', 'favourable consideration', or 'most favourable consideration'. In the case of a recommendation the matter is referred to the Secretary of the Cabinet for coordination of a response by the appropriate minister, who will communicate directly to the petitioner. Responses are reported to the House within twenty-eight days of the following session and are printed in AJHR (ibid., pp. 389–97). During 1994, 258 petitions were presented. Only one was about a matter of direct concern only to the petitioner. The others concerned general matters of public policy. Some of them led to a major inquiry by a select committee. One notable case was the 1987 inquiry into the effects on localities of post office closures (ibid., p. 392). A petition tends to be a measure of last resort. Apart from the requirement to exhaust such procedures as exist, the use of the Official Information and Ombudsmen Acts (see below) usually offer the possibility of quicker and more direct consideration and redress than petitions to Parliament.

Parliamentary Questions (PQs)

The requirement that ministers must answer questions addressed to them by other members of Parliament is a hallmark of the Westminster system of responsible government. In New Zealand questions may be for written or oral answer.[4] Oral questions may be of three types: a question of the day, a question on notice, or an urgent question. These types are differentiated by the period of notice that must be given—for urgent questions this can be a matter of minutes (McGee, 1994, p. 425).

---

4. In 1994 there were some 8100 written and 1500 oral questions (Office of the Clerk).

Questions in the House may serve several purposes. They might genuinely seek information (although generally direct approaches to ministers or organisations will serve this purpose better); they might seek to publicise a matter of public interest; they might be designed to enable a minister to direct attention to a matter for which the government claims credit; or, from the Opposition parties, they might be calculated to embarrass the government. In these latter two categories, questions often originate in the research offices of party organisations. Questions must seek factual information, not the expression of opinion. They must concern matters for which the minister to whom the question is addressed has portfolio responsibility. Whether or not the minister has responsibility can potentially be an important matter. Ministers are, for example, not responsible (under the State Sector Act 1988) for staffing decisions made by chief executives; they are, however, responsible for the general employment policies of departments and will answer questions about them. There are a number of precedents for ministers assuming *political* responsibility for matters over which they have no *legal* power, or in respect of the actions of public officials who are not subject to ministers' legal control. McGee (1994, p. 434) cites as an example ministerial responsibility for the actions of the SSC in the course of carrying out its legal functions in regard to the appointment of a chief executive.

The establishment of state enterprises under the State-Owned Enterprises Act 1986 appeared likely to narrow the scope of PQs to ministers. In practice ministers have generally been prepared to accept questions relating to individual enterprises, although often making it clear in answering that they are relaying information provided by the enterprise (ibid., p. 434). Similarly, it is clear that the responsible minister in respect of a Crown entity (see Chapter 3) is expected to answer questions about its operations.

Parliamentary questions are an important vehicle for 'keeping officials on their toes'. Officials seek to avoid embarrassment to their ministers, and the House of Representatives is obviously a very public forum. If a matter is the subject of a PQ, officials will wish to ensure not only that the minister's answer is the best available but also (in the case of oral questions) that there is adequate briefing to enable the minister to respond to supplementary questions. Bringing a matter to the attention of an MP with a view to a PQ should not be overlooked by citizens seeking to direct attention to the effect of administrative actions.

Select Committees

In 1985 a revision of the standing orders of the House of Representatives initiated by Sir Geoffrey Palmer (Palmer, 1992, p. 110) resulted in a 'total reconstruction from first principles of the system of select committees in the New Zealand Parliament' (ibid., p. 110; see also McGee, 1994; Skene, 1992). Among the most important of these changes was the empowerment, without further resort to the House, of each of the thirteen subject committees to 'examine the policy, administration and expenditure of departments and associated non-departmental government bodies'.[5] (Since 1992 all matters concerning state-owned enterprises have been the responsibility of a State

5. The committees are listed in Chapter 3 and in McGee (1994) pp. 215, 216.

Enterprises Committee.) Palmer comments: 'It is hard to exaggerate how potent such powers could be holding government to account, checking excesses, seeing that money is properly spent and looking at policy defects' (Palmer, 1992, p. 112). Although the instigator of reform has expressed some disappointment in the reluctance/inability of select committees to make full use of their powers, their importance as a mechanism for holding the executive to account should not be downplayed—and, indeed, is likely to be enhanced in an MMP Parliament.

Select committees are crucial to the law-making process, almost all bills being referred to them. The opportunity provided by select committee hearings enables citizens (whether individually or through groups) to offer views on legislative proposals, including those that impinge on the rights of individuals. In terms of time commitment, the other major function of committees is the annual cycle of examination of the government's spending plans for the current year and review of the performance for the previous year (McGee, 1994, p. 209). These two separate examinations provide opportunities for MPs to question officials on the activities of their agencies, on matters of broad administrative significance, and on the minutiae of management. Questionnaires are responded to in advance of oral hearings, and further written information is likely to be required of the CE. Hearings are held in public unless otherwise determined. The appearance of a departmental CE and senior officers before a select committee either for the *ex ante* estimates examination or the *ex post* performance review can be of critical significance in establishing the reputation of the department in Parliament and with the public. It might also provide MPs with the opportunity to pursue particular matters in the agency's administration. Select committees are, not infrequently, critical of departments in their reports to the House. (For further discussion of the processes of financial accountability, see Chapter 14.)

Select committees, principally because of the pressure of legislative and financial business, have not initiated a large number of specific inquiries over the past decade. (In 1994 nine were begun.) Nonetheless, backbench MPs have publicly indicated that they see this function developing in importance. In part, no doubt, this reflects the more volatile political environment associated with MMP. It might also owe something to the significance attached to the inquiries such as that completed in 1995 into the Office of the Race Relations Conciliator (AJHR, 1995, I. 7A).

Controller and Auditor-General

The Controller and Auditor-General is 'Parliament's watchdog', and is also the recipient of many representations from the public alleging the misuse of public resources. The independence and stature of the office of Controller and Auditor-General is a major element in the array of administrative restraints. (See also Chapter 15.)

Officers of Parliament

The first officer of Parliament was the Ombudsman, the position being created in 1962 (see below). In 1976 the Wanganui Computer Centre Privacy Commissioner was established; this position was abolished in 1993. And in 1987 the Parliamentary

Commissioner for the Environment was established. (The Controller and Auditor-General is not technically a statutory officer of Parliament, although that is likely to eventuate in the foreseeable future.) One of the distinguishing characteristics of an officer of Parliament, according to the Finance and Expenditure Committee (1989, AJHR, I. 4B), is that the position is 'created to provide a check on the arbitrary use of power by the executive'. Appointments are made by the Governor-General on the recommendation of the House, and provisions are in place (on funding, for example) to underline their independence. The Parliamentary Commissioner for the Environment 'has a wide-ranging role of inquiring into the actions of public authorities insofar as they might have an environmental impact, and auditing the procedures that public authorities themselves have in place for minimising any adverse environmental effects that might result from their activities' (McGee, 1994, p. 61). The Commissioner since the position's inception, Helen Hughes, has established a reputation as a strongly independent guardian of the interests of the environment (Bührs and Bartlett, 1993).

THE OMBUDSMEN

'The Ombudsman is Parliament's man—put there for the protection of the individual' (so said the first Ombudsman, Sir Guy Powles, on being sworn in, 1 October 1962; see Joseph, 1993, p. 123). There are now, of course, two Ombudsmen; and between 1987 and 1992 a woman, Nadja Tollemache, held the position. Nonetheless, Sir Guy's emphasis on 'the protection of the individual' and allegiance to Parliament—not the executive—remain a pithy summation of the Ombudsman's role.[6]

Over more than thirty years the jurisdiction of the office has been extended greatly. Originally concerned with government departments, coverage was widened in 1968 to include hospital and education boards; in 1975 to include local government; in 1982 to act in an independent review capacity under the Official Information Act 1982 (see below); in 1987 to make official information held by local authorities more freely available; and in 1995 to consider complaints from prisoners (Joseph, 1993, pp. 125, 126). It is significant too that, despite strenuous representations to the contrary in some cases, Parliament has maintained the jurisdiction of the Ombudsmen over state-owned enterprises (AJHR, I. 20A, 1990), Crown entities, and regional health authorities and Crown health enterprises.

Given its 'foreign' provenance (derived from Scandinavia) and initial reservations about its compatibility with the convention of ministerial responsibility, it is worth considering the reasons for the strength of the institution. Those put forward in 1984 by the second Chief Ombudsman, Sir George Laking (1987, p. 311), still seem valid:

> Its response to the challenges with which it has been faced needs to be examined against the three essential features of the office.

---

6. The position was created by the Parliamentary Commissioner (Ombudsman) Act 1962, which was replaced by the Ombudsmen Act 1975.

1. Its *independence* as a Parliamentary office not responsible to the Executive Government.[7]
2. Its *flexibility* in the conduct of investigations and in recommending remedies most calculated to achieve substantial justice as between the individual and the State.
3. Its *credibility* with the Executive Government and the public. (Emphasis in original)

To these might be added the stature of those who have held the position of Ombudsman and the respect accorded them.[8]

As originally conceived the role of the Ombudsmen might appear limited:

> to investigate any decision or recommendation, or any act done or omitted . . . relating to a matter of *administration* and affecting any person or body of persons in his or its personal capacity (s. 13(1) Ombudsmen Act 1975, emphasis added).

An assumption in 1962 was that 'administration' could be separated from 'policy', and thus the position of ministers placed beyond the reach of the Ombudsman. Despite some early tensions (Joseph, 1993, p. 126; G. Laking, 1987, p. 310), this crucial question of jurisdiction, which might otherwise have been presented to the courts for resolution, was set to one side in favour of practical understandings (G. Laking, 1987, p. 310). Powles, with the benign support of the then Prime Minister (Sir Keith Holyoake), took the view that if a decision related to an organisation within the ambit of the Act, the Ombudsman was legitimately concerned with the grounds on which it was made (Joseph, 1993, p. 126). The Ombudsmen may investigate departmental recommendations to ministers (s. 13(2) of the 1975 Act) but not the decision itself.

One of the elements in the 'flexibility' of the Ombudsmen's procedures is the ease with which a citizen may invoke them. A letter or even a telephone call is sufficient (compare the expense of litigation if judicial review is sought). An Ombudsman's investigation is informal (although backed by the power to require information or documents and to examine on oath) and, except in very exceptional circumstances, will meet with the full cooperation of the organisation under investigation. The Ombudsmen have only the power to report and make recommendations; there is no power of decision. They may recommend that the organisation consider a matter further, rectify an omission, or cancel or vary a decision. They may recommend that an administrative practice or rules be amended or that a law on which a decision was based should be reconsidered

---

7. The Ombudsmen are appointed by the Governor-General on the recommendation of the House of Representatives and hold office for a term of five years. They may be reappointed. (In 1992 the failure to reappoint Mrs Tollemache to a second term occasioned comment.) Ombudsmen may be removed from office only upon an address from the House of Representatives.

8. Sir Guy Powles (1962–75; Chief Ombudsman 1975–77); Sir George Laking (1975–77; Chief Ombudsman 1977–84); Mr Eaton Hurley (1976–84); Mr Lester Castle (1977–86; Chief Ombudsman 1984–86); Sir John Robertson (1984–86; Chief Ombudsman 1986–94); Mrs Nadja Tollemache (1987–92); Sir Brian Elwood (1992–94; Chief Ombudsman 1994–); Judge Anand Satyanand (1995–).

Table 17.1 Action on complaints to the Ombudsman for the year ended 30 June 1995

Declined, no jurisdiction	135
Declined or discontinued (s.17)	928
Resolved in course of investigation	207
Resolved informally	115
Sustained, recommendation made	12
Sustained, no recommendation made	20
Not sustained	264
Formal investigation not undertaken, explanation, advice or assistance given	773
Complaints transferred to Privacy Commissioner	3
Still under investigation 30 June	453
Total	2910

Source: Office of the Ombudsman

(Joseph, 1993, p. 129). Any of these recommendations may be made if it appears that (s. 22(1)):

> the decision, recommendation, act or omission which was the subject-matter of the investigation—
>
> (a) Appears to have been contrary to law; or
> (b) Was unreasonable, unjust, oppressive, or improperly discriminatory, or was in accordance with a rule of law or a provision of any Act, regulation, or by-law or a practice that is or may be unreasonable, unjust, oppressive, or improperly discriminatory; or
> (c) Was based wholly or partly on a mistake of law or fact; or
> (d) Was wrong.

In addition, under s. 22(2) the Ombudsmen may recommend in cases where it appears that:

> in the making of the decision or recommendation, or in the doing or omission of the act, a discretionary power has been exercised for an improper purpose or on irrelevant grounds or on the taking into account of irrelevant considerations, or that in the case of a decision made in the exercise of any discretionary power, reasons should have been given for the decision.

An indication of the complaints under the Ombudsmen Act 1975 and action taken for the year ended 30 June 1995 is given in Table 17.1. These figures do not include complaints under the Official Information Act 1982 or the Local Government Official Information and Meetings Act 1987 (of which there were some 1,250).:

On leaving office in 1994 Sir John Robertson concluded that the

> role of the office of Ombudsman will continue to be seen by the people as a sensitive and inexpensive method by which their grievances can be addressed and the extremes of maladministration corrected. It should also be seen by those who govern as a unique and special investment of democracy which can do much to improve the people's faith in public administration at all levels (Robertson, 1994, p. 4).

Some measure of the respect for the office can be seen in the way successive governments have turned to it to investigate such matters as scientology, the Security Intelligence

Service, conditions at Paremoremo prison, and the Springbok rugby tour of 1981. Sir John Robertson also presided over panels to educate the public before the electoral referendums of 1992 and 1993.

THE OFFICIAL INFORMATION ACT 1982[9]

Although chronologically later than the introduction into New Zealand of the office of Ombudsman, the Official Information Act 1982 is, in practice, often invoked as a precursor to a complaint to the Ombudsmen. Its passage into legislation was more of an event than the arrival of the Ombudsman twenty years before. Both were radical innovations; but the 1982 legislation reversed a fundamental element in the conduct of New Zealand government business (enshrined in the Official Secrets Act 1951, and one that remains in the United Kingdom): namely, that official information was the property of the government and should *not* be released unless expressly authorised. In retrospect, its emergence during the National administration of Sir Robert Muldoon (who is reported to have regarded it as a 'nine day wonder') remains surprising. In part, at least, it reflected public disillusion with the authoritarian and secretive decision-making processes of the time, particularly in respect of 'Think Big' energy projects (Gregory, 1984; Joseph, 1993, p. 142).

On the experience since the Act's passage it is possible to assert that the guiding presumption—that 'the [official] information shall be made available unless there is good reason for withholding it' (s. 5)—has had a profound impact on the style of New Zealand government. How those principally concerned with its passage, the Danks Committee and the then Attorney-General, J. K. McLay, would now judge the experience is problematic.[10] In some respects, the rationale advanced by the Danks Committee— for example, the extent of regulation of economic activity—now appears dated. But the two main objectives remain highly relevant to the conduct of political affairs:

(a) To increase progressively the availability of official information to the people of New Zealand in order—
   (i) To enable their more effective *participation* in the making and administration of laws and policies; and
   (ii) To promote the *accountability* of Ministers of the Crown and officials. ... (s. 4, Official Information Act 1982, emphasis added)

Rather than define classes of information by source (for example, by excluding Cabinet papers), the Act applies to all information held by organisations listed in the schedules to

---

9. Valuable sources for more detailed examination of the Official Information Act are the *Practice Guidelines* issued from time to time (most recently, 1995) by the Office of the Ombudsman; *Release of Official Information: Guidelines for Coordination* issued by the SSC (1992); and Eagles, Taggart, and Liddell (1992).

10. A committee chaired by Sir Alan Danks (economist and chair of the University Grants Committee) and comprising principally government officials presented two reports: *Towards Open Government* (1980) and a supplementary report containing a draft bill (1981).

the Act, however it was obtained. The Act covers government departments, state-owned enterprises, and Crown entities; local government is covered by the Local Government Official Information and Meetings Act 1987. Requests for information may be made to ministers, departments, or any organisation covered by the Act, and in general a decision on the request should be made within twenty working days (Official Information Amendment Act 1987). Documentary information may be made available in full or in part, or the request may be declined. Where information is withheld in whole or in part the applicant may request the grounds for such a decision, and the organisation concerned must inform the applicant of the right of complaint to the Ombudsmen (Joseph, 1993, p. 149).

The grounds for refusing to release information are in several categories: conclusive (s. 6), other (s. 9), and administrative (s. 18). Conclusive reasons include the likelihood that disclosure might *inter alia* prejudice security, defence, international relations, or maintenance of the law; seriously damage the economy; or endanger the safety of any person. For the purposes of this chapter the 'other' reasons in s. 9 of the Act are more interesting. These enable non-disclosure on certain grounds unless they are judged to be outweighed by considerations rendering disclosure desirable in the public interest. Non-disclosure must be considered 'necessary' in order to:

a. protect individual privacy;
b. protect trade secrets and commercial interests;
c. protect information which is subject to an obligation of confidence and where disclosure would prejudice the supply of further information;
d. avoid prejudice to measures protecting the public health or safety;
e. avoid prejudice to the substantial economic interests of New Zealand;
f. avoid prejudice to measures that prevent or mitigate loss to members of the public;
g. maintain the constitutional conventions which protect—
   • the confidentiality of communications by or with the Sovereign or her representative
   • collective and individual ministerial responsibility
   • the political neutrality of officials
   • the confidentiality of advice tendered by ministers and officials;
h. maintain the effective conduct of public affairs through
   • the free and frank expression of opinions between ministers and/or officers and employees of government departments or organisations
   • the protection of such persons from improper pressure or harassment;
i. maintain legal professional privilege;
j. avoid prejudice or disadvantage to the commercial activities of the Crown or any government department or organisation;
k. enable the Crown or any government department or organisation to carry on negotiations (including commercial or industrial negotiations); or
l. prevent the disclosure or use of official information for improper gain or advantage.

The New Zealand approach to the withholding of information has the major advantage of flexibility; and, indeed, practice has evolved principally through decisions of the

Ombudsmen on appeal (see below). On the other hand, practitioners might see virtue in a greater degree of certainty, for example, applying to classes of documents such as cabinet papers, draft legislation, or advice from officials to ministers—although there does not seem to be any widespread pressure to reduce the availability of information despite the embarrassment sometimes caused to ministers and officials and despite the apparent obstructiveness of some organisations from time to time. There is, however, a view among those who regularly seek information from public organisations that the major changes in structure and staffing of recent years (and, in some cases, the recruitment of staff from the private sector) have adversely affected institutional memory in respect of the OIA, as in other areas. It might, therefore, be timely for the government to repeat the intensive training that took place in 1982–83 (led by the SSC and the now-defunct Information Authority), and which undoubtedly assisted the smooth introduction of the Act.

One of the more controversial aspects of the Danks Report and the legislation enacted in 1982 concerned the complaints mechanism to resolve disputes when information was withheld. This function was entrusted primarily to the Ombudsmen rather than the courts (except in restricted circumstances; see Joseph, 1993, pp. 151, 152) or ministers. Ministers were, however, entitled to veto recommendations from the Ombudsmen. This power was invoked on fourteen occasions between 1983 and 1987; but, after Labour assumed office, the Act was amended in 1987 to replace the ministerial veto by an Executive Council veto (s. 32A). A minister now concerned about the release of information recommended by the Ombudsmen must, in effect, take the matter to cabinet and persuade colleagues that the criticism which would follow a veto would be outweighed by the benefit of preventing the release of particular information. The provision has not been used.

Until 1993 the Official Information Act was also the primary authority concerned with requests for personal information held by public organisations. That function has now passed to the Privacy Commissioner under the Privacy Act 1993.

At the time of writing (July 1995) the Law Commission was conducting a review of the OIA. In the words of the Minister of Justice, who requested the review, this is 'in the nature of a fine tuning exercise' rather than of principles.

JUDICIAL REVIEW[11]

Lord Wilberforce, writing about the state of administrative law in the Commonwealth, states (Wilberforce, 1986, p. ix):

> It seems to have been a common experience that, after the executive-minded approach of the 1940s, the pendulum has swung, with accelerating élan, in favour of judicial control of the executive and a widening range of decision-makers, to a point, possibly reached now and certainly coming to be visible in the UK, where a swing in the direction of restraint is due.

---

11. For more detailed treatment of judicial review in New Zealand, see Cripps et al. (1994, Chapter 9), Joseph (1993, Chapters 20–25), Taggart (1986), and Taylor (1991).

There will be different views in New Zealand about the degree to which this pendulum has swung in the direction of 'judicial control' and the extent to which it is desirable that the executive should be subject to 'the judge over your shoulder' (Crown Law Office, 1990). Certainly, it has been suggested that the New Zealand Court of Appeal, led by Sir Robin Cooke, has extended the range of the courts' powers to review executive (and perhaps, legislative) action to the point where one commentator observes that 'it is Sir Robin who is advocating revolution by mounting an open challenge to the doctrine of absolute Parliamentary sovereignty and attempting to create a new constitutional system of checks and balances which gives the Courts wider powers to review the legality of government decision-making' (Smillie, 1986, p. xii).

For at least two hundred years British courts have affirmed that it was their role and duty to uphold the rule of law over executive government.[12] Just as the scope of government has increased dramatically over that period, so too has the scope of judicial review. The implications for officials of this important aspect of administrative law are not always clear-cut but they can be far-reaching. In a judicial review case the courts may set aside a decision because of error by the public authority; but the original decision-maker may on reconsideration reach the same decision as before (Cripps et al., 1994, p. 170).

The first ground on which an administrative act or omission may be challenged in the courts is that it was *unlawful*—that the decision-maker did not have the statutory authority to make the decision. The question is whether the decision was lawful. A decision-maker acting outside legal authority is acting *ultra vires*. There are a number of circumstances that might lead a court to hold that actions or decisions have been made unlawfully:

a. the decision is made for an improper purpose (one not contemplated by legislation);
b. the decision fails to take into account certain relevant matters;
c. the decision takes into account matters which are irrelevant;
d. the decision is influenced by some factual error;
e. the decision-maker rigidly applies a pre-determined policy without regard to the particular merits of the case;
f. the decision-maker acts under dictation from someone else;
g. the decision-maker has invalidly delegated to another person a power that he or she ought to exercise or is acting pursuant to an invalid delegation (Crown Law Office, 1990).

A second ground for challenge to administrative decisions is that the decision-maker has acted *unreasonably*. (An important recent case is *Ankers* v. *Attorney-General* [1995] NZFLR 193 in which the processing and determination of benefit applications by the Director-General of Social Welfare was held to be 'unreasonable' to such an extent that it invalidated their determination.) In short, an unreasonable decision would be one that 'no sensible decision-maker, acting with due appreciation of his/her responsibilities, would have arrived at' (Crown Law Office, 1990).

---

12. *Entick* v. *Carrington* 1765 (Joseph, 1993, p. 649).

A third, and increasingly important, ground on which administrative actions may be challenged in the courts is *unfairness*. The focus is on the procedures followed by the decision-maker. Important considerations are:

a. whether the person affected has been given a fair opportunity to make representations so that all relevant considerations are before the decision-maker. This may extend to legal representation (*Badger* v. *Whangarei Refinery Expansion Commission of Inquiry* [1985] 2 NZLR 688);

b. giving prior notice of, and disclosing the reasons for, a decision (*Daganayasi* v. *Minister of Immigration* [1980] 2 NZLR 130);

c. avoidance of bias; for example, financial interest, a relationship to an interested party, or a personal prejudice towards a party;

d. consistency, including regard to 'reasonable expectations' and a duty to consult.[13]

All these considerations might loosely be described as acting in accord with principles of natural justice. More colloquially, they might be regarded as applied common sense. In exercising powers entrusted to them, officials must at all times proceed with a clear knowledge of their authority and act reasonably and fairly. In lay terms officials might need to ask themselves three questions:

a. Has the right person made the decision?
b. Have they followed the right procedures?
c. Have they made a decision they are lawfully entitled to make?

Such questions are at the heart of administrative law. The obligation of officials to consider the possibility that their actions (or failure to act) might be the subject of judicial review extends not only to the substantive dimension of officials' work but also to more mundane matters such as the recording of steps in the decision-making process and in conveying decisions. These practices have always been important elements in the administrative process; they assume even greater significance when there are incentives for officials to behave in a more entrepreneurial, risk-taking manner.

NEW ZEALAND BILL OF RIGHTS ACT 1990

The 1990 Bill of Rights Act was not the Bill initially envisaged by Sir Geoffrey Palmer and included in the White Paper published in 1985 (*A Bill of Rights for New Zealand*, 1985). Arseneau in 1990 considered that the Act, as passed, was 'an inadequate

---

13. Consultation has been defined by the Court of Appeal in these terms: 'It clearly required more than mere prior notification. If a party having the power to make a decision after consultation held meetings with the parties it was required to consult, provided those parties with relevant information and with such further information as they requested, entered the meetings with an open mind, took due notice of what they said and waited until they had had their say before making a decision: then the decision was properly described as having been made after consultation' (1 NZLR [1993] p. 672).

response' to challenges posed by Palmer himself—'matters which we must put beyond Parliament' (Arseneau, 1990, p. 37). Five years on, Palmer's own judgment (1992, p. 58) seems nearer the mark:

> The New Zealand Bill of Rights Act 1990 is a great deal more important than the legal profession and political commentators have understood. It is a very important addition to our constitutional laws. The manner in which the courts have gone about interpreting it indicates that it will be very important in future.

Critics of the New Zealand legislation point to the fact that it is not entrenched—it is 'ordinary' legislation—and that it merely affirms existing rights and freedoms (Arseneau, 1990). McLean et al. (1992, p. 90), on the other hand, argue that 'the Bill of Rights superimposes a higher constitutional dimension on top of the traditional administrative law grounds of review of discretionary authority'. And Palmer (1992, p. 58) forcefully underlines its practical implications: 'People outside government misunderstand how necessary it is to have certain obstacles in place in order to prevent enthusiastic but misguided people doing things which should not be done.'

The Act (ss. 2–3) applies to the actions of the legislative, executive, and judicial branches of government and to public authorities, and affirms the rights and freedoms contained in Part II of the Act, 'Civil and Political Rights', viz.:

- *Life and Security of the Person:* Right not to be deprived of life; Right not to be subjected to torture or cruel treatment; Right not to be subjected to medical or scientific experimentation; Right to refuse to undergo medical treatment.
- *Democratic and Civil Rights:* Electoral rights; Freedom of thought, conscience, and religion; Freedom of expression; Manifestation of religion and belief; Freedom of peaceful assembly; Freedom of association; Freedom of movement.
- *Non-Discrimination and Minority Rights:* Freedom from discrimination; Rights of minorities.
- *Search, Arrest, and Detention:* Unreasonable search and seizure; Liberty of the person; Rights of persons arrested or detained; Rights of persons charged; Minimum standards of criminal procedure; Retroactive penalties and double jeopardy; Right to justice.

For officials the implications of the Bill of Rights Act are twofold. In considering the drafting of legislation they must have regard to the provisions of the Act. In exercising powers vested in them or delegated to them, they must be careful that they do not infringe the rights and freedoms now specified in statute. In both cases they should be aware of s. 6 of the Act, which provides that 'wherever an enactment can be given a meaning that is consistent with the rights and freedoms contained in this Bill of Rights, that meaning shall be preferred to any other meaning'.

Section 7 of the Act requires the Attorney-General, when any bill is introduced to the House, to 'bring to the attention of the House of Representatives any provision in the Bill that appears to be inconsistent with any of the rights and freedoms contained in this Bill of Rights'. The Ministry of Justice vets all bills (except those of their own minister, which are considered by the Crown Law Office) for compliance with the Act.

The purpose as Palmer expressed it was 'first to ensure that the internal mechanisms of government addressed the issues seriously and with full legal analysis and second, that the political consequences of breaching the standards were brought to the fore' (Palmer, 1992, p. 60). It is known that a number of putative bills have been amended before introduction or have not proceeded because of non-compliance with the New Zealand Bill of Rights Act (ibid., p. 59). Other bills have been introduced with advice from the Attorney-General that provisions in them were inconsistent with the rights and freedoms in the Act. During the forty-third Parliament five bills (including three government bills) were treated in this manner. Ultimately, it is for the House to determine whether the legislation should be enacted (McGee, 1994, pp. 295–7).

Officials may exercise powers in a much wider range of situations than is sometimes realised. Many of the cases that have come before the courts have involved police powers, but powers that might impinge on the rights of individuals are also vested in Customs officers, immigration officials, agricultural and fisheries inspectors, persons in local or central government exercising powers under the Health Act 1956 or the Resource Management Act 1991, to name but a few. Although there is much case law defining the extent of the authority of these officials and how it may be exercised, the New Zealand Bill of Rights Act has already added new dimensions, particularly with respect to the control of discretionary power (McLean et al., 1992).

CONCLUSION

The preoccupation of the state sector reforms with efficiency and 'getting things done' could have posed threats to the protection of rights and freedoms considered valuable by New Zealanders. There has, indeed, been much criticism during the past decade of the policy-making process and, in particular, of the 'elective dictatorship' of the cabinet (Mulgan, 1992). The transition to MMP is undoubtedly, in part at least, a reaction to that trend. But it is justifiable to argue that New Zealand now has an array of political and constitutional mechanisms that provide appropriate restraints on the exercise of executive powers. As Sir Kenneth Keith (1987, p. 317) said during the early stages of the corporatisation process, 'it is safe to assume that whatever new framework of legislative and executive power is developed, it is the adequacy of any checks and balances on the exercise of that power which will decide its political acceptability'. Combined with professionalism in the public service (and other public authorities), there is good reason to believe that the structure so radically reformed since the mid 1980s is well embedded in the foundation of the law and responsible government.

conclusions

18 an assessment of the new zealand model

Public sector reform remains high on the agenda of many governments around the world (see OECD, 1994; Peters and Savoie, 1995). The continuing quest is for government that 'works better and costs less'—or, to put it colloquially, the aim is to get 'more bang for the buck'. Few countries have been more earnest, or perhaps more successful, in this endeavour than New Zealand. As outlined in previous chapters, New Zealand policy-makers since the mid 1980s have radically overhauled the organisation and management of the whole public sector. In so doing they have forged a new, distinctive model of public management and secured significant improvements in governmental efficiency, managerial accountability, and the quality of various public services.

This chapter offers some overall reflections on the nature, merits, and future of this model. More specifically, it underlines the key features of New Zealand's reforms, critically assesses their strengths and weaknesses, considers those areas where further reform might be required or where the new model has generated points of tension and difficulty, and identifies various issues requiring further research. It also discusses the lessons that the New Zealand model might have for other countries striving to build more effective, efficient, accountable, and responsive public bureaucracies. The chapter concludes with a brief analysis of the possible implications of proportional representation for the new model of public management.

SOME KEY FEATURES OF NEW ZEALAND'S PUBLIC SECTOR REFORMS

As has been argued in previous chapters, New Zealand's public management reforms are remarkable, not least for their comprehensive and integrated nature. Almost every facet of public management—institutional design, human resource management, financial management, strategic management, and so forth—has been reconfigured in some way, often radically. Moreover, most of the changes have been fashioned in accordance with a reasonably coherent analytical framework. Hence, although introduced over a period of some eight years, they have tended to be well coordinated and mutually reinforcing. Equally important, the key administrative principles underpinning the reforms have been applied with a high degree of consistency across the entire public sector, including heath care, education, trading activities, and local government. For such reasons, the recent reforms represent a paradigmatic shift or a fundamental recasting of the instruments of governance. They thus stand in sharp contrast to the incremental and more limited policy changes that had previously characterised New Zealand's approach to public management. Although other OECD countries, most notably Australia, Britain, Canada, and the USA, have embarked upon major public sector reforms since the early to mid 1980s, none have matched the scope, scale, and speed of introduction of those in New Zealand. Significantly, too, New Zealand's reforms were not undertaken in isolation but formed part of wider economic, social, and constitutional changes (e.g. the deregulation of the financial sector, the removal of subsidies and tariffs, major tax reforms, and labour market deregulation).

Although the New Zealand model embraces managerialist principles and practices that are similar to those implemented elsewhere (e.g. the decentralisation of management responsibilities, the shift from input controls to output or outcome measures, the commercialisation of many public services, the shift in emphasis from citizens to consumers, the decoupling of policy and operational responsibilities, the greater use of performance-related pay, etc.), it combines them in innovative and distinctive ways. The influence of certain bodies of economic theory, such as agency theory and transaction cost analysis, is relevant here. The impact of these theories is evident in various ways: the conception of government as a complex series of contractual relationships; the concern to ensure contestability of service provision and transparency of political interventions; the emphasis on performance specification, reporting, and monitoring; the widespread use of formal, written contracts of various kinds; and the stress on economic incentives and sanctions. Public choice theory has also been influential, notably in the way decisions on institutional design have been swayed by the concern to minimise bureaucratic and interest group capture.

Previous chapters have highlighted some of the more novel or unusual elements of the reforms in New Zealand. One of them is the use of annual performance agreements between ministers and departmental CEs. Another is the introduction of fixed-term appointments for many senior managers. Yet another is the development of a new strategic management system based on SRAs and KRAs. Distinctive, too, are many of the changes to financial management: the distinction between the ownership and purchase interests of the Crown; the distinction between outputs and outcomes and the introduction of an output-based appropriation system; the implementation of capital charges for many public organisations; the introduction of financial statements for the whole of government on a full accruals basis; and the initiatives introduced under the Fiscal Responsibility Act. Not only are these policies and practices relatively uncommon internationally but also their particular configuration in New Zealand is unprecedented. For how long New Zealand remains on the 'cutting edge' of public sector reform remains to be seen. Already, other countries are adopting aspects of the New Zealand model, and this process of emulation appears to be gathering momentum. Over time, therefore, various elements of the model might become standard practice internationally.

A particularly striking feature of the reforms in New Zealand is the fact that the changes in structure, managerial practices, and organisational culture were accomplished in a remarkably short space of time. A number of reasons for the speed of reform can be identified. Not to be overlooked is the ground prepared by earlier attempts to introduce new management practices, especially in the area of budgeting and financial management. For example, by the early 1980s accrual accounting and non-financial performance measurement were accepted as a necessary part of overall asset management, cost measurement, and external accountability. Ministers and managers were united in their dissatisfaction with input controls. When practitioner ideas were subsequently combined with prevailing economic theory, however, they assumed a new coherence and persuasive power, enabling the financial management reforms of the late 1980s to succeed where earlier attempts had failed. Similarly, there had been long-standing dissatisfaction with what were seen as cumbersome and restrictive personnel and industrial relations policies. The dissatisfaction was given a new sense of urgency because of perceived fiscal desperation. With politicians and senior officials committed to action, the public management changes were swept up in the momentum of overall economic and social reform.

Small size, a centralised, unitary system of government, a unicameral legislature, and relatively secure single-party majority governments all contributed to the relative ease and speed of New Zealand's reforms. On the one hand, they made it easier to reach consensus, at least at the elite level. On the other hand, they enabled governments to override or ignore opposition where no consensus could be secured, thereby facilitating rapid legislative enactments. Changes in organisational culture and the cross-fertilisation of ideas were facilitated by the freedom of recruitment practices created by the State Sector Act. This was particularly noticeable in the financial management area, where the flow of accountants between the public and private sectors was made easier by the existence in New Zealand of a single professional body with a single corpus of knowledge encompassing the corporate sector, the public sector, and chartered accounting firms. (In most other countries there are separate professional bodies for accountants in different sectors.) Also arising, at least in part, from small size is regular contact between accountants and economists to an extent not common internationally, enabling the two professions to cooperate in the preparation of budget-related documents. Not only has the cooperation encouraged the combination of theoretical and managerial ideas in general, but also their converging interests on particular issues—such as the need for accrual-based reports and forecasts for the whole of government—have been easier to identify and address.

The implementation of reform was further assisted in New Zealand by the particular sequencing of the change process and the mandating of key reforms via legislation. Much effort was made to ensure that the initial reforms produced visible benefits and that participants (at least at senior levels) felt comfortable with new systems before proceeding to the next stage (Ball, 1994). For example, increased efficiencies achieved during the corporatisation of state trading activities were held up as an example of what could be achieved in the core public service. The budgeting process for the government as a whole was dependent on first establishing new accounting practices in individual entities and the subsequent extension to reporting for the whole of government. Legislation articulated the new blend of managerial and theoretical ideas, required that key politicians understood the system and were publicly committed to it, and forced the momentum by setting target dates and specifying CEs' responsibilities. Finally, the overall reform process was greatly assisted by the Treasury's relative dominance within the bureaucracy and its vigorous advocacy of root and branch reform.

AN EVALUATION OF THE NEW ZEALAND MODEL

Attempts to evaluate the success of the New Zealand model to date have been hampered by a dearth of empirical data and evidence. In particular, it has been impossible to obtain consistent trend data—especially on public expenditure—amid radical restructuring and changes to the bases of measurement. In many cases there is no clear benchmark or counter-factual against which the policies can be assessed. Hence, while the large transitional costs associated with many of the reforms can be readily identified, if not calculated, it is virtually impossible to determine what the long-term costs of maintaining the previous policy regime would have been. Further, because the public management changes formed part of a much broader package of reforms, most of the new organisations have different responsibilities from those they replaced and operate in a radically altered regulatory framework. Such problems make it all the harder to isolate the particular effects, beneficial or otherwise, of changes in public management.

Even if there were a more complete and more robust database, there would still be serious methodological problems involved in assessing the costs and benefits of the changes. As pointed out elsewhere (see Boston, Martin, Pallot, and Walsh, 1991), many of the changes are not open to quantitative analysis and often even a qualitative assessment is difficult. For example, how does one assess the impact of the State Sector Act on the culture of the public service or on the process of policy-making? What effect have the numerous machinery of government changes had on staff morale? How have the introduction of performance-related pay and the move to short-term employment contracts affected productivity, innovation, and team work? And what long-term impact is the Fiscal Responsibility Act likely to have on government expenditure and revenue patterns? Clearly, even after a decade of reform in some areas, the implications of many changes are not fully apparent.

As it stands, there is surprisingly little information on the financial costs of implementing the new public management model (although most of the massive redundancy costs have been calculated). Further, assessing the effects of the changes on the quality and quantity of departmental outputs, such as policy advice, poses numerous methodological difficulties. The link between outputs and outcomes (or SRAs) is particularly hard to establish. The assessment problems have not been helped by a shortage of academic researchers in this field and the absence of a governmental monitoring unit with policy skills to undertake a systematic analysis of the reforms and to assess their outcomes.

Notwithstanding the above problems, there have been various attempts, most documented in this book, at evaluating some aspects of the New Zealand public management system. These evaluations have included reports of academics, consultants, central agencies, the Audit Office, government-appointed working parties, and over-seas commentators. On the whole, such reports have relied heavily on the opinions of senior managers and key players in the reform process. These evaluations have been mostly very favourable, citing senior managers supportive of the new managerial flex-ibility and ministers who believe that improvements in performance have resulted. Against this, the views of middle-level managers, workers at the coal face, and those displaced entirely from the workplace have not been canvassed to the same degree. Nor have the attitudes of citizens to the reforms been comprehensively assessed (although many service-oriented agencies now undertake regular client satisfaction surveys). It is thus impossible to draw detailed comparisons between elite and mass attitudes towards the reforms. However, there appears to be little support at any level within the public service, Crown entities, or local government for a return to earlier styles and systems of management.

This book has not attempted the impossible—namely, a complete, definitive, sys-tematic evaluation of the new model of public management against clearly identifiable and non-conflicting governmental objectives. Rather, it has sought to provide as full a description as possible within space limitations and to document opinions, including those of the authors, based on available evidence within New Zealand and relevant expe-rience from abroad. In doing so, it has attempted to show that however desirable the pursuit of rational approaches to public management might be, there is never a single, unambiguous solution to all the problems of governance. Up to a point, it might be possible to apply some private sector management values and practices in certain public organisations (e.g. by focusing primarily on a single main objective), and in this context the new flexibility and decision-making powers for managers have been welcomed by the more innovative managers. However, tensions between conflicting values—efficiency, due process, equity, democratic responsiveness, uniformity, diversity, cul-tural sensitivity, transparency, accountability, fiscal prudence, and so forth—are present under any model of public management. At the interface between management and pol-itics these tensions become more acute. Here, the very nature of public management involves the balancing and coordination of interdependent, but frequently conflicting, administrative values, fiscal constraints, and political imperatives.

The preceding chapters have identified the actual or potential costs and benefits associated with particular parts of the new public management approach and the questions and dilemmas that remain. Drawing on these accounts, the following summary observations and evaluations can be offered.

Institutional Design

Changes to the machinery of government, and the related dramatic downsizing of the core public sector, are perhaps the most visible expression of the administrative princi-ples underlying the new model of public management. Chief among these is the preference for single-purpose organisations with potentially conflicting functions being undertaken by separate agencies (whether public or private). Although available evidence on institutional reform in other countries has not been particularly encouraging, significant gains have been identified in New Zealand. The state trading sector has produced major improvements in productive efficiency and standards of service following the separation of commercial and non-commercial operations (see Duncan and Bollard, 1992; Spicer, Emanuel, and Powell, 1995), encouraging the government to pursue this approach in the rest of the public sector. The creation of policy ministries in areas where advice was previously patchy or non-existent (e.g. strategic advice on the environment, science, and women's issues) has improved the range of advice available to governments. Many departmental managers report that their agencies have a much sharper focus and a clearer organisational mission, and that there is less intra-organisational conflict over objectives. Senior managers in policy-oriented ministries are less distracted by the demands of operational activities. The structural changes have also contributed to the creation of a more enterprising public service culture, provided opportunities to remove poorly performing staff, and in some cases facilitated substantive policy reforms by overcoming previously entrenched departmental inertia or resistance.

Against this, the massive structural changes have imposed substantial costs. They include the direct costs of reorganisation (e.g. the costs of consultants, departmental submissions, and redundancy or redeployment), the loss of institutional memory, the costs of disruption to the ongoing business of government, and the costs to individuals and their organisations of extra work pressures, job insecurity, and loss of morale. While there has been no systematic evaluation of the cost-effectiveness of the restructuring, it is conceivable that in some instances the fiscal and social costs outweighed any subsequent longer-term gains in productive efficiency. Further, in areas where contestability is either artificial or non-existent or where efficient and effective service delivery depends on substantial inter-agency cooperation rather than competition, the merits of multiple purchasing and/or supply arrangements should not be overestimated.

The machinery of government changes also make plain that there is no one right model or ideal way of designing public bureaucracies. Likewise, they reinforce the long-held view that the quest for a unified or general theory of institutional choice is misconceived. Each structural arrangement has its own particular advantages and disadvantages, and in many cases the arguments are finely balanced. For example, against the advantages of single-purpose organisations must be weighed the disadvantages of duplication, higher transaction costs, greater problems of horizontal coordination, inter-agency conflict, a multiplicity of monitoring and review bodies, and potentially higher compliance and information costs for consumers or citizens.

While the separation of policy and operations appears to have worked satisfactorily in most cases, there is a continuing danger of advisers in policy ministries becoming detached from the communities or sectors about which they are supposed to have detailed knowledge and be in a position to offer expert advice. Furthermore, the more departmental services or outputs are contracted out to Crown entities or private providers, the greater will be the risks of a loss of core capacities (see Boston, 1995a; Kettl, 1993). Another danger is that political accountability will prove inadequate. In return for the relaxation of controls over inputs, departments are subject to considerable political scrutiny and control over performance. By contrast, the monitoring, governance, and accountability arrangements in Crown entities and the contracting sector are much less clear and in some instances remain unsatisfactory (Audit Office, 1994f). Given that the majority of government expenditure is for benefits and outputs supplied by parties other than departments, this issue is of concern. Although clarification of the accountability arrangements for Crown entities will be welcome, it is evident that Crown entities are not homogeneous and the idea that 'one size fits all' might be singularly inappropriate. In any case, institutional designers should never make the quest for organisational tidiness, uniformity, or absolute consistency an overriding priority. Each organisational form has its place in the scheme of things, depending, of course, on the functions being undertaken and the values sought. Further, whatever their particular form, it is imperative that public organisations maintain their adaptive capacity and remain responsive to changing political demands and requirements.

Devolution, Participation, and Local Government

Despite the magnitude of the public management reforms since the mid 1980s, New Zealand remains a highly centralised state. There has been relatively little genuine devolution of functions from central government to the sub-national level. There has, however, been a good deal of administrative decentralisation. At the same time, the gradual withdrawal of the state from certain areas of activity (e.g. housing and social services) has opened up opportunities for sub-national governments. Whether, and to what extent, these opportunities are taken will ultimately depend on the preferences of ratepayers in their respective jurisdictions. So far, there are few indications that territorial authorities in New Zealand are keen to expand their responsibilities, especially where significant costs might be entailed.

As in many other countries, New Zealand's reforms have placed considerable emphasis on improving responsiveness to *consumers* (see Pierre, 1995). By contrast, the reforms have demonstrated a more equivocal approach to the role and status of *citizens*. In some areas (e.g. local government, resource management, and the use of referenda), the opportunities for public participation in the governing process have been extended. However, in other areas (e.g. health care and public sector trading activities) the role of citizens has been circumscribed. The current scepticism in certain quarters over the merits of direct democratic control of public services is, of course, at the heart of the philosophy that has guided New Zealand's reforms. From the standpoint of the new public management and market liberalism, it is best to allow individuals to express their preferences for most goods and services via the market rather than via the political process (i.e. elections, petitions, lobbying, etc.). Put simply, prices, not politics, are the preferred signalling device. Competitive markets, it is argued, are efficient, albeit at times inequitable; politics, by contrast, is frequently inefficient, time-consuming, and messy. What is more, political processes often generate the wrong result—or at least the wrong result from the perspective of economic rationalists.

In New Zealand, the challenge to participatory democracy and community control has taken various forms: first, a questioning in some cases of the legitimacy of collective decision-making mechanisms and a related questioning of public solutions to societal problems; and second, a more specific effort to depoliticise various areas of public life via the marketisation of the state. How enduring the trend towards 'government by the market' (i.e. commercialisation, corporatisation, contracting out and privatisation) will be remains an open question. In many areas there can be little doubt that the public has largely accepted the new arrangements. In others, however, the desire for the continuance, or restoration, of political control remains very strong. The provision of health care is perhaps the best example.

One message that can be readily drawn from New Zealand's recent experience is that the boundaries of what is deemed to be a public or political matter remain controversial. In a democracy, the determination of such boundaries depends ultimately on the values of individuals in their capacity as citizens, not as consumers. Moreover, the values of ordinary citizens might not accord with those of the elites and might not be responsive to elite persuasion. Attempts to marketise the public sector in line with the tenets of market liberalism, therefore, will necessarily be constrained where public opinion remains hostile—all the more so under MMP. Interestingly, in this context, while the importance of local government as a direct provider of services has declined, there are indications that its role in articulating a 'vision' for communities and acting as a 'voice', often in opposition to central government, might increase.

Human Resource Management

There has as yet been no systematic evaluation of HRM policies in the public sector. The Logan report (1991) made some useful observations, but its analysis was by no means thoroughgoing. Despite this, there is no doubt that many important policy objectives have been achieved. They include the limitation of fiscal exposure in employment negotiations, downsizing, restructuring and the decentralisation of the employment relationship. A common observation from those who have lived through the reform era is that the public sector is now a completely different environment in which to work. Employees have a new kind of relationship with their superiors at all levels of the organisation. Managers exercise power more directly and obviously. If they do this fairly and objectively, they encourage loyalty and commitment to the organisation. The reverse is also true.

Decentralisation of employer authority from the SSC to CEs has been successful in forcing CEs and senior managers to assume responsibility for employment relations within their own organisation. It has led to individual departments taking initiatives to develop policies and practices that suit their particular circumstances. In addition, CEs now have the ability to involve their own employees in this process and capitalise on their expertise, which was difficult under the centrally imposed policies of the past. There have been many innovations in HRM policies, including the shift to individual and fixed-term contracts, the development of managerial competencies, more rigorous delineation of job descriptions and person specifications, the introduction of various forms of performance-based reward systems, and efforts to provide greater opportunities for effective employee influence over workplace decision-making.

The CE's role as employer has of course been qualified by the SSC's continued status as employer party for the purpose of negotiating employment conditions. This was successful as a policy instrument to limit the government's fiscal exposure. Furthermore, the continued dominance of the SSC and the PSA as the bargaining parties was vital in allowing a coordinated approach to enterprise bargaining, and it greatly facilitated the shift from a highly centralised bargaining structure to a decentralised structure based on enterprise agreements. Thus an enormous structural change was accomplished relatively easily.

But the SSC's continued dominance was not without cost. It gave rise, understandably, to tensions in the relationship between CEs and the SSC. The former increasingly felt that their ability to develop a strategic approach to HRM was compromised by their lack of control over the negotiation of employment conditions for their staff. The delegation of negotiating authority to CEs within fixed negotiating parameters since 1992 alleviates this problem but does not remove it completely.

The negotiating parameters set by the government and enforced by the SSC have ensured that employment negotiations have been protracted and difficult. On the other hand, bargaining is no longer divorced from the workplace as it once was. Employees and managers are involved in the process, understand it, and take responsibility for it. Moreover, it is now a genuine process of negotiation, unlike the pre-1988 system, which was based on a mechanistic application of private sector averages. Needless to say, there is no longer a private sector impression of state pay leadership. It is true, however, that a decentralised system still generates fairly uniform bargaining outcomes. It is difficult to see how similar organisations operating in similar environments and labour markets and under similar pressures could do otherwise, especially in just seven years.

Throughout the public sector, the aim has been to achieve the strategic integration of HRM, including EEO, with corporate objectives. Success to date has been limited by continual restructuring, the limited resources allocated to HRM, and the negotiating parameters set by the government. As a result, although departments have declared their support for the developmental humanism of the soft model of HRM—which emphasises the vital importance of developing the skills, capabilities and knowledge of employees—their actual practice has often been closer to the utilitarian instrumentalism of the hard model of HRM. This has had unavoidable and unsurprising consequences for employee commitment and morale.

Nonetheless, there have been considerable changes in the management of human resources in the public sector. The most important is the recognition that HRM is a strategic issue, and that employees should be managed accordingly with a view to recruiting and retaining good people who will be a source of competitive advantage. That strategic integration has not yet been widely achieved matters a good deal less than recognition of its importance. The same applies to EEO, where the entrenching of a new philosophy of employee diversity as a source of competitive advantage and the acceptance of the need for new policies and practices have been of more long-term importance than a precise headcount of the changing demographic profile of the public sector workforce.

Financial Management

The financial management initiatives—in particular the relaxation of input controls, the clarification of Crown and departmental responsibilities, the new model of performance reporting and the move to accrual accounting—are generally viewed as among the most successful aspects of the new public management regime. The major objectives of the financial management reforms were to improve efficiency and accountability. With respect to efficiency, New Zealand's overall economic performance has improved significantly since the early 1990s, with growth rates in the 4–5 per cent range and falling unemployment. Partly as a result of this, the country is now running a healthy fiscal surplus—for the first time in over two decades—and public expenditure has fallen as a proportion of GDP from over 40 per cent in the early 1990s to around 35 per cent in 1995. Further, a significant reduction in administrative expenditure by government departments appears to have taken place since the late 1980s. Nevertheless, it is difficult to demonstrate, in the absence of consistent trend data, how much of this improvement is due to efficiency gains generated by the public management reforms. Anecdotal evidence, however, suggests that departments are providing better services with fewer resources and that departmental management of cash and fixed assets has improved as a result of the additional information provided by accrual accounting (Ball, 1992; Morris, 1995; Scott, 1995). At the ministerial level, there can be little doubt that the capacity to prioritise and control public spending has improved (Birch, 1995; McLeay, 1995; Nethercote, Galligan and Walsh, 1993).

Nevertheless, among citizens there are concerns—some no doubt justified—that the real level of public expenditure on certain outputs has been reduced to such an extent that not only their quantity but more importantly their quality has fallen, thereby compromising public safety and other values. This is not to suggest that the NPM, or at least the version applied in New Zealand, is necessarily a 'recipe for disaster' (see Hood and Jackson, 1992). But it does underscore the fact that high-quality public management cannot be purchased cheaply and that goal-displacing behaviour by public officials is a constant risk, regardless of how sophisticated the system of performance management might be.

One of the major gains of the financial management reforms has been the vast improvement in the quantity and quality of information available to ministers. Other things being equal, this should enable them to make more informed choices about outputs, particularly if policy analysis becomes available to them in making purchase decisions. Further work is under way to improve the specification and monitoring of performance with respect to the government's ownership interest. Managers and politicians on the whole share the view that objectives have been clarified, and accountability and transparency enhanced, through the improved specification of outputs. The Audit Office, at times facing external attacks on its position as well as making an internal re-examination of its role, has been an important voice in drawing attention to the needs of Parliament and in focusing attention on the need for public accountability. Initial concerns that the output orientation might place too much emphasis on managerial accountability at the expense of accountability to Parliament and the public at large are beginning to be addressed through developments in whole-of-government budgeting and reporting, strengthened select committee processes, and work on linking the government's vision to SRAs and KRAs. The assumption is that greater transparency will result in more informed public debate and reduce political risk. Achievement of the desired end, however, will depend on Parliament, select committees, and the public at large having the necessary skills, time, resources, and motivation to make use of the enhanced information now available.

Ethos and Ethics

Traditionally, questions about the ethical dimensions of public sector management did not figure prominently in New Zealand discussions (Martin, 1994b). The public sector in New Zealand, unlike that of some other countries, has been notably free from corruption or nepotism. The principal structures and relationships—those, for example, between ministers and officials—tended to be taken for granted. The advent of the fundamental changes of the 1980s, however, raised issues common in the political debate of other countries. For example, when the State Sector Act was passed, fears were expressed that new appointment procedures for CEs could politicise the public service, that large staff turnover might weaken the 'spirit of service' (State Services Act 1962, State Sector Act 1988), and that loosening central agency controls could increase the risk of improper behaviour by public servants. Such fears have not been borne out. Despite such incidents as the resignation of a Controller and Auditor-General because of his financial circumstances, it is difficult to sustain a claim that there has been a deterioration in general standards of official conduct as a result of the reforms. Nonetheless, the measures designed to change the culture of the public sector—away from risk-averse bureaucracy to more entrepreneurial behaviour—might yet have unintended consequences. Official recognition of this danger is to be found in the State Service Commissioner's project on 'Principles, Conventions and Practice' (see Chapter 16) and the emphasis on 'professionalism'.

The changes have presented in a new form a perennial issue in democratic governments—the accountability relationship between ministers and officials. What is the status now of the classical Westminster doctrine of vicarious ministerial responsibility? On the one hand, the statutory arrangements now in place have brought about transparency—and thus improved *managerial* accountability—in New Zealand government. On the other, the fragmentation of the public sector and the experience of the last few years suggest that the acceptance of *political* responsibility by ministers has been further attenuated. If this judgment is correct, the reduction in political responsibility would need to be set against the gains in effectiveness and efficiency. It remains to be seen whether initiatives such as the Fiscal Responsibility Act will adequately address these issues of political accountability.

An associated concern is the tension, not new, between the presumptive duty of public servants to their minister and their less well-defined obligation to the 'public interest'. While the will of elected ministers must ultimately prevail, there is a legitimate expectation among citizens that public servants are imbued with an ethos that places value upon matters beyond the immediate concern of the government of the day.

Prominent among the public's expectations about the behaviour of public servants is that they should behave, particularly in the exercise of discretion, in accordance with the law and the principles of natural justice. New Zealand has a well-established array of mechanisms for the review and redress of administrative action. They are of special significance at a time when there is, perhaps, less trust than there was in the past in the institutions of government, including the public service. MMP places new pressures on a system that has been subject to severe stress for more than a decade. The parliamentary and statutory avenues for review of official behaviour will remain important. But the principal responsibility for ensuring that there is respect for the public sector will rest with its leadership—ministers, the SSC, and CEs.

UNFINISHED BUSINESS AND CONTINUING DILEMMAS

Despite the welter of reform, both ministers and senior officials recognise that there are still many important issues requiring further analysis. Additionally, the reforms are continuing to generate various concerns, and some of them are likely to require governmental responses. Matters identified in official reports as needing further work include: government-wide strategy coordination; improvements in the specification and review of performance; senior management development; the adequacy of monitoring arrangements for non-departmental outputs; and the future governance of Crown entities. Many other issues requiring attention have also been raised in the preceding chapters: the ineffectiveness of the SES; the heavy burdens placed by the new performance management regime on the State Services Commissioner; the continuing quest by Māori for greater autonomy and iwi control over the delivery of various publicly funded services; the poor representation of Māori at senior levels within the public sector; the need for clearer governmental guidelines on the nature of those services that ought not to be contracted out; the desirability of avoiding unnecessary restrictions in the role of local government; and the need for public servants to have more intensive education and training in ethics in government as part of their professional development.

Turning to HRM, one of the central issues is whether public sector HRM can shift to a model that places more emphasis on the skills of employees and the contribution they can make. A related issue is whether or not CEs will be able to take a strategic approach to HRM. Both of these will depend on CEs being relieved of the immediate issues thrown up by restructuring and on some relaxing of the fiscal constraint. Until public sector organisations are able to make this shift, the likelihood of their employees becoming a source of competitive advantage will remain problematic.

Another key issue is the future role of the SSC in HRM. Since 1988, its main HRM responsibilities have been in employment negotiations and EEO. More recently, it has taken on a role in developing and recommending a strategic approach to HRM for the public sector. There is a potential tension in the continued importance of a central agency in a decentralised HRM environment. But the government's continuing concern over its fiscal exposure means that the SSC is likely to retain a role in employment negotiations, at least in the medium term. The continuing policy commitment to EEO should ensure that the SSC retains its monitoring and developmental role for EEO. Similarly, the SSC has an important role in providing ethical leadership.

With respect to financial management, there are also various issues outstanding. First, as mentioned earlier, there is concern about the adequacy of contracting, monitoring, and accountability arrangements for benefits and outputs supplied by parties other than departments, given that they represent a large and increasing proportion of Parliament's appropriations. In particular, more thought needs to be given to the nature and materiality of risks borne by the Crown through its ownership of SOEs and Crown entities.

Second, aspects of the incentives and resource management regime, such as the degree to which decision-making powers and incentives have filtered down through departments, require further refinement. For example, the capital charge in many cases does not appear to have been imposed as a cost element in the budgets of lower-level managers.

Third, more thought needs to be given to the appropriateness of performance measures relative to their quantifiability and reliability. A complete system of public management requires clear links between outputs, outcomes, and SRAs to be established. While this is an immense (even ultimately impossible) analytical task, some move in the direction of outcome reporting is needed, not only to hold the government accountable to Parliament and the public at large, but also to impart meaning to what managers are doing. Although it is easier to hold managers accountable for *outputs*—and their discrete and quantifiable nature makes them amenable to expenditure cutting and to contracting out—the distinction between outputs and outcomes implies a separation of the political and managerial realms that is extremely difficult in practice. Present efforts to emphasise and measure more meaningfully the quality of outputs might help to link processes, outputs, and outcomes.

Whatever its role in fiscal policy or its implications for day-to-day management by government agencies, the question of public finance is one of fundamental constitutional significance. Issues such as the number and structure of appropriations, the retention of surpluses, and even the use of depreciation highlight the ongoing tension between managerial freedom and parliamentary control. Even such an apparently technical issue as the degree of sophistication and accuracy in the application of cost allocation systems, and hence in assessing whether the costs of outputs are within appropriation, is of political significance. While both public and private sector managers strive to marshal resources to meet objectives, financial managers in the public sector are constantly required to balance the interests of their organisations with the collective interests mediated through parliamentary and interdepartmental processes.

AREAS REQUIRING FURTHER RESEARCH

Although there is a growing body of research on various aspects of New Zealand's reforms, numerous areas deserve more careful scrutiny and investigation. Among them are:

a. the merits of the new system of strategic management and priority setting via SRAs and KRAs, and the linkages between KRAs and CE performance agreements;

b. the impact of some of the more recent machinery of government changes (e.g. Justice, and Agriculture and Fisheries) on policy-making and coordination, policy networks, the role of interest groups, conflict resolution, and the delivery of services;

c. the extent of contracting out across the public sector, the impact of the growth in competitive tendering and external contracting on service delivery and performance, and the quality of contract management;

d. the consequences of mainstreaming, especially in relation to service accessibility, quality, and responsiveness to Māori;

e. the impact of incentives such as capital charging on asset management;

f. the extent to which parliamentarians are making good use of the better information now available on the performance of public sector organisations, and the consequences for the scrutiny of the executive of National's loss of its parliamentary majority (in mid 1995);

g. the scope and use of political patronage, including the nature and quality of governmental appointments to the boards of Crown entities;

h. the impact of the reforms on the quality of various public services, including their accessibility, reliability and timeliness, together with the degree of choice, courtesy of staff, opportunities for redress, and levels of consumer satisfaction;

i. the issue of whether the management of change arising from organisational restructuring is being any better handled in the mid 1990s than it was in the mid to late 1980s;

j. the degree to which departments have devolved both human resource and financial responsibilities to line managers and the consequences of this devolution;

k. the particular HRM policies and practices adopted by departments, especially in the area of performance management, performance pay, recruitment and selection, and employee development; and

l. the extent to which greater 'participation' and 'accountability' (the aims of the Official Information Act 1982) are manifested in the arrangements for LATEs and Crown entities (e.g. CHEs and CRIs).

More generally, to the extent that the New Zealand model represents a 'full-blooded' version of the NPM, it comes as close as we are likely to get to furnishing an 'administrative laboratory' for testing the various hypotheses that have been advanced in relation to the likely impacts, both good and ill, of the NPM. Hood's (1990a, 1990b, 1991, 1995) continuing analyses of the NPM, in particular, deserve careful scrutiny and offer many useful points of departure for further research.

LESSONS FOR OTHER COUNTRIES

There are well-recognised risks associated with the emulation of one country's practices by another. Differences in political culture, administrative ethos, technological advancement, legal traditions and constitutional conventions all make the transfer of ideas and policies between countries a complex and hazardous business. Plainly, therefore, it would be misguided to think that the New Zealand model could be transplanted lock, stock and barrel into another jurisdiction, all the more so in the case of a developing country with limited professional expertise, fragile information systems, and high levels of petty corruption. Having said this, the administrative principles that underpin the New Zealand model are, in theory at least, all transferable; indeed, many were imported rather than home-grown. Further, most of the policy instruments or 'technology' associated with the model are also transportable. Whether such transplants are desirable, however, is another matter.

Among the many lessons of the New Zealand reforms, the following deserve highlighting (see also Ball, 1994; Hunn, 1994c; Office of the Auditor General of Canada, 1995; Scott, 1995):

a. For successful implementation, major reforms require a high level of political support, ideally of a multi-party nature. Additionally, rapid implementation will be much easier where key officials accept the need for change and endorse the main reform initiatives.

b. It is desirable to start any major reform programme with a reasonably coherent framework of ideas and clear, achievable objectives.

c. Careful consideration must be given to the ordering of the reform process, including the political desirability of being able to demonstrate positive results early in the process.

d. Although organisational restructuring is often necessary and desirable, especially in the event of major changes to an agency's purpose or mission, such restructuring can have high fiscal and social costs. Major restructuring should not, therefore, be embarked upon lightly. Further, administrative reorganisation should always be accompanied by consideration of the implications for constitutional arrangements, particularly the location of political responsibility.

e. It is possible to decentralise public sector employment relationships relatively quickly. Similarly, the transition from a highly centralised bargaining system to one based largely on enterprise or departmental bargaining can be achieved without great difficulty.

f. In certain circumstances, it is possible to downsize the public sector very considerably and in a relatively short time-frame without major industrial disruption. But it depends on a willingness to pay the price in terms of redundancy entitlements, loss of institutional memory, widespread anxiety, disrupted careers, and employee suspicion of management.

g. Any decentralisation or transfer of managerial authority must go hand in hand with improved systems of accountability, including both *ex ante* contract specification and *ex post* reporting.

h. Improving the quality and flow of information available to decision-makers is a vital ingredient in the quest for improved performance, both by individuals and organisations.

i. Financial management reform will be much more successful when integrated with overall management reform, including employment practices such as the ability of senior managers to obtain the right mix of staff and legislation making CEs responsible for financial management.

j. Under a decentralised system of management there is a corresponding need for processes to align departmental management initiatives with the collective interests of
government.

LOOKING AHEAD

As New Zealand approaches the twenty-first century, public managers face no shortage
of challenges. On the positive side of the ledger, the country's much improved economic
performance offers the prospect of a continued easing of fiscal pressures and hence
opportunities for increases, rather than yet further reductions, in budgetary allocations
for certain priority outputs. Against this, of course, there are plenty of pressing social
problems to be addressed and no lack of suggestions on how the fiscal surplus should
be spent. Additionally, the ongoing process of technological innovation will continue
to impact in various ways on how public services are delivered, and will doubtless bring
further significant changes to the work environment and employment opportunities of
many public servants. Aside from this, the organisation and management of the public
sector will continue to be affected by the process of globalisation, demographic changes,
changing immigration patterns, and the desire for a more open, consultative policy-
making process. Equally important is the need to work through the implications of the
Treaty of Waitangi for public management and to give meaningful expression to the
quest for a bicultural public service.

At the political level, the main challenge confronting the public sector, at least in the
short term, is the introduction of MMP. Various changes to the nature and process of
governance have already occurred as a result of the move to proportional representation,
and further changes are pending. Of crucial importance in this respect is the fact that
single-party majority governments are likely to be much less common in the future.
Instead, New Zealand can expect either single-party minority governments or coalition
governments (whether majority or minority in nature). Also in prospect are more frequent changes in the composition of governments and longer transitional periods
between governments. Such changes will almost certainly result in a slower, more consultative process of decision-making; indeed, this has already been apparent since the
1993 general election. Some strengthening of Parliament's role relative to that of the
executive can also be expected, with select committees undertaking more detailed scrutiny of the performance of public sector organisations. Hopefully, the effect will be to
enhance the accountability of senior managers to Parliament and to facilitate greater
political control over the bureaucracy.

For the time being at least, the new model of public management appears secure.
On the one hand, the major political parties (especially Labour and National) remain
firmly committed to the model's key legislative enactments. On the other, such parties
as are opposed to elements of the reform programme (e.g. privatisation, the Reserve
Bank Act 1989, and the Fiscal Responsibility Act 1994) will have greater difficulty
under MMP securing parliamentary majorities in support of amending legislation. In
fact, the move to MMP is full of ironies: under proportional representation public sector

reforms of the scope and scale implemented since the mid-1980s would have been much more difficult to bring about; yet, as a result of MMP, the reforms could well prove more enduring. To the extent that the role of Parliament is strengthened under MMP, electoral reform might even enhance the new model's capacity to achieve its key objectives: a more effective, efficient, responsive, and accountable public sector. Admittedly, the jury is still out, but for the present we remain optimistic.

appendix 1: a summary of new zealand's public sector reforms 1984-95

1.   Commercialisation, Corporatisation and Privatisation

1.1	User-pays introduced for many state services	1985–
1.2	Removal of almost all state-regulated monopoly rights and restrictions on state-owned companies and corporations	1984–89
1.3	Establishment of new state enterprises under State-Owned Enterprises Act (1986):	1987–90

- SOEs given primarily commercial objectives
- significant managerial autonomy, arms-length relations with ministers
- removal of controls on inputs, finance, operational scope etc.
- transparent state subsidies for non-commercial functions
- substantial rationalisation of assets and staff reductions
- improved external monitoring and accountability requirements

1.4	Restructuring to isolate natural monopoly elements of SOEs	1989–
1.5	Emphasis on light-handed regulation	
1.6	Comprehensive privatisation programme	1987–

- range of sale techniques used including partial sale of shares, partial share flotations, shares distributed to customers, the sale of usage rights (e.g. forest cutting rights), the divestiture of some physical and financial assets, etc.
- heavy reliance on competitive tendering rather than fixed price share flotations

1.7	Application of commercial imperatives to some social service providers, including hospital and related services, public housing, etc.	1992–93

2.   Machinery of Government

2.1	Separation of commercial and non-commercial functions	1987–90

- most commercial assets placed in SOEs, a few remain as agencies within government departments
- in most cases service delivery has been transferred to separate organisations (e.g. defence, education, environmental administration, health, housing, scientific research, etc.)

2.2	Separation of policy advice from service delivery functions	1987–
	• in some cases departments have been reorganised internally to ensure greater functional separation of policy advisers and service providers (e.g. agriculture, labour, justice, social welfare, etc.)	
2.3	Separation of policy advice from regulatory, review, and monitoring (e.g. education and transport)	1987–
2.4	Separation of many service delivery functions into distinct business units	
2.5	Establishment of new population-based ministries (e.g. Women's Affairs, Youth Affairs, Pacific Island Affairs, etc.)	1985–
2.6	Abolition of many quasi-governmental organisations	1986–
2.7	Establishment of 10 Crown Research Institutes	1991
2.8	Establishment of 23 Crown Health Enterprises	1993

3. Human Resource Management

3.1	Major changes to senior management of the public sector via State Sector Act (1988), including:	1988
	• new procedures for appointing departmental chief executives (CEs)	
	• CEs placed on performance-based contracts for terms of up to 5 years	
	• annual performance agreements between CEs and ministers	
	• end of unified public service; CEs become employers and thus responsible for pay fixing and conditions of employment, and all personnel functions	
	• establishment of Senior Executive Service	
3.2	Major changes to industrial relations and wage-fixing arrangements via State Sector Act, including:	1988
	• abolition of annual general adjustments and other service-wide uniform employment determinations	
	• abolition of fair relativity with private sector	
	• abolition of compulsory arbitration; final offer arbitration made available on certain conditions	
	• State Services Commission continues as employer party for bargaining purposes	
	• increased emphasis on equal employment opportunities	
3.3	General trends in HRM:	1988–
	• decentralisation of bargaining units	
	• restructuring of remuneration systems and salary scales (including ranges of rates)	
	• greater use of performance-based pay and performance management systems	
	• increased reliance on fixed-term contracts	
	• devolution of human resource management to line managers	
	• increased union membership in public service	
	• delegation of bargaining authority by Commission, with some provisos, to individual departments, Crown entities, etc.	
3.4	Employment Contracts Act (1991):	1991
	• emphasis on individual contracts rather than collective arrangements	
	• union bargaining rights made contestable	

4. Financial Management

4.1 Sweeping changes to financial management via
Public Finance Act (1989) and amendments: 1989–94
- CEs made responsible for financial management
- distinction between Crown and depts cash flows, assets
and liabilities
- introduction of accrual accounting throughout public sector
- introduction of capital charges for most public sector agencies
- distinction between the Crown's ownership and purchaser interest
- shift from input controls to output assessment
- change from programme-based to output-based appropriation
system; ministers select outputs to achieve specified outcomes,
and specify conditions (such as quantity, quality, price, and
timing of delivery)
- comprehensive new reporting requirements, including statements
of service performance
- extension in range and quality of performance indicators
- introduction of monthly Crown financial statements on an
accrual basis (similar to those for departments), including a
consolidated balance sheet and an operating statement for the
whole of the state sector
- new Estimates format

4.2 Fiscal responsibility initiatives under Fiscal Responsibility
Act (1994):   1994
- provides for regular and explicit fiscal reporting, including
an annual Budget Policy Statement at least three months
before the deadline for the budget (31 July), a Fiscal Strategy
Statement Report at the time of the budget, and comprehensive
economic and fiscal updates before each general election, etc.
- provides for parliamentary review of fiscal reports
- specifies various principles of responsible fiscal management,
such as reducing total Crown debt to prudent levels and prudent
management of the fiscal risks facing the Crown

5. Expenditure Control

5.1	Assignment of privatisation proceeds to repay public debt	1987–
5.2	User-pays principle applied to many public services	1985–
5.3	Across-the-board cuts to most government departments	1988–
5.4	Cuts in welfare benefits	1991

6. Local Government Reforms

6.1 Reorganisation and amalgamation of local authorities: 1989
- abolition of most special purpose authorities; more than
700 local authorities were reduced to fewer than 100

6.2 Corporatisation of Local Authority Trading Enterprises
(LATEs)   1989–

6.3 Sale of shares in airports, port companies and local utilities   1991–

6.4 Separation of service delivery and regulatory functions   1989–

Sources: Boston (1995b); Duncan and Bollard (1992), pp.183–7; OECD (1990), pp.78–83.

appendix 2

The New Zealand Public Service
STRIVING FOR EXCELLENCE IN SERVING NEW ZEALAND

Vision

The New Zealand Public Service will help New Zealand governments to achieve a higher quality of life, higher living standards, high employment, social equity and justice, a high quality natural environment and international respect as a member of the community of nations.

Purpose

The New Zealand Public Service, imbued with the spirit of service to the community, exists to advise the Government and implement the Government's policies and decisions to the highest possible standards of quality and with the utmost integrity in accordance with the principles of law and democracy thereby enhancing the well-being and prosperity of all New Zealanders.

Principles and Values

In an increasingly dynamic, diverse and technological world, the New Zealand Public Service should make a vital contribution to efficient and effective government. The New Zealand Public Service will:

Give free and frank advice to the government of the day, and inform and implement its decisions with intelligence, enthusiasm, energy, innovation and common sense

Demonstrate the qualities of leadership, sound judgement, fiscal responsibility and high ethical standards that attract the confidence and respect of the Government and the people of New Zealand

Establish and maintain an equitable and challenging working environment, both now and for the future, that is consistently able to respond to constant change, and trains, develops and motivates every public servant to perform to the highest levels of their ability

Ensure that people with professional management skills and the attributes of leaders are recruited and developed across the Public Service. This is to meet current and future Public Service-wide needs for high quality management and contribute to enhancing New Zealand's management resources overall

Ensure that every public servant demonstrates understanding of the collective interest of government and the special nature of the relationship between Parliament, the Crown and the Public Service in the need for apolitical, objective and professional policy advice and the custodianship of the nation's resources for future generations of New Zealanders

Act at all times within the true spirit of the law and work to maintain the stability and continuity required in a system with democratically elected government.

KO TE TOI O TE RANGI
TE TAUMATA WAIORANGA MŌ AOTEAROA

Source: State Services Commission (1994c)

References

Aaron, H. (1994) Public Policy, Values and Consciousness *Journal of Economic Perspectives* 8(2): 3–21.

Aiken, M. (1994) Parliamentary Sovereignty and Valuation Accruals: Uncongenial Conventions *Financial Accountability and Management* 10: 17–32.

Alam, M. and Lawrence, S. (1994) Evidence from the Field: Hamilton City Council *Public Sector* 17(2): 7–10.

Alford, J. (1993) Towards a New Public Management Model: Beyond Managerialism and Its Critics *Australian Journal of Public Administration* 52(2): 135–48.

Alley, R. (1992) The Powers of the Prime Minister. In Gold, 1992.

Allison, G. (1982) Public and Private Management: Are They Fundamentally Alike in All Unimportant Respects? In Lane, F. (ed) *Current Issues in Public Administration* New York, St Martin's Press.

Althaus, C. (1994) The Application of Agency Theory to Public Sector Management: A Case Study Analysis of the Separation of Policy from Delivery in New Zealand and the United Kingdom. BA (Hons) thesis, Griffith University.

Anderson, C. (1979) The Place of Principles in Policy Analysis *American Political Science Review* 73: 711–23.

Anderson, G. (1988) The Origins and Development of the Personal Grievance Jurisdiction in New Zealand *New Zealand Journal of Industrial Relations* 13(3): 257–76.

Anderson, G. (1991) The Employment Contracts Act 1991: An Employers' Charter? *New Zealand Journal of Industrial Relations* 16(2): 127–42.

Anderson, G., Brosnan, P. and Walsh, P. (1996) The New Public Management and Human Resource Management Policies: Numerical Flexibility in the New Zealand Public Sector *International Journal of Employment Studies* (forthcoming).

Arseneau, T. (1990) A Bill of Rights. In Holland and Boston, 1990.

Ashton, T. (1992) Reform of the Health Services: Weighing up the Costs and Benefits. In Boston and Dalziel, 1992.

Aucoin, P. (1990) Administrative Reform in Public Management: Paradigms, Principles, Paradoxes and Pendulums *Governance* 3: 115–37.

Audit Office (1978) *Report of the Controller and Auditor General on Financial Management in Administrative Government Departments* (Shailes Report) Wellington.

Audit Office (1988) *Report of the Controller and Auditor General: First Report for 1988 Covering— Companies, Corporations and Statutory Boards and Other Matters* Wellington.

Audit Office (1989a) *Report of the Controller and Auditor General on an Investigation into Allegations of Mismanagement against the Waitemata City Council* Wellington.

Audit Office (1989b) *Report on the Public Accounts for the Year Ended 31 March 1989* Wellington.

Audit Office (1990a) *Internal Management Plan for the Financial Year Commencing 1 July 1990* Wellington.

Audit Office (1990b) *Report of the Controller and Auditor General on Statements of Corporate Intent* Wellington.

Audit Office (1993a) Management of Physical Assets. In *Report of the Controller and Auditor General: Second Report for 1993* Wellington.

Audit Office (1993b) *The Financial Condition of Regional and Territorial Local Authorities* Wellington.

Audit Office (1994a) Accountability Arrangements for the Ministry of Transport and Related Crown Entities *Report of the Controller General: Fifth Report for 1994* Wellington.

Audit Office (1994b) Employment of Consultants by Government Departments. In Audit Office, 1994d.

Audit Office (1994c) Management of the Crown's Debt. In Audit Office, 1994d.

Audit Office (1994d) *Report of the Controller and Auditor General: Third Report for 1994* Wellington.

Audit Office (1994e) Financial Management Reforms. In *Report of the Controller and Auditor General: Fourth Report for 1994* Wellington.

Audit Office (1994f) Management of Payments on Behalf of the Crown. In *Report of the Controller and Auditor General: Fifth Report for 1994* Wellington.

Audit Office (1994g) *The Role of the Auditor General in New Zealand: A Discussion Paper* Wellington.

Audit Office (1994h) *The Employment of Local Authority Chief Executives* Wellington.

Audit Office (1994i) *Report of the Audit Office for the Year Ended 30 June 1994* Wellington.

Audit Office (1995a) *Report of the Controller and Auditor General: First Report for 1995* Wellington.

Audit Office (1995b) *Forecast Report for the Year Ending 30 June 1996* Wellington.

Audit Office (1995c) Purchasing Practices of Government Departments. In Audit Office, 1995a.

Audit Office (1995d) *Report of the Audit Office for the Year Ended 30 June 1995* Wellington.

Ball, I. (1981) *Measuring the Cost of Government Services* Wellington, New Zealand Planning Council.

Ball, I. (1992) The New Approach: Financial Management Reform *The Accountants' Journal* 71(5): 17–21.

Ball, I. (1994) Reinventing Government: Lessons Learned from the New Zealand Treasury *The Government Accountants Journal* Fall: 19–28.

Banks, J. and Weingast, B. (1992) The Political Control of Bureaucracies under Asymmetric Information *American Journal of Political Science* 36: 509–24.

Barber, B. (1984) *Strong Democracy: Participatory Politics for a New Age* Berkeley, University of California Press.

Barney, J. (1991) Firm Resources and Sustained Competitive Advantage *Journal of Management* 17(1): 99–120.

Barrington, J. (1990) Historical Factors for Change in Education. In McKinlay, 1990.

Barry, B. (1965) *Political Argument* London, Routledge and Kegan Paul.

Barry, B. (1970) *Economists, Sociologists and Democracy* London, Collier-Macmillan.

Bassett, M. (1976) *The Third Labour Government* Palmerston North, Dunmore Press.

Bassett, M. (1987) Reform of Local and Regional Government. Economic Statement, 17 December, Wellington.

Bassett, M. (1989) Reforming Local and Regional Government *Local Authority Management* 15(2): 7–10.

Beer, M., Spector, B., Lawrence, P., Mills, D. and Walton, R. (1984) *Managing Human Assets* New York, Free Press.

Bendor, J. (1988) Review Article: Formal Models of Bureaucracy *British Journal of Political Science* 18: 353–95.

Bendor, J. (1990) Formal Models of Bureaucracy: A Review. In Lynn, N. and Wildavsky, A. (eds) *Public Administration: The State of the Discipline* New Jersey, Chatham House.

Bendor, J. and Moe, T. (1985) An Adaptive Model of Bureaucratic Politics *American Political Science Review* 79: 755–74.

Benton, R. (1990) Biculturalism in Education: Policy and Practice under the Fourth Labour Government. In Holland and Boston, 1990.

Bergman, M. and Lane, J. (1990) Public Policy in a Principal–Agent Framework *Journal of Theoretical Politics* 2: 339–52.

Bertram, G. (1988) Middle-Class Capture: A Brief Survey. Paper prepared for the Royal Commission on Social Policy, Wellington.

A Bill of Rights for New Zealand: A White Paper (1985) Wellington, Government Printer.

Birch, B. (1995) Speech to Victoria University Public Policy Winter Series, Wellington, 8 August.

Blais, A. and Dion, S. (eds) (1991) *The Budget-Maximizing Bureaucrat: Appraisals and Evidence* Pittsburgh, University of Pittsburgh Press.

Blakeley, R. (1993) Managing for Quality Advice Performance. Paper presented to AIC Conference on Efficient and Effective Policy, Wellington.

Blank, R. (1994) *New Zealand Health Policy: A Comparative Study* Auckland, Oxford University Press.

Blejer, M. and Cheasty, A. (1991) The Measurement of Fiscal Deficits: Analytical and Methodological Issues *Journal of Economic Literature* 29(4): 1644–78.

Bolger, J. (1991) The Government's Vision for the Public Service. In *Proceedings of the New Zealand Public Service Senior Management Conference* Wellington.

Bolger, J. (1995a) *Towards 2010: Investing in Our Future* Wellington.

Bolger, J. (1995b) Speech to Waikato Divisional Conference of the National Party, Gisborne, 13 May.

Bollard, A. (1992) *New Zealand: Economic Reforms, 1984–91* San Francisco, ICS Press.

Bollard, A. (1994) New Zealand. In Williamson, J. (ed) *The Political Economy of Policy Reform* Washington DC, Institute for International Economics.

Booth, P. (1989) Maori Devolution: The Path to Unity or Another Tacky Affair? *North and South* June: 61–73.

Borins, S. (1988) Public Choice: 'Yes Minister' Made It Popular, But Does Winning the Nobel Prize Make it True? *Canadian Public Administration* 31: 12–26.

Boston, J. (1987) Transforming New Zealand's Public Sector: Labour's Quest for Improved Efficiency and Accountability *Public Administration* 65: 423–42.

Boston, J. (1988a) Politicians and Public Servants: New Zealand Developments Since 1984. In Clark, M. (ed) *Constitutional Transformations: Intended and Unintended* Wellington, Social Science Research Fund Committee.

Boston, J. (1988b) Democratic Theory, Devolution and Accountability. In Martin and Harper, 1988.

Boston, J. (1989a) Machinery of Government: Theory and Practice. Unpublished Paper, Victoria University of Wellington.

Boston, J. (1989b) The Treasury and the Organisation of Economic Advice: Some International Comparisons. In Easton, 1989.

Boston, J. (1990a) The Cabinet and Policy Making under the Fourth Labour Government. In Holland and Boston, 1990.

Boston, J. (1990b) Public Sector Update: Appointing a Secretary of Defence *Public Sector* 13(3): 5–6.

Boston, J. (1991) Reorganizing the Machinery of Government: Objectives and Outcomes. In Boston, Martin, Pallot, and Walsh, 1991.

Boston, J. (1992a) The Problems of Policy Coordination: The New Zealand Experience *Governance* 5(1): 88–103.

Boston, J. (1992b) The Treasury: Its Role, Philosophy and Influence. In Gold, 1992.

Boston, J. (1992c) Assessing the Performance of Departmental Chief Executives: Perspectives from New Zealand *Public Administration* 70(3): 405–28.

Boston, J. (1993) The Appointment and Accountability of Departmental Chief Executives *Public Sector* 16(2): 12–14.

Boston, J. (1994a) Purchasing Policy Advice: The Limits to Contracting Out *Governance* 6(1): 1–30.

Boston, J. (1994b) Grand Designs and Unpleasant Realities: The Fate of the National Government's Proposals for the Integrated Targeting of Social Assistance *Political Science* 46(1):1–21.

Boston, J. (1994c) Electoral Reform in New Zealand: The Implications for the Formation, Organization and Operation of the Cabinet *Australian Quarterly* 66(3): 67–90.

Boston, J. (1994d) Strategic Policy Advice: Problems, Constraints and Options. Paper presented to AIC Conference on Managing Quality Policy, Wellington.

Boston, J. (1994e) The Implications of MMP for Social Policy in New Zealand *Social Policy Journal of New Zealand* 3: 2–17.

Boston, J. (1994f) On the Sharp Edge of the State Sector Act: The Resignation of Perry Cameron *Public Sector* 17(4): 2–7.

Boston, J. (1994g) Origins and Destinations: New Zealand's Model of Public Management and the International Transfer of Ideas. Paper prepared for the Fulbright Symposium on Public Sector Management's Evolving World Trends: Learning from Others, Centre for Australian Public Sector Management, Griffith University, Brisbane, 23–24 June 1994.

Boston, J. (1995a) Inherently Governmental Functions and the Limits to Contracting Out. In Boston, 1995c.

Boston, J. (1995b) Origins and Destinations: New Zealand's Model of Public Management and the International Transfer of Ideas. In Weller, P. and Davis, G. (eds) *New Ideas, Better Government* Sydney, Allen and Unwin.

Boston, J. (ed) (1995c) *The State Under Contract* Wellington, Bridget Williams Books.

Boston, J. and Dalziel, P. (eds) (1992) *The Decent Society? Essays in Response to National's Economic and Social Policies* Auckland, Oxford University Press.

Boston, J., Martin, J., Pallot, J. and Walsh, P. (eds) (1991) *Reshaping the State: New Zealand's Bureaucratic Revolution* Auckland, Oxford University Press.

Boxall, P. (1990) Would the Good Employer Please Step Forward? A Discussion of the 'Good Employer' Concept in the State Sector Act 1988. Paper delivered to an SES seminar for senior Ministry of Transport managers, Wellington.

Boxall, P. (ed) (1995) *The Challenge of Human Resource Management: Directions and Debates in New Zealand* Auckland, Longman Paul.

Boyne, G. (1987) Bureaucratic Power and Public Policies: A Test of the Rational Staff Maximization Hypothesis *Political Studies* 35: 79–104.

Bradford, M. (1993) Purchasing Policy Advice: The New Zealand Model—Observations from a Parliamentary Perspective. Paper presented to AIC Conference on Efficient and Effective Policy, Wellington.

Bradshaw, D. (1993) Standards of Professionalism: The Community and the Public Service. In *Public Service Senior Management Conference 1993* Wellington, State Services Commission.

Braun, D. (1993) Who Governs Intermediary Agencies? Principal–Agents Relations in Research Policy-Making *Journal of Public Policy* 13(2): 135–62.

Brennan, G. and Buchanan, J. (1980) *The Power to Tax: Analytical Foundations of a Fiscal Constitution* Cambridge, Cambridge University Press.

Brennan, G. and Buchanan, J. (1985) *The Reason of Rules: Constitutional Political Economy* Cambridge, Cambridge University Press.

Britton, A. (1987) Taxpayers' Capital: The Public Sector Balance Sheet *Fiscal Studies* 8(2): 24–34.

Brook-Cowen, P. (1993) Labour Relations Reform in New Zealand: The Employment Contracts Act and Contractual Freedom *Journal of Labor Research* 14(1): 69–83.

Brookfield, F. (1992) The Governor-General and the Constitution. In Gold, 1992.

Brosnan, P. and Rea, D. (1991) An Adequate Minimum Code: A Base for Freedom, Justice and Efficiency in the Labour Market *New Zealand Journal of Industrial Relations* 16(2): 147–66.

Brosnan, P., Smith, D. and Walsh, P. (1989) *The Dynamics of New Zealand Industrial Relations* Auckland, Wiley and Sons.

Brown, E. (1995) Open Government at the Local Level. MPP Research Paper, Victoria University of Wellington.

Brown, W. (1989) Managing Remuneration. In Sisson, K. (ed) *Personnel Management in Britain* Oxford, Blackwell.

Bryson, J. and Smith-Ring, P. (1990) A Transaction-Based Approach to Policy Intervention *Policy Studies* 23: 205–29.

Buchanan, J. (1978) From Private Preferences to Public Philosophy: The Development of Public Choice *The Economics of Politics* London, Institute of Economic Affairs.

Buchanan, J. (1987) The Constitution of Economic Policy *American Economic Review* 77: 242–50.

Buchanan, J. and Tullock, G. (1962) *The Calculus of Consent: Logical Foundations of Constitutional Democracy* Ann Arbor, University of Michigan Press.

Bührs, T. (1990) The Co-ordination of Environmental Policy: An Unresolved Dilemma. Paper presented at the New Zealand Political Studies Conference, Dunedin.

Bührs, T. (1991) Strategies for Environmental Policy Co-ordination: The New Zealand Experience *Political Science* 43(2): 1–29.

Bührs, T. and Bartlett, R. (1993) *Environmental Policy in New Zealand: The Politics of Clean and Green?* Auckland, Oxford University Press.

Buiter, W. (1982) The Proper Measurement of Government Deficits: Comprehensive Wealth Accounting or Permanent Income Accounting for the Public Sector: Its Implications for Policy Evaluation and Design. National Bureau of Economic Research Working Paper No. 1013.

Burke, J. (1986) *Bureaucratic Responsibility* Baltimore, Johns Hopkins University Press.

Burns, J. (1994) A Strategic Approach to Human Resource Development: A New Opportunity for EEO. In Sayers, J. and Tremaine, M. (eds) *The Vision and the Reality: Equal Employment Opportunities in the New Zealand Workplace* Palmerston North, Dunmore Press.

Bush, G. (1980) *Local Government and Politics in New Zealand* Auckland, George Allen and Unwin.

Bush, G. (1992) Local Government: Politics and Pragmatism. In Gold, 1992.

Bushnell, P. (1989) Specifying Outputs. In *Managing Resources in the New Public Sector: Papers from the 1989 Public Sector Convention* Wellington, New Zealand Society of Accountants.

Bushnell, P. (1991) Policy Advice—Planning for Performance *Public Sector* 14: 12–16.

Bushnell, P. and Scott, G. (1988) Devolution and Accountability: An Economic Perspective. In Martin and Harper, 1988.

Cabinet Office (1994) *Cabinet Office Manual* Wellington.

Caffery, A. (1995) The Limitations of Bureaucracy: A Duty to Contract? *Public Sector* 18(1): 2–6.

Caiden, G. (1988) The Vitality of Administrative Reform *International Review of Administrative Sciences* 54: 331–58.

Caiden, G. and Truelson, J. (1988) Whistleblower Protection in the USA *Australian Journal of Public Administration* 47(2): 119–29.

Cameron, D. (1992) Institutional Management: How Should the Governance and Management of Universities in Canada Accommodate Changing Circumstances? In Cutt, J. and Dobell, R. (eds) *Public Purse, Public Purpose: Autonomy and Accountability in the Groves of Academe* Halifax, Institute for Research on Public Policy.

Campbell, C. (1983) *Governments Under Stress: Political Executives and Key Bureaucrats in Washington, London and Ottawa* Toronto, University of Toronto Press.

Campbell, C. and Peters, G. (1988) *Organizing Governance: Governing Organizations* Pittsburgh, Pittsburgh University Press.

Carpinter, P. (1993) MMP and Coalitions: Possible Effects on New Zealand's Public Service. In Hawke, 1993a.

Cawsey, T. and Inkson, K. (1992) Patterns of Managerial Job Change: A New Zealand Study *New Zealand Journal of Business* 14: 13–25.

Chan, S. and Rosenbloom, D. (1994) Legal Control of Public Administration: A Principal–Agent Perspective *International Review of Administrative Sciences* 60: 559–74.

Chandler, A. (1962) *Strategy and Structure* Cambridge, Massachusetts, MIT Press.

Chapman, R. (1972) Machinery of Government *New Zealand Journal of Public Administration* 35: 17–33.

Chapman, R. (ed) (1993) *Ethics in Public Service* Edinburgh, Edinburgh University Press.

Chatfield, M. (1974) *A History of Accounting Thought* Hinsdale, Illinois, Dryden Press.

Chen, M. and Palmer, G. (1993) *Public Law in New Zealand* Auckland, Oxford University Press.

Choat, D. (1993) Where Do They Get Their Ideas? Treasury, the Reserve Bank and the International Economics Community. Paper presented to the New Zealand Political Studies Association Conference, Christchurch.

Clarke, R. (1972) The Number and Size of Government Departments *Political Quarterly* 43: 169–86.

Cockburn, C. (1989) Equal Opportunities: The Long and Short Agenda *Industrial Relations Journal* 20(3): 213–25.

Cody, J. (1990) Devolution, Disengagement and Control in the Statutory Social Services. In McKinlay, 1990.

Committee on Official Information (1980) *Towards Open Government: General Report* Wellington, Government Printer.

Committee on Official Information (1981) *Towards Open Government: Supplementary Report* Wellington, Government Printer.

Considine, M. (1988) The Corporate Management Framework as Administrative Science: A Critique *Australian Journal of Public Administration* 47(1): 4–18.

Consumers Institute (1995) Sick Health? *Consumer* 338: 23–5.

Conybeare, J. (1984) Bureaucracy, Monopoly, and Competition: A Critical Analysis of the Budget-Maximising Model of Bureaucracy *American Journal of Political Science* 28: 479–502.

Corban, J. (1994) The Provision of Strategic Advice to Government. MPP thesis, Victoria University of Wellington.

Craig, J. (1994) Integrating HR Policies into the Strategic Plan. Address to AIC Conference on Strategic Management in the Public Sector, Wellington.

Craswell, E. and Davis, G. (1993) Does the Amalgamation of Government Agencies Produce Better Policy Coordination? In Weller, P., Foster, J. and Davis, G. (eds) *Reforming the Public Service: Lessons from Recent Experience* Melbourne, Macmillan.

Cripps, C., Eagles, I., Grantham, R., Gunasekara, G., Longdin, L. and Mapp, W. (1994) *Law in Commerce and Administration* Auckland, Palatine Press.

Crown Law Office (1990) *The Judge Over Your Shoulder* Wellington.

Cullen, R. (1986) The Victorian Senior Executive Service: A Performance Based Approach to the Management of Senior Managers *Australian Journal of Public Administration* 45: 60–73.

Culpitt, I. (1994) Bicultural Fragments—A Pakeha Perspective *Social Policy Journal of New Zealand* 2(July): 48–62.

Dakin, S. and Smith, M. (1995) Staffing. In Boxall, 1995.

Davis, G. and Gardner, M. (1995) Who Signs the Contract? Applying Agency Theory to Politicians. In Boston, 1995c.

Davis, G., Weller, P. and Lewis, C. (eds) (1989) *Corporate Management in Australian Government* Melbourne, Macmillan.

Deeks, J., Parker, J. and Ryan, R. (1994) *Labour and Employment Relations in New Zealand* Auckland, Longman Paul.

Deloitte, Haskins and Sells (1986) Submission on the State-Owned Enterprises Bill to the Government Administration Committee Wellington.

Deloitte Touche Tohmatsu (1993) *What's in an Annual Plan? A Survey of the Annual Plans of City and District Councils* Wellington.

Department of Internal Affairs (1991) *Review Functions of Community Boards* Wellington.

Department of Internal Affairs (1992a) *Public Consultation in the Local Authority Annual Planning Process* Wellington.

Department of Internal Affairs (1992b) *Reorganising Local Authority Areas* Wellington.

Department of Internal Affairs (1994a) *Local Authority Election Statistics* Wellington.

Department of Internal Affairs (1994b) *Directory of Local Government* Wellington.

Department of Internal Affairs (1994c) *Territorial Authority Service Delivery 1993–1994* Wellington.

Department of Justice (1989) *Principles for Crown Action on the Treaty of Waitangi* Wellington.

Department of Social Welfare (1992) *Report of the Department of Social Welfare for the Year Ended 30 June 1992* Wellington.

Department of Social Welfare (1994) *Report of the Department of Social Welfare for the Year Ended 30 June 1994* Wellington.

Dixon, J., Ericksen, N. and Gunn, A. (1989) Changing Environmental Administration in New Zealand: Advance or Retreat? In Hay, P., Eckersley, R. and Holloway, G. (eds) *Environmental Politics in Australia and New Zealand* Hobart, Centre for Environmental Studies, University of Tasmania.

Doig, A. (1979) The Machinery of Government and the Growth of Governmental Bodies *Public Administration* 57: 309–31.

Dollery, D. and Hamburger, P. (1993) Economic Models of Bureaucracy and the Australian Federal Budget Sector 1982 to 1992. Unpublished Paper, Economics Department, University of New England.

Donaldson, L. (1990a) The Ethereal Hand: Organizational Economics and Management Theory *Academy of Management Review* 15(3): 369–81.

Donaldson, L. (1990b) A Rational Basis for Criticisms of Organizational Economics: A Reply to Barney *Academy of Management Review* 15(3): 394–401.

Donaldson, L. and Davis, J. (1991) Stewardship Theory or Agency Theory: CEO Governance and Shareholder Returns *Australian Journal of Management* 16(1): 49–64.

Dore, R. (1983) Goodwill and the Spirit of Market Capitalism *British Journal of Sociology* 34: 459–82.

Douglas, M. (1994) New Zealand Paths to Competitive Tendering. In *Introducing Competitive Tendering in Local Government in Australia* Foundation for Local Government Education and Development Fund, Department of Management, RMIT, Melbourne.

Douglas, R. (1993) *Unfinished Business* Auckland, Random House.

Dow, G. (1987) The Function of Authority in Transaction Cost Economics *Journal of Economic Behavior and Organization* 8: 13–38.

Downs, A. (1957) *An Economic Theory of Democracy* New York, Harper and Row.

Downs, A. (1967) *Inside Bureaucracy* Boston, Little, Brown.

Duncan, I. and Bollard, A. (1992) *Corporatization and Privatization: Lessons from New Zealand* Auckland, Oxford University Press.

Dunleavy, P. (1989a) The Architecture of the British Central State. Part I Framework for Analysis *Public Administration* 67: 249–75.

Dunleavy, P. (1989b) The Architecture of the British Central State. Part II Empirical Findings *Public Administration* 67: 391–417.

Dunleavy, P. (1991) *Democracy, Bureaucracy and Public Choice* Brighton, Wheatsheaf.

Dunsire, A. (1990) Holistic Governance *Public Policy and Administration* 5(1): 4–19.

Durie, E. (1995) Justice, Biculturalism and the Politics of Law. In Wilson and Yeatman, 1995.

Durie, M. (1993) Māori and the State: Professional and Ethical Implications for a Bicultural Public Service. Paper presented to the Public Service Senior Management Conference, Wellington.

Dye, K. and Bowsher, C. (1987) Financial Statements for a Sovereign State: The Federal Government Reporting Study *Accounting Horizons* 1(1): 17–24.

Eaddy, R. (1992) The Structure and Operation of the Executive. In Gold, 1992.

Eagles, I., Taggart, M. and Liddell, G. (1992) *Freedom of Information in New Zealand* Auckland, Oxford University Press.

Earle, D. (1995) Pacific Islands Peoples in Aotearoa/New Zealand: Existing and Emerging Paradigms *Social Policy Journal of New Zealand* 4 (July): 14–23.

Earp, R. and Brown, R. (1991) The Role of Chief Executives in the Public Service. Research Paper for MBA 335, Victoria University of Wellington.

East, P. (1994) How Does the New Electoral Environment Affect the Role and Structure of the Public Sector? Keynote address to the IIR Conference on MMP: Managing the Political/ Public Sector Interface.

Easton, B. (ed) (1989) *The Making of Rogernomics* Auckland, Auckland University Press.

Easton, B. (1994) How Did the Health Reforms Blitzkrieg Fail? *Political Science* 46(2): 215–33.

Education Review Office (1994) *Effective Governance: School Boards of Trustees* Wellington.

Edwards, M. (1992) Evaluating Policy Advice: A Comment *Australian Journal of Public Administration* 51(4): 446–49.

Egeberg, M. (1988) Designing Public Organizations. In Kooiman and Eliassen, 1988.

Elkin, G. and Inkson, K. (1995) Employee Development. In Boxall, 1995.

Emmert, M. and Crow, M. (1988) Public, Private and Hybrid Organizations: An Empirical Examination of the Role of Publicness *Administration and Society* 20(2): 216–44.

Ewart, B. and Boston, J. (1993) The Separation of Policy Advice from Operations: The Case of Defence Restructuring in New Zealand *Australian Journal of Public Administration* 52(2): 223–40.

Fancy, H. (1995) *Budgeting in an MMP Environment* Wellington, Institute of Policy Studies.

Federal Accounting Standards Advisory Board (1994) *Entity and Display: Statements of Recommended Accounting and Reporting Concepts Number 2* Washington DC, Federal Accounting Standards Advisory Board.

Finance and Expenditure Committee (1989) *Report on the Public Finance Bill 1989* Wellington, House of Representatives.

Finance and Expenditure Committee (1994) *Report of the Financial Expenditure Committee on the Fiscal Responsibility Bill* Wellington, House of Representatives.

Finer, H. (1941) Administrative Responsibility in Democratic Government *Public Administration Review* 1: 335–50.

Fleras, A. (1985) Towards 'Tu Tangata': Historical Development and Current Trends in Māori Policy and Administration *Political Science* 37: 18–39.

Flint, D. (1988) *Philosophy and Principles of Auditing: An Introduction* London, Macmillan.

Foster, C. (1994) Rival Explanations of Public Ownership, Its Failure and Privatization *Public Administration* 72(4): 489–503.

Fougere, G. (1994) The State and Health Reform. In Sharp, 1994.

French, P. (1983) *Ethics in Government* Englewood Cliffs, New Jersey, Prentice-Hall.

Friedman, A. (1977) *Industry and Labour* London, Macmillan.

Friedrich, C. (1940) Public Policy and the Nature of Administrative Responsibility. In Mason, E. and Friedrich, C. (eds) *Public Policy* Cambridge, Massachusetts, Harvard University Press.

Galvin, B. (1991) *Policy Coordination, Public Sector and Government* Wellington, Victoria University Press.

Game, A. and Pringle, R. (1983) *Gender at Work* Sydney, Allen and Unwin.

Geist, B. (1981) *State Audit: Developments in Public Accountability* London, Macmillan.

Glazer, M. and Glazer, P. (1989) *The Whistleblowers: Exposing Corruption in Government and Industry* New York, Basic Books.

Gleisner, S. and Paterson, R. (1995) Rationing—The Role of Regional Health Authorities *Health Manager* 2(2): 7–11.

Gold, H. (ed) (1992) *New Zealand Politics in Perspective* 3rd ed. Auckland, Longman Paul.

Gordon, L. (1994) Is Choice a Sustainable Policy for New Zealand? In Manson, H. (ed) *New Zealand Annual Review of Education: 4* Wellington, New Zealand Council for Educational Research.

Gorringe, P. (1987) A Review Article: The Economic Institutions of Capitalism: Firms, Markets and Relational Contracting by Oliver E. Williamson *Australian Journal of Management* 12: 125–43.

Gorringe, P. (1988) Hostages, Asset Reliance and the Enforcement of Labour Contracts. Unpublished paper, Treasury.

Granovetter, M. (1985) Economic Actions and Social Structure: The Problem of Embeddedness *American Journal of Sociology* 91: 481–510.

Gregory, R. (ed) (1984) *The Official Information Act: A Beginning* Wellington, New Zealand Institute of Public Administration.

Gregory, R. (1995a) Accountability, Responsibility and Corruption: Managing the 'Public Production Process'. In Boston, 1995c.

Gregory, R. (1995b) The Peculiar Tasks of Public Management: Toward Conceptual Discrimination *Australian Journal of Public Administration* 54(2): 171–83.

Gregory, R. (1995c) Bureaucratic 'Psychopathology' and Technocratic Governance: Whither Responsibility? *Hong Kong Public Administration* 4(1): 17–36.

Guest, D. (1990) Human Resource Management and the American Dream *Journal of Management Studies* 27(4): 377–97.

Guest, D. (1992) Human Resource Management in the United Kingdom. In Towers, B. (ed) *The Handbook of Human Resource Management* Oxford, Blackwell.

Gulick, L. (1937) *Notes on the Theory of Organization* Memorandum prepared as a member of the President's Committee on Administrative Management, Washington DC.

Gunn, L. (1988) Perspectives on Public Management. In Kooiman and Eliassen, 1988.

Gustafsson, L. (1987) Renewal of the Public Sector in Sweden *Public Administration* 65: 179–91.

Guthrie, J. (1992) Public Sector Accounting: Transformations and Managerialism. Paper Presented at the AAANZ Annual Conference, Massey University, Palmerston North.

Hall, R. (1992) The Strategic Analysis of Intangible Resources *Strategic Management Journal* 13: 135–44.

Halligan, J. (1987) Reorganizing Australian Government Departments, 1987 *Canberra Bulletin of Public Administration* 52: 40–7.

Halligan, J. and Harris, P. (1978) Local Elections and Democracy. In Levine, S. (ed) *Politics in New Zealand* Sydney, George Allen and Unwin.

Hammond, T. (1990) In Defense of Luther Gulick's 'Notes on the Theory of Organization' *Public Administration* 68: 143–73.

Harbridge, R. (1993) New Zealand's Collective Employment Contracts: Update November 1992 *New Zealand Journal of Industrial Relations* 18(1): 113–24.

Harbridge, R. (1994) *Labour Market Regulation and Employment: Trends in New Zealand* Wellington, Industrial Relations Centre, Victoria University of Wellington.

Harbridge, R. and Honeybone, A. (1995) The Employment Contracts Act and Collective Bargaining Patterns: A Review of the 1994–95 Year. In Harbridge, R. and Kiely, P. (eds) *Employment Contracts: Bargaining Trends and Employment Law Update 1994–95* Wellington, Industrial Relations Centre, Victoria University of Wellington.

Harbridge, R., Hince, K. and Honeybone, A. (1995) *Unions and Union Membership in New Zealand: Annual Review for 1994* Working Paper 2/95, Industrial Relations Centre, Victoria University of Wellington.

Harbridge, R., Honeybone, A. and Kiely, P. (1994) *Employment Contracts: Bargaining Trends and Employment Law Update 1993/94* Wellington, Industrial Relations Centre, Victoria University of Wellington.

Harden, I. (1992) *The Contracting State* Buckingham, Open University Press.

Harris, B. (1992) The Constitutional Base. In Gold, 1992.

Harris, P. and Levine, S. (eds) (1992) *The New Zealand Politics Source Book* Palmerston North, Dunmore Press.

Hawke, G. (1988) *Report of the Working Group on Post Compulsory Education and Training* Wellington, Government Printer.

Hawke, G. (ed.) (1993a) *Changing Politics? The Electoral Referendum 1993* Wellington, Institute of Policy Studies.

Hawke, G. (1993b) *Improving Policy Advice* Wellington, Victoria University Press.

Hawkins, L. (1995) Purchasing Health Services *Public Sector* 18(1): 7–10.

Hayek, F. von (1979) Whither Democracy? In Hayek, F. von *Social Justice, Socialism and Democracy* London, Centre for Independent Studies.

Hayward, B. (1994) The Greening of Direct Democracy: A Reconsideration of Theories of Political Participation. Paper prepared for presentation at the XVIth World Congress of the International Political Science Association, Berlin.

Hayward, M. (1981) *Diary of the Kirk Years* Wellington, Reed and Cape Catley.

Hede, A. (1991) Trends in the Higher Civil Services of Anglo-American Systems *Governance* 4: 489–515.

Helm, D. and Smith, S. (1989) The Decentralized State: The Economic Borders of Local Government. In Helm, D. (ed.) *The Economic Borders of the State* Oxford, Oxford University Press.

Henare, D. (1995) The Ka Awatea Report: Reflections on its Process and Visions. In Wilson and Yeatman, 1995.

Henderson, A. (1990) *The Quest for Efficiency: The Origins of the State Services Commission* Wellington, Department of Internal Affairs.

Hendry, C. and Pettigrew, A. (1990) Human Resource Management: An Agenda for the 1990s *International Journal of Human Resource Management* 1(1): 17–44.

Henry, N. (1975) Paradigms of Public Administration *Public Administration Review* 35(4): 378–86.

Hensley, G. (1989) *A Structure for Border Control in New Zealand* Wellington, Domestic and External Security Secretariat.

Heymann, D. (1988) Input Controls and the Public Sector: What Does Economic Theory Offer? Paper prepared for the Fiscal Affairs Department, International Monetary Fund, Washington.

Hince, K. and Vranken, M. (1991) A Controversial Reform of New Zealand Labour Law: The Employment Contracts Act 1991 *International Labour Review* 130(4): 475–93.

Hirschman, A. (1970) *Exit, Voice and Loyalty: Responses to Decline in Firms, Organizations and States* Cambridge, Massachusetts, Harvard University Press.

Hodder, J. (1992) Judges: Their Political Role. In Gold, 1992.

Holland, M. and Boston, J. (eds) (1990) *The Fourth Labour Government* 2nd ed. Auckland, Oxford University Press.

Holmes, F. and Piddington, K. (1980) The Public and its Servants: The New Zealand Environment Re-assessed. In *State Servants and the Public in the 1980s* Wellington, Government Printer.

Hood, C. (1986) *Administrative Analysis: An Introduction to Rules, Enforcement and Organizations* Brighton, Wheatsheaf.

Hood, C. (1987) Scale Economics and Bureaucratic Giantism *Canberra Bulletin of Public Administration* 52: 56–8.

Hood, C. (1990a) Beyond the Public Bureaucracy State? Public Administration in the 1990s. Inaugural Lecture, London School of Economics.

Hood, C. (1990b) De-Sir Humphreyfying the Westminster Model of Bureaucracy: A New Style of Governance? *Governance* 3: 205–14.

Hood, C. (1991) A Public Management for All Seasons *Public Administration* 69: 3–19.

Hood, C. (1992) The 'New Public Management Model' and Its Conception of Performance Efficiency. Paper delivered to the Public Sector Convention of the New Zealand Society of Accountants, Wellington.

Hood, C. (1995) The 'New Public Management' in the 1980s: Variations on a Theme *Accounting, Organizations and Society* (forthcoming).

Hood, C. and Dunsire, A. (1981) *Bureaumetrics* Westmead, Gower.

Hood, C. and Jackson, M. (1991) *Administrative Argument* Aldershot, Dartmouth Publishing.

Hood, C. and Jackson, M. (1992) The New Public Management: A Recipe for Disaster? In Parker, D. and Handmer, J. (eds) *Hazard Management and Emergency Planning: Perspectives on Britain* London, James and James Science Publishers.

Hood, C., Huby, M. and Dunsire, A. (1984) Bureaucrats and Budgeting Benefits: How do British Central Government Departments Measure Up? *Journal of Public Policy* 4: 163–79.

Hood, C., Huby, M. and Dunsire, A. (1985) Scale Economics and Iron Laws: Mergers and Demergers in Whitehall *Public Administration* 63: 61–78.

Hoogerwerf, A. (1992) The Market as a Metaphor of Politics: A Critique of the Foundations of Economic Choice Theory *International Review of Administrative Sciences* 58: 23–42.

Horn, M. (1988) Political Economy of Public Administration. Doctoral thesis, Harvard University.

Horne, I. (1992) FMR: A Departmental Perspective *The Accountants' Journal* 71(5): 22–3.

Horner, T. (1989) Local Government Reform: Links to Public Sector Reform *Public Sector* 12(3): 2–10.

Howden-Chapman, P. (1993) Doing the Splits: Contracting in the New Zealand Health Service *Health Policy* 24: 273–86.

Howden-Chapman, P. and Ashton, T. (1994) Shopping for Health: Purchasing Health Services through Contracts *Health Policy* 29: 61–83.

Hughes, J. (1993) Personal Grievances. In Harbridge, R. (ed) *Employment Contracts: New Zealand Experiences* Wellington, Victoria University Press.

Hunn, D. (1991) Chief Executives Overview. In State Services Commission *Annual Report for the Year Ended 30 June 1991* Wellington.

Hunn, D. (1992) Commissioner's Report. In State Services Commission *Annual Report For the Year Ended 30 June 1992* Wellington.

Hunn, D. (1993) Commissioner's Report. In State Services Commission *Annual Report for the Year Ended 30 June 1993* Wellington.

Hunn, D. (1994a) *A Statement by the State Services Commissioner* 14 October.

Hunn, D. (1994b) Commissioner's Report. In State Services Commission *Annual Report for the Year Ended 30 June 1994* Wellington.

Hunn, D. (1994c) Measuring Performance in Policy Advice: The New Zealand Perspective. In OECD, *Performance Measurement in Government: Issues and Illustrations* Occasional Paper No. 5, Paris.

Hunn, D. (1994d) MMP and the Public Service. Address to MPP Seminar, Victoria University of Wellington.

Hunn, D. and Lang, H. (1989) *Review of the Prime Minister's Office and Cabinet Office* Wellington, State Services Commission.

Hunn, J. (1961) *Report on Department of Maori Affairs* Wellington.

Iles, P. and Salaman, G. (1995) Recruitment, Selection and Assessment. In Storey, 1995b.

International Federation of Accountants, Public Sector Committee (1991) *Study 1: Financial Reporting by National Governments* New York, International Federation of Accountants.

Jackson, K. (1972) *The New Zealand Legislative Council: A Study of the Establishment, Function and Abolition of an Upper House* Dunedin, University of Otago Press.

Jackson, K. (1992) Caucus: The Anti-Parliament System? In Gold, 1992.

Jacobs, K. (1994) The Management of the Health Core: A Model of Control *Health Policy* 29: 157–71.

James, C. (1992) *New Territory* Wellington, Bridget Williams Books.

James, S. (1993) The Idea Brokers: The Impact of Think Tanks on British Government *Public Administration* 71: 491–506.

Jarman, A and Kouzmin, A. (1993) Public Sector Think Tanks in Inter-Agency Policy Making: Designing Enhanced Governance Capacity *Canadian Public Administration* 26: 499–529.

Jennings, S. and Cameron, R. (1987) State-Owned Enterprise Reform in New Zealand. In Bollard, A. and Buckle, R. (eds) *Economic Liberalisation in New Zealand* Auckland, Allen and Unwin.

Jensen, M. and Meckling, W. (1976) Theory of the Firm: Managerial Behaviour, Agency Costs and Ownership Structure *Journal of Financial Economics* 3: 305–60.

Jewson, N. and Mason, D. (1986) The Theory and Practice of Equal Opportunities Policies: Liberal and Radical Approaches *Sociological Review* 34(2): 307–34.

Johnson, E. (1995) Total Quality Management and Performance Appraisal: To Be or Not To Be? In Boxall, 1995.

Johnson, R. (1994) The National Interest, Westminster and Public Choice *The Australian Journal of Agricultural Economics* 38(1): 1–30.

Jones, G. (1977) Responsibility and Government. Inaugural Lecture, London School of Economics.

Jones, G. and Stewart, J. (1983) *The Case for Local Government* 2nd ed. London, George Allen and Unwin.

Jones, S. (1990) Iwi and Government. In McKinlay, 1990.

Joseph, P. (1993) *Constitutional and Administrative Law in New Zealand* Sydney, Law Book.

Joskow, P. (1985) Vertical Integration and Long-term Contracts: The Case of Coal-Burning Electric Generating Plants *Journal of Law, Economics and Organization* 1: 33–80.

Kawharu, I. (1989) *Waitangi: Maori and Pakeha Perspectives of the Treaty of Waitangi* Auckland, Oxford University Press.

Kay, J. (1993) *Foundations of Corporate Success: How Business Strategies Add Value* Oxford, Oxford University Press.

Kay, N. (1992) Markets, False Hierarchies and the Evolution of the Modern Corporation *Journal of Economic Behavior and Organization* 17: 315–34.

Keith, K. (1987) Open Government in New Zealand *Victoria University of Wellington Law Review* 17(4): 333–43.

Kelman, S. (1987) 'Public Choice' and Public Spirit *The Public Interest* 87: 80–94.

Kelsey, J. (1990) *A Question of Honour? Labour and the Treaty, 1984–1989* Wellington, Allen and Unwin.

Kelsey, J. (1991) Rogernomics and the Treaty of Waitangi. PhD thesis, University of Auckland.

Kelsey, J. (1993) *Rolling Back the State* Wellington, Bridget Williams Books.

Kemp, P. (1990) Next Steps for the British Civil Service *Governance* 3: 186–96.

Kernaghan, K. (1993) Promoting Public Service Ethics: The Codification Option. In Chapman, R. (ed) *Ethics in Public Service* Edinburgh, Edinburgh University Press.

Kessler, I. (1993) Performance Pay. In Sisson, K. (ed) *Personnel Management in Britain* 2nd ed. Oxford, Blackwell.

Kettl, D. (1988) *Government by Proxy: (Mis?) Managing Federal Programs* Washington DC, Congressional Quarterly Press.

Kettl, D. (1993) *Sharing Power: Public Governance and Private Markets* Washington DC, Brookings Institution.

Kilroy, S. (1995) State Services Shaken by Chapman Affair *Dominion* 4 May: 7.

Kirk, A. (1988) *Report of Strategos Consulting on the New Zealand Audit Office* Wellington, Strategos Consulting.

Kooiman, J. and Eliassen, K. (eds) (1988) *Managing Public Organizations: Lessons from Contemporary European Experience* London, Sage.

Kymlicka, W. (1989) *Liberalism, Community and Culture* Oxford, Oxford University Press.

Laking, G. (1987) The Ombudsman in Transition *Victoria University of Wellington Law Review* 17(4): 307–17.

Laking, R. (1987) Social Policy and the Future of Bureaucracy. In von Tunzelman, A. and Johnston, J. (eds) *Responding to the Revolution* Wellington, Government Printing Office.

Laking, R. (1994) *Senior Manager Origins Survey* Unpublished Paper, Ministry of Housing.

Laking, R. (1995) Reward Strategies: Diversity in Pay and Terms and Conditions: A New Zealand Case Study. Paper presented at the joint conference of the Government of South Africa and the Commonwealth Association for Public Administration and Management on Encouraging Diversity within a Unified Public Service, Cape Town.

Lally, M. (1992) Capital Charge Regime: Economic Rhetoric or Rationality? *The Accountants' Journal* 71(1): 54–5.

Lane, J. (ed) (1987) *Bureaucracy and Public Choice* London, Sage.

Lane, J. (1988) Public and Private Leadership. In Kooiman and Eliassen, 1988.

Lange, D. (1988) *Tomorrow's Schools—The Reform of Education Administration in New Zealand* Wellington, Department of Education.

Laugesen, M. and Salmond, G. (1994) New Zealand Health Care: A Background *Health Policy* 29(1/2): 11–23.

Laughrin, D. (1988) *Identifying and Developing Potential Senior Executive Service Staff: A Report on the Study of Options for Future State Services Commission Activity* Wellington, State Services Commission.

Legge, K. (1995) HRM: Rhetoric, Reality and Hidden Agendas. In Storey, 1995b.

Legislation Advisory Committee (1990) *Public Advisory Bodies* Wellington.

Levett, A. (1988) Devolution and the Social Services. In Martin and Harper, 1988.

Levine, H. and Henare, M. (1994) Mana Māori Motuhake—Māori Self-Determination *Pacific Viewpoint* 35(2): 193–209.

Levine, S., Rainbow, S. and Roberts, J. (1987) Ministers and Public Servants—Attitudes to Policy Making. Paper presented at the Australasian Political Studies Conference, Auckland.

Levinthal, D. (1988) A Survey of Agency Models of Organization *Journal of Economic Behavior and Organization* 9: 153–85.

Lewis, G. (1991) A Departmental Perspective: Effect of the Regime *The Accountants' Journal* 70(9): 27–8.

Lewis, N. (1993) The Citizen's Charter and Next Steps: A New Way of Governing? *Political Quarterly* 64(4): 316–35.

Lindblom, C. (1979) Still Muddling, Not Yet Through *Public Administration Review* 39: 517–26.

Lippman, W. (1956) *The Public Philosophy* New York, Mentor Books.

Lipson, L. (1948) *The Politics of Equality* Chicago, University of Chicago Press.

Lister, P., Rivers, M. and Wilkinson, A. (1991) The Management of Change: The Social and Personnel Perspective. In Boston, Martin, Pallot, and Walsh, 1991.

Local Government Association (1993a) *Charter for Local Government on Social Justice Issues, Community Development and Social Services* Wellington.

Local Government Association (1993b) *Draft Protocol: Statement of Principles* Wellington.

Logan, B. (1991) *Review of State Sector Reforms* Wellington, Steering Group.

Longdin-Prisk, M. (1986) Setting Legal Limits to Government Borrowing *New Zealand Universities Law Review* 12(2): 160–77.

Lough, N. (1990) *Today's Schools: A Review of the Education Reform Implementation Process* Wellington, Government Printer.

Lovell, R. (1992) Citizen's Charter: The Cultural Challenge *Public Administration* 70(2): 395–404.

Macaskill, S. (1994) Management, Manipulation, or Mousetrap. Address to Society of Local Government Managers, Auckland.

McCallum, B. (1994) *Report on the Audit of the Administration of the Audit Office Consequent on the Resignation of Mr J. T. Chapman as Controller and Auditor General on 10 October 1994* Wellington, McCallum, Peterson and Co.

McCubbins, M., Noll, R., and Weingast, B. (1987) Administrative Procedures and Political Control *Journal of Law, Economics and Organization* 3: 243–77.

McCulloch, B. (1991) A Charge for Government Departments: What is it All About? *The Accountants' Journal* 70(9): 21–3.

McCulloch, B. and Ball, I. (1992) Accounting in the Context of Financial Management Reform *Financial Accountability and Management* 8(1): 7–12.

McDonald, P. and Sharma, A. (1994) Towards Work Teams Within a New Zealand Public Service Organization. Paper presented to the 1994 International Conference on Work Teams, University of North Texas.

McDowell, B. (1991) *Ethical Conduct and the Professional's Dilemma: Choosing Between Service and Success* New York, Quorum Books.

McGee, D. (1992) The House of Representatives. In Gold, 1992.

McGee, D. (1994) *Parliamentary Practice in New Zealand* 2nd ed. Wellington, GP Publications.

McGuire, T. (1981) Budget-Maximising Governmental Agencies: An Empirical Test *Public Choice* 36: 313–22.

Mackenzie, W. (1966) Foreword. In Normanton, E. *The Accountability and Audit of Governments* Manchester, Manchester University Press.

McKinlay, P. (ed.) (1990) *Redistribution of Power? Devolution in New Zealand* Wellington, Victoria University Press.

McKinlay, P. (1994) Local Government Reform: What was Ordered and What has been Delivered. Unpublished paper, Wellington.

McLaren, I. (1974) *Education in a Small Democracy—New Zealand* London, Routledge.

McLaren, R. (1989) Organizing Government Departments: Experience from Saskatchewan *Canadian Public Administration* 32: 462–9.

McLean, D. (1989) Submission on the Defence Bill 1989 to the Foreign Affairs and Defence Committee. Wellington.

McLean, I. (1986) Review Article: Some Recent Work on Public Choice *British Journal of Political Science* 16: 377–94.

McLean, J., Rishworth, P. and Taggart, M. (1992) The Impact of the Bill of Rights on Administrative Law. In *The New Zealand Bill of Rights Act 1990: Papers Presented at Seminars held by Legal Research Foundation* Auckland, Legal Research Foundation.

McLeay, E. (1991) Two Steps Forward, Two Steps Back: Maori Devolution, Maori Advisory Committees and Maori Representation *Political Science* 43(1): 30–46.

McLeay, E. (1995) *The Cabinet and Political Power in New Zealand* Auckland, Oxford University Press.

MacLeod, R. (1992) Crown Financial Statements: Breaking New Ground *The Accountants' Journal* 71(5): 29–30.

McMillan, J. (1994) Whistleblowing Initiatives: An Overview. In N. Preston, 1994.

McRae, T. (1994) *A Parliament in Crisis: The Decline of Democracy in New Zealand* Wellington, Shieldaig Publications.

Malcolm, L. and Barnett, P. (1994) New Zealand's Health Providers in an Emerging Market *Health Policy* 29: 85–100.

Mansbridge, J. (1990) Self-Interest in Political Life *Political Theory* 18: 132–53.

Mansfield, H. (1969) Federal Executive Reorganization: Thirty Years of Experience *Public Administration Review* 29: 332–45.

Maori Affairs Committee (1994) *1994/95 Estimates Vote Maori Affairs* Wellington.

March, J. and Olson, J. (1983) Organizing Political Life: What Administrative Reorganization Tells Us About Government *American Political Science Review* 77: 281–96.

Marginson, P., Armstrong, P., Edwards, P. and Purcell, J. (1993) The Control of Industrial Relations in a Large Company: Initial Analysis of the Second Company-Level Industrial Relations Survey. In *Warwick Papers in Industrial Relations: No. 45* Coventry, University of Warwick.

Martin, J. (1988a) *A Profession of Statecraft?* Wellington, Victoria University Press.

Martin, J. (1988b) Foreword. In Martin and Harper, 1988.

Martin, J. (1990) Remaking the State Services. In Holland and Boston, 1990.

Martin, J. (1991a) *Public Service and the Public Servant* Wellington, State Services Commission.

Martin, J. (1991b) Devolution and Decentralization. In Boston, Martin, Pallot, and Walsh, 1991.

Martin, J. (1994a) The Role of the State in Administration. In Sharp, 1994.

Martin, J. (1994b) Ethics in Public Service: The New Zealand Experience. In N. Preston, 1994.

Martin, J. (1994c) A New Ethics Regime for the Public Service. Paper presented to the AIC conference on Public Accountability in the MMP Environment.

Martin, J. (1995a) Contracting and Accountability. In Boston, 1995c.

Martin, J. (1995b) Democracy and Duty: The New Zealand Way. In Woldring, K. (ed) *Business Ethics in Australia and New Zealand: Essays and Cases* Melbourne, Thomas Nelson.

Martin, J. and Harper, J. (eds) (1988) *Devolution and Accountability* Wellington, New Zealand Institute of Public Administration.

Mascarenhas, R. (1991) State-Owned Enterprises. In Boston, Martin, Pallot, and Walsh, 1991.

Mazengarb's Employment Law (1995) Wellington, Butterworths.

Memon, A. (1993) *Keeping New Zealand Green: Recent Environmental Reform* Dunedin, University of Otago Press.

Messervy, P. (undated) Equal Employment Opportunities: A Strategy for Radical Change or a Screen for Liberal Justice? Unpublished Paper, Wellington.

Metcalfe, L. (1993) Public Management: From Imitation to Innovation *Australian Journal of Public Administration* 52(3): 292–304.

Miller, G. and Moe, T. (1983) Bureaucrats, Legislators, and the Size of Government *American Political Science Review* 77: 297–322.

Minister of Māori Affairs (1988a) *He Tirohanga Rangapu: Partnership Perspectives* Government Discussion Paper. Wellington, Government Printer.

Minister of Māori Affairs (1988b) *Te Urupare Rangapu: Partnership Response* Government Policy Statement. Wellington, Government Printer.

Minister of State Services (1986) *Pay-fixing in the State Sector* Wellington, Government Printer.

Ministerial Advisory Committee on a Māori Perspective for the Department of Social Welfare (1986) *Puao-te-Ata-tu (Day Break)* Wellington, Department of Social Welfare.

Ministerial Planning Group (1991) *Ka Awatea* Wellington, Office of the Minister of Maori Affairs.

Minnery, J. (1988) Modelling Coordination *Australian Journal of Public Administration* 47: 253–62.

Mitchell, W. (1988) Virginia, Rochester, and Bloomington: Twenty-Five Years of Public Choice and Political Science *Public Choice* 56: 101–19.

Moe, R. (1987) Exploring the Limits of Privatization *Public Administration Review* 47: 453–60.

Moe, T. (1984) The New Economics of Organization *American Journal of Political Science* 28: 739–75.

Moe, T. (1990) Political Institutions: The Neglected Side of the Story *Journal of Law, Economics and Organization* 6: 213–53.

Moe, T. (1991) Politics and the Theory of Organization *Journal of Law, Economics and Organization* 7: 106–29.

Morel, M. (1992) Ethics in the Public Service *Service* March/April.

Morris, R. (1994) The Pricing of Policy Advice: The Proposed Cabinet Benchmark. Paper presented to AIC Conference on Managing Quality Policy, Wellington.

Morris, R. (1995) Public Sector Management—Looking Back and Looking Forwards. Paper presented to the IIR conference on Public Sector Financial Accounting and Management Wellington.

Morton, R. (1994) Radical Reform of the Maori Affairs Portfolio: Has It Benefited Maori? Research Paper for MAPP 510, Victoria University of Wellington.

Morton, R. (1995) The Political Economy of Public Policy on Treaty of Waitangi Settlements. MPP Research Paper, Victoria University of Wellington.

Mosher, F. (1981) *Democracy and the Public Service* 2nd ed. New York, Oxford University Press.

Moss, L. (1990) Picot as Myth. In Middleton, S., Codd, J. and Jones, A. (eds) *New Zealand Education Policy Today: Critical Perspectives* Wellington, Allen and Unwin/Port Nicholson Press.

Mulgan, R. (1989) *Maori, Pakeha and Democracy* Auckland, Oxford University Press.

Mulgan, R. (1990) The Changing Electoral Mandate. In Holland and Boston, 1990.

Mulgan, R. (1992) New Zealand—An Elective Dictatorship? In Gold, 1992.

Mulgan, R. (1994) *Politics in New Zealand* Auckland, Auckland University Press.

Musolf, L. and Seidman, H. (1980) The Blurred Boundaries of Public Administration *Public Administration Review* 40: 124–30.

Nagel, J. (1987) *Participation* Englewood Cliffs, New Jersey, Prentice-Hall.

Nethercote, J. Galligan, B. and Walsh, C. (eds) (1993) *Decision-Making in New Zealand Government* Canberra, Federalism Research Centre.

New Zealand Business Roundtable (1995) *Local Government in New Zealand: An Overview of Economic and Financial Issues* Wellington.

New Zealand Government (1992) *Financial Statements of the Government of New Zealand for the Six Months Ended 31 December 1991* Wellington.

New Zealand Institute of Local Government Managers (1992) *Local Government Handbook 1992* Wellington.

New Zealand Society of Accountants (1987) *Statement of Public Sector Accounting Concepts* Wellington.

New Zealand's Top Fifty Local Bodies (1993) *Management* April: 33–45.

Niskanen, W. (1971) *Bureaucracy and Representative Government* Chicago, Rand McNally.

Nixon, A. (1988) Devolution and the Social Services. In Martin and Harper, 1988.

Norman, R. (1995) New Zealand's Reinvented Government—Experience of Public Sector Managers *Public Sector* 18(2): 22–5.

OECD (1987a) *Administration as Service: The Public as Client* Paris.

OECD (1987b) *Strengthening the Cohesiveness of Policy Making* Paris.

OECD (1994) *Governance in Transition: Public Management Reforms in OECD Countries* Paris, (draft).

Office of the Auditor General of Canada (1995) *Towards Better Governance: Public Service Reform in New Zealand (1984–94) and Its Relevance to Canada* Ottawa.

Office of Treaty Settlements (1994) *Crown Proposals for the Settlement of Treaty of Waitangi Claims: Detailed Proposals* Wellington.

Officials Coordinating Committee on Local Government (1988a) *Reform of Local and Regional Government: Discussion Document* Wellington, Department of Internal Affairs.

Officials Coordinating Committee on Local Government (1988b) *Funding Issues: A Discussion Document* Wellington, Department of Internal Affairs.

Olson, M. (1965) *The Logic of Collective Action* Cambridge, Massachusetts, Harvard University Press.

Olson, M. (1982) *The Rise and Decline of Nations: Economic Growth, Stagflation and Social Rigidities* New Haven, Connecticut, Yale University Press.

Orange, C. (1987) *The Treaty of Waitangi* Wellington, Allen and Unwin/Port Nicholson Press.

O'Reilly, T. and Wood, D. (1991) Biculturalism and the Public Sector. In Boston, Martin, Pallot, and Walsh, 1991.

Orr, G. (1964) *Report on Administrative Justice in New Zealand* Wellington, Government Printer.

Osbaldeston, G. (1989) *Keeping Deputy Ministers Accountable* Toronto, McGraw-Hill Ryerson.

Osborne, D. and Gaebler, T. (1993) *Reinventing Government* New York, Plume.

O'Toole, B. and Jordan, G. (eds) (1995) *Next Steps: Improving Management in Government?* Aldershot, Dartmouth Publishing.

Ouchi, W. (1979) Conceptual Framework for the Design of Organizational Control Mechanisms *Management Science* 25(9): 833–48.

Oxenbridge, S. (1994) Health Sector Collective Bargaining and the Employment Contracts Act: A Case-Study of Nurses *New Zealand Journal of Industrial Relations* 19(1): 17–34.

Oxley, H., Maher, M., Martin, J., Nicoletti, P. and Alonso-Gamo, P. (1990) *The Public Sector: Issues for the 1990s* Working Paper No. 90, Department of Economics and Statistics, OECD.

Painter, M. (1981) Central Agencies and the Coordination Principle *Australian Journal of Public Administration* 40: 265–80.

Painter, M. (1987) *Steering the Modern State: Changes in Central Co-ordination in Three Australian State Governments* Sydney, Sydney University Press.

Painter, M. (1988) Public Management: Fad or Fallacy? *Australian Journal of Public Administration* 47: 1–3.

Pallot, J. (1990) The Nature of Public Assets: A Response to Mautz *Accounting Horizons* 4(2): 79–85.

Pallot, J. (1991) Financial Management Reform. In Boston, Martin, Pallot, and Walsh, 1991.

Pallot, J. (1994) The Development of Accrual-Based Accounts for the Government of New Zealand *Advances in International Accounting* 7: 287–308.

Palmer, G. (1979) *Unbridled Power? An Interpretation of New Zealand's Constitution and Government* Wellington, Oxford University Press.

Palmer, G. (1987) *Unbridled Power: An Interpretation of New Zealand's Constitution and Government* 2nd ed. Auckland, Oxford University Press.

Palmer, G. (1988) Political Perspectives. In Martin and Harper, 1988.

Palmer, G. (1992) *New Zealand's Constitution in Crisis: Reforming Our Political System* Dunedin, John McIndoe.

Palmer, K. (1993) *Local Government Law in New Zealand* 2nd ed. Sydney, Law Book.

Parata, H. (1994) Mainstreaming: A Maori Affairs Policy? *Social Policy Journal of New Zealand* 3: 40–51.

Parry, G., Moyser, G. and Day, N. (1992) *Political Participation and Democracy in Britain* Cambridge, Cambridge University Press.

Paterson, J. (1988) A Managerialist Strikes Back *Australian Journal of Public Administration* 47: 287–95.

Pearson, D. (1990) Community. In Spoonley, P., Pearson, D. and Shirley, I. (eds) *New Zealand Society* Palmerston North, Dunmore Press.

Perrow, C. (1986a) Economic Theories of Organization *Theory and Society* 15: 11–145.

Perrow, C. (1986b) *Complex Organizations: A Critical Essay* New York, Random House.

Perry, J. (1988) Making Policy by Trial and Error: Merit Pay in the Federal Service *Policy Studies Journal* 17: 389–405.

Peters, B. (1992) Government Reorganization: A Theoretical Analysis *International Political Science Review* 13: 199–217.

Peters, B. and Savoie, D. (1995) *Governance in a Changing Environment* Montreal and Kingston, McGill-Queen's University Press.

Peters, T. (1993) *Liberation Management: Necessary Disorganization for the Nanosecond Nineties* London, Macmillan.

Petersen, J. (1993) The Economics of Organization: The Principal–Agent Relationship *Acta Sociologica* 36: 277–93.

Picot Report. See *Taskforce to Review Education Administration 1988*.

Pierre, J. (1995) The Marketization of the State: Citizens, Consumers, and the Emergence of the Public Market. In Peters and Savoie, 1995.

Pilgrim, C. (1992) Can We Be Held Responsible? The Exercise of Employer Responsibilities by New Zealand School Boards of Trustees. Paper presented to the Australian Association for Research in Education/New Zealand Association for Research in Education joint conference on Educational Research: Discipline and Diversity, Deakin University.

Pitt, D. and Smith, B. (1981) *Government Departments: An Organizational Perspective* London, Routledge and Kegan Paul.

Plumptre, T. (1988) *Beyond the Bottom Line: Management in Government* Halifax, Institute for Research on Public Policy.

Polaschek, R. (ed) (1956) *Local Government in New Zealand* Wellington, New Zealand Institute of Public Administration.

Polaschek, R. (1958) *Government Administration in New Zealand* London, Oxford University Press.

Pollitt, C. (1984) *Manipulating the Machine* London, Allen and Unwin.

Pollitt, C. (1995) Charters: The Citizen's New Clothes? *Hong Kong Public Administration* 3(2): 167–76.

Pops, G. (1988) Ethics in Government: A Framework of Analysis. In Bowman, J. and Elliston, F. (eds) *Ethics, Government, and Public Policy: A Reference Guide* Westport, Connecticut, Greenwood Press.

Potter, J. (1988) Consumerism and the Public Sector: How Well Does the Coat Fit? *Public Administration* 66(2): 149–64.

Powell, I. (1989) The Emergence and Development of Fair Relativity as a State Pay-fixing Criterion in New Zealand *New Zealand Journal of Industrial Relations* 14(1): 53–81.

Powell, I. (1995) Negotiating Collective Contracts for Senior Doctors in Crown Health Enterprises: Resolving Ideological Divides and Achieving Enhancements. Paper presented at the Third International Employment Relations Association Conference, University of Waikato.

Pratt, J. and Zeckhauser, R. (eds) (1985) *Principals and Agents: The Structure of Business* Boston, Harvard Business School Press.

Pratt, M. (1992) Capital Charge Regime: Technical Rationality and Legitimation of Monopoly Rents *The Accountants' Journal* 71(8): 50–1.

Prebble, M. (1987) Some Foundations for Social Policy Analysis. Unpublished paper, Wellington.

Preston, D. (1994) Creating the Right Environment for Policy Advice Development. Paper presented to AIC Conference on Managing Quality Policy, Wellington.

Preston, N. (ed) (1994) *Ethics for the Public Sector: Education and Training* Annandale, New South Wales, Federation Press.

Price Waterhouse (1993) *Capital Charging Regime for Government Departments—Survey of Benefits and Current Issues* Wellington, Price Waterhouse Management Consultants.

Probine, M. (1990) Everybody's Business. Address to the PSA National Conference, Wellington.

Probine, M. (1994) The State Sector Act: Lessons from the Recent Past *Public Sector* 17(4): 12–14.

Public Expenditure Committee (1984) *Report on the Format and Content of the Estimates and the Public Accounts* Wellington, House of Representatives.

Public Service Consultative Committee (1946) *Report of the Public Service Consultative Committee on Salaries* Wellington, Government Printer.

Puketapu, I. (1982) Reform from Within. In Burns, C. (ed) *The Path to Reform* Wellington, New Zealand Institute of Public Administration.

Purcell, J. (1989) The Impact of Corporate Strategy on Human Resource Management. In Storey, J. (ed.) *New Perspectives on Human Resource Management* London and New York, Routledge.

Purcell, J. (1995) Corporate Strategy and Its Link with Human Resource Management Strategy. In Storey, 1995b.

Purcell, J. and Ahlstrand, B. (1989) Corporate Strategy and the Management of Employee Relations in the Multi-divisional Company *British Journal of Industrial Relations* 27(3): 398–417.

Pusey, M. (1991) *Economic Rationalism in Canberra* Melbourne, Cambridge University Press.

Quiggan, J. (1987) Egoistic Rationality and Public Choice: A Critical Review of Theory and Evidence *Economic Record* 63: 10–21.

Radbone, I. (1988) The Reality of Administrative Reform in South Australia *Canberra Bulletin of Public Administration* 57: 50–9.

Rae, K. (1991) Industrial Relations for New Zealand Teachers. Paper presented at the New Zealand Conference on Educational Administration, Kohia Teachers Centre, Auckland.

Randle, D. (1985) *Industrial Relations in the Public Sector* Wellington, Industrial Relations Centre, Victoria University of Wellington.

Rangihau, J. et al. *See* Ministerial Advisory Committee on a Māori Perspective for the Department of Social Welfare (1986)

Rasmussen, R., Deeks, J. and Street, M. (1995) The Entrepreneurial Worker: Changes to Work and Contractual Relationships. Paper presented to the International Employment Relations Association Third Annual Conference, University of Waikato.

Rees, R. (1985a) The Theory of Principal and Agent: Part 1 *Bulletin of Economic Research* 37(1): 1–26.

Rees, R. (1985b) The Theory of Principal and Agent: Part 2 *Bulletin of Economic Research* 37(2): 75–95.

Reid, M. (1994) Local Government—Service Delivery or Governance? *Public Sector* 17(2): 2–6.

Renfrow, P. (1989) Corporate Management and the Senior Executive Service: An American and Australian Comparison. In Davis, Weller, and Lewis, 1989.

Review Committee (1994) *Review of the Department of Justice: Stage One Report* Wellington.

Rhodes, R. (1988) *Beyond Westminster and Whitehall: The Sub-Central Governments of Britain* London, Routledge.

Ringer, J. (1991) *An Introduction to New Zealand Government* Christchurch, Hazard Press.

Roberts, J. (1987) *Politicians, Public Servants and Public Enterprise: Restructuring the New Zealand Government Executive* Wellington, Victoria University Press.

Roberts, J. (1991) The Possibilities of Accountability *Accounting Organizations and Society* 16(4): 355–68.

Robertson, J. (1974) Legislation in the Public Sector. In Howells, J., Woods, N. and Young, F. (eds) *Labour and Industrial Relations in New Zealand* Carlton, Vic., Pitman.

Robertson, J. (1990) *Ethics in the Public Sector: The Role of Parliament and Officers of Parliament (A New Zealand Viewpoint)* Paper presented to the National Conference of the Royal Australian Institute of Public Administration, Brisbane.

Robertson, J. (1994) *Report of the Chief Ombudsman on Leaving Office* Wellington.

Robson, P. (1988) Equal Employment Opportunities and the State Sector Act. Circular Memorandum to Chief Executives. Wellington, State Services Commission.

Rodger, S. (1988) State Sector Bill: Public Service No Longer Relevant *Public Sector* 10(4): 2–4.

Rolfe, J. (1990) The Formulation of Defence Policy in New Zealand. Paper prepared for the New Zealand Political Studies Association Conference, Dunedin.

Rolfe, J. (1993) *Defending New Zealand: A Study of Structures, Processes and Relationships* Wellington, Victoria University Press.

Roseveare, J. (1994a) The Independent Responsibilities of Departmental Chief Executives. MPP Research Paper, Victoria University of Wellington.

Roseveare, J. (1994b) The Managerial Responsibilities of Departmental Chief Executives *Public Sector* 17(3): 7–9.

Roseveare, J. (1994c) Chief Executives and Statutory Independence *Public Sector* 17(4): 8–11.

Rowat, D. (1963) Canada's Royal Commission on Government Organization *Public Administration* 41: 193–205.

Royal Commission of Inquiry (1962) *The State Services in New Zealand* Wellington, Government Printer.

Rutherford, B. (1983) *Financial Reporting in the Public Sector* London, Butterworths.

Ryan, R. (1995) *Workplace Reform—Towards an Indigenous Definition* Wellington, Industrial Relations Centre, Victoria University of Wellington.

Sako, M. (1991) The Role of 'Trust' in Japanese Buyer–Supplier Relationships *Ricerche Economiche* 45: 449–74.

Salmond, G., Mooney, G. and Laugesen, M. (eds) (1994) *Health Policy* Special Issue: Health Care Reform in New Zealand 29(1/2).

Sarr, P. (1993) The Work of the Department of Conservation in Fulfilling Its Obligations Under the Treaty of Waitangi. Research Paper for MAPP 510, Victoria University of Wellington.

Schaffer, B. (1958) Theory and Practice in the Machinery of Government *Public Administration* 17: 353–68.

Schaffer, B. (1962) Brownlow or Brookings: Approaches to the Improvement of the Machinery of Government *New Zealand Journal of Public Administration* 24: 37–63.

Scharpf, F. (1986) Policy Failure and Institutional Reform: Why Should Form Follow Function? *International Social Science Journal* 108: 179–89.

Schumpeter, J. (1979) *Capitalism, Socialism and Democracy* London, George Allen and Unwin.

Schwartz, H. (1994) Public Choice Theory and Public Choices: Bureaucrats and State Reorganization in Australia, Denmark, New Zealand, and Sweden in the 1980's *Administration and Society* 26(1): 48–77.

Scott, C. (1988) Funding Issues, Devolution and Accountability. In Martin and Harper, 1988.

Scott, C. (1992) Review of the Purchase of Policy Advice from Government Departments *Public Sector* 15(2): 19–24.

Scott, C. (1994) Reform of the New Zealand Health Care System *Health Policy* 29(1/2): 25–0.

Scott, G. (1990) More Accountability Will Ensure Better Returns *NBR Weekly Magazine* 24 August: 25–6.

Scott, G. (1994) Submission on the Fiscal Responsibility Bill to the Finance and Expenditure Committee Wellington.

Scott, G. (1995) *Government Reform in New Zealand* Washington DC, International Monetary Fund.

Scott, G., Bushnell, P. and Sallee, N. (1990) Reform of the Core Public Sector: The New Zealand Experience *Governance* 3(2): 138–67.

Scott, G. and Gorringe, P. (1989) Reform of the Core Public Sector: The New Zealand Experience *Australian Journal of Public Administration* 48: 81–92.

Scott, K. (1962) *The New Zealand Constitution* London, Oxford University Press.

Self, P. (1977) *Administrative Theories and Politics* London, George Allen and Unwin.

Self, P. (1985) *Political Theories of Modern Government: Its Role and Reform* London, Allen and Unwin.

Self, P. (1989) What's Wrong with Government? The Problem of Public Choice *Political Quarterly* 61: 23–35.

Self, P. (1993) *Government by the Market? The Politics of Public Choice* London, Macmillan.

Sen, A. (1977) Rational Fools: A Critique of the Behavioural Foundations of Economic Theory *Philosophy and Public Affairs* 6: 317–44.

Sen, A. (1987) *On Ethics and Economics* Oxford, Basil Blackwell.

Shailes Report. *See* Audit Office, 1978.

Sharp, A. (1990) *Justice and the Maori* Auckland, Oxford University Press.

Sharp, A. (ed.) (1994) *Leap into the Dark: The Changing Role of the State in New Zealand Since 1984* Auckland, Auckland University Press.

Sharp, A. (1995) Why be Bicultural? In Wilson and Yeatman, 1995.

Sharpe, L. (1977) Whitehall—Structures and People. In Kavanagh, D. and Rose R. (eds) *New Trends in British Politics: Issues for Research* London, Sage.

Shepherd, S. (1994) Accounting in the Public Sector: A Political Economy Approach. MCA thesis, Victoria University of Wellington.

Silver, N. (1995) Rationale and Politics in the Restructuring of the Ministry of Defence. MA thesis, University of Auckland.

Simon, H. (1947) *Administrative Behavior* New York, Macmillan.

Simon, H. (1991) Organizations and Markets *Journal of Economic Perspectives* 5(2): 25–44.

Sisson, K. (1995) Human Resource Management and the Personnel Function. In Storey, 1995b.

Skene, G. (1992) Parliament: Reassessing its Role. In Gold, 1992.

Smillie, J. (1986) Introduction. In Taggart, 1986.

Smith, B. (1985) *Decentralization: The Territorial Dimension of the State* London, George Allen and Unwin.

Smith, M., Marsh, D. and Richards, D. (1993) Central Government Departments and the Policy Process *Public Administration* 71: 567–94.

Smith, V. (1995) Contracting for Social and Welfare Services: The Changing Relationship between Government and the Voluntary Sector in New Zealand. MPP Research Paper, Victoria University of Wellington.

Spann, R. (1973) *Public Administration in Australia* Sydney, Government Printer.

Spicer, B., Emanuel, A., and Powell, M. Transforming Government Enterprises: Managing Radical Organisational Change in Deregulated Environments. Unpublished manuscript, Centre for Research in Public Management, University of Auckland.

Spicer, J., Trlin, A. and Walton, J. (1994) *Social Dimensions of Health and Disease: New Zealand Perspectives* Palmerston North, Dunmore Press.

Stack, J. (1995) The New Zealand Transport Sector Model *Public Sector* 18(2): 2–7.

State Services Commission (1986) *Maori Affairs Department: Overseas Borrowing Initiatives* Wellington.

State Services Commission (1988) *Sharing Control: A Policy Study of Responsiveness and Devolution in the Statutory Social Services* Report of the Steering Group of Permanent Heads from the Task Group on Devolution, Wellington, Government Printer.

State Services Commission (1989) *Guidelines for Preparing Chief Executives Performance Agreements* Wellington.

State Services Commission (1990) *Code of Conduct* Wellington.

State Services Commission (1991) *Review of the Purchase of Policy Advice from Government Departments* Wellington.

State Services Commission (1992a) *Equal Employment Opportunities: Progress in the Public Sector as at June 1991* Wellington, EEO Section, SSC.

State Services Commission (1992b) *The Policy Advice Initiative: Opportunities for Management* Wellington.

State Services Commission (1993) *Briefing Papers for the Incoming Government* Wellington.

State Services Commission (1994a) *Guidelines for Preparing 1994/95 Chief Executive Performance Agreements* Wellington.

State Services Commission (1994b) *Review of the Medium to Long Term Role of Te Puni Kōkiri*, Wellington.

State Services Commission (1994c) *The Senior Public Servant* Wellington.

State Services Commission (1994d) *Annual Report for the Year Ended 30 June 1994* Wellington.

State Services Commission (1994e) *Equal Employment Opportunities: Progress in the Public Service as at June 1993* Wellington.

State Services Commission (1994f) *Review of Accountability Requirements: Report of the Working Party to the Advisory Group* Wellington.

State Services Commission (1995a) *Chief Executive Performance Agreement: Guidelines and Proforma 1995/96* Wellington.

State Services Commission (1995b) *Equal Employment Opportunity Planning and Reporting Requirements* Wellington.

State Services Commission (1995c) *Public Service Principles, Conventions and Practice* [series of papers] Wellington.

State Services Commission (1995d) *Working Under Proportional Representation: A Reference for the Public Service* Wellington.

State Services Commission (undated) *A Draft Model for Strategic Human Resource Development in the State Sector* Wellington.

Statistics New Zealand (1995) *Labour Market: 1994* Wellington, Statistics New Zealand.

Stella, P. (1989) Toward Defining and Measuring the Fiscal Impact of Public Enterprises. IMF Working Paper WP/898/76.

Stewart, J. (1993a) Rational Choice Theory, Public Policy and the Liberal State *Policy Sciences* 26: 317–30.

Stewart, J. (1993b) The Limitations of Government by Contract *Public Money and Management* 13: 7–12.

Stoker, G. (1991) *The Politics of Local Government* 2nd ed. Basingstoke, Macmillan.

Storey, J. (1987) Developments in Human Resource Management: An Interim Report. In *Warwick Papers in Industrial Relations: No. 17* Coventry, University of Warwick.

Storey, J. (1992) *Developments in the Management of Human Resources* Oxford, Blackwell.

Storey, J. (1995a) Human Resource Management: Still Marching On, or Marching Out? In Storey, 1995b.

Storey, J. (ed) (1995b) *Human Resource Management: A Critical Text* London and New York, Routledge.

Storey, J. and Sisson, K. (1993) *Managing Human Resources and Industrial Relations* Buckingham, Open University Press.

Strategos Consulting (1989a) *Department of Justice: Resource Management Review* Wellington, Government Printer.

Strategos Consulting (1989b) *New Zealand Defence: Resource Management Review 1988* Wellington, Government Printer.

Strategos Consulting (1989c) *New Zealand Police: Resource Management Review* Wellington, Government Printer.

Strategos Consulting (1989d) *Review of the Ministry of Agriculture and Fisheries* Wellington, Strategos Consulting.

Sullivan, A. (1990) Devolution: Reform or Rhetoric? Paper prepared for the New Zealand Political Studies Association Conference, Dunedin.

Sullivan, M. (1991) From Personal Tragedy to Social Oppression: The Medical Model and Social Theories of Disability *New Zealand Journal of Industrial Relations* 16: 255–72.

Taggart, M. (ed.) (1986) *Judicial Review of Administrative Action in the 1980s: Problems and Prospects* Auckland, Oxford University Press.

Tahi, B. (1995) Biculturalism: The Model of Te Ohu Whakatupu. In Wilson and Yeatman, 1995.

Tanner, R. (1993) Integrated Policy Development: Case Study—The Social Assistance Reform Committee. Paper presented to AIC Conference on Efficient and Effective Policy, Wellington.

Taskforce to Review Education Administration (1988) *Administering for Excellence—Effective Administration in Education* Wellington, Department of Education.

Taylor, G. (1991) *Judicial Review: A New Zealand Perspective* Wellington, Butterworths.

Te Puni Kōkiri (1993) *Mauriora Ki Te Ao: An Introduction to Environmental and Resource Management Planning* Wellington.

Te Puni Kōkiri (1994a) *Ngā Mahi Auraki: Summary of Mainstreaming* Wellington.

Te Puni Kōkiri (1994b) *Nga Tau e Rua Ki Muri: The First Two Years* Wellington.

Thomas, R. (1993) *Teaching Ethics: Government Ethics* Cambridge, Centre for Business and Public Sector Ethics International Press.

Thompson, S. and Wright, M. (eds) (1988) *Internal Organisation, Efficiency and Profit* Oxford, Philip Allan.

Thynne, I. (1988) New Zealand. In Rowatt, D. (ed) *Public Administration in Developed Democracies* New York, Marcel Dekker.

Tiebout, C. (1956) A Pure Theory of Local Expenditures *Journal of Political Economy* 64: 416–24.

Treasury (1967) *Financial Planning and Control: Report of the Study Group on Treasury Procedures* Wellington, Government Printer.

Treasury (1984) *Economic Management* Wellington, Government Printer.

Treasury (1987) *Government Management: Volumes I and II* Wellington, Government Printer.

Treasury (1994) Fiscal Responsibility Act: Brief Overview *FM Report 8* Wellington.

Treasury (1995) *Purchase Agreement Guidelines with Best Practices for Output Performance Measures* Wellington.

Treasury and Civil Service Committee (1994) *The Role of the Civil Service, Volume 1* London, HMSO.

Trebilcock, M. (1995) Can Government Be Reinvented? In Boston, 1995c.

Tremaine, M. (1991) Equal Employment Opportunity and State Sector Reform. In Boston, Martin, Pallot, and Walsh, 1991.

Tritter, J. (1994) The Citizen's Charter: Opportunities for Users' Perspectives? *Political Quarterly* 65(4): 397–414.

Trotman, I. (1988) New Zealand Public Sector Reform. An address to the Senior Executive Residential Program, New South Wales Government.

Trotman, I. (1993) Evolution of Review Practices in the State Services Commission *Evaluation Journal of Australia* 5(1): 3–17.

Trotman, I. and Jones, N. (1993) Review of Public Service Chief Executive Performance in New Zealand. In *Proceedings of the National Evaluation Conference* Brisbane, Australasian Evaluation Society.

Tullock, G. (1965) *The Politics of Bureaucracy* Washington DC, Public Affairs Press.

Tullock, G. (1984) A (Partial) Rehabilitation of the Public Interest Theory *Public Choice* 42: 89–99.

Tyler, B. (1989) Accountability in the New Public Sector. In *Managing Resources in the New Public Sector: Papers from the 1989 Public Sector Convention* Wellington, New Zealand Society of Accountants.

Uhr, J. (1987) Rethinking the Senior Executive Service: Executive Development as Political Education *Australian Journal of Public Administration* 46: 20–36.

Upton, S. (1991) *Your Health and the Public Health: A Statement of Government Health Policy* Wellington, Government Print Books.

US General Accounting Office (1991) *Government Contractors: Are Contractors Performing Inherently Governmental Functions?* Washington DC, GOA/GGD–92–11.

Vinde, P. (1967) *The Swedish Civil Service* Stockholm, Swedish Ministry of Finance.

Vinde, P. and Petri, G. (1978) *Swedish Government Administration* Stockholm, The Swedish Institute.

Vining, A. and Weimer, D. (1990) Government Supply and Government Production Failure: A Framework Based on Contestability *Journal of Public Policy* 10: 1–22.

Waaka Consultancy (1990) *A Report on EEO (Maori) and a Bi-cultural Approach to Government* Rotorua, Waaka Consultancy.

Wakelin, R. (1994) An Assessment of the 1993 Health Reforms: Issues of Accountability. Paper for MAPP 510, Victoria University of Wellington.

Waller, M. (1992) Evaluating Policy Advice *Australian Journal of Public Administration* 51(4): 440–46.

Walsh, P. (1988a) Accountability and the Industrial Relations Climate. In Wylie, C. (ed.) *Proceedings of the First Research into Educational Policy Conference* Wellington, New Zealand Council for Educational Research.

Walsh, P. (1988b) The Struggle for Power and Control in the New Corporations: The First Year of Industrial Relations in the State-Owned Enterprises *New Zealand Journal of Industrial Relations* 13(2): 179–89.

Walsh, P. (1989) A Family Fight? Industrial Relations Reform under the Fourth Labour Government. In Easton, 1989.

Walsh, P. (1990) Conditions of Employment in Tomorrow's Schools: Industrial Relations and Personnel Policies in the Education Sector. Paper presented to the Second Research into Education Policy Conference, New Zealand Council for Educational Research, Wellington.

Walsh, P. (1991a) The State Sector Act 1988. In Boston, Martin, Pallot, and Walsh, 1991.

Walsh, P. (1991b) Pay-fixing Reform in the New Zealand Public Service, 1912–1948 *New Zealand Journal of History* 25(1): 18–40.

Walsh, P. (1991c) Industrial Relations and Personnel Policies under the State Sector Act. In Boston, Martin, Pallot, and Walsh, 1991.

Walsh, P. (1992) The Employment Contracts Act. In Boston and Dalziel, 1992.

Walsh, P. (1993a) Has the Evil been Remedied? The Development of Public Sector Unionism in New Zealand. In Walsh, P. (ed.) *Pioneering Labour History: Essays in Honour of Bert Roth* Palmerston North, Dunmore Press.

Walsh, P. (1993b) Managerialism and Collective Bargaining in the New Zealand Public Sector. In Gardner, M. (ed.) *Human Resource Management and Industrial Relations in the Public Sector* Melbourne, Macmillan.

Walsh, P. and Dickson, J. (1994) The Emperor's New Clothes: The Uncertain Fate of Equal Employment Opportunities in the New Zealand Public Sector, 1988–1992 *New Zealand Journal of Industrial Relations* 19 (1): 35–53.

Walsh, P. and Fougere, G. (1989) Fiscal Policy, Public Sector Management and the 1989 Health Sector Strike *New Zealand Journal of Industrial Relations* 14(3): 219–29.

Walsh, P. and Ryan, R. (1993) The Making of the Employment Contracts Act. In Harbridge, R. (ed.) *Employment Contracts: New Zealand Experiences* Wellington, Victoria University Press.

Walsh, P. and Wetzel, K. (1993) Preparing for Privatization: Corporate Strategy and Industrial Relations in New Zealand's State-Owned Enterprises *British Journal of Industrial Relations* 31(1): 57–74.

Watson, G. (1985) Ministerial Responsibility and the Maniototo Irrigation Scheme *Otago Law Review* 6: 158–74.

Webb, J. and Liff, S. (1988) Play the White Man: The Social Construction of Fairness and Competition in Equal Opportunities Policies *Sociological Review* 36: 532–50.

Webster, M. (1989) A Study of the Evolution of the New Zealand Public Service since 1935. Unpublished paper, Victoria University of Wellington.

Weingast, B. (1984) The Congressional-Bureaucratic System: A Principal–Agent Perspective (With Application to the SEC) *Public Choice* 4: 147–91.

Weller, P. (1991) Amalgamated Departments—Integrated or Confederated? Establishing Criteria for Evaluating Machinery of Government Changes *Canberra Bulletin of Public Administration* 65: 41–7.

West, A. (1994) Public Service is Independent of Public Servants *Public Sector* 17(2): 26–8.

Wettenhall, R. (1986) *Organizing Government: The Uses of Ministries and Departments* Sydney, Croom Helm.

Whitcombe, J. (1990a) The Accountability Relationship between Chief Executive and Minister under the State Sector Act. MPP thesis, Victoria University of Wellington.

Whitcombe, J. (1990b) The New Zealand Senior Executive Service *Canberra Bulletin of Public Administration* 61: 153–57.

Wilberforce, Lord (1986) Foreword. In Taggart, 1986.

Wildavsky, A. (1978) A Budget for All Seasons? Why the Traditional Budget Lasts *Public Administration Review* 38: 501–9.

Wildavsky, A. (1979) *Speaking Truth to Power: The Art and Craft of Policy Analysis* Boston, Little, Brown.

Williams, M. (1995) Justice Towards Groups: Political not Juridicial *Political Theory* 23(1): 67–91.

Williamson, J. (1994) The Christchurch Case Study on Competitive Tendering. In *Introducing Competitive Tendering in Local Government in Australia* Foundation for Local Government Education and Development Fund, Department of Management, RMIT, Melbourne.

Williamson, O. (1975) *Markets and Hierarchies* New York, Free Press.

Williamson, O. (1985) *The Economic Institutions of Capitalism: Firms, Markets, Relational Contracting* New York, Free Press.

Williamson, O. (1991) Comparative Economic Organization: The Analysis of Discrete Structural Alternatives *Administrative Science Quarterly* 36: 269–96.

Williamson, O. (1992) Markets, Hierarchies, and the Modern Corporation: An Unfolding Perspective *Journal of Economic Behavior and Organization* 17: 335–52.

Wilson, J. (1989) *Bureaucracy: What Government Agencies Do and Why They Do It* New York, Basic Books.

Wilson, M. and Yeatman, A. (eds) (1995) *Justice and Identity: Antipodean Practices* Wellington, Bridget Williams Books.

Wistrich, E. (1992) Restructuring Government New Zealand Style *Public Administration* 70: 119–35.

Woldring, K. (ed.) (1995) *Business Ethics in Australia and New Zealand: Essays and Cases* Melbourne, Thomas Nelson.

Wood, B. (1989) Principal–Agent Models of Political Control of Bureaucracy *American Political Science Review* 83: 965–78.

Wood, R. (1989) Performance Appraisal in the Reform of Public Sector Management Practices. Working Paper 89–007, Australian Graduate School of Management, University of New South Wales.

Wood, R. (1991) Performance Pay and Related Compensation Practices in Australian State Public Sector Organisations. In *PUMA Occasional Papers* Paris, OECD.

World Economic Forum (1993) *World Competitiveness Report* Lausanne, IMD (International Institute for Management Development).

Wright, P. and McMahan, C. (1992) Theoretical Perspectives for Strategic Human Resource Management *Journal of Management* 18(2): 295–320.

Wylie, C. (1994) *Self-Managing Schools in New Zealand: The Fifth Year* Wellington, New Zealand Council for Educational Research.

Yeatman, A. (1987) The Concept of Public Management and the Australian State in the 1980s *Australian Journal of Public Administration* 47: 341–53.

Index